Lecture Notes in Computer S

Commenced Publication in 1973
Founding and Former Series Editors:
Gerhard Goos, Juris Hartmanis, and Jan van Leeuwen

Trond Aalberg   Christos Papatheodorou
Milena Dobreva   Giannis Tsakonas
Charles J. Farrugia (Eds.)

Research and Advanced Technology for Digital Libraries

International Conference on Theory and Practice
of Digital Libraries, TPDL 2013
Valletta, Malta, September 22-26, 2013
Proceedings

 Springer

Volume Editors

Trond Aalberg
Norwegian University
of Science and Technology
7491 Trondheim, Norway
E-mail: trond.aalberg@idi.ntnu.no

Milena Dobreva
University of Malta
MSD2280 Msida, Malta
E-mail: milena.dobreva@um.edu.mt

Charles J. Farrugia
National Archives of Malta
RBT1043 Rabat, Malta
E-mail: charles.j.farrugia@gov.mt

Christos Papatheodorou
Ionian University
49100 Corfu, Greece
E-mail: papatheodor@ionio.gr

Giannis Tsakonas
University of Patras
26504 Patras, Greece
E-mail: john@lis.upatras.gr

ISSN 0302-9743   e-ISSN 1611-3349
ISBN 978-3-642-40500-6   e-ISBN 978-3-642-40501-3
DOI 10.1007/978-3-642-40501-3
Springer Heidelberg New York Dordrecht London

Library of Congress Control Number: 2013945880

CR Subject Classification (1998): H.2.8, H.3, I.7, H.2, I.2, H.4, H.5

LNCS Sublibrary: SL 3 – Information Systems and Application, incl. Internet/Web
and HCI

Typesetting: Camera-ready by author, data conversion by Scientific Publishing Services, Chennai, India

Printed on acid-free paper

Springer is part of Springer Science+Business Media (www.springer.com)

Preface

Over the human life span, 17 years is a period that marks the long transition from infancy into maturity. Definitely, conference maturity is not to be measured with the same metrics, but looking back in the areas of establishment and growth of the European Conference on Research and Advanced Technology for Digital Libraries, started in 1997, it is valid to ask what makes this conference special? We will argue that one of the unique impacts of this conference on the digital library domain is in the quality of sharing it offers and in its particular role to inspire. While its first editions helped the establishment and the professional recognition of the digital library community, it is a great compliment to this community that this domain sprouted in a whole range of new areas, which grew strong and now meet at their specialized well-established events - digital curation and preservation, metadata, or evaluation of information services to mention just a few.

This year the conference took place in Valletta, Malta, during September 22–26, 2013, and it had the challenging task of reconnecting its community in a climate of economic austerity. Once again, the conference called for sharing and inspiration: the general theme "Sharing Meaningful Information" addressed the challenges of interoperability and long-term preservation in the environment of the Web of data. The location of the conference is possibly the first sign of the integrative role it plays. Selecting Malta, where practitioners are involved in digital library work, but research in this area is still making its first steps, will definitely give a chance to strengthen the local capacity.

The conference invited submissions in a wide range of research topics, clustered in four broader areas: Foundation; Infrastructures; Content; and Services. The formulation of the topics once again aimed to bring into the conference a range of interdisciplinary methods, and to engage with it the academic and practitioner communities. The keynote speakers at this conference edition presented two different points of view on digital libraries in the context of the main conference theme. Prof. Christine L. Borgman explored the research aspect of use of digital resources looking into "Digital Scholarship and Digital Libraries: Past, Present, and Future" while Prof. Sören Auer addressed "What Can Linked Data Do for Digital Libraries?". Further, the conference hosted two panels looking at cooperation within our community: "COST Actions and Digital Libraries: Between Sustaining Best Practices and Unleashing Further Potential" and "e-Infrastructures for Digital Libraries... the Future."

Following the established tradition, the conference started with the Doctoral Consortium and a set of six tutorials. The tutorials were split into three morning and three afternoon sessions forming a set of three streams: a first stream that is applied and introductory of relevance to professionals, a second focusing on metadata, and a third one on technical aspects on the system end. A novelty this year was the cooperation with the iSchools community through G-WiS, the Global Workshop of iSchools, which was organized in parallel to the DC. A joint session of TPDL2013 DC and G-WiS showcased the potential avenues in DL education to all young researchers. Further accompanying events included six workshops held after the main conference track. This year we had the joy of welcoming three new workshops ("Practical Experiences with CIDOC CRM and its Extensions," "Moving Beyond Technology: iSchools and Education in Data Curation" and "Linking and Contextualizing Publications and Datasets") beside the three well-known and established workshops that are held in conjunction with TPDL (2nd International Workshop on Supporting Users Exploration of Digital Libraries, 3rd International Workshop on Semantic Digital Archives, 12th European Networked Knowledge Organisation Systems Workshop).

The Program Committee took care of the evaluation of all submissions, following the well-established model involving independent review of each contribution by three or more members of the Program Committee, and facilitation for the discussion by a Senior Program Committee member. The selection process once again was extremely competitive resulting in an acceptance rate of 24%. From the 158 submissions, 24 were accepted as full papers, 13 as short papers, 22 as posters, and 8 as demonstrations. This year, however, was marked by a substantial increase in the diversity of the countries of origin of submissions, which included 40 countries compared to 26 for the conferences in 2011 and 2012. The submissions also covered practically all the conference topics, with the following attracting the highest number of submissions: interoperability and information integration, digital library architectures, information retrieval and browsing, interfaces to digital libraries, user behavior analysis and modelling, linked data and its applications, data mining from networked information, Semantic Web issues in digital libraries, digital curation, and preservation and evaluation of online information environments.

We were also very fortunate to have the outstanding support of Mounia Lalmas and Laszlo Kovacs (Workshop Chairs), Jaap Kamps and Hussein Suleman (Tutorial Chairs), José Borbinha and Claus-Peter Klas (Poster and Demo Chairs), Ingo Frommholz (Demo Chair), Marcos Andre Gonçalves and Stefan Gradmann (Doctoral Consortium Chairs). The inspiration from our Honorary Chair, Constantino Thanos, and from the discussions in the Steering Committee of the conference, also need a special mention, as well as the outstanding local support of Charles J. Farrugia, Organization Chair.

The support from the Ministry for Finance of Malta, the visibility partnership with the COST programme of the EC, and the contributions of our sponsors and supporters deserve our particular gratitude, because they enhanced what this conference was all about – sharing meaningful information.

September 2013

Trond Aalberg
Christos Papatheodorou
Milena Dobreva
Giannis Tsakonas

Organization

TPDL 2013 was organized by the University of Malta in partnership with COST – European Cooperation in Science and Technology.

Organizing Committee

General Chairs

Milena Dobreva — University of Malta, Malta
Giannis Tsakonas — University of Patras, Greece

Honorary Chair

Constantino Thanos — ISTI-CNR, Italy

Program Chairs

Trond Aalberg — Norwegian University of Technology and Science, Norway
Christos Papatheodorou — Ionian University, Greece

Organization Chair

Charles J. Farrugia — National Archives, Malta

Workshop Chairs

Mounia Lalmas — Yahoo! Labs, Spain
Laszlo Kovacs — MTA SZTAKI, Hungary

Poster and Demo Chairs

José Borbinha — Instituto Superior Técnico, Portugal
Claus-Peter Klas — FernUniversität in Hagen, Germany

Tutorial Chairs

Jaap Kamps — University of Amsterdam, The Netherlands
Hussein Suleman — University of Cape Town, South Africa

Publicity Chair

William Zammit — University of Malta, Malta

Panel Chair

Ingo Frommholz — University of Bedfordshire, UK

Doctoral Consortium Chairs

Marcos Andre Gonçalves	Universidade Federal de Minas Gerais, Brazil
Stefan Gradmann	KU Leuven, Belgium

Senior Program Committee

Maristella Agosti	University of Padua, Italy
David Bainbridge	University of Waikato, New Zealand
José Borbinha	Instituto Superior Técnico, Technical University of Lisbon and INESC-ID, Portugal
George Buchanan	City University London, UK
Donatella Castelli	CNR-ISTI, Italy
Panos Constantopoulos	Athens University of Economics and Business, Greece
Schubert Foo	Nanyang Technological University, Singapore
Edward Fox	Virginia Polytechnic Institute and State University, USA
Richard Furuta	Texas A&M University, USA
Marcos Andre Gonçalves	Universidade Federal de Minas Gerais, Brazil
Stefan Gradman	KU Leuven, Belgium
Yannis Ioannidis	University of Athens and "Athena" Research Center, Greece
Sarantos Kapidakis	Ionian University, Greece
Laszlo Kovacs	MTA SZTAKI, Hungary
Gary Marchionini	UNC-Chapel Hill, USA
Carlo Meghini	CNR ISTI, Italy
Michael L. Nelson	Old Dominion University, USA
Erich Neuhold	University of Vienna, Austria
Andreas Rauber	Vienna University of Technology, Austria
Heiko Schuldt	University of Basel, Switzerland
Timos Sellis	RMIT University, Australia / National Technical University of Athens, Greece
Ingeborg Torvik Sølvberg	Norwegian University of Science and Technology, Norway
Nicolas Spyratos	University of Paris South, France
Constantino Thanos	ISTI-CNR, Italy
Pertti Vakkari	University of Tampere, Finland
Herbert Van de Sompel	Los Alamos National Laboratory, USA

Program Committee

Eneko Agirre	University of the Basque Country, Spain
Thomas Baker	DCMI, USA
Christoph Becker	Vienna University of Technology, Austria
Maria Bielikova	Slovak University of Technology in Bratislava, Slovakia
Pável Calado	Instituto Superior Técnico, Technical University of Lisbon and INESC-ID, Portugal
José H. Canós	Universitat Politècnica de València, Spain
Vittore Casarosa	ISTI-CNR, Italy
Lillian Cassel	Villanova University, USA
Timothy Cole	University of Illinois at Urbana-Champaign, USA
Gregory Crane	Tufts University, USA
Fabio Crestani	University of Lugano, Switzerland
Sándor Darányi	University of Borås, Sweden
Theodore Dalamagas	IMIS "Athena" Research Center, Greece
Marco de Gemmis	Università di Bari, Italy
Makx Dekkers	Independent consultant, Spain
Giorgio Maria Di Nunzio	University of Padua, Italy
Boris Dobrov M.V.	Lomonosov Moscow State University, Russia
Martin Doerr	ICS-FORTH, Greece
Fabien Duchateau	Université Claude Bernard Lyon 1, France
Erik Duval	K.U. Leuven, Belgium
Floriana Esposito	Università di Bari, Italy
Nicola Ferro	University of Padua, Italy
Pierluigi Feliciati	Università degli Studi di Macerata, Italy
Ingo Frommholz	University of Bedfordshire, UK
Norbert Fuhr	University of Duisberg-Essen, Germany
Manolis Gergatsoulis	Ionian University, Greece
David Giaretta	STFC, UK
C. Lee Giles	Pennsylvania State University, USA
Julio Gonzalo	Universidad Nacional de Educación a Distancia, Spain
Jane Greenberg	University of North Carolina at Chapel Hill, USA
Bernhard Haslhofer	Cornell University, USA
Annika Hinze	University of Waikato, New Zealand
Jen Shin Hong	National Chi Nan University, Taiwan
Jane Hunter	University of Queensland, Australia
Antoine Isaac	Europeana / VU University Amsterdam, The Netherlands
Jaap Kamps	University of Amsterdam, The Netherlands

Michael Khoo	Drexel University, USA
Ross King	AIT Austrian Institute of Technology, Austria
Claus-Peter Klas	FernUniversität in Hagen, Germany
Martin Klein	Los Alamos National Laboratory, USA
Alberto Laender	Universidade Federal de Minas Gerais, Brazil
Carl Lagoze	University of Michigan, USA
Mounia Lalmas	Yahoo! Labs Barcelona, Spain
Birger Larsen	Royal School of Library and Information Science, Denmark
Ronald Larsen	University of Pittsburgh, USA
Ray Larson	University of California, Berkeley, USA
Patrick Le Boeuf	Bibliothèque Nationale de France, France
Ee-Peng Lim	Singapore Management University, Singapore
Maria Teresa Linaza	VICOMTech, Spain
Clifford Lynch	CNI, USA
Zinaida Manžuch	Vilnius University, Lithuania
Bruno Martins	Instituto Superior Técnico, Technical University of Lisbon and INESC-ID, Portugal
Erwin Marsi	Norwegian University of Science and Technology, Norway
Natasa Milic-Frayling	Microsoft Research Ltd., UK
Reagan Moore	University of North Carolina at Chapel Hill, USA
Wolfgang Nejdl	L3S / University of Hannover, Germany
Ragnar Nordlie	Oslo and Akershus University College of Applied Sciences, Norway
Kjetil Nørvåg	Norwegian University of Science and Technology, Norway
Pasquale Pagano	ISTI-CNR, Italy
Maggy Pezeril	University of Montpellier, France
Nils Pharo	Oslo and Akershus University College of Applied Sciences, Norway
Dimitris Plexousakis	FORTH-ICS, Greece
Edie Rasmussen	University of British Columbia, Canada
Cristina Ribeiro	DEI-FEUP and INESC LA, University of Porto, Portugal
Thomas Risse	L3S Research Center, Germany
Laurent Romary	INRIA / HUB-IDSL, France
Mike Rosner	University of Malta, Malta
Seamus Ross	University of Toronto, Canada
Ian Ruthven	University of Strathclyde, UK
Raivo Ruusalepp	Tallinn University, Estonia
J. Alfredo Sánchez	UDLAP, Mexico
Robert Sanderson	Los Alamos National Laboratory, USA

Chris Staff	University of Malta, Malta
Michalis Sfakakis	Ionian University, Greece
Mário J. Silva	Instituto Superior Técnico, Technical University of Lisbon and INESC-ID, Portugal
Maria Śliwińska	The International Center for Information Management Systems and Services (ICIMSS), Poland
Frank Shipman	Texas A&M University, USA
Cassidy Sugimoto	Indiana University Bloomington, USA
Shigeo Sugimoto	University of Tsukuba, Japan
Hussein Suleman	University of Cape Town, South Africa
Tamara Sumner	University of Colorado at Boulder, USA
Atsuhiro Takasu	National Institute of Informatics, Japan
Manfred Thaller	Universität zu Köln, Germany
Yin-Leng Theng	Nanyang Technological University, Singapore
Anastasios Tombros	Queen Mary University of London, UK
Sascha Tönnies	University Braunschweig, Germany
Chrisa Tsinaraki	Technical University of Crete, Greece
Douglas Tudhope	University of South Wales, UK
Yannis Tzitzikas	University of Crete / FORTH-ICS, Greece
Titia van der Werf	OCLC Research, USA
Thomas Wilson	University of Borås, Sweden
Felisa Verdejo	Universidad Nacional de Educación a Distancia, Spain
Iris Xie	University of Wisconsin-Milwaukee, USA
Panayiotis Zaphiris	Cyprus University of Technology, Cyprus
Maja Žumer	University of Ljubljana, Slovenia

Additional Reviewers

Yasmin Alnoamany
Dimitris Gavrilis
Ilya Markov
Massimiliano Assante
Giorgos Giannopoulos
Dana McKay
Nikos Bikakis
Morgan Harvey
Luis Meneses
Lina Bountouri
Michal Holub
Panagiotis Papadakos
Thilo Böhm
Giacomo Inches

Domenico Redavid
Leonardo Candela
Angela Italiano
João Rocha da Silva
Gianpaolo Coro
Eleftherios Kalogeros
Gianmaria Silvello
Soheil Danesh
Haridimos Kondylakis
Jakub Šimko
Evangelia Daskalaki
Hannes Kulovits
Kostas Stefanidis
Nicola Di Mauro

Monica Landoni
Md. Sultan
Ovo Dibie
Egoitz Laparra
Maria Theodoridou
Pavlos Fafalios
João Correia Lopes
Thanasis Vergoulis
Luigi Fortunati
Parvaz Mahdabi
Peter Wittek

Organizing Committee

Luke Attard Bason	University of Malta, Malta
Malcolm Bonello	University of Malta, Malta
Stanislava Gardasevic	National Library of Serbia, Serbia
Marie-Grace Gauci	University of Malta, Malta
Krassimira Ivanova	IMI BAS, Bulgaria
Anna Kristina Micallef-Ampong	Library, University of Malta, Malta
Josephine Mifsud	Library of MCAST, Malta
Leonidas Papachristopoulos	Ionian University, Greece
Giuseppina Vullo	University of Pavia, Italy

Sponsors

Ministry for Finance – Government of Malta
Malta Tourism Authority
OntoText
Emerald
OCLC
CERIS Information Policies in Science
Facet Publishing
Inmark
ERCIM
IGI Global
X23 The Primate
IEEE TCDL
Heritage Malta

Digital Scholarship and Digital Libraries

Christine L. Borgman

Past, Present, and Future
University of California, Los Angeles

Abstract. In a few short decades, the practices of scholarship have been transformed by the use of digital resources, tools, and services. Some shifts are obvious, such as seeking, reading, and publishing research online, often to the exclusion of print. Other shifts are subtle, such as data being viewed as research products to be disseminated. Research objects are more atomized, yet aggregated in new ways. Digital technologies offer opportunities to innovate in scholarly practice, collaboration, and communication. Innovation in digital libraries is necessary to advance digital scholarship. The talk will present a set of challenges for 21st century research and practice drawn from Prof. Borgman's forthcoming book, tentatively titled "Big Data, Little Data, No Data".

What can Linked Data do for Digital Libraries?

Sören Auer

Universität Leipzig

Abstract. The paradigm of publishing and interlinking structured data on the Web got quite some traction recently. In this talk we will give an overview on recent developments in the Linked Data realm. We will have a look on how Linked Data can contribute to making Digital Libraries and the rich, qualitative content therein more accessible, inter-connected and attractive. As the Web evolves from a medium for document exchange to increasingly facilitating data exchange, Digital Libraries will also evolve from document repositories to knowledge hubs. We will discuss some challenges and opportunities on that road.

Table of Contents

Digital Curation

Mining and Extraction

Architectures and Interoperability

Interfaces to Digital Libraries

Semantic Web

Information Retrieval and Browsing

Preservation

Posters

Demos

Panels

Tutorials

Sustainability of Digital Libraries: A Conceptual Model

Gobinda G. Chowdhury

Centre for Information and Knowledge Management, University of Technology Sydney,
P.O. Box 2007, Sydney, Australia
gobinda.chowdhury@uts.edu.au

Abstract. Major factors related to the economic, social and environmental sustainability of digital libraries have been discussed. Some research in digital information systems and services in general, and digital libraries in particular, have been discussed to illustrate different issues of sustainability. Based on these discussions the paper, for the first time, proposes a conceptual model and a theoretical research framework for sustainable digital libraries. It shows that the sustainable business models to support digital libraries should also support equitable access supported by specific design and usability guidelines that facilitate easier, better and cheaper access, support the personal, institutional and social culture of users, and at the same time conform with the policy and regulatory frameworks of the respective regions, countries and institutions.

Keywords: digital libraries, sustainability, social sustainability, economic sustainability, environmental sustainability.

1 Introduction

Sustainability "creates and maintains the conditions under which humans and nature can exist in productive harmony, that permit fulfilling the social, economic and other requirements of present and future generations."[1]. However, achieving sustainability in all its three forms, viz. economic sustainability, social sustainability and environmental sustainability, is a major challenge because often measures taken for achieving one form of sustainability affect the other forms of sustainability. This paper discusses all the three forms of sustainability in the context of digital libraries. It then identifies some factors that have implications on each form of sustainability. Examples of some current research are used, not exhaustively to review the developments in the specific fields per se but to illustrate the cases, for the economic and social sustainability issues of digital libraries. Similarly the paper draws upon some current research in green IT and cloud computing to illustrate some issues of environmental sustainability that are relevant for digital libraries. Based on these discussions this paper, for the first time, proposes a new model for sustainable digital libraries, and a theoretical framework for study and research in this area.

---

[1] http://www.epa.gov/sustainability/basicinfo.htm

T. Aalberg et al. (Eds.): TPDL 2013, LNCS 8092, pp. 1–12, 2013.

2   Sustainability of Digital Libraries

Sustainable information refers to resources that facilitate integration of all the three parts of sustainable development – social, economic and environmental sustainability, and it contributes to the strengthening of the processes in which society is transformed according to the ideals of sustainable development [1]. Overall, the concept of sustainability has not been researched well within the mainstream information science in general and in the context of digital libraries in particular [1,2].

In order to study the sustainability of digital libraries, it is necessary to identify the challenges that are associated with the design, delivery, access and use of digital information. Again, the issues of sustainability can be considered in the context of the major factors influencing the lifecycle of information – from creation to management, use/re-use, and disposal (when required, for example disposal of analogue information resources and also disposal of computing infrastructure and equipment in the context of digital libraries) [3]. In the context of digital libraries,

- the target for the economic sustainability is to ensure cheaper, easier and better access to digital information. The success can be achieved by building a sustainable business model as well as taking measures for reductions in the creation, distribution and access to information; and also by taking measures for reductions in the user time and efforts for contextual discovery, access and use of information;
- the target for the social sustainability is to ensure equitable access to information in order to build a better (well informed) and healthy society; the success can be achieved by measures to increase the accessibility and usability as well impact of digital libraries in every sphere of life and society; and
- the target for the environmental sustainability is to ensure reductions in the environmental impact of digital information; the success can be achieved by reducing the greenhouse gas (GHG) emissions throughout the lifecycle of digital libraries.

These factors are interrelated, and none should be considered in isolation. For example, rapidly changing ICT infrastructure and information design to deal with digital content and data will have implications for all the three forms of sustainability of digital libraries: (1) on the economic sustainability because of the increasing costs, increasing levels of efforts or specific needs for ICT equipment for access to information, etc. (2) on the social sustainability because of changes in the level of equitable access, and effects on the users' work and culture, and perhaps causing more social exclusion, and (3) environmental sustainability in terms increase in the GHG emissions due to quick changes in, and disposal of, the ICT infrastructure, and so on. Furthermore there are a number of external factors that form the foundations of digital libraries, such as the emerging ICT infrastructure and policies; changing web, social networking and mobile technologies; intellectual property rights (IPR), privacy and security issues, etc. Often these factors play a significant part in each area of sustainability and thus affecting the overall sustainability of digital libraries.

Some past research have indirectly touched upon different forms of sustainability of digital information services. For example, a number of alternative business models for information have been studied in the context of e-books and e-journal subscription models in libraries, and also in the context of open access models (see for example, [4]). Similarly there have been many evaluation studies focusing on the impact of digital library services. A significant amount of research has taken place in the broad area of user studies as well as digital literacy, social inclusion, etc. in the context of digital libraries (for a review see [5]). Recently Chowdury [2,6-8] has discussed the environmental aspects of digital information systems and services. However, to date very little research has been done addressing all the three forms of sustainability and the factors that influence the sustainability of digital libraries, their implications as well as their interrelationships in the context of digital library development [3].

3   Economic Sustainability of Digital Libraries

As stated earlier in the paper, the target for the economic sustainability is to ensure cheaper, easier and better access to digital information through a sustainable funding model. Thus for digital libraries, economic sustainability can be achieved by:

1. Building a sustainable business model supporting the economic, technological and manpower resources for the design, delivery and management for cheaper and easier access to digital content and data in order to meet the present and future needs of the user community, and
2. A sustainable model for providing the economic, technological as well as intellectual support for preservation of digital content and data.

Although it has been talked about in several publications, economic sustainability of digital libraries still remains a challenge requiring further research and studies [9].

3.1   A Sustainable Business Model for Digital Libraries

While some digital libraries are based on commercial models, i.e. they require payment or subscriptions for access, many digital libraries have appeared over the past decade or so that are free at the point of use. Such digital libraries are funded by:

1. governments, e.g. the US National Science Foundation providing support for the National Science Digital Library, or the National Library of Medicine as part of the US National Institute of Health providing funds for PubMed;
2. specific countries/institutions or consortia for example, various EU countries providing support for Europeana, or specific institutional repositories; and
3. charities, e.g. the Wellcome Library funded by the Wellcome Trust.

However, sustainable funding is still a major issue for many digital libraries. A recent report on the funding of Europeana notes that it has raised €2.1 million since 2008 from Ministries of Culture & Education across Europe but it is becoming increasingly difficult to get further commitment from governments and institutions. The report points out that Europeana has a funding gap for 2011, 2012 and 2013 of €1.2 million[2]. Most other digital libraries face a similar funding crisis.

---

[2] http://pro.europeana.eu/documents/844813/851970/Funding+Gap+Paper.pdf

The open access (OA) movement that emerged in the early 1990s with the establishment of the open archive known as arXiv.org (formerly xxx.lanl.gov) gave a significant boost to digital library development. However, a sustainable business model for open access has yet to appear. Developments through the green route to open access that is based on self-archiving of research papers, has given rise to thousands of institutional repositories but its uptake has been slow due a variety of reasons ranging from the lack of a sustainable funding model for institutions, lack of interests from publishers and authors in participating in the process, the complex workflow and copyright clearance process, duplication of efforts, and so on. Huge amounts of discussions and debates are currently going on around the world on this. Moreover, different institutions follow different practices for creation of institutional repositories. A recent survey of the funding and deployment of institutional repositories [10] notes that:

- institutions that mediate submissions incur less expense than institutions that allow self-archiving,
- institutions that offer additional services incur greater annual operating costs than those who do not, and
- institutions that use open source applications have lower implementation costs but have comparable annual operating costs with institutions that use proprietary software.

The gold route to open access has also suffered from a sustainable business model. Recently the UK government has taken a radical step by accepting the Finch Report [11] and making recommendations based on this through the UK Research Councils (RCUK) for implementation of a model with article processing charges (APCs) to support the gold route to OA. The report and RCUK OA policies recommend APCs as the main vehicle for supporting open access. It is proposed that the UK Research Councils and other public sector funding bodies should establish more effective and flexible arrangements to meet the costs of OA. The Finch Report recommends a funding of £50-60 million per year to support OA to research publications in the UK.

3.2   Long-Term Access: Digital Preservation

Sustainable digital preservation is a societal concern and transcends the boundaries of any content domain, and therefore all parts of society such as the national and international agencies, funders and sponsors of data creation, stakeholder organizations, and individuals have roles in achieving sustainability [13]. However, the DPimpact Study [12] noted that the memory institutions had very limited funding for digital preservation. According to Dobreva & Ruusalepp [14], the economic and social sustainability of digital preservation has not been a major area of digital preservation research. The EU SHAMAN project [15] proposed an Enterprise Architecture-based approach that enables the accommodation of digital preservation concerns in the overall architecture of an organization with the justification that although the preservation of content is not a main business requirement, it is required to enable the actual delivery of value in the primary business. Overall a sustainable funding model for digital preservation has yet to appear.

4   Social Sustainability of Digital Libraries

Broadly speaking social sustainability may be defined as the maintenance and improvement of well-being of current and future generations [16]. However, the concept of well-being can be defined differently in different contexts ranging from the equity of access to essential services for healthy lifestyle and well-being, to democratic and informed citizenship, to promotion and sharing of positive relations and culture, and so on. Many indicators of sustainable development have been proposed (see for example, [17,18]), but broadly speaking for digital libraries the main goal of social sustainability is to ensure equitable access and use of digital information in every sphere of life and society. Access is a rather broad term here that includes all the activities related to discovery, access and use/re-use of information for day-to-day business, pleasure, well-being, knowledge and understanding, and so on. A number of parameters are associated with the social sustainability of digital libraries that have direct or indirect influence on equitable access, such as:

1.   HIB (human information behavior) and IS&R (information seeking and retrieval) issues;
2.   Information and digital literacy issues;
3.   Accessibility and usability issues including access to ICT and internet, digital library software and interface issues; and
4.   Policy and legal issues.

4.1   HIB and IS&R Issues

HIB and IS&R have remained the two most widely researched areas of information science for the past few decades giving rise to several models in information science in general (for details see, [19-21]) and in the context of digital libraries in particular [22,23]. These models discus various personal, contextual, social, cultural and technological issues that influence access to, and use of, digital libraries.

As discussed in the previous section, open access has become a major agenda among governments and research funding bodies. However, still there are some major cultural issues that need to be overcome in order to make it a success. For example, one may argue that the Finch Report [11] and RCUK OA policies (discussed earlier) based on the APCs, may create a situation where publication of a research paper may be decided not only by the quality but the affordability of the authors and institutions to pay the APCs of a target journal. Furthermore, national research assessment exercises like the REF in UK, ERA in Australia, are still very much guided by the assessment of quality of research in journals and conferences with high impact factors. These assessment measures may affect the social sustainability of open systems.

Although it is generally recognised that open access research outputs get more access, and therefore more citations, there is still a lack of evidence as to how open access output compare with ranked commercial journals and conferences in terms of their long-term research impact. This remains a major factor affecting the social sustainability of open access information and open scholarship, that will have implications on the social sustainability of digital libraries. So, a number of parameters interplay towards the social sustainability of digital libraries, and to date no systematic research has taken place to study these parameters and their inter-relationships.

4.2   Information and Digital Literacy Issues

Like human information behaviour, information literacy has also remained a major area of research in information studies. There are other related areas of research like digital literacy, digital divide, social inclusion, etc. Access to, and effective use of, digital libraries can be significantly affected by poor information and digital literacy skills of people [5]. A November 2012 BBC news[3] reports that 16 million people in Britain, i.e. about one in four, or one in three in the adult British population, do not have the basic Internet skills. It may be safely assumed that this is not an isolated case and many countries in the world have comparable, or even worse, information and digital literacy skills causing social exclusion. In the context of digital libraries, social exclusion may be caused by a number of factors ranging from the lack of adequate access to ICT infrastructure and services, to lack of digital and information skills that are the pre-requisites for successful access to, and use of, digital library services.

4.3   Accessibility and Usability Issues

Access to, and effective use of, digital libraries can be significantly affected by digital divide that is often manifested by [24]:

- the social divide which is characterized by the difference in access between diverse social groups
- the global divide which is characterized by the difference in terms of access to the Internet technologies, and
- the democratic divide which is characterized by the different applications and uses of digital information in order to engage and participate in social life.

There are different indicators for assessing these different manifestations of digital divide, and these are not only prevalent in the developing world, but also among various communities within the developed nations. For example, more than a third of the US households do not have a broadband connection yet, and only about two-thirds of the 27 EU countries have a broadband connection at home [24]. So, the vision of the Europeana digital library, to provide digital information and culture to everyone in Europe, still cannot be fully utilized because two-thirds of the EU homes do not yet have a broadband connection. The situation in the third world countries is even worse.

Usability of digital libraries is often affected by the user needs and expectations that are set, often wrongly, by the search engines. In a usability study of the Europeana digital library it was noted that young users' information needs and search strategies and expectations were quite different from those of more matured users [25]. The study further noted that many younger users wanted to be able to download,

---

[3] http://www.bbc.co.uk/news/technology-20236708

annotate and share digital objects. The latter is a relatively new phenomenon which is caused by the recent proliferation of the easy-to-use search engine services that have created a different set of expectations, especially amongst the younger users.

4.4   Policy and Legal Issues

Digital library development is influenced by several policy issues. For example, the recent policies of various research funding bodies with regard to open access can have a significant impact on the economic and social sustainability of digital libraries. Research and funding bodies and institutions in many countries now support the motto of open access and encourage researchers to self-archive their published research papers, some even make it compulsory. For example, the public access policy of the US National Institute of Health (NIH) states that:

> *"all investigators funded by the NIH submit or have submitted for them to the National Library of Medicine's PubMed Central an electronic version of their final, peer-reviewed manuscripts upon acceptance for publication, to be made publicly available no later than 12 months after the official date of publication."*[4]

Wellcome Trust have also introduced a similar open access policy that:

> *"requires electronic copies of any research papers that have been accepted for publication in a peer-reviewed journal, and are supported in whole or in part by Wellcome Trust funding, to be made available through PubMed Central (PMC) and Europe PubMed Central (Europe PMC) as soon as possible and in any event within six months of the journal publisher's official date of final publication"*[5]

The newly introduced OA policy of the European Commission[3] stipulates that as of 2014, all research papers produced with funding from EU Horizon 2020 will have to be freely accessible to the public. The process of self-archiving has given rise to several specialized open access repository services like PubMed Central, and has given rise to institutional repositories at many specific institutional levels. However, the overall take up of self-archiving has been slow because of a lack of consistent policy issues and some legal challenges.

The gold OA model has been adopted by many journals whereby they have introduced article processing charges (APCs), and there are now some hybrid journals that follow both the subscription and APC-based open access model. Some funding bodies have introduced inclusion of APCs within their research funding models. For example, the OA policy of the Wellcome Trust states that the Trust, where appropriate, will provide their research grant holders with additional funding, through their institutions, to cover open access charges. The European Commission recommends the following two options for open access[6]:

---

[4] http://publicaccess.nih.gov/policy.htm
[5] http://www.wellcome.ac.uk/About-us/Policy/Policy-and-position-statements/WTD002766.htm
[6] http://europa.eu/rapid/press-release_IP-12-790_en.htm

- Gold open access where research papers will be made immediately accessible on-line by the publisher and the researchers will be eligible for reimbursement of the APCs from the Commission; or
- Green open access where researchers will make their research papers available through an open access repository no later than six months after publication (or 12 months for articles in the fields of social sciences and humanities).

A number of social, institutional and cultural issues are involved here. For example, it is not clear how the APC model of gold OA will be implemented, and similarly how the self-archiving of research papers will be adopted by the academics and researchers across all the education and research institutions and disciplines.

Access to, and use of, digital information is very much hindered due to the inappropriate, and often stringent, intellectual property rights (IPR) and complex digital rights management (DRM) issues. This was identified in several studies (see for example, [26,27,28]). Considering the various recommendations of the Hargreaves Review [28], the UK Government commissioned a feasibility study that recommended the development of a *Copyright Hub* to serve a number of functions including [29]:

- Information and copyright education;
- Registries of rights;
- A marketplace for rights - licensing solutions; and
- Help with the orphan works problem.

The report concluded that a number of issues existed with copyright licensing making them unfit for the digital age [29]. However, it will be interesting to see how the new IP laws influence the publishing industry and digital libraries.

5   Environmental Sustainability of Digital Libraries

Digital libraries are based on a variety of ICT infrastructure that run various information systems and services and the overall lifecycle of a digital library. ICT have a profound impact on the environment causing about 2% of global greenhouse gas emissions (GHG) emissions [7,8]. The information services sector, by virtue of making extensive use of ICT infrastructure and equipment make a significant amount of GHG emissions. In 2010 Google's overall consumption of electricity was reported to be 2.26 million MWh [30]. This is equivalent to emissions from about 11 power stations in Britain [7]. Another estimate shows that about one billion Google search is conducted every day, and thus even on a conservative estimate, one billion grams or 1,000 tonnes of CO_2 (carbon dioxide, a measure used to show GHG emissions) is emitted only for Google search every day [31]. This does not include the client-side ICT and energy usage figures. It is estimated that the Internet consumes between 170 and 307 GW (GigaWatt) of electricity which is equivalent to 1.1–1.9% of the total energy usage of humanity [32]. The HE institutions (HEIs) in the US produce 121 million tonnes of CO_2 in a year which is equivalent to nearly 2% of total annual

GHG emissions in the US, or about a quarter of the entire State of California's annual emissions [33]. It is estimated that in 2008-2009, HEIs in the UK alone used nearly 1,470,000 computers, 250,000 printers and 240,000 servers; and it is estimated that there would be 500,000 tonnes of CO_2 emissions from this electricity use [34].

Some data related to the environmental impact of information services based on print and digital content is provided by Chowdhury [8]. Studies also show that use of modern technologies like cloud computing, can reduce both the economic and environmental impact of digital information [2]. In the UK, the Joint Information Systems Committee (JISC) is promoting the idea of using the cloud computing technology for providing data and information access services for the HEIs that can reduce the environmental costs of information services, and the ICT infrastructure costs. Some US universities are also taking similar initiatives in developing cloud-based systems for managing research data and information [35]. In The Netherlands, SURFnet is also taking several measures to promote the use of cloud computing for higher education and research.

Thus cloud-based information services can improve the environmental sustainability of digital libraries and information services [2,7]. However, a number of social and user related issues are also associated with cloud-based information services, e.g., access and management issues related to sensitive data and content, information behaviour of users in relation to remote access to data and content; institutional and user culture and practices in relation to access and use of remote digital content and data, and so on. To date no research has addressed all of these issues in tandem in relation to digital libraries, and specific user communities and contexts [2,7].

6   A Sustainability Model for Digital Libraries

Figure 1 presents a sustainability model for digital libraries. This model can be used to build a general framework for research and development in digital libraries. At the core, the model shows that a digital library connects users with digital content and data by using appropriate ICT. Recent research (e.g. Chowdhury [2,7]) shows that a cloud-based architecture can help us build green information services with significant environmental, and perhaps some economic, benefits. Although further research is needed to justify the overall economic and environmental gains from cloud architecture, based on the current trends, the model proposes a cloud-based architecture for digital libraries for providing access to linked content and data.

However, a sustainable digital library needs sustainable funding models that support various social sustainability measures and also meet the environmental sustainability requirements. The model shows that appropriate measures should be taken to achieve each form of sustainability that enhances or supports the other forms of sustainability. The model also shows some areas of research to attain sustainability.

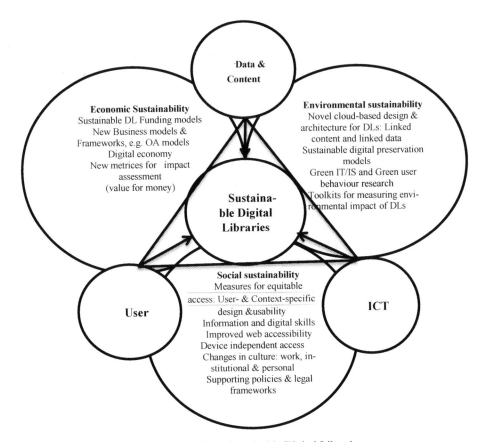

Fig. 1. A Model for Sustainable Digital Libraries

7   Conclusion

In order to build sustainable digital libraries, attention should be paid to all the areas viz. economic, social and environmental sustainability. The generic model shows that sustainable business models to support digital libraries should also support easy and equitable access supported by specific design and usability guidelines that facilitate easier, better and cheaper access, support the personal, institutional and social culture of users, and at the same time conform with the policy and regulatory frameworks of the respective regions, countries and institutions. Similarly, the model shows that green IT, green IS and cloud computing will help to achieve environmental sustainability but this should also meet the requirements of the business/funding models and also the social requirements by providing user- and context-specific access to linked content and data. Overall, the model can serve as a starting point for future research and development with a holistic view of digital libraries, and the various factors that have implications on all the three forms of sustainability.

References

1. Nolin, J.: Sustainable information and information science. Information Research 15(2) (2010), http://informationr.net/ir/15-2/paper431.html (retrieved August 8, 2011)
2. Chowdhury, G.G.: Building sustainable information services: A Green IS research agenda. Journal of the American Society for Information Science and Technology 63(4), 633–647 (2012)
3. Chowdhury, G.G.: Sustainability of digital information services. Journal of Documentation (accepted, 2013)
4. Houghton, J., Rasmussen, B., Sheehan, P., Oppenheim, C., Morris, A., Creaser, C., Greenwood, H., Summers, M., Gourlay, A.: Economic implications of alternative scholarly publishing models: exploring the costs and benefits. JISC (2009), http://ie-repository.jisc.ac.uk/278/3/EI-ASPM_Report.pdf
5. Liew, C.L.: Digital library research 1997-2007: Organisational and people issues. Journal of Documentation 65(2), 245–266 (2009)
6. Chowdhury, G.G.: Carbon footprint of the knowledge sector: what's the future? Journal of Documentation 66(6), 934–946 (2010)
7. Chowdhury, G.G.: An agenda for green information retrieval research. Information Processing and Management 48(6), 1067–1077 (2012)
8. Chowdhury, G.G.: How digital information services can reduce greenhouse gas emissions. Online Information Review 36(4), 489–506 (2012)
9. Collier, M.: Sustainability of digital libraries: economic and business planning. In: Law, D. (ed.) Libraries in a Digital Age: Fundamentals and Latest Thinking. The Biomedical & Life Sciences Collection. Henry Stewart Talks Ltd., London (2012), http://hstalks.com
10. Burns, C.S., Lana, A., Budd, J.M.: Institutional repositories: exploration of costs and value. D-Lib Magazine 19(1/2) (2013), http://www.dlib.org/dlib/january13/burns/01burns.html
11. Finch, J.: Accessibility, sustainability, excellence: how to expand access to research publications. Report of the Working Group on Expanding Access to Published Research Findings (2012), http://www.researchinfonet.org/publish/finch
12. DPimpact, Socio-economic Drivers and Impact of Longer Term Digital Preservation. Final Report (2009), http://cordis.europa.eu/fp7/ict/telearn-digicult/dpimpact-final-report.pdf
13. Blue Ribbon Task Force on Sustainable Digital Preservation and Access, Sustainable economics for a digital planet: ensuring long-term access to digital information. Final report (2010), http://brtf.sdsc.edu/biblio/BRTF_Final_Report.pdf
14. Dobreva, M., Ruusalepp, R.: Digital preservation: interoperability ad modum. In: Chowdhury, G.G., Foo, S. (eds.) Digital Libraries and Information Access: Research Perspectives, pp. 193–215. Facet Publishing, London (2012)
15. SHAMAN Reference Architecture, EU FP7 Large Scale Integrated project. Final report (2102), http://shaman-ip.eu/sites/default/files/SHAMAN-REFERENCE%20ARCHITECTURE-Final%20Version_0.pdf
16. Mak, M.Y., Peacock, C.J.: Social Sustainability: A Comparison of Case Studies in UK, USA and Australia. In: 17th Pacific Rim Real Estate Society Conference, Gold Coast, January 16-19 (2011), http://www.prres.net/papers/Mak_Peacock_Social_Sustainability.pdf

17. Hutchins, M.J., Gierke, J.S., Sutherland, J.W.: Decision making for social sustainability: a lifecycle assessment approach. In: IEEE International Symposium on Technology and Society, ISTAS 2009, May 18-20, pp. 1–5 (2009)
18. Hutchins, M., Sutherland, J.W.: An exploration of measures of social sustainability and their application to supply chain decisions. Journal of Cleaner Production 16(15), 1688–1698 (2008)
19. Wilson, T.: On user studies and information needs. Journal of Documentation, Special publication, 174–186 (2009)
20. Ruthven, I., Kelly, D. (eds.): Interactive information seeking, behaviour and retrieval. Facet Publishing, London (2011)
21. Ingwersen, P., Järvelin, K.: The turn: integration of information seeking and retrieval in context. Springer, Dordrecht (2005)
22. Wilson, T.D., Maceviciute, E.: Users' interactions with digital libraries. In: Chowdhury, G.G., Foo, S. (eds.) Digital Libraries and Information Access: Research Perspectives, pp. 113–128. Facet Publishing, London (2012)
23. Dobreva, M., O'Dwyer, A. (eds.): User studies for digital library development. Facet Publishing, London (2012)
24. Chowdhury, G.G., Chowdhury, S.: Information users and usability in the digital age. Facet Publishing, London (2011)
25. Dobreva, M., Chowdhury, S.: A User-Centric Evaluation of the Europeana Digital Library. In: Chowdhury, G., Koo, C., Hunter, J. (eds.) ICADL 2010. LNCS, vol. 6102, pp. 148–157. Springer, Heidelberg (2010)
26. Chowdhury, G.G.: . Towards the conceptual model of a content service network. In: In: Globalizing academic libraries vision 2020, Proceedings of the International Conference on Academic Libraries, Delhi, October 5-8, pp. 215–220. Delhi Mittal Publications (2009)
27. Chowdhury, G.G., Fraser, M.: Carbon footprint of the knowledge industry and ways to reduce it. World Digital Libraries 4(1), 9–18 (2011)
28. Hargreaves, I.: Digital opportunity: a review of intellectual property and growth. An Independent Report (2011), http://www.ipo.gov.uk/ipreview-finalreport.pdf
29. Hooper, R., Lynch, R.: Copyright works: streaming copyright licensing for the digital age. UK Intellectual Property Office (2012), http://www.ipo.gov.uk/dce-report-phase2.pdf
30. Albanesius, C.: How much electricity does Google consume each year? PCMag.com (2011), http://www.pcmag.com/article2/0,2817,2392654,00.asp
31. Gombiner, J.: Carbon footprinting the internet. Consilience: The Journal of Sustainable Development 5(1), 119–124 (2011)
32. Raghavan, B., Ma, J.: The energy and emergy of the internet. In: Proceedings of the ACM Workshop on Hot Topics in Networks (Hotnets), Cambridge, MA (November 2011), http://www.cs.berkeley.edu/~jtma/papers/emergy-hotnets2011.pdf
33. Sinha, P., Schew, W.A., Sawant, A., Kolwaite, K.J., Strode, S.A.: Greenhouse gas emissions from US institutions of higher education. Journal of Air & Waste Management Association 60(5), 568–573 (2010)
34. James, P., Hopkinson, L.: Green ICT: managing sustainable ICT in education and research (2009), http://www.jisc.ac.uk/publications/programmerelated/2009/sustainableictfinalreport.aspx (retrieved August 8, 2011)
35. Foster, I.: Research data lifecycle management as a service (2011), http://www.columbia.edu/~rb2568/rdlm/Foster_UChicago_RDLM2011.pdf

Quality Assessment in Crowdsourced Indigenous Language Transcription

Ngoni Munyaradzi and Hussein Suleman

Department of Computer Science, University of Cape Town,
Cape Town, South Africa
ngoni.munyaradzi@uct.ac.za, hussein@cs.uct.ac.za

Abstract. The digital Bleek and Lloyd Collection is a rare collection that contains artwork, notebooks and dictionaries of the indigenous people of Southern Africa. The notebooks, in particular, contain stories that encode the language, culture and beliefs of these people, handwritten in now-extinct languages with a specialised notation system. Previous attempts have been made to convert the approximately 20000 pages of text to a machine-readable form using machine learning algorithms but, due to the complexity of the text, the recognition accuracy was low. In this paper, a crowdsourcing method is proposed to transcribe the manuscripts, where non-expert volunteers transcribe pages of the notebooks using an online tool. Experiments were conducted to determine the quality and consistency of transcriptions. The results show that volunteers are able to produce reliable transcriptions of high quality. The inter-transcriber agreement is 80% for |Xam text and 95% for English text. When the |Xam text transcriptions produced by the volunteers are compared with a gold standard, the volunteers achieve an average accuracy of 64.75%, which exceeded that in previous work. Finally, the degree of transcription agreement correlates with the degree of transcription accuracy. This suggests that the quality of unseen data can be assessed based on the degree of agreement among transcribers.

Keywords: crowdsourcing, transcription, cultural heritage.

1   Introduction

The digital Bleek and Lloyd Collection [10] is a collection of scanned notebooks, dictionaries and artwork that document the culture and beliefs of the indigenous people of Southern Africa. The notebooks, specifically, contain 20000 pages of bilingual text that document the stories and languages of speakers of the now-extinct |Xam and !Kun languages. These notebooks were created by linguistics researchers in the mid-1800s and are the most authoritative source of information on the then indigenous population. Figure 1 shows a typical page from one of the notebooks.

Transcriptions of the scanned notebooks would make the text indexable and searchable. It would also enable translation, text-to-speech and other forms of processing that are currently not possible. Manual translation is a possibility but

T. Aalberg et al. (Eds.): TPDL 2013, LNCS 8092, pp. 13–22, 2013.

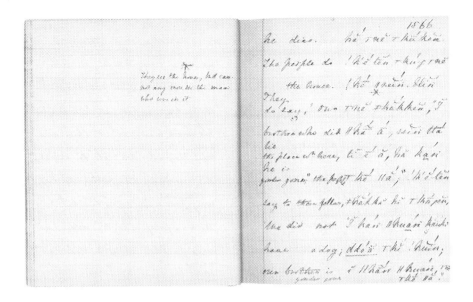

Fig. 1. Sample page from Bleek and Lloyd notebooks

this is an expensive solution and not one that can easily be adapted to similar problems for other digital collections and other forms of document processing, especially in resource-constrained environments.

An alternative is presented by the Citizen Cyberscience movement [4], where ordinary citizens are recruited to volunteer their time and/or computational resources to solve scientific problems, often with benefit to the public. Such problems include mapping of roads in rural Africa and monitoring of disease spread, (e.g., FightMalaria@Home). In typical projects, each volunteer is given one or more small tasks via a Web interface and these tasks are collated to solve a larger problem.

This project is based on the premise that the preservation of cultural heritage is of importance to ordinary citizens, who could therefore be recruited as volunteers to transcribe handwritten documents. The Bossa [2] framework for distributed/volunteer thinking was used to develop a transcription application.

This paper investigates the feasibility and accuracy of volunteer transcription, as one example of an intellectually-intensive tasks in digital libraries, and how it compares to computational techniques like machine learning.

The rest of this paper is structured as follows: Section 2 discusses the background and related work that serves as a foundation and motivation for the approach used in this research; Section 3 describes the Bossa volunteer framework used to harness distributed human computation power; Section 4 focuses on the analysis of the initial results; and Section 5 draws conclusions and discusses future work.

2   Related Work

Crowdsourcing (or volunteer thinking) has been applied to solve various problems related to information search and discovery. Volunteer thinking may be defined as crowdsourcing with volunteers, as opposed to paid workers.

Shachaf [9] investigated the quality of answers on the Wikipedia Reference Desk, and compared it with library reference services to determine whether volunteers can outperform expert reference librarians. Their results show that both systems provide reference services at the 55% accuracy level. Overall, the volunteers outperform the expert librarians – this is significant because the volunteers are amateurs and not paid for their services. The individual responses submitted by volunteers were comparable to those of librarians, but the amalgamated responses from volunteers produced answers that were similar or better than those of expert librarians.

Clickworkers [6] is an example of a citizen science project, set up by NASA, where volunteers identify and classify the age of craters on Mars images. The objectives of such citizen science projects include determining if volunteers are ready and willing to contribute to science and if this new way of conducting science produces results that are as good as earlier established methods. Ongoing work by Callison-Burch [3], Nowak [8] and others has shown that both questions can be answered in the affirmative.

reCAPTCHA[1] is a snippet transcription tool used for security against automated programs. reCAPTCHA is used to digitize books, newspapers and old time radio shows. This service is deployed in more than 44 000 websites and has been used to transcribe over 440 million books, achieving word accuracies of up to 99% [11]. The tasks are, however, very small and there is a strong motivation to complete them successfully as failure prevents access to whatever resource is being protected by reCAPTCHA. This is not typical of transcription projects.

The work by Causer and Wallace [5] in the Transcribe Bentham project gives an enlightening picture of the effort required to successfully create awareness about a transcription project and costs involved. Early reported results in 2012 were promising but the project included the use of professional editors and thus relied on project funding to ensure quality. In contrast, this paper investigates what level of quality can be achieved solely by volunteers and automated postprocessing techniques.

Williams [12] attempted to transcribe the Bleek and Lloyd notebooks solely using machine learning techniques, by performing a detailed comparison of the best known techniques. Using a highly-tuned algorithm, a transcription accuracy of 62.58% was obtained at word level and 45.10% at line level. As part of that work, Williams created a gold standard corpus of |Xam transcriptions [13], which was used in the work reported on in this paper.

In summary, there have been numerous attempts at transcription, with a focus on the mechanics of the process. This paper, instead, focuses on the assessment of transcription accuracy, which is further in the context of a language that is

---

[1] http://www.google.com/recaptcha

unfamiliar to volunteers. The mechanics were greatly simplified by use of the Bossa toolkit, as discussed in the next section.

3   Bossa Framework

The Berkeley Open System for Skill Aggregation (Bossa) [2] is an open source software framework for distributed thinking - where volunteers complete tasks online that require human intelligence. Bossa was developed by David Anderson[2], and is part of the larger Berkeley Open Infrastructure for Network Computing (BOINC) framework - BOINC is the basis for volunteer computing projects such as SETI@Home [1]. The Bossa framework is similar to the Amazon Mechanical Turk but gives the project administrator more control over the application design and implementation. Unlike the Mechanical Turk, Bossa is based on the concept of volunteer work with no monetary incentives.

The framework simplifies the task of creating distributed thinking projects by providing a suite of common tools and an administrative interface to manage user accounts and tasks/jobs. A well-defined machine interface in the form of a set of PHP call-back functions allows for the interconnection with different custom applications.

For each application, a core database with important application details is pre-populated and can be expanded with application-specific data. The programmer can then define the actual task to be performed as a Web application, and link this to the call-back functions. These callback functions determine how the tasks are to be displayed, manage issuing of further tasks and what happens when a task is completed or has timed out.

The Transcribe Bleek and Lloyd project used a Web application that defined each page of text to be transcribed as a single task. Volunteers were presented with a Web interface where the original text was displayed and they were asked to enter their transcriptions, with special characters and diacritics entered using a visual palette. This palette-oriented editing interface was adapted from earlier work by Williams [12]. Figure 2 shows the transcription interface.

4   Evaluation

An evaluation of transcription accuracy was conducted by: checking the consistency of multiple transcriptions; comparing transcriptions to a known gold standard; and correlating consistency with accuracy.

4.1   Transcription Similarity Metric

The Levenshtein distance [7] or edit distance is a measure of the similarity between strings. It can be defined as the minimum cost of transforming string X into Y through basic insertion, deletion and substitution operations. This

---

[2] http://boinc.berkeley.edu/anderson/

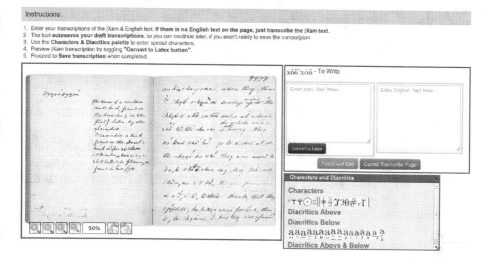

Fig. 2. Bossa-based interface for transcription of pages

method is popularly used in domains of pattern recognition and error correction. This method is not suitable to solve certain problems as the method is sensitive to string alignment; noisy data would significantly affect its performance. The method is also sensitive to string lengths; shorter strings tend to be more inaccurate, if there are minor errors, than longer strings. Yujian and Bo [14] note that, because of this, there is need for a normalized version of the method.

Notation-wise, Σ represents the alphabet, Σ^Λ is the set of strings in Σ and $\lambda \notin \Sigma$ denotes the null string. A string $X \in \Sigma^\Lambda$ is represented by $X = x_1 x_2 ... x_n$, where x_i is the ith symbol of X and n is the length of the string calculated by taking the magnitude of X across $x_1 x_2 ... x_n$ or $|X|$. A substitution operation is represented by $a \rightarrow b$, insertion by $\lambda \rightarrow a$ and deletion by $b \rightarrow \lambda$. $S_{x,y} = S_1 S_2 ... S_u$ are the operations needed to transform $X \rightarrow Y$. γ is the weight function equivalent to a single edit transformation that is non-negative, hence the total cost of transformation is $\gamma(S_{x,y}) = \Sigma_{j=1}^{u} \gamma(S_j)$

The Levenshtein distance is defined as:

$$LD(X,Y) = min\{\gamma(S_{a,b})\} \tag{1}$$

Yujian and Bo [14] define the normalized Levenshtein distance as a number within the range 0 and 1, where 0 means that the strings are different and 1 means that they are similar.

$$NLD(X,Y) = \frac{2 \cdot LD(X,Y)}{\alpha(|X| + |Y|) + LD(X,Y)} \tag{2}$$

where $\alpha = max\{\gamma(a \rightarrow \lambda), \gamma(\lambda \rightarrow b)\}$

4.2   Inter-transcriber Agreement

The normalized Levenshtein distance metric was used to measure transcription similarity or inter-transcriber agreement amongst users who have transcribed the same text. The inter-transcriber agreement can be used to assess reliability of the data from volunteers or consistency in the transcriptions.

Transcription similarity or inter-transcriber agreement is calculated at line level. The overall similarity among documents can be trivially calculated using the compound sum of each individual line in a document. During the data collection phase, each individual page was transcribed by up to three unique volunteers. From the individual transcriptions, each line is compared with the other two for similarity.

The minimum, average and maximum similarity values were calculated independently for the English and |Xam text.

English Text. Figure 3 is a plot of the minimum, average and maximum similarity for each transcription of English text. The blue, red and green data points represent the maximum, average and minimum values respectively. The transcriptions have been sorted on average similarity to clearly show clusters of similar values.

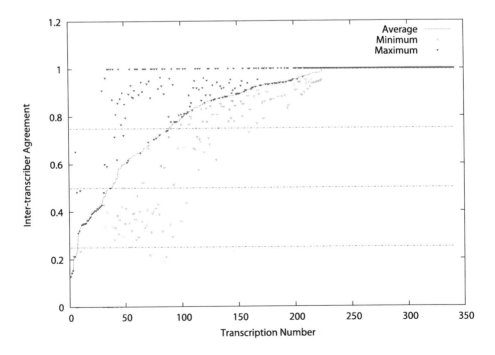

Fig. 3. Inter-transcriber similarity for English text

A total of 371 transcriptions were plotted in Figure 3. Single transcriptions or perfect correspondences are indicated by the convergence at an agreement value of 1. Approximately one third of the transcriptions (225-371) result in perfect agreement, while another one third (100-224) have at least 80% agreement. For higher levels of agreement, the variance in values is also low. For the lowest one third of the transcriptions (1-99), there is a higher variance but the appearance of many high maximum values suggest that 2 transcriptions have high agreement while the third is an outlier.

The results show that volunteers (non-experts) are able to produce English transcriptions that are reliable and consistent, with an overall similarity measure of $\mu = 0.95$ for all the transcriptions.

|Xam Text.** Figure 4 is a plot of the minimum, average and maximum for each transcription of |Xam text. The blue, red and green data points represent the maximum, average and minimum values respectively. The transcriptions have been sorted on average similarity to clearly show clusters of similar values.

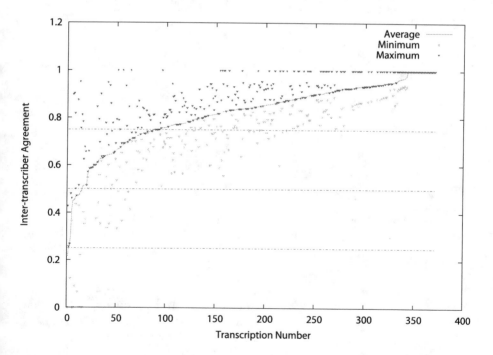

Fig. 4. Inter-transcriber similarity for |Xam text

A total of 412 transcriptions were plotted in Figure 4. Single transcriptions or perfect correspondences are indicated by the convergence at an agreement value of 1, and only account for approximately 10% of the transcriptions. However, about 80% of transcriptions (80-412) have an agreement value of at least 75%. The variance is also relatively low and there are few transcriptions with small agreement values.

As before, the results show that volunteers (non-experts) are able to produce |Xam transcriptions that are reliable and consistent, with an overall similarity measure of $\mu = 0.80$ for all the transcriptions.

4.3 Transcription Accuracy

In this experiment, the Bleek and Lloyd transcription gold standard (Corpus-G) [13] was used as a comparison for the transcriptions produced by the crowd-sourced volunteers (Corpus-V). Transcription accuracy was measured by calculating the normalized Levenshtein distance between two strings. A total of 186 transcriptions were used.

Table 1 depicts the transcription accuracy distribution. 34.41% of the transcriptions have an average accuracy higher than 70%, while 40.86% have an accuracy between 51% and 69%. 14.51% of the transcriptions have an accuracy between 36% and 50%, and the remaining 8.60% have an accuracy lower than 35%. The global average accuracy is 64.75%.

Table 1. Accuracy Distribution for Corpus-V with Corpus-G

Accuracy	DataPoints	Percentage
0.70 - 1.00	64	34.41%
0.51 - 0.69	76	40.86%
0.36 - 0.50	27	14.51%
0.00 - 0.35	16	8.60%

The average accuracy is therefore substantially higher than previous studies at line level and marginally higher than previous studies at word level. In addition, this accuracy was obtained on the basis of the "wisdom of the crowd" rather than highly optimized algorithms.

Correlation of Inter-transcriber Agreement and Accuracy. The final experiment considered whether inter-transcriber agreement correlates with accuracy. Inter-transcriber agreement can be calculated mechanically during processing of tasks while accuracy can only be computed based on an existing gold standard. Thus, if there is a correlation, it suggests that inter-transcriber agreement could be used as an alternative metric to accuracy for non-training data.

Figure 5 is a box-and-whisker plot of the correlation, with agreement levels separated into 10 discrete bands. The graph shows clearly that there is a linear relationship between average inter-transcriber agreement and transcription accuracy. Thus, greater agreement among transcriptions of a line of text may

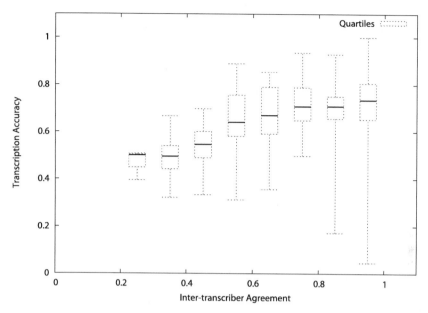

Fig. 5. Correlation between inter-transcriber similarity and accuracy

translate to a higher level of accuracy and this could be exploited in the crowd-sourcing application by, for example, injecting additional jobs into the queue if inter-transcriber agreement is low.

5   Conclusions

This paper considered the feasibility of volunteer thinking for the transcription of historical manuscripts, with a focus on quality of transcriptions.

The experiments have demonstrated that: (a) transcriptions produced by volunteers have a high degree of similarity, suggesting that the transcriptions are reliable and consistent; (b) the acccuracy of transcriptions produced by volunteers is higher than that obtained in previous research; and (c) a high degree of consistency correlates with a high degree of accuracy.

Thus, it may be argued that is possible to produce high quality transcriptions of indigenous languages using volunteer thinking. Furthermore, this technique should be considered to complement or as an alternative approach for other heritage preservation tasks where the "wisdom of the crowd" may produce comparable or better results.

Future work related to transcription includes the use of language models for suggestion, correction and merging of transcriptions; and result merging to produce synthetically-derived transcriptions with potentially higher levels of accuracy.

Acknowledgements. This research was partially funded by the National Research Foundation of South Africa (Grant numbers: 85470 and 83998), the Citizen Cyberscience Centre and University of Cape Town.

The authors acknowledge that opinions, findings and conclusions or recommendations expressed in this publication are that of the authors, and that the NRF accepts no liability whatsoever in this regard.

References

1. Anderson, D.P., Cobb, J., Korpela, E., Lebofsky, M., Werthimer, D.: SETI@home: An Experiment in Public-Resource Computing. Communications of the ACM 45(11), 56–61 (2002)
2. Bossa, http://boinc.berkeley.edu/trac/wiki/bossaintro
3. Callison-Burch, C.: Fast, cheap, and creative: evaluating translation quality using amazons mechanical turk. In: Proceedings of the 2009 Conference on Empirical Methods in Natural Language Processing, EMNLP 2009, vol. 1, pp. 286–295. Association for Computational Linguistics, Stroudsburg (2009)
4. Catlin-Groves, C.L.: The Citizen Science Landscape: From Volunteers to Citizen Sensors and Beyond. International Journal of Zoology, 2012, Article ID 349630, 14 pages (2012), doi:10.1155/2012/349630
5. Causer, T., Wallace, V.: Building a volunteer community: results and findings from Transcribe Bentham. Digital Humanities Quarterly 6(2) (2012)
6. Kanefsky, B., Barlow, N.G., Gulick, V.C.: Can Distributed Volunteers Accomplish Massive Data Analysis Tasks? In: Lunar and Planetary Institute Science Conference Abstracts. Lunar and Planetary Inst. Technical Report, vol. 32, p. 1272 (March 2001)
7. Levenshtein, V.I.: Binary codes capable of correcting deletions, insertions, and reversals. Soviet Physics Doklady 10(8), 707–710 (1966)
8. Nowak, S., Rüger, S.: How reliable are annotations via crowdsourcing: a study about inter-annotator agreement for multi-label image annotation. In: Proceedings of the International Conference on Multimedia Information Retrieval, MIR 2010, pp. 557–566. ACM, New York (2010)
9. Shachaf, P.: The paradox of expertise: Is the wikipedia reference desk as good as your library? Journal of Documentation 65(6), 977–996 (2009)
10. Suleman, H.: Digital libraries without databases: The Bleek and Lloyd collection. In: Kovács, L., Fuhr, N., Meghini, C. (eds.) ECDL 2007. LNCS, vol. 4675, pp. 392–403. Springer, Heidelberg (2007)
11. Von Ahn, L., Maurer, B., McMillen, C., Abraham, D., Blum, M.: RECAPTCHA: Human-based character recognition via web security measures. Science 321, 1465–1468 (2008)
12. Williams, K.: Learning to Read Bushman: Automatic Handwriting Recognition for Bushman Languages. MSc, Department of Computer Science, University of Cape Town (2012)
13. Williams, K., Suleman, H.: Creating a handwriting recognition corpus for bushman languages. In: Xing, C., Crestani, F., Rauber, A. (eds.) ICADL 2011. LNCS, vol. 7008, pp. 222–231. Springer, Heidelberg (2011)
14. Yujian, L., Bo, L.: A normalized Levenshtein distance metric. IEEE Transactions on Pattern Analysis and Machine Intelligence 29(6), 1091–1095 (2007)

Defining Digital Library

Armand Brahaj[1,2], Matthias Razum[1], and Julia Hoxha[3]

[1] FIZ Karlsruhe, 76344 Eggenstein-Leopoldshafen, Germany
{name.surname}@fiz-karlsruhe.de
[2] Humboldt-Universität zu Berlin, 10099 Berlin, Germany
[3] Albanian Institute of Science, Tirana, Albania
julia.hoxha@ais.al

Abstract. This paper reflects on the range of the definitions of digital libraries demonstrating their extent. We analyze a number of definitions through a simplified intensional definition method, through which we exploit the nature of the definitions by analyzing their respective genera and attributes. The goal of this paper is to provide a synthesis of the works related to definitions of digital library, giving a fine-grained comparative approach on these definitions. We conclude that, although there are a large number of definitions, they are defined in overlapping families and attributes, and an inclusive definition is possible.

Keywords: Digital Library, Definition, Evaluation of Digital Libraries.

1   Introduction

The field of digital libraries (DL) has been for many years an avenue of extensive research and practical implementations. Despite the wide-ranging developments, the term "digital library" remains ambiguous and varies between different communities. Part of the ambiguity originates from the shared perceptions related to the concepts "digital" and "library", but this has not spared the specialists who, approaching the problem from different backgrounds, bring their own conceptualization of a digital library.

The definition of DL is also an interesting topic because of its impact in the evaluation process. The connection between the evaluation and definition of the term has been advocated by Saracevic [1], who highlights the importance of DL definition in the evaluation process. Significant contributions in this regard have been introduced by the "Digital Library Reference Model" [2] proposed by DELOS. The topic is part of investigative research works such as [3] [4] [5]. These claims are also supported by Borgman [6] which points out that from a research perspective there are no attempts to introduce new definitions of DLs, but rather studies which synthesize already existing definitions. From the practice perspective she argues that there are additional needs such as evaluation metrics, which tend to introduce new definitions. The methods and metrics for the evaluation of DLs may vary according to whether these are viewed as institutions, information systems, new technologies, collections, or as services.

Motivated by the multitude of the various DL definitions, as well as their importance in further implementations and evaluation frameworks, this paper reflects on the range of the existing definitions demonstrating their respective extent. The work is based on an analysis of the nature of the genera and attributes across different

T. Aalberg et al. (Eds.): TPDL 2013, LNCS 8092, pp. 23–28, 2013.

definitions. It is not the intent of the paper to introduce yet another digital library definition, but rather to provide a synthesis of the works related to the definitions of the digital library (in Section 3). Furthermore, we present an analysis of the definitions based on a fine-grained comparative approach (Section 4), concluding with the findings of the analysis and insights on the future use of the term.

2   Related Work

Discussions on the term "digital libraries" have been central to many scholarly communication activities since the notion came to existence. While the term dominates today in practice and research, the library community has used several different terms in the past [10]. Although with some resistance, the term "digital library" soon dominated and became widely accepted. Borgman [6] discussing the term concludes that its usage is problematic since it confuses the boundaries between electronic collections and institutions. She predicts that *"neither community is likely to surrender the term in favor of another. .. The failure to define the terms slows the development of theory, research and practice"* [6]. Careful approach in using the term has also been advised by Lynch [11]. Just as Borgman he regarded the term problematic considering the complex relation between the libraries as institutions and electronic collections. Harter [9] attempts to enclose the distance between traditional and DLs arguing that the latest should have the properties of a traditional library. Cleveland in [10] stresses the technical aspects of DLs as a step beyond the traditional library.

Significant contributions in the analysis of digital library have been done through the DELOS initiative in the Digital Library Manifesto [2]. The Manifesto lead to the development of a reference document that captured key concepts involved in a DL. Manifesto's analysis considers three types of relevant "systems" in this area: Digital Library as a virtual organization, Digital Library System as a specific interface system, and Digital Library Management System which is a software layer supporting administration. Their choice of separating these three concepts was a step ahead in avoiding confusion and the use of the notions interchangeably in literature.

In our quest to address the issues of the many different definitions we rely solely on the already existing definitions in attempt to show the extent of the concept. We do not analyze the definitions in the context of specific communities, but focus on the broad vision of digital libraries. Similar attempts are noted in [7] where he encourages a synthesis of definition.

3   Digital Library

3.1   Defining the Definition

> *Define: To state the precise meaning*
> *of a word or sense of a word [12]; To specify distinctly*

A simple search for the definition of digital libraries in academic articles will yield more than a dozen results leading instinctively to the questions: Why are so many definitions for the same concept? Should the definitions be unique when related to a unique concept?!

We start our analysis by considering first the definition as a concept per se. The word *define,* as many other words used in the scientific terminology, derives from

Latin in the form *definire* and it is composed of the prefix *de-* and root *finire*. The prefix *de-* usually means "out of" or "away from." For example, *deplete* literally means "out of full" or "away from full". The meaning of deplete is close to *empty*. Just the same, *despera* means literally "out of hope".

The root *finire* indicates the extent of something, the limit as opposed to the word infinite. Deriving from the information above, the word *define* means away from the end/boundaries of something; putting an end to something as in enclosing; or as in showing its boundaries. Still, the meaning of the word *define* is not *confine*. While confine is more about keeping something restricted, the word define is about showing the potential *extent* of a concept. Following this reasoning, the many definitions that can be found on the term "digital library" are attempting to show the potential *extent* of DLs and also provide an overview of main components.

Definitions have also a well-organized form. A definition is a passage describing the meaning of a term, an object or a concept. Basically, in a definition we have [21]:

- a *definiendum* – the object of our definition,
- a *genus* – the family where the definition takes place
- and one or more *differentia* – distinguishable attributes

The above analysis of a definition will be the basis of the next section. If we take as an example the definition: *"A digital library is an online system that stores media assets, and provides services for retrieving and presenting this content to humans or other online systems"* then, the *"digital library"* is called the **definiendum;** *Online system* is the **genus;** *Stores media assets* and *provides services* are the **differentiae**.

In order to exploit the extent of DLs, we have used an analysis based on genus and differentia for a number of definitions found in scholar articles and institutional dictionaries. The method is also known as *intensional definition* [13] and it gives the meaning of a term by specifying all the properties required to derive that definition, i.e., the necessary and sufficient conditions for belonging to the set being defined.

We have applied this analysis to a list of prominent definitions on digital libraries. Even though we claim that this paper provides an exhaustive coverage of works that contain definitions of digital library, we are aware that potentially there can be other definitions which could be appended to our analysis. Some of the extracted genera and the differentiae are illustrated in Table 1 together with the respective definitions. An extensive datasets and definitions used in our analysis can be found at [8].

Table 1. Analysis of Digital Library definitions, partial dataset

Digital Libraries are organizations that provide the resources, including the specialized staff, to select, structure, offer intellectual access to, interpret, distribute, preserve the integrity of, and ensure the persistence over time of collections of digital works so that they are readily and economically available for use by a defined community or set of communities[14]	Genus	Organization
	Differentia	Provide resources and specialized staff to: - select collections of digital work - structure collections of digital work - offer intellectual access to collections of digital work - interpret collections of digital work - distribute collections of digital work - preserve the integrity of digital work - ensure persistence over time of digital work collections

Definition		Extraction
An informal definition of a digital library is a managed collection of information, with associated services, where the information is stored in digital formats and accessible over a network[15]	Genus	Managed collection
	Differentia	Associated services Information is stored in digital format Information accessible over network
Digital library is "a focused collection of digital objects, including text, video, and audio, along with methods for access and retrieval, and for selection, organization, and maintenance of the collection[16]	Genus	Focused collection
	Differentia	Methods for access and retrieval of collection
Digital libraries .... viewed as systems providing a community of users with coherent access to a large, organized repository of information and knowledge [17]	Genus	Systems
	Differen-	Provide community with access to large, organized information
A digital library is a distributed technology environment which dramatically reduces barriers to the creation, dissemination, manipulation, storage, integration, and reuse of information by individuals and groups. [18]	Genus	Distributed Environment
	Differen-	Reduces barriers to information: creation, manipulation, storage, reuse
A digital library is an integrated set of services for capturing, cataloging, storing, searching, protecting, and retrieving information. [19]	Genus	A group of Services
	Differentia	These services enable: capturing, cataloging, searching, protecting, retrieving, information
A "digital library" is fundamentally a resource that reconstructs the intellectual substance and services of a traditional library in digital form. [7]	Genus	Resource
	Differentia	Reconstruct the intellectual substance Reconstructs the services of a traditional library in digital form
A possibly virtual organization that comprehensively collects, manages, and preserves for the long term rich digital content, and offers to its user communities specialized functionality on that content, of measurable quality and according to codified policies [2]	Ge-	Virtual organization
	Differentia	Collects, manages and preserves digital content; Offers specialized content functionality to user communities and according to codified policies

3.2   Synthesis of the Definitions

We have considered a number of definitions on digital library and applied an analysis of the definition to each of them. The result is an extraction of genera and differentia in each definition. After analyzing the genera extracted from the definitions, we realized that the genera can be grouped under four main concepts: Collection, Service, Organization, and System

As illustrated in Table 2, most of the definitions bind digital libraries to Collections. It is also interesting to find out that most of the definitions that relate digital library to Collections highlight specifications of collections, such as focused collection, managed collection or organized collection. The requisite to explicitly specify collections shows a bond of the concept with specific perceptions related to usability

Table 2. Genera of digital libraries grouped in four groups

Collections	Services	Organization	Systems
- Organized collections	- Library services	- Organization	- Systems
- Managed collection	- Dynamic federated	- Operational organi-	- Tools
- Focused collection	structures	zation	- Electronic resources
- Electronic resources	- Information sto-	-Socio-technical	- Database on hyper-
- Collection of collections	rage	systems	text environment
- Collection of information	- Retrieval systems	- Virtual organization	- Environment
objects	- Distributed envi-		- Library
- Collection of documents	ronment		- Socio-technical
in electronic format	- Collection of		systems
- Resource	services		- Networks of tech-
	- Group of services		nology

and added value. The terminology still varies in different definitions, sometime focusing on the extension of library services, sometime on interoperability (dynamic federated structures), and in other cases on information storage and information retrieval systems. Surprisingly, few definitions regard digital libraries as *Organizations*, although many properties tend to push toward this family. A more abstract genus is found in defining DLs as *Systems* leaving space for technical interpretations.

Just as the genera of the DL overlap, so do the differentia found in different definitions. Our analysis on the attributes provides a first attempt towards generalization and categorization. It is interesting to notice the occurrence of these attributes in the list of candidate properties which are needed in the evaluation of digital libraries as proposed by Saracevic [1]. Many of the attributes can also be seen as mapped inside the *main concepts* of the DELOS's Digital Library Universe. Their analysis is an interesting direction for future research.

Recalling the meaning of the term definition itself (Section 4.1) as the potential ex-tent of a concept, as well as the observed overlap between the genera and differentia found among the existing definitions of digital library, we strongly argue that this collection of genera and differentia constitutes a basis for an inclusive definition of DL.

4   Conclusions

The use of the term 'digital library' is very broad. Digital libraries have evolved dynamically over the past two decades, and such has the use of the term. Digital libraries are no longer theoretical constructs, but reality. They are driven by user groups or communities. Each of them focuses on their specific usage scenarios, leading to the existing variety of definitions. In most of the definitions evaluated in this work, community- and scenario-specific requirements are not expressed as genera, but rather as attributes found in differentia. Separating the manifold of attributes from the overarching concepts of 'collection', 'service', 'organization', and 'service' allows us to provide a framework for existing and future definitions of the term 'digital library'. Every definition should reflect those concepts. This does not necessarily mean that all four concepts must be part of the definition. Depending on the concrete usage scenario, one or more genera might be left out intentionally. However, given the prominence of these genera throughout all evaluated existing definitions, they provide a valid guideline for future work.

For this paper, we did not analyze the attributes found in the differentia of the evaluated definitions in greater detail. A rather cursory grouping produced the following, non-definitive list: Intellectual Access, Service Management, Information Structuring, Collection Management, Digital Accessibility, Permanent Access, Supplement to conventional library collections, Economic Perspective, Technical Capabilities. A more systematic and accurate grouping is an avenue for future work.

Although we initially started this work with the conception that the term 'digital library' is ill-defined and maybe even misleading, the results of the analysis showed that it is based on four abstract concepts, that are then concretized with community- and scenario-specific attributes.

References

1. Saracevic, T.: Digital library evaluation: Toward evolution of concepts. Library Trends 49(2), 350–369 (2000)
2. Candela, L., et al.: The DELOS Digital Library Reference model. Foundations for digital Libraries (Version 0.98) (2008)
3. Fuhr, N., et al.: Evaluation of digital libraries. International Journal on Digital Libraries 8(1), 21–38 (2007)
4. Xie, H.I.: Users' evaluation of digital libraries (DLs): Their uses, their criteria, and their assessment. Information Processing & Management 44(3), 1346–1373 (2008)
5. Khoo, M., MacDonald, C.: An Organizational Model for Digital Library Evaluation. In: Gradmann, S., Borri, F., Meghini, C., Schuldt, H. (eds.) TPDL 2011. LNCS, vol. 6966, pp. 329–340. Springer, Heidelberg (2011)
6. Borgman, C.L.: What are digital libraries? Competing visions. Informacion Processing Management 35, 227–243 (1999)
7. Seadle, M., Greifeneder, E.: Defining a digital library. Library Hi Tech (2007)
8. Brahaj, A., Razum, M., Hoxha, J.: Dataset of definitions related to Defining Digital Libraries. Figshare (2013), http://dx.doi.org/10.6084/m9.figshare.707337
9. Harter, S.P.: What is a digital library? Definitions, content, and issues. In: International Conference on Digital Libraries and Information Services for the 21st Century (1996)
10. Cleveland, G.: Digital Libraries: Definitions, Issues and Challenges. In: UDT (1998)
11. Lynch, C.A.: Accessibility and integrity of networked information collections. Congress of the United States, Office of Technology Assessment, Washington, DC (1993)
12. American Heritage, American Heritage® Dictionary of the English Language, 4th edn. (2003), http://www.thefreedictionary.com/define (accessed 2013)
13. Cook, R.T.: Intensional Definition. In: In A Dictionary of Philosophical Logic, p. 155. Edinburgh University Press (2009)
14. DLF (1998), http://old.diglib.org/about/dldefinition.htm (accessed 2013)
15. Arms, W.: Digital Libraries. M.I.T. Press (2000)
16. Witten, I.H., et al.: How to build a digital library. Morgan Kaufmann (2009)
17. Lynch, C., Garcia-Molina, H.: Interoperability, scaling, and the digital libraries research agenda. In: Iita Digital Libraries Workshop (1995)
18. Fox, E.A.: Source Book on Digital Libraries. Virginia Tech, Virginia (1993)
19. WTEC Hyper-Librarian, WTEC Principles of Digital Libraries (1999), http://www.wtec.org/loyola/digilibs/04_02.htm (accessed 2013)
20. Ojha, R.C., Aryal, S.: Digital Libraries: Challenges and Opportunites. Infolib (2010)
21. Copi, I.M., Cohen, C.: Introduction to Logic, 91h ed (1994)

E-Books in Swedish Public Libraries: Policy Implications

Elena Maceviciute and Tom D. Wilson

Swedish School of Library and Information Science, University of Borås,
Allégatan 1, Borås, Sweden
elena.maceviciute@hb.se, tom.wilson@hb.se

Abstract. The aims of the paper are: review the situation of e-books delivery in the Swedish public libraries (as it looked at the end of 2012); identify the barriers that public libraries encounter in providing access to e-books; highlight the policy-related problems of e-book provision through public libraries. A survey was carried out in October, 2012 of all public libraries in Sweden. 291 questionnaires were issued. 185 were completed, response rate was 63.3%. The provision of an e-book service has arisen as a result of either demand or an ideological belief that the ethos of democratic values and equality of access requires libraries to offer material in all media. Librarians find the situation of e-books provision through libraries unsatisfactory: the provider of titles removes them from the catalogue without warning or explanation, there are too few titles for children and students, and access to popular titles is delayed.

Keywords: e-books, public libraries, information policy, Sweden.

1 Introduction

Sweden is among the top countries with regard to the penetration of broadband, internet, mobile technology, and internet usage in global surveys. The Swedish Statistical Bureau stated that 93% of Swedish population aged 16-74 had internet access at home in 2011 [1, p. 247]. According to ITU data, internet penetration in Sweden is 92.9% (third place in the world after Iceland and Norway) and the literacy rate is 99% [2]. But the picture is different if we look at e-book production and use in Sweden. According to Bohlund [3] e-books accounted for only 1% of book production in Sweden in 2011, while Nordicom figures show that only 0.5% of Swedish readers use an e-book on an average day [4]. The provision of e-books in Sweden is dominated by one provider Elib, which has a monopoly position as a result of being established by a consortium of the country's four major publishers. The model that Elib offers to public libraries includes a firm sum for each loan of an e-book (20 SEK= approx. €2.4). This is an attractive model for less popular books, but is increasingly expensive for popular titles.

These figures and models relate to only one type of e-books published by commercial publishers and distributed in the market for profit. Economic copyright for these books is in force and is held by authors or publishers. Most of these e-books have printed equivalents. There are other types of e-books: digitised books or digital

T. Aalberg et al. (Eds.): TPDL 2013, LNCS 8092, pp. 29–34, 2013.
© Springer-Verlag Berlin Heidelberg 2013

copies of the texts free of copyright or those that are in copyright but distributed freely by authors or producers. This presentation deals only with the first category, i.e., commercially distributed e-books.

In 2011 the National Library of Sweden produced a report mapping the problems of e-books in Swedish library activities [5]. The report stated that there was no problem with the acquisition and provision of e-books in academic libraries.

The report provided proof of scarcity of the content in local languages in e-book format and the lack of a convenient business model [5, p. 21-23]. Despite this the latest statistics show that, in 2012, e-book loans from public libraries have increased 65% in comparison with 2011 and 289% in comparison with 2009. [6, p. 27].

A team from the SSLIS has conducted a census with all Swedish public libraries regarding their work with e-books and the problems arising from this novel activity.

The aims of this short paper are:

- To review the situation of the e-books' delivery to the users in the Swedish public libraries (as it looked at the end of 2012)
- To identify the barriers that public libraries encounter in providing access to e-books to their users
- To highlight the policy-related problems of the e-books provision through public libraries in Sweden.

2   Research Method

A survey was carried out in October, 2012 of all public libraries in Sweden. A total of 291 questionnaires was issued and 225 or 77.3% began to complete the questionnaire. 185 fully completed it, an effective response rate, after three follow-up messages, of 63.6%. The SurveyMonkey online survey service was used for the study. The percentages reported below are the percentage of people responding to a specific question.

The questionnaire was composed of 35 mainly closed questions, in Swedish, with some open questions or follow-up questions that allowed for open responses. The questions were grouped into 11 categories, as follows: Introduction, Policy for handling e-books, Access to e-books, License agreements with suppliers, Inclusion of e-books in the library catalogue, User training, How does e-book provision affect the relationship with the existing book suppliers, Assessment of user demand and satisfaction, The need for a library consortium for e-book purchases, Provision of e-books in Swedish, Future intentions (if e-books were not provided at present) .

3   The State of E-Book Service Provision in Swedish Public Libraries

3.1   The E-Book Service Presence and Marketing

Ninety-five per cent of libraries indicated that they offered an e-book service to their users; however, only 19 or 9.6% of those answering the question (i.e., 197) claimed to have a formally documented policy underpinning the e-book service. Seventy percent (14) of those who did have a policy declared that it was publicly available and nine respondents indicated a Website address as the location of the policy while one sent a document file to the investigators. In most cases, however, the *policy* was simply a statement of the availability of e-books and the rules governing their lending.

When asked what factors determined the decision to offer e-books, the responses commented on the demand from readers, the need to develop services appropriate in the 21st century, the fact that an e-book is simply another medium and should be offered just as print books are offered, and, importantly for some, the opportunity was offered to participate in county-wide collaborations in the provision of e-books. A number also commented that the service was a way of attracting new readers to the library. A typical response was:

The library will of course provide all kinds of media formats. Complement to the printed book, allowing more borrowers to read the book at the same time, no queues. Meet borrowers' requirements that we offer new technology, new media formats. Give borrowers the opportunity to test new ways of reading.

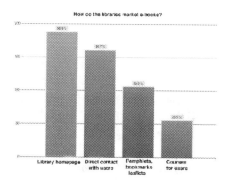

Fig. 1. Marketing means

As Fig. 1 shows, the most common way of marketing the service was through the library's Website (99%), followed by direct contact with the users and the issuing of brochures, bookmarks and other documentation. Courses on the use of e-books were offered by a substantial minority of libraries – 29%.

3.2   The Work with the Users of E-Book Services

Although Sweden is a highly computer-literate country, for many people the e-book is a novel phenomenon. Not surprisingly, therefore, almost half of the respondents reported offering user-education of some kind.

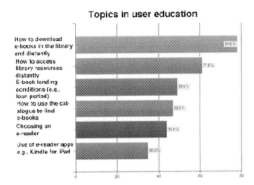

Fig. 2. User education: subjects

Most commonly, users were taught how to download the e-books when in the library, and remotely and how to use library resources in general at a distance. More than half of the libraries also gave instruction on how to use the catalogue to locate e-books, how to select an appropriate e-reader, and the conditions under which e-books could be borrowed. A smaller proportion (40%) gave instruction on the use of apps such as the Kindle app for the iPad.

Only three libraries reported having carried out any reader satisfaction study in relation to e-books and only one of these reported the results, which were that readers were highly satisfied with the service. Ninety-eight per cent of the libraries responding to the question (i.e., 179 out of 182) had carried out no survey, but 91.4% of respondents intended to do so.

3.3   The Barriers to Efficient E-Book Service

E-book provision in Swedish public libraries is done through agreements with the provider, Elib. This is no doubt an efficient means of provision from the point of view of the publishers, but it presents severe problems from the perspective of the librarians. They feel very strongly that this mode of provision does not enable them to perform their normal professional responsibilities for the selection of material for their readers: they can only accept what the consortium chooses to make available. Furthermore, popular titles may not be made available in e-book form until months after the initial release, if at all, and titles may be withdrawn from the catalogue without notice. The librarians made comments such as:

We cannot decide what we want to buy, what literature we want to promote and offer to borrowers. It feels awful to be dependent on the vendor.

The publishers keep certain books in quarantine and remove the titles willy-nilly. The title choice is very small for adults and virtually non-existent for children and young people.

The librarians also do not have bibliographical control over the catalogue, since the user is transferred from the library's Web page to the Elib site and all the bibliographical data is at that site. Sixty-eight percent of the respondents attempted to deal with this by entering details of the available e-books into their own catalogues, usually simply transferring the data made available by Elib, but, in some cases (only 17%), creating additional meta-data. We have here the emergence of a kind of hybrid digital library; one that is partly under the control of the library and partly under the control of the e-book provider.

Librarians have expressed the great dissatisfaction with the present pricing model for e-books. Almost 86% of respondents said that there was a need for a library consortium to be created to supply e-books. Sixty-nine per cent of respondents felt that the means for the supply of e-books in Swedish was less than satisfactory and when asked what should be done to improve things, said, in effect, that ways should be found to overcome the limitations of the current system. Suggestions included:

National agreement on different pricing model, state aid.

A wider range from the publishers' side, digitization of older titles, no waiting period for new titles...

Abolish the waiting period for new books in Swedish. Get an agreement that enables even translated titles to be offered.

More e-book providers would increase competition and hopefully improve the range. Another hope is that the smaller publishing companies could enter the market.

In particular, access to literature for young people is quite poor. Since children use iPads and computers one-to-one in the school, this is a problem.

4   Discussion and Conclusions

The provision of an e-book service in Sweden has arisen as a result of either user demand or an ideological belief that democratic values and equality of access requires libraries to offer material in all media. But this position has some disadvantages: first, there is a lack of formal policy for service provision. By this we mean that no goals or objectives of service provision are set and there is no evaluation process to determine whether the goals are being satisfied.

A barrier to cost efficient service delivery lies in the fact that an e-book is treated as a digital file and, consequently, the public lending right act in Sweden does not apply to e-books. This is one reason why Elib can charge the SEK 20 for each loan directly to the library. There is the additional issue that an e-book is not bought by the library, but is licensed for use. It seems that marketing and user education is not active because of this lending cost to libraries.

The results of the survey reveal that librarians find this situation unsatisfactory: they find the operations of Elib in the provision of titles to be arbitrary, with titles being removed from the catalogue without warning or explanation, with too few titles for children and students, and with delays in access to popular titles. The establishment of a monopoly of this kind is believed to inhibit the entry of small publishers into the e-book market.

The latest statistics of library use in Sweden show a significant decline in loans of printed books, newspapers and journals, including the loans of children's books in public libraries. The increase in the loans of e-books does not compensate for this decrease [6, p. 27]. One of the reasons for this decrease may be this lack of suitable e-content in public libraries.

This is a considerable issue that has to be taken into account by the Parliament in adopting the library law with legal provisions for better access to media. The present proposal states that public libraries should ensure access free of charge to all literature regardless of publication form, but there is nothing that could change the conditions of e-book acquisition for public libraries [7]. The opposition and library community has already suggested changes to the Government proposal suggesting that the law should clearly state library responsibility to provide access without payment to all media, not only "literature". The demand is expressed for a clear national library strategy that will help to make access to library services equal for everyone. The proposals should be debated in early autumn by the Swedish Parliament.

Given the trends, discussed earlier, it seems highly improbable that the present situation in Sweden will persist. More libraries will be able to buy e-books directly from publishers from abroad and the pressure on Swedish publishers to adapt to this situation will be irrepressible. The leading role and initiatives of the National Library of Sweden will become more significant. The government's policies are likely to take more notice of the concerns of librarians and educational institutions in the light of the recent statistics reported above.

Acknowledgments. Our thanks go to all the librarians who participated in the survey. The study was carried out with the support of the Swedish Library Association. We also acknowledge the support of Swedish Research Council.

References

1. CSB: Privatpersoners Användning av Datorer och Internet (Usage of computers and internet by private persons). Stockholm (2012),
   http://www.scb.se/statistik/_publikationer/
   LE0108_2011A02_BR_IT01BR1201.pdf (retrieved May 26, 2013)
2. Internet World Stats: Top 50 Countries with the Highest Internet Penetration Rate (2011),
   http://www.internetworldstats.com/top25.htm (retrieved May 28, 2013)
3. Bohlund K. Faktabanken, http://forlaggare.se/faktabank (retrieved May 26, 2013)
4. Facht U. Aktuell Statistik om E-böcker, http://www.nordicom.gu.se/common/stat_xls/2189_3090_E-bokstatistik_antologi_2012.pdf (retrieved May 28, 2013)
5. Kungliga Biblioteket: När Kommer Boomen? En Kartläggning av E-boken i Sverige ur ett Biblioteksperspektiv. (When will the boom happen? A survey of the e-book in Sweden from a library perspective.) Svensk Biblioteksföreningen, Stockholm (2011)
6. National Library of Sweden. Bibliotek 2012. Kungliga biblioteket, Stockholm (2013)
7. Regeringens proposition 2012/13:147. Ny bibliotekslag,
   http://www.riksdagen.se/sv/Dokument-Lagar/Forslag/
   Propositioner-och-skrivelser/Ny-bibliotekslag_H003147/
   ?html=true (retrieved May 29, 2013)

On the Change in Archivability
of Websites Over Time

Mat Kelly, Justin F. Brunelle, Michele C. Weigle, and Michael L. Nelson

Old Dominion University, Department of Computer Science
Norfolk VA, 23529, USA
{mkelly,jbrunelle,mweigle,mln}@cs.odu.edu

Abstract. As web technologies evolve, web archivists work to keep up
so that our digital history is preserved. Recent advances in web technologies have introduced client-side executed scripts that load data without
a referential identifier or that require user interaction (e.g., content loading when the page has scrolled). These advances have made automating
methods for capturing web pages more difficult. Because of the evolving
schemes of publishing web pages along with the progressive capability of
web preservation tools, the *archivability* of pages on the web has varied
over time. In this paper we show that the archivability of a web page
can be deduced from the type of page being archived, which aligns with
that page's accessibility in respect to dynamic content. We show concrete
examples of when these technologies were introduced by referencing mementos of pages that have persisted through a long evolution of available
technologies. Identifying these reasons for the inability of these web pages
to be archived in the past in respect to accessibility serves as a guide for
ensuring that content that has longevity is published using good practice
methods that make it available for preservation.

Keywords: Web Archiving, Digital Preservation.

1 Introduction

The web has gone through a gradient yet demarcated series of phases in which
interactivity has become more fluid to the end-user. Early websites were static.
Adoption of JavaScript allowed the components on a web page to respond to
users' actions or be manipulated in ways that made the page more usable. Ajax
[9] combines multiple web technologies to give web pages the ability to perform
operations asynchronously. The adoption of Ajax by web developers facilitated
the fluidity of user interaction on the web. Through each phase in the progression
of the web, the ability to preserve the content displayed to the user has also
progressed but in a less linear trend.

A large amount of the difficulty in web archiving stems from the crawler's
insufficient ability to capture content related to JavaScript. Because JavaScript
is executed on the client side (i.e., within the browser after the page has loaded),
it should follow that the archivability could be evaluated using a consistent replay medium. The medium used to archive (normally a web crawler tailored

T. Aalberg et al. (Eds.): TPDL 2013, LNCS 8092, pp. 35–47, 2013.
© Springer-Verlag Berlin Heidelberg 2013

for archiving, e.g., Heritrix [21]) is frequently different from the medium used to replay the archive (henceforth, the *web browser*, the predominant means of replay). The crawler creates the web archive, which is processed by a replay system (e.g., Internet Archive's Wayback Machine [26]), which is then accessed by an end-user through the web browser medium (e.g., the user accesses Wayback's web interface). This inconsistency between the perspective used to capture the pages versus the perspective used to view the stored content [11] introduces difficulty in evaluating the web resources' potential to be archived (henceforth the *archivability*). Further discrepancies in the capabilities of the crawler versus the web browser make archivability difficult to measure without manual inspection.

The success of preservation of a web page is defined by how much of the originally displayed content is displayed on replay. The success of a consistent replay experience when the original experience contained a large amount of potential user interactivity (and more importantly, the loading of external resources not initially loaded) might not rely on the level of interactivity able to be re-experienced at replay. The success of this experience is dependent on whether all of the resources needed to properly display the web page on replay were captured at the time of archiving and are loaded when the archive is replayed.

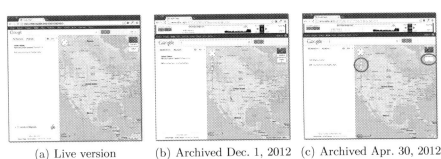

(a) Live version   (b) Archived Dec. 1, 2012   (c) Archived Apr. 30, 2012

Fig. 1. Google Maps is a typical example where the lack of completeness of the archive is easy to observe. Figure 1(a) shows how the web page should look. The map in the middle has interactive UI elements. An archived version of this page (Figure 1(c)) is missing UI elements (circled), and the interaction does not function. Figure 1(b) shows a recently archived (December 1, 2012) version that gives the façade of functionality when, in fact, resources on the live web are being loaded.

The nature of the execution of the archiving procedure is often to blame for not capturing resources loaded at runtime that not only manipulate the Document Object Model (DOM) but also load subsequent representations of resources. These subsequently loaded representations are often captured [21] if their location is able to be extracted from the static code by a crawler, but a problem occurs when their loading is latent or triggered by user interaction. An example of this can be seen in the Internet Archive's capture of Google Maps[1] (Figure 1). When this archive is replayed, everything that was presented to the

---

[1] http://maps.google.com

user (i.e., the crawler) at time of archiving is displayed. None of the trademark panning or user interface (UI) elements function in a manner similar to the live version (Figure 1(a)) of the same page. The resources, however, appear to be correctly loaded (Figure 1(c)), though the asynchronous JavaScript calls are never fired because of the broken UI elements. Versions of a page recently archived (Figure 1(b)) appear to have all resources required for interactivity, and the page performs as expected, but upon inspection of the URIs, all reference the live web and not the resources at the archive.

Contrasting the completeness of the archive of an interactive website with one from a simpler website that does not contain interactive elements or the loading of external resources via JavaScript further exemplifies that this trait is to blame for archive incompleteness. For example, a page containing only HTML, images, and CSS is likely to be completely represented in the archive when preserved with an archival tool like Heritrix. In this paper we will show that the archivability of a website, given the state of the art of archiving tools, has changed over time with the increased usage of resource-loading JavaScript and the increased accessibility of websites. Further, we will examine the incapability of crawlers and archiving tools in capturing this content and what can be done to remedy their shortcomings and increase the archivability of problematic web pages.

2   Related Work

Many components contribute to the archivability of a web page ranging from reliability of the mechanism used to archive to the frequency at which the mechanism is run. Ainsworth et al. utilized web directories like DMOZ, Delicious, Bitly and search engine results to determine how much of the web is archived [2]. McCown et al., in earlier work, developed strategies for resurrecting web pages from the archives but mainly considered those with static resources (including JavaScript) [16]. McCown also touched on the sources used to recreate lost websites (of particular interest, using Internet Archive's) and the long tail effect on the unlikelihood of domain specific sites to be able to be resurrected using the larger archives as a source [17]. Mohr set the basis for the Internet Archive's Heritrix, while introducing incremental crawling into the tool's repertoire of capability [25].

As JavaScript has been the source of many problems in archiving, particularly since the web has become more dynamic, it is useful to note prior attempts relating to JavaScript and archivability. Likarish [14] developed a means of detecting JavaScript with certain facets (namely malicious code via deobfuscation) using Machine Learning techniques and Heritrix. Livshits et al. took on some of the complexities of JavaScript, including attributes only available at runtime and thus normally limited to be experience by the client [13,15,20,28]. Bergman described the quantity of resources we are unable to index (the "deep Web") [5], which has significantly increased with the advent of resources being loaded only at runtime. Ast proposed approaches to capture Ajax content using a conventional web crawler (i.e., one not used for preservation) [3].

3   Why JavaScript Makes It Difficult

A user or script normally browses the web using a user agent. In the case of a user, this is normally a web browser. Initially, web browsers were inconsistent in implementation. This inconsistency eventually was the impetus for creating web standards to remedy the guesswork developers had to do to ensure that the display was as desired. The layout engine is the component of a web browser that is responsible for rendering HTML, the structural portion of a web page. Along with the structure, there is also a stylistic portion (implemented via CSS) and a behavioral portion (implemented in JavaScript) on the client-side.

As the layout engines of modern browsers evolved, the JavaScript rendering engine lagged behind, causing the behavioral functionality of web pages to perform inconsistently among users. This was particularly noticeable when Ajax-based websites became common. To simplify the process of obtaining the data quickly and without worry about behavior, many crawlers and scrapers do not include a JavaScript rendering engine, opting to only grab the HTML and any embedded resources and rely on the user's layout engine to render the fetched data at a later date. This is problematic in that some resources' location on the web might be built at runtime or included in the page because of Java-Script DOM manipulation. In the case of a crawler, this might be negligible, as the resource will still be hot-linked and thus included when the web page is "replayed". For crawlers intended for preservation, however, the archive must be self-contained and thus, for a complete archive, these resources must be captured and their locations rewritten to be accessible at time of replay.

Early versions of Heritrix had limited support for JavaScript. The crawler's parsing engine attempted to detect URIs in scripts, fetch the scripts and recursively repeat this process with the intention of ensuring maximum coverage of the archive creation process. Recently, Heritrix was rewritten to be built on top of PhantomJS[2], a headless WebKit (the layout engine used by Google Chrome, Apple Safari, etc.) with JavaScript support, which greatly increases the potential for accurate JavaScript processing and the likelihood that all resources required to replay a web page are captured by a crawler.

4   Archivability of Sites in Respect to Type

We stated in our recent work that web pages of links shared over Twitter were less archivable than those selected to be preserved by the collection-based Archive-It service [6]. Interestingly, many of the websites on Archive-It are governmental. Many of those on Twitter are commercially-based. Unlike commercial websites, governmental websites are mandated to conform to web accessibility standards for content. From this, it can be extrapolated that the more accessible a website is, the more archivable it is. Further, certain features of JavaScript (e.g., the reliance of it being enabled to show content) may make a page generally less accessible.

---

[2] http://phantomjs.org/

The markup (HTML) of a web page is rarely a hindrance to a website being captured. The difference in interpretation of markup among various users, for instance, does not make the code more or less accessible. Semantic markup, as encouraged by Section 508, WAI specifications, and other organizations that advocate accessible web development practices does affect how end-users see the content. Even if the content displayed is hidden from view, it is still likely present and thus preserved, making variance in markup replay a moot point.

In contrast to markup, behavior (usually JavaScript) can contend what content resides in the markup. If certain behaviors are not invoked, certain content may never make it to the markup, thus compromising the degree at which the content that should be archived is archived.

5   Experimental Setup

We used the Memento Framework [27] to query mementos with a reliable date-time association. Using a URI convention and the HTTP Accept-Datetime header, archives can be queried for the approximate time desired and the closest result will be returned.

5.1   Gauging Accessibility

While Section 508 gives suggestions on how websites should comply to be considered accessible, other organizations (namely the World Wide Web Consortium (W3C) through the Web Content Accessibility Guidelines (WCAG)) give concrete ways for developers to evaluate their creations to make them more accessible [7]. Hackett et al. go in-depth on the accessibility of archives on a pre-Ajax corpus (from 2002) and enumerate very specific features that make a page accessible in the legal sense. Much of this information is beyond the scope of this study. Other efforts were made following the document's release on a metric to evaluate web accessibility [22], but also fail to consider an asynchronous web.

As stated in Section 4, the markup of a web page is not problematic for crawlers to capture. To understand the role that JavaScript plays in hindering comprehensive web archiving by crawlers, it is useful to examine the WCAG Principles of Accessibility [7] and remark on where issues would occur for a crawler. JavaScript, specifically, affects a page's accessibility by hiding information from view (perceivability), only working if all components of the script are present (operability), and frequently playing a critical role in a page being useable (robustness).

5.2   Fetching Data

The initial experiment was to test the archivability of web sites whose presence in the archive has persisted over a long period of time. These can be described as the "stubby head" juxtaposed to McCown's "long tail" of sites that are preserved.

```
 1: function GetMemsWithYearInterval(mementoURIs)
 2:     M ← mementoURIs[1]                                          ▷ Get First Memento
 3:     lastDate ← extractDate(M)
 4:     lastDateTest ← lastDate
 5:     for m = 2 → length(mementoURIs) do
 6:         testingDate ← extractDate(mementoURIs[m])
 7:         testingDate = extractDate(mementoURIs[m])
 8:         if lastDate + oneYear ≤ testingDate then
 9:             if |lastDate − testingDate + oneYear| ≥
10:                 |lastDateTested − lastDate + oneYear|  then
11:                 lastDate ← mementoURIs[m − 1]
12:             else
13:                 lastDate ← mementoURIs[m]
14:             end if
15:             push(M,mementoURIs[m])
16:         else
17:             lastDateTested ← testingDate
18:         end if
19:     end for
20:     return M
21: end function
```

Fig. 2. Pseudocode to get mementos from a timegate at a temporal distance of one year per memento or as close as possible with the first memento as the pivot

Alexa[3] has gathered the traffic of many of these sites and ranked them in descending order. This ranking currently exists as Alexa's Top 500 Global Sites[4]. We first attempted an approach at gathering data by querying the archives (namely, Internet Archive's Wayback) for past Top lists[5] but found that the location of this list was inconsistent to the present one and some of the sites in past top 10 lists remained present in the current list. We used a simple scraping scheme to grab the paginated list but that turned up pornographic sites by the third page on the 2012 list so we kept it to the top few sites to remain representative, unbiased, and to reduce the likelihood of including sites without longevity.

For each of these web sites, the TimeMap was acquired from Internet Archive using the URI convention "`http://api.wayback.archive.org/list/timemap/link/URI`" (where *URI* is the Fully Qualified Domain Name of the target site) to produce output like Figure 3. From this TimeMap we chose mementos with a one year spread.

The URI of each memento was passed to a PhantomJS script, and the HTTP codes of each resource as well as a snapshot were taken. A memento[6] for `google.com` with the Memento-Datetime 20110731003335, for example, produces a line break delimited list of the subsequent HTTP codes and respective URIs dereferenced to assemble the page. Here, we noticed that subsequent requests for the resources yielded resources from the live web. We tailored the PhantomJS script to rewrite the URIs to hit the Wayback Machine instead[7]. This produces an identical display (part of the Wayback UI was programatically hidden) but with resource requests that access archived content. The last step was repeated but with PhantomJS sent the directive to capture the page with JavaScript off.

---

[3] `http://www.alexa.com`

[4] `http://www.alexa.com/topsites`

[5] `http://web.archive.org/web/20090315000000*/http://www.alexa.com/topsites`

[6] `http://api.wayback.archive.org/memento/20110731003335/http://google.com`

[7] e.g., `http://web.archive.org/web/20110731003335/http://google.com`

```
<http://api.wayback.archive.org/list/timebundle/http://cnn.com>; rel="
    timebundle",
<http://cnn.com>; rel="original",
<http://api.wayback.archive.org/list/timemap/link/http://cnn.com>; rel="
    timemap"; type="application/link-format",
<http://api.wayback.archive.org/list/timegate/http://cnn.com>; rel="timegate
    ",
<http://api.wayback.archive.org/memento/20000620180259/http://cnn.com/>; rel
    ="first memento"; datetime="Tue, 20 Jun 2000 18:02:59 GMT",
<http://api.wayback.archive.org/memento/20000621011731/http://cnn.com/>; rel
    ="memento"; datetime="Wed, 21 Jun 2000 01:17:31 GMT",
<http://api.wayback.archive.org/memento/20000621140928/http://cnn.com/>; rel
    ="memento"; datetime="Wed, 21 Jun 2000 14:09:28 GMT",
...
<http://api.wayback.archive.org/memento/20061227222050/http://www.cnn.com>;
    rel="memento"; datetime="Wed, 27 Dec 2006 22:20:50 GMT",
<http://api.wayback.archive.org/memento/20061227222134/http://www.cnn.com/>;
    rel="memento"; datetime="Wed, 27 Dec 2006 22:21:34 GMT",
<http://api.wayback.archive.org/memento/20061228024612/http://www.cnn.com/>;
    rel="memento"; datetime="Thu, 28 Dec 2006 02:46:12 GMT",
...
<http://api.wayback.archive.org/memento/20121209174923/http://www.cnn.com/>;
    rel="memento"; datetime="Sun, 09 Dec 2012 17:49:23 GMT",
<http://api.wayback.archive.org/memento/20121209174944/http://www.cnn.com/>;
    rel="memento"; datetime="Sun, 09 Dec 2012 17:49:44 GMT",
<http://api.wayback.archive.org/memento/20121209201112/http://www.cnn.com/>;
    rel="last memento"; datetime="Sun, 09 Dec 2012 20:11:12 GMT"
```

Fig. 3. A sample abbreviated (for space) TimeMap for cnn.com

From the top 10 websites on Alexa for 2012, some websites had a robots.txt restriction. The number of mementos obtained by using the code in Figure 2 and applying the URI transformation produces the following quantity of mementos, ordered corresponding to Alexa's 2012 ranking (Table 1).

Table 1. Alexa's 2012 Top 10 websites and available mementos

Alexa Rank	Web Site Name	Available Mementos
1	Facebook.com	no mementos robots.txt exclusion
2	Google.com	15 mementos 1998 to 2012
3	YouTube.com	7 mementos 2006 to 2012
4	Yahoo.com	16 mementos 1997 to 2012
5	Baidu.com	no mementos robots.txt exclusion
6	Wikipedia.org	12 mementos 2001 to 2012
7	Live.com	15 mementos 1999 to 2012
8	Amazon.com	14 mementos 1999 to 2012
9	QQ.com	15 mementos 1998 to 2012
10	Twitter.com	no mementos robots.txt exclusion

That the content of some of these websites is not preserved (namely Facebook and Twitter) by institutions has been addressed by multiple parties [1, 4, 12, 18, 19]. All of these websites may not exhibit traits of un-archivability, as previously imagined. The root domain, in this case, may not be representative of the extent at which a web site (contrasted to web page) utilized un-archivable practices. One particular site that has succumbed to the effects of unarchivability due partially to both its longevity and publishing medium is YouTube. Crook [8] went

(a)   (b)

Fig. 4. A YouTube memento from 2006 shows a subtle distinction in display when JavaScript is enabled (Figure 4(a)) and disabled (Figure 4(b)) at the time of capture. The Ajax spinner (above each "loading" message in Figure 4(b)) is never replaced with content, which would be done were JavaScript enabled on capture. When it was enabled, the script that gathers the resources to display (blank squares in the same section of the site in Figure 4(a)) is unable to fetch the resources it needs in the context of the archive. The URIs of each of these resources (the image source) is present as an attribute of the DOM element but because it is generated post load, the crawler never fetches the resource for preservation.

into detail about the issues in preserving multimedia resources on the web, and Prellwitz documented how quickly this multimedia degrades [23], so highlighting this website for analysis would be useful in remedying one of the many reasons that it is not sufficiently preserved.

Using the procedure described earlier in this section, we captured screen shots and HTTP requests for one memento per year of YouTube.com. While there have been efforts in attempting to capture the multimedia on this site in a reliable way (e.g., TubeKit [24]), our concern is less about executing a focused crawl and more on analyzing the results of what has been done in the past. The simpler case here of lack of archivability is observable from the homepage. In each of the cases of capturing a screen shot (Figure 4) of the memento with and without JavaScript, there is variance on the "Recently Viewed" section of the website. This part of the website is Ajax-driven, i.e., after the page has loaded, the content is fetched. A crawler could retain the JavaScript that fetches the resources and attempt to grab a copy of the resources contained within and loaded at runtime but this particular script takes a moment post-load to load and display the images that represent links to videos. This is better explained by Figure 4(a), which is representative of the memento with JavaScript enabled. The content necessary to display this section was preserved due to its reliance on runtime execution. Figure 4(b) shows the same memento fetched with JavaScript off. The place-holder Ajax "spinner" demonstrates that the JavaScript to overwrite the DOM elements is present in the archive and executable but the resources needed to fully build this web page do not exist in the archive.

Contrast this to five years later (2011) when a redesign of YouTube that is heavily reliant on Ajax fails. When loading this memento[8] into Wayback via a web browser, the JavaScript errors in Figure 5(b) appear in the console. This memento (Figure 5(a)) exhibits leakage [10].

---

[8] http://api.wayback.archive.org/memento/20110420002216/http://youtube.com

The lack of aesthetic of the 2011 YouTube memento is a result of the CSS files (first line of Figure 5(b)) returning an HTTP 302 with the final URI resulting in a 404, as evidence in the log file that accompanies the Figure 5(a) screenshot during the annual memento collection process. By examining the JavaScript log, we noted that a causal chain prevented subsequent resources from being fetched. JavaScript is fairly resilient to runtime errors and oftentimes will continue executing so long as a resource dependency is not hit[9]. The progressive increase of Ajax on YouTube over time has caused a longer chain of failures than the 2006 example. Testing this same procedure on a website that persisted from before Ajax existed until today yet chose to rely on it at one time would test whether its inclusion greatly reduced the archivability.

(a)

```
GET http://web.archive.org/web/20121208145112cs_/http://s.ytimg.com/yt/cssbin
    /www-core-vfl_OJqFG.css 404 (Not Found) www.youtube.com:15
GET http://web.archive.org/web/20121208145115js_/http://s.ytimg.com/yt/jsbin/
    www-core-vfl8PDcRe.js 404 (Not Found) www.youtube.com:45
Uncaught TypeError: Object #<Object> has no method 'setConfig' www.youtube.
    com:56
Uncaught TypeError: Cannot read property 'home' of undefined www.youtube.com
    :76
Uncaught TypeError: Cannot read property 'ajax' of undefined www.youtube.com
    :86
Uncaught TypeError: Object #<Object> has no method 'setConfig' www.youtube.
    com:101
Uncaught ReferenceError: _gel is not defined www.youtube.com:1784
Uncaught TypeError: Object #<Object> has no method 'setConfig' www.youtube.
    com:1929
Uncaught TypeError: Cannot read property 'home' of undefined www.youtube.com
    :524
GET http://web.archive.org/web/20130101024721im_/http://i2.ytimg.com/vi/1
    f7neSzDqvc/default.jpg 404 (Not Found)
```

(b)

Fig. 5. The 2011 capture of this YouTube.com memento demonstrates the causal chain that occurs when a resource is not captured

6   A Reinforcing Case

A second example where the change in archivability over time is much more dramatic can be found in the NASA website[10]. As a government funded agency,

---

[9] This is by design of the interpreted language but appears to go against the fast-fail software philosophy.

[10] http://www.nasa.gov

```
<script language="javascript" type="text/javascript" src="flash.js"></script>
<script language="javascript" type="text/javascript">
function flashURL(id) {
  //Flash Redirect URL
  window.location.href = 'index.html';
}
</script>
```

(a)

```
var fstr = '';
if(hasFlash(6)) {
        fstr+='<object id="screenreader.swf">...</object>';
        window.status = 'Flash 6 Detected...';
} else {
        fstr+='...To view the enhanced version of NASA.gov, you must have
            Flash 6 installed....';
}
with(document) { open('text/html'); write(fstr); close(); }
```

(b)

Fig. 6. In 2003, `nasa.gov` introduced code (abbreviated here) into their website that checked the capability of the user's web browser and showed or hid content. The link to enter the website regardless of the user's browser capability, here, is generated with JavaScript. This would cause the content to not be displayed were the user's browser incapable or if client-side scripting were disabled in the user's browser preferences.

is advised to comply with the aforementioned accessibility standards. The same procedure (Section 5) of creating a collection of annual mementos was used to obtain screenshots (Figure 8), HTTP logs, and the HTML of the memento. Mementos ranging from 1996-2006 were available and retained, a sampling that sufficiently spanned the introduction of dynamism into the web.

The mementos from 1996 through 2002 show table-based websites devoid of JavaScript. In 2003, JavaScript was introduced into the markup (Figure 6(a)). Checkpoint 6.3[11] of the Web Content Accessibility Guidelines [7] mandates that pages remain usable when programmatic objects are present on the page but not necessarily supported by the user. This is to ensure all content on a page is accessible. Lack of accessibility directly correlates with unarchivability. Normally, providing an alternate means of viewing the page's content would suffice were the link to "Enter NASA" regardless of the incompatibility, but even the single relevant link on the page (with the other being a link to install Flash) is generated by a script (Figure 6(b)). From the 2004 to 2006 snapshots on, in lieu of testing for Flash, the ability to progress into the site is no longer offered but rather a message stating that JavaScript is required and a means to access instructions to enable it is the sole content supplied to the crawler. Observing the count of the resources required to construct a memento (Figure 7(a)) gives further evidence that both accessibility and archivability suffered between 2004 and 2006.

Relying solely on the number of resources fetched to determine where a site's reliance on unarchivable technologies lies is not foolproof, but it is a good guide to identify problematic pages. Were a crawler to encounter this drastic change and if the changed count was sustained, this should be noted as evidence of

---

[11] http://www.w3.org/TR/WCAG10/wai-pageauth.html#tech-scripts

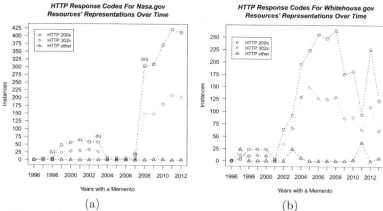

(a)   (b)

Fig. 7. The number of resources required to construct the page (Figure 7(a)) has a noticeably absent lull that corresponds to Figure 8. The preservation of the White House web page (Figure 7(b)) exhibits a different problem yet is briefly similar in that the count drastically changed. The sudden change in 2011 is the result of a set of CSS files not reaching the crawler horizon, which may have had implications on subsequent resource representations (embedded within the CSS) from being preserved.

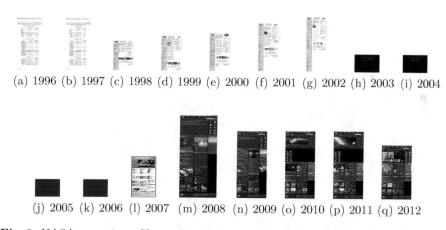

(a) 1996 (b) 1997 (c) 1998 (d) 1999 (e) 2000 (f) 2001 (g) 2002 (h) 2003 (i) 2004

(j) 2005 (k) 2006 (l) 2007 (m) 2008 (n) 2009 (o) 2010 (p) 2011 (q) 2012

Fig. 8. NASA over time. Changes in design and thus the technologies used is easily observable between Figures 8(b) and 8(c), 8(g) and 8(h), 8(k) and 8(k), and 8(l) and 8(m)

potential problems. On a comparable note, the same procedure was run on another government website where this deviation from web standards would be the least likely to surface, whitehouse.gov. A similar dip can be seen in Figure 7(b) in 2010. Examining the screen shot and log of HTTP codes, it is evident that a subset of CSS files were not preserved by the crawler. A preserved web page resembling this problem is not one necessarily related to the crawler's inability to fetch components of a page embedded in JavaScript but rather, the URI was not persistent enough to endure the time to reach Heritrix's horizon (the point at which it is preserved) once placed on the frontier (list of URIs to be preserved).

7   Conclusions

The archivability of websites has changed over time in different ways for different classes of websites. While JavaScript is partially to blame for this, it is more a problem that content is not accessible. Lack of accessibility makes content more difficult for crawlers to capture. Websites that are trend leaders, unfortunately, set a bad precedent for facilitating archivability. As this trend continues, tools are being created (Heritrix 3) that are archiving inaccessible websites. Recognizing techniques to make the archiving process easier by those that want their content preserved is a first step in guiding web development practices into producing web sites that are easier to preserve.

References

1. Twitter Donates Entire Tweet Archive to Library of Congress (2010), http://www.loc.gov/today/pr/2010/10-081.html
2. Ainsworth, S.G., Alsum, A., SalahEldeen, H., Weigle, M.C., Nelson, M.L.: How Much of the Web is Archived. In: Proceeding of the 11th Annual International ACM/IEEE Joint Conference on Digital Libraries (JCDL), JCDL 2011, pp. 133–136. ACM, New York (2011)
3. Ast, P., Kapfenberger, M., Hauswiesner, S.: Crawler Approaches And Technology. Graz University of Technology, Styria, Austria (2008), http://www.iicm.tugraz.at/cguetl/courses/isr/uearchive/uews2008/Ue01%20-%20Crawler-Approaches-And-Technology.pdf.
4. Bass, J.: Getting Personal: Confronting the Challenges of Archiving Personal Records in the Digital Age. Master's thesis, University of Winnipeg (2012)
5. Bergman, M.: White Paper: the Deep Web: Surfacing Hidden Value. Journal of Electronic Publishing 7(1) (2001)
6. Brunelle, J.F., Kelly, M., Weigle, M.C., Nelson, M.L.: Losing the Moment: The Unarchivability of Shared Links (submitted for publication)
7. Chisholm, W., Vanderheiden, G., Jacobs, I.: Web Content Accessibility Guidelines 1.0. Interactions 8(4), 35–54 (2001)
8. Crook, E.: Web Archiving in a Web 2.0 World. The Electronic Library 27(5), 831–836 (2009)
9. Garrett, J.: Ajax: A New Approach to Web Applications (2005), http://www.adaptivepath.com/ideas/ajax-new-approach-web-applications
10. Brunelle, J.F.: Zombies in the Archives (2012), http://ws-dl.blogspot.com/2012/10/2012-10-10-zombies-in-archives.html
11. Kelly, M.: An Extensible Framework For Creating Personal Archives Of Web Resources Requiring Authentication. Master's thesis, Old Dominion University (2012)
12. Kelly, M., Weigle, M.C.: WARCreate - Create Wayback-Consumable WARC Files from Any Webpage. In: Proceedings of the 12th Annual International ACM/IEEE Joint Conference on Digital Libraries (JCDL), Washington, DC, pp. 437–438 (June 2012)

13. Kıcıman, E., Livshits, B.: AjaxScope: A Platform for Remotely Monitoring the Client-Side Behavior of Web 2.0 Applications. In: Proceedings of Symposium on Operating Systems Principles (2007)
14. Likarish, P., Jung, E.: A Targeted Web Crawling for Building Malicious Javascript Collection. In: Proceedings of the ACM First International Workshop on Data-Intensive Software Management and Mining, DSMM 2009, pp. 23–26. ACM, New York (2009)
15. Livshits, B., Guarnieri, S.: Gulfstream: Incremental Static Analysis for Streaming JavaScript Applications. Technical Report MSR-TR-2010-4, Microsoft (January 2010)
16. McCown, F., Diawara, N., Nelson, M.L.: Factors Affecting Website Reconstruction from the Web Infrastructure. In: Proceedings of the 7th Annual International ACM/IEEE Joint Conference on Digital Libraries (JCDL), pp. 39–48 (2007)
17. McCown, F., Marshall, C.C., Nelson, M.L.: Why Websites Are Lost (and How They're Sometimes Found). Communications of the ACM 52(11), 141–145 (2009)
18. McCown, F., Nelson, M.L.: What Happens When Facebook is Gone. In: Proceedings of the 9th Annual International ACM/IEEE Joint Conference on Digital Libraries (JCDL), pp. 251–254. ACM, New York (2009)
19. Meyer, E.: Researcher Engagement with Web Archives-Challenges and Opportunities. Technical report, University of Oxford (2010)
20. Meyerovich, L., Livshits, B.: Conscript: Specifying and Enforcing Fine-Grained Security Policies for Javascript in the Browser. In: 2010 IEEE Symposium on Security and Privacy (SP), pp. 481–496. IEEE (2010)
21. Mohr, G., Kimpton, M., Stack, M., Ranitovic, I.: Introduction to Heritrix, an Archival Quality Web Crawler. In: Proceedings of the 4th International Web Archiving Workshop (IWAW 2004) (September 2004)
22. Parmanto, B., Zeng, X.: Metric for Web Accessibility Evaluation. Journal of the American Society for Information Science and Technology 56(13), 1394–1404 (2005)
23. Prellwitz, M., Nelson, M.L.: Music Video Redundancy and Half-Life in YouTube. In: Gradmann, S., Borri, F., Meghini, C., Schuldt, H. (eds.) TPDL 2011. LNCS, vol. 6966, pp. 143–150. Springer, Heidelberg (2011)
24. Shah, C.: Tubekit: a Query-based YouTube Crawling Toolkit. In: Proceedings of the 8th Annual International ACM/IEEE Joint Conference on Digital Libraries (JCDL), p. 433. ACM (2008)
25. Sigurðsson, K.: Incremental Crawling with Heritrix. In: Proceedings of the 5th International Web Archiving Workshop, IWAW 2005 (2005)
26. Tofel, B.: 'Wayback' for Accessing Web Archives. In: Proceedings of the 7th International Web Archiving Workshop, IWAW 2007 (2007)
27. Van de Sompel, H., Nelson, M.L., Sanderson, R., Balakireva, L.L., Ainsworth, S., Shankar, H.: Memento: Time Travel for the Web. Technical Report arXiv:0911.1112 (2009)
28. Vikram, K., Prateek, A., Livshits, B.: Ripley: Automatically Securing Web 2.0 Applications Through Replicated Execution. In: Proceedings of the 16th ACM Conference on Computer and Communications Security, pp. 173–186. ACM (2009)

Checking Out: Download and Digital Library Exchange for Complex Objects

Scott Britell[1], Lois M.L. Delcambre[1], Lillian N. Cassel[2], and Richard Furuta[3]

[1] Dept. of Computer Science, Portland State University, Portland, OR
{britell,lmd}@cs.pdx.edu
[2] Dept. of Computing Sciences, Villanova University, Villanova, PA
lillian.cassel@villanova.edu
[3] Dept. of Computer Science and Engineering, Texas A&M University,
College Station, TX
furuta@cse.tamu.edu

Abstract. Digital resources are becoming increasingly complex and are being used in diverse ways. For example, educational resources may be cataloged in digital libraries, used offline by educators and students, or used in a learning management system. In this paper we present the notion of "checking out" complex resources from a digital library for offline download or exchange with another digital library or learning management system. We present a mechanism that enables the customization, download and exchange of complex resources. We show how the mechanism also supports digital library and learning management system exchange formats in a generic fashion with minimal overhead. We also show how checkouts grow linearly with respect to the complexity of the resources.

1 Introduction

A common claim among designers and implementers of digital libraries is that a particular system or library will facilitate reuse of resources. But the complexity of the resources is often quite limited. While many systems support structured resources similar to their analog counterparts—books with chapters and pages or journals with volumes and articles—more complex structure is often not supported. But in some domains, such as education, resources can have rich and varied structure. A large number of educational digital libraries host educational resources but the complexity of structure in these libraries is often limited.

These complex objects often share components in ways unlike traditional digital library (DL) resources. An instructional item may be used in several curricula in different ways. For example, a video explaining the solar system may be used as advanced material for younger students and as introductory material for older students; the video may be given to students to watch on their own and learn in a self-directed manner or used as discussion material by a teacher in a class. Also, when one teacher uses another's course materials, they often choose a subset of the materials and may reorder them to suit their situation.

T. Aalberg et al. (Eds.): TPDL 2013, LNCS 8092, pp. 48–59, 2013.

Another issue is that no single application is suitable to support every use of a digital resource. Increasingly schools are using learning management systems (LMS) to store student grades and assignments as well as instructional materials for courses. But LMSs are often limited in their ability to share content between different instances of a single course, much less between different courses and even less so between courses in different schools. Teachers are also using content management systems (CMS) such as Wordpress[1] and Drupal[2] to host their curricula online. CMSs allow users to create complex resources tailored to their particular content. Yet, a complex resource may not be sharable outside a given CMS other than by using the URL of a given webpage. Lastly, resources are often needed offline when school districts limit students' Internet access.

In this paper we present a mechanism that enables the customization, download and exchange of complex resources from an educational digital repository built using the Drupal CMS. By using canonical structures—a system for complex heterogeneous structure integration—users can easily select and reconfigure content and then export it to a number of different formats including SCORM [4] (for use in an LMS), the DSpace [11] Simple Archive Format, the educational repository EdRepo[3], and a download format that can be used offline behind school firewalls or online as a simple website. We also show how the size of the representation of the complex objects in each of these formats scales linearly in the number of resources in an object regardless of complexity.

2 Related Work

A number of digital libraries host educational materials, for example DLESE[4], MERLOT[5], and NSDL[6], and provide features such as curation and commenting. Many of these libraries support metadata exchange using traditional DL mechanisms such as the Open Archives Initiative Protocol for Metadata Harvesting (OAI-PMH) [3] and the Metadata Encoding and Transmission Standard (METS) [2] to exchange various forms of metadata like Dublin Core[7] or Learning Object Metadata [1]. While metadata exchange is useful for federated search over multiple libraries it does not solve the problem of resource exchange.

A number of projects have combined metadata and resource exchange in digital libraries, such as that of Van de Sompel et al. [12], Bell and Lewis [6], the Greenstone exchange center [5], the StoneD [13] project, and the Open Archives Initiative Object Reuse and Exchange (OAI-ORE) [10] standard. While these projects address the problem of interoperability they are often limited in the complexity of resources that can be exchanged and are not designed to exchange resources with non-digital library systems.

---

[1] http://wordpress.org

[2] http://drupal.org

[3] http://edrepo.sourceforge.net/

[4] http://www.dlese.org

[5] http://www.merlot.org

[6] http://nsdl.org

[7] http://dublincore.org

LMS mechanisms such as the Sharable Content Object Reference Model (SCORM) [4], the Learning Object Discovery and Exchange (LODE)[8] project, or proprietary exchange mechanisms, like Moodle's[9] GIFT or XML formats, allow for LMS exchange. Additionally, Learning Object Repositories, like Equella[10] and xpLor[11], have been created to enable sharing of educational resources among LMSs. While these all allow exchange between LMSs they do not provide compatibility with DLs. We see our work as being one possible bridge between the DL and LMS ecosystems by creating generic mechanisms to export content in any of the formats acceptable by these systems.

3 Background

The Ensemble project[12] has built and maintains a digital library portal that provides access to digital library collections related to computing education. Ensemble harvests metadata records from independent collections via OAI-PMH and hosts collections in the portal itself. Metadata records from Ensemble are then provided to the NSDL.

One of the collections developed by the Ensemble project is STEMRobotics[13] —a repository of middle and high school robotics curricula. STEMRobotics is not an LMS; it is a public website designed to facilitate the sharing of curricula and learning objects among educators and students.

STEMRobotics allows content authors to create curricula with various structures corresponding to their various teaching styles and methods. The structure often has meaningful semantics. For example, a single instructional item may be used as a primary instructional material in one lesson; a differentiated instructional material in another; or a tutorial in a third. The repository was built using the Drupal CMS which allows users to define custom content types and relationships between them. Working with the content authors, we have defined a number of different structures. The authors have then added content as HTML directly by using a WYSIWYG editor, by attaching files, or by entering links to external resources.

While Drupal allows us to create varied structures it also presents the challenge of how to provide functionality generically across these structures. To address this challenge we created *canonical structures*—common structural patterns —and mappings from the canonical structures to the Drupal structures [9]. Examples of canonical structures include a parent-part aggregation hierarchy as well as the instructional-material-for and assessment-for relationships. We have developed a number of functionalities based on canonical structures such as

---

[8] http://www.imsglobal.org/lode.html
[9] http://moodle.org/
[10] http://www.equella.com
[11] http://www.blackboard.com/sites/xplor/infographic.html
[12] http://computingportal.org
[13] http://stemrobotics.cs.pdx.edu

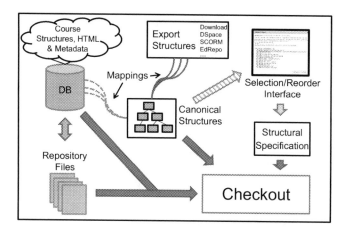

Fig. 1. The system architecture of the checkout tool is shown here

navigation and clone widgets as well as mechanisms for transmitting complex structure to other systems via OAI-PMH and OAI-ORE [7,8].

STEMRobotics hosts a large curriculum, called STEM Robotics 101. The course comprises eleven units, where each unit has a number of lessons and each lesson has instructional materials and assessments. The course has an associated professional development program for teachers that encourages them to select, clone, extend, and modify the original curriculum. To date, this course has been cloned seven times where each teacher uses all or a subset of the original resources in a variety of customizations. As more teachers have adopted some or all of this curriculum, we have been asked to provide mechanisms for download and exchange—what we call *checkout* in this paper—such that these materials can be used offline, behind school firewalls, or in LMSs. This checkout capability is built generically based on our prior work using canonical structures.

4 Checking Out

The architecture of the checkout mechanism is shown in Figure 1. On the left side of the figure are the the the two main components of the Drupal repository. The database component (DB) stores information about all the resources including their metadata, HTML, and paths to attached files. Files attached to resources are stored in the server filesystem. Canonical structures are mapped to the course structures in the DB (green/dashed lines in Figure 1) and are used by generic widgets such as navigation and the selection and reorder widget described below.

To begin a checkout, a user browses to a resource in the collection (here we use the STEMRobotics 101 curricula described above) and clicks a checkout button. The user is then presented with a selection and reordering interface shown at the top right of Figure 1 and shown in detail in Figure 2. The interface extends the navigation interface from the repository which is defined with

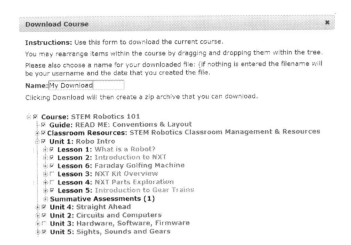

Fig. 2. The selection and reorder interface is shown where a subset of a course has been selected and units and lessons have been reordered via the drag-and-drop interface

canonical structures and their mappings to the course structures in the Drupal DB. The navigation interface is extended by adding checkboxes to each resource. A user may rearrange the order of units, lessons, and materials or move lessons between units or materials between lessons by dragging and dropping them in the interface. When a resource is moved, all of the children of that resource are also moved. In Figure 2 we show how Unit 4 has been moved ahead of Units 2 and 3 and Lesson 6 has been moved ahead of Lessons 3, 4, and 5. We also show that Unit 3 and Lessons 3 and 4 were not included in this checkout. The rules regarding which resources may be dragged into other resources is governed by the semantics of the original curricular structure enabled by the canonical structures and mappings; a detailed explanation of the rule mechanism is beyond the scope of this paper.

Once a user has made their reordering and selection choices, the interface allows them to name their checkout and choose whether they would like to download or exchange their resources. The system then captures the user's choices in the *structural specification* (shown in the middle of Figure 1). This specification records the timestamp and username of the person creating the checkout as well as the resources selected for checkout and how they have been ordered.

As exchange formats have varying structures, for example hierarchical formats like XML or more complex structures like OAI-ORE, we implemented our checkout functionality in a generic fashion. We specified export structures, like we did for the course structures in Drupal, and created mappings between the export structures and the canonical structures (red/solid lines at the top middle in Figure 1).

Using the structural specification in conjunction with the export format mappings and the repository content (DB and files), we produce export packages for each mapped system (shown in the bottom right of Figure 1). The structural

Fig. 3. The directory structure of the download checkout archive

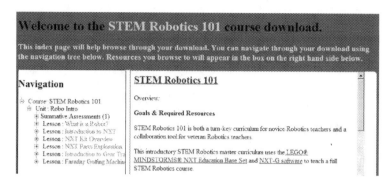

Fig. 4. A downloaded checkout from the repository contains a navigation tree to browse the complex resource. Resource content is displayed in the iframe on the right.

specification is stored so that it can be used at a later time to re-checkout the curricula. Thus, a single structural specification can be used to checkout the resource multiple times for one or more target formats. For example, a user who downloaded a course may at a later time reuse that structural specification to create a SCORM package.

4.1 Download

The download option for checkout creates a zip archive that can be downloaded and extracted on a user's computer for offline or firewalled access. The archive contains all HTML files for resources selected by the user and attached files for those resources which are stored in a resource directory within the "node" directory shown in Figure 3. In each resource directory we also materialize a metadata file in XML. The checkout mechanism also builds index and dl-at-a-glance HTML files to help the user browse their downloaded resources. The index file is shown in Figure 4. The dl-at-a-glance file shows an expanded version of the navigation tree adorned with additional metadata information such as the author and subject headings.

On the left hand side of the index page, a navigation tree details the structure of the downloaded complex resource. This tree is based on the structural specification created by the user as well as the canonical structures and mappings used in the repository for the navigation tree. The right side of the index page contains an iframe that loads a resource when it is clicked on in the tree. All of the links in the download are relative so the archive can be browsed on a computer, offline. The archive may also be extracted on a webserver as a self-contained website.

To reduce the delay when a zip archive is created, we materialize the HTML and XML metadata files whenever a resource is created or modified in the repository. These files are stored using a directory structure on the server that is the same as the download structure. Symbolic links are also created to reference files attached to resources. The materialization of this DB content avoids the cost of generating them every time a resource is checked out and the symbolic links avoid the cost of maintaining multiple copies of files.

Using the server-side directory structure and the structural specification, the checkout mechanism dynamically generates the index, dl-at-a-glance and the zip archive at the time of download.

4.2   Exchange

We describe here the three exchange targets we implemented. We explore both LMS and digital library exchange.

SCORM. We implemented SCORM exchange, because it has been adopted by most major LMS providers and thus allows our users to bring content into their LMSs. A SCORM package allows the content to be in a (complex) user-defined structure which is defined in the manifest of the package. We reuse the server-side directories defined above and add a directory of shared Javascript and CSS files used by SCORM runtimes to navigate through a SCORM package.

The manifest of the SCORM package defines the structure of the package in an XML format. The hierarchical structure of the SCORM manifest is mapped to our canonical structures. The structural specification produced by the selection and reorder interface is used to dynamically generate the manifest at checkout time using the mapping. The checkout mechanism then creates the zip file dynamically in the same fashion as the download archive.

Figure 5 shows the checkout specified in Figure 2 as a SCORM package. Each sub-resource of the complex resource is defined as a self-contained Shareable Content Object (SCO) and the links between the SCOs are defined in the manifest. Each SCO contains the HTML from STEMRobotics as well as any attached files of those resources.

DSpace. While not directly requested by our users, we chose to explore integration with DSpace due to its wide adoption. DSpace lists over 1400 instances on their website[14] and is designed with the goals of making digital library use and administration easy [11]. As a proof-of-concept, we used a limited form of exchange using the DSpace Simple Archive Format (SAF) to create a packaged checkout—a more complex exchange could use OAI-ORE as described in Section 3, above.

---

[14] http://www.dspace.org/

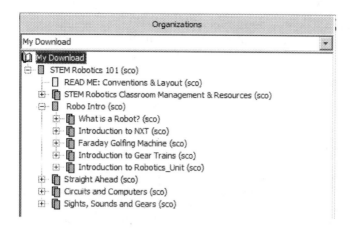

Fig. 5. The rearranged and selected course from Figure 2 has been checked out as a SCORM package—shown here in a SCORM player

Each resource in the SAF archive has its own directory containing the resource files, a metadata file, and a contents file listing all the files of the resource. On the server, we leverage the structure already created for download by creating a new directory of symbolic links to the download directory structure as well as creating the contents file at the same time we generate files for download.

SAF allows us to create a complex object as a single DSpace collection embedding the structure of the object in the metadata files of each resource using the Dublin Core relation and sub-relation fields as described in our previous work [8]. The metadata files are generated at checkout time based on the structural specification of the checkout.

EdRepo. EdRepo[15] was designed to allow teachers to store educational materials on the web and provides an OAI-PMH provider to share resources with other digital libraries and portals. EdRepo supports the logical unit of modules of educational resources which may be related to other modules. We created two styles of exchange; one that mapped each complex sub-resource of a complex resource to a module in EdRepo; and one that flattened a complex resource into a single module.

EdRepo does not currently have an import mechanism so we created an archive package that can be extracted in an EdRepo directory containing the checked out files and an SQL script that can be run to populate an EdRepo database with the metadata and structure of the resources. EdRepo contains a simplified directory structure compared to the other systems—all materials are stored in a single materials directory and the filenames are hashed. We accommodate this by creating a directory of symbolic links to all of the resources in our site—where the name of the symbolic link is the hashed filename.

---

[15] http://edrepo.sourceforge.net

At checkout, the structural specification is used to generate the SQL script. In the multiple related modules style we used the canonical structure mapping described above for SCORM checkout. In the flat style, we created a mapping from the resource hierarchy to a flat list of resources that disregards the complexity of the resource. The SQL script inserts information about each resource including metadata information and the hashed name of all the resources.

5   Evaluation

We tested our checkout mechanism using the STEMRobotics repository. STEMRobotics contains over 1500 resources in a variety of complex structures. We evaluated the storage overhead necessary to materialize resources for checkout and the size of checkout packages in relation to the complexity of resources.

As described in the previous section, each of the checkout mechanisms materializes some aspect of the repository to increase the speed of the check out. Table 1 shows the differing amounts of storage used on our server by each type of checkout as well as the repository itself. We see that the largest amount of materialized data is used for the HTML of each resource. This HTML is then used by all of the checkout mechanisms. While we materialized metadata for both download and DSpace, the download metadata contained fields not used by DSpace. This resulted in a larger amount of data used for download even though we also materialized the "contents" file for each resource for DSpace. The EdRepo checkout uses less space than both download and DSpace since it stores metadata in a more compact, non-XML, format. We also see that SCORM uses the least amount of storage since it only has to store shared javascript and css files and does not materialize any of the metadata. It is notable that even in the worst case, download, the storage necessary is still two orders of magnitude less than the storage used by the original site.

Next we looked at how the various checkout mechanisms scale with respect to the complexity of the checked out resource. This test was performed by selectively choosing resources from the STEM Robotics 101 curriculum. This curriculum consists of 533 individual resources in 11 units. We first selected the resources not in any unit and then added one unit to each successive checkout. "EdRepoFlat" and "EdRepoTree" refer to the flattened and complex styles of EdRepo exchange formats. Figure 6 shows how the size of checkouts increases as the number of resources in the checkout increases. We see that the size increases linearly with the number of resources in the checkout. This size is also dependent on the size of the attached resources in a repository. If a resource had a large attached movie it would skew these results, for example. STEM Robotics 101 has a fairly consistent

Table 1. Additional server storage necessary for each type of download as well as the size of all the files in the repository

Repository	HTML	Download	DSpace	EdRepo	SCORM
2G	17.5M	14.8M	14.3M	9.8M	80K

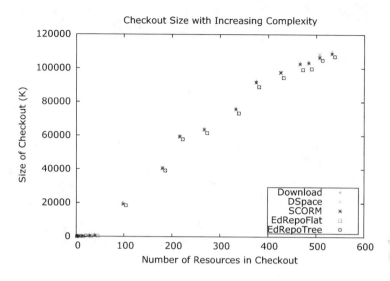

Fig. 6. As the complexity of a checkout increases the corresponding size of the download increases linearly

Table 2. Checkout sizes in KB as shown in the graph in Figure 6 for selections of units of an 11 unit course

Units	Download	DSpace	SCORM	EdRepoFlat	EdRepoTree
			Checkout Destination		
1	19,848	19,172	19,300	18,524	18,524
2	41,088	40,356	40,508	39,144	39,144
3	60,052	59,296	59,448	57,832	57,832
4	64,208	63,436	63,568	61,616	61,060
5	76,328	75,516	75,648	73,248	73,248
6	92,400	91,556	91,736	89,000	89,000
7	98,244	97,376	97,584	94,472	94,472
8	103,336	102,448	102,636	99,264	99,264
9	103,908	103,004	103,192	99,708	99,708
10	107,104	108,212	106,404	104,760	104,760
11	109,412	110,616	108,700	106,984	106,984

attachment size, although the later units tend to have smaller resources which explains the sub-linear trend near the end of the plot.

Notice that the size of the flat and complex styles of EdRepo exchange formats differ by less than a kilobyte since the structure is embedded in the SQL insert statements in the file. The EdRepo exchange formats are also slightly smaller than the other formats since they do not contain the extra directory structure or the separate metadata files. Table 2 shows the data presented in Figure 6. We see in the table that the minor difference in size between the formats is negligible.

Initial user feedback has been positive with anecdotal feedback like "great update" and "awesome" from the beta-testers who used the checkout feature. The feature will be released to our entire user base this summer during our annual STEM Robotics 101 professional development sessions.

6   Conclusions and Future Work

We have shown how download and exchange mechanisms can support complex structures. We have also shown how to transmit and transform that structure such that it can be used in several target systems. We have shown how the size of the exchange mechanisms scales linearly in relation to the complexity of complex objects.

We have also shown how additional exchange formats can be added with minimal storage overhead to a system. For larger repositories or for a system with a large number of target exchange systems, it may be necessary to implement mechanisms where only frequently used resources are materialized while others are generated dynamically at checkout. We leave this exploration to future work.

This paper has focused on repositories built using the Drupal CMS. We plan to release our modules back to the Drupal community so that anyone building a Drupal DL or LMS can use these features. We plan to add full sequencing and ordering of SCORM packages to our interface. We are also working to allow content in any of the exchange formats described in this paper to be imported into a Drupal repository. This two-way exchange will allow us to reuse LMS and DL materials in more ways and also allow us to track how exported resources have been reused.

While the current prototype is built using Drupal, these ideas may be applied to any repository or CMS that supports complex structure. As future work, we are exploring porting our mechanisms to other digital libraries and content management systems.

We are also working on ways to inform users of resource reuse using the structural specifications described in Section 4. By capturing how users select and reorder content we can provide information to content authors on how their resources are being used. When content in the repository changes, we can also use the structural specifications to notify users who have checked out those resources of those changes.

We are working to expand the number of exchange formats that we work with. We are continuing our prior work with OAI-ORE beyond metadata transmission as well as exploring transmission using METS.

Acknowledgments. This work was supported in part by the National Science Foundation grants 0840668 and 1250340. We would like to thank our collaborators and content authors, including Randy Steele, author of STEM Robotics 101.

References

1. IEEE LTSC — WG12 — Final LOM Draft Standard,
   http://ltsc.ieee.org/wg12/20020612-Final-LOM-Draft.html
2. Metadata Encoding & Transmission Standard,
   http://www.loc.gov/standards/mets/
3. Open Archives Initiative Protocol for Metadata Harvesting,
   http://www.openarchives.org/pmh/
4. SCORM, http://www.adlnet.gov/capabilities/scorm
5. Bainbridge, D., Ke, K.Y.J., Witten, I.H.: Document level interoperability for collection creators. In: ACM/IEEE-CS Joint Conference on Digital Libraries - JCDL 2006, p. 105. ACM Press, New York (2006)
6. Bell, J., Lewis, S.: Using OAI-PMH and METS for exporting metadata and digital objects between repositories (2006),
   http://cadair.aber.ac.uk/dspace/handle/2160/203
7. Britell, S., Delcambre, L., Cassel, L., Fox, E., Furuta, R.: Exploiting canonical structures to transmit complex objects from a digital library to a portal. In: ACM/IEEE-CS Joint Conference on Digital Libraries - JCDL 2012. ACM Press, New York (2012)
8. Britell, S., Delcambre, L.M.L., Cassel, L.N., Fox, E.A., Furuta, R.: Enhancing Digital Libraries and Portals with Canonical Structures for Complex Objects. In: Zaphiris, P., Buchanan, G., Rasmussen, E., Loizides, F. (eds.) TPDL 2012. LNCS, vol. 7489, pp. 420–425. Springer, Heidelberg (2012)
9. Britell, S., Delcambre, L.M.L.: Mapping Semantic Widgets to Web-based, Domain-specific Collections. In: Atzeni, P., Cheung, D., Ram, S. (eds.) ER 2012. LNCS, vol. 7532, pp. 204–213. Springer, Heidelberg (2012)
10. Lagoze, C., Van de Sompel, H., Nelson, M.L., Warner, S., Sanderson, R., Johnston, P.: Object Re-Use & Exchange: A Resource-Centric Approach. CoRR abs/0804.2 (2008)
11. Smith, M., Barton, M., Branschofsky, M., McClellan, G., Walker, J.H., Bass, M., Stuve, D., Tansley, R.: DSpace. D-Lib Magazine 9(1) (January 2003)
12. Van de Sompel, H., Nelson, M.L., Lagoze, C., Warner, S.: Resource Harvesting within the OAI-PMH Framework. D-Lib Magazine 10(12) (December 2004)
13. Witten, I.H., Bainbridge, D., Tansley, R., Huang, C.Y., Don, K.J.: StoneD: A bridge between Greenstone and DSpace (2005),
    http://researchcommons.waikato.ac.nz/handle/10289/996

Profiling Web Archive Coverage
for Top-Level Domain and Content Language

Ahmed Alsum[1], Michele C. Weigle[1],
Michael L. Nelson[1], and Herbert Van de Sompel[2]

[1] Computer Science Department, Old Dominion University, Norfolk, VA USA
{aalsum,mweigle,mln}@cs.odu.edu
[2] Los Alamos National Laboratory, Los Alamos, NM USA
herbertv@lanl.gov

Abstract. The Memento aggregator currently polls every known public web archive when serving a request for an archived web page, even though some web archives focus on only specific domains and ignore the others. Similar to query routing in distributed search, we investigate the impact on aggregated Memento TimeMaps (lists of when and where a web page was archived) by only sending queries to archives likely to hold the archived page. We profile twelve public web archives using data from a variety of sources (the web, archives' access logs, and full-text queries to archives) and discover that only sending queries to the top three web archives (i.e., a 75% reduction in the number of queries) for any request produces the full TimeMaps on 84% of the cases.

Keywords: Web archive, query routing, memento aggregator.

1 Introduction

The web archive life cycle started with crawling the live web, then preserving for future access [1]. The global archived web corpus is distributed between various web archives around the world. Every archive has its own initiative to crawl and preserve the web [2], and these rules control its selection policy to determine the set of URIs for the web archive to crawl and preserve [3].

However, neither the selection policy nor the crawling log may be publicly available. This means that there is no way to determine what has been planned nor actually archived. This challenges our ability to search for a URI in the archives. For example, the British Library Web Archive is interested in preserving UK websites (domains ending with .uk or websites existing in the UK)[1], so searching it for The Japan Times[2] may not return anything because that URI is not in the BL's selection policy. Furthermore, although www.bbc.co.uk is covered in the BL web archive, a request for this page from the year 2000 should not be sent to the BL because it did not begin archiving until 2007.

---

[1] http://www.bl.uk/aboutus/stratpolprog/coldevpol/index.html
[2] http://www.japantimes.co.jp/

T. Aalberg et al. (Eds.): TPDL 2013, LNCS 8092, pp. 60–71, 2013.

Table 1. List of Web archives under experiment

	Archive Name	FullText search	Website
IA	Internet Archive		web.archive.org
LoC	Library of Congress		www.loc.gov/lcwa
IC	Icelandic Web Archive		vefsafn.is
CAN	Library & Archives Canada	x	www.collectionscanada.gc.ca
BL	British Library	x	www.webarchive.org.uk/ukwa
UK	UK Gov. Web Archive	x	webarchive.nationalarchives.gov.uk
PO	Portuguese Web Archive	x	arquivo.pt
CAT	Web Archive of Catalonia	x	www.padi.cat
CR	Croatian Web Archive	x	haw.nsk.hr
CZ	Archive of the Czech Web	x	webarchiv.cz
TW	National Taiwan University	x	webarchive.lib.ntu.edu.tw
AIT	Archive-It	x	www.archive-it.org

For each web archive, we can determine a set of characteristics that distinguish the archive from other archives and provide an insight about the archive content, e.g., the age of the archived copies and the supported domains for crawling. This profile enables the user to select the archives that may have the required URI at the specific "datetime". The application of this could be that the user-agent or the web archive could redirect the request based on the requested URI characteristics to another web archive that may have the URI. Also, the profile may help to determine the missing portion of the web that needs more coverage.

Ainsworth et al. [4] showed that between 16% - 79% of the web has been archived. The experiment was conducted between 13 archives and search engine caches. The results showed that the maximum number of archives that responded to the same URI was only 10 archives, so there was no single URI that appeared in all of the archives.

In this paper, we performed a quantitative study to create profiles for 12 web archives around the world (see Table 1). To build these profiles, we use a dataset constructed from URIs for the live web, fulltext search of the archives themselves, and access logs of the archives. We evaluated the constructed profiles in query routing between the various archives.

The rest of the paper is organized as follows. Section 2 describes the related work. Section 3 defines the archive profile characteristics. Section 4 defines the URI samples. Section 5 describes the experiment set and the results. Section 6 evaluates the usage of the profile in query routing. Section 7 concludes with a summary and future work for this study.

2   Related Work

The general web archiving procedures have been studied by Masanés [3], Brown [1], and Brüger [5]. Evaluating the current status of web archives has been studied in various research. Shiozaki and Eisenschitz [2] published a questionnaire survey conducted between 16 national libraries to justify the web archiving activities in the national libraries. Niu [6,7] evaluated several web archives to study the selection, acquire, and access techniques of the web archives. Niu limited her study to web archives with an English interface.

National libraries have published their web archiving initiatives in various studies, for example, National Library of France [8], Portuguese web archive [9], National Library of the Czech Republic [10], National Taiwan University [11], National Archives of Australia [12], and China Web InfoMall [13].

Memento [14] is an extension for the HTTP protocol to allow the user to browse the past web as the current web. The memento $(URI - M)$ is a snapshot for the original resource $(URI - R)$ as it appeared in the past and was preserved by a web archive. The time that the memento was observed (or captured) by an archive is known as *Memento-Datetime*. The TimeMap is a resource from which a list of URIs of mementos of the original resource is available. A Memento Aggregator [15] provides a single TimeMap for multiple archives. The Memento Aggregator depends on various proxies [16] that provide Memento support for third-party servers and non-memento compliant web archives.

3   Archive Profile

An archive profile is a set of characteristics that describe the content of the web archive. The goal of this description is to give a high-level overview about the web archive. This overview will help the user, other archives, or third party services to select the best web archive in case selection between different archives is required. Examples of these rules include the following:

- **Age:** describes the age of the holding of the web archive. It is defined by the Memento-Datetime of the oldest memento in the archive. It may differ from the web archive starting date. For example, Portuguese Web Archive project started in 2007 but they included preserved materials that captured before 1995[3].
- **Top-Level Domain (TLD):** describes the supported hostnames and top-level domains by the web archive. Some web archives have a special focus that will consider specific domains only. For example, Library and Archives Canada have focused on the .gc.ca TLD.
- **Language:** describes the supported languages by the web archive. It varies depending on the motivation of the web archive creation. The Internet Archive has a wide range of languages, while the Icelandic web archive focuses on content in the Icelandic language.
- **Growth Rate:** describes the growth of the web archive corpus in the number of original URIs and mementos through time.

---

[3] http://sobre.arquivo.pt/how-to-participate/supplying-historical-portuguese-web-contents

4   URI Dataset Samples

We prepared various URI sample sets to profile the web archives. We sampled URIs from three sources: live web, archive holding, and archive access logs.

Open Directory (DMOZ)[4] is used for URIs on the live web. Recording web archives' fulltext search responses represent what the web archives have already acquired. Finally, sampling from user requests to the Internet Archive and Memento Aggregator represents what the users are looking for in the past. In all the samples, we used the hostname to create a top-level URI. For example, `http://example.org/a/b.html` will be `example.org`. Each sample has unique hostnames, however the different samples may have an overlap of hostnames.

4.1   Sampling from the Web

DMOZ is an open source web directory that is built by user submissions of URIs. We selected DMOZ because it is well-represented in web archives [4]. We created three samples from DMOZ data:

- **DMOZ Random Sample:** We randomly sampled 10,000 URIs from the total directory of more than 5M URIs.
- **DMOZ Controlled (TLD):** We classified the DMOZ directory's URIs by the TLD. For each TLD, we randomly selected 2% of the available hostnames or 100 hosts whichever is greater. We limited the study to a specific set of TLDs that are distributed around the world. The total number of URIs in this sample was 53,526 URIs.
- **DMOZ Controlled (Language):** DMOZ provides a specific list of URIs per language. We extracted these URIs and selected randomly 100 URIs from each language. The study focused on a limited set of languages that represent the world. The total number of URIs in this sample was 2,300 URIs.

4.2   Sampling from the Web Archive

Most of the web archives provide fulltext search in addition to URI-lookup or collection browsing. We used the fulltext search to discover the hidden content of the web archives by submitting various queries and recording the responses.

This sample aims to calculate the overlap between the different archives and avoid biasing for archives that use DMOZ as a URI source (such as the Internet Archive). In order to reach a representative sample, we used two sets of queries:

- **Top 1-Gram:** The first set of queries terms was extracted from Bing Top 100k words as they appeared in April 2010[5]. We randomly sampled 1000 terms where most of them were in English.

---

[4] `http://www.dmoz.org`
[5] `http://web-ngram.research.microsoft.com/info/BingBodyApr10_`
`Top100KWords.zip`

Table 2. Total number of unique hostnames returned from the query terms

	Top Query Languages search									Total	Top 1-Gram
	chi	eng	fre	ger	ita	jpn	kor	por	spa		
AIT	26	2066	3512	3837	3321	119	2	2434	2141	12617	3953
BL	163	2354	2350	2240	2068	225	131	1940	2056	6430	3187
CAN	49	800	804	646	601	77	113	580	514	1351	1107
CR	54	706	697	703	701	74	19	599	600	1599	1201
CZ	363	1782	1578	1695	1519	577	114	1310	1278	6081	3360
CAT	28	2775	2496	2448	2280	209	129	2164	2429	8996	4241
PO	91	2460	3603	3081	3113	53	69	3267	3177	14126	5004
TW	357	178	176	165	157	106	7	198	119	1004	354
UK	0	2698	2009	2049	2046	0	0	1903	1871	8261	3431

- **Top Query Languages:** The second set of queries was taken from Yahoo! Search query logs for nine languages[6]. This dataset has the 1000 most frequent web search queries issued to Yahoo Search in nine different languages. As the query terms are not limited to the search engine languages, they may have other languages especially English (e.g., Apple was one of the top query terms in Japanese). We filtered each file manually to include the designated language only and exclude the common terms (e.g., Obama, Facebook).

We issued each query to all web archives that support fulltext search (see table 1)[7], then we recorded the top 10 results, and filtered by the hostname only. Table 2 shows the total number of unique hosts returned by querying each query set from the archive. The total column has the total number of unique hosts that were retrieved by each archive. The total column provides an indication of the size of the web archive.

4.3   Sampling from Users' Requests

The third sample came from users' requests to the past web as recorded by the log files.

- **IA Wayback Machine Log Files:** IA Wayback Machine (WM) [17] is the access interface for the Internet Archive, and has 240B+ URIs[8]. WM receives more than 90M+ hits per day [18]. We selected log files for one week from (Feb 22, 2012 to Feb 26, 2012). We used only the requests to mementos or TimeMaps. For each memento or TimeMap, we extracted the original resource. We then sampled 1,000 URIs randomly from this list.
- **Memento Aggregator Logs:** we sampled 100 unique hosts from the LANL Memento aggregator[9] logs between 2011 to 2013.

---

[6] http://webscope.sandbox.yahoo.com/catalog.php?datatype=l
[7] UK Gov. Web Archive has a problem in searching with unicode characters.
[8] http://blog.archive.org/2013/01/09/updated-wayback/
[9] http://mementoproxy.lanl.gov/

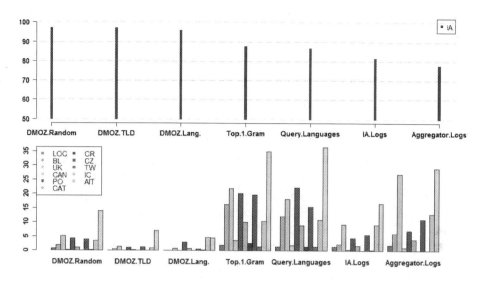

Fig. 1. Coverage histogram for all samples, IA on the top and all other archives below

5   Experiment and Results

For each hostname in the sample set (e.g., example.org), we converted it into
a URI (i.e., http://example.org). We used the Memento proxies to retrieve the
TimeMap for each URI. We recorded each memento with its Memento-Datetime.
The coverage is the percentage of URIs that were found in each archive related
to the sample size. In a future study, we will include other measurements such
as the number of mementos per URI, the total number of mementos per archive,
and the archive density [4].

Coverage: Figure 1 shows the coverage for each sample through the archives.
The results show IA, shown in the top graph, has the best coverage for all
samples, ranging from 79% to 98%. IA covered DMOZ samples with more than
95% because DMOZ is used as a URI source for IA. The bottom graph shows the
coverage for the rest of the archives. UK, PO, CZ, and IC show good coverage
for specialized archives.

Cross Coverage: Figure 1 also shows that the web archives have a good coverage for the Top 1-Gram and Query Languages samples. This is because each
archive contributed a part of the URIs to the samples as shown in table 2. Table
3 shows the details of the coverage across archives. The table lists the URIs'
source archives (as appeared in Table 2) on the rows and the queried archive on
the columns. We can conclude the following from the table:

1. The overlap between the web archives and IA is high, which means that IA
   is effectively a superset for all the archives.

Table 3. The coverage percentage across the archives for fulltext search samples

Source	Target Archive											
	IA	AIT	BL	CAN	CR	CZ	CAT	PO	TW	UK	IC	LoC
AIT	89.48	**84.83**	5.23	0.27	0.01	10.49	4.42	12.6	0.47	19.17	12.88	2.29
BL	93.61	35.13	**76.78**	0.26	0	10.25	3.57	12.57	0.49	40.99	11.96	1.46
CA	84.13	26.12	0.94	**78.93**	0	3.91	0.12	1.59	0.04	7.24	1.71	0.57
CR	96.36	11.96	2.54	0	**52.93**	4.61	1.68	3.71	0.29	5.96	4.00	0.32
CZ	91.26	13.66	3.27	0.23	0	**82.95**	2.01	6.84	0.34	7.50	6.94	1.23
PA	80.58	21.50	3.42	0.11	0.02	5.53	**39.47**	8.74	0.11	10.83	7.60	1.22
PO	82.45	21.20	3.69	0.08	0.02	7.10	3.55	**58.94**	0.14	11.14	10.23	1.29
TW	93.00	18.92	2.72	0.52	0	5.08	0.88	4.79	**67.89**	8.17	3.90	1.40
UK	81.87	35.82	14.13	0.27	0.05	12.68	6.09	17.92	0.47	**40.85**	18.07	2.34

2. The overlap between the archives and each other is low, which means they are covering different portions of the web. The highest overlap was between BL and UK because both are focusing on UK domains.
3. The web archives may have inconsistent interfaces between fulltext search and URI-lookup, as the overlap between the archive and itself is less than 100% (highlighted in bold in table 3). For example, querying BL with URIs that have been extracted from the BL fulltext search returned only 75%. One reason may be that we removed the URI path from the extracted URI, i.e., if fulltext search returned (www.example.com/a/b.html), we will use (www.example.com) in the sample set. For the collection based archive, the curator may be interested in a specific URI and not the hostname itself. For example, you can extract `http://www.icsc.org.uk/index.html` from BL by searching for the term "Consumer Sciences", but there are no mementos for `http://www.icsc.org.uk/`. Another reason is that the web archive may index the entire crawled corpus and make it available through fulltext search (including the embedded resources). These embedded URIs may not be available through the URI-lookup interface. For example, Croatian Web Archive responds with embedded videos from `youtube.com` that can not be discovered using the URI-lookup.

Top-Level Domain Distribution: Figure 2 shows the coverage of each TLD sample (columns) by the web archives (rows). "*White*" means the archive has 0% of this TLD, "*Black*" means the archives returned 100% of the sample TLD. The results show that IC, PO, CAT, TW, CZ, CR have good coverage for their national domains, and IC, PO, and UK extend their crawling beyond these domains. This behavior has been elaborated by studying the distribution of successfully retrieved URIs from each archive. Figure 3(b) shows the top TLD per archive from both the fulltext search and the DMOZ TLD sample. There is a high correlation between both interfaces. The results show that even though the national archives work perfectly on their domains, they are not restricted to these domain only. CAN is the only closed archive for its domain. TW supports a set of regional domains (i.e., .cn, .jp, and .sg). Figure 4 illustrates the top archives per domain. It shows IA and AIT have high level coverage over the

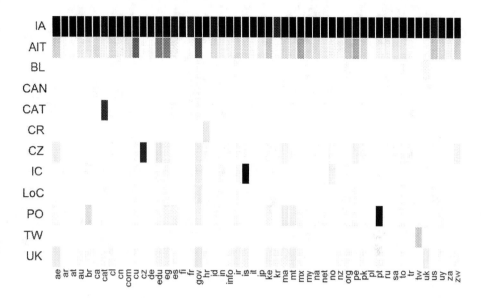

Fig. 2. Heat map of archive coverage for TLD samples

other archives for the general domains, however the national archives are doing similar or better for their domains (e.g., CAT for .cat and IC for .is).

Language Distribution: Figure 5 shows the coverage for each web archive divided by the language. CAT, IC, TW, and PT show good coverage for their languages.

Growth Rate: Figure 6 shows the growth rate for each archive through time. The growth rate is accumulated and normalized for the number of mementos and the number of new URIs added each month. The figure shows both LOC and CAN covered a limited period of time, then they stopped their crawling activities as their number of new URIs does not increase. CZ and CAT stopped adding new URIs a few years ago, but they are still crawling more mementos through time. This figure also gives an idea about the start date for each archive. For example, IA and PO are the only archives that began before 2000.

Reflecting on the findings presented in this section, it is clear that IA is large, with mementos for 90% of the dataset, and AIT and PO are in second place with 10%. This could be due in part to a bias in the dataset toward IA holdings, with logs from the Wayback Machine and the Memomento Aggregator as well as from DMOZ, a known seed URI site for IA. Although we attempted to include content from a variety of archives, producing an unbiased dataset is difficult [4]. Another possible explanation is simply that IA and PO have the oldest holdings, as both of them carried mementos from 1996.

There are surely other public web archives that exist that we simply did not know of. Some regions of the world do not appear to have active, public web archiving projects such as India and Africa. There are on going projects for the Arabic content by Bibliotheca Alexandrina and Latin America by the

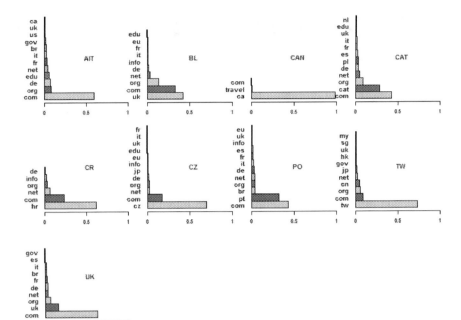

(a) The distribution of TLD per archive (Fulltext search).

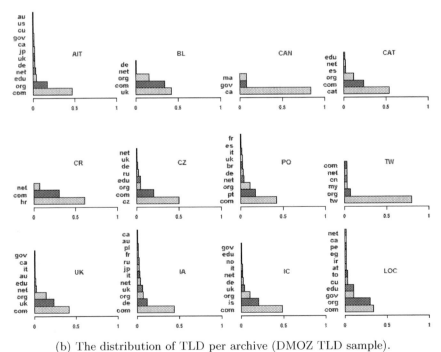

(b) The distribution of TLD per archive (DMOZ TLD sample).

Fig. 3. The distribution of the TLD through the archives

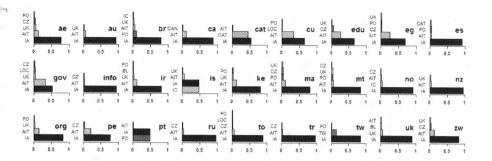

Fig. 4. Top-level domains distribution across the archives

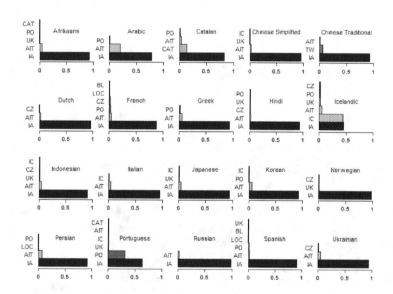

Fig. 5. Languages distribution per archive using DMOZ Language sample

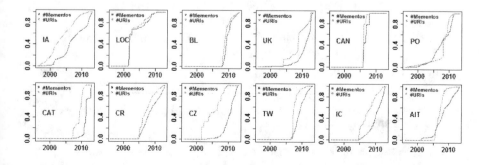

Fig. 6. Web Archive's corpus growth rate for URIs and Mementos

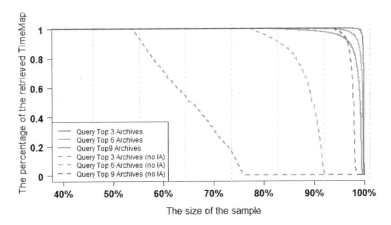

Fig. 7. Query routing evaluation using TLD profile

University of Texas[10]. Finally, starting at about 2005 there appears to be a watershed moment for web archiving, when many projects begin to significantly grow their collections.

6   Evaluation

The profiles of web archives could be used in optimizing query routing for the Memento Aggregator. In order to quantify the success of the new profile, we applied ten-fold cross-validation. We used TLD information (from Figure 4) to create a general profile for the relationship between TLDs and archives. For each URI, we queried the aggregator with a different level of confidence using the top 3, top 6, and top 9 archives based on the requested URI's TLD.

We define the success criteria as how many URIs we get from a TimeMap when we select the top archives only. For example, if using the top 3 archives retrieved 10 mementos and using the full TimeMap (all 12 archives) retrieved 15 mementos, we computed success as 0.67. Figure 7 shows the normalized results for each case. We ran the experiment with all 12 archives and then repeated it IA.

The results show that we were able to retrieve the complete TimeMap in 84% of the cases using only the top 3 archives. This increased to 91% when using the top 6 archives.

Excluding IA, we were still able to get the complete TimeMap using the top 3 archives in 52% of the cases. We assume each web archive query costs the same time for serving the request. In future work, we will profile the performance of responding to web archive queries.

7   Conclusions

In this paper, we proposed an automatic technique to construct profiles for web archives. The results showed that the Internet Archive is the largest and widest

---

[10] http://lanic.utexas.edu/project/archives/

in coverage. The national archives have good coverage of their domains and languages, and some of them extend their selection policies to cover more domains. The evaluation of using the profile in query routing retrieved the complete TimeMap in 84% of the cases using only the top 3 archives.

In a future study, we plan to profile more characteristics such as: *robots respect*, *crawling frequency*, and *crawling depth*. Also, we will use fulltext search to profile more characteristics in addition to the URI-lookup. In the evaluation, we will include more characteristics and increase the coverage of the sample URIs.

References

1. Brown, A.: Archiving websites: A practical guide for information management professionals, 1st edn. Facet, London (2006)
2. Shiozaki, R., Eisenschitz, T.: Role and justification of web archiving by national libraries: A questionnaire survey. Journal of Librarianship and Information Science 41, 90–107 (2009)
3. Masanès, J.: Web archiving. Springer, Heidelberg (2006)
4. Ainsworth, S.G., AlSum, A., SalahEldeen, H., Weigle, M.C., Nelson, M.L.: How much of the Web is Archived? In: Proceedings of the 11th Annual International ACM/IEEE Joint Conference on Digital Libraries, JCDL 2011, pp. 133–136 (2011)
5. Brügger, N.: Archiving Websites. In: General Considerations and Strategies, 1st edn. The Center for Internet Research, Aarhus N (2005)
6. Niu, J.: Functionalities of Web Archives. D-Lib Magazine 18 (2012)
7. Niu, J.: An Overview of Web Archiving. D-Lib Magazine 18 (2012)
8. Aubry, S.: Introducing Web Archives as a New Library Service: The Experience of the National Library of France. LIBER Quarterly 20, 179–199 (2010)
9. Gomes, D., Nogueira, A., Miranda, J.A., Costa, M.: Introducing the Portuguese Web Archive Initiative. In: Proceedings of 8th IWAW (2008)
10. Vlcek, I.: Identification and Archiving of the Czech Web Outside the National Domain. In: Proceedings of 8th IWAW (2008)
11. Chen, K., Chen, Y., Ting, P.: Developing National Taiwan University Web Archiving System. In: Proceedings of 8th IWAW (2008)
12. Heslop, H., Davis, S., Wilson, A.: An Approach to the Preservation of Digital Records. Technical report, National Archives of Australia (2002)
13. Yan, H., Huang, L., Chen, C., Xie, Z.: A New Data Storage and Service Model of China Web. In: Proceedings of 4th IWAW (2004)
14. Van de Sompel, H., Nelson, M.L., Sanderson, R.: HTTP framework for time-based access to resource states – Memento (2011),
    https://datatracker.ietf.org/doc/draft-vandesompel-memento/
15. Sanderson, R., Shankar, H., AlSum, A.: Memento Aggregator source code (2010),
    https://code.google.com/p/memento-server
16. Sanderson, R.: Memento Tools: Proxy Scripts (2010),
    http://www.mementoweb.org/tools/proxy/
17. Tofel, B.: 'Wayback' for Accessing Web Archives. In: Proceedings of 7th IWAW (2007)
18. AlNoamany, Y., Weigle, M.C., Nelson, M.L.: Access Patterns for Robots and Humans in Web Archives. In: Proceedings of the 13th ACM/IEEE-CS Joint Conference on Digital Libraries, JCDL 2013 (2013)

Selecting Fiction in Library Catalogs:
A Gaze Tracking Study

Janna Pöntinen and Pertti Vakkari

University of Tampere, Finland
{janna.pontinen,pertti.vakkari}@uta.fi

Abstract. It is studied how readers explore metadata in book pages when selecting fiction in a traditional and an enriched online catalog for fiction. The associations between attention devoted to metadata elements and selecting an interesting book were analyzed. Eye movements of 30 users selecting fiction for four search tasks were recorded. The results indicate that although participants paid most attention in book pages to content description and keywords, these had no bearing on selecting an interesting book. Author and title information received less attention, but were significant predictors of selection.

1   Introduction

Nearly half of the adults had read fiction in 2008 in the U.S. [14], and 80 % of adults in Finland in 2010 [16]. The public library is a major medium for readers to access fiction [16], and most of the books borrowed are fiction. In the Netherlands, its share of all borrowed books was 73 % in 2005 [7], and in Finland 67 % in 2010 [8].

The proportion of fiction books in electronic form is increasing. In e-bookshops selecting books takes place totally in an electronic environment. Readers will face the same development in the public libraries. Library catalogs facilitate accessing fiction through metadata. When fiction is available in libraries in electronic form selecting books based on metadata is linked with browsing and reading text in the books.

Library users are in favor of browsing bookshelves instead of library catalogs for selecting reading [5, 9]. E-book collections do not facilitate as functioning browsing as physical collections do [6]. Therefore, it is necessary to study how readers select books by using metadata in order to inform designing of metadata for fiction searching. Adkins and Bossaler [1] argue that online catalogs are effective in known author or known title searches, but not as effective in supporting browsing books. They call for studies on actual fiction searching practices of readers using electronic catalogs to determine how those readers make book selection decisions.

There are lots of studies on selecting fiction in physical collections [5], but very few focusing on the use of electronic catalogs in finding fiction [1]. The scarce evidence on fiction searching in online catalogs hints that it is more important to inspect the result list than to query for finding good novels. When readers looked for good novels without a clear goal in an online catalog, effort invested in examining result lists and book metadata was positively associated with finding interesting novels, whereas effort in querying had no bearing on it [12]. This result hints that

T. Aalberg et al. (Eds.): TPDL 2013, LNCS 8092, pp. 72–83, 2013.

result page and metadata examination is important for search success. This speaks for analyzing how readers select fiction books using online catalogs.

The aim of this study is to analyze how readers select fiction in online public library catalogs. It is compared whether there are differences in the selection between an enriched catalog for fiction compared to a traditional one. We study how readers explore individual web pages of books when selecting fiction: 1) How many times and how long were various metadata elements in a book page visited during selection? 2) To what extent readers found interesting fiction? 3) Is there an association between the metadata elements visited and finding interesting fiction?

2   Related Research

Next we briefly introduce relevant studies on selecting fiction in public libraries, and on gaze-tracking.

Based on a representative survey of adult population in Finland, Mikkonen and Vakkari [9] analyzed readers' methods of accessing fiction in public libraries. The most common method was known title or author search, which was used often by 57 % of the respondents. It was followed by browsing the shelves (29 %) and skimming the returned loans (27 %). As can be inferred from [9], both known item (author or title) search and browsing are the two major tactics for selecting books in public libraries. By interviewing 500 library users in the UK, Spiller [17] found that 54 % searched novels by title or author's name, and the rest 46 % by browsing in the library. 78 % of fiction searches were carried out by combining these two methods.

If public library users were not aware of the author when browsing, they selected books most commonly based on text on the back cover (88 %) describing the book and its author. The next common attributes, text passages of the book (33 %), cover (31 %) and tittle (22 %), were less common criteria in selection [17].

In all, the findings hint that readers need mostly information on the content of the book for selection, and when browsing they observe most metadata, which provides most information about the content of the book for borrowing decision.

Gaze-tracking has gained popularity in studies on the distribution of searchers' visual attention in search result pages. This technique measures how frequently and how much time participants pay attention to various areas of interest on result pages and on landing pages [3]. Eye movements are generally composed of fixations and saccades. A fixation is a time span of at least 80-100 ms, during which the eye steadily gazes at one point. A saccade is a rapid, ballistic eye movement from one fixation to the next. Visual information is generally only perceived during fixations, not during saccades. Fixations and gaze duration has been used as indicators of attention and cognitive processing in studies on HCI [3]. In studies on information searching the number and duration of fixations have been used as indicators of attention by users to specific areas of search result lists and web pages [2].

Eye-tracking reveals that searchers fixate on the few first items in the result list; the higher the rank of the item, the shorter the arrival time and the more time is devoted on examining it [4]. Users tend also to pay attention first to the upper left region of web pages, and spend proportionally most time fixating on it. Users pay very little attention to the right side of web pages [3].

The amount of information provided in the form of snipped length improved significantly performance for informational tasks but degraded performance for navigational tasks [4]. The proportion of time devoted to titles instead of snippets decreased in the case of long snippets in informational tasks. It may be that a long snippet provides so much information about the page that attention to the title is not so important as in the case of shorter snippets [4].

In [2] was examined how searchers' visual behavior was related to the use of relevance criteria in selecting items in result lists. Searchers made more fixations and spent more time fixating on information related to topicality, scope, user background and quality compared to other relevance criteria like resource type or recency.

3   Research Design

3.1   Search Tasks

Our search tasks simulated typical situations in selecting fiction in public libraries:

1. Your friend interested in reading suggests that you should familiarize yourself with the production of the novelist Joel Haahtela. Select a novel by Haahtela, which appeals to you.
2. Search for a novel about friendship, which you would like to read.
3. You would like to familiarize yourself with authors and novels unfamiliar to you. Select two works by an author not familiar to you.
4. You are leaving for a vacation trip. Find a good novel to read during the trip.

In the first task the name of the author is known. *Author search* is the most common method of searching novels in public libraries [5, 9, 17]. Author search functioned also as an easy task for the participants to start with and familiarize themselves with the system used. The second task was a *topical search*, where the reader wishes to find a novel on a particular theme. This method was identified in [13]. The aim of the third task was to generate *browsing*, which is a popular method of choosing fiction [5, 9, 17]. By instructing participants to select works unfamiliar to them we tried to exclude the possibility that they would choose in all tasks books known to them. The fourth task simulated a situation when seeking for a good read. The aim was to let the participant select a book of her/his liking without limiting it by author, theme or familiarity [13, 15]. We call this task *vacation reading*.

In usability tests it is recommended that the first task should be easy so that the participants relax and receive a feeling of success in the test. It is also recommended that the last task should be relatively easy, so that the participants would be motivated until the end of the test [11]. Therefore, all our participants performed author search as the first task. Also the third task was performed as third by all participants, because we did not want to place that kind of demanding task as the last one. The order of topical search and vacation reading task varied so that the former was the last task for 12 participants and the latter for 18 participants.

3.2   Online Catalogs

The catalogs compared were Kirjasampo (http://www.kirjasampo.fi), which is an enriched networked service for fiction literature (Sampo), and Satakirjastot (http://www.satakirjastot.fi), which is a traditional online public library system (Sata).

Sampo is a fiction portal based on the semantic web. In the database, in addition to bibliographic information, content and context information is also indexed. The database employs functional content-centered indexing, ontological vocabularies and the networked data model of linked data [10]. The Finnish fiction ontology Kaunokki is used for indexing the works in the database. The portal also includes information about authors, current news on fiction literature, and recommendations.

Sampo has two basic functionalities, searching and browsing. Searching includes the possibility of using text or cover image queries. Users may also utilize book recommendations at the main page or select books through fellow users bookshelves. As a result of text querying a list of categories "author, person or other actor", and various "genres" like novels, short stories or cartoons are provided. After having clicked a category, the user is provided with brief information about the book including the title, cover image and a few keywords. By clicking a book title the user is transferred to the information page of the book, which includes the following metadata: author, title, keywords from facets genre, theme, figures, time and place and other keywords, a content description (typically from the back of the book), a sample text passage, publication data, cover image, possible presentation by other readers, and "see also" recommendations.

Table 1. The major characteristics of Kirjasampo (Sampo) and Satakirjasto (Sata)

Characteristics		Sampo	Sata
Searching	Quick search	Yes	Yes
	Advanced search	No	Yes
	Image search	Yes	No
	Browsing	Yes	Yes, after querying
Book Page In-formation	Author, title	Yes, always	Yes, always
	Keywords	Yes, often	Yes, often
	Content description	Yes, often	Yes, seldom
	Publication data	Yes, always	Yes, always
	Cover image	Yes, often	Yes, seldom
Other		Bookshelves, Tip of the day, Literary news, Book reviews, Recommendations	Library class

The browsing interface provides the user with the possibility to wander through the context of a work and through it to other works. Besides allowing one to walk the semantic network through the actors, books and keywords, the interface also provides recommendations, which automatically locate interesting semantically related content to the currently viewed work [10].

Sata is a traditional public library online catalog providing users with quick search, advanced search and browsing options. Searching starts with querying. In quick search, users key in search terms in a textbox, whereas in advanced search they may limit the search also by the type of literature (fiction – non-fiction), author, title, keywords, or other bibliographic information. The result list is organized by material type such as books or CDs. In the list the user should click the link "book" in order to explore the list of books retrieved. The list includes the following metadata from each book: author, title, material type, publication year and library class. A click on a book title leads to the book page containing metadata title, author, publication data, keywords from the fiction thesaurus Kaunokki. The upper right corner includes more recent books, a cover image and a link to the content description of the story.

In Sampo users may end up on a book page without querying, e.g. by browsing via links, whereas in Sata one query is a minimum requirement for accessing a book page. In general, book pages in Sampo include more information about the books compared to Sata. The systems are presented in Table 1.

3.3   Participants

We recruited participants by posting announcements on mailing lists for students of information studies and of literature. We used also snowball sampling by asking participants to mediate information to their friends about the test.

There were 30 participants in the experiment: 24 were females and 6 males. 23 were students: 12 from information studies and 11 from literature; the rest were professionals. The number of fiction books read during the last 12 months varied between 1-50, the average being 16. Of the participants, 19 borrowed fiction in the public library at least once a month and about half of them had searched for fiction in an online catalog at least once a month. Almost all the participants assessed their computer skills as at least good, and 17 of them as excellent.

We used between subjects design, assigning 15 participants to Sampo and 15 to Sata. It is necessary to check that there are no between group differences in variables, which may influence the distribution of attention in the book pages. A t-test revealed only one significant difference: the users of Sata borrowed fiction in the public library significantly more frequently compared to the users of Sampo ($p=.029$). There were no differences between the groups in the distribution of gender, age, in the number of novels read, self-assessed computer skills or in the frequency of searching fiction in library catalogues ($p>.05$). It is likely that the difference in the borrowing frequency does not have an influence on the results of eye-tracking between the groups.

None of the participants had used Sata, whereas two had used Sampo. It is likely that this does not bias the results.

3.4   Data Collection

Pretests were conducted for assessing the test arrangements and questionnaires. The actual tests took place in a gaze-tracking laboratory in September 2012. During searching participants' eye movements were captured by Tobii T60 eye-tracker. The device included a 17inch screen with the gaze-tracking mechanism. It allowed for the users' free head motion. Before each session users' eyes were calibrated to the screen to ensure the accuracy of recording. Minimum duration for fixation was set to 100 milliseconds, because it is considered as the minimum duration for a fixation [4]. The sampling data rate was 60Hz. There was no time limit for performing the search tasks.

We collected information by three questionnaires. The first one elicited before the test, users' background information like gender, book reading, library use and computer skills. After each task participants rated on a five-point scale how interesting the novel selected was (very interesting, fairly interesting, marginally interesting, could not find one, cannot say), and indicated the most decisive element in the metadata influencing their selection. The test was finished by a questionnaire eliciting users' assessments of the online catalogs used. In the end of the test, users received a cinema ticked for compensation.

The result lists in Sampo downloaded slowly. We informed participants about this and asked patience in searching. It is likely that the users of Sampo did not browse so many book pages as they would have done if the system had responded swiftly. This does not bias, however, the results of attention devoted to the pages, when they have been opened.

3.5   Analysis

We focus on the selection of novels in the book pages opened. The unit of observation is a book page, i.e. landing page from the result list, which contains the metadata of a particular book. We defined five areas of interest (AOI) for the metadata in each book page. They were 1) author and title, 2) keywords, 3) content description, 4) publication data, and 5) cover image.

For each of these areas the number of visits, total visit duration and the proportion of visit duration in an AOI of the total visit duration in all AOI were measured. A visit is defined as the interval of time between the first fixation on the AOI and the next fixation outside the AOI. If during a task the participant returns to the same AOI, then the new fixations on the AOI will be included in the calculations of the metric. Thus, this variable measures the duration of all visits within an AOI. Visit count measures the number of visits within an AOI. The number of visits indicates to what extent an AOI draws attention, and the total visit duration within an AOI indicates how central it is in the selection of books. Like fixation length and frequency, visit metrics, total duration in particular, can be considered as an indicator of attention and cognitive processing be it due to interest or difficulties in comprehension [4].

4   Results

Users opened 217 book pages in Sampo and 207 in Sata (p>.05). The average time spent on a book page was significantly longer in Sampo (23.5 sec) compared to Sata (13.5 sec) (p=.000).

4.1   The Frequency and Duration of Visits in Metadata

The largest number of visits were paid to keywords (Table 2). They were visited equally in both systems (c. 2.7; p=.92). After keywords, in Sata publication data was most frequently visited (2.48) followed by author/title data (1.46), content description (0.95) and cover (0.41). In Sampo, the corresponding order was content description (1.81), cover (1.43), author/title (1.05) and publication data (0.96). The difference between the systems was significant in the number of visits in author/title data (p=.014), content description (p=.000), publication data (p=.000) and cover (p=.000).

Table 2. The average number of visits in AOI

AOI	Sampo		Sata	
	n	Avrg	n	Avrg
Author and title	216	1.05	205	1.46
Keywords	216	2.68	186	2.70
Content description	182	1.81	20	0.95
Publication data	216	0.96	205	2.48
Cover image	178	1.43	114	0.41

Keywords excluded, users devoted most frequently attention in Sampo to content description and cover image, and less to author/title data and publication data. In Sata their popularity was vise versa: publication data and author/title data draw most frequently attention, whereas content description and cover were less frequently visited. The differences between these groups within the systems were statistically significant (paired-samples t-test p<.05).

Table 3. Total visit duration in AOI (Sec)

AOI	Sampo		Sata	
	n	Avrg	n	Avrg
Author and title	216	1.12	205	1.52
Keywords	216	5.14	186	5.03
Content description	182	12.04	19	13.13
Publication data	216	2.01	205	2.45
Cover image	177	1.92	114	0.38

The total visit duration in author/title data, publication data and content description was slightly longer in Sata compared to Sampo, while vising keywords took somewhat more time in Sampo (Table 3). However, the differences were not statistically significant. The only significant difference was in the visit duration in cover image, which took 1.92 sec in Sampo, but only 0.38 sec in Sata. Very small differences in the total visiting time in various AOI between the systems imply that users devoted as much attention to the same metadata regardless of the system.

In both systems, most time was devoted to content description, 12.04 sec in Sampo and 13.13 sec in Sata. This was twice as much as devoted to the second metadata element, keywords (5.14 vs. 5.03 sec), and four-five times more as devoted to the third one, publication data (2.01 vs. 2.45 sec). Although the total visit duration in Sata was longest in content description, the number of users visiting that metadata was only 19 compared to the 182 visitors in Sampo. Therefore, it is likely that other, more commonly visited metadata elements are more important in selecting books in Sata.

4.2 Modeling the Selection of Fiction

The participants were able to select for each task interesting books. In both systems the distribution of books on various levels of interest was similar (Chi^2: p=.69) (Table 4). About two thirds of the book pages browsed were uninteresting in both systems. The absolute number of non-interesting pages was about the same implying that there were no difference in the effort invested in browsing both systems. In all, there were no differences in selecting interesting reading between the systems.

Table 4. The distribution of book ratings (%)

Rating	Sampo (n=221)	Sata (n=213)
Very interesting	17	14
Fairly interesting	16	20
Marginally interesting	1	1
Not interesting	66	65
Total	100	100

Next we analyze how attention devoted to metadata in book pages was associated with the interest scores of books. The scoring was from four (very interesting) to zero (not interesting). We compare whether there are differences in the models explaining variation in book scores between the systems. The technique of modeling is linear regression analysis using stepwise variable selection. The variables used in modeling were the frequency and duration of visits in AOI in book pages. We also calculated the proportion of visit duration in an AOI of the total visit duration in all AOI.

For Sampo estimation produced a model with four variables significantly contributing to the interest scores of books (Table 5). It explained c. 30 % of the variation in the scores. The frequency of cover visits was clearly the strongest predictor of book scores (β=0.31), followed by the number of author/title visits (β=0.19), the proportion of the author/title visit duration of the total visit duration in all metadata items (β=0.18), and the proportion of keyword visit duration of the total visit duration in all metadata items (β=-0.16).

The model for Sampo indicates that 1) the more frequently readers visit book cover, and 2) the more frequently they visit author/title metadata and 3) the larger share these visits take of the total duration of visits in all metadata, and 4) the smaller the proportion of visit duration in keywords of all metadata visits, the more interesting is the book that is selected. It seems that a decision leading to the selection of an interesting book is based on visiting frequently on book cover, and on looking for a proportionally long time and frequently at the author/title information. Spending proportionally long time on keywords decreases the odds of selecting a good book. In addition to glancing at the cover frequently, devoting attention to author/title and not to keywords predicts selecting an interesting book.

Table 5. Multiple regressions on book scores in Sampo (n=221)

Step	Variable introduced	β	β	β	β
1	Book cover visit #	0.45***	0.41***	0.41***	0.31**
2	Author/title visit duration %		0.26***	0.24***	0.18*
3	Keyword visit duration %			-0.15*	-0.16*
4	Author/title visit #				0.19*
R		0.453	0.518	0.540	0.558
R^2		0.205	0.268	0.291	0.311
Adj. R^2		0.200	0.259	0.278	0.293
R^2 change		0.205***	0.063***	0.023*	0.020*
Model F		40.7***	28.8***	21.4***	17.5***

Note: * = $p \leq 0.05$; ** = $p \leq 0.01$; *** $p \leq 0.001$

The model estimated for Sata included five variables significantly contributing to the book scores (Table 6). These variables explain c. 32 % of the variation in interest scores. The predictors in the model were the proportion of author/title visit duration of the total visit duration in all metadata (β=0.41), the frequency of publication data visits (β=0.37), the duration of publication data visits (β=0.25), the frequency of author/title visits (β=-0.24) and the duration of cover visits (β=0.17).

Table 6. Multiple regressions on book scores in Sata (n=213)

Step	Variable introduced	β	β	β	β	β
1	Publication data visit #	0.42***	0.37***	0.23*	0.21*	0.37**
2	Author/title visit duration %		0.29***	0.31***	0.32***	0.41***
3	Publication data visit duration			0.24*	0.25*	0.25*
4	Cover visit duration				0.17*	0.17*
5	Author/title visit #					-0.24*
R		0.418	0.507	0.544	0.569	0.591
R^2		0.175	0.257	0.296	0.324	0.349
Adj. R^2		0.167	0.243	0.276	0.298	0.318
R^2 change		0.175***	0.083***	0.039*	0.028*	0.025*
Model F		22.6***	18.4***	14.7***	12.5***	11.1***

Note: * = $p \leq 0.05$; ** = $p \leq 0.01$; *** $p \leq 0.001$

The model for Sata indicates that 1) the greater the duration of author/title visits of all visits in metadata, 2) but the smaller the number of those visits, and 3) the greater the number and 4) duration of visits in publication data, and 5) the longer the duration of visits in cover, the more interesting book is selected. Chances for selecting an interesting book in Sata increased if users focused their attention proportionally most to a limited amount of author/title data, glanced frequently at publication data and devoted attention to book cover. In Sata users' selections are based on processing mostly author/title information and glancing frequently at publication metadata.

The models predicting interest scores differed between the systems. Their explanatory power was about the same, 32 % in Sata and 30 % in Sampo. The models had two common variables concerning author/title visits. Interestingly, content description did not contribute significantly to selecting fiction, although it took the greatest amount of attention in terms of visit duration. The conclusion is based on information from Sampo. There were too few users (n=19) visiting content description in Sata for the multivariate analysis.

5   Discussion and Conclusions

This is the first eye-tacking study analyzing how users observe metadata when selecting fiction in online catalogs. The study extends our knowledge to what extent users pay attention to metadata items in book pages, and how the modes of this attention contribute to selecting interesting novels in a traditional online catalog and an enriched online catalog for fiction.

There were no differences in the duration of visits in the metadata elements between the systems except book cover. It seems that in selecting fiction users devoted as much attention to the same metadata elements regardless of the system. However, in Sampo visits in book cover lasted significantly longer compared to Sata. The position of metadata items in both interfaces was about similar with the exception of cover image and content description. In Sampo cover image was located in the upper left corner, and in Sata in the upper right corner of the page. It is known that the upper left region in a web page is observed first, and proportionally most time is spent on fixating it. Users pay very little attention to the right side of web pages [3]. It seems that this regularity holds also in selecting fiction in book pages.

The pattern of visiting frequency in metadata differed between the systems. In Sata publication data and author/title data draw most frequently attention, whereas content description and cover image were less frequently visited. The pattern was vice versa in Sampo. This difference may in part be due to the differences in the position of these elements in the book pages. The better position of cover image and content description, but less favorable position of title/author data in Sampo compared to Sata may to some degree explain the differences in the patterns of visit frequency [cf. 3].

There were no differences between the systems in the number or in the grades of interest of the books selected. However, the average time spent on a book page selecting novels was significantly longer in Sampo compared to Sata. Thus, the users of Sampo had to invest more effort in selecting an interesting book compared to Sata.

We build a model for both systems for explaining the variation in the interest scores of books selected. The models differed somewhat. First, neither included variables representing content description and attention to keywords contributed negatively to finding books in Sampo. However, users spent considerably more time in visiting these metadata types compared to other types. Thus, although users devoted most attention to content description and keywords, they either had no bearing, or a negative effect on the selection of fiction.

Second, author/title visits had a significant but differing role in book selection in both systems. A proportionally long total visiting time in the author/title metadata consisting of infrequent visits in Sata, but of frequent visits in Sampo predicted finding an interesting novel. Thus, firm attention to author/title data in Sata, but glancing it frequently in Sampo produced success in selecting novels. In Sampo also glancing frequently book cover, but devoting minimal attention to keywords during visits contributed to finding an interesting novel. In Sata long and frequent visits in publication data also predicted successful book selection. It seems that in addition to author/title data, in the selection the users of Sampo leaned on cover image, whereas the users of Sata leaned on publication data. It is likely that the more common availability and the better position of cover images in Sampo compared to Sata explain in part the differences in the selection process.

The crucial role of author and title is surprising, when three of our four tasks aimed at selecting a novel not likely familiar to the participants. One would have expected that the content description of books as a more extensive information source had contributed more to selection compared to other metadata, author/title, in particular.

The remarkable role of author and title and the minimal role of content description contradict the findings on fiction selection in physical libraries. When browsing, readers most commonly select books based on text on the back cover, and then on passages of the book or cover, and less commonly on title [17]. In physical libraries readers inspect first external attributes of books, which trigger their interest like title or cover image, and then focus on internal attributes like passages in the book, which facilitate borrowing decisions [5]. Deviating from this, our results hint, that in online catalogs users base their choice on external attributes of books, i.e. author/title information, whereas the only internal attribute provided, i.e. content description is not crucial in selection. This causal interpretation is tentative, because from the time devoted to metadata it is difficult to infer, whether it led to the acceptance or rejection of the book. This requires more detailed empirical analysis for validation.

When users browse in libraries to find fiction, they commonly use author's name as a selection criterion. They choose titles unknown to them from known authors [5, 15]. Although in three of our four tasks the aim was to trigger browsing for unknown books, it may be that users to some extent combined author search with browsing [cf. 17]. It is also natural to pick a book by a familiar author known to write good novels, if it pops up in the result list.

To conclude, there were no differences between the systems in the ratings of books selected. However, the average time spent on a book page selecting books was significantly longer in the system designed for searching fiction. Thus, a system devoted to fiction search did not outperform a typical public library catalog. The position of metadata items in the interfaces seemed to explain to a certain extent the attention devoted to them. Unexpectedly, those metadata elements, which got least attention, predicted best the selection of novels, author/title, in particular. It is likely, that when browsing readers prefer selecting novels unknown to them but written by a known author. The next step in our study is to elaborate the results by search tasks; and analyze how readers' perceptions of the utility of metadata elements are associated to the attention devoted to them and to search success.

References

1. Adkins, D., Bossaller, J.E.: Fiction access points across computer-mediated book information sources. LISR 29(3), 354–368 (2007)
2. Balatsoukas, P., Ruthven, I.: An eye tracking approach to the analysis of relevance judgments on the web. JASIST 63(9), 1728–1746 (2012)
3. Buscher, G., Cutrell, E., Morris, M.: What do you see when you are surfing? In: Proceedings of the 27th International Conference on Human Factors in Computing Systems, pp. 21–30. ACM, New York (2009)
4. Cutrell, E., Guan, Z.: What are you looking for? An eye-tracking study of information usage in web search. In: Proceedings of the ACM HCI 2007 Conference on Human Factors in Computing Systems, pp. 407–415. ACM, New York (2007)
5. Goodall, D.: Browsing in the public libraries. In: LISU Occasional Paper No 1. Library and Information Statistics Unit, Loughborough (1989)
6. Hinze, A., McKay, D., Vanderschanz, N., Timpany, C., Cunningham, S.: Book selection behavior in the physical library: implications for ebook collections. In: Proceedings of JCDL 2012, pp. 305–314. ACM, New York (2012)
7. Huysmans, F., Hillebrink, C.: The future of the Dutch public library: Ten years on. SCP, The Hague (2008)
8. Library Statistics Finland 2010
9. Mikkonen, A., Vakkari, P.: Readers' search strategies for accessing books in public libraries. In: Proceedings of the 4th IIIX Symposium, pp. 214–233. ACM, New York (2012)
10. Mäkelä, E., Hypén, K., Hyvönen, E.: Improving Fiction Literature Access by Linked Open Data -Based Collaborative Knowledge Storage - the BookSampo Project. In: 78th IFLA General Conference and Assembly, Helsinki (2012),
    http://conference.ifla.org/ifla78
11. Nielsen, J.: Usability Engineering. Academic Press, Boston (1993)
12. Oksanen, S., Vakkari, P.: Emphasis on examining results in fiction searches contributes to finding good novels. In: Proceedings of JCDL 2012, pp. 199–202. ACM, New York (2012)
13. Pejtersen, A.M.: The Bookhouse: Modelling user's needs and search strategies as a basis for system design. Risø report M-2794. Roskilde Risø National Laboratory (1989)
14. Reading on the rise. A new chapter in the American literacy. National Endowment for the Arts' (2008), http://www.nea.gov/research/ReadingonRise.pdf (retrieved March 27, 2012)
15. Ross, C.S.: Making choices: What readers say about choosing books to read for pleasure. The Acquisition Librarian 13, 5–21 (2001)
16. Serola, S., Vakkari, P.: The role of public libraries in citizens' activities. Publications of the Ministry of Education and Culture 21 (2011), http://www.minedu.fi/export/sites/default/OPM/Julkaisut/2011/liitteet/OKM21.pdf (retrieved March 27, 2012)
17. Spiller, D.: The provision of fiction for public libraries. J Libr. 12(4), 238–266 (1980)

Social Information Behaviour in Bookshops: Implications for Digital Libraries

Sally Jo Cunningham[1], Nicholas Vanderschantz[1], Claire Timpany[1],
Annika Hinze[1], and George Buchanan[2]

[1] University of Waikato, New Zealand
{sallyjo,vtwoz,ctimpany,hinze}@waikato.ac.nz
[2] City University London, United Kingdom
george.buchanan.1@city.ac.uk

Abstract. We discuss here our observations of the interaction of bookshop customers with the books and with each other. Contrary to our initial expectations, customers do not necessarily engage in focused, joint information search, as observed in libraries, but rather the bookshop is treated as a social space similar to a cafe. Our results extend the known repertoire of collaborative behaviours, supporting further development of models of user tasks and goals. We compare our findings with previous work and discuss possible implications of our observations for the design of digital libraries as places of both information access and social interaction.

Keywords: participant observation, social space, collaborative information behaviour, book-based social networking.

1 Introduction

Investigations of human behaviour in physical bookshops and libraries have resulted in valuable insights into user needs and tasks in digital libraries [6,8]. Most previous work focused on academic libraries, where the library users are likely to be engaged in information searches to support specific tasks. This paper looks instead at information behaviour in commercial bookshops, to extend our understanding of physically sited information behaviour beyond academic collections. We focused on the non-fiction sections of the bookshops to create a level of comparability to behaviours identified in academic libraries.

A bookstore is, of course, a store. Stores are understood to be a social places frequented in the company of friends and family. Consequently, the difference between patrons visiting academic libraries and customers shopping bookstores is that the former tend to engage with the collection on their own, while the latter often visit in groups. This paper explores the behaviour of pairs or small groups of bookshop customers by conducting ethnographic participant-observations in five bookshops.

Previous studies in libraries and bookshops observed the social interactions of people searching with others [4] or using the bookshop café as a social space [23]. Other studies analysed collaborative *use* of books [5] and ebooks [15]. However,

T. Aalberg et al. (Eds.): TPDL 2013, LNCS 8092, pp. 84–95, 2013.

there is very scant knowledge about book selection undertaken in the context of a group. To the best of our knowledge no studies have analysed the practical implications of this collaborative behaviour for digital library environments.

Using observation methods similar to those applied in earlier library and bookshop studies [6,22] allows us to compare insights. In this study we found that behaviours of bookshop patrons are identifiably different to those of library patrons. Not all observed customers appeared to have specific information needs, but seemed to treat the bookshop as a physical space for social interactions, often occurring in tandem with book selection. Many book-related group interactions observed within the physical space are currently not supported in digital libraries. The contribution of this paper lies in an analysis of how the observed book and social interactions may be transferred into the digital library environment.

2   Related Work

Collaborative information work has been long established as an area of interest in digital libraries [24]. While the pursuit of individual information needs remains a complex area, fundamental research on information seeking behaviour, reading and group work has repeatedly demonstrated the critical role of the collaborative discovery, selection and reading of texts [15]. Current models of collaborative information behaviour do not explicitly address collaborative document selection (in the virtual or physical environment), [8,20]. As our focus here is on group information behaviour in bookstores, this related work section looks at collaborative information behaviour research as applied in physical document collections, current support for book-based social networking, and issues for group members' maintaining a sense of each other's presence in a physical or digital environment.

2.1   Collaborative Information Behaviour

Of the few naturalistic studies of behaviour in bookshops and libraries, even fewer address collaboration in browsing and searching for books. For example, Bryant et al. [4] examine collaborative behaviour, but primarily in the use of books rather than their selection. A study of children in bookshops uncovered considerable collaboration in browsing, selection, and reading [7], where the interactions appear to be initiated to enhance enjoyment of the bookshop experience (rather than to achieve greater efficiency or precision in book selection).

The majority of ethnographic, qualitative research on collaboration in a library setting has often focused on interaction between library staff and library patrons [17]. In this work, we focus instead on interactions between bookshop customers primarily with each other, but also at times in their interactions with bookshop assistants. Investigations of collaboration in work teams have been primarily longitudinal and focus on information search, information dissemination within the group, and information use [19,21]. These studies come to a fine-grained understanding of complex behaviour in one specific team. We examine selection and browsing only, over a short time span for each set of collaborators.

2.2 Book-Based Social Networking

At present, shared experience of reading in the digital environment is often typified by book-based social networking sites such as librarything.com, goodreads.com and shelfari.com. These systems are web applications that focus on cataloguing one's own personal digital library. All have forums, the ability to rate, recommend or review the books, and make use of social networking tools like Facebook, Twitter, and email.

Existing ebook reading software (e.g., Kindle, Kobo and Inkling) offer similar social networking links to share and comment on the content of a book. These comments are open to all readers (i.e., owners) of the ebook and are proprietary to a specific software publisher. Online book clubs are found on a mixture of dedicated sites (e.g., socialbooks.com) and private blogs (e.g., www.cornflowerbooks.co.uk) that provide meeting places to discuss books. The book-based social networking activities focus on post-purchase or post-loan group activities. Academic research on these tools is limited. However, there is an equal need to understand reading outside of the digital fold, and we focus particularly on pre-purchase activities in bookshops.

2.3 Social Presence

Social presence refers to the sense of 'being with' other individuals: the "sense of shared space, shared engagement and shared (inter)activity" [3] as two or more people occupy the same physical or virtual environment. Social presence exists on a continuum, with the affordances of that environment determining the degree of each individual's potential for awareness of others. Face-to-face physical interaction is assumed to be the gold standard for supporting social presence, as that mode encompasses the full bandwidth of verbal and non-verbal (e.g., gesture, body language, facial expression) communication.

When people are together physically, they often maintain a sense of awareness of each other even though they are not in direct line of sight. Given that one of the goals of this paper is to investigate how to transfer the behaviour from the physical to the digital world, we will also consider techniques for maintaining awareness for other people in the digital world: specifically, ambient awareness. Baharin & Mühlberger [2] describe "Atomic Interaction" as "the creation and maintenance of contact without the creation and transfer of content." In the physical world we do this when visiting a café or shop, and in the digital world when using video conferencing (ie. Skype) and instant messaging (ie. Twitter, Facebook).

3 Study Method

3.1 Observation Methodology

To investigate customer behaviour in bookshops, we conducted anonymous observations at five bookshops. We observed the activities of groups of two or more customers as they interacted with each other and the store's books. Where possible, each group was followed from entry to exit, for a full picture of each visit. The criterion for selecting a group for observation was that one or more member actively browsed the shelves (not socializing, drinking coffee etc.). To avoid too wide a spread of genre, the observations focused on non-fiction reading, as it is best covered in existing literature. Manual notes were taken in situ, and later transcribed for analysis.

3.2   Participant Sample

Forty two observations were taken at five bookshops that represented different sizes, specialistations and locations. Four stores were in New Zealand and one in the USA. Of the four New Zealand bookstores, shop A is an upscale second-hand bookshop in an urban centre location (18 observations), shop B the bookshop of a research university (4 obs.), shop C is a large chain bookshop in a central business district (3 obs.), and D is a specialist art and architecture bookshop (1 observation). Shop E is a large chain bookshop located in a popular mall in a mid-sized city in the USA (16 obs.). Observations were conducted separately by three of the researchers; they occurred both on weekends and working days, and in the evenings and the afternoons.

The 42 observed groups included a total of 94 people (56 female, 38 male). These groups, hereafter referred to as G1 to G42, comprised of 9 groups of female customers, 24 groups of male & female customers, 2 groups of male customers and one group with a male customer with unknown associates. There were six parent/child groups, and a total of nine children. No children were observed without adults. Group size ranged from two to five people (35 in groups of two, 3 of three, 1 of four and 2 of five, and 1 group of unknown size). The duration of the observations varied from 1 to 64 minutes, with a mean of 11 minutes. The estimated age of customers included thirty-seven 18-29 year olds, nineteen 30-39 year olds, nineteen 40-49 year olds, eight 50-59 year olds. No data was recorded for two customers.

4   Results

4.1   Observed Patterns of Bookshop Visits

We identified three main patterns of interaction that occurred within the groups over the observed duration of their visit to the bookshops.

Social Interaction (24 Instances): Customers were observed engaging predominantly in social interactions such as chatting, waiting for a friend, passing time and dating, while browsing for and sampling books.

Example of Social Interaction (G4). A couple in their early 20's in the Graphic Novel section. This pair had a large format (bigger than A4) book "The Batman Films" which was on display. He flipped through the book as they both looked. After 5min he sat down on a sofa and she stood beside him and looked while he flipped. She then crouched next to sofa. Their interaction involved pointing to images as they turned page-by-page, exploring together, though not reading the text. He reads aloud, following the lines with his finger then explained some backstory to her. She goes away, he stays and keeps looking page-by-page. She comes back and sits next to him, it appears she had bought a book. He reads, and explains more background, she asks questions while they flip. After about 5min they put the book away and left the shop.

This social interaction between the couple seemed to be a means of him introducing her to an interest of his (Batman movies). In another instance of a social interaction (G7), two customers told each other about their countries of origin using travel books as props. Here the interactions appeared to be more about getting to know each other, with the books as tools to facilitate the conversation.

Collaborative Search (8 Instances): The conventional conception of collaborative information seeking is a group of people engaging in a search to accomplish a shared task. The behaviour of some observed groups seemed to fit into this pattern: we observed indications of shared information need. We observed customers engaging in shared search for books where only one of the party seemed to have an information need and the others were helping in the search for a book.

Example of Collaborative Search (G6). A man and a woman in their 20s searched together for books. She began in the 'Top 100' section of the shop: she picks up a book and looks at the back and front, then flips through and returns it. She walks along the shelf looking until she gets to Travel Guides where she stops next to him. They talk about the books, he holds one and flips through, she turns pages of a second book. They compare the indexes, searching for information on a specific location. They laugh. She grabs a third book, he points to the content and reads out parts. They look at the backs of the books, then walk away without any books.

As with other groups, this pair appeared to have a shared goal for searching for specific information. Groups accomplished collaboration in search by different means. Typically, group members stayed near each other, browsing the same section. Potentially relevant books were examined and either handed to the other person (G9), or examined together, side by side (G6). In other instances of collaborative search, we noted groups referring to bibliographic data for comparison, such as table of contents, front matter and covers. The physical act of pointing, flipping and turning the book synchronously so that both partners may review the material visually in real time appears to be an important aspect of this type of interaction.

Independent Search (11 Instances): Each customer in these groups seemed to follow individual motivations for browsing in the bookshop. They searched independently, occasionally sharing their finds.

Example of Independent Search (G8). Two women in their 20s visiting multiple sections of the store. Despite seeming to have independent search goals, they repeatedly interacted. 1st woman "I'm gonna run around this corner and try to find the book I want, it's a book about cooking for a baby" and while she scans the shelves, the 2nd woman reads text messages. The 1st woman gave a running commentary of her search to the 2nd woman, who continues to text. She half-pulls several books before moving to find another section. Failing to find the section she wants, she asks a shop assistant who takes her to the section and helps her find the book. She explains her choice of which book to get saying "this one is bigger, I get more". The 2nd woman now has a book and reads it to the first. The 1st woman pulls a book, showing it to the 2nd; they laugh, return the book and leave. The 1st woman buys 2 books, the 2nd one.

Each of these individuals were searching for different books, yet both shared their discoveries and spoke with each other about the process. This type of shared experience seemed have the purpose of a social gathering as well as searching for specific material. This was seen with groups and pairs of adults as well as with groups of mixed age visitors, i.e. families or adults and children. We observed both verbal and nonverbal communication with synchronous and asynchronous interactions.

4.2   Observed Sharing Behaviours

We also observed the following sharing behaviours between customers, which occurred within the patterns described above. Patterns of bookshop visits describe at a macro level the overall type of interaction between the individuals within the group. The observed sharing behaviours below occur at the micro level.

One customer reads aloud to another one as the second one continues their activity, e.g., he reads to her while they are comparing the books (G6 as described above); she scans display books, he is reading and shuffling near her. He reads a passage to her, she keeps scanning books, (G11, couple with child).

Customer shows or points to a part of a book that one of the customers is holding. G11: after reading aloud, he shows her the book content; G14 is in the gardening section, she reads and shows him a page: "I like how they do this..."

Customers talk about a topic inspired by the books around them: Couple G15 standing back in isle and scan and talk, don't pull or touch; two women (G39) stand in Philosophy section, they look at the titles and discuss several concepts in philosophy.

Customer passes a book to another: in three groups with children (G11,G16,G9) a book was passed between parent and child: one finds a book and passes it to the other for inspection; G36: Girl to Dad: "Can you pass down The Naughtiest Girl?".

Customer looks over the shoulder of another customer: typically the first person is reading, while a second person is busy otherwise (e.g. reading, browsing, texting), the second person finishes their activity to see what the first person is focussing on, e.g., G37: woman leafs through book, man looks over her shoulder. This interaction is more passive than "showing" or "pointing"; it is initiated by the observer.

Customers point to books on shelves during a discussion, e.g., she shows him a book in her hand and points out one on a shelf: "This whole stand and only one book on Corgi's!" (G18); a man takes another couple to corner of the store, explains that he knew that these books were there because he saw them the last time he visited.

Customers text or talk on the phone, sometimes seems to be related to books, sometimes not, e.g., G16: a woman on phone went outside (we assume conversation was not related to books); G12: found a book and phoned to talk about that book.

Questions about process: group members ask how the other's search is proceeding; G11: woman: "Did you find anything?".

Customers told each other what they were doing, sometimes in reaction to a question, but often unprompted, e.g., G29: "Well, I'm going to get [this book]!"

Reading together: father and son (G13) are sitting on the floor, father opens the book to the middle, looks at photos, leafs forward. Son: "What's that?" father: "A creature" Son: "What?" Father: "A gross Alien".

Searching together: couple G23 in the diet section, she: "There's gotta be another one here; mamma has one that's blue".

Customers chatted while standing between the bookshelves. Conversation might or might not be related to books, e.g. G35 (Mother, Granddaughter family group) Girl looks for books, they all talk about her reading those books when she was younger.

Verbal versus Non-verbal Interactions

The observed shared behaviours can be distinguished into verbal (e.g. read aloud) and non-verbal interactions (e.g., pointing). The focus of an interaction was observed to revolve around a shared book (e.g. when reading together), be about different books (e.g., when comparing books) or not be related to any particular book (e.g., chatting). Non-book interactions were verbal in all observed instances (11). When behaviours revolved around the same book the interactions were close to evenly divided between verbal (19) and non-verbal (17). When involving different book, interactions were predominantly verbal (21) rather than non-verbal (3).

Group members usually enter the shop together and frequently go together to a specific set of shelves. They rarely explicitly directed each other to another area of the shop. Instead one person would "drift" to a near-by section of shelves, while the other continued browsing and then caught up after a short while. There are subtle physical cues in facial expression and body language that people can interpret subconsciously to understand the mood and the level of engagement of the other people in the group.

Bookshop as a Social Space

Bookshops are locations for people to enjoy each other's company and to socialise, as well as being used for locating information. Bookshops share aspects of both libraries and stores. At the same time, people behave more freely than they would in a library. For example, in a mother-daughter group G34, Mum starts dancing to the music and gets Daughter to dance as well, and they dance to the middle of the shop. Bookshops can be a backdrop for talking about personal matters. At times the books serve as props to further the conversation. For example, a pair in group G7 introduced themselves to each other using books of their home countries, New Zealand and Thailand ("this is called 90 mile beach", "So here is the central part of Bangkok").

Here and in Section 4.1 we have noted that interactions within the bookshop environment may not be directly related to searching for books, or indeed the bookshop was used as a means to pass time. If digital libraries successfully serviced this social activity around reading, then we may be likely to see a similar kind of incidental social activity that is not directly book related. This aspect will be expanded in the next section.

5   Discussion

We now demonstrate how our findings lead to new requirements for the further development of digital libraries. This idea that collaborative practices in DLs require investigation is not new: Twidale et al. [24] stated that "although the digital library threatens collaborative activities, it also opens up new opportunities that are presently prevented by the physical constraints of digital libraries". That research was executed in the context of a library rather than a bookshop. Consequently, many of the participants in that study exhibited clear information needs, which this was not apparent in our observations. This suggestts that digital libraries need to cater for both task-oriented and 'serendipitous' information searching behaviours.

Research in digital libraries and human-computer interaction has investigated the design of collaborative reading systems. Raffle et al [18] investigated collaborative reading between an adult and child in different locations, while Pearson et al. [15], studied co-located users with individual devices reading a single document. Some of Pearson's co-located behaviours mirror ours, with readers physically pointing out specific passages to another. In the case of co-located users this sort of interaction is easily supported by natural gesture. When readers remotely collaborate, the challenge is to design for equally intuitive and light-weight sharing.

5.1   Affordances of Digital Book Sharing Environments

Sharing between people in a physical bookshop is typically synchronous while book sharing in a digital environment may more likely be asynchronous (cf. [24]). Fig. 2 compares the support for the sharing behaviours we observed in physical stores (see Sect. 4.2), in different digital environments. In the figure, + indicates full support for the observed social behaviours, o indicates partial support, and – no support. Note that partial support may indicate that a behaviour that would be synchronous in the bookshop may be supported only asynchronously in the system. We make the assumption that system users are not co-located (i.e., each is using a computer).

As indicated by Fig. 2, traditional digital libraries and ereaders, on the whole, do barely support collaborative book search/interaction. In particular, it is difficult with these technologies to pass a book, point to a set of books, show or point to content, read out loud, or "look over a shoulder." Dedicated systems such as cloudbooks, family story play, merely address singular aspects of a shared bookshop experience. Shared wishlists (e.g. as offered by Amazon) have a different focus (information instead of shared experience) and fall short of many of the criteria.

Many of the social networks and web applications in the lower part of Figure 2 are not inherently book-focussed. However, many of the users of these latter digital tools use them to discuss books they have read, are reading, or intend to read.

The purpose of the systems in the upper part of Figure 1 is to support an individual in locating interesting documents, and possibly managing that relevant subset of the larger collection. The systems at the bottom part, typified by message and voice services like Skype, or social networks like Facebook or LibraryThing, could support discussion or sharing of material. At present, DL systems provide a limited awareness both of an immediate social circle and of the wider enviroment. These two factors were a continual feature of group dynamics in the physical bookshop.

No single system currently supports the user in both sets of behaviours. A 'complete' solution could be created by 'gluing' together individual systems that support selected features. However, this would have significant engineering problems, and would likely be brittle, inefficient and not transferable between different DL systems. In terms of engineering, and interaction quality, a single intentionally-designed system is much more likely to provide an optimal solution. The optimal framework for this is a fruitful line for future research. A further constraint is that an effective design will, likely, use nearly subliminal, ambient feedback, rather than explicitly depict social information.

		read aloud	show content	talk about books	pass books	look over shoulder	point to shelved item	text/talk on phone	question about process	tell what they are doing	reading together	searching together	chatting
book focus	digital library	-	-	-	-	-	-	-	-	-	-	-	-
	ebook reader	-	-	+	-	-	-	-	-	o	o	-	o
	cloudBooks	-	+	-	-	+	-	-	-	-	-	+	-
	family story play	+	-	o	-	-	-	-	-	-	+	-	o
	shared wishlist	-	-	-	-	-	o	-	-	-	-	-	-
social focus	video/audio messaging	+	+	+	+	+	-	+	+	+	+	+	+
	text-based messaging	-	-	+	-	-	-	o	+	+	-	+	+
	social networks	-	-	+	-	-	-	-	o	o	-	o	o
	book-based social networking	-	-	+	-	-	-	-	o	o	-	o	o
	blogs	-	-	+	-	-	-	-	o	o	-	o	o

Fig. 1. Support for social book interactions (+ strong support, o partial support, - no support)

While the sharing of books and shared review of books in a physical environment is tactile and natural, in a digital environment, where two readers may not be co-located, the interaction is not as intuitive. Insights gained in this study into patterns of engagement with physical book collections may be transferable to e-books to create more effective display and search systems and how sharing books is conducted within these digital spaces. Digital libraries, ebook collections and digital search systems only seem to support asynchronous collaboration methods (e.g., email or social bookmarking). Support for synchronous collaboration will need to be investigated.

5.2   Interaction Constraints

Earlier research in collaborative information behaviour primarily focused on students and academic staff at university libraries, and on formal work groups (e.g., in healthcare [19] or the military [16]). The assumptions for collaborative groups in these domains is that they have specific, often ongoing, information needs, the documents located in the search can be matched to that information need in a relevance assessment, and the documents used to complete a common group task. These assumptions do not necessarily hold in a commercial bookstore: members of the group might have a common task and information need to fulfil; or only one group member has an identified need that the others are assisting in fulfilling; or each member might have a separate information need that the others might, or might not, assist with as they shop together; or indeed, none of the group members have a specific need but instead look for 'something interesting' or simply aim to kill time.

Support for formal work must often necessarily include cognitively and, perhaps, interactively 'heavy-weight' actions. This is a consequence of complexity: group members must not only individually locate useful material, but must also disseminate the document through the group and maintain an 'interwoven situational awareness' [21] of the other group members' understanding of the state of the task and information gathered to date. To avoid ambiguity, and costly consequences in long-term activity, an 'upfront' cost of attention is worthwhile, even if uncertain factors, like intention, require explicit articulation.

In contrast, support for the informal, transitory and less directed behaviours observed in bookshops must be 'light-weight'. The individual group members' understandings of the others' objectives appear less formed, but also inherently less consequential and across short timespans. Each member's motivations and goals may change frequently as the brief shopping period progresses. Mutual understanding of each other's general interests and tastes are grounded in shared social and personal backgrounds, rather than in formal relationships for accomplishing specific tasks. A light-weight approach would build on the shared implicit understandings by not forcing formal recording of inherently fluid personal preferences.

5.3   Bookshops as Third Places

Oldenburg's [14] notion of "third places" has been described as "a place of refuge other than the home or workplace where people can regularly visit and commune with friends, neighbours, co-workers, and even strangers" [13]. From our observations, the bookshop constitutes a "third place" which people regularly visit with families and friends: e.g. in family group, when it was time to leave, Dad called out "Come on you lot, we're coming back tomorrow" (G36). The social activity that starts around, but extends beyond, books (see Sec. 4.2) may enable a similar status for digital libraries.

This finding is partially speculative, is supported by research that demonstrates a similar effect when facets of the bookshop environment were brought in to physical libraries [1]. Furthermore, Trager [23] notes that "mega-bookstores" are deliberate, not accidental, social spaces. Such bookshops are designed to be welcoming and comfortable, including sofas, tables to sit and drink coffee and play areas for children. The important social aspect of these reading and purchasing spaces is carefully manufactured. Only one of the five bookstores in our observations was one of these "mega-bookstores" yet similar social interactions were occurring across all five stores despite four not being specifically designed to facilitate this behaviour. We mirror Trager's finding that customers often do not come with specific information needs, but are happy to browse, or use books to facilitate conversations within a social space.

Current DL systems do not support or achieve the sense of a third place. Social interaction and collaborative functionality are weak or non-existent. The best examples include seeing download rates for books (e.g., in the ACM DL) or the passages of books anonymously highlighted by others (e.g., Kindle reader). There is some evidence that digital library users value these supports, however slight, for creating a sense of the existence of a larger group of readers [25]. However, the primary experience of the digital library is that of an isolated user with only tangential awareness of the activities of others.

6   Conclusions

In this study both observations were conducted of customers and their interactions when selecting books within a physical bookshop. Our most significant insight is that people do more than look for information in bookshops: there is a significant social and recreational aspect to the experience. Engagement with the books themselves seems to be relatively indirect and based more heavily on browsing than on searching.

It appears that the social interactions in which the groups engaged during book selection may be "collaborative grounding" behaviour [9] – i.e., the individuals seeking to reinforce the appropriateness of the book being selected. This however, seems to be conducted in a different manner than that observed in library observations. The "collaborative grounding" in a bookshop seemed to be conducted in a less direct manner, where the interaction appeared to be more social in nature.

Current support for the broad spectrum of activities that support this collaborative grounding in DL systems appears limited, nor is there a ready solution by coopting other technologies from elsewhere. The physical space of the bookshop can help us hypothesise what features may be most appropriate in a digital environment for the collaboration of socially motivated groups of people and their collaborative assessment of books. Further work is needed to consolidate and theorise the current gap in our understanding of, and support for, social activity in and around reading.

References

1. Aabø, S., Audunson, R.: Use of library space and the library as place. Library & Information Science Research 34(2), 138–149 (2012)
2. Baharin, H., Mühlberger, R.: Living with the sound of the past: experiencing sonic atomic interaction using the sound diary. In: Procs. 10th Intl. Conf. NZ Chapter of the ACM's Special Interest Group on Human-Computer Interaction, pp. 101–104. ACM (2009)
3. Barden, P., et al.: Telematic dinner party: Designing for togetherness through play and performance. In: Procs. Designing Interactive Systems, pp. 38–47. ACM press (2012)
4. Bohley, K.T.: "Browsing madness" and global sponsors of literacy: The politics and discourse of deterritorialized reading practices and space in Singapore. Journal of Audience and Reception Studies 8(2), 85–119 (2011)
5. Bryant, J.E., Matthews, G., Walton, G.: Academic libraries and social learning space: A case study of Loughborough University Library, UK. Journal of Librarianship and Information Science 41(1), 7–18 (2009)
6. Buchanan, G., McKay, D.: In the Bookshop: Examining Popular Search Strategies. In: Proceedings of ACM/IEEE JCDL 2011 Ottawa, Canada, pp. 269–278. ACM (2011)
7. Cunningham, S.J.: Children in the physical collection: Implications for the digital library. Procs. American Society for Information Science and Technology 48(1), 1–10 (2011)
8. Hinze, A., McKay, D., Vanderschantz, N., Timpany, C., Cunningham, S.J.: Book selection behavior in the physical library: implications for ebook collections. In: Procs. ACM/IEEE Joint Conference on Digital Libraries, pp. 305–314 (2012)
9. Hertzum, M.: Collaborative Information Seeking: The Combined Activity of Information Seeking and Collaborative Grounding. Information Processing & Management 44(2), 957–962 (2008)
10. Hyldegard, J.: Collaborative information behavior–exploring Kuhlthau's Information Search Process model in a group-based educational setting. Information Processing & Management 42, 276–298 (2006)
11. McKay, D., Hinze, A., Heese, R., Vanderschantz, N., Timpany, C., Cunningham, S.J.: An Exploration of ebook Selection Behavior in Academic Library Collections. In: Zaphiris, P., Buchanan, G., Rasmussen, E., Loizides, F. (eds.) TPDL 2012. LNCS, vol. 7489, pp. 13–24. Springer, Heidelberg (2012)

12. McKay, D., Buchanan, G., Vanderschantz, N., Timpany, C., Cunningham, S.J., Hinze, A.: Judging a book by its cover: interface elements that affect reader selection of ebooks. tba, OzCHI (2012b)

13. Mehta, V., Bosson, J.K.: Third places and the social life of streets. Environment and Behavior 42(6), 779–805 (2010)

14. Oldenburg, R.: The Great Good Place: Cafes. Coffee Shops, Community Centers, Beauty Parlors, General Stores, Bars, Hangouts, and How They Get You Through the Day (1989)

15. Pearson, J., Owen, T., Thimbleby, H.T., Buchanan, G.: Co-reading: investigating collaborative group reading. In: Procs. JCDL 2012, pp. 325–334. ACM Press (2012)

16. Precop, P.: A qualitative study of collaborative information seeking. Journal of Documentation 58(5), 533–547 (2002)

17. Procter, R., Goldenberg, A., Davenport, E., McKinlay, A.: Genres in support of collaborative information retrieval in the virtual library. Interacting with Computers 10(2), 157–175 (1998)

18. Raffle, H., et al.: Family story play: reading with young children (and elmo) over a distance. In: Procs. ACM SIGCHI, pp. 1583–1592. ACM Press (2010)

19. Reddy, M., Spence, P.R.: Collaborative information seeking: a field study of a multidisciplinary patient care team. Info. Processing & Management 44(1), 242–255 (2008)

20. Shah, C.: Toward collaborative information seeking (CIS). In: JCDL Workshop on Collaborative Information Retrieval (2008), http://workshops.fxpal.com/jcdl2008/submissions/tmpE1.pdf

21. Sonnonwald, D.H., Pierce, L.G.: Information behavior in dynamic group work contexts: Interwoven situational awareness, dense social networks and contested collaboration in command and control. Inf. Processing and Management 36, 461–479 (2000)

22. Timpany, C., Alqurashi, H., Hinze, A., Cunningham, S.J., Vanderschantz, N.: Shared browsing and book selection in an academic library. In: Workshop on Collaborative Information Seeking, San Antonio, TX (in press, 2013)

23. Trager, K.D.: Reading in the borderland: An ethnographic study of serious readers in a mega-bookshop café. The Communication Review 8(2), 185–236 (2005)

24. Twidale, M., Nichols, D.M., Paice, C.D.: Browsing is a Collaborative Activity. Information Processing and Management 33(6), 761–783 (1997)

25. Winget, M.: Social Reading and Its Implications for Preservation. Preservation, Digital Technology & Culture 42(1) (in press, 2013)

Do User (Browse and Click) Sessions Relate to Their Questions in a Domain-Specific Collection?

Jeremy Steinhauer[1], Lois M.L. Delcambre[1],
Marianne Lykke[2], and Marit Kristine Ådland[3]

[1] Portland State University, Department of Computer Science, Portland, OR, U.S.A.
`{jsteinha,lmd}@cs.pdx.edu`
[2] Aalborg University Nyhavnsgade 14, Room 3-16, 9000 Aalborg, Denmark
`mlykke@hum.aau.dk`
[3] Dept. of Library and Information Science, Oslo University College, Oslo, Norway
`marit-kristine.adland@hioa.no`

Abstract. We seek to improve information retrieval in a domain-specific collection by clustering user sessions as recorded in a click log and then classifying later user sessions in real-time. As a preliminary step, we explore the main assumption of this approach: whether user sessions in such a site relate to the question that they are answering. The contribution of this paper is the evaluation of the suitability of common machine learning measurements (measuring the distance between two sessions) to distinguish sessions of users searching for the answer to same or different questions. We found that sessions for people answering the same question are significantly different than those answering different questions, but results are dependent on the distance measure used. We explain why some distance metrics performed better than others.

1 Introduction

With the advent of the Internet, collections often allow searching and browsing. And sites often have logs that capture browse moves in addition to queries and clicksthroughs. We are interested in using sessions in such a log for domain-specific sites to personalize search results to improve information retrieval.

Researchers have attempted to personalize search results based on profiles, ratings, and web usage logs. Many researchers have used machine learning to cluster users based on the similarity of their behavior [1-7]. Based on the cluster to which a user belongs, they predict items in a collection that might be of interest to that user (collaborative filtering). However, we have found no studies that directly address the fundamental viability of using click logs with these machine learning techniques. In particular, few have reported the effects of various distance measures or ways of representing user actions on the overall performance of the clustering. In this paper we address the suitability of machine learning techniques to cluster web usage logs via these research questions:

1. How well can we distinguish between users searching for answers to the same questions from users searching for answers to different questions?

T. Aalberg et al. (Eds.): TPDL 2013, LNCS 8092, pp. 96–107, 2013.

2. Does question similarity affect the ability to tell these two types of sessions apart?
3. Does question difficulty (measured by average session length) affect the ability to tell them apart?

We conducted a user study where we asked participants to find the answer to a set of ten questions; each question was answered by fifty users. We selected existing questions from various Internet question-answering sites appropriate for our domain and we analyzed the pair-wise similarity of the questions we used.

We describe related work in Section 2, the methods we used for gathering and analyzing our data in Section 3, and our data analysis in Section 4. In Section 5, we discuss our result and describe what can be done to build on our work.

2   Related Work

Much work using machine learning techniques with web logs focuses on web search engine logs of queries and click-through data, without a user's full search and browse history. Also, researchers use machine learning techniques without verifying that any benefit they might derive comes from an actual correspondence between clicks and users' information needs [1-7].

Similar to our work, Strehl et al. [8] performed a systematic analysis of distance measures for the purposes of improving information retrieval. They tested the ability of clustering algorithms to group similar pages together. They tested some of the same distance measures we do using page content as their feature vector (instead of user sessions) and evaluated the performance of various clustering algorithms with varying distance measures, whereas we evaluated the distance measures directly.

Some work has analyzed raw query and click-through logs to understand user information needs and behaviors. Jansen et al. [9] used Excite click logs to identify trends in user searching mistakes. Ageev et al. [10] gathered logs of users answering a set of hard to answer questions. Both of these studies used click logs to compare user search sessions, neither used machine learning distance metrics and only Ageev et al. used both search and browse behaviors of user. Note that we are not attempting to identify or classify user behavior or information needs; our users have known information needs (i.e., the questions that we provided for them).

Pallis et al. [11] evaluated clustering algorithms based on Web user sessions by examining clusters and trying to infer what each cluster represents. While their validation method is similar to ours, the authors did their validation after the application of clustering algorithms. We are interested in the applicability of these types of machine learning techniques based purely on the session data, before any clustering techniques have been applied.

3   Methods

Here we describe how we selected questions for users to answer, the study design, the user session model, and the distance metrics we evaluated.

Questions. We selected the American Cancer Society's website (cancer.org) as our domain-specific collection. We gathered 141 questions from cancer forums, the question and answer sections of cancer sites, and question asking sites such as Yahoo! Answers. We determined that 120 of these questions could be answered using cancer.org by attempting to find the answers to the questions using cancer.org.

An oncologist listed which cancer types, if any, were associated with each question. A lay person estimated the difficulty of each question, on a scale from 1 to 5, based on how long it took to find the answer using cancer.org. To determine the relatedness of questions based on criteria other than cancer type, we assessed questions for general topics; 15 topics were chosen. These topics were associated with each question when appropriate. For example the question: "Where do ampullary cancers normally start?" was associated with the topic *detection*.

We determined question distance scores between questions using two measurements. The first pairwise question distance measure is based on the percentage of overlap of related cancer types between a pair of questions. If T_1 and T_2 are the cancer types associated with question Q_1 and Q_2 in the pair and $C=T_1 \cap T_2$, the question distance score $QDist_{ct}$ is:

$$QDist_{ct}(Q_1, Q_2) = 1 - \frac{|C|}{((|T_1| + |T_2|)/2)}. \tag{1}$$

For this measure, 0 means that the questions have the same associated cancer type(s) and 1 means they have no cancer types in common.

The second question distance measure, $QDist_{tfidf}$, compares term vectors for the questions. Text of a question is concatenated with the associated cancer types (from the oncologist) and the associated topics (determined manually, as described above). Stop words are removed and the Porter stemming algorithm is applied. The questions are turned into term vectors where each position in the vector represents a term, with a position for all unique terms found in the questions, cancer types and topics (a value > 0 in a position means the question has that term associated with it). Term vectors are weighted using the TF-IDF score for each term. The cosine distance measure is used to determine the distance between each pair of questions' term vectors. (The $QDist_{tfidf}$ score is also on a scale from 0 to 1 where 0 is the same and 1 is completely different).

We programmatically selected 40 questions (4 sets of 10) to use in the study. To test a range of similarities, we selected three sets of four similar questions, three sets of three similar questions and three sets of two similar questions (27 in total), such that within a set the questions were similar but were not similar to any of the other questions. Then we chose 13 questions that were not similar to any other question. We used a greedy algorithm that chose questions from the larger sets of similar questions, then the smaller sets, and finally the set of different questions. Questions were put into 4 sets of 10 such that within each group all questions were pairwise dissimilar – to prevent a training effect from users knowing where to find information. Each set had at least one question from each of the 5 difficulty levels.

Question distance was determined by our second method described above. A question pair with a score from 0 to .65 exclusive were considered similar and from

.85 to 1 were considered different. These boundaries were set such that the algorithm could pick 40 questions while maximizing the gap between the scores of the two groups. Our highest scoring (i.e. least similar) pair that was still deemed similar with distance score of .63 was:

- What is retinoblastoma?
- In what age range is retinoblastoma most commonly found?

Our lowest scoring pair deemed different, with a similarity score of .86, was:

- Can one still have children after testicular cancer?
- Can chemotherapy or radiation cause anemia?

Study. We based our study on one by Ageev et al. [9] which was designed as a question answering game to encourage participation. Each participant in our study was given a set 10 questions to answer using only cancer.org and only the interface we provided. We used a proxy server and captured the user's click stream.

We used Amazon's Mechanical Turk to recruit 200 participants. Google's CAPTCHA test was used to ensure that the participants were people. The participants were randomly divided into 4 groups of 50. Each group was given one of the predefined sets of 10 questions. Participants were presented questions one at a time, in random order. They also were given a frame set to the homepage of cancer.org at the start of each new question to be used for answering the question. Participants were given 45 minutes to answer the questions. They were paid one dollar (an amount on the high end for Mechanical Turk compensation [12]) for following the rules and participating. The top 25% of users, based on the number of correct answers given, earned an additional dollar. (This incentive payment is the part that makes it a game). Correct answers were first determined ahead of time by searching cancer.org and were expanded, if needed, by examining the final page of users' sessions to see if we could find a correct answer. (We were fairly lenient as correctness of an answer was not used in our measurements only for determining compensation).

We eliminated sessions for which there was only one page hit other than the homepage (the first page in every session), unless the correct answer was obviously on that page. Such users may have already known the answer, used an outside source, or simply guessed. We kept sessions where users answered the question incorrectly or not at all as long as they met our selection criteria.

We divided user clicks into individual sessions where one session consisted of the pages viewed by one user answering one question. We eliminated page clicks associated with the game, such as question submissions, and cancer.org's homepage since it appeared in every session. We standardized the escaping of characters in URLs and we manually analyzed URLs in our logs to determine pages that had different URLs but referred to the same page either by redirects or by standard URL conventions.

User Session Model. We modeled each session S as a vector of pages where each position, S_i, in the vector represents one page in the set of all unique pages viewed in the course of the study (our corpus). We used four ways to determine the values at each position of the vector.

Binary represents whether or not a page was viewed in the session.

$$\forall\, S_i \in S\!: \text{Binary}(S_i) = \begin{cases} 1 \text{ if the page was viewed} \\ 0 \text{ otherwise} \end{cases} \tag{2}$$

Frequency represents the number of times a page was viewed in the session.

$$\forall\, S_i \in S\!: \text{Frequency}(S_i) = \#\text{ of time } S_i \text{ was viewed in } S \tag{3}$$

PFISF, Page Frequency times Inverse Sessions Frequency, a weighting formula we defined based on TF-IDF, gives a larger score to pages that have been viewed by fewer sessions. It takes the frequency value for S_i from (3) and divides it by the number of sessions in which S_i has appeared, F_i.

$$\forall\, S_i \in S\!: \text{PFISF}(S_i) = \text{Frequency}(S_i) * \frac{1}{F_i} \tag{4}$$

Tail weighting reflects the idea that later pages tend to be more important. We used a linear formula: the closer to the end of the user's sessions, the higher the weight. Let $\text{pos}(S_i)$ be the position of the page S_i in the user's session (if a page appeared more than once, the later page position is used).

$$\forall\, S_i \in S\!: \text{Tail}(S_i) = \text{pos}(S_i)/|S| \tag{5}$$

Distance Measurements. We investigated the ability to discriminate between sessions using the following standard machine learning distance measures, provided by Mahout, an open source machine learning tool from Apache:

- Cosine Vector (cos)
- Euclidean (euc)
- Manhattan (man)
- Squared Euclidean (sqe)
- Tanimoto (tan)

These distance measures take two vectors and compute a distance score of 0 for identical vectors with increasing scores as the vectors become farther apart.

4   Results

Here we report basic statistics of the Mechanical Turk data set. Then we analyze the data with respect to our research questions.

Table 1. Averaged data for questions used in the Mechanical Turk study

	Avg.	Std. Dev.	Min	Max
Sessions	50	0	50	50
Accepted	30.75	4.25	15	39
Time spent	68.2 s	36.7 s	7.6 s	171.7 s
Clicks	4.45	1.37	1.69	8.41

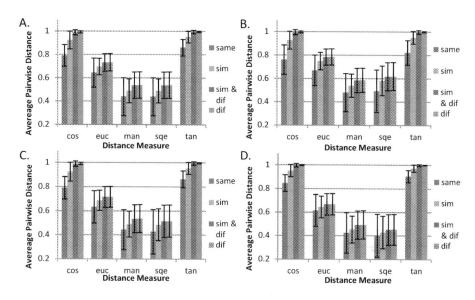

Fig. 1. Averages with standard deviation of pairwise distances calculated for each distance measure and weighting group by TF-IDF based similarity. Different graphs represent different weightings: A. binary, B. tail, C. frequency, D. PFISF.

Mechanical Turk Study Data. 200 participants completed our study in 4 hours. Table 1 shows averages per question from the Mechanical Turk study. We had a 61.50% acceptance rate (30.75/50) based on our criteria for an acceptable session, as described in Section 3. This acceptance rate is a little below what others have reported [11], but not atypical for Mechanical Turk studies.

Session lengths (clicks) varied with a minimum of 1.69 and a maximum of 8.41. We used session length to determine question difficulty; this data shows a range of difficulties as we had hoped.

Research Question 1: Same versus Different Questions. Our first research question investigated whether standard machine learning distance measures could differentiate between sessions of people answering the same questions and sessions of people answering different questions. We also analyzed how different user sessions models affected that ability. Fig. 1 shows average pairwise distances grouped by similarity determined by QDist$_{tfidf}$ score for each user session model and distance measure. Colors of bars represent pairwise distances between sessions answering questions that are all: the same (same); similar, 0-.65 QDist$_{tfidf}$ score (sim); not the same (sim & dif); and different .85-1 QDist$_{tfidf}$ score (dif). All session distances have been normalized before averaging by dividing by the max value. Error bars in the figure represent a single standard deviation. (Note, we refer back to this figure when we discuss the effect similarity has on our ability to differentiate similar questions in the next subsection.)

To compare the distance between pairs of sessions answering the same question (same) and the distance between pairs of sessions not answering the same question (sim & dif) consider the first and third bar in each grouping. This comparison shows that the distance measurements fall into two groups, regardless of user session model. For cosine vector (cos) and tanimoto (tan), we see a clean separation between same and sim & dif questions; there is no overlap in the error bars. A T-Test comparing these two sets shows the difference is highly significant; with average scores of 2.29E-13; the combination of cosine vector distance and a frequency weighting perform the best with a score of 6.18E-16. The second group consists of distance measures Euclidean (euc), Manhattan (man), and squared Euclidean (sqe). For this group, we see nearly completely overlapping error bars and with an average T-Test score of 0.0146. While this result is still significant it is 11 orders of magnitude less significant than the other group.

Research Question 2: Similarity. Our second research question was: what effect does the similarity between questions have on our ability to differentiate between sessions from users answering the same question and sessions of users answering different questions? Look again at Fig. 1: in each grouping compare the second column (sim), the average distance between sessions for people answering similar questions, 0-.65 using $QDist_{tfidf}$ and the fourth column (dif), the average distance between sessions for people answering different questions, .85-1 using $QDist_{tfidf}$. As one might expect, sim is closer in value to same (column 1), regardless of weighting or distance measure, than dif is to same. We again see the same two groups of differently performing distance measures. For tan and cos, the error bars somewhat overlap; using the T-Test, the difference between same questions and similar questions is still strongly significant with an average score of 8.68E-5: Cosine vector and PFISF performed the best, 1.57E-5. For the other group (euc, sqe, and man), except for one instance, the error bar for sim is contained in the error bar for same, and there was no significant difference, T-Test scores averaging .309; the one outlier was euc with tail weighting which was barely significant, 0.0469.

Fig. 2 shows the average pairwise distance between sessions for all pairs of questions plotted against their $QDist_{tfidf}$ scores: 0 for same, 0-.65 for similar, and .85-1 for different. For the rest of the paper, we use cosine vector and Euclidean as representatives of the two classes of distance measures and we limit ourselves to the PFISF- the best performing user session model. In graph 2A (cosine vector), for similar points, we see an upward trend as we move from left to right. A line fitted to these points had a positive slope and an R^2 value of .191. While not significant, this result still suggests that as question pairs are deemed less similar, their sessions tend to be farther apart (have fewer page clicks in common).

Fig. 2A has some outliers: the red square and two blue diamonds well below the others. The question pair for the similar question outlier (red square) is:

- What is retinoblastoma?
- In what age range is retinoblastoma most commonly found?

These questions are about an uncommon cancer for which there is relatively little information on the cancer.org website. So it is not surprising that questions related to this cancer might hit the same pages.

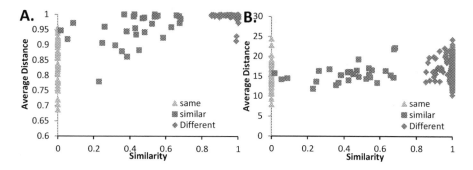

Fig. 2. Question distances, QDist$_{tfidf}$, compared with average session distances, A. cosine vector. B. Euclidean, weighted with PFISF.

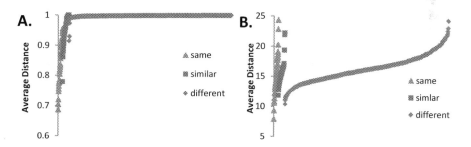

Fig. 3. Average session distances, A. cosine vector and B. Euclidean, weighted with PFISF and separated into QDist$_{tfidf}$ similarity groups and ordered by average session distance.

The two outliers in the different question pair range (blue diamonds) reflect a shortfall of our TF-IDF distance metric. One question was the same in these two question pairs and the other two questions were considered similar (the same question and the other two were consider different hence the classification as different). The question that was the same between the pairs was:

- How long does it take for a normal cell to become cancerous after it starts changing?

The other two questions in the pairs deemed similar to each other were:

- When does a tumor become cancerous?
- Are all tumors cancerous?

We can see that all of these questions are quite similar, especially the question found in both pairs and the first of the other two. However, the only term that they have in common that is not a stop word is cancerous. This term stems to cancer which appears quite often in our questions and therefore has a low TF-IDF score. These are also general questions that do not have a specific cancer type associated with them; thus neither of our question similarity measures served to indicate that these questions are similar.

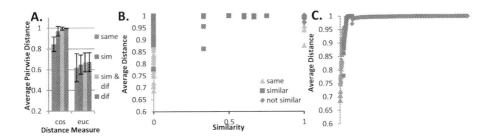

Fig. 4. The same graphs from Fig. 1, 2, and 3 using the cancer type distance, $QDist_{ct}$, and co-sine vector distance (and Euclidean distance in 4A) with PFISF weighting.

Fig. 2B clearly shows the Euclidean distance measure having trouble differentiating between same, similar and different questions. All three groups of questions pairs (same, similar, different) have a similar range of distance score.

Fig. 3 shows the average pairwise distance of sessions for all question pairs sorted from closest to farthest divided into three groups: same, similar and different. For cosine vector (3A), the same and similar groups are distributed fairly evenly within their range, with same appearing mostly below similar. Different questions are all mostly clustered near the top, with only a few points having a slightly closer distance score. The graph of the Euclidean data (3B) continues to show the distance measure performing poorly.

Fig. 4 shows results for the other similarity measure we implemented, $QDist_{ct}$, based on cancer type which we described in Section 3. Here we see three graphs, A, B and C, that correspond to Fig. 1, 2, and 3. Since the results for $QDist_{ct}$ were quite similar to the results for the $QDist_{tfidf}$ with regard to distance measure performance and the effect of the   user session model, we only show data for PFISF weighting and the cosine vector distance measure except for 4A where we include the Euclidean distance measure.

Fig. 4A shows a similar result to what we saw in Fig. 1; we still see that same questions are discernible from dif & sim questions with T-Test scores of 7.42E-16 and 1.01E-09 for cosine vector respectively. We also still see the same difference in performance between the two classes of distance measure.

Fig. 4B compares average session distance per question pair and question distance using cancer types, $QDist_{ct}$. The graph shows us that $QDist_{ct}$ is less nuanced than $QDist_{tfidf}$ (Fig. 2); few data points are in the middle meaning that most of the questions either had the same associated cancer types or had no types in common.

Fig. 4C gives a better feel for where the data lies. When we compare Fig. 4C to 3A, we see that both question distance measures classify the majority of low scoring session distances (sessions with more pages in common) as same or similar. However, we see that $QDist_{ct}$ classifies many more question pairs as similar where the session distance score is large (sessions have less in common). This result explains why there is less distinction between column 2 (sim) and 4 (dif) in 4A than in 1D.

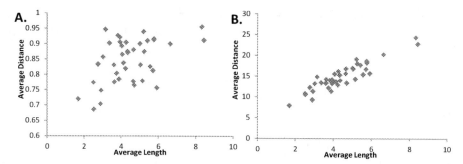

Fig. 5. A comparison of average distance and length for same questions for cosine vector, A, and Euclidean, B, distance measures

Research Question 3: Difficulty. Our final research question was: how does question difficulty affect the ability of distance measures to discriminate between questions? Recall that we measure a question's difficulty as the average number of page views taken for users to answer that question.

Fig. 5 shows average distance between sessions for user's answering the same questions plotted against the average length of sessions for those questions. Fig. 5A shows the results for cosine vector. Here we see very little correlation between question difficulty and distance between sessions. There is a slight upward slope to the line as the number of page clicks goes up but the R^2 value of a line fitted to the data is .22, meaning only 22 percent of the variance can be attributed to it.

In contrast when we look at the same graph for the Euclidean distance measure we see a much stronger correlation between question difficulty and average distance between sessions. As questions increase in difficulty, they also increase in average distance between sessions. A line fitted to this data had an R^2 of .84. This result is surprising to us since we assumed that as sessions got longer there would be more of a chance for sessions to have pages in common which would lead to a lower average distance.

5   Discussion and Future Work

We found that machine learning metrics were able to differentiate between sessions from people answering the same question and different questions. Moreover we found that that ability was greatly influenced by the distance measure used and marginally affected by how we weighted session vectors. To explain why some distance measures perform radically better than others, we defined the following property.

Property – Two sessions that hit the same page should be closer together than sessions that have no pages in common.

For example consider the following 3 vectors:

```
1 0 0 0
1 0 1 1
0 1 0 0
```

For vectors of page views, we believe it makes sense for vectors 1 and 2 to be considered closer than vectors 1 and 3. Failure to adhere to this property will result in short sessions with little in common being closer than long sessions with more overlap. This property holds for the cosine vector and Tanimoto distance measures, but does not hold in all cases for Euclidean, Manhattan, and squared Euclidean. We see this in Fig. 5B where we see a strong correlation between length of session and distances between sessions. We believe this is why those distance measure perform poorly for our data.

We observed that when we separated similar questions from different questions, regardless of which similarity metric we used, our ability to differentiate same from similar was somewhat less but still possible. Both same and similar questions had a lot of variance in terms of average difference and had a fairly even distribution within that range. What is interesting about this result is that the amount of overlap between user sessions seems dependent on the question itself. It could be the case for same and similar questions, that the ability to tell them apart using our methods is affected by the number of pages available about the question in the collection. This certainly seems to be the case when we consider the outlier we identified in the similar range in Section 4. By looking at outliers, we also observed that there were some limitations of our question distance measure. However, TF-IDF is used extensively in the information retrieval community and the limitations are well understood. They did not appear to impact our results other than explaining a few outliers.

It should be noted that, while this study used real questions from actual users and user sessions of real people looking for the answers to those questions, this is still a controlled experiment. This type of question answering behavior is very likely not the only type of behavior on a site. Even for question answering, users often do not have well-formulated questions, such as the ones we provided. Further, they may have multiple unrelated information needs in the same session. These challenges should be addressed if one were to use these techniques on actual user session data.

Other interesting work that could be done with our data is to see what effect the correctness of a user's answer has on the distance between sessions. One could also examine whether sessions with the correct answers found the answer on the same page. It is entirely possible if two (or more) pages have the answer for a question, there could be two (or more) paths for finding those pages leading to sessions that are completely different but found the answer to the same question. This possibility could affect our current study by making average pairwise distances between same questions farther apart.

Future work could include enumerating more properties of distance measures for our type of data to further refine our choice of metric or to inform the development of a new one. We may also apply what we have learned about distance measures and representations of session vectors to real log data where user intentions are unknown. Such an effort could be used to enhance search or to suggest pages for users based on historical user access and the perceived information need of the current user. We are also interested in considering the structure of the website and how it relates to user sessions, in addition to just looking at the click log.

Acknowledgements. We acknowledge the support of the Danish Cancer Society and Mr. Tor Øyan, our contact, and support from the National Science Foundation, award 0812260. Any opinions, findings, and conclusions or recommendations expressed in this publication are those of the author(s) and do not necessarily reflect the views of the NSF. We thank Ms. Tesca Fitzgerald, Ms. Suzanna Kanga, Ms. Flery Decker, and Jonathon Britell, MD, Board Certified Oncologist.

References

1. Mobasher, B., Cooley, R., Srivastava, J.: Automatic personalization based on Web usage mining. Communications of the ACM 43(8), 142–151 (2000)
2. Beeferman, D., Berger, A.: Agglomerative clustering of a search engine query log. Presented at the Proceedings of the International Conference on Knowledge Discovery and Data Mining, pp. 407–416 (2000)
3. Wang, W., Zaïane, O.R.: Clustering web sessions by sequence alignment. In: Proceedings of the 13th International Workshop on Database and Expert Systems Applications, pp. 394–398 (2002)
4. Nasraoui, O., Frigui, H., Joshi, A., Krishnapuram, R.: Mining Web access logs using relational competitive fuzzy clustering. In: Proceedings of the Eight International Fuzzy Systems Association World Congress, vol. 1, pp. 195–204 (1999)
5. Joshi, A., Krishnapuram, R.: On mining web access logs. DTIC Document (2000)
6. Li, C.: Research on Web Session Clustering. Journal of Software 4(5), 460–468 (2009)
7. Chi, E.H., Pirolli, P., Chen, K., Pitkow, J.: Using information scent to model user information needs and actions and the Web. In: Proceedings of the SIGCHI Conference on Human Factors in Computing Systems, pp. 490–497 (2001)
8. Strehl, A., Ghosh, J., Mooney, R.: Impact of similarity measures on web-page clustering. In: Workshop on Artificial Intelligence for Web Search (AAAI 2000), pp. 58–64 (2000)
9. Jansen, B.J., Spink, A., Saracevic, T.: Real life, real users, and real needs: a study and analysis of user queries on the web. Information Processing & Management 36(2), 207–227 (2000)
10. Ageev, M., Agichtein, Q.G.D.L.E.: Find it if you can: a game for modeling different types of web search success using interaction data. In: Proceedings of the 34th International ACM SIGIR Conference on Research and Development in Information, SIGIR, vol. 11, pp. 345–354 (2011)
11. Pallis, G., Angelis, L., Vakali, A.: Validation and interpretation of Web users' sessions clusters. Information Processing & Management 43(5), 1348–1367 (2007)
12. Buhrmester, M., Kwang, T., Gosling, S.D.: Amazon's Mechanical Turk A New Source of Inexpensive, Yet High-Quality, Data? Perspectives on Psychological Science 6(1), 3–5 (2011)

Digital Libraries for Experimental Data: Capturing Process through Sheer Curation

Mark Hedges and Tobias Blanke

Centre for e-Research, Department of Digital Humanities, King's College London, UK
{mark.hedges,tobias.blanke}@kcl.ac.uk

Abstract. This paper presents an approach to the 'sheer curation' of experimental data and processes of a group of researchers in the life sciences, which involves embedding data capture and interpretation within researchers' working practices, so that it is automatic and invisible to the researcher. The environment described does not capture just individual datasets, but the entire workflow that represents the 'story' of the experiment, including intermediate files and provenance metadata, so as to support the verification and reproduction of published results. As the curation environment is decoupled from the researchers' processing environment, a provenance graph is inferred from a variety of domain-specific contextual information as the data is generated, using software that implements the knowledge and expertise of the researchers.

1 Introduction

Digital library and repository systems are increasingly being used for the curation and publication of research data in various domains and various forms [1][2]. This paper presents a particular approach to data curation in the fields of biophysics and structural biology, an approach that addresses the need to capture, not just the individual datasets generated in the course of an experiment, but the entire process through which they were captured, generated and analysed – the workflow that tells the story of the experiment, and allows its results to be validated or reproduced.

A particular challenge that the work had to address is that all data capture and processing takes place 'in the wild', that is to say in an personalised environment of tools and data on the researcher's desktop that is entirely decoupled from the repository, following a workflow that is highly unpredictable at a detailed level, its flow of control depending on the (inaccessible) personal decisions of the researcher. While it would be possible to ingest the set of files generated during processing into a repository, it would not be at all clear what all this data meant, as the story of the experiment is represented by a variety of implicit information whose significance will have been lost in this *post hoc* model of curation.

This paper presents a 'sheer curation' approach in which curation activities are integrated with minimal disturbance into the normal workflow of the researchers, so that it occurs automatically and invisibly to them. A lightweight

T. Aalberg et al. (Eds.): TPDL 2013, LNCS 8092, pp. 108–119, 2013.

client 'scavenges' information from the researcher's work area – specifically, any changes at the file system level – and transfers any new or modified files to the repository. Here, the ingest software uses a range of contextual information to position the file within the workflow and to infer its relationships to other data objects in the repository, thus building up a graph of digital objects that represent the process of the experiment. In this way, we bridge the gap between the *ad hoc* and independent environment of the researcher's lab desktop, and the curated, sustainable, environment of the digital library. We also extend the existing sheer curation model to take into account process and provenance as well as the data objects themselves.

The paper is organised as follows: after a survey of related research in Section 2, we described the context of the work – the scientists' research practices and the challenges that they raise for curation – in Section 3. We then present our approach to addressing these challenges in Section 4, and finish by describing our current conclusions and future work in Section 5.

2   Related Work

Significant work has been undertaken on the use of digital libraries to curate research data, where by *curation* of data we understand an active process of managing, preserving and adding value to it with a view to its future use [3]. The UK Digital Curation Centre's (DCC) curation lifecycle [4] addresses the planning of curation activities and processes, although this approach is concerned with a macroscopic view of processes and institutional descriptions, whereas our work seeks to describe the individual information objects and their relationships. [3] discusses digital curation in research, with a particular focus on inter-disciplinary research. The work described in this paper is also based on the close collaboration between scientists and information specialists, which offered particular challenges to developing an appropriate information model. [3], however, concentrates on information architecture, rather than the research processes themselves, which are our focus.

In recent years, there have been renewed efforts among digital curators to establish new methods of performing digital curation from the outset. The limiting factor among researchers is that they have time to meet only their own immediate, short-term requirements, and – even when willing – they typically have insufficient resources, whether in terms of time, expertise or infrastructure, to spend making their datasets reusable by others [5][6]. One approach to this challenge has been termed *sheer curation*[1], in which curation activities are integrated into the workflow of the researchers creating or capturing data. The word 'sheer' is used in the sense of the 'lightweight and virtually transparent' way in which these activities are integrated with minimal disruption[2]. Such an

---

[1] By Alistair Miles of the Science and Technology Facilities Council.
[2] http://alimanfoo.wordpress.com/2007/06/27/zoological-case-studies-in-digital-curation-dcc-scarp-imagestore/, Accessed 18 March 2013.

approach depends on data capture being embedded within the researchers' working practices, so that it is automatic and invisible to the researcher.

Sheer curation is based on the principle that effective data management at the point of creation and initial use lays a firm foundation for subsequent data publication, sharing, reuse, curation and preservation activities. For example, the SCARP project[3], during which the term *sheer curation* was coined, carried out several case studies in which digital curators engaged with researchers in a range of disciplines, with the aim of improving data curation through a close understanding of research practice [7] [8]. Other examples, this time from the business world, are provided by [9], which discusses the role of sheer curation in the form of distributed, community-based curation of enterprise data. Sheer curation may be contrasted with *post hoc* curation, which only takes place *after* the period during which the digital objects are created and primarily used. However, the sheer curation model has been relatively little discussed in the scientific literature; in this paper we extend the concept to take account of process and provenance as well as the data itself.

Data provenance is a particular kind of metadata that describes the derivation history of digital objects. It is widely applied in the digital library community as a way of documenting the activities that occur during the lifecycle of a digital object [10], and in the e-Science community as a way of recording the scientific process with a view to verifying or reproducing it [11]. The Open Provenance Model (OPM) is an emerging standard for modelling provenance that aims to enable the digital representation of the provenance of any object, whether itself digital or not, in a generic manner so as to support the exchange of provenance information between different systems, the building of common tools etc. [12]. This abstract model may be serialised in XML [13], and also in a more lightweight fashion as an OWL-DL ontology called OPMV (Open Provenance Model Vocabulary) [14]. More recently, the W3C Provenance Working Group issued the PROV Ontology (PROV-O)[4], a series of documents defining conceptual data model and vocabulary for describing provenance; this was issued after the work described here had been carried out, although it will be taken into consideration in future work.

3   Context

3.1   Research Environment and Practices

The specific research use cases addressed by our work were in the fields of biophysics and structural biology, a multidisciplinary area that involves interaction and collaboration across research groups, as well as with industrial partners such as pharmaceutical companies. While researchers from five separate research groups were interviewed, for the implementation and evaluation described here

---

[3] http://www.dcc.ac.uk/projects/scarp
[4] http://www.w3.org/TR/prov-o/

we focused our efforts on two of these, macromolecular crystallography and biological nanoimaging, which we describe here briefly to provide a context for what follows.

Macromolecular crystallography involves determining the structure of large molecules, such as proteins, using X-ray diffraction. In high-level terms, an X-ray beam is directed at a crystal of the substance under investigation from many angles, resulting in a set (typically 360) of diffraction images. Each image contains several hundred spots, whose location and intensity are determined using specialised software; this information is combined (also using specialised software) to produce a model of the atomic co-ordinates of the protein. This process involves many steps, and the flow of the process depends on multiple decisions taken by the researcher. Moreover, this flow is not linear; it involves dead ends and repetitions, e.g. when a processing step is deemed not to have worked and is repeated with modified parameters. All of this generates large numbers of interim files, and while a small number of the resulting files are published – for example, PDB files in the Protein Data Bank[5] – the vast majority are not currently retained by the researchers, at least not in any curatable form.

Biological nanoimaging involves the use of microscopy to capture high resolution images of biological samples, for two broad research purposes: on the one hand, to develop new methods of and algorithms for digital imaging and processing of biological specimens, and on the other, to carry out research into cell and tissue structures using existing methods. In addition to 2D images, the data include pseudo-3D representations constructed from horizontal sections, or *in vivo* imaging, in which a sample is imaged in a time series. The same datasets may be processed many times using different analysis techniques, and many raw images are involved when developing new analysis tools. Again, the majority of the information generated in these processes is not currently curated or retained.

The research practices clearly vary as regards detail, even within a research group; however, common patterns emerged from our use case analyses, and at a very high level, the processes we encountered may be broken down as follows:

1. An initial stage in which raw data is captured from experimental equipment in a laboratory.
2. A (potentially large) number of steps in which the data is processed and analysed, using a variety of software tools, and where typically the output from one stage serves as input to the next.
3. Publication of outputs, which may include limited amounts of data as well as journal articles.

Compared to "big science" such as physics or astronomy, the datasets are not large. A typical experiment in macromolecular crystallography generates about 10 GB. A simple nanoimaging experiment generates a few GB, long-term *in vivo* imaging in the region of 50 GB. Many of the files generated are small text files; the issues addressed here arise from the difficulty of interpreting individual files, and the complexity of relationships between files, rather than their size *per se*.

---

[5] http://www.wwpdb.org/docs.html

3.2 Objectives

The outputs of the research practices that we examined were restricted to traditional scientific articles, together with a limited set of derived data objects or other digital outputs. The additional information that was generated during the workflow, which represents the 'story' of the experiment and the provenance of the published results, was not retained. However, this provenance is viewed as a key component of recording research processes, as it allows researchers – both those who carried out the research and those who read or reuse their results – to understand the origin of published results, to verify the processes through which the results were obtained, to examine these processes for defects, and potentially to repeat the work and reproduce the results [11].

From the data curation perspective, recent research has demonstrated that carrying out digital curation and preservation activities in the *early* stages of data creation is cost-effective in comparison with the potential loss that can be incurred through the destruction of data, for example because of the need to recreate the data, or the loss of an organisation's reputation [15]. On the one hand, decisions taken during the early stages of a digital object's lifecycle frequently have consequences for the preservation strategies that can be applied at a later date; on the other hand, if digital objects are being preserved so that they can be reused in an informed manner, account has to be taken of the different practices of researchers across disciplines and the different characteristics of the data they create or gather [16].

The broad objectives of our work were thus driven by both scientific and curatorial imperatives, and may be summed up as follows:

- To capture automatically data provenance and curation metadata that is available at the point of data creation, during the execution of the workflow itself, but which could not be extracted later in a generic preservation environment.
- To implement data and metadata capture mechanisms that are, as far as possible, 'non-invasive', that is which operate invisibly to the researcher and require no (or very little) change to researchers' normal practice.
- To model within a digital library environment not just individual datasets and their metadata, but entire experimental workflows, represented as compound objects that incorporate data, metadata and provenance.

3.3 Challenges

The targeted researchers typically carry out their processing on a single desktop or laptop computer, once the raw data has been copied over from the lab environment, and at the end of an experiment the associated data files, including all intermediate files, reside in the local file system within a directory dedicated to that experiment. If the contents of this directory were deposited in a generic preservation environment, it would be possible to carry out a certain amount of digital preservation, for example, extracting metadata about individual files, or recording the relationships between objects represented in the directory structure; however, the significance of the data would not be at all clear from the information available. The story of the experiment is represented implicitly in a number of ways, for example the location of files in the directory hierarchy, metadata embedded in binary files, filenames, the contents of log files, and in other opaque sources of information. The semantics of the collection as a whole is lost in such a *post hoc* curation model, and it is unlikely that the researcher would have the time or the ability to explain it in great detail.

In a sheer curation model, this information is captured as far as possible at the point of data creation, when a variety of domain-specific contextual information is still available. The context in which any such system would have to operate raises a number of challenges, however. Firstly, the broad process of experiment, processing and curation spans multiple independent 'environments': capture of the raw data typically occurs in a laboratory, for example using a microscope and camera; this data, together with any metadata captured by the laboratory equipment, is transferred to the researcher's desktop computer where all subsequent processing and analysis takes place; finally, any curation activity takes place in a separate digital repository environment.

The processing environment is not at all predictable or tightly controlled; it is in fact a very 'messy' environment of interactive tools and data located on the researcher's desktop. For practical, organisational, reasons – computers attached to the lab equipment were stand-alone and not networked – in the work to date we have addressed only the part of the process that begins with the transfer of raw data to the processing environment, after initial data capture. Nevertheless, the work described here operated across two quite distinct and independent environments, which were entirely decoupled from one another. On the one hand, there is the desktop environment where the data processing and analysis takes place, within the researcher's department and under the researcher's control. On the other hand, there is the curatorial environment, which is typically managed at an institutional level. A major challenge was thus to bridge the gap between the 'wild', *ad hoc* and independent environment of the researcher's desktop, and the managed and curated environment of the digital library.

While the processing that occurs on the researcher's desktop constitutes a workflow in the broad sense of this term, the situation is quite different from the more ordered, automated workflows that are constructed using workflow engines or frameworks that allow such processes to be built up from smaller components. In such cases, the workflow framework has by its nature access to information at the level of these components: which are being called, what are their parameters, and how they are combined. Examples of integrating provenance plug-ins in such cases are provided by the Taverna workbench itself [17], and the rule engine incorporated into the iRODS software [18].

In the environment addressed in this paper, no such workflow framework is present; all tools involved are executed at the operating system level. In addition, the workflows are highly interactive, with control of flow largely in the hands of the researcher. At each stage, the researcher invokes and responds to desktop-based tools, selects parameters based on their prior experience and the results of the process so far, and examines outputs, before deciding whether to repeat an operation with different parameters, or to move on to another stage. Another challenge is presented by the *unpredictability* of the workflow. While, for a particular type of experiment, the structure of these research processes follows certain general patterns, they are highly unpredictable at a detailed level, partly as a result of their interactive nature. The flow of control frequently depends on the researcher's personal judgement and decisions, which are in general inaccessible and cannot themselves be captured directly.

Moreover, the individual tools used by the researchers are typically developed by people working within the discipline, either by researcher communities themselves, or by suppliers of laboratory equipment, and they are designed to operate in the researchers' local environment using data that is accessible via the local file system (although there are some web-based services). The tools might thus be outside the control or influence of the repository staff, who are thus obliged to take them as they come; it is not possible to integrate and provenance- or metadata-capture services within them.

4   Implementation

4.1   Overall Approach

The overall framework used to implement a sheer curation approach involved three main components:

- A lightweight client application, installed on the researcher's desktop computer, that 'scavenges' information about changes on the local file system and transfers information about any new or updated files (as well as the files themselves) to the curation environment.
- Repository ingest software that uses contextual information around an ingested file to interpret the current stage of the workflow and infer the file's relationships to other objects in the repository, thus building up a representation of the workflow within the repository.
- A repository system that manages all digital objects and their relationships.

The client monitors the local file system for changes, and each time that a file is created or modified within the directory associated with the experiment, this file is transferred to the data repository, together with metadata describing the type of action (creation or update), original pathname and timestamp; in terms of the OAIS model, this corresponds to the Submission Information Package for this particular object. In the curation environment, this information is interpreted and used as the basis for creating digital objects, extracting domain-specific metadata from the objects, and inferring relationships between objects, which are then ingested into the data repository.

Much of this processing is concerned with analysing the information that is available and exploiting it to infer the details of the researcher's workflow. Although this workflow cannot be monitored directly, within a particular category of scenario (in our case, either macromolecular crystallography or nanoimaging) its structure broadly speaking may be predicted, in terms of the potential *patterns* that it may exhibit. Certain types of files are expected at certain stages, and are known to be related to certain other types of files. Moreover, a workflow generates as a by-product abundant information that can be used to infer inter-object relationships, for example in file headers and log files. This requires a detailed understanding of the researchers' workflows, which was elicited through a series of interviews. The logic of the researchers' processing workflows was then implemented in domain-specific modules within the repository's ingest software.

A generic preservation environment, which has encoded within it no understanding of the experiments being carried out, will be unable to interpret fully the context or nature of many of the files generated during processing, as these will appear simply as files in a directory structure, the semantics of the collection as a whole having been lost. However, this information is highly important for subsequent curation, preservation, sharing, reuse, and publication of the data objects, even when it does not benefit directly their creators and primary users. In our sheer curation environment, we incorporate domain-aware processing to extract the implicit semantics, and thus build up provenance graphs that represent the steps of the processing and the relationships between files. Once this information has been extracted and stored, it can be transferred without loss to other, more generic, preservation environments. We now consider how this information is represented in the repository, and examine in more detail how these representations are constructed.

4.2   Representing Research Processes in the Repository

The workflows are modelled using OPM, specifically the OPMV ontology [14]. The three fundamental types of entity in OPM are *artifact*, an 'immutable piece of state, which may have a physical embodiment in a physical object, or a digital representation in a computer system'; *process*, an 'action or series of actions performed on or caused by artifacts, and resulting in new artifacts'; and *agent*, a 'contextual entity acting as a catalyst of a process, enabling, facilitating, controlling, affecting its execution'.

In our implementation, artifacts correspond to files generated during the processing (and in some cases to aggregate objects comprising sets of related files), processes correspond to steps in the researcher's workflow – the individual actions taken by the researcher, such as the execution of a command or script, and agents either to the tools or scripts used or to human researchers. Entities may be connected to one another by a variety of relationship types. OPM represents data provenance by a directed graph, where the node types correspond to OPM entities, and the arcs indicate the nature of the causal dependency relationships between the nodes; in our case, the basic relationships are that *agents* control *processes* that take *artifacts* as input and generate other *artifacts*.

In the implementation, each of these entities corresponds to a digital object within the repository system, which was based on the Fedora Commons software[6]. For process and agent entities, these objects contained only metadata and relationships. Relationships were held in the RELS-EXT datastream of the objects, using the standard Fedora approach to representing relationships, and thus the abstract OPM model mapped naturally onto our implementation.

4.3   Building the Provenance Graph

When a new or updated file is notified to the repository ingest service, the first step is to identify the type of file, where *type* is understood in more granular terms that simply file format. Essentially, each category of experiments addressed has associated with it a typology of files that corresponds to their functional positions within the workflow. As well as using more general file-identification registries, such as PRONOM, the file-recognition stage carries out a range of specific checks to identify the file within this typology, for example on the basis of file suffix, header information, or internal structure.

Once the file type is determined, the ingest service extracts metadata for that object. Again, this combines generic metadata (such as PREMIS preservation metadata) with additional services for extracting domain-specific metadata associated with files of that type.

Once the digital object corresponding to the file – comprising various metadata as well the content – has been created, the next step is to determine the *relationships* that object has with other objects, already in the repository, that belong to the same experimental workflow. Each file type has a separate Java class containing logic that encapsulates the potential relationships that such a file type can have, given its place in the workflow.

Note that, while *artifacts* correspond to files that are directly ingested, objects in the repository corresponding to *processes* and *agents* do not correspond to concrete data objects, and their existence and relationships are inferred on the basis of ingested data files. Thus if a file is ingested that is associated with a specific stage in the processing (e.g. as an output or log file), and the corresponding *process* or *agent* is not yet in the repository, it is created along with the corresponding relationships.

Figure 1 shows an example OPM fragment corresponding to an individual step – namely 'sorting reflection data' – from a crystallography experiment. The full graph consists of a number of such fragments chained together, linked by files that are involved in two or more steps, typically as output and input respectively.

Some simplifying assumptions were possible. In all the scenarios addressed, the scientist works through the processing of an experiment at the same desktop machine. This simplified the implementation by allowing us to focus on capturing the researcher's process, restricting ourselves to looking at information flow in one direction only – from the desktop to the data repository – during the processing of the data. A further simplification was made possible by the fact that a researcher works on an experiment in a dedicated directory, so that all files derived during processing are saved in the file hierarchy within that directory.

---

[6] http://fedora-commons.org/

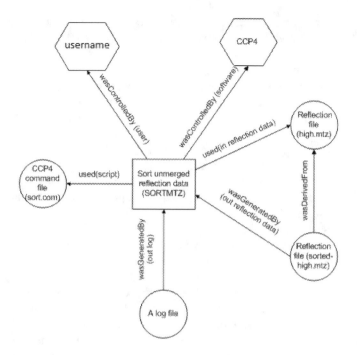

Fig. 1. Fragment of provenance graph generated during ingest

Of course, the researcher could in principle sabotage this approach by moving files to other directories or by renaming files at random.

The close involvement of researchers was a key aspect of the work. Firstly, the information specialists needed to obtain a clear and detailed understanding of the researchers' data, processes and tools, so that this expertise could be incorporated into the ingest software. Secondly, a key idea behind sheer curation is that it should be integrated with the researchers' processes in as non-invasive a way as possible. Thirdly, services for access to and reuse of these specialised datasets need to be aligned very closely with the ways, possibly equally specialised, in which the communities would want to use them. As a consequence, instead of a loose partnership between the scientists and information specialists, these different areas of knowledge and expertise were closely integrated. Indeed, one of the major issues encountered was the difficulty and effort involved in the information specialists gaining sufficient understanding of the science.

5   Conclusions and Future Work

In the case studies addressed to date, the environment in which the data processing takes place is very unpredictable and 'untidy'; however, it cannot in general be assumed that scientific data processing occurs in integrated environments that are subject to close monitoring and control. Indeed, the kind of environment considered here, in which much of the processing is only loosely coupled to the curation environment, occurs in other disciplines where researchers work as individuals or in small groups, and the data processing is very much an interactive process. Such automated approaches to capturing the progression from raw data to published results have the potential for broader application.

One significant issue with the approach described here is that to implement the software that analyses the files being ingested and makes inferences about the workflow requires a quite detailed understanding of the researchers' work, tools and data, as in essence it involves embedding this knowledge within the logic of the software. This knowledge has to be elicited from researchers via user-engagement activities that may require a significant degree of effort and expense, particularly when the development team has no background knowledge of the discipline in question. Subsequent work will attempt both to apply the approach to other use cases, and to determine how generalisable it is, and thus to address its economic aspects and justification.

User interaction with the repository is an area where more research remains to be carried out. A conventional repository interface that allows a user to browse through files, or to search for files by metadata elements, is not very useful; individual files, taken out of the context of the workflow, are of little interest, and the metadata associated with these files is mostly highly technical and not appropriate for searching. From our engagement with researchers, we determined that, while a user may search on attributes of experiments to find examples of interest, once they have fixed upon one they are more likely to want to 'drill down' into it in a way that corresponds to their conception of how the experiment took place, in terms of processing steps and the files generated at each step.

Initially we investigated the use of the underlying RDF representation of the provenance graphs as a natural basis for such a graphical user interface; however, as these graphs may contain several thousand nodes, this had the effect of swamping the user with information that could not easily be navigated. This conclusion reflects existing work on the drawbacks of exposing raw RDF structures to users [19]. Although the users appreciated the principle of a graph-based interface, from their point of view not all nodes were equal. Some files were much more significant than others, and these files, together with the *processes* that correspond to the processing steps, were the main components of the researcher's mental map of the workflow. Other files – such as log files and scripts – were of interest primarily when examining an individual processing step in detail; an interface that reflected these priorities proved far more useful, and provides a basis for further work. Another avenue will be to use graph databases such as Neo4j[7] for managing and interacting with the provenance data; these technologies may provide a more effective basis for user interaction with graph-based information.

References

1. Greenberg, J., White, H.C., Carrier, S., Scherle, R.: A metadata best practice for a scientific data repository. Journal of Library Metadata 9(3-4), 194–212 (2009)

---

[7] http://www.neo4j.org/

2. Monastersky, R.: Publishing frontiers: The library reboot. Nature 495, 430–432 (2013)
3. Beagrie, N.: Digital curation for science, digital libraries, and individuals. International Journal of Digital Curation 1(1), 3–16 (2006)
4. Higgins, S.: The DCC curation lifecycle model. International Journal of Digital Curation 3(1), 134–140 (2008)
5. Shearer, K.: Survey of digital preservation practices in Canada, Library and Archives Canada. Technical report (2009)
6. Key Perspectives Ltd. Data dimensions: disciplinary differences in research data sharing, reuse and long term viability. SCARP Synthesis Study. Technical report (2010)
7. Lyon, E., Rusbridge, C., Neilson, C., Whyte, A.: Disciplinary approaches to sharing, curation, reuse and preservation, DCC SCARP final report. Technical report (2010)
8. Whyte, A., Job, D., Giles, S., Lawrie, S.: Meeting curation challenges in a neuroimaging group. The International Journal of Digital Curation 1(3) (2008)
9. Curry, E., Freitas, A., O'Riin, S.: The role of community-driven data curation for enterprises. In: Wood, D. (ed.) Linking Enterprise Data, Part 1, pp. 25–47. Springer US, Boston (2008)
10. PREMIS data dictionary for preservation metadata v. 2.1. Technical report (2011)
11. Simmhan, Y., Plale, B., Gannon, D.: A survey of data provenance in e-science. SIGMOD Record 34(3), 31–36 (2005)
12. Moreau, L., Clifford, B., Freire, J., Futrelle, J., Gil, Y., Groth, P., Kwasnikowska, N., Miles, S., Missier, P., Myers, J., et al.: The Open Provenance Model core specification (v1. 1). Future Generation Computer Systems 27(6), 743–756 (2011)
13. Moreau, L., Groth, P.: Open Provenance Model (OPM) XML Schema Specification (2010), http://openprovenance.org/model/opmx-20101012
14. Zhao, J.: Open Provenance Model Vocabulary Specification (2010), http://purl.org/net/opmv/ns-20101006
15. Rumsey, A.S. (ed.): Sustainable economics for a digital planet: Ensuring long-term access to digital information, final report of the Blue Ribbon Task Force on Sustainable Digital Preservation and Access. Technical report (2010)
16. Borgman, C.L.: Scholarship in the digital age: Information, infrastructure, and the Internet. MIT Press, Cambridge (2007)
17. Belhajjame, K., Wolstencroft, K., Corcho, O., Oinn, T., Tanoh, F., William, A., Goble, C.: Metadata management in the Taverna workflow system. In: 8th IEEE International Symposium on Cluster Computing and the Grid, CCGRID 2008, pp. 651–656 (2008)
18. Weise, A., Hasan, A., Hedges, M., Jensen, J.: Managing provenance in iRODS. In: Allen, G., Nabrzyski, J., Seidel, E., van Albada, G.D., Dongarra, J., Sloot, P.M.A. (eds.) ICCS 2009, Part II. LNCS, vol. 5545, pp. 667–676. Springer, Heidelberg (2009)
19. Schraefel, M.C., Karger, D.: The pathetic fallacy of RDF. In: International Workshop on the Semantic Web and User Interaction (SWUI), vol. 2006 (2006)

Metadata Management and Interoperability Support for Natural History Museums

Konstantinos Makris, Giannis Skevakis, Varvara Kalokyri,
Polyxeni Arapi, and Stavros Christodoulakis

TUC/MUSIC, Lab. of Distributed Multimedia Information Systems and Applications,
Technical University of Crete, University Campus, 73100, Chania, Greece
{makris,skevakis,vkalokyri,xenia,stavros}@ced.tuc.gr

Abstract. Natural History Museums (NHMs) are a rich source of knowledge about Earth's biodiversity and natural history. However, an impressive abundance of high quality scientific content available in NHMs around Europe remains largely unexploited due to a number of barriers, such as: the lack of interconnection and interoperability between the management systems used by museums, the lack of centralized access through a European point of reference like Europeana, and the inadequacy of the current metadata and content organization. The Natural Europe project offers a coordinated solution at European level that aims to overcome those barriers. This paper presents the architecture, deployment and evaluation of the Natural Europe infrastructure allowing the curators to publish, semantically describe and manage the museums' Cultural Heritage Objects, as well as disseminate them to Europeana.eu and biodiversity networks like BioCASE and GBIF.

Keywords: digital curation, preservation metadata, Europeana, BioCASE.

1   Introduction

Natural History Museums (NHMs) are unique spaces that have only recently come to comprehend the effectiveness of the learning opportunities they offer to their visitors [9]. Their scientific collections form a rich source of knowledge about Earth's biodiversity and natural history. However, an impressive amount of high quality content available in NHMs around Europe remains largely unexploited due to a number of barriers, such as: the lack of interconnection and interoperability between the management systems used by museums, the lack of centralized access through a European point of reference like Europeana, as well as the inadequacy of current content organization and the metadata used.

The Natural Europe project [15] offers a coordinated solution at European level that aims to overcome the aforementioned barriers, making the natural history heritage available to formal and informal learning processes. Its main objective is to improve the availability and relevance of environmental cultural content for education and life-long learning use, in a multilingual and multicultural context. Cultural heritage content related to natural history, natural sciences, and natural/environmental

T. Aalberg et al. (Eds.): TPDL 2013, LNCS 8092, pp. 120–131, 2013.

preservation is collected from six Natural History Museums around Europe into a federation of European Natural History Digital Libraries, directly connected with Europeana.

It is clear that the infrastructure offered by Natural Europe needs to satisfy a number of strong requirements for metadata management, and establish interoperability with learning applications, cultural heritage and biodiversity repositories. Towards this end, the Natural Europe project offers appropriate tools and services that allow the participating NHMs to: (a) uniformly describe and semantically annotate their content according to international standards and specifications, as well as (b) interconnect their digital libraries and expose their Cultural Heritage Object (CHO) metadata records to Europeana.eu and biodiversity networks (i.e., BioCASE [2] and GBIF [10]).

This paper presents the Natural Europe Cultural Environment, i.e. the infrastructure and toolset deployed on each NHM allowing their curators to publish, semantically describe, manage and disseminate the CHOs that they contribute to the project.

2   The Natural Europe Cultural Environment (NECE)

The Natural Europe Cultural Environment (NECE) is a node in the cultural perspective of the Natural Europe project architecture [13]. It refers to the toolset deployed at each participating NHM, consisting of the Multimedia Authoring Tool (MMAT) and its underlying repository that facilitate the complete metadata management life-cycle: ingestion, maintenance, curation, and dissemination of CHO metadata. NECE also specifies how legacy metadata are migrated into Natural Europe.

In the context of Natural Europe, the participating NHMs provide metadata descriptions about a large number of Natural History related CHOs. These descriptions are semantically enriched with Natural Europe shared knowledge (shared vocabularies, taxonomies, etc.) using project provided annotation tools and services. The enhanced metadata are aggregated by the project, harvested by Europeana (to become available through its portal) and exploited for educational purposes. Furthermore, they are exposed to the BioCASE network, contributing their high quality content to biodiversity communities.

The following sections present MMAT along with its underlying repository (i.e., CHO Repository), identifying their basic architectural components and their internal functionality.

2.1   The MultiMedia Authoring Tool (MMAT)

The Multimedia Authoring Tool (MMAT) is the first step towards allowing the connection of digital collections with Europeana. It is a multilingual web-based management system for museums, archives and digital collections, which facilitates the authoring and metadata enrichment of cultural heritage objects. Moreover, it establishes the interoperability between museums and Europeana and the seamless ingestion of legacy metadata. MMAT supports a rich metadata element set, the Natural Europe CHO Application Profile [14], which is a superset of the Europeana Semantic Elements (ESE) [8] metadata format, as well as a variety of the most popular multimedia formats. The development of the Natural Europe CHO Application Profile was an iterative process involving the NHMs' domain experts and the technical partners of the project, driven by the needs and requirements of the stakeholders and the application domain. The main features of MMAT include the publication of multimedia objects, the semantic linkage of the described objects with well-established controlled vocabularies, and the real-time collaboration among end-users with concurrency control mechanisms. Additionally, it provides the means to directly import the museums' legacy metadata for further enrichment and supports various types of users with different access rights.

MMAT adopts the Google Web Toolkit (GWT) [11] technology, which enables the web applications to perform part of their business logic into the client side and part on the server side. The client side refers to business logic operations performed within a web browser running on a user's local computer, while the server side refers to the operations performed by a web server running on a remote machine. The overall architecture of MMAT is presented in Fig. 1.

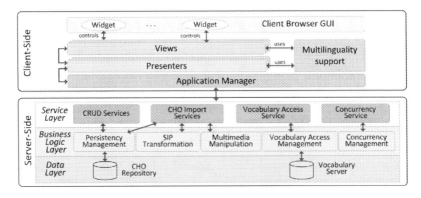

Fig. 1. MMAT Architecture

The **Client Side** is responsible for the interaction with the user, the presentation of the information as well as the communication with the server when needed. It follows the Model-View-Presenter (MVP) [16] design pattern and accommodates modules with discrete roles in managing and delivering/fetching content and metadata from/to the Client Browser GUI to/from the Server Side. The main modules on the Client Side are described below.

- The *Client Browser GUI* refers to the Graphical User Interface presented to the user's web browser. It consists of a composite widget set, each of which aggregates multiple simple widgets (e.g., tables, labels, buttons, textboxes, menus etc.) and serving a specific purpose.
- The *View* modules control composite widgets and are responsible for their layout. They dispatch user action events to their corresponding Presenters for processing.
- The *Presenter* modules are responsible for controlling Views and handling user actions (e.g., user clicks). They communicate with the Service Layer on the Server Side through the Application Manager.

- The *Application Manager* acts as a centralized point of control, handling the communication between the Presenters and the server side by making calls to the services exposed in the Service Layer, and notifying Presenters for their responses.
- The *Multilinguality Support* module handles the translation of the user interface elements. While the tool loads on the client's browser, the translation corresponding to the user language preferences is transferred along with the user interface components.

The **Server Side** of MMAT follows a multi-layered architecture consisting of the following layers:

- The *Service Layer* controls the communication between the client and server logic by exposing a set of services to the client side components. These services comprise the middleware concealing the application's business logic. The basic system services are: (a) the CRUD Service, facilitating the creation, retrieval, update and deletion of a CHO, a CHO record/collection, a user etc., (b) the CHO Import Service, supporting the ingestion of XML metadata records to the CHO Repository through the Persistency Management module, (c) the Vocabulary Access Service, enabling the access to taxonomic terms, vocabularies, publicly sourced authority files of persons, places, etc., through the Vocabulary Access Management module, and (d) the Concurrency Service, providing the basic methods for acquiring/releasing/refreshing locks on a CHO record/collection.
- The *Business Logic Layer* contains the business logic of the application and separates it from the Data Layer and the Service Layer. It consists of five basic modules: (a) the Persistency Management module, managing the submission/retrieval of information packages to/from the CHO Repository, (b) the SIP Transformation Module, transforming XML metadata records to Submission Information Packages (SIPs), (c) the Multimedia Manipulation Module, creating thumbnails and extracting metadata from media files used for the creation and enrichment of CHO records, (d) the Vocabulary Access Management Module, providing access to indexed vocabularies and authority files residing on the Vocabulary Server, and (e) the Concurrency Management Module, applying a pessimistic locking strategy to CHO record/collection metadata in order to overcome problems related to the concurrent editing by multiple users.
- The *Data Layer* accommodates external systems that are used for persistent data storage. Such systems are the CHO Repository and the Vocabulary Server of the Natural Europe federal node [13].

2.2   The CHO Repository

The CHO Repository handles both content and metadata and adopts the OAIS Reference Model [12] for the ingestion, maintenance and dissemination of Information Packages (IPs). To this end, it accommodates modules for the ingestion, archival, indexing, and accessing of CHOs, CHO records/collections etc. This functionality refers to a complete information preservation lifecycle, where the producer is the MMAT and the consumers are the MMAT, the harvester application of the Natural Europe federal node and the BioCASE network.

Fig. 2 presents the overall architecture of the CHO Repository with emphasis to the internal software modules (i.e., Ingest Module, Archival Module, Indexing Module, and Access Module), employed by the repository.

The **Ingest Module** is responsible for the ingestion of an information package (i.e., CHOs, CHO records/collections, and user information) in order to store it as a new Archival Information Package (AIP) to the repository, or to update/delete an already existing AIP. Any submitted information package should be validated and processed in order to identify and create the required AIPs that should be transferred for archival. The only actor on this module is the MMAT, which serves as a SIP producer.

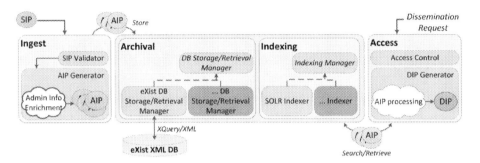

Fig. 2. CHO Repository Architecture

The **Archival Module** receives AIPs from the Ingest Module for storage purposes, as well as AIP retrieval requests from the Access Module for dissemination purposes. In order to support storage and retrieval operations, it employs a DB Storage/Retrieval Manager component which is implemented in a flexible way for supporting any DBMS (relational, XML, etc.). A dedicated eXist DB Storage/Retrieval Manager has been implemented, supporting database specific storage and retrieval operations in an eXist XML DB instance, using XQuery/XML. After the storage, update, or deletion of an AIP, the Archival Module notifies the Indexing Module of the changes.

The **Indexing Module** receives AIPs from the Archival Module in order to build and maintain AIP index structures, as well as AIP retrieval requests from the Access Module for dissemination purposes. In order to support both the maintenance and retrieval index operations, it employs an Indexing Manager component which is flexibly implemented to support any search platform. Currently, a dedicated Apache SOLR Indexer component has been implemented, supporting platform specific maintenance and retrieval operations.

The **Access Module** provides a number of services allowing Dissemination Information Package (DIP) consumers (i.e., the MMAT, the harvester application of the Natural Europe federal node and the BioCASE network) to request and receive information stored in the CHO Repository. It provides functionality for receiving information access requests, while applying access control policies through the Access Control component. Furthermore, it exploits any available indices maintained by the Indexing module, in order to retrieve the requested AIPs. The AIPs retrieved from the Archival and/or Indexing Modules are passed to the DIP Generator component so as to be further processed for creating the final DIP that will be delivered to the DIP consumer. Additionally, the Access Module offers an OAI-PMH interface, allowing NHMs to expose their metadata in order to be harvested by the Natural Europe federal node and subsequently to Europeana. Finally, it implements the Bio-CASE protocol, enabling the connection to biodiversity networks like BioCASE and GBIF.

3   The Metadata Management Life-Cycle Process

The complete life-cycle process that NECE defines for the NHM metadata management comprises four phases: (a) pre-ingestion phase, (b) ingestion phase, (c) maintenance phase, and (d) dissemination phase.

During the **pre-ingestion phase (preparatory phase)** each NHM selects the CHO records/collections that will be contributed to the project and ensures that they will be appropriately migrated into Natural Europe. This includes:

— Web publishing of the CHOs, along with their respective thumbnails (e.g., using MMAT), making them accessible to end users.
— Metadata unification of existing CHO descriptions by preparing XML records conforming to the Natural Europe CHO Application Profile.

During the **ingestion phase** any existing CHOs and CHO descriptions are imported to the Natural Europe environment. The latter are further enriched through a semantic annotation process.

— MMAT provides functionality for loading metadata conforming to the Natural Europe CHO Application Profile, as well as CHOs into its underlying repository. Afterwards, museum curators have the ability to inspect, modify, or reject the imported CHO descriptions. Fig. 3 presents an indicative screenshot of this tool.
— As far as the ingestion through the normal metadata curation/annotation activity is concerned, MMAT allows museum curators to maintain (create/view/modify/enrich) CHO metadata. This is facilitated by the access and concurrency control mechanisms, ensuring security, integrity, and consistency of the content.

The **maintenance phase** refers to the storage and management of CHOs and CHO metadata using MMAT and the CHO Repository.

The **dissemination phase** refers to the controlled provision of the maintained metadata to third party systems and client applications. Such systems are the Natural Europe federal node, the BioCASE network etc.

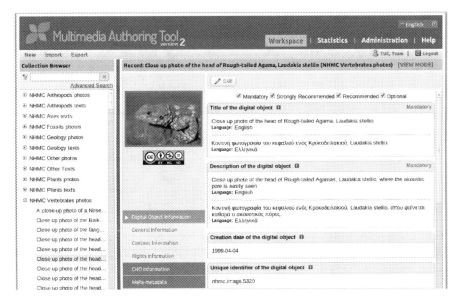

Fig. 3. The Multimedia Authoring Tool in use

4   Connection of the Natural Europe Cultural Environment with BioCASE

The Biological Collection Access Service for Europe (BioCASE) [2] is a transnational network of biological collections of all kinds. BioCASE enables widespread unified access to distributed and heterogeneous European collections and observational databases using open-source, system-independent software and open data standards/protocols.

In order for data providers to connect to this network, they have to install the Bio-CASE Provider Software. This software offers an XML data binding middleware for publishing data residing in relational databases to BioCASE. The information is accessible as a web service and retrieved through BioCASE protocol requests. The BioCASE protocol is based on the ABCD Schema [1], which is the standard for access and exchange of data about specimens and observations. The ABCD Schema is rather huge, offering nearly 1200 different concepts.

Fig. 4 presents an overview of the BioCASE architecture. On the top left resides the BioCASE portal, backed up by a central cache database, accessing information from the data providers (bottom). The BioCASE Provider Software (wrapper) is attached on top of each provider's database, enabling communication with the Bio-CASE portal and other external systems (e.g., GBIF). This wrapper is able to analyze BioCASE protocol requests and transform them to SQL queries using some predefined mappings between ABCD concepts and table columns. The SQL queries are executed over the underlying database and the results are delivered to the client after being transformed to an ABCD document.

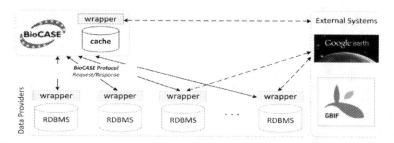

Fig. 4. BioCASE architecture

Although BioCASE supports a variety of relational databases, it does not support non-SQL databases (e.g., XML DBMS). This is also the case of MMAT, which is backed up by an eXist XML Database. To address this problem, we have built a customized wrapper on top of the data providers' repositories (Fig. 5). The wrapper is able to analyze BioCASE protocol requests and transform them to XQueries, exploiting mappings between the Data Provider's schema and the ABCD schema. Towards this end, a draft mapping of the Natural Europe CHO Application Profile to ABCD was produced based on BioCASE practices [3]. The XQueries are executed over the providers' repositories and the results are delivered to the client after being transformed to an ABCD document. The above approach was implemented and successfully tested with a local BioCASE portal installation, retrieving CHOs from all federated node CHO Repositories[1].

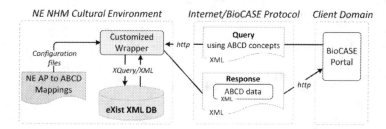

Fig. 5. Connecting Natural Europe Cultural Environment with BioCASE

5   Deployment, Use and Evaluation

The MMAT and the CHO Repository have been deployed on each Natural History Museum participating in the project, allowing the curators to publish, semantically describe, manage and disseminate the CHOs they will contribute to the project[2].

By today (3rd year of the project), a large number of CHOs have been published by each NHM using MMAT, as presented in Table 1. Till the end of the project the total number of CHOs (2nd column) for each NHM will be reached.

---

[1] http://natural-europe.tuc.gr/biocase
[2] A demo version of MMAT is available at: http://natural-europe.tuc.gr/mmat

Table 1. Number of CHOs published and to be published by each NHM using MMAT

Museum	Published CHOs	Remaining CHOs	TOTAL
Natural History Museum of Crete (**NHMC**)	2611	1399	**4010**
National Museum of Natural History – University of Lisbon (**MNHNL**)	1708	902	**2610**
Jura-Museum Eichstätt (**JME**)	1172	478	**1650**
Arctic Center (**AC**)	302	178	**480**
Hungarian Natural History Museum (**HNHM**)	3134	1076	**4210**
Estonian Museum of Natural History (**TNHM**)	1923	0	**1923**

Improvements of the user-interface and the search functionalities have been made after continuous feedback from museum partners in a number of tool releases. Heuristic evaluation of the MMAT was performed, while extensive usability studies have been and will be performed in a number of curator workshops organized by the participating NHMs.

5.1   Heuristic Evaluation

The heuristic evaluation of the Multimedia Authoring Tool was performed by a team of inspectors comprised of 5 current Masters in Human Computer Interaction (HCI) graduates with background and experience in fields such as Computer Science and Information Technology in the context of the HCI course of the Electronic and Computer Engineering Dept. of the Technical University of Crete. In this course, the students had to perform usability evaluation on several products including MMAT. The evaluation was based on Jakob Nielsen's heuristics; 88 errors (9 major) were detected and fixed[3].

5.2   Curator Workshops

A number of curator workshops were organized by the NHMs [17], attracting participants from different professions (presented in Table 2), while more are planned for the current year of the project.

Table 2. Core data of curators participated in the workshops

NHM	Participants	Gender		Mean age	Profession
		M	F		
AC	1	1	0	40	Curator
JME	1	1	0	28	Communication
NHMC	7	3	4	46	Curators, Librarian
MNHNL	7	5	2	41	Curators, zoological curator, biologist, Post Doc, Digital resource manager
TNHM	10	4	6	48	Curators
HNHM	14	5	9	45	Researchers, Curators, Librarian

---

[3] Results of the Heuristic Evaluation (in Greek):
http://natural-europe.tuc.gr/mmat/heuristic

The participants of the workshops carried out by AC, JME, NHMC, TNHM and HNHM were asked about their experience with metadata. Twenty out of thirty three curators had already described items from their collection using metadata. However, most of the workshop participants had seldom or never used any tool to upload multimedia files from their museum collections or manage museum digital collections. In addition, the exploitation of digital collections in education is new for the majority of curators. Regarding the MNHNL curator workshop, all participants had already worked with databases, while most of them occasionally search for or use digital resources from other NHMs (e.g., getting suggestions about metadata management or doing scientific research).

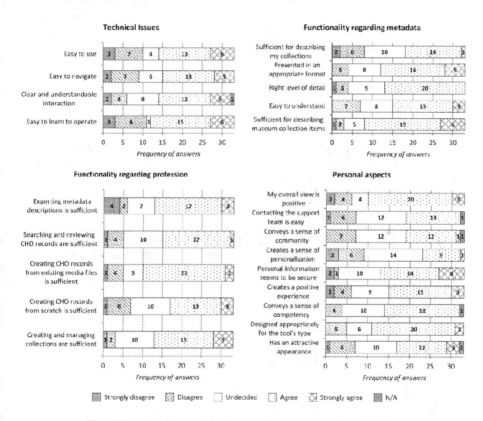

Fig. 6. Results of the satisfaction questionnaire regarding MMAT

After interacting with MMAT, the participants of the NHMC, JME, HNHM, AC and TNHM workshops were administered the satisfaction questionnaire. The results are presented in four parts (Fig. 6): Technical issues, functionality regarding metadata, functionality regarding profession and personal aspects.

- **Technical Issues:** MMAT was rated positively by the majority of the curators of the NHMC, JME, HNHM, AC and TNHM workshops. Twenty one of the participants found the MMAT easy to learn to operate and only six identified the interaction with the system as not clear/understandable.

- **Functionality Regarding Metadata:** In general, the use of metadata elements related to MMAT was rated as satisfying; only three of the curators found that the elements are not sufficient for describing their collections items.
- **Functionality Regarding Profession:** The functionality regarding the profession of curation is generally satisfying. Creation of CHO records/collections is sufficient. Exporting metadata, searching and reviewing CHO records were rated adequately.
- **Personal Aspects:** The overall impression of the tool was positive. Most of the curators felt competent using MMAT and secure in providing their personal information.

6   Related Work

CollectiveAccess [5] is a web-based multilingual cataloguing tool for museums, archives and digital collections. It allows integration of external data sources and repositories for cataloguing and supports the most popular media formats. Although CollectiveAccess supports a variety of metadata standards (Dublin Core, PBCore and SPECTRUM, etc.), direct support for the ESE specification is not provided. Moreover, CollectiveAccess does not implement any harvesting protocol (e.g., OAI-PMH), making impossible to publish the content to Europeana's web portal. Finally, the current version of CollectiveAccess lacks any importing mechanism, crucial in the case of museums having already described their cultural content with metadata in legacy or internal (museum specific) formats.

Collection Space [4] is a web-based application for the description and management of museum collection information. Collection Space does not support the ESE specification and its metadata dissemination mechanisms are limited (REST-API). Moreover, it does not support any harvesting protocol.

Custodea [6] is a system mainly intended for historical and cultural institutions that need to deal with digitization. Custodea covers harvesting of digital content and representations, data transformation, creation and storage of metadata, vocabulary management, publishing and provision of data for Europeana and other institutions. However, the front-end application is desktop-based, which greatly complicates the collaboration of museum curators.

Finally, none of the above tools provides out-of-the-box support for connection to any biodiversity network (e.g., BioCASE, GBIF).

7   Conclusion and Future Work

We presented the architecture, deployment and evaluation of the infrastructure used in the Natural Europe project, allowing curators to publish, semantically describe, and manage the museums' CHOs, as well as disseminate them to Europeana and to biodiversity networks, e.g. BioCASE and GBIF. This infrastructure consists of the Multimedia Authoring Tool and the CHO Repository. It is currently used by six European NHMs participating in the Natural Europe project, providing positive feedback regarding the usability and functionality of the tools. A large number of CHOs has already been published and more are to be published till the end of the project. A long term vision of the project is to attract more NHMs to join this effort.

We are currently developing a semantically rich cultural heritage infrastructure for NHMs, as a proof of concept, by supporting EDM [7]. This will give a Semantic Web perspective to the Natural Europe cultural content. Towards this end, the Natural Europe cultural metadata records will be semantically enriched with well-known vocabularies and thesaurus like Geonames, DBpedia, GEMET and CoL/uBio. Part of this procedure is going to be performed through automatic processes by exploiting existing web services. Object aggregations will be created and the semantically enriched metadata records will be transformed to EDM.

Acknowledgements. This work has been carried out in the scope of the Natural Europe Project (Grant Agreement 250579) funded by EU ICT Policy Support Programme.

References

1. ABCD Schema, http://wiki.tdwg.org/ABCD/
2. BioCASE, http://www.biocase.org/
3. BioCASE practices,
   http://wiki.bgbm.org/bps/index.php/CommonABCD2Concepts
4. CollectionSpace, http://www.collectionspace.org
5. CollectiveAccess, http://www.collectiveaccess.org/
6. Custodea, http://www.custodea.com/en/home
7. Europeana Data Model Definition V.5.2.3, http://pro.europeana.eu/documents/900548/bb6b51df-ad11-4a78-8d8a-44cc41810f22
8. Europeana Semantic Elements Specification V.3.4.1, http://pro.europeana.eu/documents/900548/dc80802e-6efb-4127-a98e-c27c95396d57
9. Falk, J.H., Storksdieck, M.: Using the Contextual Model of Learning to Understand Visitor Learning from a Science Center Exhibition. Wiley InterScience (2005)
10. Global Biodiversity Information Facility (GBIF), http://www.gbif.org/
11. Google Web Toolkit (GWT), http://code.google.com/intl/el-GR/webtoolkit/
12. ISO 14721:2003 Open Archival Information System (OAIS) Reference Model, http://www.iso.org/iso/iso_catalogue/catalogue_tc/catalogue_detail.htm?csnumber=24683
13. Makris, K., Skevakis, G., Kalokyri, V., Gioldasis, N., Kazasis, F.G., Christodoulakis, S.: Bringing Environmental Culture Content into the Europeana.eu Portal: The Natural Europe Digital Libraries Federation Infrastructure. In: García-Barriocanal, E., Cebeci, Z., Okur, M.C., Öztürk, A. (eds.) MTSR 2011. CCIS, vol. 240, pp. 400–411. Springer, Heidelberg (2011)
14. Natural Europe Cultural Heritage Object Application Profile, http://wiki.natural-europe.eu/index.php?title=Natural_Europe_Cultural_Heritage_Object_Application_Profile
15. Natural Europe Project, http://www.natural-europe.eu
16. Potel, M.: MVP: Model-View-Presenter. The Taligent Programming Model for C++ and Java (1996)
17. Sattler, S., Bogner, F.: D6.2 Integrated Pilot Evaluation Report. Natural Europe Project (Ref. No 250579, Area CIP-ICT-PSP.2009.2.5 – Digital Libraries) (2013)

A Curation-Oriented Thematic Aggregator

Dimitris Gavrilis[1], Costis Dallas[1,2,3], and Stavros Angelis[1]

[1] Digital Curation Unit – IMIS, Athena Research Centre, Athens, Greece
[2] Department of Communcation, Media and Culture, Panteion University, Athens, Greece
[3] Faculty of Information, University of Toronto, Toronto ON, Canada
{d.gavrilis,c.dallas,s.angelis}@dcu.gr

Abstract. The emergence of the European Digital Library (Europeana) presents the need for aggregating content using a more intelligent and effective approach, taking into account the need to support potential changes in target metadata schemas and new services. This paper presents the concept, architecture and services provided by a curation-oriented, OAIS-compliant thematic metadata aggregator, developed and used in the CARARE project, that addresses these challenges.

Keywords: Digital curation, metadata aggregator, Europeana, CARARE, workflows, metadata enrichment.

1 Introduction

The European Digital Library (Europeana) has been established through the aggregation of heterogeneous content from multiple content providers, which needs to be delivered reliably and consistently, using a commonly agreed metadata schema, typically by means of collaborative metadata mapping and delivery projects based on national or thematic aggregators. The CARARE - Connecting Archaeology and Architecture in Europeana project [1,2], completed in January 2013, delivered successfully over 2 million records (ca. 10% of Europeana's total content) from over 22 different providers, related to European archaeological and architectural monuments and their representations (photos, 3D models). The project had to deal with changes in the target metadata schema from ESE (Europeana Semantic Elements) to the new and still evolving EDM (Europeana Data Model) schema [3], and to meet demanding delivery requirements.

An important factor for overcoming these challenges was the adoption of an innovative workflow and system architecture, based on the implementation of a curation-aware, OAIS-compliant true digital repository capable of supporting comprehensive metadata ingestion, curation, preservation, transformation and harvesting services. The paper introduces the major features of this system and summarizes its usefulness.

2 CARARE Metadata Workflow

The workflow implemented in the CARARE project ensures that heterogeneous archaeological and architectural metadata from multiple providers gets transformed to

T. Aalberg et al. (Eds.): TPDL 2013, LNCS 8092, pp. 132–137, 2013.

the intermediary CARARE schema adopted by the project, using an appropriate transformation system (e.g., MINT [4] or Repox [5]), is ingested into the MoRe metadata
aggregator where they benefit from various curation and preservation services, and is
then delivered to the Europeana digital library via an OAI-PMH service (Fig. 1).

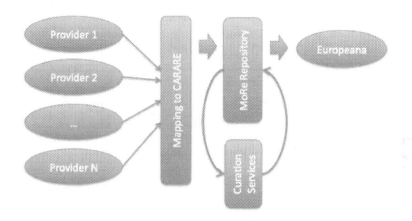

Fig. 1. Metadata workflow in the CARARE project

3   Monument Repository (MoRe) Metadata Aggregator

In order to manage all information submitted by multiple content providers to Europeana a digital repository was introduced, departing from earlier practice in Europeana aggregation. The mission of the repository was to provide:

a.   Versioning support for subsequent ingestion of the same digital objects
b.   Preservation services
c.   Curation services, including metadata enrichment

A true repository-based approach, such as implemented by CARARE for the first time
in the context of Europeana aggregation, has the advantages of: a) ensuring continuous
availability of all metadata ingested to date, thus making it possible to perform actions at
repository level, collection level, or content provider level, and b) isolating ingestion
from subsequent steps, thus significantly saving effort at the interface with content providers. This also helps manage properly the submission of new versions of original metadata, enrichment with dynamically evolving linked data, and future changes in information delivery environment. The system designed and developed for this purpose was
based on Mopseus [6], a digital repository developed by the Digital Curation Unit-IMIS,
Athena Research Centre on top of the widely used Fedora system [7].

3.1   MoRe Repository Architecture

The core of the repository architecture (Fig. 2) consists of a layer of services that
receive information packages, pre-process them, and store the resulting datastreams in

a Fedora installation. The indexes of those datastreams are stored in a MySQL database, and maintained in synchronization with Fedora. A set of curation services, inspired by a micro-services approach [8], are running alongside with the repository, orchestrated by a workflow processing engine. Most services operate at the datastream level, although there are some that only use the MySQL database indexes (e.g. for new information discovery, such as for records of monuments that are in close geographical proximity). The information supplied by content providers is stored and preserved, curated, transformed and made ready for publication by MoRe.

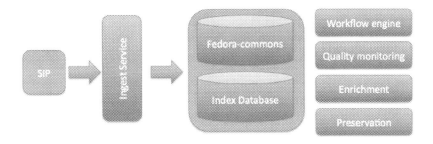

Fig. 2. MoRe metadata aggregator repository architecture

The MoRe repository is fully OAIS-compliant, as the procedures established and information packages ingested, stored and disseminated through it adhere to the OAIS model [9]. The repository core services layer, along with the micro-services layer, were developed in Java and are running under an Apache Tomcat server. The services of MoRe are:

a. Indexing Service. Indexing is a fundamental repository service. MoRe comes with its own indexing mechanism which uses a descriptive XML document to define not only which parts of the metadata will be indexed, but also the structure of the SQL database that they will be indexed to. This approach simplifies, and in part automates, the work of other services such as the quality monitoring service.

b. Quality Monitoring Service. Quality monitoring is an essential part of MoRe, ensuring that content owners are informed about, and thus can control effectively, the status of metadata objects ingested. The quality of the information is measured in diverse ways, summarized per collection or even per submission package, as it is not feasible to inspect each information item separately. Some of the quality attributes monitored are:

1.   Metadata completeness
2.   Duplication of parts of information objects
3.   Element-attribute proper completion

c. Ingestion Service. Being OAIS compliant, the MoRe metadata aggregator handles information packages following precise specifications as regards content and structure of Submission Information Packages (SIPs). SIPs are ingested using a RESTful protocol which allows submission of a large number of digital objects (including multiple datastreams per digital object). Content owners initially map internal metadata into records compliant to CARARE schema, an intermediary schema aimed at capturing a rich representation of architectural and archaeological assets and related digital resources [2], using a transformation tool such as MINT [4] or Repox [5]. To ensure preservation and provenance, each metadata record is followed by its native schema and XSLT transformation document. For each CARARE object, all this information is accompanied by a technical metadata XML file and is encapsulated in one file (ZIP format is used).

Fig. 3. Structure of Submission Information Packages (SIP) in MoRe

d. Curation Services. Curation services monitor information objects and perform curation tasks, including enrichment, that aim to improve content quality. Each particular curation action corresponds to an intended effect concerning the resulting metadata records (Table 1).

Table 1. Curation actions in MoRe and intended effect

Action	Effect
Element & attribute cleaning	Homogeneity
De-duplication	Information item identification
Element & attribute fill	Improved completeness
Relation add	Enriched information
Spatial transform	Homogeneity

Specific examples of curation actions in CARARE satisfy particular goals/effects:

a. Setting the language attributes (e.g. el,gre, GR to el) provides homogeneity to resulting records. In general, this ensures provision of better services for end users.
b. Spatial information was encoded using different coordinate reference systems, and had to be transformed (WGS84 was used as the output coordinate system).
c. In several cases, information had to be added to a record by MoRe, such as a relation that denotes rights usage, a language attribute, or its format type.

e. Workflow Engine. The workflow used to execute curation services is especially important. Services that perform cleaning and simple element filling (with little built-in logic) are executed first. Complex services (with more intelligent logic built in) such as adding relations, performing de-duplication of records, etc. are executed afterwards, so as to use the fullest possible input data in order to provide better results.

f. Preservation Services. Preservation services are responsible for maintaining the metadata of the records provided to the repository, enabling their revision, versioning and validation. Each curation action that modifies content, generates new content or in any way modifies existing information, produces a new datastream version that is stored in Fedora along with its PREMIS event log [10]. A PREMIS event log is maintained across the entire collection.

The Submission Information Package specification requires that each CARARE item is accompanied by its native record, the XSLT document that was used to transform between them and the administrative metadata associated with the record. All these data are ingested as separate datastreams under the same item in the repository along with the appropriate PREMIS event (which is generated during ingest). Conformance with the above preservation model ensures that all AIP managed by MoRe can record the entire lifecycle of each individual digital object.

4   Conclusions

During the 3-year CARARE project, over two million digital records were ingested, curated and delivered using the Monument Repository (MoRe) metadata aggregator with the architecture presented in this paper. CARARE records are now fully available in the Europeana digital library. They are also accessible through a mapping interface, and through a landing page providing access to an ORE aggregation offering a composite view of each heritage asset with related digital resources.

To achieve its objectives, the CARARE project had to overcome multiple challenges, related to: a) harmonization between heterogeneous, complex metadata, b) optimization of the ingestion and delivery process in the light of continuous modifications of the target schema, c) fitness-for-purpose regarding discovery and display of geographically-located cultural heritage objects, d) control over the integrity and authenticity of metadata, allowing for their long term preservation and access, and e) efficiency with regard to large-scale, time-intensive processing of metadata from ingestion to delivery, including the handling of very large batch submissions.

To meet these challenges, CARARE introduced MoRE, a curation-aware, OAIS-compliant true digital repository designed for metadata aggregation. The solution adopted allows handling changes in the target metadata schema without having to resort to re-ingestion from primary collections. Curation services improve metadata consistency and ensure effective de-duplication, geographic placement, and linking between heritage assets, related digital resources, and external linked data. Preservation services support metadata quality monitoring, ensure integrity and authenticity of evolving objects, and allow their continued access and use beyond the end of the project. The pertinence of the solution adopted was clearly manifested during the project, most notably in managing the shift of Europeana from ESE to evolving versions of EDM, including the subsequent addition of elements such as edm:Place, which was applied by MoRe retrospectively on already ingested metadata.

Further work on the MoRe aggregator is currently underway, aiming at leveraging cloud technologies, and at incorporating information objects beyond metadata, SKOS-based vocabulary services, historic name gazeteers, and multiple intermediary schemas and workflows.

Acknowledgments. This paper presents work in CARARE – Connecting Archaeology and Europeana, a best practice network co-funded by the SIP programme of the European Commission (Grant Agreement no. 250445). Authors express thanks to Panos Constantopoulos and colleagues at the Digital Curation Unit-IMIS, Athena Research Centre, as well as to CARARE partners, for useful insights, collaboration and feedback.

References

1. Hansen, H.J., Fernie, K.: CARARE: Connecting Archaeology and Architecture in Europeana. In: Ioannides, M., Fellner, D., Georgopoulos, A., Hadjimitsis, D.G. (eds.) EuroMed 2010. LNCS, vol. 6436, pp. 450–462. Springer, Heidelberg (2010)
2. Papatheodorou, C., Dallas, C., Ertmann-Christiansen, C., Fernie, K., Gavrilis, D., Masci, M.E., Constantopoulos, P., Angelis, S.: A New Architecture and Approach to Asset Representation for Europeana Aggregation: The CARARE Way. In: García-Barriocanal, E., Cebeci, Z., Okur, M.C., Öztürk, A. (eds.) MTSR 2011. CCIS, vol. 240, pp. 412–423. Springer, Heidelberg (2011)
3. Doerr, M., Gradmann, S., Hennicke, S., Isaac, A., Meghini, C., van de Sompel, H.: The Europeana Data Model (EDM). In: World Library and Information Congress: 76th IFLA General Conference and Assembly, pp. 10–15 (2010)
4. Kollia, I., Tzouvaras, V., Drosopoulos, N., Stamou, G.: A systemic approach for effective semantic access to cultural content. Semantic Web 3(1), 65–83 (2012)
5. Reis, D., Freire, N., Manguinhas, H., Pedrosa, G.: REPOX – A Framework for Metadata Interchange. In: Agosti, M., Borbinha, J., Kapidakis, S., Papatheodorou, C., Tsakonas, G. (eds.) ECDL 2009. LNCS, vol. 5714, pp. 479–480. Springer, Heidelberg (2009)
6. Gavrilis, D., Papatheodorou, C., Constantopoulos, P., Angelis, S.: Mopseus – A Digital Library Management System Focused on Preservation. In: Lalmas, M., Jose, J., Rauber, A., Sebastiani, F., Frommholz, I. (eds.) ECDL 2010. LNCS, vol. 6273, pp. 445–448. Springer, Heidelberg (2010)
7. Lagoze, C.: Fedora: An architecture for complex objects and their relationships. International Journal on Digital Libraries 6(2), 124–138 (2006)
8. Abrams, S., Kunze, J., Loy, D.: An Emergent Micro-Services Approach to Digital Curation Infrastructure. International Journal of Digital Curation 5(1) (2010)
9. Consultative Committee for Space Data Systems, NASA: Reference Model for an Open Archival Information System (OAIS). CCSDS Secretariat, NASA, CCSDS 650.0-B-1 (September 2007)
10. Caplan, P., Guenther, R.S.: Practical preservation: The PREMIS experience. Library Trends 54(1), 111–112 (2005)

Can Social Reference Management Systems Predict a Ranking of Scholarly Venues?

Hamed Alhoori and Richard Furuta

Center for the Study of Digital Libraries and
Department of Computer Science and Engineering
Texas A&M University, USA
{alhoori,furuta}@tamu.edu

Abstract. New scholarly venues (e.g., conferences and journals) are emerging as research fields expand. Ranking these new venues is imperative to assist researchers, librarians, and research institutions. However, rankings based on traditional citation-based metrics have limitations and are no longer the only or the best choice to determine the impact of scholarly venues. Here, we propose a venue-ranking approach based on scholarly references from academic social media sites, and we compare a number of citation-based rankings with social-based rankings. Our preliminary results show a statistically significant correlation between the two approaches in a number of general rankings, research areas, and subdisciplines. Furthermore, we found that social-based rankings favor open-access venues over venues that require a subscription.

Keywords: Scholarly Venues, Ranking, Digital Libraries, Bibliometrics, Altmetrics, Impact Factor, Readership, Social Reference Management, Citation Analysis, Google Scholar Metrics.

1 Introduction

Rankings play a vital role in daily life. Students use rankings to select top universities, graduate students use rankings to select the best jobs, patients use rankings to select hospitals, and travelers use rankings to plan their vacations. Rankings of scholarly venues are often used in academia and research. Despite the concerns and objections regarding venue rankings, they continue to be used to identify major scholarly hubs. Researchers agree that these hubs should be assessed based on academic quality. The top scholarly venues have an influence on research. Prestigious journals use the rankings for publicity, librarians use them for subscription decisions, researchers use them for publication decisions, and universities use them for academic hiring, promotions, and funding decisions.

The impact of scholarly venues is typically measured using citation analysis. A major measure used in ranking scholarly venues is the controversial 'impact factor', which has its own limitations. Moreover, research articles, especially those published in conferences, are limited in terms of length, so authors may not be able to cite all the related references. Various usage-based metrics, such as readership [1], downloads,

T. Aalberg et al. (Eds.): TPDL 2013, LNCS 8092, pp. 138–143, 2013.
© Springer-Verlag Berlin Heidelberg 2013

comments, and bookmarking statistics, have been proposed and used to measure the impact of articles and journals, and each has its benefits and limitations [2].

Researchers often use social reference management systems to store and discover scholarly articles. By storing references online, researchers can archive their research interests without limits. Therefore, the statistics for these online digital libraries are strong indicators of researchers' interests and may reflect more accurate interests than statistics about downloads or views.

In this study, we propose and investigate a social-based approach to ranking scholarly venues. We compare our method of venue-ranking with various citation-based ranking approaches and find several strong positive relationships. We also investigate the effects of open-access venues on rankings. This paper is structured as follows: We discuss the related work in Section 2. In Section 3, we describe the experiments, data collection, and methodology. In Section 4, we present and discuss our results. In Section 5, we conclude and highlight some of the future work.

2   Related Work

Although the impact factor is a well-known method for ranking scholarly venues, it suffers from citation delay [3], differs according to discipline [4], and may not be available for emergent venues. The Science Journal Ranking (SJR) indicator [5] has been proposed as an alternative to the impact factor. The SJR indicator considers the quantity and quality of citations. A number of journal-ranking approaches have used the PageRank algorithm, including the SJR indicator and Eigenfactor [6]. The h-index, expert survey [7], and publication power approach [8] have also been used to rank venues.

Zhuang et al. [9] used program committee characteristics to discover and rank conferences. Yan et al. [10] defined two approaches to rank academic venues, a seed-based approach that used author meta-data and a browsing-based approach that used both the citation and author meta-data. Martins et al. [11] used a large number of features with machine learning techniques to assess the quality of scientific conferences. Rahm et al. [12] found that conferences could have a higher impact factor than journals. Google Scholar joined the effort to rank venues when it announced Scholar Metrics, which ranks top scholarly venues in several disciplines and languages, ordered by their five-year h-index.

Bollen et al. [13] concluded that "the notion of scientific impact is a multi-dimensional construct that cannot be adequately measured by any single indicator". Alhoori and Furuta [14] found that social reference management systems significantly affect the scholarly activities of researchers. Social-based approaches have been used to assist in evaluating the scientific impact in several projects such as Altmetrics[1], Article-Level Metrics[2], and Usage Factor[3]. Li et al. [15] compared Web of Science citation counts and CiteUL-ike/Mendeley readership counts on a limited sample of articles published in *Nature* and *Science* and found significant correlations between the two rankings. Kraker et al. [16]

---

[1] http://altmetrics.org/manifesto/
[2] http://article-level-metrics.plos.org/
[3] http://www.projectcounter.org/usage_factor.html

found a significant relationship between Mendeley references and SCImago's impact index, which is SCImago's version of the impact factor. They also found differences among disciplines and indicators that results improve with number of references available.

3   Experiments

We crawled CiteULike and downloaded 554,023 files, in which each file contains a reference to an article and the users who have added it to their digital libraries. We used only the files that contained details of either conferences or journals, for a final sample of 407,038 files. We then extracted the details of venues and collected a total of 1,317,336 postings of researcher–article pairs and a total of 614,361 researcher–venue pairs. We defined three social-based metrics and used them in venue-ranking:

1. **Readership:** The number of researchers who have added references from a venue to the social reference management system.
2. **Article Count:** The number of unique articles from a single venue that were added to the social reference management system.
3. **Active Researchers Rating (ARR):** We defined active researchers as those who added twenty or more venues to their digital libraries. We used a weighted sum to increase the importance of newly added references. Equation (1) was used to compute the ARR for venue v.

$$ARR(v) = \sum_{i=1}^{n} \sum_{w=m}^{1} w \log (v_w + 1) \tag{1}$$

The outer summation of the ARR totals the individual ratings for n researchers. In the inner summation, v_w denotes the number of references from a specific venue that a researcher added to his or her digital library during a particular year, out of all the m years that the researcher followed venue v. Weight w increased the importance of newly added references. The ARR favors researchers who have followed venues for several years over researchers who have added numerous references from venues for a few years. The log minimized the effect of adding many references.

We first compared Google's h5-index with our social-based rankings. Google Scholar's current h5-index includes research articles published between 2007 and 2011 and indexed in Google Scholar as of November 2012. To compare our social-based rankings with Google's h5-index, we selected the articles that were published and added to CiteUlike between 2007 and 2011. Our question was whether a correlation exists between social metrics from CiteULike and Google's h5-index for the indicated time span. We repeated the same strategy with the other citation-based rankings. For example, Eigenfactor score, which uses Web of Knowledge citations, was released in 2011 and includes articles published between 2006 and 2010. Therefore, in this instance, we used a dataset of articles that were published and added to CiteULike between 2006 and 2010.

We used Spearman's rank correlation coefficient, ρ (rho), to compare our social-based rankings with different citation-based rankings, such as Google's h5-index, SCImago's h-index, the Thomson Reuters Impact Factor, the Eigenfactor score, and total citations. We began with citation-based rankings and mapped the corresponding values from the social-based rankings.

4   Results and Discussion

We first compared the general citation-based rankings of the top 100 venues with our social-based rankings. We found a strong positive relationships ($p < 0.01$), as shown in Table 1. There was no significant correlation between the social metrics and the impact factor or the impact index.

Table 1. Correlations between citation-based metrics and social metrics for the top 100 venues

Citation-based metric	Readership	ARR	Article count
SCImago h-index	0.581	0.566	0.534
Google's h5-index	0.336	0.354	0.349
Eigenfactor score	0.688	0.669	0.665
Total citations	0.675	0.625	0.632

We then compared the top twenty venues among different research areas using Google's h5-index and social-based metrics. We found significance relationships in some areas, as shown in Table 2. In Tables 2 and 3 below, we use * to represent ($p<0.05$) and ** to represent ($p<0.01$).

Table 2. Correlations between Google's 5h-index and social metrics for different research areas

Research area	Readership	ARR	Article count
Health & Medical Sciences	0.647 **	0.672**	0.642**
Humanities, Literature & Arts	0.368	0.471	0.200
Life Sciences & Earth Sciences	0.788 **	0.768 **	0.735 **

We also compared Google's h5-index with the social metrics for some subdisciplines in engineering and computer science, as shown in Table 3.

Table 3. Correlations between Google's 5h-index and social metrics for some engineering and computer science subdisciplines

Subdiscipline	Readership	ARR	Article count
Automation & Control Theory	0.567 *	0.382	0.466
Bioinformatics & Computational Biology	0.814 **	0.700 **	0.706 **
Educational Technology	0.575 *	0.512 *	0.374
Library & Information Science	0.761 **	0.769 **	0.754 **
Robotics	0.532 *	0.482	0.460 *

No significant relationships were found between Google's h5-index and social-based rankings in some areas, such as arts and humanities, and some subdisciplines, such as artificial intelligence. However, we found a significant relationship between SCImago's h-index and the readership ranking in arts and humanities ($p < 0.05$) and in artificial intelligence ($p < 0.01$). Surprisingly, and in most cases when compared with the citation-based rankings, the readership rankings had higher correlations than the ARR. The article count usually had weaker correlations than did readership and ARR.

As shown in Table 1, it is clear that social metrics are an effective way to measure the popularity of venues because they have a strong positive correlation with the total number of venue citations. Social metrics can also measure the quality of venues, as they are strongly positively correlated with quality ranking methods, such as Eigenfactor scores. Tables 2 and 3 show differences in correlations among various research areas; these differences could be due to varied levels of online scholarly activity. Moreover, such differences may also relate to unequal distributions of research communities across social reference management systems, or to the existence of research communities that are not active in such online systems. We experimented with two social-based metrics that resemble the impact factor, but we did not find any strong correlation. For the first metric, we divided the readership of a venue by article count, and for the second metric, we divided the ARR by article count.

Finally, we investigated whether the venue-ranking approach (citation-based or social-based) was related to the type of access to venues (subscription or open access). We compared the top 20 venues in Google's h5-index with the top 20 venues in readership and ARR rankings. We included hybrid and delayed access venues in the open-access venue category. There were more open-access venues in the readership and ARR rankings than in the citation-based rankings. We did not find a significant relationship for the readership ranking. However, using the ARR, we found 13 open-access venues but only 6 in Google's h5-index; a Chi-squared test determined there was a significant positive relationship ($X^2 = 4.9123$, $p < 0.05$) between the venue-ranking approach and the type of access to venues.

5   Conclusions and Future Work

In this study, we investigated the relationship between ranking methods for scholarly venues that use traditional citation-based metrics and our proposed social-based metrics. We found statistically significant correlations between the two approaches, with disciplinary differences. Our results suggest that social reference management systems have the potential to provide an early intellectual indicator of the influence of scholarly venues, while reducing the limitations of citation-based metrics.

In the future, we will investigate whether there is a set of social-based metrics that can measure the influence of scholarly venues in all research areas, or if each research area needs to define its own metrics. We plan to explore how the data from different social reference management systems differ and whether they measure similar or different impact of research.

Acknowledgement. This work has been supported under the grant ID NPRP 4 – 029 – 1 – 007 for the project entitled "Establishing a Qatari Arabic-English Digital Library Institute", 2011-2014, which is funded by the Qatar National Research Fund (QNRF).

References

1. Darmoni, S.J., Roussel, F., Benichou, J., Thirion, B., Pinhas, N.: Reading factor: a new bibliometric criterion for managing digital libraries. Journal of the Medical Library Association, JMLA 90, 323–327 (2002)
2. Neylon, C., Wu, S.: Article-Level Metrics and the Evolution of Scientific Impact. PLoS Biology 7(6) (2009)
3. Brody, T., Harnad, S., Carr, L.: Earlier Web usage statistics as predictors of later citation impact: Research Articles. Journal of the American Society for Information Science and Technology 57, 1060 (2006)
4. Rinia, E., Van Leeuwen, T., Bruins, E., Van Vuren, H., Van Raan, A.: Citation delay in interdisciplinary knowledge exchange. Scientometrics 51, 293–309 (2001)
5. González-Pereira, B., Guerrero-Bote, V.P., Moya-Anegón, F.: A new approach to the metric of journals' scientific prestige: The SJR indicator. Journal of Informetrics 4, 379–391 (2010)
6. Bergstrom, C.: Eigenfactor: Measuring the value and prestige of scholarly journals. CRL News 68, 314–316 (2007)
7. Serenko, A., Dohan, M.: Comparing the expert survey and citation impact journal ranking methods: Example from the field of Artificial Intelligence. Journal of Informetrics 5, 629–648 (2011)
8. Holsapple, C.W.: A Publication Power Approach for Identifying Premier Information Systems Journals. Journal of the American Society for Information Science 59, 166–185 (2008)
9. Zhuang, Z., Elmacioglu, E., Lee, D., Giles, C.L.: Measuring conference quality by mining program committee characteristics. In: Proceedings of the 7th ACM/IEEE-CS Joint Conference on Digital Libraries, pp. 225–234. ACM (2007)
10. Yan, S., Lee, D.: Toward alternative measures for ranking venues. In: Proceedings of the 7th ACM/IEEE-CS Joint Conference on Digital Libraries, pp. 235–244. ACM (2007)
11. Martins, W.S., Gonçalves, M.A., Laender, A.H.F., Pappa, G.L.: Learning to assess the quality of scientific conferences. In: Proceedings of the 9th ACM/IEEE-CS Joint Conference on Digital Libraries, pp. 193–202. ACM (2009)
12. Rahm, E., Thor, A.: Citation analysis of database publications. ACM SIGMOD Record, 48–53 (2005)
13. Bollen, J., Van de Sompel, H., Hagberg, A., Chute, R.: A principal component analysis of 39 scientific impact measures. PloS One 4, e6022 (2009)
14. Alhoori, H., Furuta, R.: Understanding the Dynamic Scholarly Research Needs and Behavior as Applied to Social Reference Management. In: Gradmann, S., Borri, F., Meghini, C., Schuldt, H. (eds.) TPDL 2011. LNCS, vol. 6966, pp. 169–178. Springer, Heidelberg (2011)
15. Li, X., Thelwall, M., Giustini, D.: Validating online reference managers for scholarly impact measurement. Scientometrics 91, 461–471 (2011)
16. Kraker, P., Körner, C., Jack, K., Granitzer, M.: Harnessing user library statistics for research evaluation and knowledge domain visualization. In: Proceedings of the 21st International Conference Companion on World Wide Web - WWW 2012 Companion, pp. 1017–1024. ACM (2012)

An Unsupervised Machine Learning Approach to Body Text and Table of Contents Extraction from Digital Scientific Articles

Stefan Klampfl[1] and Roman Kern[1,2]

[1] Know-Center GmbH
[2] Knowledge Technologies Institute, Graz University of Technology
Graz, Austria
{sklampfl,rkern}@know-center.at, rkern@tugraz.at

Abstract. Scientific articles are predominantly stored in digital document formats, which are optimised for presentation, but lack structural information. This poses challenges to access the documents' content, for example for information retrieval. We have developed a processing pipeline that makes use of unsupervised machine learning techniques and heuristics to detect the logical structure of a PDF document. Our system uses only information available from the current document and does not require any pre-trained model. Starting from a set of contiguous text blocks extracted from the PDF file, we first determine geometrical relations between these blocks. These relations, together with geometrical and font information, are then used categorize the blocks into different classes. Based on this logical structure we finally extract the body text and the table of contents of a scientific article. We evaluate our pipeline on a number of datasets and compare it with state-of-the-art document structure analysis approaches.

1 Introduction

As the growth of the global volume of scientific literature reaches unprecedented levels, there is an increasing demand for automated processing systems that support both librarians and researchers in managing collections of scholarly articles. The tasks of these systems range from the extraction of meta-data of a paper to the extraction of the table of contents and the body text, as well as named entities and facts contained therein. An important prerequisite for these tasks is the analysis of the document structure, which is commonly distinguished into a physical or logical layout [1]. Even though today most articles are digitally produced as PDF files, this remains a challenging problem because most of them do not contain structural information, but only provide the rendering information of individual text fragments.

Here we describe a processing pipeline that performs logical layout analysis from a scientific article in PDF format and uses this information to extract its body text and table of contents. A demonstration of the system can be accessed online[1], and the source code is available under an open source license[2]. The physical structure is provided by

---

[1] http://knowminer.at:8080/code-demo/index.html
[2] https://www.knowminer.at/svn/opensource/projects/code/trunk

T. Aalberg et al. (Eds.): TPDL 2013, LNCS 8092, pp. 144–155, 2013.

an open source tool[3] that builds upon the output of the PDFBox[4] library and that produces a set of contiguous text blocks. Our pipeline performs three main steps: First, two geometrical relations between text blocks are extracted: the reading order and the block neighbourhood (section 3). Second, the blocks are categorized into different logical labels based on their bounding boxes and font information (section 4). This categorization stage also makes use of the geometrical relations above. Finally, we extract the body text, consisting of the section headings and the main text, and the table of contents as a tree with the section headings as nodes (section 5).

These individual steps are solved using clustering techniques and heuristics. Apart from the categorization of meta-data blocks, which we reused from previous work [2], our system works completely unsupervised and model-free and uses only information provided by the current document. This sets our approach apart from a number of related studies that use a pre-trained supervised model (e.g., [3,4,5]). A performance comparison shows that for a set of articles from the biomedical domain we outperform the approach in [5] in our tasks (section 6).

2 Related Work

Document structure analysis has been a well-studied research problem for a quite some time (see [1] for a review). Early work approached the problem with mostly rule-based systems that operated on scanned document images or the output of OCR. With the advent of PDF as the dominating format for scientific articles, researchers began to analyze documents directly in digital form. We restrict our discussion of related work to a number of more recent articles on this topic.

A recent paper [6] describes an open source system for analysing PDF publications in the biomedical domain. This system uses heuristics to extract text blocks from the PDF and a rule-based method to classify these blocks into "rhetorical" categories. This categorization stage achieves a very good overall performance, but requires the user to specify a separate rules file for every different journal layout. The authors also evaluate the main text flow, but do not detail any efforts in determining the reading order.

The authors of [7] present a comprehensive system for the structure extraction of PDF books, which is used within a commercial e-book software. They perform a categorization of text blocks through a combination of heuristics, clustering, and supervised learning. Their approach is rather similar to ours, in particular, we build upon the same decoration detection method [8]. They calculate the reading order of blocks by computing the optimal matching in a bipartite graph, using not only positional information, but also the rendering order and the text content of blocks. Furthermore, they extract the document hierarchy from the book's table of contents section in a rule-based manner.

Other work targeted the extraction of certain aspects of PDF documents, such as meta-data [9] or tables [10]. A popular supervised learning method for structure analysis are Conditional Random Fields (CRFs) [3]. One example is the ParsCit system [4], which uses a combination of heuristics and CRFs for reference parsing. A related system is SectLabel [5], which builds upon the feature sets defined for ParsCit to detect

---

[3] Available at the same SVN location.

[4] http://pdfbox.apache.org/

the logical structure of whole scientific documents, and which categorizes the individual lines of a raw input text file. We use this system for comparison in our evaluation (section 6).

3   Extracting Relations between Text Blocks

We extract two geometrical relations between the text blocks on a page that serve as additional information in the categorization stage. The first relation is the *reading order*, the order in which blocks on a page are supposed to be read by humans, the second is a simple geometrical neighbourhood relation.

Reading Order. The reading order on a given page is defined as a specific permutation of all text blocks on that page. We follow the approach of Aiello et al. [11], who defined the *BeforeInReading* relation as a Boolean combination of binary relations for intervals in X and Y direction, which states for any pair of bounding boxes whether the first one occurs at some point (not necessarily immediately) before the other in a column-wise reading order (see Figure 5 in [11] for the exact definition). In addition to [11], we also define the *BeforeInRendering* relation that tells whether a block is rendered at some time before another block in the PDF. We incorporate both relations into a single partial ordering of blocks by specifying a directed graph with an edge between every pair of blocks for which at least one of the two relations hold. We then perform topological sort on this graph by sorting the nodes by the number of outgoing edges in descending order; the first node in this sorted list is the first node in the reading order on that page. We remove that node and all edges connecting this node, resort the nodes by the number of remaining outgoing edges, and select the next node for the reading order. This is repeated until all nodes of the graph have been removed, yielding a permutation of the blocks on the page as the reading order (see Fig. 1A).

More sophisticated methods for reading order detection have been defined [7,12], but we found that our simplifications yield satisfying results for scientific documents and once the reading order is restricted to blocks containing the main document text in a later stage.

Block Neighborhood. We employ a simple straightforward algorithm that searches for the nearest neighbour of each block on the page in each of the four main directions, viz., top, bottom, left, and right. This yields a directed neighbourhood graph of blocks on the page, since this relation is not necessarily symmetric (see Fig. 1B).

For our setup, we found this neighbourhood relation more usable than using a Voronoi diagram computed for the centres of the blocks (as in [11]) because the latter often results in blocks being connected that are quite distant to each other, especially small blocks like page numbers or short headings.

4   Categorization of Text Blocks

The categorization of text blocks is implemented as a sequential pipeline of *detectors* each of which labels a specific type of block. Apart from the meta-data detectors they

A B C

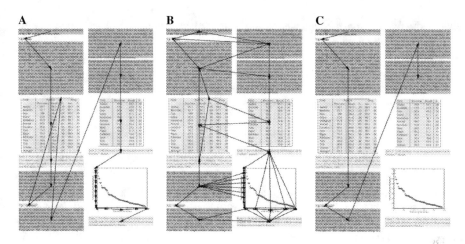

Fig. 1. Sample snapshots of our processing pipeline. All panels show the same document page with the extracted text blocks categorized into different classes (denoted by different colors). The reading order (A) and block neighbourhood (B) is determined first for all blocks on the page, later the reading order is post-processed to contain only the body text (C).

are completely model-free and unsupervised. We derive the categories only from information provided by the current document: they only use the labels given by previous detectors, the geometric information of the text blocks, their content including font information, as well as the block relations extracted before.

Meta-Data. To detect meta-data blocks, which contain information about the published article, e.g., the title, the journal, or the abstract, we reused previously published work [2] which uses sequence classifiers to detect the following types of meta-data blocks: *Title*, *Journal*, *Author*, *Affiliation*, *Email*, and *Abstract*. The details of this approach are beyond the scope of this paper; the interested reader is referred to [2].

Decorations. Decoration blocks contain information such as authors, titles, and page numbers and occur repeatedly at the border of each page, mostly inside headers and footers, but sometimes also at the left or right edge of the page. We adopt the work in [8], which is based on associating top and bottom lines across neighbouring pages based on both their content and their position on the page. This is considered one of the standard header/footer detection methods [7].

We use a slightly modified variant of the approach in [8] that is applicable to text blocks instead of lines. For each page, we sort all blocks on the page in four different orders: from top to bottom, from bottom to top, from left to right, and from right to left. In each ordering we consider the first 5 blocks, and for each block we calculate the maximum similarity to the 5 blocks on both the next and previous page. This similarity score is a value in the range $[0, 1]$ and given by the product between the content and the geometric similarity. The former is calculated from the normalized edit distance between the two content strings, where digits are replaced with "@" chars. The geometric similarity is the area of the intersection between the two bounding box rectangles divided by the larger of the two bounding boxes.

A block is labelled as *Decoration* if its score exceeds some predefined threshold (here, 0.25). The relatively low threshold allows for some noise in the block extraction stage, for example, on different pages of the same document headers might be extracted as a single or multiple blocks.

Captions. Captions are text blocks usually located directly above or below a figure or table explaining its contents. To detect a *Caption* block we simply check whether its first word equals one of certain predefined keyword (viz., "Table", "Tab", "Tab.", "Figure", "Fig", "Fig.") and the second word contains a number (optionally followed by a punctuation, such as ":" or "."). This simple heuristic has been found sufficient for previous work [10,7].

Main Text. We identified the following properties of text blocks containing the main text of most scientific articles: i) they are left-aligned to a limited number of x coordinates (typically the number of columns), ii) they have a similar width (if the text is justified, the width is virtually identical), iii) the font of the majority of characters inside the block is the same for all main text blocks, and iv) the majority of lines in the document belong to the main text.

In order to capture the similarities expressed by properties i) and ii), we applied hierarchical agglomerative clustering (HAC) on all blocks of a document in the two-dimensional feature space defined by the left x coordinate and the width of the blocks. As inter-cluster distance we used "single link"; as the distance between two blocks we used standard Euclidean distance, however, for two blocks with a different majority font we set the distance to positive infinity. This accounts for property iii) and basically ensures that such pairs of blocks end up in different clusters, or, equivalently, all blocks inside one cluster share the same majority font.

HAC merges blocks bottom-up with decreasing similarity and stops once a distance threshold is reached. We chose 10 as the distance threshold, however, this parameter is not too critical; it should be large enough to allow for some variability for the alignment of blocks inside a column, but small enough not to merge blocks across columns or very short blocks. In the next step we sort the resulting clusters by their total size in *lines* in decreasing order, such that according to property iv), the largest clusters should contain the main text blocks. We iterate over this sorted list of clusters and label the contained blocks as *Main text*, until we encounter either a large change in the average width of blocks (larger than a threshold $\Theta_{width} = 5$), or a simultaneous change in font size and cluster size (the portion of all document lines changes by more than $\Theta_{size} = 0.1$). The reason for the second criterion is that main text may consist of more than one font size, but we include blocks of different font size only if there is a substantial amount of text.

The flexibility of the clustering algorithm deals with small disalignments, e.g., slightly indented blocks such as enumerations or lists, but some layouts might require a tuning of the threshold parameters. Main text blocks remain undetected mainly if their width substantially deviates from the normal column width, e.g., when text floats around a figure spanning 1.5 columns, or when the main text spans the whole page width on the first page of the paper, while being set in two columns for the remaining part.

Headings. The heading detection is based on the previous labelling of main text blocks and uses additional information provided by the block relations, reading order and block neighbourhood. A necessary condition for a text block to be considered as a heading is that it occurs either immediately before a main text block in the reading order or is the top neighbour of a main text block. Furthermore, a candidate heading block has to be either left- or centre-aligned to the following main text block. Additionally, each of the following conditions must be met: i) the text starts with either a number or an uppercase character, ii) apart from an optional numbering it consists of at least one non-whitespace letter, iii) it has a maximum number of lines (here: 3), iv) the majority font size is at least as large as for the neighbouring main text block, v) the distance to the neighbouring text block is lower than a threshold (here: 4 times the size of a line of the current heading block candidate). If these conditions are satisfied for unlabelled blocks, they are labelled as *Heading*. A main text block is allowed to be relabelled, if in addition the majority font is bold or italic.

Sparse Blocks and Tables. The remaining blocks contain various document elements such as references, footnotes, formulas, and texts in figures and tables. According to [10] we labelled these blocks as *Sparse* blocks if (1) their width was smaller than 2/3 of the average width of a main text block, or (2) there exists a gap between two consecutive words in the block that is larger than than two times the average width between two words in the main text. Starting from a table caption (recognized by checking if it starts with a keyword such as "Table") neighbouring sparse blocks (defined by the block neighbourhood) are recursively labelled as *Table* blocks if their vertical distance does not exceed a threshold of 2.5 times the average line height of the document main text.

5   Body Text and Table of Contents Extraction

Once the text blocks have been categorized we can now extract the body text and the table of contents of the given document. The body text is given by the sequence of section headings and main text blocks in the extracted reading order. The table of contents is determined by creating a tree structure of headings using hierarchical clustering.

Body Text Extraction. The first step in extracting the body text from the document is to post-process the reading order, which has been originally determined from all blocks, to contain only section headings and main text blocks. This is achieved by a straightforward sequential filtering (see Fig. 1C). Additionally we remove sections titled "Abstract", "Acknowledgments", "References", "Bibliography", or "Supporting Information" from the body text: once we encounter a heading with this content we remove this block and all immediately following main text blocks until the next heading block. The body text is then composed by a simple concatenation of the contents of the remaining blocks in the sequence of the reading order.

Furthermore, we resolve hyphenations by removing hyphens "-" and concatenating the split word parts if they are the result of a proper English hyphenation. For each line of a main text block that ends with a hyphen we apply the hyphenation on the concatenated word using a list of hyphenation patterns taken from the TeX distribution, and if the line split occurs at one of the proposed split points we resolve the hyphenation. As we repeat this check across main text blocks, hyphenations are also resolved across columns and pages.

Table of Contents Extraction. The task of the table of contents (TOC) extraction is to recreate the structure of the scientific article and to identify the hierarchy of sections. The output of this process is a tree of headings for the individual sections. We use the blocks labelled as headings as the starting point for the TOC extraction. Our approach is divided intro three stages: i) grouping of heading with similar formatting, ii) order the groups according to the heading level and iii) use the sequence information within the article and the order of groups to create a hierarchy.

In the first stage of the algorithm we group headings of similar formatting. We use the HAC clustering algorithm, where the distance function is a weighted sum of the differences of the mean character height and of the mean number of characters of two clusters. More precisely, $d(c_1, c_2) = \frac{|\overline{h_{c_1}} - \overline{h_{c_2}}|}{\min(\overline{h_{c_1}}, \overline{h_{c_2}})} + 0.1 \frac{|\overline{l_{c_1}} - \overline{l_{c_2}}|}{\max(\overline{l_{c_1}}, \overline{l_{c_2}})}$, where $\overline{h_{c_i}}$ denotes the average height of a character and $\overline{l_{c_i}}$ the average character count of a heading in cluster c_i. The distance between two clusters is set to infinity if one of the following criteria is met: i) two headings are directly adjacent, ii) either one of the clusters is made up exclusively upper-case characters, iii) the difference in mean character heights differs by more than $\max(stdev(h_{c_1}), stdev(h_{c_2})) + 0.01$, or iv) the level of the numbering that precedes the heading text differs.

The input for the second stage is the list of clusters that contain at least a single heading. These clusters are ordered according to their assumed heading level by the following precedence rules: i) number of prefix segments, ii) difference in mean character height, iii) preference of all upper-case clusters. The output then is a sequence of headings where the ranking defines the heading level.

The final stage takes the ranked list and produces a TOC tree by exploiting the sequence information. Starting from an empty tree with a single root node all headings are iterated in the sequence of how they appear within the article. The first heading is added as a child to the root node. If the level of the current heading is higher than that of the preceding heading it is added as a direct child of the root node. If its level is lower it is added as a sibling to the last heading of the same level. By enforcing a valid tree hierarchy this approach corrects some errors made during the first two stages.

6   Evaluation

First, we evaluate the quality of the block categorization on the GROTOAP dataset, which consists of labelled segmentations of scientific documents into zones. Second, the performance of the main text and heading extraction is assessed on the PubMed dataset, which provides a structured XML file along with each PDF document. The main text evaluation is based on a modified edit distance and indirectly measures the quality of

Table 1. Contingency table of blocks evaluated on the GROTOAP dataset. Columns correspond to our labels, rows correspond to GROTOAP labels. Boldface entries denote equivalent labellings.

	Decoration	Caption	Main	Heading	Table	Sparse	unlabelled
abstract	0	0	6	1	0	50	25
body	6	25	**3707**	1188[*]	8	377	278
keywords	0	0	2	1	0	6	17
correspondence	0	0	0	0	0	9	4
figure_caption	0	**437**	0	0	2	106	45
table_caption	2	**167**	0	0	8	14	5
equation_label	10	0	0	0	0	183	0
page_number	**819**	0	0	0	0	26	0
unknown	3	3	76	66	345	366	377
table	14	1	2	4	**3700**	1790	46
copyright	5	0	7	0	0	75	90
type	1	0	0	0	0	101	1
author	0	0	0	2	0	4	3
editor	0	0	0	0	0	18	1
references	2	0	379[†]	37	0	375	516
title	0	0	0	1	0	2	6
figure	2	1	0	0	7	3706	89
dates	0	0	0	0	0	7	64
equation	0	0	2	32	0	491	3
bib_info	**1158**	0	2	3	0	115	59
affiliation	0	0	5	4	0	48	44
Total	2022	634	4188	1339	4070	7869	1673

[*] In the ground truth dataset, headings are part of the body zone of the following paragraph.
[†] We do not yet detect special reference blocks.

the detected reading order. Finally, we determine the correctness of the extracted tables of contents on the same dataset using an edit distance measure on trees.

Block Categorization. We evaluate the block categorization on the GROTOAP dataset [13]. This dataset consists of 113 documents from various open access journals in digital form as well as their geometric hierarchical structure in XML format. It provides a ground truth for both the segmentation of document pages into contiguous text blocks and their labelling. In a related paper the same authors use this dataset to evaluate their own block extraction and meta-data categorization process [14].

This dataset provides a rather fine-grained labelling of the various text blocks (see row headings in Table 1). Since their block extraction method is different from ours it sometimes yields a different granularity of text blocks: blocks might be merged or split compared to the ground truth segmentation. For the alignment of our extracted labels with the ground truth labels we choose the simple strategy that for each extracted block we search for the corresponding ground truth zone that has the maximum overlapping area and compare the two labels. Note, that this might result in smaller ground truth zones not being used for comparison at all, or larger zones to be compared multiple times.

The resulting contingency table is shown in Table 1. Decoration blocks are mostly paired with zones labelled as *page_number* or *bib_info* (usually the journal name or other publishing information), which typically occur in headers or footers of documents. Decorations are mislabelled if a block with similar content accidentally repeats at almost the same position on neighbouring pages (e.g., equation numbers, table elements).

Table 2. Performance of main text and heading extraction compared to the output of ParsCit (SectLabel) evaluated on a random subset of 1000 documents from the PubMed dataset. Main text performance is defined in terms of the relative number of insert and delete operations necessary to reproduce the ground truth text. "Raw" indicates performance without hyphenation resolution. ParsCit requires raw text as input, generated by PDFBox and Poppler.

Body text:						
	Micro-			Macro-		
	Precision	Recall	F1	Precision	Recall	F1
Main text	**0.873**	**0.969**	**0.918**	**0.950**	**0.961**	**0.945**
Main text (raw)	0.871	**0.969**	0.917	0.947	**0.961**	0.944
ParsCit (PDFBox)	0.741	0.963	0.838	0.787	0.960	0.857
ParsCit (Poppler)	0.711	0.926	0.804	0.757	0.925	0.827

Headings:						
	Micro-			Macro-		
	Precision	Recall	F1	Precision	Recall	F1
Headings	**0.748**	**0.771**	**0.760**	**0.837**	**0.768**	**0.779**
ParsCit (PDFBox)	0.403	0.227	0.290	0.392	0.269	0.299
ParsCit (Poppler)	0.417	0.219	0.287	0.421	0.259	0.300

Caption blocks are mostly assigned to figure and table captions; blocks of the body text are sometimes erroneously labelled if their text starts with one of the caption keywords. Main text blocks largely correspond to zones labelled *body*; depending on the font size, the reference section might be part of the main text or not. Most headings also overlap with a *body* zone; the reason for that is that in the ground truth dataset headings are typically merged to the *body* zone of the following paragraph. A large part, but not all of the sparse blocks inside tables have been correctly identified as table blocks, indicating room for improvement by further work on table recognition. As expected, the remaining sparse blocks are mostly composed of small text blocks inside figures, equations and their labels, and parts of the main text which are aligned differently from the standard columns, e.g., lists or insets.

Body Text and Headings. We use a dataset of 1000 randomly selected documents from PubMed[5], a free database created by the US National Library of Medicine holding full-text articles from the biomedical domain together with a standard XML markup that rigorously annotates the complete content of the published document.

We evaluate the quality of the extracted main text (the content of heading and main text blocks in the reading order, see section 5) by comparing it to the concatenated string of characters contained in the body part of the ground truth XML. We remove all whitespace characters in both strings and determine their similarity by a variant of the Levenshtein distance that counts the number of insertions and deletions (but not of substitutions) necessary to transform the extracted text into the actual text. Given these numbers we define precision and recall for the main text as $P_{text} = 1 - D/\max(N, M)$ and $R_{text} = 1 - I/\max(N, M)$, respectively, where D and I are the number of deletions and insertions and N and M are the lengths of the two strings. Intuitively, a low

---

[5] http://www.ncbi.nlm.nih.gov/pubmed/

number of deletions means that most of the extracted text is contained in the true body text in the right order, thus having a high precision. Analogously, if the number of insertions is small most of the true body text is extracted, leading to a high recall. This evaluation not only depends on the correct labelling of main text and heading blocks, but also the correct reading order, as shuffling text pieces results in reduced precision and recall values.

Since the dataset contains a range of different article types, including book reviews, abstracts, and product presentations, we included only those documents into the analysis which contain a body text and at least one section header. It can be seen in Table 2 that most of the main text is extracted correctly. Insertions (decreased recall) typically occur when main text blocks are miscategorized as e.g., captions or sparse blocks. A typical case for deletions (decreased precision) is that parts of the reference section get included into the main text although they are not part of the ground truth text. We also evaluated the effect of resolving hyphenations ("raw" in Table 2) and found that it is below 1% in precision and obviously does not affect recall.

In the PubMed dataset headings are contained within the *title* tag of a *sec* section. For the evaluation of the extracted headings we collect the texts from the blocks labelled as heading and compute standard precision and recall. Table 2 shows that performance values are around 80%. One source of error here is that the ground truth does not distinguish between normal section headings and paragraph headings, which we do not extract since they are not offset from, but part of the following main text block.

We compared our performance to a state-of-the-art system for logical structure detection, SectLabel [5] from the ParsCit package[6]. This system takes a raw text file as input and uses a trained CRF model to classify individual lines into different categories, in particular *bodyText*, *sectionHeader*, *subsectionHeader*, and *subsubsectionHeader*. We applied SectLabel on the output of two standard pdf-to-text tools, PDFBox and Poppler[7], and evaluated the extracted main text and section headings on the same subset of the PubMed dataset. Table 2 shows the performance values obtained on both the main text and the heading extraction. On the main text, which is obtained by concatenating the contents of the *bodyText* tags, a reasonable recall is achieved, however, typically more than the actual body text is categorized as such. The performance on headings is substantially lower.

Table of Contents. For the table of contents evaluation we use the same dataset as for the evaluation of the heading labelling. We filter the test articles from the PubMed dataset to contain only documents with available section information and no duplicate heading names, resulting in 633 documents. To measure the quality of the TOC extraction we compute the minimal tree edit distance in comparison to the heading tree from PubMed, calculated by the Zhang-Shasha algorithm[8] [15]. A distance of zero indicates that the algorithm exactly recreated the TOC tree.

Errors in the TOC extraction might originate in i) the block extraction stage (e.g., blocks which do not exactly contain the heading text), ii) the block categorization stage (e.g., heading blocks which are not labelled as such), or iii) in errors introduced by the

---

[6] http://wing.comp.nus.edu.sg/parsCit/
[7] http://poppler.freedesktop.org/
[8] https://github.com/timtadh/zhang-shasha

Table 3. Performance of the table of contents extraction on the PubMed dataset measured as the average tree edit distance. Different scenarios highlight the influence of different types of errors (see text). The best performance is achieved when errors introduced by the block extraction and the categorization stages are removed. The results are compared to the TOC created from the ParsCit (SectLabel) output applied to the text output of PDFBox and Poppler.

	TOC ext. error iii)	TOC ext. Block cat. errors ii) & iii)	TOC ext. Block cat. Block ext. errors i) - iii)	ParsCit (Poppler)	ParsCit (PDFBox)
Mean tree edit distance	0.25	2.15	5.18	13.59	13.42
Number of articles	308	308	633	633	633

TOC extraction itself. In the evaluation we allow up to four extra characters at the front (or back) of the extracted heading, as for example the heading numbering is sometimes not part of the ground truth. In Table 3 the achieved performance of our approach is compared to the ParsCit algorithm using its default settings. We report three runs for our system to demonstrate the impact of the different types of errors. For about half of the documents (305) all heading blocks have been correctly extracted. Here our TOC extraction algorithm produces results very close to the ground truth with an average edit distance of considerably less than 1 (the edit distance was 0 for about 89% of these articles). Including errors from the block categorization stage raises the average edit distance by about 2, and errors introduced by the block extraction stage again add roughly the same amount. Even with all sources of errors considered, the performance of our system is considerably better than the ParsCit approach.

7   Discussion and Conclusions

We have developed an unsupervised processing pipeline that performs logical layout analysis and extracts the body text and the table of contents from a scientific article given as a PDF file, from which we extract the text stream using PDFBox. The problem with this and other tools is that the information provided about individual characters in the PDF is inherently noisy, for example, height and width information might be wrong, or information about the font of some characters might be missing. This implicit noise affects every stage of our system, and we believe that its performance could be considerably improved if this low-level information would be more reliable.

On the other hand, our evaluation shows that the performance of our system, which makes use of the formatting and layout of the article, is considerably better than the SectLabel algorithm from the ParsCit system, which operates on plain text only and which we plugged in with the off-the-shelf CRF model. It has already been shown in [5] that the inclusion of rich document features would significantly improve the detection of the logical structure. Another reason for the large performance deterioration could be that the statistics of PubMed documents are substantially different from those documents for which the SectLabel system was trained. A similar observation was made in [6], where this system is also discussed. We would like to further investigate this in future work, where we plan to compare our unsupervised pipeline to a fully supervised classification model.

Acknowledgments. The presented work was in part developed within the CODE project funded by the EU FP7 (grant no. 296150) and the TEAM IAPP project (grant no. 251514) within the FP7 People Programme. The Know-Center is funded within the Austrian COMET Program - Competence Centers for Excellent Technologies - under the auspices of the Austrian Federal Ministry of Transport, Innovation and Technology, the Austrian Federal Ministry of Economy, Family and Youth and by the State of Styria. COMET is managed by the Austrian Research Promotion Agency FFG.

References

1. Mao, S., Rosenfeld, A., Kanungo, T.: Document structure analysis algorithms: A literature survey. Proceedings of SPIE 5010(1), 197–207 (2003)
2. Kern, R., Jack, K., Hristakeva, M., Granitzer, M.: TeamBeam - Meta-Data Extraction from Scientific Literature. In: 1st International Workshop on Mining Scientific Publications (2012)
3. Peng, F., McCallum, A.: Accurate Information Extraction from Research Papers using Conditional Random Fields. In: HLTNAACL 2004, vol. 2004, pp. 329–336 (2004)
4. Councill, I.G., Giles, C.L., Kan, M.Y.: ParsCit: An open-source CRF Reference String Parsing Package. In: Proceedings of LREC, vol. 2008, pp. 661–667. Citeseer, European Language Resources Association, ELRA (2008)
5. Luong, M.T., Nguyen, T.D., Kan, M.Y.: Logical structure recovery in scholarly articles with rich document features. International Journal of Digital Library Systems 1(4), 1–23 (2011)
6. Ramakrishnan, C., Patnia, A., Hovy, E., Burns, G.A.: Layout-Aware Text Extraction from Full-text PDF of Scientific Articles. Source Code for Biology and Medicine 7(1), 7 (2012)
7. Gao, L., Tang, Z., Lin, X., Liu, Y., Qiu, R., Wang, Y.: Structure extraction from PDF-based book documents. In: Proceedings of the 11th Annual International ACM/IEEE Joint Conference on Digital Libraries, pp. 11–20 (2011)
8. Lin, X.: Header and Footer Extraction by Page-Association. Proceedings of SPIE 5010, 164–171 (2002)
9. Granitzer, M., Hristakeva, M., Knight, R., Jack, K., Kern, R.: A Comparison of Layout based Bibliographic Metadata Extraction Techniques. In: WIMS 2012 - International Conference on Web Intelligence, Mining and Semantics, pp. 19:1–19:8. ACM, New York (2012)
10. Liu, Y., Mitra, P., Giles, C.L.: Identifying table boundaries in digital documents via sparse line detection. In: Proceeding of the 17th ACM Conference on Information and Knowledge Mining, CIKM 2008, pp. 1311–1320. ACM Press (2008)
11. Aiello, M., Monz, C., Todoran, L., Worring, M.: Document understanding for a broad class of documents. International Journal on Document Analysis and Recognition 5(1), 1–16 (2002)
12. Malerba, D., Ceci, M., Berardi, M.: Machine learning for reading order detection in document image understanding. Machine Learning in Document Analysis, 45–69 (2008)
13. Tkaczyk, D., Czeczko, A., Rusek, K.: GROTOAP: ground truth for open access publications. In: Proceedings of the 12th ACM/IEEE-CS Joint Conference on Digital Libraries, pp. 381–382 (2012)
14. Tkaczyk, D., Bolikowski, L., Czeczko, A., Rusek, K.: A Modular Metadata Extraction System for Born-Digital Articles. In: 2012 10th IAPR International Workshop on Document Analysis Systems, pp. 11–16 (March 2012)
15. Zhang, K., Shasha, D.: Simple Fast Algorithms for the Editing Distance between Trees and Related Problems. SIAM Journal on Computing 18(6), 1245–1262 (1989)

Entity Network Extraction
Based on Association Finding and Relation Extraction

Ridho Reinanda[1,2], Marta Utama[1], Fridus Steijlen[2], and Maarten de Rijke[1]

[1] ISLA, University of Amsterdam, The Netherlands
{r.reinanda,derijke}@uva.nl, marta.utama@gmail.com
[2] Royal Netherlands Institute of Southeast Asian and Caribbean Studies
steijlen@kitlv.nl

Abstract. One of the core aims of semantic search is to directly present users with information instead of lists of documents. Various entity-oriented tasks have been or are being considered, including entity search and related entity finding. In the context of digital libraries for computational humanities, we consider another task, network extraction: given an input entity and a document collection, extract related entities from the collection and present them as a network. We develop a combined approach for entity network extraction that consists of a co-occurrence-based approach to association finding and a machine learning-based approach to relation extraction. We evaluate our approach by comparing the results on a ground truth obtained using a pooling method.

1 Introduction

Today's increasing digitization and curation of humanities content in digital libraries gives rise to a new and interesting set of opportunities. In computational humanities, re-searchers are particularly interested in applying computational methods and algorithms to gain insight from this kind of data [16]. One interesting and urgent problem is ex-tracting and analyzing networks of entities from unstructured, possibly noisy text such as (archival) newspaper articles. Recognizing such entities (person, organization, or lo-cation) and discovering how they are connected to each other benefits computational humanities researchers asking questions about network and entities, for example in un-derstanding the network of an elite politician and its dynamics [9].

We view entity network extraction task as a form of semantic search. Our working hypothesis is that having entities and related entities presented in the form of a network is more useful than returning a large list of documents and forcing users to go through each and every one of them to manually identify the connections. For our purposes a network is a graph with a main entity together with a set of related entities as nodes, with edges connecting these nodes. A connection between two nodes denotes that there is a relationship between these two entities according to evidence found in the text. In our computational humanities application scenario, our users use a manually constructed English corpus of newspaper articles about Indonesia collected over a 10 year period. This amounts to 140,263 articles, mostly consisting of politics and economy articles. Fig. 1 shows (part of) an entity network automatically extracted from the corpus. The query entity is "BJ Habibie," a former president of Indonesia. Because the query entity

T. Aalberg et al. (Eds.): TPDL 2013, LNCS 8092, pp. 156–167, 2013.

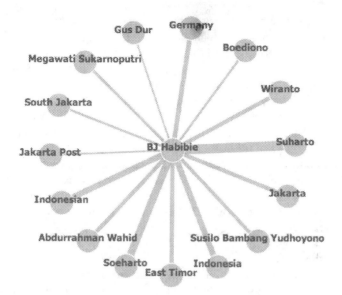

Fig. 1. A sample network retrieved in response to "BJ Habibie" as query entity. The thickness of the links depicts the association strength as represented in the document collection.

is a popular person, he is related to many other entities in the text. We rank the entity relations based on a scoring method, and build the network from top ranked entities only. We use an English-language corpus with Indonesian politics as the primary topic, but our approach also works on other languages with minor changes in the pipeline (utilizing respective linguistic tools). Our approach does not rely on domain-specific pattern extraction, so it is adaptable to other topics or domains as well.

The closest benchmarking task to our proposed task is the related entity finding (REF) task that was considered at TREC 2009, 2010 and 2011 [2]. Related entity finding works as follows: given a source entity, a target page, a narration of the relation of interest, one has to give a ranked list of entities and their home page that engage in this relation with the source. Our task is different from the REF task in the sense that we only have the names of the entities; no sample homepage, and no narration. Furthermore, we are not interested in a single specific relation, but in all possible relationships.

In this paper we address the task of extracting an entity network from text in two ways: (1) by discovering associations between entities through statistical or information-theoretic measures, and (2) by performing relation extraction and building a network using the relationships discovered. We contrast these two approaches and also consider a combination of the two types of approach based on pairwise learning-to-rank [13].

2 Related Work

Entity Network Extraction as Semantic Search. Previous research has dealt with extracting various kinds of network from document collections. Referral Web [14] takes a person name as input and finds people related to this person on the Web by using an external search engine. Referral Web uses the number of pages where two person names co-occur to measure the degree to which they are related.

Merhav et al. [17] perform extraction of relational networks of entities from blog posts. This is done by first creating entity pairs, clustering those entity pairs, and later labeling these clusters with the nature of the relationship. Elson et al. [7] extract social networks from literary fiction. The networks are derived from dialogue interactions, thus the method depends on the ability to determine whether two characters are in a conversation. Their approach involves name chunking, quoted speech attribution, and conversation detection. Tang et al. [21] extract social networks of academic researchers. After entities are identified and disambiguated, they provide a shortest-path search mechanism that links the researchers and their publications as a network.

Association Measures. Association measures can be used to describe the relationship between two words or concepts. There are various ways to measures associations or relatedness. We distinguish between the following types: frequency-based, distance-based, distributional similarity/feature-based, and knowledge-based measures.

Frequency-based measures rely on the frequency of word co-occurrences and the (unigram) frequency of each word. These include measures that are derived from probability theory or information theory, for example Chi-Square, Pointwise Mutual Information, and Log Likelihood Ratio [6]. Distance-based measures rely on the distance between words in the text. Co-dispersion, introduced in [22], is one such measure.

Feature-based or distributional similarity measures describe the relatedness between two words or concepts based on the distribution of words around them. These are measures based on extracting a number of features for each entity, and then comparing the feature vectors for different entities. One example is by using cosine similarity to determine the relatedness of two entities based on linguistic features, such as neighboring words, part-of-speech tag, etc. [6]. Knowledge-based measures are measures that use on ontology, thesaurus, or semantic network to determine the relatedness between words or concepts [18].

Relation Extraction. In relation extraction, we want to extract relations between entities such as persons, organizations, and locations. *Supervised* methods view the relation extraction task as a classification task. Features are extracted from entity pairs and a classifier is trained to determine whether a pair of entities is related. There are various groups of methods: feature based methods, in which syntactic and semantic features are extracted from the text, and string kernel methods, where the whole string is passed as a feature and string kernel functions are used to recognize the richer representations of the structure within the strings to determine whether two entities are in a relation.

Semi-supervised methods are often based on pattern-based extraction algorithms. The core idea is bootstrapping, in which one tries to extract patterns iteratively, using newly found patterns to fuel later extraction steps. DIPRE [4] starts with a small set of entity pairs; the system then tries to find instances of those seeds. With newly found instances, the relation is generalized. Snowball [1] uses the same core idea. Snowball starts with a seed set of relations and attaches confidence scores to them; it uses inexact matching to cope with different surface structures. TextRunner [8] learns relations, classes, and entities from text in a self-supervised fashion. The system starts by generating candidate relations from sentences, then uses constraints to label candidates as positive or negative examples to feed a binary classifier.

Since labeling and annotating a corpus to create relation examples is an expensive and time-intensive procedure, there is increasing attention for *unsupervised* or *weakly-supervised* approaches to relation extraction. With distant supervision [19], indirect examples in the form of relations from a knowledge base such as Freebase and DBPedia are used. From these relation tuples, instances of relations in the form of sentences in the corpus are searched. From these sentences, text features are extracted that are then used to train classifiers that can identify relations.

Our work differs from the related work described above in the following important ways. Firstly, in building the network, we also look at measures to determine the score of the related entities. Secondly, we experiment with alternative association measures, i.e., distance-based ones. Thirdly, while relation extraction methods usually train a specific classifier for each predefined relation type, we train a generic relation classifier on linguistic features. To the best of our knowledge, we are the first to consider combining association finding and relation extraction to extract an entity network from text.

3   Method

Task Description. The task of network extraction is as follows: given a corpus and an input entity as a query, we must return a list of related entities, along with scores that can be used to rank them. The scores can be used for visualization purposes, and can be interpreted as the strength of association between the entities, or number of pieces of evidence supporting an extracted connection.

Pipeline. In the preparation stage, we enrich each document with linguistic annotations. We perform the following types of linguistic processing: tokenization, part-of-speech tagging, sentence splitting, constituency parsing, and named entity recognition with the Stanford NLP tools [15]. We later construct an index out of these documents and their linguistic annotations.

Our main pipeline consists of the following steps: (1) query construction, (2) document selection, (3) entity extraction, (4) candidate scoring, and (5) candidate ranking.

(1) Query Construction. For each query entity e, we construct the query q, a phrase query that will be used in searching the index.

(2) Document Selection. For retrieval purposes in the search step, we use Lucene,[1] which combines a boolean model and vector space model. After obtaining the search results, we use all of the returned documents in the next step.

(3) Entity Extraction. For every document in the search result, we extract pairs of entities (x, y) that co-occur within the same sentence. We then filter these pairs of entities, to only consider pairs that contain the query entity e.

In filtering the pair of entities, we follow the rule-based inexact matching scheme used in expert finding [3], but we adapt the rules to suit our task:

---

[1] http://lucene.apache.org

- EXACT MATCH returns a match if x is mentioned exactly the same as query entity e.
- LAST NAME MATCH returns a match if x is the last name of the query entity e.
- FIRST NAME MATCH returns a match if x is the first name of the query entity e.

(4a) Candidate Scoring – Association Measure. A score is assigned for each entity pair based on association measures. We compute the association strength by several *frequency based measures*: pair frequency, pointwise mutual information (PMI), and Jaccard. In the following equations, $f(x, y)$ denotes the frequency of two entities appearing together in the same sentence, $f(x)$ is the unigram frequency of entity x within the set of selected documents, and $f(y)$ is the unigram frequency of entity y within the set. Pair frequency is computed as follows: $PF(x, y) = f(x, y)$. Pointwise mutual information is computed as follows: $PMI(x, y) = \log \frac{f(x,y)}{f(x)f(y)}$. The Jaccard measure is computed as follows: $Jaccard(x, y) = \frac{f(x,y)}{f(x)+f(y)-f(x,y)}$. Both document-level and sentence-level frequency are used as evidence in counting the frequency. With document-level frequency as evidence, $f(x, y)$ is basically the document frequency of entity pairs.

We also experiment with *distance-based measures*, first by simply using the average distance of two entities. Here distance means the number of tokens separating two entities. With M denoting mean, we define the *inverse mean distance* (IMD) as follows: $IMD(x, y) = \frac{1}{M(dist_{xy1},...,dist_{xyn})}$, where $dist_i$ is the linear word distance at the pair occurrence i.

An alternative to linear word distance is dependency distance. To get a dependency distance, we first need to perform dependency parsing [10] on sentences containing the entity pair. The result of this parsing is a dependency tree. Entities are not stored in a single node in a parse tree, but broken down into component words. We define dependency distance as the number of edges between the head word of entity x to the head word of entity y. We find the shortest path between these two head word nodes, and use the number of edges as distance. We then simply subsitute dependency distance as $dist$ in the previous equation to compute the dependency-based IMD.

Based on the preliminary observation that simply using pair frequency performs quite well, we propose the following measure: $PF.IMD(x, y) = PF(x, y) \times IMD(x, y)$. This measure takes into account both frequency and average distance. The intuition behind this is that a good relation will spread across a lot of documents with small dependency distance.

(4b) Candidate Scoring – Relation Extraction. We use sentences containing the pairs of entities as text snippets. We extract the following features from each text snippet: named entity types, dependency distance, linear distance, typed dependencies (conjunction, noun modifier, or preposition), dependency trigram/bigram, and punctuation type between entities. Sentence level features are also extracted: number of tokens, the presence of quotes, and number of entities within the sentences. We avoid using lexical features in order to have a domain-independent, generic classifier.

We use a portion of our ground truth to train and tune a SVM classifier [20]. For every pair of entities that is extracted, we run the classifier to determine whether their snippets describe that the two entities are related. The snippets that are classified as

Table 1. Entity network extraction methods considered in the paper

Method	Description
pf-doc	Document-level pair frequency
pmi-doc	Document-level PMI
pf-sen	Sentence-level pair frequency
pmi-sen	Sentence-level PMI
jaccard-doc	Document-level Jaccard
jaccard-sen	Sentence-level Jaccard
imd-lin	Inverse mean distance, linear
imd-dep	Inverse mean distance, dependency
pf-doc.imd-dep	Document-level PF.IMD, dependency
pf-sen.imd-dep	Sentence-level PF.IMD, dependency
rel-conf	Relation confidence
rel-support	Relation support
rel-conf.rel-support	Relation confidence.support
ensemble-all	Ensemble of all methods
ensemble-freq	Ensemble of frequency methods
ensemble-dist	Ensemble of distance methods
ensemble-freq.dist	Ensemble of frequency and distance methods
ensemble-rel	Ensemble of relation extraction methods
ensemble-top-4	Ensemble of top 4 methods from feature selection
ensemble-top-6	Ensemble of top 6 methods from feature selection
ensemble-top-8	Ensemble of top 8 methods from feature selection
ensemble-top-10	Ensemble of top 10 methods from feature selection

correct relations will serve as *support* instances to the relation. We score the entity pairs based on how many support instances remain after the classification. We also calculate the *confidence* score of a pair, defined as the number of snippets detected as relations over all the snippets extracted containing the pair. We define another score as combination: *support.confidence*.

(5) Candidate Ranking. We simply rank entity pairs based on their score.

Combination Methods. As we will see below, the network extraction methods that we consider behave quite differently. Because of this, we also experiment with learning to rank for combining rankings produced by various methods. Specifically, we use RankSVM [13], a pairwise learning to rank algorithm. Scores from various network extraction methods are used to build an ensemble ranking model. We try different combinations of ensembles. First, training an ensemble using scores from all methods, and also ensembles built from each family of methods. We also experiment with ensembles based on automatic feature selection. We use a filtering approach, ranking features by importance, using randomized trees [11]. Randomized regression trees are built from subsamples of the training data. Feature importance is computed based on the number of times a feature is selected as decision node in the randomized trees [20]. We use the top 4, 6, 8, and 10 features from this feature selection step to build our ensembles.

Network Extraction Methods Compared. All in all, we consider the methods listed in Table 1 for extracting networks.

4   Experimental Setup

Research Questions. We aim to answer the following research questions. (RQ1) How do the methods based on association measures and relation extraction compare? (RQ2) Can we combine these various scoring methods in an ensemble to improve the performance? (RQ3) How does performance differ across different queries?

Dataset. We use a corpus manually constructed by social historians, from web articles during the period between 2000 and 2012.[2] The corpus contains 140,263 articles about Indonesia and South East Asia. These are mainly news articles from English language media based in Indonesia such as Jakarta Post and Jakarta Globe. Some articles from international media such as The Washington Post and The New York Times are also included. The articles are from diverse topics: politics, economy, cultural events, etc. Some of the named entities of the type organization and location appear in the their English version. An example of this case is "Badan Intelijen Negara" (BIN), which appears in the text both as "BIN" and "State Intelligence Agency."

Ground Truth. We prepare our ground truth by using a pooling strategy (similar to TREC [12]). We select 35 query entities that are known to occur in our corpus, run all entity network extraction methods listed in Table 1 and pool the top 10 related entities from each method. In the assessment step, pairs (query entity, related entity) are presented to three assessors (domain experts) along with supporting text snippets. The assessors' task is to decide whether the two entities are directly related based on the text snippets containing the pair. The assessors are not given a strict definition of a relation. In case of disagreement, the majority vote determines the final assessment. We reach 80 percent average pairwise agreement between the assessors, with a kappa value of 0.60.

Evaluation Metrics and Significance Testing. We use recall, precision and F-measure as a way to evaluate the performance of our entity network extraction methods. In this task, recall is the fraction of correct relations retrieved over all relations in our ground truth. Precision is the fraction of correct relations over the retrieved relations. We mainly look at the performance in the top ten and thirty entities returned. For significance testing, we use a paired t-test with $\alpha = 0.05$.

5   Results

We run our entity network extraction approach on the query entities with various scoring methods. Table 2 shows the results of extracting the top-10 and 30 related entities.

Methods Comparison. To answer RQ1, we look at the performance of the non ensemble methods. Overall, we can see that `pf-doc`, simply counting the number of documents in which the pair of entities co-occur, already provides a decent performance. Using the sentence count, `pf-sen`, further improves the performance. The `Jaccard` measures, both at the document and sentence count, perform slightly worse than `pf`. The `pmi-doc` and `pmi-sen` methods both perform significantly worse than the baseline.

---

[2] Access to the dataset and ground truth can be facilitated upon request.

Table 2. Results of the entity network extraction methods at top-10 and top-30 related entities. Significance is tested against the baseline with $\alpha = 0.05$.

Method	R@10	P@10	F@10	Method	R@30	P@30	F@30
pf-doc (baseline)	0.506	0.544	0.478	pf-doc (baseline)	0.775	0.324	0.435
pmi-doc	0.365▼	0.321▼	0.295▼	pmi-doc	0.613▼	0.245▼	0.333▼
pf-sen	0.519	0.558	0.491	pf-sen	0.785	0.329	0.441
pmi-sen	0.328▼	0.309▼	0.281▼	pmi-sen	0.609▼	0.241▼	0.327▼
jaccard-doc	0.520	0.529	0.468	jaccard-doc	0.763	0.318	0.427
jaccard-sen	0.483	0.529	0.460	jaccard-sen	0.763	0.323	0.431
imd-lin	0.434	0.355▼	0.350▼	imd-lin	0.670▼	0.257▼	0.354▼
imd-dep	0.425	0.366▼	0.347▼	imd-dep	0.685▼	0.268▼	0.367▼
pf-doc.imd-dep	0.516	0.515	0.461	pf-doc.imd-dep	0.803	0.334	0.449
pf-sen.imd-dep	0.519	0.524	0.465	pf-sen.imd-dep	0.815	0.342	0.459
rel-conf	0.365▼	0.326▼	0.312▼	rel-conf	0.712▼	0.277▼	0.381▼
rel-support	0.489	0.501	0.452	rel-support	0.795	0.332	0.446
rel-conf.rel-support	0.443▼	0.429▼	0.398▼	rel-conf.rel-support	0.777	0.321	0.433
ensemble-all	**0.569**	**0.564**	**0.507**	ensemble-all	0.822▲	0.343	0.461▲
ensemble-freq	0.544	0.552	0.490	ensemble-freq	0.772	0.321	0.431
ensemble-dist	0.504	0.498	0.447	ensemble-dist	0.800	0.333	0.448
ensemble-rel	0.544	0.541	0.486	ensemble-rel	**0.825▲**	**0.346▲**	**0.465▲**
ensemble-freq.dist	0.470	0.475▼	0.431	ensemble-freq.dist	0.788	0.328	0.442
ensemble-top-4	0.409	0.315▼	0.321▼	ensemble-top-4	0.685▼	0.262▼	0.362▼
ensemble-top-6	0.439	0.349▼	0.351▼	ensemble-top-6	0.703▼	0.271▼	0.374▼
ensemble-top-8	0.548	0.535	0.484	ensemble-top-8	0.818▲	0.341	0.459
ensemble-top-10	0.555	0.549	0.494	ensemble-top-10	0.820▲	0.342	0.460▲

PMI yields the worst performance compared to all other methods. When we look at the actual relations returned by pmi-doc and pmi-sen, we find that it is prone to extracting rare co-occurrences of entities. As a consequence, errors in the preprocessing stage (e.g., named entity recognition errors) sometimes appear in the results. Distance-based methods also perform worse than the baseline. Relying on distance alone, two entities that only appear once within close distance can easily be favored over the ones that appear more often.

We take a closer look by comparing the top-10 results of pf-doc and imd-dep on query entity "BJ Habibie." In Table 3 correctly related entities are shown in bold face.

On this particular query, pf-doc clearly outperforms imd-dep. Almost all of the non-related entities retrieved by imd-dep in the table appear with the query entity in the same sentence as *enumerations* (e.g., listings of people attending a particular event). In a dependency parse tree, this type of co-occurrence will appear with dependency distance of 1, with *conjunction* as the dependency type. It is interesting to note that by using average distance instead of frequency, we successfully retrieve relations that do not occur often in the text. The two relations: "IPTN" (company founded by BJ Habibie), and "Watik Pratiknya" (a friend of BJ Habibie) are the kind of relations that are less frequently present in our corpus, since news articles are more likely to describe event-based stories instead of giving description of one's family or friends.

Table 3. Comparing `pf-doc` and `imd-dep`

pf-doc	imd-dep
Suharto	Taufik Kiemas
Soeharto	Wahid
Indonesian	Megawati Soekarnoputri
Indonesia	**IPTN**
Germany	Emil Salim
Abdurrahman Wahid	**Watik Pratiknya**
Wiranto	Sudi Silalahi
East Timor	Soehardjo
Jakarta	Xanana Gusmao
Susilo Bambang Yudhoyono	Sarwono Kusumaatmadja

As we have seen, replacing frequency by distance has its own advantages and disadvantages. We proceed to look at the performance of our proposed method `pf.imd`, which combines frequency and distance. This combination yields some improvement over the baseline at top-30 results, but the improvement is not significant.

With `rel-conf`, the relations that are detected by the machine learning method, but only found in one sentence, can outweigh relations that appear in many sentences. This explains why `rel-support` has a better performance, even outperforming both `pf-doc` and `pf-sen` for the top-30 results. The method `rel-support`, which can be viewed as a filtered version of `pf`, classifies text snippets before counting the frequency. This provides a more reliable way of counting the pair frequency. However, when we see the per-query results, the classifier does not always work, leading to a lower average performance compared to `pf-doc` and `pf-sen` (for the top-10 results).

Next, we contrast the results of a relation extraction method, `rel-support` with `pf-doc`, again for the query "BJ Habibie." The relations are listed in Table 4. For this query, the filtering effect of the relation extraction classifier manages to improve the results. The resulting ranking introduces three new entities (all related) and pushes out one non-related entity.

Table 4. Comparing `rel-support` with `pf-doc`

pf-doc	rel-support
Suharto	**Suharto**
Soeharto	Abdurrahman Wahid
Indonesian	**Indonesian**
Indonesia	**Megawati Soekarnoputri**
Germany	**Soeharto**
Abdurrahman Wahid	**Germany**
Wiranto	**Susilo Bambang Yudhoyono**
East Timor	**Boediono**
Jakarta	**ICMI**
Susilo Bambang Yudhoyono	**Golkar**

Ensemble Methods. To answer RQ2, we contrast the results of our ensemble methods against the non-ensemble ones. Table 2 shows that most ensemble methods give improvements over the baseline. Indeed, the overall best performance is achieved using ensemble methods. The improvements are statistically significant at top 30 related entities (`ensemble-all` and `ensemble-rel`, and `ensemble-top-10`). Simply using all of the methods in one ensemble can give a good performance. Ensembles of methods within the same family do not perform as well as combining method from various families. An exception to this is `ensemble-rel`, which only combines relation extraction methods scores.

Interestingly, the tree-based feature selection returns the following as top-6 features: `imd-lin`, `jaccard-sen`, `relation-conf`, `jaccard-sen`, `pmi-sen`, and `imd-dep`. Using these top-4 and top-6 features in an ensemble results in poor performance. As we observed above, three of these scoring methods are among the worst performing methods, thus combining them without adding (many) other scoring functions reinforces the weaknesses.

Score Differences between Entities. To answer RQ3, we average the performance of all methods on each query. As shown in Fig. 2, the performance varies. Some entities appear frequently in the dataset, therefore having more possible candidates and more possible types of context and relations. However, there does not seem to be a direct correlation with entity network extraction performance.

What went wrong with the worst performing queries? The person in query-24, "J Kristiadi," is a political observer. Most sentences mentioning him in the text are statements containing his observation about other entities, while only two describing actual relations to his affiliations. On this extreme case, most methods fail. For query-26, most of the snippets consist of mentions of the query with other entities in the form of enumerations. The snippets of query-29 also contain speech statements about other entities, along with invalid snippets created due to sentence splitting errors.

As shown in Fig. 2, query-11 has the highest average performance. The person in query-11, "Edy Harjoko," is a military commander. Most snippets in the text mention his rank or role in the organization (i.e., "TNI Chief of General Affairs Edy Harjoko"). There is almost no direct/indirect speech found in the snippets of this query. The snippets of query-23 also consist of a lot "head of" and "founder of" mentions. The next best performing query contains a lot of snippets in the form of appositions (e.g., "who founded . . . "). Overall, we can say that these queries have more reliable snippets.

Error Analysis. We further analyze the errors made by most methods. In particular, we look at the bottom-10 query entities for which the worst performance is observed. By inspecting the supporting text snippets, we discover several types of error, mostly caused by the type of sentence that are used to extract the co-occurrence.

One of the most common cases is sentences containing *indirect/direct speech*, in which one entity mentions other entities. The fact that one entity mentions another entity does not necessarily mean that they have a direct connection. The low performing queries tend to have more of this type of sentence than other queries, as we have shown with query-24.

Another common case of errors are *enumerations*. As we have described above, enumerations of entities do not necessarily mean that the entities enumerated are related.

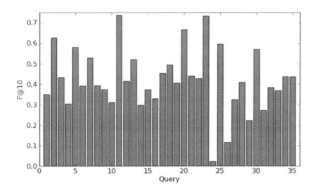

Fig. 2. Extraction performance per query (in F@10)

We observe that in our document collection most enumerations are ad-hoc, i.e., listing a number of entities that attend a certain event. When the text snippets returned for a query entity contain many enumerations, we tend to get a lower performance.

6   Conclusions

Today, more humanities content are archived and made available in digital libraries. We have presented the task of entity network extraction from text that can be applied to these types of contents. The task is studied in the context of a computational humanities application scenario. Our approach introduces an information retrieval pipeline that involves document search, entity extraction, and entity pairs scoring based on multiple scoring functions. We explore various methods for scoring extracted entity pairs, based on co-occurrences or relation extraction. In our experiments, we find that these methods display different behaviors. Combining them in a learning to rank ensemble successfully improves the performance.

As to future work, upon analyzing the results, we have discovered common errors related to certain sentence types that affect most methods' performance. Detecting in-direct/direct speech as well as enumerations, and automatically filtering them out, is an interesting next step to improve the effectiveness of our approaches.

Additionally, to help users of the extracted networks interpret and contextualize the results, we aim to explore the usefulness of automatically linking the newspaper archive from which the networks have been extracted to other archives, similar to [5].

Acknowledgments. This research was supported by the European Community's Seventh Framework Programme (FP7/2007-2013) under grant agreements nr 258191 (PROMISE Network of Excellence) and 288024 (LiMoSINe project), the Netherlands Organisation for Scientific Research (NWO) under project nrs 640.004.802, 727.011.-005, 612.001.116, HOR-11-10, the Center for Creation, Content and Technology (CCCT), the BILAND project funded by the CLARIN-nl program, the Dutch national program COMMIT, the ESF Research Network Program ELIAS, the Elite Network Shifts project funded by the Royal Dutch Academy of Sciences (KNAW), as well as the Netherlands eScience Center under project number 027.012.105.

References

[1] Agichtein, E., Gravano, L.: Snowball: extracting relations from large plain-text collections. In: DL 2000, pp. 85–94. ACM, New York (2000)

[2] Balog, K., Serdyukov, P., de Vries, A.P.: Overview of the TREC 2011 entity track. In: TREC 2011 Working Notes. NIST (2011)

[3] Balog, K., Fang, Y., de Rijke, M., Serdyukov, P., Si, L.: Expertise retrieval. Foundations and Trends in Information Retrieval 6(2-3), 127–256 (2012)

[4] Brin, S.: Extracting patterns and relations from the world wide web. In: Atzeni, P., Mendelzon, A.O., Mecca, G. (eds.) WebDB 1998. LNCS, vol. 1590, pp. 172–183. Springer, Heidelberg (1999)

[5] Bron, M., Huurnink, B., de Rijke, M.: Linking archives using document enrichment and term selection. In: Gradmann, S., Borri, F., Meghini, C., Schuldt, H. (eds.) TPDL 2011. LNCS, vol. 6966, pp. 360–371. Springer, Heidelberg (2011)

[6] Chaudhari, D.L., Damani, O.P., Laxman, S.: Lexical co-occurrence, statistical significance, and word association. In: EMNLP 2011, pp. 1058–1068. ACL, Stroudsburg (2011)

[7] Elson, D.K., Dames, N., McKeown, K.R.: Extracting social networks from literary fiction. In: ACL 2010, pp. 138–147. ACL, Stroudsburg (2010)

[8] Etzioni, O., et al.: Open information extraction from the web. Commun. ACM 51(12), 68–74 (2008)

[9] Farkas, G.: Essays on Elite Networks in Sweden: Power, social integration, and informal contacts among political elites. PhD thesis, Stockholm University (2012)

[10] Finkel, J.R., Grenager, T., Manning, C.: Incorporating non-local information into information extraction systems by gibbs sampling. In: ACL 2005, pp. 363–370. Association for Computational Linguistics, Stroudsburg (2005)

[11] Geurts, P., Ernst, D., Wehenkel, L.: Extremely randomized trees. Mach. Learn. 63(1), 3–42 (2006)

[12] Harman, D.K., Voorhees, E.M. (eds.): TREC: Experiment and Evaluation in Information Retrieval. MIT Press (2005)

[13] Joachims, T.: Training linear SVMs in linear time. In: KDD 2006, pp. 217–226. ACM, New York (2006)

[14] Kautz, H., Selman, B., Shah, M.: Referral web: Combining social networks and collaborative filtering. Commun. ACM 40(3), 63–65 (1997)

[15] Klein, D., Manning, C.D.: Accurate unlexicalized parsing. In: ACL 2003, pp. 423–430. ACL, Stroudsburg (2003)

[16] Lunenfeld, P., Burdick, A., Drucker, J., Presner, T., Schnapp, J.: Digital Humanities. MIT Press (2012)

[17] Merhav, Y., Mesquita, F., Barbosa, D., Yee, W.G., Frieder, O.: Extracting information networks from the blogosphere. ACM Trans. Web 6(3), 11:1–11:33 (2012)

[18] Milne, D., Witten, I.H.: An effective, low-cost measure of semantic relatedness obtained from wikipedia links. In: AAAI 2008 (2008)

[19] Mintz, M., Bills, S., Snow, R., Jurafsky, D.: Distant supervision for relation extraction without labeled data. In: ACL 2009, pp. 1003–1011. ACL, Stroudsburg (2009)

[20] Pedregosa, F., et al.: Scikit-learn: Machine learning in Python. Journal of Machine Learning Research 12, 2825–2830 (2011)

[21] Tang, J., Zhang, D., Yao, L.: Social network extraction of academic researchers. In: ICDM 2007, pp. 292–301. IEEE Computer Society, Washington, DC (2007)

[22] Washtell, J., Markert, K.: A comparison of windowless and window-based computational association measures as predictors of syntagmatic human associations. In: EMNLP 2009, pp. 628–637. ACL, Stroudsburg (2009)

Word Occurrence Based Extraction
of Work Contributors from Statements of Responsibility

Nuno Freire

The European Library, Europeana Foundation
Willem-Alexanderhof 5, 2509 LK The Hague, Netherlands
nfreire@gmail.com

Abstract. This paper addresses the identification of all contributors of an intellectual work, when they are recorded in bibliographic data but in unstructured form. National bibliographies are very reliable on representing the first author of a work, but frequently, secondary contributors are represented in the statements of responsibility that are transcribed by the cataloguer from the book into the bibliographic records. The identification of work contributors mentioned in statements of responsibility is a typical motivation for the application of information extraction techniques. This paper presents an approach developed for the specific application scenario of the ARROW rights infrastructure being deployed in several European countries to assist in the determination of the copyright status of works that may not be under public domain. Our approach performed reliably in most languages and bibliographic datasets of at least one million records, achieving precision and recall above 0.97 on five of the six evaluated datasets. We conclude that the approach can be reliably applied to other national bibliographies and languages.

Keywords: named entity recognition, information extraction, national bibliographies, library catalogues, copyright.

1   Introduction

National bibliographies comprehensively record every publication in a country, under the auspices of a national library or other governmental agency. Depending on the country, every publisher is required to send a copy of its published works to the legal deposit agency, or in other countries, a national organization actively collects all publications. Given that the publisher domain is very heterogeneous, and that in a country thousands of publishers may exist, national bibliographies are effectively the only point where every publication of an intellectual work can be traced. This fact has motivated the use of national bibliographies in processes of intellectual property rights clearance.

National bibliography catalogues are created to mainly fulfill the information requirements of library management and library users. The process of rights clearance brings new requirements for these bibliographic data sources. This paper addresses a specific requirement for the identification of all contributors of an intellectual work, when they are recorded in the data but in unstructured form, such as natural language text or simple textual expressions. National bibliographies are very reliable on

T. Aalberg et al. (Eds.): TPDL 2013, LNCS 8092, pp. 168–179, 2013.
© Springer-Verlag Berlin Heidelberg 2013

representing the first author of a work, but frequently, secondary contributors are not represented in structured form. They reside in the bibliographic records under the statements of responsibility. These statements usually contain information about authorship, editors, photographers, translators, and others involved in creating the work. In printed books, the statement of responsibility is typically present on the title page and, according to the Anglo-American Cataloguing Rules [1], the statement of responsibility is transcribed by the cataloguer exactly as it appears in the book.

The digitization activities being undertaken worldwide, particularly those addressing works that may not be in public domain, present a strong motivation for the identification of all contributors of a work, so that the publication status of the work may be determined. While in many cases, it is possible to automatically determine the publication status of a work, if all work contributors are not taken into account, the task of rights clearance is performed on incomplete information, which could lead to incorrect results, with potentially unfair to either libraries or rights holders.

The identification of work contributors mentioned in statements of responsibility is a typical motivation for the application of information extraction techniques. This paper presents an approach developed in the scope of the ARROW rights infrastructure[1]. ARROW stands for Accessible Registries of Rights Information and Orphan Works, and it consists in a network of organizations that are establishing a single framework to combine and provide access to rights information by creating a seamless service across a distributed network of national databases. This infrastructure provides access to information that will assist in determining the copyright status of works, and provides valuable tools for libraries and other organizations to identify and contact rights holders, in seeking rights clearance for the use of content.

This paper will proceed in Section 2 with a description of the challenges presented by statements of responsibility for performing the recognition of the names of work contributors. Section 3 summarizes the state of the art in entity recognition, and Section 4 follows with a description of our approach and details of its implementation. Section 5 presents the evaluation procedure and the obtained results. Section 6 concludes and discusses future work.

2   The Problem

Statements of responsibility present a scenario with particular characteristics for the application of information extraction. To make all contributor data available for automatic processing, this information needs to be represented in structured form, therefore it must be recognized from statements of responsibility through named entity recognition techniques.

The available named entity recognition techniques, when applied to statements of responsibility, are unable to reliably identify these entities. These techniques are dependent on the lexical evidence provided by grammatically well-formed sentences. In statements of responsibility, such lexical evidence is often not available, since the

---

[1] http://www.arrow-net.eu/

statements may consist in simple textual references to contributors and roles, often abbreviated. The following are some examples of statements of responsibility taken from bibliographic records from catalogues of national libraries:

- *"French Canadian freely arranged by Katherine K. Davis".*
- *"ed. by Peter Noever ; with a forew. by Frank O. Gehry; and contrib. by Coop Himmelblau."*
- *"W. Lange, A.C. Zeven and N.G. Hogenboom, editors"*
- *"by Pamela and Neal Priestland"*
- *"translated by Alexander Pope, with notes and introduction by the Rev. Theodore Alois Buckley ... and Flaxman's designs".*
- *"Ernst Theodor Amadeus Hoffmann. Mit Holzstichen von Andreas Brylka"*
- *"Vicente Aleixandre ; estudio previo, selección y notas de Leopoldo de Luis"*

In these examples we can observe the heterogeneity of the textual structure of statements of responsibility. For the purpose of our approach, the desired output result of the entity recognition process is the identification of the person names existing in the statements. In the examples above, the name "Katherine K. Davies" should be extracted from the first statement. In the second statement, three names should be extracted: "Peter Noever", "Frank O. Gehry" and "Coop Himmelblau".

This paper addresses this problem, and makes the following contributions:

- A novel technique for the recognition of person names in statements of responsibility. Although we studied a much focused problem, this technique has the application potential for other bibliographic data elements containing similar text.
- This work is in itself a case study of performing named entity recognition in the absence of lexical evidence.
- The results of this research also contribute with evidence for the application of statistical methods of word occurrence to support named entity recognition operations.

3   Related Work on Named Entity Recognition

The Named Entity Recognition task refers to locating atomic elements in text and classifying them into predefined categories such as the names of persons, organizations, locations, expressions of time, quantities, etc. [2]. Initial approaches were based on manually constructed finite state patterns and/or collections of entity names [2]. However, named entity recognition soon was considered as a typical scenario for the application of machine learned models, because of the potential availability of many types of evidence, which form the model's input variables [3]. Current solutions can reach an F-measure accuracy of around 0.90 in well-formed text, thus a near-human performance [2].

However, previous work suggested that current NER techniques underperform when applied to texts existing within bibliographic data [4, 5, 6, 7]. Most research on NER has focused mainly on natural language processing, involving text tokenization, part-of-speech classification, word sequence analysis, etc. Recognition with these techniques is therefore language specific and dependent of the lexical evidence given by grammatically well-formed text that, in bibliographic data, may not be available.

Although not addressing the same type of data as we do, we can find approaches used in other contexts that also perform NER in text containing little or no lexical evidence. In [8], an approach is described for performing information extraction on a particular kind of unstructured and ungrammatical text posted on the World Wide Web, such as item auction posts or online classifieds. The aim of this approach however is to extract a structured data record from each post, assuming that each post contains multiple attribute values of one entity. It is thus, not applicable to our scenario.

Other works, addressing NER in text without lexical evidence, focused on search engine queries [9, 10]. In such works, the problem is defined assuming the existence of one main entity per query, and a specific technique for such cases is adopted, based on query logs or user sessions and topic models. We find the topic model approach to be not generally applicable for NER in to the data we are studying, since it assumes the existence of only one main entity per data element value.

Our recent work on named entity recognition in digital library metadata [11] is closely related to the problem of this paper. However, due to the particular characteristics of the application scenario we address in this paper, which will be further explained in the Section 4, we did not find the machine learning based approach of [11] to be immediately applicable, although many of its conclusions about what kind of evidence may be used to recognize named entities are the basis of the design of the approach described in this paper.

4 The Approach

The design of our approach is greatly influenced by our application scenario. Since the approach was to be applied in national bibliographies of several European countries, it needed to be easily applicable on different languages. Another relevant issue influencing the design of this approach was its application in rights infrastructures. The output of an automatized rights clearance process, such as the one applied in ARROW, must be able to provide information explaining the final result. This supporting information is essential for safeguarding the interests of the rights holders and of libraries undertaking digitization projects, in case of future legal dispute. Therefore, for its application in rights clearance processes, the outcome of the contributor recognition operation should also be explainable, that is, the system must be able to provide a minimum justification why a name was recognized, and considered for the rights clearing process.

These two factors discouraged the design of an approach based on machine learning. The requirement to support several languages would make the solution too expensive, given the need to create training data sets for every language. In addition, while some machine learning algorithms can provide human understandable explanations of their results, such as decision trees, the state of the art sequence labelling algorithms applied in named entity recognition do not provide these kinds of explanations.

Our approach is designed to take advantage of structured data within national bibliographies, which allows for the analysis of the frequency of word occurrences in names of persons, and in other textual data. By basing the approach on word occurrence frequency, we bypass the need for building training sets, and are able to provide simpler explanations of the name recognition results.

To better illustrate our approach we will describe it in the process of its application to recognize the work contributors present in statements of responsibility within a complete national bibliography. However, as will be shown later, after the initial extraction of word occurrences, the approach can be applied to bibliographic records not present in the national bibliography.

These are the main steps of our approach:

1. An iteration is performed on all records in the national bibliography, and the titles and names of persons are collected from structured fields. For example, in MARC21 titles are collected from fields 245 (Title Statement), 240 (Uniform Title), etc. The names of persons are collected from fields 100 (Main Entry - Personal Name), 600 (Subject Added Entry - Personal Name) and 700 (Added Entry - Personal Name).

2. The field values are tokenized, and the occurrences of each word are counted, resulting in dictionaries containing all words found in the fields values and their respective occurrence count. Four of these dictionaries are built:

    a. Words in titles
    b. Words in person's surnames
    c. Words in other parts of person's names, than the surname
    d. Words that appear in lowercase in person names (such as "von" in German names, or "de" in Portuguese names, for example).

3. In order to devise an approach independent of the size of national bibliography, the word occurrences in the dictionaries are normalized as follows.

    a. For each dictionary, the mean word occurrence, and its standard deviation are calculated.
    b. The frequency of the words in the dictionaries are changed from absolute values to values which are relative to the arithmetic mean of the word frequencies in the dictionary. The relative value is expressed as the distance from the mean, using the standard deviation as unit, as follows. Let D denote a dictionary, let w denote a word in D, let n_w denote the absolute frequency of w, let $\bar{D}$ denote the arithmetic mean of D, and $\sigma(\bar{D})$ the standard deviation of $\bar{D}$. The relative frequency is define as follows:

$$RelativeFrequency(w, D) = \frac{(n_w - \bar{D})}{\sigma(\bar{D})} \tag{1}$$

4. After all dictionaries are built and normalized, the records in the national bibliography are processed for recognition of contributors in the statements of responsibility. For each record the following process is applied:

   a. The record is checked for the existence of a statement of responsibility. If the record does not contain the statement, no further processing is done on it.

   b. The text of the statement of responsibility is tokenized.

   c. The person names are extracted (a detailed description of this step is provided later in this section).

   d. The recognized names are compared against the names of the contributors present in the structured fields of the record. If no similar name exists in the record, the contributor is added to the record in a structured data field.

The tokenization, performed in steps 2 and 4.a of the process is performed at word level. No sentence tokenization is performed, since in many cases well-formed sentences are not present in statements of responsibility, thus the results of sentence tokenization could make harder the recognition of the names. Word tokenization is performed in a language independent way, according to the word breaking rules of UNICODE [12]. The decision to apply a language independent tokenization was based on our observations that punctuation was sometimes used with different meanings than in well-formed natural language text.

The recognition of the person names uses the results of the tokenization step and compares the sequence of tokens with the dictionaries built in steps 1 to 3. If sequences of tokens are located according to some defined patterns, a name is recognized. Fig. 1 presents these patterns in Augmented Backus–Naur Form [13], using value-ranges based on the dictionaries previously built, and comparing the number of word occurrences across the dictionaries.

For the definition of the value-ranges, let F denote the dictionary built from all first names found in the national bibliography, let S denote the dictionary built from all surnames found in the national bibliography, let L denote the dictionary built from all words that appear in lowercase in person names found in the national bibliography, let W denote the dictionary built from all word from titles within the national bibliography, and let α denote a configurable threshold for word frequency comparisons:

- *first-name:* the set formed by every word $w \in F$ that satisfies the following condition:

$$max\big(RelativeFrequency(w, F), RelativeFrequency(w, S)\big) > 0$$
$$\wedge$$
$$\frac{max\big(RelativeFrequency(w, F), RelativeFrequency(w, S)\big)}{RelativeFrequency(w, W)} < \alpha \quad (2)$$
$$\wedge$$
$$RelativeFrequency(w, W) < \alpha$$

- *non-ambiguous-word-first-name:* the set formed by every word $w \in F$ that satisfies the condition for the value set *first-name* and the following condition:

$$max\big(RelativeFrequency(w, F), RelativeFrequency(w, S)\big) > 3$$
$$\vee \qquad \qquad (3)$$
$$RelativeFrequency(w, W) < \alpha$$

- *surname:* the set formed by every word $w \in S$ that satisfy the condition in Equation 2.
- *non-ambiguous-surname:* the set formed by every word $w \in S$ that satisfies the condition in Equation 2 and Equation 3.
- *non-capitalized-name:* the set formed by every word $w \in L$ that satisfies the condition in Equation 2.
- *non-ambiguous-non-capitalized-name:* the set formed by every word $w \in L$ that satisfies the conditions in Equation 2 and Equation 3.
- *initial:* one single Latin letter followed by a period

In the equations above, the variable α allowed us to establish a threshold for relative word frequency comparisons between person names and titles in the name recognition process. The value for α was determined by experimentation on real data by measuring its impact on the recognition results in the evaluation dataset, which will be described in Section 5.1. For the actual recognition system used for ARROW, we apply the value $\alpha=29$.

```
person-name =
  (initial / non-ambiguous-first-name /
    non-ambiguous-surname / non-ambiguous-non-capitalized-name)
    *(initial / first-name / surname / non-capitalized-name) surname
  / non-ambiguous-surname
```

Fig. 1. Possible sequences used to locate person names

5   Evaluation

This section describes the experimental setup for the evaluation of our approach and the obtained results. It will follow with the description of the data sets used for evaluation, and then describe the evaluation procedure, and it finalizes with the obtained results.

5.1   Evaluation Data Sets and Procedure

The evaluation of our approach was performed in catalogues the national libraries that maintain the national bibliography of their corresponding country. The approach was evaluated in six European countries that are available in the ARROW rights infrastructure, or that are currently being implemented in ARROW. Six main languages were covered by these national bibliographies: English, German, Dutch, Greek, Italian and French.

While the complete catalogues were used to build the dictionaries of words that underlie our approach, the evaluation focused on the analysis of a sample of records in each national bibliography. The sample of records used for the evaluation where chosen randomly from records of the national bibliographies that contained statements of responsibility.

The statements of responsibility in the evaluation samples were manually annotated. References to persons, as contributors of the works, were located in the statements and tagged. The size of the catalogues, the number of records with statement of responsibility and the total number of referred persons in the statements are shown in Table 1. In total, 1329 statements of responsibility were used, and these contained 2104 references to persons.

Table 1. National library catalogues and evaluation samples

Catalogue	Total records	Main language	Evaluation sample	
			Statements of responsibility	Referred Persons
British Library	13.4 million	English	205	328
German National Library / Deutsche Nationalbibliothek	9.4 million	German	200	378
Koninklijke Bibliotheek / National Library of the Netherlands	3.2 million	Dutch	200	335
Εθνική βιβλιοθήκη της Ελλάδος / National Library of Greece	0.4 million	Greek	297	379
Istituto Centrale per il Catalogo Unico / Central Institute for the Union Catalogue of Italian Libraries	12.4 million	Italian	224	297
Bibliothèque royale de Belgique / Koninklijke Bibliotheek van België / Royal Library of Belgium	1 million	French and Dutch	203	387
		Total:	**1329**	**2104**

For the evaluation method we have chosen to evaluate using two methods: the *exact-match* and the *partial-match* methods, which have been used in several named entity recognition evaluation tasks [14, 15, 16]. In the *exact-match* method, a person name is only considered correctly recognized if it is exactly located as in the manual annotation. Recognition of only part of the name, or with words that are not part of the name, is not considered correct. In the *partial-match* method, a person name is only considered correctly recognized if it matches at least a portion of the manual annotation.

Using both evaluation methods is relevant in the context of ARROW, where the extracted information is used for different purposes, such as querying publisher and rights holder's databases, or for visual inspection by a person. Knowing how the recognition system performs under these two evaluation methods provides important support for making decisions in the design of the rights clearance workflows.

No baseline was defined for the evaluation of our approach since in previous work it has been shown that named entity recognition techniques designed for grammatically well-formed text underperform in these kinds of text [4, 5, 6, 7]. In addition, we could not find a comparative technique that would cover the full range of languages we evaluated our approach on.

5.2   Evaluation Results

In combination with the exact and partial matching methods, we used two metrics to measure the results of our approach: precision (the percentage of correctly identified named entities in all named entities found); and recall (the percentage of named entities found compared to all existing named entities).

Table 2 presents the measured results on each catalogue, and the overall result across all catalogues. Overall, the results were very good, and show that the technique can be used reliably in rights clearing processes, as well as for other applications. For the application of the approach in ARROW, we were particularly interested in the results of precision and recall of the partial-match metric, which were both above 0.95. However, the typical values were actually better on five of the six catalogues, with values above 0.97.

A much lower result was obtained in the catalogue of the national library of Greece. Although the evaluation methodology did not allow identifying the cause of the poorer results, this dataset has distinct characteristics from the other datasets. First, this catalogue was the smallest in number of records, with 0.4 million records, which could affect the comprehensiveness of the words included in the built dictionaries, and also have an impact in the statistical significance of the word usage statistics. Second, this catalogue uses the Greek alphabet while all others used the Latin alphabet.

Our further observation of the cases where the person names were not correctly recognized, pointed to three major types of error:

- Foreign person names negatively affected recall. They were often not recognized because they were not often found in other records of the catalogue.
- Names of persons used in names of organizations negatively affected precision. The system recognized those names as a person while they refer to organizations.
- Two persons with same surname mentioned together negatively affected recall. As for example, in the following statements:
  o "hrsg. von *Volker* und *Michael Kriegeskorte*"
  o "by *Pamela* and *Neal Priestland*"

Table 2. Evaluation results

Dataset	Exact match metric		Partial match metric	
	Precision	**Recall**	**Precision**	**Recall**
British Library	0.981	0.979	0.991	0.991
German National Library / Deutsche Nationalbibliothek	0.975	0.934	0.992	0.992
Koninklijke Bibliotheek / National Library of the Netherlands	0.973	0.875	0.977	0.979
Εθνική βιβλιοθήκη της Ελλάδος / National Library of Greece	0.656	0.414	0.758	0.868
Istituto Centrale per il Catalogo Unico / Central Institute for the Union Catalogue of Italian Libraries	0.97	0.896	0.971	0.973
Bibliothèque royale de Belgique / Koninklijke Bibliotheek van België / Royal Library of Belgium	0.981	0.959	0.981	0.982
Overall:	**0.948**	**0.837**	**0.958**	**0.963**

Future work should address these cases for further improvement of the results. The cases of foreign names may be addressed by introducing a dictionary built from a more comprehensive source of names of persons, such as the Virtual International Authority File (VIAF). The names of organizations are also to be addressed, not only for the difficulties they pose for the recognition of person names, but because they are also relevant to be recognized for rights infrastructures, therefore they should be addressed in depth in future work. The third kind of error, when two persons with same surname are mentioned together, may possibly be addressed by further elaborating the recognized patterns presented in Fig. 1 of Section 4.

6　Conclusions and Future Work

This paper presented an approach for the recognition of person names in statements of responsibility from bibliographic records of national bibliographies. The approach was designed for the specific application scenario of the ARROW rights infrastructure being deployed in several European countries to assist in the determination of the copyright status of works that may not be under public domain.

Good results were obtained from the evaluation of our approach. The approach performed reliably in most languages and bibliographic datasets of at least one million records, achieving precision and recall above 0.97 on five of the six evaluated datasets. Only the results obtained on the Greek national bibliography were not satisfactory. Although the evaluation methodology did not allow identifying the cause of these results, the dataset has distinct characteristics from the others: it has a smaller size, a different alphabet, and a different language. We consider that the approach can be reliably applied to other national bibliographies and languages, but an evaluation of the results should always be performed.

The evaluation of the approach also revealed typical cases for which the recognition of the names is not performed correctly, and that can be addressed in future work. This work may also be extended in functionality, by adding support to the recognition of organization names, and also to support the recognition of the role of the recognized contributors (illustrator, editor, etc.) which is also frequently mentioned in statements of responsibility.

Acknowledgments. We would also like to acknowledge the work of Marcela Strelcova, Chiara Latronico and Eva Kralt-Yap from The European Library in the annotation of the evaluation dataset. We would also like to acknowledge the work of the participants in ARROW Plus project, who contributed to all the work described in this paper. In particular, we would like to acknowledge the contributions of Associazione Italiana Editori, the University of Innsbruck for their support in the testing and validation of this work.

This work was carried out in the ARROW Plus project, a best practice network funded under the European Commission's Competitiveness and Innovation Framework Programme, grant agreement number 270942.

References

1. Joint Steering Committee for Revision of AACR: Anglo-American Cataloguing Rules, 2nd edn. (2005) ISBN: 978-1-85604-570-4
2. Nadeau, D., Sekine, S.: A survey of named entity recognition and classification. Linguisticae Investigationes 30 (2007)
3. McCallum, A., Freitag, D., Pereira, F.: Maximum entropy Markov models for information extraction and segmentation. In: International Conference on Machine Learning (2000)
4. Martins, B., Borbinha, J., Pedrosa, G., Gil, J., Freire, N.: Geographically-aware information retrieval for collections of digitized historical maps. In: 4th ACM Workshop on Geographical information Retrieval (2007)
5. Freire, N., Borbinha, J., Calado, P., Martins, B.: A Metadata Geoparsing System for Place Name Recognition and Resolution in Metadata Records. In: ACM/IEEE Joint Conference on Digital Libraries (2011)
6. Sporleder, C.: Natural Language Processing for Cultural Heritage Domains. Language and Linguistics Compass 4(9), 750–768 (2010)
7. King, P., Poulovassilis, A.: Enhancing database technology to better manage and exploit Partially Structured Data. Technical report, University of London (2000)
8. Michelson, M., Knoblock, C.: Creating Relational Data from Unstructured and Ungrammatical Data Sources. Journal of Articial Intelligence Research 31, 543–590 (2008)
9. Guo, J., Xu, G., Cheng, X., Li, H.: Named Entity Recognition in Query. In: 32nd Annual ACM SIGIR Conference (2009)
10. Du, J., Zhang, Z., Yan, J., Cui, Y., Chen, Z.: Using Search Session Context for Named Entity Recognition in Query. In: 33rd Annual ACM SIGIR Conference (2010)
11. Freire, N., Borbinha, J., Calado, P.: An approach for Named Entity Recognition in Poorly Structured Data. In: Simperl, E., Cimiano, P., Polleres, A., Corcho, O., Presutti, V. (eds.) ESWC 2012. LNCS, vol. 7295, pp. 718–732. Springer, Heidelberg (2012)

12. The Unicode Consortium, Unicode Text Segmentation (2010),
    http://www.unicode.org/reports/tr29/
13. Crocker, D., Overell, P.: Augmented BNF for Syntax Specifications: ABNF. RFC Editor (2008)
14. Sang, T.K., Erik, F.: Introduction to the CoNLL-2002 Shared Task: Language-Independent Named Entity Recognition. In: Proceedings Conference on Natural Language Learning (2002)
15. Sang, T.K., Erik, F., De Meulder, F.: Introduction to the CoNLL-2003 Shared Task: Language-Independent Named Entity Recognition. In: Proceedings Conference on Natural Language Learning (2003)
16. Grishman, R., Sundheim, B.: Message Understanding Conference - 6: A Brief History. In: Proceeding of the International Conference on Computational Linguistics (1996)

Evaluating the Deployment of a Collection of Images in the CULTURA Environment

Maristella Agosti[1], Marta Manfioletti[1], Nicola Orio[2], and Chiara Ponchia[2]

[1] Department of Information Engineering, University of Padua, Italy
{agosti,manfioletti}@dei.unipd.it
[2] Department of Cultural Heritage, University of Padua, Italy
nicola.orio@unipd.it, ponchiachiara1@studenti.unipd.it

Abstract. The paper reports on the effort of reconsidering the characteristics of the IPSA online collection of illuminated images created for specialised users, involving the redesigning of the interaction functions to make the online collection of interest for new and diverse user categories. The effort is part of the design and development of a new adaptive and dynamic environment that aims at increasing user engagement with cultural heritage collections and which is taking place in the context of the European CULTURA project[1].

Keywords: Cultural heritage systems, IPSA collection of illuminated images, CULTURA environment, archives, illuminated manuscripts, user engagement with cultural heritage collections.

1   Introduction

In our era the development of the internet and information technologies has assured access to a constantly increasing amount of knowledge for an unprecedented number of people. This easy access to information, the sources and reliability of which are uncertain, sets a new challenge for knowledge providers such as universities and libraries that have to reach the widest amount of end-users with high quality information. The main aim of these kinds of institutions should be not only to foster research and create new knowledge, but also to disseminate it to the benefit of the whole population. The accomplishment of this difficult task requires continuous interaction with end-users in order to draw a profile of the different user communities, to understand their interests, needs and expectations, and to make cultural contents more engaging and attractive for them.

In the context of the European project CULTURA[2], which aims to increase user engagement with cultural heritage collections through the development of a new adaptive and dynamic environment, we decided to open up IPSA[3], an online collection of illuminated images purposely created for specialised users, to new user categories

---

[1] http://cordis.europa.eu/projects/rcn/97304_en.html
[2] http://www.cultura-strep.eu/
[3] http://ipsa.dei.unipd.it/en_GB/

T. Aalberg et al. (Eds.): TPDL 2013, LNCS 8092, pp. 180–191, 2013.

such as students, users with an interest in art and the general public. This effort required our research team to face challenging issues concerning the characterisation of the new user categories involved and brought about meaningful thoughts and ideas that are helpful for similar challenging research projects.

2   Evaluations of the IPSA Digital Archive

IPSA (*Imaginum Patavinae Scientiae Archivum* - Archive of images to support the study of scientific research at Padua University) is a digital archive of illuminated manuscripts that includes both astrological codices and herbals produced mainly in the Veneto region, in Northern Italy, during the XIV and XV centuries. The online archive was created specifically for professional researchers in History of Illumination to allow them to compare the illuminated images held in the collection and verify the development of a new realistic way of painting closely associated with the new scientific studies that were flourishing at the University of Padua in the XIV century, particularly thanks to the teaching of Pietro d'Abano [1]. Disclosing new relationships between images is one of the main purposes of research in art history, because it brings further knowledge on a painter or an illuminator, on a work of art, or on a whole specific artistic period. According to this particular user requirement, in IPSA professional researchers are provided with tools that allow them to link and annotate images, so they are able to keep track of their considerations on the illuminations and their relations [2]. Selecting from a drop-down menu, professional researchers can choose between five different kinds of relation:

- **Copied in:** the subject of the oldest image is quite faithfully re-proposed in the newer image;
- **Same tradition of:** the two illuminations show subjects belonging to the same iconographic tradition; this kind of relation is valid both for images markedly distant from one another in time and for images close to one another in time;
- **Not related to:** the two illuminations show subjects belonging to different iconographic traditions;
- **Siblings:** the two illuminations were copied from the same model;
- **Similar to:** the two illuminations show some analogies, but it is not possible to further specify the kind of relation existing between them.

Furthermore, researchers can annotate the link, specifying the reason for their choice, or with other remarks on the two illuminations that they decide to link together. From this concise description, it can be easily understood that IPSA is a very specialist collection. This made the process of opening it up to new user categories with different interests and less knowledge on the topic even more challenging.

We decided to start our research with a series of interactions with undergraduate and postgraduate students in Humanities, not necessarily in History of Art. We involved undergraduate students in History and Preservation of Cultural Heritage, postgraduate students in Communication Strategies, in Management of Archival and

Bibliographic Heritage and in Modern Languages. We chose such a heterogeneous sample because we thought that users with a different cultural background would be more likely to focus their attention on details that may have not been considered by Computer Scientists or Art Historians.

We decided to start the evaluation campaign with students because we believed that they constitute the first step to approaching different kind of users, as they are half-way between professional users and the general public. Actually, the students involved were not acquainted with the IPSA collection or with History of Illumination in general, but they had a certain interest in the field of Humanities research, in the case of postgraduate students they had already developed a research methodology, and they generally had a reasonable knowledge of information technology tools.

The first interaction with students was carried out in November and December 2011. We developed a series of simple tasks to make students interact with the system for at least one hour. A task oriented experience was considered the best means of getting valuable feedback from users, because from previous evaluation campaigns with professional researchers it was noted that the lack of motivation in using the system may reduce the effort put into learning how to use it, and this inevitably reduces the quality of the interaction. When we decided to involve the student community, we knew we needed to design at least two tasks that would require the students to interact with the system in different ways [3]. To get further feedback, after each trial, students were asked to answer an evaluation questionnaire prepared specifically for the occasion by a team of psychologists from the University of Graz [4], which has a long experience in such evaluations and which is a partner of the CULTURA project involved in the evaluation process.

The evaluation was divided into two parts carried out within two weeks, so we were able to make some basic improvements to the system based on the advice provided by the students between the first and the second session. For example, we developed a more practical and faster way to present the illuminations to the users. Indeed, some of the manuscripts held in the collection have hundreds of illuminations that in the initial version of the interface IPSA required some time to be loaded. From the first trial of the evaluation it was evident that download time was evaluated as negative by non professional users, who tend to browse many items from the collection while scholars have a more focused approach to the collection and did not highlight any latency issue. Therefore, in the second trial the images were shown divided into smaller groups, and the loading was faster and more engaging for non-specialist users. The second session was preceded by a short explanation on the basic concepts of History of Illumination and the IPSA collection, its purposes and meaning. We noticed that a better comprehension of the collection, particularly of the goals of the IPSA project, gave more motivation to the students, who found the exploration of the collection more satisfactory.

In April 2012 we carried out further interaction sessions with students, presenting the modified and improved version of IPSA. As we had verified that dividing the evaluation within a short amount of time is a good way to create a fruitful interaction process with the users, we decided to divide the trial into two parts also on this occasion [5]. 77 people were involved: 53 master students and 24 undergraduate students.

The interaction brought about new changes that further improved IPSA acceptability and usability by non-professional users, such as a relevant change to the interface between the first and the second trial with the insertion of a drop-down menu at the bottom of the wall of images that allows an intuitive search through all the illuminations contained in the manuscript of interest. Another issue during the first trial was the creation of a link between two images. In the previous version of the system, the setting of a link was not intuitive enough to be used by non-professional users. The user had to start from the illumination of interest and do a search to find a second image of interest. Throughout the entire process, a box with the status of the operation was displayed at the top of the page. For professional researchers in History of Illumination and History of Art, who are used to working with images, it is easier to recall the initial illumination, and generally they already have a research path in mind, so they are able to find a second illumination of interest more quickly. For non-professional users, finding the second image may require different searches and a certain amount of time, so in the meanwhile they may not recall the image with which they started. Following the observations of the students involved in the evaluations, the operation status box was enlarged and, what is most useful, it now shows the thumbnails of the selected starting-image, some help text, and large explicative buttons for completing the link, or for deleting the operation. The new way of creating a link was presented in the second trial and received favourable feedback. Moreover, students felt that their opinion was effectively taken into account, and hence were more motivated to carry out the second part of the trial.

During the first two years of the CULTURA project, 107 students were involved in the evaluation campaign, a remarkable number of users that provided us with precious information on how the system is perceived by non-professional users. One of the most relevant things that emerged from questionnaires and further discussion with the participants in the evaluation trials is the need of non-professional users to be guided through such a specialist collection as IPSA. Particularly, lack of confidence towards the collection generates the desire for a more collaborative environment, in which users can share their opinions and reflections, and benefit from the help of expert users. This is why students would also like to be able to open their research from the collection to the Web, in order to easily gather more information to fulfil the purpose of their research. Another important outcome was the need for a simplified interface that allows quick and easy access to the resources of the database. Finally, we noticed that when students were given time to freely interact with the system, they showed particular attention to the Renaissance illuminations held in the collection. This happened probably because Renaissance is the best-known artistic period in Italy and the most studied in high school, so for the students involved in the evaluation Renaissance illuminations were easier to appreciate and to relate to their personal cultural background.

All the considerations made thanks to this interaction led to the IPSA deployment in the CULTURA environment, as described in the following paragraph.

3   IPSA Deployment in the CULTURA Environment

Between May and October 2012 a subset of metadata from the IPSA collection was selected to be imported in the CULTURA environment for use as a case study to test the new environment and its functions. This new environment was named IPSA@CULTURA to underline that IPSA content was being used with tools and services making up part of the CULTURA environment[4].

CULTURA provides a service-oriented architecture, where the user can interact with a number of functions that have been developed and are maintained by partners of the project [6]. The portal was developed using Drupal[5] by the research group of the Trinity College Dublin [7], which also developed the search functions, while our group provides two services. The first of these is an annotation service that allows users to add content to the illustrations and their metadata and share them with all users or a selected group of users. Annotations can also be used to create an explicit link between two illustrations, allowing the user an alternative way of expressing a relation between two illustrations, a feature which was also possible with the first implementation of IPSA. The second service our research group provides regards accessing the high-quality images of the manuscripts, which are automatically watermarked tracking the user ID that is replicated on the digital image background together with additional information about the collection and about the copyright owner.

Another important service is provided by Commetric, a company based in Sofia and specialised in social network visualisation. The visualisation tool allows users to explore the network of connections among metadata, for instance to find all the manuscripts that contain a given illustration or to explore the production in different geographical regions. This service, together with the possibility of annotating links between objects in the collection, is completely in line with the user requirements gathered during the first evaluation, because they also allow non-specialised users to navigate within the collection, either by following links annotated by other users, or by exploring the visual representation of the entity network.

Because evaluation plays a central role in the CULTURA approach, the user can also directly access an online survey developed by the University of Graz. This made it possible to match the qualitative impressions on IPSA@CULTURA with the user activity logs.

The first evaluation of IPSA@CULTURA was carried out in December 2012 with a group of 110 postgraduate students majoring in Linguistics and Communications Theories. As in the previous evaluation with students, they were asked to interact with the system for approximately one hour, accomplishing some easy tasks that made them use all the CULTURA tools: advanced search, annotations, bookmarks and two different kinds of visualisation.

Annotations (Fig. 1) can be private or public, or shared only with one group of people. This allows users not only to keep track of their thoughts on the illuminations, but also to share their thoughts if they want to compare them with those of other users, ask for advice or give suggestions. Shared annotations are a valuable tool for research groups, as people can work remotely and share their progress only with other members of their research group.

---

[4] http://kdeg.cs.tcd.ie/ipsa/
[5] http://drupal.org/

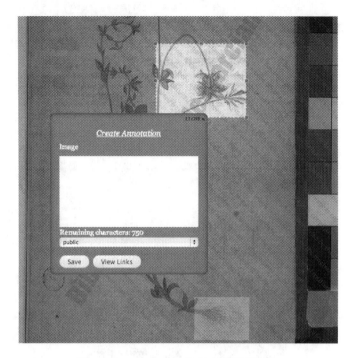

Fig. 1. Annotations in IPSA@CULTURA

Visualise IPSA Collection

absenço's and absinthium's and artemisia's and assenzio: medico ne illustra
le proprietà a un giovane's works

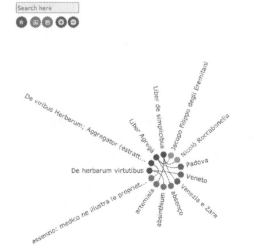

Fig. 2. "The wheel" in IPSA@CULTURA

Visualisations represent another useful tool, particularly for non-professional users, because they allow the connections between the manuscripts and the illuminations of the collection to be checked in a single glance. The visualisations (Figs. 2-3) also provide links to other online informative resources such as Wikipedia, Google, or Bing, thus addressing the need of non-professional users to get further information on the cultural context and content of the collection.

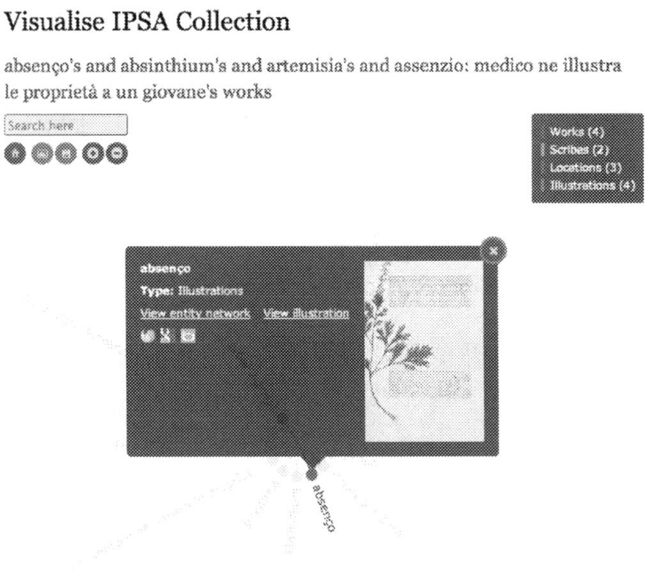

Fig. 3. By clicking on each dot of the visualisation, further information can be obtained through the entity network and links to other websites

Tasks were structured as follows: firstly, each student was assigned a plant name and had to search for an illumination containing that plant, and then annotate it with personal observations. Afterwards, they had to choose one of the two possible visualisations, and by doing so, they verified if the same plant is represented in other manuscripts. If this was the case, they had to select at least one more illumination, and to annotate or bookmark it.

As in the previous evaluation with students, the participants expressed the desire for an introductory explanation of the characteristics of the collection, and the need to be guided in the exploration of the database. As a result, they were particularly delighted with the annotations tool, since it constitutes a way to share one's impressions with other users and to ask for their opinion, and a means for professional researchers to register useful recommendations and indications for non-professional users. This generates a problem concerning the authority of the annotations, so many of the students observed the need to have users sign their annotations. In this regard the annotation tool also tracks the ID of the user who created an annotation, but during the evaluation exercise we had to create a number of test accounts which by their nature provided no information about the users.

The desire for a simple interface emerged as well, and since for some of them visualisations were not clear, they proposed the use of icons to indicate the different entities in the network, such as a book for text, a pen for author, and so on.

Finally, students proposed connecting the system to social networks, and this is not surprising at all, since social networks are hugely widespread, especially among young people.

After testing the CULTURA environment with other students, the following step was to verify whether this new system, which already takes into account the needs and desires of the student community, will turn out to be engaging and interesting for the general public as well, but without losing its effectiveness as a research tool for professional users. That is why we planned three additional evaluation exercises, the first of which involved interested users from the general public: this is described in Section 4. The second and the third evaluation exercises are scheduled for April and September 2013, and they will involve non-domain professional users and postgraduate students with different fields of expertise attending a European Master. The organisation of these evaluations is described in Section 5.

4   Interaction with Members from the General Public

For the first interaction session with people belonging to the general public, we chose to involve people with no specific knowledge in History of Art, but with an interest towards Cultural Heritage and historical monuments. With these criteria in mind, we contacted the *Salvalarte* association[6], which is a voluntary association of individuals who share a great interest in History of Art and Cultural Heritage in general. The goal of the association is to protect and preserve Italian historical monuments, and to foster better knowledge on Italian cultural heritage among the general public. There are many chapters of the association in different cities of Italy. The Paduan section was founded 15 years ago, and currently has approximately 80 volunteers. They work for free to allow visitors to access many Paduan monuments that otherwise would be closed to the public. They also organise courses and seminars on History of Art topics. Recently, some volunteers collaborated in a research project on the study and the preservation of the ancient archive documents regarding two important Paduan monuments, the *Ospedale di San Francesco* and the *Scuola Grande della Carità*.

For this evaluation, we decided not to have a task-oriented experience, because we wanted to recreate the realistic situation of a member of the general public who finds the webpage of CULTURA by chance, either while doing other research or just browsing the internet without any specific goal in mind. So we just showed IPSA@CULTURA and its tools to Salvalarte members, and then we asked them to explore the collection and try to use all the tools, and then tell us their impressions, especially what they liked more and what they would have changed.

Because many of Salvalarte members have a limited knowledge of English, one of the main requests was an Italian version of the interface of the web application. They also showed a lack of confidence with IT tools, so they need a simplified interface with clear explanations on how to use the system. In this regard, a tutorial of the most

---

[6] http://www.legambiente.it/contenuti/campagne/salvalarte (in Italian).

important CULTURA environment functionalities would probably be the best solution, as this would also address students' requirements.

Concerning content issues, Salvalarte members already had a basic knowledge of History of Art, but still they needed an introduction to the collection. Nonetheless, once they were taught to use the CULTURA environment tools and they were given all the preliminary information about the collection, they were able to browse it and to appreciate its content.

It must be noted that they seemed to particularly enjoy the manuscripts strictly related to the history of Padua, as all the interviewees were born in Padua or have been living in Padua for many years. This is similar to what happened with those students that were especially attracted by Renaissance illuminations: users that are not browsing the collection for academic research purposes are more interested in something they are already acquainted with, even if they do not have a deep knowledge of the topic. They are more gratified because they feel they already have a little competence about the collection, and are more motivated to look for new information to integrate their knowledge of it. This is why Salvalarte members appreciated the links to external websites: because they were often looking for more information resources on the illuminations they were observing. Through the links to external websites, they could easily and quickly obtain all the data they needed to further understand the collection, and to better place the manuscripts or the illuminations they liked in their correct historical and art-historical period.

5   Discussion

As previously reported, the two evaluation exercises of IPSA@CULTURA present a number of common outcomes that help us to understand how non-specialised users consider the IPSA digital archive, and to figure out possible solutions to make it more accessible to the general public.

First of all, both students and Salvalarte members showed greater interest towards the collection when they realised they could connect elements of the collection to their own experience: e.g. the history of their native city or their high school studies in History of Art. So it is very likely that an introduction to IPSA that highlights the collection connections with Paduan and Italian history can attract user attention. This holds good for every Humanities collection: end-users get more involved if they know the purposes of the original project and if they can relate some elements of the collection to their own personal experience and cultural background.

Another outcome concerns users' requests to provide more preliminary information on the digital content. Since it was developed for domain professional users, who are chiefly interested in images, IPSA provides only a basic set of descriptive metadata. This information, although relevant and congruent with library standards, was considered insufficient. Users asked for more involvement with the digital content by being provided with access to additional information, such as the research results produced by specialists.

These outcomes are completely in line with the trends in dissemination of cultural heritage. The application of 3D technology to interact with digital artefacts and navigate inside virtual spaces, the development of serious games for dissemination purposes, the increasing exploitation of portable and interactive devices – including users' portable devices – all suggest that the cultural content itself is not sufficient to raise interest among the general public.

To this end, we believe that an effective way to improve the involvement of members of the general public is to exploit the experience and the knowledge of professional users who are interacting with the same digital archive. Scholars have always played the role of "mediators" between artistic content and the public. Experts select the artefacts that are to be disseminated to the general public, study them in detail, and provide in-depth description of their artistic and historical relevance. Direct access to online collections may prevent the general public from taking advantage of the results of scientific research, thus without the benefit of mediated access. The request from students to have an introduction to the IPSA collection and to the research methods on illuminated manuscripts supports this point of view.

A possible solution, which we are developing further, is the use of pathways inside the collection that are created using all the available services. These pathways, which are in the form of narratives, can be thought as simple lectures where the users are invited to follow a number of guided tours inside the collection. At each step the system provides a concise description of the actual research goal, highlights the relevant aspects that might be hidden by the large amount of information accessed by the user at each step, and supports the exploration of the digital content through a number of predefined queries. Since narratives are added to the original system, users are still free to follow different directions, make new queries, use different tools or simply navigate the collection according to their particular interests. One of the goals of narratives is to highlight the richness of the available digital content, which may be difficult to retrieve for non-experts.

Fig. 4. Screen shot of the initial page of the lesson block of the narrative on the development of botanical illustrations in Italy

The creation of a particular narrative, which can be selected by the user at any moment during the interaction, needs to be designed and prepared by professional users. This was done in our initial experiments of creating some complete thematic paths across the IPSA@CULTURA collection, showing that the approach is feasible. Figure 4 shows the initial page of a lesson block on the development of botanical illustrations in Italian illuminated manuscripts.

The usage of narratives is expected to improve user involvement with the digital content, and its impact will be seen in a few months, because in upcoming months we will have more interaction sessions with different groups of users.

6   Future Work

To continue to collect useful feedbacks from the users, an additional evaluation will take place with users visiting the CoLab centre of the University of Parma, Italy. CoLab is a cross-department research centre for learning and digital publishing support [8]. It organises workshops on e-learning, digital publishing, digital humanities, and in general topics related to information technology applied to teaching and learning. To organise the interaction with CoLab we are currently working with one of the researchers in charge of the centre, who is also responsible for the International Master in Digital Library Learning (DILL) [9]. In fact the evaluation exercise will involve students attending the Master which is a two-year international master's programme that aims to provide elite information professionals with the skills and competencies to navigate the rapidly evolving world of digital libraries. It takes into account both the technical and the organisational issues involved in digital libraries, developing criteria and methods that exploit the strengths of digital libraries in a socio-economic and interdisciplinary manner. DILL is offered in cooperation with Oslo and Akershus University College of Applied Sciences (Norway), Tallinn University (Estonia), and the University of Parma (Italy)[7]. Students are therefore requested to spend at least one semester at each institution. The first semester starts with a summer school, and takes place in Oslo. The second semester students are in Tallinn. The third semester contains a second summer school, and takes place in Parma. In the third semester students are also required to do an international internship. In the final semester, students can choose in which country they would like to write their Master thesis. The evaluation excercise is going to take place in Parma during the third semester.

Involving students coming from different European countries and attending an International Master will surely enrich our user studies. Up to now we have involved Italian users, who, although with different cultural backgrounds, obviously share the same national identity. Especially the Salvalarte group is a local association, strongly linked to the city context. Thanks to the interaction with DILL students, we will move from a local perspective to a European perspective. Particularly, we will be able to verify what parts of the IPSA collection can be interesting for European users, and if the tools are user-friendly enough to help users to browse a collection which they are completely unfamiliar with and which they cannot relate to their personal experience, or to their city or national history.

---

[7] http://dill.hioa.no/

Acknowledgements. The work reported has been partially supported by the CULTURA project (reference: 269973) within the Seventh Framework Programme of the European Commission.

References

1. Mariani Canova, G.: Per Cultura: le immagini dei manoscritti della scienza a Padova dal Medioevo al Rinascimento. Atti e Memorie dell'Accademia Galileiana di Scienze, Lettere ed Arti. Vol. CXXIV , pp. 81–90 (2011-2012)
2. Agosti, M., Ferro, N., Orio, N.: Annotating illuminated manuscripts: an effective tool for research and education. In: Marlino, M., et al. (eds.) Proc. 5th ACM/IEEE-CS Joint Conference on Digital Libraries (JCDL 2005), pp. 121–130. ACM Press, New York (2005)
3. Ponchia, C.: Engaging the User: Elaboration and Execution of Trials with a Database of Illuminated Images. In: Agosti, M., Esposito, F., Ferilli, S., Ferro, N. (eds.) IRCDL 2012. CCIS, vol. 354, pp. 207–215. Springer, Heidelberg (2013)
4. Nussbaumer, A., Hillemann, E.-C., Steiner, C.M., Albert, D.: An Evaluation System for Digital Libraries. In: Zaphiris, P., Buchanan, G., Rasmussen, E., Loizides, F. (eds.) TPDL 2012. LNCS, vol. 7489, pp. 414–419. Springer, Heidelberg (2012)
5. Agosti, M., Manfioletti, M., Orio, N., Ponchia, C., Silvello, G.: The Evaluation Approach of IPSA@CULTURA. Presentation at the 9th Italian Research Conference on Digital Libraries (IRCDL 2013) (2013), http://www.dis.uniroma1.it/~ircdl13/?q=node/43
6. Hampson, C., Agosti, M., Orio, N., Bailey, E., Lawless, S., Conlan, O., Wade, V.: The CULTURA Project: Supporting Next Generation Interaction with Digital Cultural Heritage Collections. In: Ioannides, M., Fritsch, D., Leissner, J., Davies, R., Remondino, F., Caffo, R. (eds.) EuroMed 2012. LNCS, vol. 7616, pp. 668–675. Springer, Heidelberg (2012)
7. Hampson, C., Lawless, S., Bailey, E., Yogev, S., Zwerdling, N., Carmel, D., Conlan, O., O'Connor, A., Wade, V.: CULTURA: A Metadata-Rich Environment to Support the Enhanced Interrogation of Cultural Collections. In: Dodero, J.M., Palomo-Duarte, M., Karampiperis, P. (eds.) MTSR 2012. CCIS, vol. 343, pp. 227–238. Springer, Heidelberg (2012)
8. Tammaro, A.M., Valla, S., Longhi, E.: The Co-Laboratory: A tool for research and education at the University of Parma (2009),
   http://rse.academia.edu/TammaroAnnaMaria/Papers
9. Virkus, S., Tammaro, A.M.: Models of academic cooperation in European LIS Education (2005), http://rse.academia.edu/TammaroAnnaMaria/Papers

Formal Models for Digital Archives: NESTOR and the 5S

Nicola Ferro and Gianmaria Silvello

Department of Information Engineering, University of Padua, Italy
{ferro,silvello}@dei.unipd.it

Abstract. Archives are a valuable part of our cultural heritage but despite their importance, the models and technologies that have been developed over the past two decades in the Digital Library (DL) field have not been specifically tailored to them. This is especially true when it comes to formal and foundational frameworks, as the Streams, Structures, Spaces, Scenarios, Societies (5S) model is.

Therefore, we propose an innovative formal model, called NEsted SeTs for Object hieRarchies (NESTOR), for archives, explicitly built around the concepts of context and hierarchy which play a central role in the archival realm. We then use NESTOR to extend the 5S model offering the possibility of opening up the full wealth of DL methods to archives. We provide account for this by presenting two concrete applications.

1 Introduction

Nowadays, the scope of Digital Libraries (DLs) goes far beyond the realm of traditional libraries and also encompasses other kinds of cultural heritage institutions, such as archives and museums. Nevertheless, these institutions are quite different from several points-of-view: they have different internal organizations and traditions; their resources are different in nature, structure, and descriptions; and their users have different information needs which call for different access methods to resources [18].

Archives are not simply constituted by a series of objects that have been accumulated and filed with the passing of time but they represent the trace of the activities of a physical or juridical person in the course of their business which is preserved because of their continued value over time [2].

To this end, archives keep the *context* in which their records have been created and the network of relationships between them in order to preserve their informative content and provide understandable and useful information over time [8]. The fundamental characteristic of archives resides in their *hierarchical organization*. This expresses the *context* – i.e. the relationships and dependencies between the records of the archive – by using what is called the *archival bond* [4] and it distinguishes archives from other objects in the realm of cultural heritage – e.g. books – which in general are perceived as individual, repeatable and unrelated entities. Archives are in fact made up of series which, in turn, can be organized in sub-series formed of archival units, such as files, registers and so on [17].

T. Aalberg et al. (Eds.): TPDL 2013, LNCS 8092, pp. 192–203, 2013.

In this article we highlight the central role of formal models for the DL, because integration and cooperation between these models can turn into a real case of interoperability between the different facets of DL, including their community, methodology and technology. In this context a model for archives is sorely needed to formally define their characteristics and to prove that general DL methods and technologies can be embodied in this field and respect archival practice.

Therefore, we propose an innovative formal model for archives built around the notion of *archival bond* and *hierarchy*. The proposed model, called NEsted SeTs for Object hieRarchies (NESTOR), is based on the idea of expressing the hierarchical relationships between objects through the inclusion property between sets, in place of the binary relation between nodes exploited by the tree.

The set data models composing NESTOR are well-suited for archival practice; indeed, the idea of "set" shapes the concept of archival division which is a "container" comprising distinct elements that have some properties in common. An archive from the physical point-of-view resembles a Chinese boxes structure as there are boxes, folders, sheets, etc. contained one inside the other. Nested sets are closer to this view of reality than trees are. Indeed, although archival practice commonly considers archives as trees, a tree is actually a higher level abstraction than the nested sets as it only focuses on structural relationships; conversely, NESTOR comprises both the structure and the content of the archive.

DLs benefit from the existence of sophisticated formal models, such as the Streams, Structures, Spaces, Scenarios, Societies (5S) model [7,9], which allow us to formally describe them and to prove their properties and features. Despite the importance of archives, so far there has been no attempt to develop a dedicated formal model, built around their peculiar constituents. Nor can we exploit the 5S model as it is for archives because, as we will discuss later on, it needs some kind of extension and tailoring.

To this end, we exploit NESTOR to formally extend the 5S model to define a *digital archive* as a specific case of digital library. This defines an actual bridge between these two formal models which: (i) allows archives to exist and interact with other realities (i.e. libraries and museums); (ii) provides archives the possibility of exploiting the full wealth of DL technologies and methods; and, (iii) enables integrated access to heterogeneous contents.

As concrete accounts of this, we briefly describe how these formal models can be applied to overcome well-known issues in the archival field. We present two applications, the former regards the interoperability between digital archives and we formally exploit the Open Archives Initiative Protocol for Metadata Harvesting (OAI-PMH)[1] to give a concrete account of how DL technologies can be adopted with archives. The latter one shows how the archives modeled with NESTOR can form compound digital objects made available as Linked Open Data (LOD) [10] on the Web adopting the Open Archives Initiative Object Reuse and Exchange (OAI-ORE)[2] as a working framework.

---

[1] http://www.openarchives.org/pmh/

[2] http://www.openarchives.org/ore/

The paper is organized as follow: Section 2 provides some background on digital archives. Section 3 describes the NESTOR Model and the 5S Model. Section 4 shows how the 5S model can be extended via NESTOR. Section 5 describes how the extended 5S addresses concrete issues in the DL realm. Finally, 6 draws some final remarks.

2   Digital Archives: Background

Archival descriptions have to reflect the peculiarities of the archive, retain all the evidential value of a record, and keep trace of the provenance and original order in which resources have been collected and filed by archival institutions [2,8]. They have to be organized in a hierarchical way to express the relationships and dependency links between the records of the archive in order to retain the archival bond [4]. Therefore, archival descriptions produced according to the International Standard for Archival Description (General) (ISAD(G)) [11] take the form of a tree. The principles of ISAD(G) are put into action by the Encoded Archival Description (EAD) standard [19] for encoding archival descriptions.

EAD reflects the archival structure and holds relationships between entities in an archive. In addition, EAD encourages archivists to use collective and multilevel description, and because of its flexible structure and broad applicability, it has been embraced by many repositories. On the other hand, EAD allows for several degrees of freedom in tagging practice, which may turn out to be problematic in the automatic processing of EAD files, since it is difficult to know in advance how an institution will use the hierarchical elements.

EAD represents an archive as a monolith and every description is embedded in the archival structure. This means that *content and structure are interlinked in the same XML file* and they cannot be handled separately. A direct consequence is that in a distributed environment where it is necessary to exchange data between repositories we are forced to exchange the archive as a whole. Indeed, we cannot share a specific piece of information – e.g. the descriptions of the documents belonging to a specific "series" – without extracting it from the EAD file and losing in this way the structural information retained thanks to the nested tags in the EAD itself [21]. This leads to difficulties in fully exploiting the OAI-PMH within the archives [16].

Furthermore, EAD presents some difficulties both for the expert user (i.e. the archivists who find the "complexity of EAD itself to be a deterrent to implementation" [21]) and the general user who has to consult and interpret the archival data without specific knowledge of archival theory and practice. The main difficulty is related to the reconstruction of the archival context starting from an element buried in the hierarchy; this difficulty related to the data model on which EAD is based may be reflected in a similar difficulty and disorientation for the user in the perception of the context which supply the information needed to satisfy the her/his information requirements.

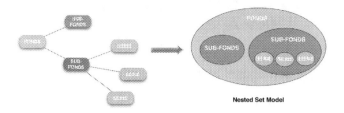

Fig. 1. An archive modeled by means of the NS-M

Lastly, when we need to relate one or more digital objects to their archival descriptions represented as metadata, EAD introduces some more limitations. Indeed, EAD allows for the linkage of only one digital object with an archival description (i.e. through the `<dao>` tag); if we need to link a bunch of digital objects with a description, we need to use the so-called digital wrappers which complicate the structure of EAD and limit its share-ability, interoperability [15] and the possibility of expose archives as LOD on the Web [5].

3 Formal Models for Digital Libraries and Archives

3.1 Overview of the NESTOR Model

NESTOR [6] is defined by two set data models – i.e. the Nested Sets Model (NS-M) and the Inverse Nested Sets Model (INS-M) – which are independent but complementary one to the other. For space reasons, in this context we present only the NS-M and its applications. INS-M provides different modeling features w.r.t. the NS-M, but its use as well as its integration with the 5S model can be derived by following the methodologies we present for the NS-M.

To illustrate the basic ideas behind NESTOR, let us consider an archive composed of six divisions: a fonds, two sub-fonds, and three series. As shown in Figure 1, the NS-M adopts a bottom-up approach: (i) each set corresponds to an archival division; (ii) the innermost sets are the leaves of the hierarchy, e.g. the series; (iii) you create supersets as you climb up the hierarchy, e.g. the sub-fonds and fonds. We can see that the NS-M is well-suited for bottom-up descriptive activities where the archivist does not know in advance the archive s/he is going to describe. In this case, s/he starts to study the documents and decides how to put them together in order to form an archival division, thus the archival hierarchy is built from the bottom. We call it bottom-up approach because in this case dividing the documents into archival divisions is an iterative process: the archivist starts from the whole set of documents (i.e. the fonds) and s/he defines the subsets (i.e. subfonds, series, etc.) by construction, analysing the documents one by one.

Formally, we define the NS-M as a collection of subsets where specific conditions must hold.

Definition 1. *Let A be a set and let C be a collection of subsets of A. Then C is a **Nested Sets Collection** (NS-C) if:*

$$A \in \mathcal{C}, \tag{3.1}$$

$$\forall H, K \in \mathcal{C} \mid H \cap K \neq \emptyset \Rightarrow H \subseteq K \vee K \subseteq H. \tag{3.2}$$

Therefore, we define a NS-C as a collection of subsets where two conditions must hold. The first condition (3.1) states that set A which contains all the subsets of the collection must belong to the NS-C itself. The second condition states the intersection of every couple of sets in the NS-C is not the empty-set only if one set is a proper subset of the other one. This definition formally defines how an archive can be modeled by means of the NS-M as shown in Figure 1. The collection of subsets $\mathcal{C}$ is the considered archive; the first condition says that there is a set – i.e. the "fonds" – which contains all the subsets – i.e. "subfonds", "series", etc. – of the archive. The second condition says that two subsets such as two "series" cannot have common elements, thus their intersection is always empty.

3.2 Overview of the 5S Model

The Streams, Structures, Spaces, Scenarios, Societies (5S) [7,9] is a formal model and draws upon the broad DL literature in order to have a comprehensive base of support. It was developed largely bottom up, starting with key definitions and with elucidation of the DL concepts from a minimalist approach. It is built around five main concepts: (i) *streams* are sequences of elements of an arbitrary type, e.g. bits, character, images, and so on; (ii) *structures* specify the way in which parts of a whole are arranged or organized, e.g. hypertexts, taxonomies, and so on; (iii) *spaces* are sets of objects together with operations on those objects that obey certain constraints, e.g. vector spaces, probabilistic spaces, and so on; (iv) *scenarios* are sequences of related transition events, for instance, a story that describes possible ways to use a system to accomplish some functions that user desires; and, (v) *societies* are sets of entities and relationships between them, e.g. humans, hardware and software components, and so on.

Starting from these five main concepts, it provides a definition for a minimal DL which is constituted by: (i) a repository of digital objects; (ii) a set of metadata catalogs containing metadata specifications for those digital objects; (iii) a set of services containing at least services for indexing, searching, and browsing; and, (iv) a society.

While these broad concepts can be also in common with archives, when you look at the specific way in which they are formally defined, you realize that the definitions cannot be straightforwardly applied to the archives case without at least some extension as we discuss in the next section.

4   Extending the 5S Model via NESTOR

The 5S model needs some kind of extension to be tailored to the specific case of archives. The notion of *descriptive metadata specification*[3] (definition 12 [9, p. 292]) is suitable either for representing, for each archival division, a descriptive metadata – e.g. a metadata describing a series, a sub-fonds, or an archival unit – or for representing the archive as a whole, as it happens in the case of EAD.

When it comes to the definition of *metadata catalog* (definition 18 [9, p. 295]), there is no means to impose a structure over the descriptive metadata in the catalog. Therefore, if you use separate *descriptive metadata specifications* for each archival division, as in the former case, this would prevent the possibility of expressing the relationships between these archival divisions, i.e. you would lose the possibility of retaining the archival bond. This means that an archive cannot be properly modeled throughout the 5S model without losing one of its main properties.

Moreover, in a *metadata catalog*, there is no means to associate (sub–)parts of the *descriptive metadata specifications* to the *digital objects* (definition 16 [9, p. 294]) that they describe, but you can only associate a whole descriptive metadata to a whole digital object.

Therefore, if you represent an archive as a whole with a single *descriptive metadata specification*, as in the latter case, it would not be possible to associate (sub-)parts of that descriptive metadata to the different digital objects corresponding to the various archival divisions; this does not allow the definition of compound digital objects and it is a barrier towards the adoption of the LOD paradigm in the archival context as discussed in Section 5.2. Furthermore, this strongly limits the interoperability between digital archives and the possibility of sharing archival metadata with variable granularity.

Our extension to the 5S model is thus organized as follows:

- using the notion of *structure* (definition 2 [9, p. 288]), we introduce the notion of **NESTOR structure**, as a structure that complies with the constraints of NS-M;
- using the notion of *metadata catalog*, we introduce the notion of **NESTOR metadata catalog**, as a metadata catalog that exploits a NESTOR structure to retain the archival bonds;
- using the notion of *digital library* (definition 24 [9, p. 299]), we introduce the notion of **digital archive**, as a digital library where at least one of the *metadata catalogs* is a NESTOR metadata catalog.

Definition 2. *Let $\mathcal{C}$ be a Nested Set Collection (NS-C) on a set A. A **NESTOR structure**(A) is a structure $(NS\text{-}G, L, \mathcal{F})$, where L is a set of label values, $\mathcal{F}$ is a labeling function, and $NS\text{-}G = (V, E)$ is a directed graph where $\forall v_j \in V, \exists! \, J \in \mathcal{C} \wedge \forall e_{j,k} \in E, \exists! \, J, K \in \mathcal{C} \mid K \subseteq J$.*

---

[3] In this section, we use italics to highlight definitions taken from the 5S model.

Definition 2 applies to the definition of NS-M (i.e. Definition 1) ensuring that the resulting structure complies with the NS-M[4]. Note that the set of label values L and the labeling function $\mathcal{F}$ are not strictly needed for the NS-M, but they can be useful in the context of the 5S and this feature, in turn, may extend the NS-M with semantic possibilities.

The definition of *metadata catalog* in the 5S model can be expressed as follows. Let H be a set of handles to *digital objects* and M a set of *descriptive metadata specifications*, then a *metadata catalog* is a function $DM : H \times 2^M$.

Definition 3. *Let H be a set of handles to digital objects and M a set of descriptive metadata specifications, a metadata catalog DM is a* **NESTOR metadata catalog** *if:*

$$\forall h_i \in H \mid \exists M_i \in 2^M \ \wedge \ DM(h_i) = M_i \Rightarrow |M_i| = 1 \qquad (4.1)$$

$$\exists \ \text{NESTOR structure}(M) \qquad (4.2)$$

Condition 4.1 imposes that, if exists, there is only one *descriptive metadata specification* for a given *digital object* because, in archival practice, every single metadata describes a unique archival division, being it a level in the archive or a digital object [11]. Condition 4.2 ensures that the relationships between the different archival divisions are compliant with the *descriptive metadata specifications* in M.

Definition 4. *A* **digital archive** *$(\mathcal{R}, DM, \text{Serv}, \text{Soc})$ is a digital library where*

- $\mathcal{R}$ *is a repository;*
- *at least one of the metadata catalogs in the set of metadata catalogs DM is a NESTOR metadata catalog;*
- *Serv is a set of services containing at least services for indexing, searching, and browsing;*
- *Soc is a society.*

Definition 4 extends the definition of *digital library* in the 5S model requiring that at least one of the *metadata catalogs* is a NESTOR one, i.e. there exists at least one *metadata catalog* capable of retaining the archival bonds. This definition has several consequences. Firstly, more than one NESTOR metadata catalogs can be present in the same digital archive, thus making it possible to express different archival descriptions over the same set of *digital objects*. This extends the current practice in which a system for managing an archive is usually capable of managing only one description of the archive, thus giving only one point-of-view on the material held [3,12]. Secondly, you can mix NESTOR and not-NESTOR metadata catalogs which allows for the seamless integration of different visions of the managed *digital objects* within the same digital archive. This opens up the possibility of exploiting the whole breadth of methodologies and tools available in the DL field with the archives.

---

[4] This definition can be extended to enclose also the INS-M if needed.

5 Applications of the 5S Model Extended via NESTOR

The extension of the 5S model via NESTOR represents an actual bridge between these two formal models which allows the archives to live and cooperate with other methodologies initially not built for archives. A first application shows how OAI-PMH can now be employed by the archives without changing its internal functioning and broadening its functionalities. A second example shows how this theoretical framework can be employed for exposing archives through the LOD paradigm realized by means of OAI-ORE.

5.1 Employ OAI-PMH within Digital Archives

OAI-PMH is the *de-facto* standard for metadata exchange in DLs [1,14] and it has also been modeled by means of the 5S model allowing for "the specification and automatic generation of DL applications" [9]. In the 5S model, Data and Service providers are represented as (electronic) *Societies*; the communications between these providers are *Streams*; the sets, metadata, and schemas are *Structures*; and, each request-response pair (e.g. harvesting the records belonging to specific sets) is associated with a *Scenario* [9, p. 283].

The 5S model formally specifies OAI-PMH by defining its components and services allowing us to know in advance how the harvesting service works in the library context. NESTOR does not provide a formalization of OAI-PMH, thus there is no formal way of defining the harvesting procedure for digital archives. A formal definition of OAI-PMH in the archival context is needed to know if archival properties and constraints are respected when the data are shared via harvesting in distributed environments.

As we have previously seen, OAI-PMH cannot be properly employed with digital archives modeled and realized with EAD files; to this end, we exploit the extended 5S to propose a general solution for modeling the archives, thus overcoming the limitations of EAD and enabling a full exploitation of OAI-PMH. To do this we exploit the set organization of OAI-PMH; indeed, OAI-PMH can organize records into OAI-sets, each one identified by a `setSpec` which is unique handle for a set within the repository. OAI-set organization may be hierarchical expressed thanks to the `setSpec` field using a colon [:] separated list indicating the path from the root of the set hierarchy to the respective node. This feature is used to map an archive modeled by the NS-M into an OAI-PMH set organization respecting all the archival constraints; for a detailed description of the mapping procedure refer to [6].

As an example, let us consider the archive represented by the NS-C in Figure 1. As we can see in Figure 2, each set composing this nested set structure is mapped into an OAI-Set with a proper `setSpec`; the set called "fonds" is mapped into an OAI-set with $<$ setspec $>$ 0001 $<$ /setspec $>$. This set has two subsets that are mapped into two OAI-sets: $<$ setspec $>$ 0001 : 0002 $<$ /setspec $>$ and $<$ setspec $>$ 0001 : 0003 $<$ /setspec $>$ and so on for the other sets.

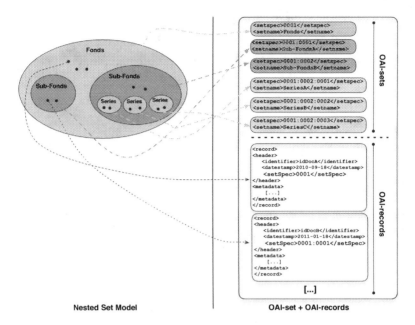

Fig. 2. An archive represented as a NS-C mapped into OAI-PMH

We can see that the hierarchical relationships and thus the inclusion order between the sets is maintained by the OAI-sets and each single archival description is mapped into a metadata belonging to an OAI-set. With this model we can exchange metadata and sets with variable granularity being able to reconstruct their original context. The extended 5S model allows us to formally employ OAI-PMH within the archives where the 5S is used to model the protocol and its features and NESTOR is used to model the archives within the protocol which allows us to respect the archival practice also when there is the necessity of sharing data in a distributed environment.

5.2   Expose Archives as LOD on the Web

Currently, archival practice is moving towards the definition of complex relationships between the resources of interest as well as the constitution of compound digital objects. To this end archives can take advantage of using the LOD paradigm which eases the access to the resources, enhances the interoperability by moving the focus from the systems managing the data to the data themselves, and provides additional and flexible representations of archival resources. In the context of the DL, the LOD paradigm can be instantiated by means of Open Archives Initiative Object Reuse and Exchange (OAI-ORE) which has a precise focus in the representation and management of compound digital objects.

In order to exploit OAI-ORE within the archives there is the need to model the archival structure – which is the mean to retain all the archival characteristics such as the archival bond – into OAI-ORE. The 5S models OAI-ORE as

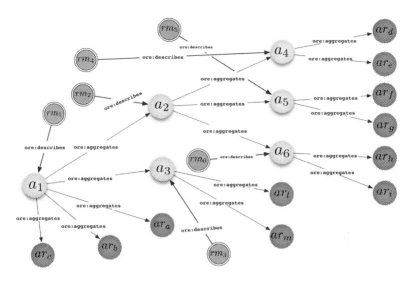

Fig. 3. The archive shown in Figure 1 mapped into an OAI-ORE instance

a *Structure* [13]; this very model extended via NESTOR allows us to impose conditions on the 5S *Structure* – i.e. by defining it as a *NESTOR Structure* (Definition 2) – thus creating OAI-ORE instances accordingly to the archival practice.

To model an archive throughout OAI-ORE we have to consider the features of this framework (refer to [20] for a detailed description) which are: Aggregations (i.e. A) composed of Aggregated Resources (i.e. AR), Resource Maps (i.e. RM) which are materializations of the Aggregations, and Proxies (i.e. P) which allows the definition of relationships between Aggregated Resources. Another important feature is the possibility of defining *Nested Aggregations* which enables the definition of Aggregations of Aggregations. Thanks to this feature, an order (i.e. $\prec_a$) exists between Aggregations: for all $a_i, a_j \in A$ we say that $a_i \prec_a a_j$ if and only if the Aggregation a_i is aggregated by a_j.

We can represent an archive by means of OAI-ORE by modeling it as a NS-C and then defining a mapping between this NS-C and an OAI-ORE instance exploiting the conditions defined by the *NESTOR structure*. So, starting from a the NS-M representation of an archive, the intuitive mapping idea is that every set $H \in \mathcal{C}$ becomes an Aggregation $a_h \in A$ and consequently, every resource $r_t \in R$ belonging to H becomes an aggregated resource $ar_t \in AR$ aggregated by a_h as shown in Figure 3 where the archive of Figure 1 is mapped into an OAI-ORE instance. Furthermore, for every pair of sets $\{H, K\} \in \mathcal{C}$ such that $H \subseteq K$, it is possible to create a pair of aggregations $\{a_h, a_k\} \in A$ such that $a_h \prec_a a_k$ where $\prec_a$ is the order relation defined above[5].

Every set in the NS-C is mapped into an Aggregation in the OAI-ORE model materialized by a Resource Map which in the 5S model is a modeled as a

---

[5] Further details about the formal mapping can be found in [5].

Structure and in the extended 5S model is modeled as a *NESTOR Structure*. The inclusion order between the sets is maintained by the relation defined between the Nested Aggregations of OAI-ORE. Every resource belonging to a given set H in the NS-C is mapped into Aggregated Resources belonging to the Aggregation mapped from H. Note that OAI-ORE proxies allows us to handle complex relationships between metadata and digital objects in an aggregation. Therefore, we can map a NS-C into a correspondent OAI-ORE instance ruled by the definition of NESTOR Structure in the extended 5S model.

This procedure makes it possible to model and describe the archives from scratch by means of OAI-ORE while allowing archivists to easily express relationships between archival metadata and digital objects. Archival principles are preserved and still have primary importance for understanding archival resources; at the same time, OAI-ORE offers the possibility of defining new relationships between the resources enabling the definition of new services over the archives. Furthermore, this methodology provides a means to define archival compound objects that can be shared with the systems which already employ OAI-ORE and that can be exposed as LOD on the Web.

6   Final Remarks

The 5S model has been built around the most general concepts but without specifically dealing with the peculiar features of the archives. This hampers the possibility of fully exploiting and applying them for defining a theory for digital archives, intended as digital libraries with specific characteristics that fit in the archival domain.

The archival domain deserves a formal theory as well and this theory has to be reconciled with the more general theories for DL in order to disclose to archives the full breadth of methodologies which have been developed in the DL field.

To this end, we have introduced a formal model, called NESTOR and we extended the 5S model through it in order to introduce the notion of digital archive as a specific case of digital library complying with archival constraints. Finally, we applied this extension to two concrete cases showing how we can overcome current issues with state-of-the-art digital archive solutions.

References

1. Bell, J., Lewis, S.: Using OAI-PMH and METS for exporting metadata and digital objects between repositories. Program: Electronic Library and Information Systems 40(3), 268–276 (2006)
2. Cook, T.: Archival Science and Postmodernism: New Formulations For Old Concepts. Archival Science 1(1), 3–24 (2001)
3. Discovery, E., Shaw, S., Reynolds, P.: Creating the Next Generation of Archival Finding Aids. D-Lib Magazine 13(5/6) (May/June 2007)
4. Duranti, L.: The Archival Bond. Archives and Museum Informatics 11(3–4), 213–218 (1997)

5. Ferro, N., Silvello, G.: Modeling Archives by means of OAI-ORE. In: Agosti, M., Esposito, F., Ferilli, S., Ferro, N. (eds.) IRCDL 2012. CCIS, vol. 354, pp. 216–227. Springer, Heidelberg (2013)
6. Ferro, N., Silvello, G.: NESTOR: A Formal Model for Digital Archives. Information Processing & Management (in print, 2013), http://dx.doi.org/10.1016/j.ipm.2013.05.001
7. Fox, E.A., Gonçalves, M.A., Shen, R.: Theoretical Foundations for Digital Libraries: The 5S (Societies, Scenarios, Spaces, Structures, Streams) Approach. Morgan & Claypool Publishers, USA (2012)
8. Gilliland-Swetland, A.J.: Enduring Paradigm, New Opportunities: The Value of the Archival Perspective in the Digital Environment. Council on Library and Information Resources (2000)
9. Gonçalves, M.A., Fox, E.A., Watson, L.T., Kipp, N.A.: Streams, Structures, Spaces, Scenarios, Societies (5S): A Formal Model for Digital Libraries. ACM Transactions on Information Systems (TOIS) 22(2), 270–312 (2004)
10. Heath, T., Bizer, C.: Linked Data: Evolving the Web into a Global Data Space. In: Synthesis Lectures on the Semantic Web: Theory and Technology. Morgan & Claypool Publishers, USA (2011)
11. International Council on Archives. In: ISAD(G): General International Standard Archival Description, 2nd edn., International Council on Archives, Ottawa (1999)
12. Kaplan, D., Sauer, A., Wilczek, E.: Archival description in OAI-ORE. Journal of Digital Information 12(2) (2011)
13. Kozievitch, N.P., da S. Torres, R.: Describing OAI-ORE from the 5S Framework Perspective. In: Chowdhury, G., Koo, C., Hunter, J. (eds.) ICADL 2010. LNCS, vol. 6102, pp. 260–261. Springer, Heidelberg (2010)
14. Lagoze, C., Van De Sompel, H., Nelson, M., Warner, S.: The Open Archives Initiative Protocol for Metadata Harvesting – Version 2.0 (December 2008), http://www.openarchives.org/OAI/openarchivesprotocol.html
15. University of California. California Digital Library. CDL Guidelines for Digital Objects. Version 2.0. Technical report, 34 pages (January 2011)
16. Prom, C.J., Habing, T.G.: Using the Open Archives Initiative Protocols with EAD. In: Hersh, W., Marchionini, G. (eds.) Proc. 2nd ACM/IEEE-CS Joint Conference on Digital Libraries (JCDL 2002), pp. 171–180. ACM Press, New York (2002)
17. Ridener, J.: From Polders to Postmodernism: A Concise History of Archival Theory. Litwin Books (2009)
18. Ross, S.: Digital Preservation, Archival Science and Methodological Foundations for Digital Libraries. New Rev. Inf. Netw. 17(1), 43–68 (2012)
19. Society of American Archivists. Encoded Archival Description: Tag Library, ver. 2002. Society of American Archivists (2003), http://www.loc.gov/ead/tglib/
20. Van de Sompel, H., Lagoze, C.: Interoperability for the Discovery, Use, and Re-Use of Units of Scholarly Communication. CTWatch Quarterly 3(3) (2007)
21. Yako, S.: It Complicated: Barriers to EAD Implementation. American Archivist 71(2), 456–475 (2008)

Evaluating the SiteStory Transactional Web Archive with the ApacheBench Tool

Justin F. Brunelle[1,2], Michael L. Nelson[2], Lyudmila Balakireva[3],
Robert Sanderson[3], and Herbert Van de Sompel[3]

[1] The MITRE Corporation, Hampton, VA 23666
jbrunelle@mitre.org
[2] Old Dominion University, Department of Computer Science, Norfolk VA, 23529
{jbrunelle,mln}@cs.odu.edu
[3] Los Alamos National Laboratory, Los Alamos, NM 87544
{ludab,rsanderson,herbertv}@lanl.gov

Abstract. Conventional Web archives are created by periodically crawling a Web site and archiving the responses from the Web server. Although easy to implement and commonly deployed, this form of archiving typically misses updates and may not be suitable for all preservation scenarios, for example a site that is required (perhaps for records compliance) to keep a copy of all pages it has served. In contrast, transactional archives work in conjunction with a Web server to record all content that has been served. Los Alamos National Laboratory has developed SiteStory, an open-source transactional archive written in Java that runs on Apache Web servers, provides a Memento compatible access interface, and WARC file export features. We used Apache's ApacheBench utility on a pre-release version of SiteStory to measure response time and content delivery time in different environments. The performance tests were designed to determine the feasibility of SiteStory as a production-level solution for high fidelity automatic Web archiving. We found that SiteStory does not significantly affect content server performance when it is performing transactional archiving. Content server performance slows from 0.076 seconds to 0.086 seconds per Web page access when the content server is under load, and from 0.15 seconds to 0.21 seconds when the resource has many embedded and changing resources.

Keywords: Web Archiving, Digital Preservation.

1 Introduction

Web archiving is an important aspect of cultural, historical, governmental, and institutional memory. The cost of capturing Web-native content for storage and archiving varies and is dependent upon several factors. The cost of manual Web archiving has prompted research into automated methods of digital resource capture. The traditional method of automatic capture is the Web crawler, but recent migrations toward more personalized and dynamic resources have rendered crawlers ineffective at high-fidelity capture in certain situations. For example, a

T. Aalberg et al. (Eds.): TPDL 2013, LNCS 8092, pp. 204–215, 2013.

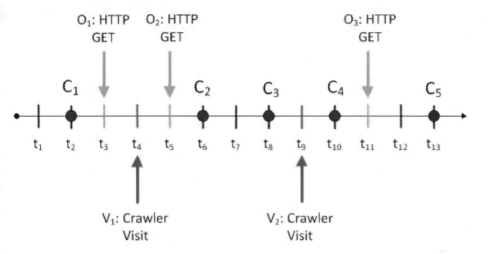

Fig. 1. User and crawler accesses control the archival interval, capturing each returned representation

crawler cannot capture every representation of a resource that is customized for each user. Transactional archiving can, in some instances, provide an automatic archiving solution to this problem.

1.1 Transactional Archiving

The purpose of a transactional archive (TA) is to archive every representation of a resource that a Web server disseminates. A client does an HTTP GET on a URI and the Web server returns the representation of the resource at that time. At dissemination time, it is the responsibility of TA software to send to an archive the representation sent to the client. In this way, *all* representations returned by the Web server can be archived. If storing all served representations is costly (e.g., a high-traffic site with slowly changing resources), it is possible to optimize a TA in a variety of ways: store only unique representations, store every n^{th} representation, etc.

Figure 1 provides a visual representation of a typical scenario where a page P is both changed and access at irregular intervals. This scenario assumes an arbitrary page that will be called P changes at inconsistent intervals. This timeline shows page P changes at points C_1, C_2, C_3, C_4, and C_5 at times t_2, t_6, t_8, t_{10}, and t_{13}, respectively. A user makes a request for P at points O_1, O_2, and O_3 at times t_3, t_5, and t_{11}, respectively. A Web crawler (that captures representations for storage in a Web archive) visits P at points V_1 and V_2 at times t_4 and t_9, respectively.

Since O_1 occurs after change C_1, an archived copy of C_1 is made by the TA. The Web crawler visits V_1 captures C_1, and makes a copy in the Web archive. In servicing V_1 or O_1, an unoptimized TA will store another copy of C_1 at t_4

and an optimized TA could detect that no change has occurred and not store another copy of C_1.

Change C_2 occurs at time t_6, and C_3 occurs at time t_8. There was no access to P between t_6 and t_8, which means C_2 is lost – an archived copy exists in neither the TA nor the Web crawler's archive. However, the argument can be made that if no entity observed the change, should it be archived? Change C_3 occurs and the representation of P is archived during the crawler's visit V_2, and the TA will also archive C_3. After C_4, a user accessed P at O_3 creating an archived copy of C_4 in the TA.

In the scenario depicted in Figure 1, the TA will have changes C_1, C_3, C_4, and a conventional archive will only have C_1, C_3. Change C_2 was never served to any client (human or crawler) and is thus not archived by either system. Change C_5 will be captured by the TA when P is accessed next.

1.2   SiteStory

Los Alamos National Laboratory has developed SiteStory[1], an open-source transactional Web archive. First, mod_sitestory is installed on the Apache server that contains the content to be archived. When the Apache server builds the response for the requesting client, mod_sitestory sends a copy of the response to the SiteStory Web archive, which is deployed as a separate service. This Web archive then provides Memento-based access to the content served by the Apache server with mod_sitestory installed, and the SiteStory Web archive is discoverable from the Apache Web server using standard Memento conventions (see Section 4 of [14]).

Sending a copy of the HTTP response to the archive is an additional task for the Apache Web server, and this task must not come at too great a performance penalty to the Web server. The goal of this study is to quantify the additional load mod_sitestory places on the Apache Web server to be archived.

2   Prior Work

Extensive research has been done to determine how Web documents change on the Web. Studies of "wild" pages (such as Cho's work with crawlers [4] or Olston's work in recrawl scheduling [10]) have shown that pages change extremely frequently.

Prior research has focused on crawlers and robots to find pages and monitor their change patterns [3, 6, 17]. These crawlers follow the links on pages to discover other pages and archive and recrawl the discovered pages over time to compile an archive. This method is unsuitable for an intranet that is closed to the public Web; crawlers cannot access the resources of archival interest [8]. As a way to have finer control over the archival granularity, transactional archiving should be used. Transactional archiving implementations include TTApache [5]

---

[1] http://mementoWeb.github.com/SiteStory/

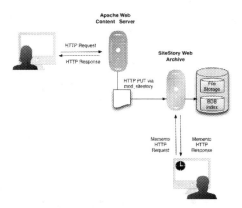

Fig. 2. SiteStory consists of two parts: mod_sitestory which is installed on the Apache server to be archived, and the transactional archive itself. Image taken from the SiteStory GitHub at `http://mementoWeb.github.com/SiteStory/`.

and pageVault [7]. These implementations were also shown not to substantially increase the access time seen by Web users; pageVault saw an increase of access time from 1.1 ms to 1.5 ms, and TTApache saw a 5-25% increase in response time, depending on requested document size.

Memento is a joint project between Old Dominion University and Los Alamos National Laboratory. The Memento Framework defines HTTP extensions that allow content negotiation in the dimension of time [15, 16]. When used with Memento-aware user agents like MementoFox [11], users can set a desired date-time in the past and browse the Web as it existed at (or near) that datetime. Un-like other, single-archive applications like DiffIE [12,13], Past Web Browser [9], or Zoetrope [1], Memento provides an multi-archive approach to presenting the past Web. Integrating multiple Web archives can give a more complete picture of the past Web [2].

3   Experiment Design

SiteStory was tested with a variety of loads on a variety of resources. Three different tests were run during the experiment.

3.1   Experiment Machines

The SiteStory benchmarking experiment was conducted with a pre-release version of SiteStory installed on a machines referred to as PC1. PC1 has a single core 2.8 GHz processor, ran the prefork version of the Apache 2 Web server, and the mod_sitestory-enabled Apache server provided content from `localhost:8080`. The SiteStory archive was installed as a separate service at `localhost:9999`. Although the developers have experimented with optimizations discussed in Section 1.1, SiteStory currently archives all returned representations regardless of whether the representation has changed or not.

3.2 Experiment Runs

Three separate experiments were run on PC1. The first experiment tests the throughput of a content server enabled with SiteStory software. The second experiment performs a series of accesses to 100 static resources to test the access rates, response times, and round trip times possible. The third experiment performs a series of accesses to 100 dynamic, constantly changing set of 100 resources to demonstrate a worst-case scenario for SiteStory – everything is archived on each access.

3.3 Connection Handling: ab

This first experiment to measure the differences in throughput when SiteStory is running and when SiteStory is turned off was run twice a day for 45 days, resulting in 90 data points. The experiment uses the ab (ApacheBench) tool[2], with a total of N connections made with a concurrency of C connections, where N and C are specified by the user. The ab utility records the response, throughput, and other server stats during a test. Essentially, the ApacheBench utility issues HTTP GET requests for content to establish a benchmark for performance.

Three different HTML resources were targeted with this test: a small, medium, and large file of sizes 1kB, 250 kB, and 700 kB. We used combinations of N=(1,000, 10,000, 100,000, 216,000) and C=(1, 100, 200, 450) as parameters to the ab utility. We chose the file sizes, connection, and concurrency values to match the values observed in our study of MITRE's Corporate Intranet. For simplicity and brevity, this report discusses the runs of 10,000 connections with concurrencies 1 and 100, and runs of 216,000 connections with concurrencies 1 and 100. This subset of results illustrates typical results of all other tests.

We modified the three resources between each set of connections to ensure the resource is archived each run. To modify the resources, we ran a script to update a timestamp displayed on each page and change the image that was embedded in the page. These modifications would ensure that not only the image was changed and able to be re-archived, but the surrounding HTML was changed, as well. Since SiteStory re-archives content whenever a change is detected, each test run results in each resource being re-archived. It is essential to make sure the resource is re-archived to observe the effect of an archival action on the content server performance.

We ran each ab test twice: once while SiteStory was turned on, and once while it was turned off. This shows how SiteStory affects the content server performance. A subset of the results are provided in Figure 3. The red lines represent the runs in which SiteStory was turned off, while the blue lines represent the runs in which SiteStory was turned on. Each entry on the x-axis represents an independent test run. The y-axis provides the amount of time it took to execute the entire ab run. The horizontal lines represent the averages over the entire experiment. The dotted, vertical green lines indicate machine restart times due to

---

[2] http://httpd.apache.org/docs/2.0/programs/ab.html

power outages. The power outages were noted to show when a cache and memory resets may have occurred that could impact the performance of the machines.

To illustrate how SiteStory affects the content server's performance, please reference Figure 3 that portrays the changes in the total run time of the ab test when SiteStory is on (actively archiving served content) and off (not archiving served content).

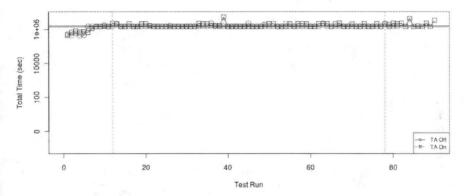

(a) Total run time for the ab test with 10,000 connections and 1 concurrency.

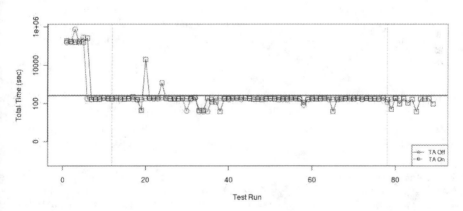

(b) Total run time for the ab test with 10,000 connections and 100 concurrency.

Fig. 3. Total run time for 10,000 Connections

3.4   100 Static Resources: Clearing the Cache

The second experiment uses the `curl` command to access 100 different HTML resources, none of which change. After running the ab tests in Section 3.3, a theory was formulated that a reason for some of the anomalies was from server caching. This additional test shows the effect of clearing the server cache on SiteStory by accessing a large number of large files in sequence. This access essentially thrashes the server cache. Each resource has text, and between 0 and 99 images (the 0th resource has 0 images, the 1st resource has 1 image, etc.). These resources were generated by a Perl script that constructed 100 different HTML pages and embedded between 0-99 different images in the generated resources. The resources were created with different sizes, and different numbers of embedded resources to demonstrate how SiteStory affects content server performance with a variety of page sizes and embedded images.

Figure 4 demonstrates the accesses of the 100 resources. The dark blue and red lines indicate the average run time for accessing a resource (in seconds). The filled areas around the lines are the standard deviation (σ) of the observations over the duration of the experiment.

3.5   100 Changing Resources: Worst-Case Scenario

We ran the same experiment from Section 3.4 in which each resource changes between runs to provide a "worst case scenario" of data connections vs. archiving and run time. We executed a script in between each run in which each resource was updated to make SiteStory archive a new copy of the resource. This means that each access resulted in a new archived copy of each resource. The results of this run are shown in Figure 5(a).

Note that Figure 5 show a "burdened" system. An artificial user load was induced on the servers to simulate a production environment in which many users are requesting content. A script was run during the test that made curl calls to the server pages to induce the load. Figure 5 shows the impact of SiteStory operating in a burdened environment.

4   Results

This section explores the results of the tests, from which we conclude whether or not SiteStory affects its host content server in an acceptable manner.

4.1   ab Results

For the ApacheBench tests described in Section 3.3, several obvious patterns emerge. Primarily, there is little separation between the total run times of the ab tests when SiteStory is on and when SiteStory is off. One can observe only minor differences in the plotted results. The results differ very little between any given run of the tests, and the averages across the experiment are almost identical in all tests. In the run of N=10,000 and C=1, the average total run times were 6.156 seconds when SiteStory was off, and 6.214 seconds when SiteStory was on. In the run of N=10,000 and C=100, the average total run time was 2.4 seconds when SiteStory was off, and 2.42 seconds when SiteStory was on. In the run of N=216,000 and C=1, the average run time was 8.905 seconds when SiteStory was off, and 8.955 seconds when SiteStory was on. In the run

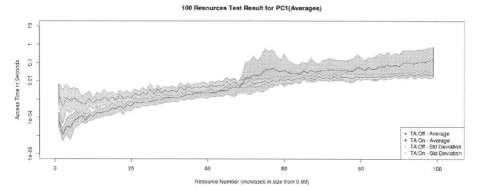

(a) Total access time for the 100 static resources on PC1.

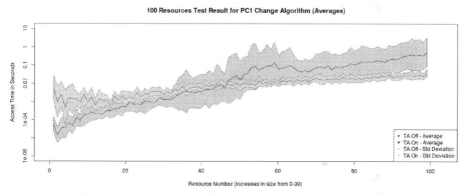

(b) Total access time for the 100 changing resources on PC1.

Fig. 4. 100 resources accessed on PC1. Resource n has n embedded images.

of N=216,000 and C=100, the average total run time was 4.698 seconds when SiteStory was off, and the average total run time was 4.706 when SiteStory was on. This indicates SiteStory does not significantly affect the run time of the ab statistics, and therefore does not affect the performance of the content server with regard to content delivery time.

Additionally, C=1 resulted in more consistent executions across each run whereas the runs with C=100 are more inconsistent, as indicated by the spikes in runtime. This could potentially be because of server caching, connection limitations, or even machine memory restrictions. The runs of C=100 also begin with a much longer total run time before dropping significantly and leveling out at runs 9 and 10. This is due to additional processes running on the experiment machines that induced extra load in runs 1-8. However, the spikes and inconsistencies do not affect a single run, and do not affect only the runs in which SiteStory is on or those when SiteStory is off. As such, these anomalies are disregarded since they affect both runs.

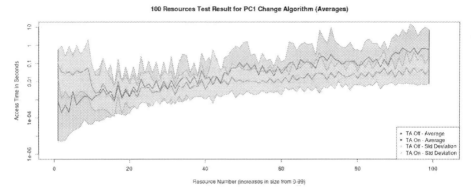

(a) Total access time for the 100 static resources on a burdened PC1.

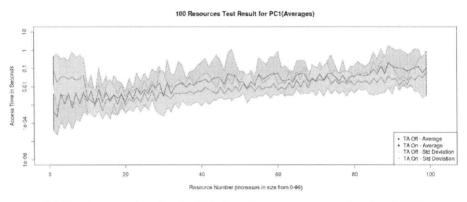

(b) Total access time for the 100 changing resources on a burdened PC1.

Fig. 5. 100 resources accessed on a burdened PC1. Resource n has n embedded images.

Finally, the runs of 216,000 connections take much longer to complete than the runs of 10,000 connections – specifically, 2.736 seconds longer, on average. This is intuitive since more connections should take longer to run. Additionally, the runs of C=1 take 3.9 seconds longer than the runs of C=100. By executing more connections in parallel, the total run time is intuitively shorter.

The ab test provides evidence that SiteStory does not significantly affect server content delivery time. As such, a production server can implement SiteStory without users observing a noticeable difference in server performance.

4.2   100 Resource Results

The runs of the 100 resources are more interesting, and provide a deeper insight into how SiteStory affects the server's performance than the ab test. This section examines the results of both the static and changing resource tests, as they provide interesting contrasts in performance. The results are listed in Table 1.

When comparing the unchanging vs changing resources (such as Figure 4(a) vs. 4(b)), it is apparent that σ is, on average, two times higher for the changing resources than the unchanging resources. (The average σ for unchanging resource is 0.0839 and 0.1680 for changing resources.) Additionally, the average access times when SiteStory is off remains approximately the same when the resources change or remain the same. The interesting result is that the average access time increases from 0.15 seconds per GET to 0.21 seconds per GET for the changing resources when SiteStory is on. This is intuitive considering SiteStory needs to re-archive the accessed content during an access when the resource changes.

The most important observation in Figures 4(a) and 5(b) is that the run time of this test is approximately 0.5 seconds higher on average when SiteStory is on vs. when SiteStory is off. This number is reached by comparing the difference in average run time for each test when SiteStory is on vs. off. For each on-off pair, the average difference was taken to reach the approximate 0.5 second difference across all tests. That is, the difference between the average run times of the tests in Figures 4(a) when SiteStory is running (red) vs when SiteStory is off (blue) is 0.08 seconds. When the same comparison is performed across all tests and the average of these results is taken, an overall impact of SiteStory on server performance is realized.

Each figure begins with SiteStory off taking more time than when SiteStory is on, but this can be attributed to experiment anomaly or similar server access anomaly. Inevitably, the run time when SiteStory is on becomes slower than when SiteStory is off as the resource size increases. This demonstrates that the performance difference of a server when SiteStory is on vs. off is worse when there is a large amount of embedded resources, such as images. PC1's average page access time increases by, on average, 0.006 seconds per embedded image. One could come to the conclusion that servers providing access to image-laden resources would see the biggest performance decrease when utilizing SiteStory.

Table 1. 100 Resource Test Results

Case	Avg. Unburdened Run Time	Unburdened σ	Avg. Burdened Run Time	Burdened Burdened σ
		Static Resources		
SS Off	0.121	0.0254	0.192	0.2021
SS On	0.206	0.1811	0.292	0.3103
		Changing Resources		
SS Off	0.132	0.0346	0.225	0.2174
SS On	0.354	0.4244	0.292	0.6137

5   Conclusions

In this work, we stress tested and benchmarked a pre-release version of SiteStory with the ApacheBench (ab) utility. Our experiment environment replicates resource sizes and access loads observed in MITRE's Corporate Intranet. The results of this study show that SiteStory does not significantly affect the performance of a server. While different servers and different use cases cause different performance effects when SiteStory is archiving content, the host server is still able to serve sites in a timely manner. The type of resource and resource change rate also affects the server's performance – resources with many embedded images and frequently changing content are affected most by SiteStory, seeing the biggest reduction in performance.

SiteStory does not significantly increase the load on a server or affect its ability to serve content – the response times seen by users will not be noticeably different in most cases. However, these graphs demonstrate the impact of SiteStory on performance, albeit small – larger resources with many embedded resources take longer to serve when SiteStory is on as opposed to when SiteStory is off due to the increased processing required of the server. However, the significant finding of this work is that SiteStory will not cripple, or even significantly reduce, a server's ability to provide content to users. Specifically, SiteStory only increases response times by a fraction of a second – from 0.076 seconds to 0.086 seconds per access when the server is under load, and from 0.15 seconds to 0.21 seconds when the resource has many embedded and changing resources. These increases will not be noticed by human users.

Acknowledgments. This work is supported in part by NSF grant 1009392 and the Library of Congress. A Corporate Case Study to investigate the feasibility of a transactional archive in a corporate intranet was funded by a Fiscal Year 2011 Innovation Grant from the MITRE Corporation. MITRE employees Jory T. Morrison and George Despres were integral to the MITRE Innovation Grant and Case Study.

References

1. Adar, E., Dontcheva, M., Fogarty, J., Weld, D.: Zoetrope: interacting with the ephemeral web. In: Proceedings of the 21st Annual ACM Symposium on User Interface Software and Technology, pp. 239–248. ACM (2008)
2. Ainsworth, S., Alsum, A., SalahEldeen, H., Weigle, M.C., Nelson, M.L.: How much of the Web is archived? In. In: JCDL 2011: Proceedings of the 11th Annual International ACM/IEEE Joint Conference on Digital Libraries, pp. 133–136 (2011)
3. Brewington, B., Cybenko, G., Coll, D., Hanover, N.: Keeping up with the changing Web. IEEE Computer 33(5), 52–58 (2000)
4. Cho, J., Garcia-Molina, H.: The evolution of the web and implications for an incremental crawler. In: Proceedings of the 26th International Conference on Very Large Data Bases, pp. 200–209 (2000)
5. Dyreson, C.E., Lin, H.-L., Wang, Y.: Managing versions of Web documents in a transaction-time Web server. In: Proceedings of the 13th International Conference on World Wide Web, WWW 2004 (2004)
6. Fetterly, D., Manasse, M., Najork, M., Wiener, J.: A large-scale study of the evolution of web pages. Software: Practice and Experience 34(2), 213–237 (2004)
7. Fitch, K.: Web site archiving: An approach to recording every materially different response produced by a Website. In: 9th Australasian World Wide Web Conference, pp. 5–9 (July 2003)

8. Hagedorn, K., Sentelli, J.: Google Still Not Indexing Hidden Web URLs. D-Lib Magazine 14(7) (August 2008),
   http://dlib.org/dlib/july08/hagedorn/07hagedorn.html
9. Jatowt, A., Kawai, Y., Nakamura, S., Kidawara, Y., Tanaka, K.: Journey to the past: Proposal of a framework for past web browser. In: Proceedings of the Seventeenth Conference on Hypertext and Hypermedia, pp. 135–144. ACM (2006)
10. Olston, C., Pandey, S.: Recrawl scheduling based on information longevity. In: Proceeding of the 17th International Conference on World Wide Web, pp. 437–446. ACM (2008)
11. Sanderson, R., Shankar, H., Ainsworth, S., McCown, F., Adams, S.: Implementing Time Travel for the Web. Code4Lib Journal 13 (2011)
12. Teevan, J., Dumais, S.T., Liebling, D.J.: A longitudinal study of how highlighting web content change affects people's web interactions. In: Proceedings of the 28th International Conference on Human Factors in Computing Systems, CHI 2010 (2010)
13. Teevan, J., Dumais, S.T., Liebling, D.J., Hughes, R.L.: Changing how people view changes on the web. In: UIST 2009: Proceedings of the 22nd Annual ACM Symposium on User Interface Software and Technology, pp. 237–246 (2009)
14. Van de Sompel, H., Nelson, M.L., Sanderson, R.: HTTP framework for time-based access to resource states – Memento draft-vandesompel-memento-06 (2013),
    http://tools.ietf.org/pdf/draft-vandesompel-memento-06.pdf
15. Van de Sompel, H., Nelson, M.L., Sanderson, R., Balakireva, L.L., Ainsworth, S., Shankar, H.: Memento: Time Travel for the Web. Technical Report arXiv:0911.1112 (2009)
16. Van de Sompel, H., Sanderson, R., Nelson, M.L., Balakireva, L.L., Shankar, H., Ainsworth, S.: An HTTP-Based Versioning Mechanism for Linked Data. In: Proceedings of the Linked Data on the Web Workshop (LDOW 2010) (Also available as arXiv:1003.3661) (2010)
17. Wolf, J.L., Squillante, M.S., Yu, P.S., Sethuraman, J., Ozsen, L.: Optimal crawling strategies for web search engines. In: WWW 2002: Proceedings of the 11th International Conference on World Wide Web, pp. 136–147 (2002)

Exploring Large Digital Library Collections Using a Map-Based Visualisation

Mark Hall[1] and Paul Clough[2]

[1] Department for Computer Science
University of Sheffield
Sheffield, UK
m.mhall@sheffield.ac.uk
[2] Information School
University of Sheffield
Sheffield, UK
p.d.clough@sheffield.ac.uk

Abstract. In this paper we describe a novel approach for exploring large document collections using a map-based visualisation. We use hierarchically structured semantic concepts that are attached to the documents to create a visualisation of the semantic space that resembles a Google Map. The approach is novel in that we exploit the hierarchical structure to enable the approach to scale to large document collections and to create a map where the higher levels of spatial abstraction have semantic meaning. An informal evaluation is carried out to gather subjective feedback from users. Overall results are positive with users finding the visualisation enticing and easy to use.

1 Introduction

Access to current Digital Library (DL) services is primarily provided through the use of a search box and a query-response mode of interaction [20]. However, there are a number of situations when this is insufficient [21,28] and where users would benefit from a richer user-interface to interact with [30]. For example, when users do not have clearly defined information needs [36]; when users have complex search tasks [33]; or when they want to gain an overview over a collection [15]. This has led to the design of browsing and exploration functionalities, including thesaurus-based search improvements [23,31], document clustering [27] or the use of concepts arranged hierarchically in facets [12,34]. All approaches have been shown to improve the user's search experience for exploration activities.

However, they are still primarily focused on improving the search experience and less on supporting overviewing and exploratory browsing tasks. Visualisations have been suggested as alternatives that would focus more on these two tasks and a number of visualisation techniques have been developed. The visualisations support the browsing experience [2], but struggle to scale to large collections and in the best cases support displaying a few thousand to tens of thousand of documents. This is either because there are computational limits

T. Aalberg et al. (Eds.): TPDL 2013, LNCS 8092, pp. 216–227, 2013.
© Springer-Verlag Berlin Heidelberg 2013

restricting the number of documents that can realistically be processed, or because there is a limit to the amount of information that can be displayed before the visualisation becomes unusable.

In this paper we present a novel approach to generating map-based visualisations for DLs that overcomes both these limitations. We achieve this by integrating hierarchical structure information, taken from a thesaurus that the documents have been mapped to, into the spatialisation process. This has three major advantages: first, it makes it possible to generate a map-based visualisation for collections with hundreds of thousands of documents; second, the hierarchical information means that the resulting map is not overloaded and remains usable with such a large collection; third: all structures shown on the map have an explicit semantic meaning, addressing issues of spatial-metaphor mis-use raised by [8]. The paper is structured as follows. Section 2 describes related work on collection overviews and information visualisation; Section 3 presents our approach to generating a 2D map-based visualisation of the concept or semantic space; Section 4 provides the results of an initial evaluation of the visualisation and Section 5 concludes the paper and provides directions for future research.

2   Background

2.1   Exploration of Digital Collections

In recent years approaches have been proposed for visualising document collections and providing overviews of the contents in order to support users with information exploration and discovery [14,10]. The objective is to allow the user to gain an overview of the themes within an entire document collection which can provide a starting point for subsequent searches, especially if users are unfamiliar with the contents of a collection or are unable to formulate queries due to limited domain knowledge. A number of past studies have shown that visualising document collections can aid users with exploration [35,2].

Overviews can vary from visualisations that display the individual documents in a collection and their relationships (i.e. the *document space*) to displays that show themes or topics associated with the contents of the documents (i.e. the *semantic space*). The design of overviews typically follows the principle of overview-then-details: providing zoomed out views of the collection and then allowing users to zoom in and inspect documents [32]. Various forms of visualisation have been used in the past, including spring-based visualisations [25], fish-eye views, 2D and 3D spatial visualisations [18,24], network structures and hierarchical and tree-based visualisations of topics and documents [5,3,13,14]. However, a common problem with visualisations is scaling them to deal with large collections and making them usable and understandable to users. For 2D or 3D spatialisation techniques [18,24] the scaling limit is imposed by the computational complexity of the algorithms. For graph-based visualisations [25,5,3] the limit is defined by the amount of information that can be displayed before the visualisation becomes overloaded and unusable. The novel algorithm presented in the next section overcomes both these issues through the creation of a hierarchically structured 2D map.

2.2 Spatial Metaphors for Information Visualisation

One type of visualisation that has been used in multiple domains is a 2D map which aims to spatially represent the contents of a document collection on maps or landscapes (a process known as *spatialisation*). These map-style visualisations are based on a spatial metaphor whereby similar documents (or themes) are clustered together and placed physically nearer to each other. They have been used for a range of applications, including providing thematic clustering of search results [1] and document collections [8], helping software developers make sense of large repositories of source code [17], allowing users to explore music libraries where "islands" on the map represent different genres or styles of music [26], and visualising user traffic on the Internet radio station last.fm [22].

Visualisations based on maps are often seen as a good metaphor in the sense that users of such systems are likely able to relate to the visualisation in a similar way they relate to maps derived from spatial data. However, Fabrikant et al. [8] argue that the spatial metaphor is often mis-used and that representing non-spatial information on maps or landscapes might not be as intuitive to users as one might think. For example the "islands" in [26], or contour lines in self-organizing maps [18], imply a spatial extent of the labelled concepts in the map, however all they actually represent is the spatial density of the individual documents. Thus documents belonging to a topic could lie outside of the "islands", breaking the spatial metaphor. To address this issue all spatial structures that our algorithm generates have a semantic meaning and observe basic geographic principles. Thus a boundary on our map denotes the border of a semantic area (in our case a topic in the thesaurus), just as a boundary on a geographic map denotes the border of a spatial object (such as a town or country). Similarly where areas in our map are contained within other areas, there is a part-of relationship between the contained object and the container, just as on a geographic map. This should ensure that people's common-sense assumptions about geography [7] are in line with how the semantic map works.

3   Hierarchical Spatialisation Algorithm

The novel Hierarchical Spatialisation Algorithm (HSA) presented in this paper requires as its input a thesaurus, a collection of documents, and a mapping of the documents into the thesaurus. From these it generates a hierarchical, semantic map using the six-step pipeline shown in Fig. 1. The first three steps (Tree pruning, Item pruning, Vectorisation) pre-process the thesaurus into the structure required for the main spatialisation algorithm. The next two steps (Spatialisation, Positioning) create the spatialisation of the thesaurus and the documents in the collection. The last step (Post-processing) creates the final map outline.

Fig. 1. High-level workflow of the hierarchical spatialisation algorithm

3.1   Pre-processing

The HSA requires that the thesaurus is a tree-structure and that documents are only found in the leaf nodes of the thesaurus. The pre-processing steps ensure that the thesaurus conforms to both criteria by first removing any multi-path structures and then pushing all documents into the leaf topics, creating new leaf topics where required. In addition to the structural requirements, the spatialisation algorithm also requires that all documents and topics have TFIDF vectors that define their position in the document space, and that are calculated in the third pre-processing step.

The restriction to tree-structures and that documents must be in the leaf nodes are limitations in the current implementation of the core spatialisation algorithm. However, Yu et al. [37] clearly demonstrate that thesauri with multiple paths to documents perform better in exploration tasks, as they increase the likelihood of the user finding any one path to the documents they are interested in. Thus work is currently ongoing to extend the core spatialisation algorithm to work with thesauri that are directed acyclical graphs.

Tree pruning ensures that the thesaurus is a pure tree, using a top-down, breadth-first algorithm that finds the highest location (closest to the root topic) for each topic in the thesaurus (Fig. 2). For each topic the pruning algorithm iterates over its child topics. If a child-topic has not yet been seen, then it is marked as "seen" (Fig. 2, b). If a child-topic is already marked as "seen" (Fig. 2, c) then the parent-child relationship is pruned, ensuring that each topic is placed at the highest location in the tree (Fig. 2, d).

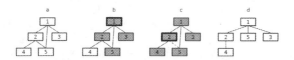

Fig. 2. Example of pruning a DAG hierarchy, the topic being processed is marked with a thick border. a) the original hierarchy where topic 5 has two parents; b) processing topic 1 and marking its children as "seen"; c) processing topic 2, topic 5 has already been "seen" and is thus removed from topic 2; d) the final thesaurus tree for spatialisation.

The highest location metric was chosen due to two criteria. First, a topic higher in the thesaurus is easier and faster to find. Second, a flatter thesaurus is better suited to the two-dimensional representation in the map. This heuristic was chosen as it worked best for our test collection and for other collections, different heuristics might work better. With the future transition to supporting DAGs in the spatialisation, the question of which heuristic to use will become moot.

Item Pruning. After pruning the topic structure, the topic-document mappings also have to be pruned to ensure that each document belongs to only one topic. Items belonging to multiple topics, are removed from all non-leaf parent topics (Fig. 3, a). If after that step an document still has multiple parent topics, then it is assigned to the topic that is deepest in the hierarchy (Fig. 3, b). The justification being that a topic deeper in the hierarchy is likely to be more specific and thus provide a better fit for the document. If there are multiple parent topics at the same depth, then the document is randomly assigned to one. Only leaf topics may contain documents, thus for all non-leaf topics that contain documents a new child-topic is added with the original topic's label. All of the original topic's documents are then moved into the new child-topic (Fig. 3, c).

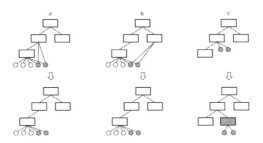

Fig. 3. Item pruning examples. a) pruning from non-leaf topics; b) pruning from higher-level topics; c) creating of an additional leaf node.

Vectorisation. Items and topics are defined by TFIDF vectors calculated based on the documents' title, description, and subject keywords. To create the bag-of-words for each document, its title and description are tokenised and stop-worded, while the subject keywords are used as-is. Words that occur less than 5 times in the collection or in more than half of the documents in the collection are filtered. A single IDF vector is calculated based on all documents' bag-of-words. Then each document's TFIDF vector is calculated based on its bag-of-words and the IDF vector. For each topic the bag-of-words is created by combining the bag-of-words of all documents that belong to that topic or to one of the topic's descendants. The topic's TFIDF vector is then calculated based on the combined bag-of-words. As this leads to very large TFIDF vectors, for each topic only the 30 highest-scoring words are used for the final TFIDF vector. The threshold of 30 words was determined empirically, with a smaller number leading to indistinguishable topic vectors, while higher numbers created additional noise without improving topic distinguishability.

3.2   Hierarchical Spatialisation

The core spatialisation algorithm uses a depth-first, bottom-up process to generate the documents' and topics' spatialisations (Fig. 4). Starting at the leaf nodes each topic is processed using the spatialisation algorithm described below. For leaf topics it is the documents that are spatialised, while for all other topics it is their child topics that are spatialised. After the documents or child-topics are spatialised the convex hull around them is calculated as the initial outline of the topic. This initial outline is then buffered in order to ensure that there is spatial separation between the topics. The buffered outline will be referred to as the topic's footprint. The centroid of the footprint is stored with the topic, as it is required for generating the final document placement.

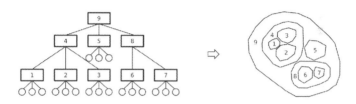

Fig. 4. Sample thesaurus hierarchy and the resulting spatialisation. The order in which the topics are processed is indicated by the numbers.

The algorithm achieves scalability to large collections through the ability to parallelise the process, as topics that are not in a parent-child relationship can be processed independently and concurrently. In the example in Fig. 4 the leaf topics 1, 2, 3, 5, 6, and 7 can all be processed in parallel. The same goes for topics 4 and 8. The only constraint in the parallelisation is that in order to be able to process a topic, all its child topics have to have been spatialised, as the spatialisation requires the child topics' footprints. Thus for example topic 4 can only be processed after topics 1, 2, and 3 have been spatialised. The scalability can be seen in the evaluation (Sect. 4), where a collection with approximately half a million documents is spatialised.

Spatialisation. Items or topics are spatialised based on the TFIDF vectors calculated in the pre-processing step. By default the initial spatialisation is calculated using Multi Dimensional Scaling (MDS) [16]. However, if the number of elements to spatialise is larger than a given threshold α ($\alpha = 2000$ was used in the maps shown in this paper), then the elements are assigned co-ordinates randomly. While not ideal, it ensures that arbitrary numbers of elements can be processed in a realistic time-frame. At this point in the process both documents' and topics' locations are represented by points, the topics' spatial extents will integrated into the spatialisation at a later point.

One of the drawbacks of MDS is that if there are elements that are very different from the majority of elements to be spatialised, then this leads to a degenerate spatialisation with a large cluster of points very closely positioned and the outliers at a distance (Fig. 5). To make the closely positioned points distinguishable on the map they have to be moved apart, however a simple linear scaling would result in maps with large amounts of empty space as the distance to the outliers would increase as well.

Fig. 5. Degenerate MDS with a large cluster of very densely located points and two outliers

To address this problem the MDS spatialisation is transformed into a more compact representation (Fig. 6). First the Delaunay triangulation [6] for the MDS points plus a virtual point at $(0, 0)$ is calculated using QHull[1] (Fig. 6, b). Due to the properties of the Delaunay triangulation, each point will be linked to its nearest neighbours in all directions. Then, for each point, the final co-ordinates p are calculated from the MDS co-ordinates m and the distance d from the $(0,0)$ point in the neighbourhood graph using equation 1. $\frac{m}{\|m\|}$ is the unit vector of m, a vector of length 1 that points in the same direction as the original vector m. Multiplying the unit vector by the distance d creates a concentric set of final co-ordinates for each point (Fig. 6, c), that maintains the qualitative spatial layout of the MDS spatialisation.

$$p = \frac{m}{\|m\|} \cdot d \tag{1}$$

Points are placed in the order of their distance d, thus the inner circle will be created first and then the outer circles added consecutively. The concentric spatialisation of the elements reduces the quantitative relationship between the point distance in the document vector space and the two-dimensional locations to a qualitative representation, however, the core principle that closer means more similar is maintained.

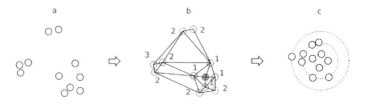

Fig. 6. The core spatialisation steps. a) the initial result of the MDS; b) the Delaunay triangulation with the neighbourhood distances; c) the final concentric spatialisation.

---

[1] http://www.qhull.org

When spatialising a set of topics, the topics' footprints have to be taken into account. To do this, each topic's footprint is placed so that its centroid is at point p. It is then checked if the footprint overlaps with other footprints that have already been placed and if it has then d is increased until it no longer overlaps. This results in a concentric spatialisation of the footprints where the footprints' boundaries touch, but do not overlap.

Final Positioning. To enable scalability the spatialisation algorithm processes each level in each sub-tree of the thesaurus independently. The result of the independent processing is that the topic footprints are not within the footprints of their parent topic and the documents are also not located within their topic's footprint (Fig. 7). To correct this the topics and documents are moved into their final position using the offset between their parent topic's footprint's current centroid and the centroid calculated when the footprint was created. This is performed in a top-down, depth-first manner, ensuring that each topic or document is moved only once, guaranteeing optimum performance.

Fig. 7. On the left the placement of the footprints after the spatialisation, with footprints stacked above each other. At this point spatial containment does not indicate topical containment. On the right the spatialisation after final positioning and now spatial containment means topical containment.

3.3   Post-processing

After the spatialisation is completed, the topics' footprints will in most cases be touching their neighbours' footprints, which makes it harder to visually distinguish them. To correct this the algorithm removes the buffering added in the spatialisation process, ensuring sufficient distance between the topic outlines and creating the final map shown in Fig. 8.

4   Evaluation

Information visualisations are inherently complex to evaluate and multiple evaluation approaches exist [29,9,4]. We focus on user experience as opposed to evaluating aspects such as visual data analysis and reasoning, collaborative data analysis, or work practices [19]. The goal is to elicit subjective feedback and opinions on using the map in an undirected "exploring" context, to assess the intuitiveness, utility, and usability of the map[19]. This cannot replace a full formal evaluation, but gives an initial indication of the visualisation's usability.

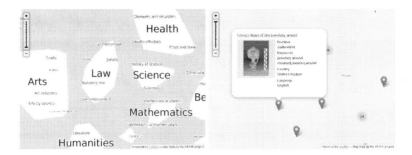

Fig. 8. On the left the initial overview over the map. On the right a zoomed-in showing individual documents and document clusters.

The HSA was evaluated using a collection of 547,780 documents taken from the English sub-set of Europeana[2], together with an automatically generated thesaurus [11] consisting of 27,049 topics covering all documents. Without parallelising any parts of the algorithm, the HSA required two days of processing on standard desktop PC, clearly demonstrating that it scales to large collections.

10 participants were shown the map and instructed to spend five to ten minutes exploring it. Leaflet[3] together with TileLite[4] were used to generate an interactive, digital map that provided the same interaction patterns as common on-line maps such as Google Maps. They were then asked to assess the system using a modified version of the the System Usability Scale (SUS) [4] that focuses on evaluating interactive digital maps, together with three quantitative questions derived from [19]. Additionally they were asked three qualitative questions.

Table 1. The SUS score is out of a hundred, with 0 being "unusable" and 100 "perfect usability". The other questions are between "1" (bad) and "5" (good).

Question	1st Quart.	Median	3rd Quart.
SUS Total Score	70	81.25	91.88
How understandable is the map?	4	4.5	5
Would you use the map again?	4	4.5	5
Did you generally know where in the map you were?	3	3.5	4

The participants spent an average 5 minutes 45 seconds exploring the map and a summary of their quantitative responses is shown in Table 1. Overall the results show that the participants felt comfortable using the map to explore the collection, although issues with orientation within the map remain. The qualitative answers support these conclusions, with comments including "The freedom of movement among topics" and "Overview of the topics", but also "Some text was overlapped" and "Need to double click to zoom in - took me a while to figure this out".

---

[2] The European Digital Library – http://www.europeana.eu
[3] http://leafletjs.com/
[4] https://bitbucket.org/springmeyer/tilelite/wiki/Home

5   Conclusions

In this paper we describe a novel spatialisation algorithm that can scale to hundreds of thousands of documents and provides an intuitive map-based visualisation that can be used to hierarchically navigate themes in a document collection. This is possible by exploiting the hierarchical relationships between topics in a thesaurus that is attached to the documents. An informal evaluation shows that the resulting map succeeds in its goal of providing an enticing interface for getting an initial overview over the collection and exploring it. The 2D map would also be suitable for presenting collection overviews on mobile devices with limited screen space and when using a more tactile form of interaction. The visualisation has been deployed in the PATHS project[5], demonstrating its integration into a larger digital cultural heritage exploration system.

A number of areas to explore in future work remain. The foremost is to perform a more formal evaluation to determine the maps performance in the "overviewing" and "undirected exploring" tasks and comparing it to established interfaces such as faceted search or tag-clouds. A second major area is how to continuously update the map as the underlying collection changes, without having to re-calculate the whole map. Finally the cartographic styling of the map needs to be investigated to ensure that users understand it correctly.

Acknowledgements. The research leading to these results was supported by the PATHS project (http://paths-project.eu) funded by the European Community's Seventh Framework Programme (FP7/2007-2013) under grant agreement no. 270082.

References

1. Andrews, K., Gutl, C., Moser, J., Sabol, V., Lackner, W.: Search result visualisation with xfind. In: Proceedings of Second International Workshop on User Interfaces to Data Intensive Systems, UIDIS 2001. IEEE Computer Society (2001)
2. Butavicius, M.A., Lee, M.D.: An empirical evaluation of four data visualization techniques for displaying short news text similarities. International Journal of Human-Computer Studies 65(11), 931–944 (2007)
3. Carey, M., Heesch, D., Rüger, S.: Info navigator: A visualization tool for document searching and browsing. In: 9th International Conference on Distributed Multimedia Systems (DMS) (March 2003)
4. Çöltekin, A., Heil, B., Garlandini, S., Fabrikant, S.I.: Evaluating the effectiveness of interactive map interface designs: A case study integrating usability metrics with eye-movement analysis. Cartography and Geographic Information Science 36(1), 5–17 (2009)
5. Chen, C., Cribbin, T., Kuljis, J., Macredie, R.: Footprints of information foragers: Behaviour semantics of visual exploration. International Journal of Human-Computer Studies 57(2), 139–163 (2002)

---

[5] http://www.paths-project.eu

6. Delaunay, B.: Sur la sphère vide. Izvestia Akademii Nauk SSSR, Otdelenie Matematicheskikh i Estestvennykh Nauk 7, 793–800 (1934)
7. Egenhofer, M.J., Mark, D.M.: Naive geography. In: Kuhn, W., Frank, A.U. (eds.) COSIT 1995. LNCS, vol. 988, pp. 1–15. Springer, Heidelberg (1995)
8. Fabrikant, S.I., Montello, D.R., Mark, D.M.: The natural landscape metaphor in information visualization: The role of commonsense geomorphology. Journal of the American Society for Information Science and Technology 61, 253–270 (2010)
9. Forsell, C., Johansson, J.: An heuristic set for evaluation in information visualization. In: Proceedings of the International Conference on Advanced Visual Interfaces, AVI 2010, pp. 199–206. ACM, New York (2010)
10. Greene, S., Marchionini, G., Plaisant, C., Shneiderman, B.: Previews and overviews in digital libraries: Designing surrogates to support visual information seeking. Journal of the American Society for Information Science and Technology 51(4), 380–393 (2000)
11. Hall, M.M., Clough Paul, D., Fernando, S., Stevenson, M., Soroa, A., Aguirre, E.: Automatic generation of hierarchies for exploring digital library collections (forthcoming)
12. Hearst, M.A.: Clustering versus faceted categories for information exploration. Communications of the ACM 49(4), 59–61 (2006)
13. Hearst, M.A.: Search User Interfaces, 1st edn. Cambridge University Press, New York (2009)
14. Herrmannova, D., Knoth, P.: Visual search for supporting content exploration in large document collections. D-Lib Magazine 18(7/8) (2012)
15. Hornbæk, K., Hertzum, M.: The notion of overview in information visualization. International Journal of Human-Computer Studies 69(7-8), 509–525 (2011)
16. Kruskal, J.B.: Multidimensional scaling by optimizing goodness of fit to a nonmetric hypothesis. Psychometrika 29(1), 1–27 (1964)
17. Kuhn, A., Erni, D., Nierstrasz, O.: Embedding spatial software visualization in the ide: An exploratory study. In: Proceedings of the 5th International Symposium on Software Visualization, SOFTVIS 2010, pp. 113–122. ACM, New York (2010)
18. Lagus, K., Kaski, S., Kohonen, T.: Mining massive document collections by the websom method. Information Sciences, 163(1-3), 135 – 156 (2004), Soft Computing Data Mining
19. Lam, H., Bertini, E., Isenberg, P., Plaisant, C., Carpendale, S.: Seven guiding scenarios for information visualization evaluation. Technical report, Department of Computer Science, University of Calgary (2011)
20. Liew, C.L.: Online cultural heritage exhibitions: A survey of information retrieval features. Program: Electronic Library and Information Systems 39(1), 4–24 (2005)
21. Marchionini, G.: Exploratory search: From finding to understanding. Communications of the ACM 49(4), 41–46 (2006)
22. Mashima, D., Kobourov, S.G., Hu, Y.: Visualizing dynamic data with maps. In: Proceedings of the 2011 IEEE Pacific Visualization Symposium, PACIFICVIS 2011, pp. 155–162. IEEE Computer Society, Washington, DC (2011)
23. Milne, D.N., Witten, I.H., Nichols, D.M.: A knowledge-based search engine powered by wikipedia. In: Proceedings of the Sixteenth ACM Conference on Conference on Information and Knowledge Management, pp. 445–454. ACM (2007)
24. Newton, G., Callahan, A., Dumontier, M.: Semantic journal mapping for search visualization in a large scale article digital library. In: Second Workshop on Very Large Digital Libraries at ECDL 2009 (2009)

25. Olsen, K.A., Korfhage, R.R., Sochats, K.M., Spring, M.B., Williams, J.G.: Visualization of a document collection: The vibe system. Information Processing & Management 29(1), 69–81 (1993)
26. Pampalk, E., Rauber, A., Merkl, D.: Content-based organization and visualization of music archives. In: Proceedings of the Tenth ACM International Conference on Multimedia, MULTIMEDIA 2002, pp. 570–579. ACM, New York (2002)
27. Pirolli, P., Schank, P., Hearst, M.A., Diehl, C.: Scatter/gather browsing communicates the topic structure of a very large text collection. In: Proceedings of the SIGCHI Conference on Human Factors in Computing Systems: Common Ground, pp. 213–220. ACM (1996)
28. Pirolli, P.: Powers of 10: Modeling complex information-seeking systems at multiple scales. Computer 42(3), 33–40 (2009)
29. Plaisant, C.: The challenge of information visualization evaluation. In: Proceedings of the Working Conference on Advanced Visual Interfaces, AVI 2004, pp. 109–116. ACM, New York (2004)
30. Rao, R., Pedersen, J.O., Hearst, M.A., Mackinlay, J.D., Card, S.K., Masinter, L., Halvorsen, P.-K., Robertson, G.C.: Rich interaction in the digital library. Communications of the ACM 38(4), 29–39 (1995)
31. Shiri, A.A., Revie, C., Chowdhury, G.: Thesaurus-enhanced search interfaces. Journal of Information Science 28(2), 111–122 (2002)
32. Shneiderman, B., Feldman, D., Rose, A., Grau, X.F.: Visualizing digital library search results with categorical and hierarchical axes. In: Proceedings of the Fifth ACM Conference on Digital Libraries, pp. 57–66. ACM (2000)
33. Singer, G., Norbisrath, U., Lewandowski, D.: Ordinary search engine users carrying out complex search tasks. Journal of Information Science (2012)
34. Stoica, E., Hearst, M.A., Richardson, M.: Automating creation of hierarchical faceted metadata structures. In: Human Language Technologies: The Annual Conference of the North American Chapter of the Association for Computational Linguistics (NAACL-HLT 2007), pp. 244–251 (2007)
35. Westerman, S.J., Cribbin, T.: Mapping semantic information in virtual space: dimensions, variance and individual differences. International Journal of Human-Computer Studies 53(5), 765–787 (2000)
36. White, R.W., Kules, B., Drucker, S.M., Schraefel, M.C.: Introduction. Communications of the ACM 49(4), 36–39 (2006)
37. Yu, J., Thom, J.A., Tam, A.: Ontology evaluation using wikipedia categories for browsing. In: Proceedings of the Sixteenth ACM Conference on Information and Knowledge Management, pp. 223–232. ACM (2007)

AugDesk. Fusing Reality with the Virtual in Document Triage. Part1: Gesture Interactions

Fernando Loizides[1], Doros Polydorou[1], Keti Mavri[1],
George Buchanan[2,*], and Panayiotis Zaphiris[1]

[1] Cyprus University of Technology
[2] City University London
{fernando.loizides,doros.polydorou,keti.mavri,
panayiotis.zaphiris}@cut.ac.cy,
george.buchanan.1@city.ac.uk

Abstract. In this paper we present the first version of AugDesk, an affordable augmented reality prototype desk for sorting documents based on their relevance to an information need. The set-up is based on the findings from previous work in conjunction with a user-centred iterative design process to improve both the software and hardware configuration. In this initial version of the prototype the documents automatically appear on a table from an overhead projector and the user can control the movement and selection of these documents by using gestures, identified from a Microsoft Kinect Sensor. The first part of our work included recording users' actions to identify the most popular interactions with virtual documents on a table and integrating these into AugDesk.

1   Introduction and Motivation

An action that is undertaken daily by scholars is that of triaging academic documents to identify their possible relevance to an information need. This includes querying an online search engine which returns thousands of web pages in a results list or an academic search engine which returns a corpus of potentially relevant documents. It is then up to the individual information seeker to manually 'sift' through the search results and make a relevance decision on the available documents. This process is constantly changing as new technologies are developed. For example, the introduction of smaller screen devices, as well as the multiple-display desktop has given new possibilities and interaction capabilities to the seeker [1,4].

Wanting to promote a more natural way of interaction, we attempted to explore the richness of physical space by building upon a concept proposed by Hiroshi Ishii more than a decade ago [6]. Taking advantage of newly released and affordable technologies such as the Microsoft Kinect and the Leap Motion[1] system, we attempted to recreate a version of metaDESK specifically for the

---

* Corresponding author.
[1] See https://www.leapmotion.com/

T. Aalberg et al. (Eds.): TPDL 2013, LNCS 8092, pp. 228–234, 2013.

task of academic document triage. By investigating dedicated works from across disciplines such as psychology, sociology, philosophy [5,7] and more recently HCI [3] it is clear that there is a paradigm shift taking place, leading computer interactions away from traditional Graphical User Interfaces and flat 2D screens. So far investigations upon natural gesture interactions (out of the context of entertainment and gameplay) are introduced in scenarios of convenience such as mundane navigation of menus and maps. By simulating a scenario where the user is sitting on a physical desk, surrounded by familiar physical objects and ubiquitous technology we expect that the user will be able to sort through large amounts of digital information in ways which resembles ,more closely, our natural physical modalities.

We begin by presenting a pilot study which identified basic common interactions that users preferred with the system. We then continue to describe the working prototype software as well as the hardware set-up we used.

2   Interaction Pilot Study

The initial study in our iterative design methodology required participants to 'show us' their most intuitive interactions. In order to elicit these actions in a way that could be reproduced by the Kinect sensor, we set up our participants in the same conditions that they would be when using AugDesk. Since the interactions were not implemented yet, the table was projected with the AugDesk background and a physical document was placed in front of the participant that was to be considered the 'working document'; in other words the document that the interactions would be used for. All the participants were familiar with using touch screen technology. Since it is widely accepted that using this technology is ubiquitous we did not filter out these participants which may affect the interactions. For this reason we chose to place a physical document on the table rather than a projection of a document that would have encouraged a touch interaction approach rather than to utilise the 3 dimensional physical space. 10 participants, 5 male and 5 female, all right-handed, were asked to demonstrate which physical actions they would use for a predefined set of interactions such as 'Enlarge Document' and 'Decrease Document Size' (See Figure 1). The participants gestures were then recorded using a Kinect sensor with a 3 dimensional co-ordinate point system which recorded the participant's joint locations at 24 frames per second. An HD video camera also recording the exact gesture so as to confirm the validity of the data recorded by our Kinect sensor.

Below we present the most common gestures as recorded by the Kinect sensor from our participants. At least five of the ten participants needed to reproduce an interaction (judged by visual inspection by three investigators) in order for us to accept it and integrate the action into the AugDesk. We do not accept the interactions as being the best fit for the task at this point, something that needs to be determined by user testing; these actions constitute a starting point for us to develop the system and begin experimentation. A visual list of these actions can be seen in Figure 2.

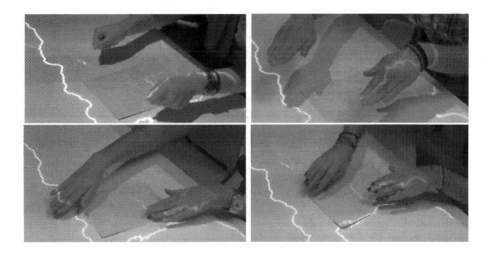

Fig. 1. Most Popular Zooming Gestures (Stretch and Condense)

Select Document from List. The first action is to select a document from the results list located on the left of the screen. The most common interaction here was for the user to move the left hand toward the pile of document on the left in an up-and-down arc fashion and pull the document in front of him while almost touching the table.

Next Page Navigation. We asked users to tell us how they would choose to navigate to the next page as each document can currently only show one page at a time. The user places the hand almost touching the table on the document in front of him and moves the hand to the left a distance of over 20cm without vertical distance alteration.

Previous Page Navigation. We asked users to tell us how they would choose to navigate to the previous page in a document. The user places the hand almost touching the table on the document in front of him and moves the hand to the right a distance of over 20cm without vertical distance alteration.

Enlarge (Zoom In) Document. We asked our users how they would enlarge the document in order to zoom in on the material. The user places both hands almost touching the table surface at the two edges of the document. The right hand is usually placed on the top right part of the document and the left hand is placed on the bottom left of the document. The user then moves the hands away from each other. The action is similar to the 'zoom in' on a touch screen device but we see it produced on a larger scale using gestures.

Scale Down (Zoom Out) Document. We asked our users how they would decrease the size of the document in order to zoom out of the material. The user places both hands almost touching the table surface close to the two edges of the document. The right hand is placed on the top right quadrant of the document

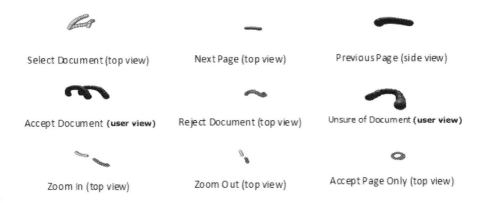

Fig. 2. Most popular 3D gestures for common actions as captured by a Kinect sensor on participants wrist joints (presented from the optimal camera angle for easier viewing)

and the left hand is placed on the bottom left quadrant of the document. The user then moves the hands closer to each other. The action is similar to the 'zoom out' on a touch screen device but we see it produced on a larger scale using gestures.

Accept Document. We asked our users to show us what they would do when they deemed a document to be relevant to the information need and would like to select it to read later. The most popular action was to move the document higher up in front of the user, either by using one hand or both hands. The action could either be using an arc fashion to move the document or simply by sliding it forward.

Reject Document. When asked to show us how a document would be rejected if deemed not relevant, users would "throw it away" off the table by sliding it to the right bottom part of the table to the right side of the user.

Unsure of Document. When studying the actions of user during document triage using physical documents, Buchanan and Loizides discovered that users often place some documents in a pile representing a 'undecided' pile [2]. This are documents that may possibly be looked at later in order to make a more informed decision on. We asked our participants to show us what they would do when they are not sure about the relevance of a document and are likely to want to view it later. The most popular behaviour was to place the document back into the pile rather than having an individual pile. We hypothesise that this behaviour (which is currently at odds with the behaviour from previous work) will possibly change when a user test will happen with the interactions integrated into the system.

Accept Page Only. We also wanted to test for an interaction that would allow the user to accept and save only one page; namely the page that is currently in view. The most common gesture was to circle the document, either by a larger circle using the palm of ones hand or by using a finger to circle the page. The second scenario, could not be detected by the Kinect sensor (but was captured by the camera recording) since the wrist joint did not move during the interaction.

3   AugDesk System Description

The three main parts of this system (See Figure 3 (a)) are: 1) A physical desk 2) A projector 3) a camera 4) a Kinect sensor (soon to be replaced by the more suitable Leap motion system). The physical desk is not a flat 2D surface but rather a desk populated with physical objects that interact with the digital ecosystem. The software prototype is created with VVVV[2], a graphical/textural programming environment designed to facilitate easy development of media environments for physical interfaces and motion graphics. The Kinect sensor is integrated into the environment and by closely monitoring the hand joints of the users we can perform gestural analysis and project a representation of the hand position and orientation on the desk.

The physical desk is split using a projection into 4 sections (See Figure 3 (b)). On the left side of the desk, we have a list of papers which are under review. Currently, we have the first page being shown, with the title and the abstract highlighted for quick browsing. When a paper is selected, it 'locks' in the middle bottom part of the desk on an inclined surface (for an easier viewing angle for the user to read the information). Moving to the next or previous page is achieved by the gentle movement of a hand to the left (previous page) or the right (next page). If the user decides that this paper is suitable, then he/she can push it towards the 'relevant documents' section. If the user decides that this paper is not suitable, then by moving his/her hand towards the physical waste basket, located on the floor on the right side of the user, the system identifies that the current paper is no longer needed and deletes it from the on table contents. Finally, if the user is not sure yet whether the paper is suitable or not, he/she can gently move it back to the results list for further/future consideration. The spatial area on the desk of the sections 'relevant documents', and 'unsure' are determined by physical objects which are placed on the table by the user. These physical objects (currently an open file folder for 'relevant documents' along with the waste basket for 'not relevant' documents) are tracked by a camera vision system. When the user is done with the selection process, by placing his/her phone on a pre-defined space on the desk, the system forwards all the selected papers to the user. Currently, this is achieved by sending all the files on a dropbox[3] folder synchronized to the account of the user. All the information is projected and mapped on the surface from a projector sitting on top of the system and the hand gestures are captured by the Kinect sensor. As there is no finger recognition with the Kinect system, a decision has been made to shift the technology to the leap motion sensor as soon as it becomes available. This system is ready and operational and it serves as a good prototype to get feedback and make improvements.

---

[2] `vvvv.org`

[3] `https://www.dropbox.com/`

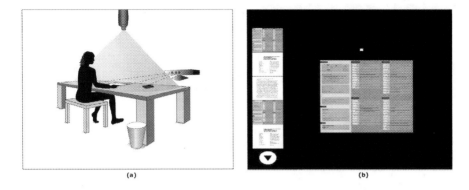

Fig. 3. (a): the setup for AugDesk. (b): the projection displayed.

4   Conclusions and Future Work

In this paper we began investigating how to integrate the virtual with the physical in a common everyday process of looking through academic documents. We presented an initial study that identified natural preferred interactions by users within a virtual environment and continued by describing the architecture in terms of hardware as well as software of the initial version of AugDesk, a dedicated novel, portable, low cost system for document triage. Using an iterative design process we aim to develop the system further and test with a larger participant group as to the usability of the gestures and the entire system in general. Furthermore, we aim to test the system with both left handed as well as right handed individuals to experiment for differences. We hypothesise that all the different user groups will behave similarly in interaction but will vary more in the needs for actions. Finally, we aim to try and reduce the cost as well as increase the mobility of the system by using different technologies such as pico projectors. Lastly, we wish to investigate how AugDesk can be used to facilitate collaborative information seeking for multiple users.

References

1. Bae, S., Badi, R., Meintanis, K., Moore, J.M., Zacchi, A., Hsieh, H., Marshall, C.C., Shipman, F.M.: Effects of display configurations on document triage. In: INTER-ACT 2005. LNCS, vol. 3585, pp. 130–143. Springer, Heidelberg (2005)
2. Buchanan, G., Loizides, F.: Investigating document triage on paper and electronic media. In: Kovács, L., Fuhr, N., Meghini, C. (eds.) ECDL 2007. LNCS, vol. 4675, pp. 416–427. Springer, Heidelberg (2007)
3. Dourish, P.: Where the action is: The foundations of embodied interaction. MIT Press, Cambridge (2001)
4. Loizides, F., Buchanan, G.R.: Performing document triage on small screen devices. part 1: Structured documents. In: Proceedings of the Third Symposium on Information Interaction in Context, IIiX 2010, pp. 341–346. ACM, New York (2010)

5. Merleau-Ponty, M.: Phenomenology of Perception. trans. Colin Smith, London (2005)
6. Ullmer, B., Ishii, H.: The metadesk: models and prototypes for tangible user interfaces. In: Proceedings of the 10th Annual ACM Symposium on User Interface Software and Technology, UIST 1997, pp. 223–232. ACM, New York (1997)
7. Ziemke, T.: Whats that thing called embodiment. In: Proceedings of the 25th Annual Meeting of the Cognitive Science Society, pp. 1305–1310. Lawrence Erlbaum, Mahwah (2003)

The Role of Search Interface Features during Information Seeking

Abdigani Diriye[1], Ann Blandford[2], Anastasios Tombros[3], and Pertti Vakkari[4]

[1] Carnegie Mellon University, Pennsylvania, USA
[2] University College London Interaction Centre, University College London, UK
[3] Department of Computer Science, Queen Mary University London, UK
[4] School of Information Sciences, University of Tampere, Finland
adiriye@cs.cmu.edu, a.blandford@ucl.ac.uk,
tassos@eecs.qmul.ac.uk, ti.vakkari@uta.fi

Abstract. In this paper, we examine the role search interface features play in information seeking across different categories and complexities of search tasks. We present a system called Search Buddy that provides features to enable exploration, filtering and browsing of information. Differing categories and complexities of search tasks were studied through qualitative and quantitative methods. We find specific user patterns in the frequency, points and context of search interface usage. This study highlight the potential value of contextualizing interface features to the type of task and stage of information seeking.

1 Introduction

A variety of interface features exist to help search engine and digital library users search, browse and find useful information. Examples include related searches, document summaries and query autocomplete. Each of these are intended for different purposes and play different roles in the user's information seeking.

System designers and researchers have several design approaches in their toolbox to help them construct search engine and digital library interfaces: for example the eight "golden rules" for interface design; the user-centered design process; task analysis; and interface design patterns like Yahoo's and Endeca's. Given these tools, we find that there is little theoretical work that puts forward a solid explanation to how different search engine and digital library interface features are used or what their role or importance is. To design and construct supportive search interfaces, we need to understand more about the utility of these interface features. In this paper we present a user study that examines the role of interface features on peoples information seeking.

2 Background

Search interfaces and search tasks are well studied topics. Search tasks vary in terms of complexity, clarity, and the search activities involved. A number of

T. Aalberg et al. (Eds.): TPDL 2013, LNCS 8092, pp. 235–240, 2013.

studies show these factors invariably affect how searchers interact with information [4] [6]. Studies into different search interfaces have found features on search engine and digital library interfaces like faceted navigation are useful for browsing tasks [9]; query autocomplete have been shown to be perceived as useful for well-defined tasks [8]; and related searches are known to be useful for complex tasks [3]. Research has also looked at the relationship between search tasks and search interfaces. Washington carried out a field study that looked at how search interface features support jobs tasks at a large public institution [7], and found that depending on the task at hand, users want additional content or different layouts. Divoli and Medelyan conducted a qualitative study evaluating the usefulness of digital library interface features by bioscientists [2], and came to the conclusion that there are preferences for certain search features over others. Paul and Morris developed a collaborative search system that supports sensemaking via several activity views [5], and found their participants used different search views for different collaboration modes and task types. Vakkari et al. analyzed how information searching and IR is connected with tasks [6]. They found that different task stages affect peoples search tactics, term selections and relevance judgements. More recently, Diriye et al. in [1] carried out work that explored the relationship between search tasks and search interfaces and found that interfaces have an impact on information seeking.

Some work has been carried out on search interfaces and search tasks, but there still is a dearth of work that closely examines their relationship. This paper extends previous work by: (i) examining the role and utility of search interface features; and (ii) studying several different search interface features.

3   System Design

We constructed a rich and highly interactive search interface that enables all the major search activities involved in known-item and complex and exploratory search tasks such as lookup, browsing and learning [4]. Search Buddy provides a search box and list of search results that provide the user with the ability to lookup and navigate documents; search filters and related searches on the left-hand pane to assist in browsing, filtering, identification and exploration; and "starter pages", a novel feature that promotes learning by presenting documents that are of a general nature. The search interface features designed support different kinds of search actions and activities. In Figure 1, we see a screenshot of the search interface. Search Buddy works by retrieving search results using the Bing API. The search filters are generated by using the search result captions (i.e. the title, snippet and URL) to generate labels for topics latent in the search results. The Lingo clustering algorithm was used to organize search results into topics. The related searches, found on the left-hand side, are scraped from Google, and the starter pages were created by identifying authoritative and popular resources.

Fig. 1. Screenshot of the Search Buddy interface. 1= search box; 2 = search filters; 3 = related searches; 4 = starter pages; 5 = recommended sites; 6 = search result caption.

4 Study Design

The study had a 2 x 2 factorial design: two different categories of search tasks (known-item and exploratory) and two different levels of complexity (low and high). We developed a rich search interface to provide a diverse range of search actions and activities during usage. We decided to focus on only one search interface as our interest lay in studying how the search interface was used during information seeking. We collected qualitative and quantitative data using questionnaires, interviews, eye-tracking and system logs, and we logged our participants interactions at the search feature-level and the task-level.

4.1 Methodology

Each user study lasted up to an hour, and our participants were paid £7 each for their time. A Graeco Latin square design was used to permute the search tasks. The study procedure began with the participant being informed of the aim of the study, afterwards, each participant was asked to select a search tasks from each of the four categories of search tasks and rate them, and explain how they plan on completing the task. They would then perform the task whilst using the Tobii eye-tracking machine; gather information to address the task into a text file; complete a questionnaire on how useful and helpful the search features were; and finally provide feedback on the rationale behind their usage of the search features. After the study, each participant was required to fill out an exit questionnaire comparing the search features for the different search tasks. Finally, the participant was thanked and paid for their time.

4.2   Participants

We recruited 24 participants via a university participant pool. The participants ages ranged from $18 - 51$ (mean $= 27.1$ years) and our sample comprised 8 males and 16 females. The participants all expressed familiarity with popular search engines like Google, Yahoo and Bing, and reported having at least 6 years of online searching experience (mean $= 8.8$ years), and they all rated their computer proficiency between average and excellent.

5   Results

The data is focused around two core themes: 1) the impact the search tasks have on information seeking; and 2) the usage and impact of the search features during the search tasks.

5.1   Perceptions of Search Features

After each search task, our participants were asked to complete a questionnaire eliciting their perceptions on how useful, helpful and important the search features were during the search task. Statistical analysis revealed that there were significant differences between the search features (all: $F_{3,22} = 16.432$, p $<.000$), but our participants could not perceive any differences between the search tasks (all: $F_{3,22} <1.480$, p $<.158$). This means despite the fact that some search features were perceived as more or less useful for certain search tasks, this trend was not apparent for all search tasks.

Search Interface Feature Usage. According to the data from our system logs, that specific search feature usage was not statistically significant across any of the search tasks (starter pages: $F_{3,23} = 1.319$, p $= .275$; related searches: $F_{3,23} = 1.668$, p $= .182$; search filters: $F_{3,23} = 1.470$, p $= .238$). But, there were significant differences in the total usage of search interface features for each search task (total: $F_{3,23} = 4.334$, p $= .049$). What this means is that though we could not find a relationship between specific search features and specific search tasks, there was an increase in the number of search support features used as the search task became more complex and exploratory. We also found a significant difference between the number of queries and documents selected across the different search task (queries: $F_{3,23} = 8.029$, p $<.001$; docs selected: $F_{3,23} = 12.604$, p $<.001$).

Points of Search Interface Usage. Using our system logs and screen recording, we examined the points in time search features were used.We can also see in the figure a peak in the usage for the search box. 50% of the queries formulated via the search box was concentrated in the $2^{nd} - 4^{th}$ minutes of our participants search tasks, whereas usage of the search filter and related searches remained steady across the entire duration of the search tasks. A chi-squared test showed these figures were significant ($\chi_2 = 113.6$, p $<.017$). This data highlights the

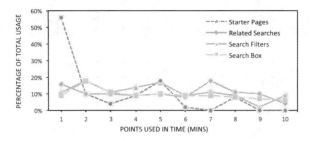

Fig. 2. Time intervals search features were used across all the search tasks

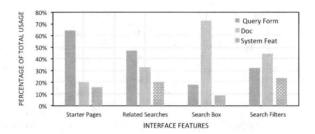

Fig. 3. Preceding user actions prior to use of interface features

differences in how these system features were used amongst our participants across the search tasks. The starter pages were found to be mostly used at the start of the search tasks to find general information, and subsequently used less frequently when more specific information was required. Other features like the search filters and related searches were utilized throughout the search task.

Context of Usage. Our system logs and screen recording reveal search features were used after leaving a document, manually formulating a query, or after using other search features. In Figure 3, we present the frequency of usage. The starter pages and search box were associated with specific contexts. Queries were reformulated using the search box feature after our participants would leave a document over 73% of the time. The most popular sequence of search behaviours involved returning from a document and then reformulating the query using the search box feature. Similar search sequences were evident for the starter pages. 64% of usage of the starter pages occurred after the searcher had formulated a query. In all, search features like the search box and starter pages can be context and search stage specific, whereas features like the search filters and related searches were used uniformly across the different search stages and contexts.

6   Discussion

The findings in this paper verify search features are context and search stage specific: search interface features like the search box and starter pages were used heavily at the start of the search tasks, and within specific contexts like after a query reformulation or document selection. Other search features like the search filters and related searches were more flexible and used uniformly across the different search stages and contexts. This indicates that search features play different roles on the user interface. Some search features like the starter pages and search box are search stage-specific features that are useful at certain points during information seeking or search contexts; other search features like the search facets and search filters are search stage *agnostic* features, and afford the user a generic set of search actions and activities at any stage of their information seeking.

Although we did not find significant differences in how useful, helpful or important the search features were perceived to be across the different search tasks, we did find significant differences in how frequently the search features were used. The data reveals that as the search tasks became more complex and exploratory, and required more search action and strategies to complete, the total number of search features used on the features increased.

In the post-task interviews our participants identified using the search features based on the attributes of the search task they were undertaking, or as a result of their search habits, and in some cases as a fallback mechanism when the search box and search results failed to help them find relevant information. This further substantiates the finding that search features support as well as impede information seeking [1].

Our findings have implications for the design of search interfaces: interface features have been shown to be search stage and search task sensitive, this puts the case forward for adaptive interfaces that present interface features that suit a user's particular search context and stage. This could be search contexts where the system deciphered the user is engaged in like look-up or identification, and thus promotes the use of certain interface features like search filters, or cases where the users search tasks appears to be exploratory or informational, and so search features like starter pages or related searches are promoted.

References

1. Diriye, A., Blandford, A., Tombros, A.: When is System Support Effective? In: Information Interaction in Context, IIiX 2010 (2010)
2. Divoli, A., Medelyan, A.: Search interface feature evalua-tion in biosciences. In: HCIR 2011, Google, Mountain View, CA, USA (2011)
3. Fowkes, H., Beaulieu, M.: Interactive searching behavior: Okapi experiment for TREC-8. In: Proc. BCS-IRSG, pp. 47–56 (2000)
4. Marchionini, G.: Exploratory search: from finding to understanding. Commun. ACM 49(4), 41–46 (2006)
5. Paul, S.A., Morris, M.R.: CoSense: enhancing sensemaking for collabora-tive web search. In: Proc. of CHI, pp. 1771–1780 (2009)
6. Vakkari, P., Pennanen, M., Serola, S.: Changes of search terms and tactics while writing a research proposal. Inf. Process. Manage., 445–463 (2003)
7. Washington, A.: Discussing Design: How search interface features support job tasks in an institutional repository. In: Proc. of AMCIS (2006)
8. White, R.W., Bilenko, M., Cucerzan, S.: Studying the use of popular destinations to enhance web search interaction. In: Proc. of SIGIR 2007, pp. 159–166 (2007)
9. Yee, K.-P., Swearingen, K., Li, K., Hearst, M.: Faceted Metadata for Image Search and Browsing. In: CHI 2003(2003)

Users Requirements in Audiovisual Search: A Quantitative Approach

Danish Nadeem[1], Roeland Ordelman[1,2], Robin Aly[1], and Erwin Verbruggen[2]

[1] University of Twente, Enschede, The Netherlands
[2] Netherlands Institute for Sound and Vision, Hilversum, The Netherlands

Abstract. This paper reports on the results of a quantitative analysis of user requirements for audiovisual search that allow the categorisation of requirements and to compare requirements across user groups. The categorisation provides clear directions with respect to the prioritisation of system features from the perspective of the development of systems for specific, single user groups and systems that have a more general target user group.

1 Introduction

A key component for the "business model" that allows the significant investment in restoration, conservation and digitisation of audiovisual content is to enable its access. The data quantities that audiovisual archives are dealing with on the one hand, and the needs for content descriptors that vary depending on the access requirements of different user groups on the other hand, force archives to re-evaluate their annotation strategies and access models. Advanced search technology on top of automatic content analysis and social tagging strategies plays an important role in these access models but its implementation can only be successful provided that it aligns well with user needs.

In this paper we zoom in on the requirements that users have when they engage into searching an audiovisual archive using advanced search technology. Typically, user requirement studies use qualitative methods (e.g., [2]), transaction log analysis (e.g., [4]) or investigated specific parts of a system such as browsing interfaces for a digital library consisting of videos [8]. Although qualitative user studies provide valuable insights into the diversity of requirements specific to users, content features or system parts, it is usually difficult to translate the results directly into guidelines that help development and implementation. Therefor, we deploy a *quantitative* approach that allows us to categorise user requirements according to different user groups and to prioritise the implementation of system features for each group. We anticipate here on the assumption that each group may require its own specific implementation of the system.

In order to structure the needs of different groups of users and allow a quantitative comparison of groups, we use the so-called "concept mapping" method [11,5] that combines a structured data collection approach with various types of data analyses such as multidimensional scaling (MDS) [7] and hierarchical cluster analysis (HCA) [3]. Concept mapping has been applied to a wide range of topics, such as the needs analysis for social recommendation system [10], defining the concepts of mobile learning [1] and the evaluation and design of digital libraries [9]. This paper reports on this quantitative approach.

T. Aalberg et al. (Eds.): TPDL 2013, LNCS 8092, pp. 241–246, 2013.
© Springer-Verlag Berlin Heidelberg 2013

2   Method

Concept mapping consists of two phases: first, the idea generation phase, followed by the sorting and rating of the ideas. In the idea generation phase, participants are asked to provide their individual ideas –also referred to as "statements"– about a particular topic. In our study those statements represent requirements. In the sorting and rating phase, participants are provided with the statements generated by all of the participants. The task is then to order the statements, e.g., on the basis of importance as perceived by the individual participant of the study. In addition, participants are instructed to group statements into categories and provide for each category a meaningful label, i.e., a textual description of the category. The criteria for categorising statements are left to the participant.

When different groups of participants are selected to take part in the study –e.g., based on gender or profession–, appreciation of statements and correlations between groups of statements can be compared across these groups.

For our study we slightly change the standard procedure of the concept mapping method. Instead of asking participants to generate ideas on audiovisual search, we use a list of 71 "ideas" collected in previous requirements studies [6] on audiovisual search in interview sessions, group elicitation sessions using mock-ups, and on-line surveys focusing on the different user groups. The reason for following this approach is that we estimate that by leaving the generation of statements to the participants, we run the risk of ending up with a sparse list of statements due to the unfamiliarity of participants with audiovisual search. By introducing the main concepts of audiovisual search and showing participants mock-ups and prototype systems, this unfamiliarity issue could be solved during earlier studies, but such an approach is logistically not feasible for the concept mapping study.

We translated the 71 requirements from the interview and elicitation sessions into comprehensive statements. As it is important that the statements are self-explanatory and unambiguous for individuals that are not acquainted with audiovisual search technology, we convert the technically oriented formulation of requirements into a form that is understandable for non-experts.

2.1   User Groups and Participants

We differentiate into three groups –broadcast professionals, academic researchers and journalists, and home users– based on a study on use scenarios and user goals (targets) related to the use of audiovisual access technology that took place in the course of the earlier requirements studies mentioned above. Within the group that we label as media professionals we identify broadcast professionals, focusing on searching for relevant audiovisual content for *reuse*. As the target goal of the academic educators (*educate*) may include targets from both the journalist group (*investigate*) and academic research group (*research*) we leave out academic educators. The target for the home users we label as *entertainment/edutainment*.

In total 47 representatives from each of the three user groups take part in the concept mapping study. For the broadcast professionals group, we invited 15 individuals, 14 scholars from the humanities and 3 journalists represent the "academic researchers and journalists" group and a total of 15 home users matching a pre-defined profile – familiarity with computer work (using applications such as Facebook and YouTube) but without any background knowledge on audiovisual search technology– participate.

2.2 Rating Procedure

We use a web-interface to present the statements in random order and tell the participants that the statements were generated by asking potential users the following trigger question: *What would you like from a system when you are searching for videos?* We then ask the participants to categorise the statements according to perceived similarity, providing them with the following instructions: first read through the complete list of statements; then, categorise the statements by either creating a new category for a statement, or moving a statement to an already created category; make sure that every statement is put somewhere; finally, label each category with a description that represents the category as good as possible.

Participants are free to sort the statements into as many groups as they like although they are informed that in most cases using 10-20 groups should work out well. After sorting the statements, we ask the participants to rate each of the statements according to *desirability* on a scale between 1 and 5 where 1 means undesirable and 5 means very desirable.

3   Results

3.1   Requirements Categorisation

Using the category labels created by participants in combination with an analysis of the keywords that are present within the statements, we identify 10 categories of user requirements, listed in the left column of Table 1.

In Figure 1 the 10 categories are visualised with labels for the individual categories. The amount of layers (e.g., one layer for the category "Search recommendation" and three layers for "Search accuracy") give a visual indication of the desirability of the statements in the particular categories.

The average rating for each of the categories is provided in the right column of Table 1. The category *User-defined search functions* has only four statements but each statement is rated high so that it achieves the highest overall rating. This suggests that this category of requirements is very important for system development. When we look at the statements connected to this category, it is interesting to note that from a technical point of view these requirements relate to different aspects of search: ordering of results, application of filters and the use of Boolean operators during search. This suggests that during system development the implementation of these requirements should not be addressed in isolation.

The high ranking of the category "Help functions" also stands out. When looking at the individual statements of this category however, we see that the category label may be misleading. With "Help functions" one may expect system functionalities within this category such as represented by the statement: "The system should include a help

Table 1. Categories and their average rating

Category	Average Rating
User-defined search functions	4.49
Help functions	4.30
Advanced search options	4.13
Search accuracy	3.99
User personal search history	3.95
Browser friendliness	3.74
Save search history	3.73
Feedback, share and social media	3.60
Search recommendation	3.31
Technical features	3.13

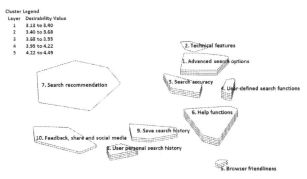

Fig. 1. Visualisation of a 10-category map with category labels. The layers give a visual indication of the average desirability rating for that category.

manual that explains how to use the system". However, the requirements in this category rather point to a smooth, clear and transparent functioning of the system: results that load quickly, being able to view and navigate through the videos, transparent about filters that are active, alternatives for spelling mistakes, consistent results for a query, a clear and user-friendly interface, and of course also guidance for using the system via manuals.

In the light of the discussion about the re-evaluation of annotation strategies and access models in audiovisual archives, the high ranking of requirements related to "Advanced search functionalities" is interesting. The statements in this category indicate that users are eager to make use of complex search strategies for searching, are interested in alternative access-points to the collections such as persons (who is speaking, who appears) and events, and are willing to deploy alternative types of annotations such as speech transcripts. However, according to the category labelled with "Technical features" users seem to have less interest in searching on the basis of annotations that are often associated with technical metadata such as shot types, camera movement and black and white versus colour.

Fig. 2. Comparison of requirement category ranking of academics/journalists vs. broadcast professionals (a) and of broadcast professionals vs. home users (b)

3.2 User Group Comparison

To compare the ranking of requirement categories across the identified user groups we compute the correlation of requirements categories between groups. Figure 2 (a) shows for the academic researchers and the broadcast professionals the average desirability of requirement categories. Although the correlation between the two groups is relatively high ($r = 0.83$) it is clear that some categories are ranked rather differently, such as the category "User personal search history" that is highly desired by the academics group and less by the broadcast professionals. In contrast and as expected, broadcast professionals are more interested than academics in searching the more technical features of videos.

Similarly, Figure 2 (b) illustrates how broadcast professionals compare with home users with respect to the ranking of requirement categories. The correlation between these two groups is again relatively high ($r = 0.78$). The most notable differences between the groups are the substantially higher rating of browser friendliness (e.g., working on various brands and on mobile devices) and personal search history (e.g., saving search histories) by home users, and again the higher preference for searching technical information with the broadcast professionals.

4 Conclusion and Future Work

In this paper we report on the results of a quantitative analysis of user requirements for audiovisual search. We apply a method referred to as concept mapping to structure requirements that were obtained using a combination of qualitative requirement studies, and compare these across three types of users: home users, academic researchers and journalists, and broadcast professionals.

The analysis provides us with a ranked list of 10 categories defined by users that give clear directions with respect to the prioritisation of system features from both an individual and a multiple user group perspective. For example, the study reveals the relative importance for all user groups of three aspects of a search system: (i) the proper handling of basic search functions such as Boolean search, filtering and result presentation,

(ii) the clear, smooth, consistent and transparent functioning of the system as a whole, and (iii) the availability of advanced search options with alternative access-points to the collections.

With respect to the comparison of different user types, we found that broadcast professionals compare better with academics and journalists than with home users, and that a category such as *Technical features* are typically desired by broadcast professionals. On the other hand, a category such as *Help functions* is more desired by home users and academics compared to broadcast professionals.

Acknowledgments. The work reported in this paper was funded by the EU Project AXES (FP7-269980) and the Dutch national program COMMIT.

References

1. Börner, D., Glahn, C., Stoyanov, S., Kalz, M., Specht, M.: Expert concept mapping study on mobile learning. Campus-Wide Information Systems 27(4), 240–253 (2010)
2. Cunningham, S.J., Nichols, D.M.: How people find videos. In: JCDL, pp. 201–210 (2008)
3. Everitt, B.: Cluster Analysis, 2nd edn. Halsted Press, A Division of John Wiley and Son, New York (1980)
4. Huurnink, B.: Search in Audiovisual Broadcast Archives. PhD thesis, University of Amsterdam (2010)
5. Kane, M., Trochim, W.: Concept Mapping for Planning and Evaluation. Sage Publication, Thousand Oaks (2007)
6. Kleppe, M., Kemman, M., Beunders, H.: User Requirements Report V1. In EU Project No. 269980 AXES (2011), http://www.axes-project.eu/wp-content/uploads/2011/10/ AXES-D1.2.pdf
7. Kruskal, J.B., Wish, M.: Multidimensional Scaling. Sage University Paper Series on Quantitative Applications in the Social Sciences, vol. 31. Sage Publications (1978)
8. McKay, D., Shukla, P., Hunt, R., Cunningham, S.J.: Enhanced browsing in digital libraries: Three new approaches to browsing in greenstone. Int. J. on Digital Libraries 4(4), 283–297 (2004)
9. Mead, J.P., Gay, G.: Concept mapping: An innovative approach to digital library design and evaluation. SIGOIS Bull. 16(2), 10–14 (1995)
10. Nadeem, D., Stoyanov, S., Koper, R.: Using concept mapping for needs analysis for a social support system in learning network. iJIM 5(1), 41–46 (2011)
11. Trochim, W.: An introduction to concept mapping for planning and evaluation. In: Trochim, W. (ed.) A Special Issue of Evaluation and Program Planning, vol. 12, pp. 1–16 (1989)

Hierarchical Structuring of Cultural Heritage Objects within Large Aggregations

Shenghui Wang[1], Antoine Isaac[2], Valentine Charles[2], Rob Koopman[1],
Anthi Agoropoulou[2], and Titia van der Werf[1]

[1] OCLC Research, Leiden, The Netherlands
[2] Europeana Foundation, The Hague, The Netherlands

Abstract. Huge amounts of cultural content have been digitised and
are available through digital libraries and aggregators like Europeana.eu.
However, it is not easy for a user to have an overall picture of what is
available nor to find related objects. We propose a method for hierarchically structuring cultural objects at different similarity levels. We
describe a fast, scalable clustering algorithm with an automated field
selection method for finding semantic clusters. We report a qualitative
evaluation on the cluster categories based on records from the UK and
a quantitative one on the results from the complete Europeana dataset.

1 Introduction

More and more Cultural Heritage (CH) content is being digitised and made
available through digital libraries and aggregators such as Europeana.eu and
the new Digital Public Library of America (`dp.la`). These aggregators provide
access to large numbers of heterogeneous Cultural Heritage objects (CHOs), *e.g.*,
Europeana gathers over 26 million objects (books, sound recordings, movies...)
contributed by over 2,200 institutions from all over Europe.

Metadata plays a crucial role for these aggregations, which are largely relying on mappings from the original metadata, created by providers in many
different formats and vocabularies, to a shared vocabulary like the *Europeana
Semantic Elements* (ESE). However, aggregating metadata from heterogeneous
collections raises quality issues such as uneven granularity of the descriptions,
ambiguity between original and derivative versions of the same object, even
duplication if different providers give access to a same object. Also, simple,
common-denominator vocabularies like ESE are inappropriate for capturing *internal semantic links* between objects (*e.g.*, parts of an object, adaptations of a
work, objects representing others) or *external links* to contextual entities (*e.g.*,
places or persons related to an object). Both types of link could benefit services
like Europeana by enabling a wider range of search and browsing options, as for
example in [10].

There are many efforts in the cultural domain to enable and encourage the
provision of richer and interoperable metadata, *e.g.*, CIDOC-CRM[1] and the

---

[1] http://www.cidoc-crm.org/

T. Aalberg et al. (Eds.): TPDL 2013, LNCS 8092, pp. 247–259, 2013.

new Europeana Data Model (EDM).[2] And yet, many providers do not have the resources to enhance their metadata in the way envisioned by these approaches, especially for links spanning *across* different collections. *Data enrichment* in aggregations such as Europeana is therefore valuable.

Meanwhile, keyword-based search is still the main access and navigation mechanism for such aggregations. Recommendations for similar object browsing are often provided, *e.g.*, one can "Explore further" in Europeana, using Solr's default "MoreLikeThis" function.[3] Still, in such facilities it is difficult for a user to have an overall picture of what is available or to find objects with different levels of relatedness. Researchers have started looking at automatically identifying related CHOs [2,3,7]. However, the existing work has mostly focused on one dimension of similarity despite the multidimensional characteristics of the cultural domain. For example, a portrait of one person could be linked to other portraits of the same person, or to portraits of the people who held the same office. Moreover, it often stayed at a small scale and could not process datasets as large as Europeana's.

This paper presents a feasibility experiment on semantic linking for a general, large cultural aggregation. We focus on *internal* links between objects from the aggregated collections, with a specific eye on enabling better-quality "similar object" browsing. The issue bears similarity with "FRBRization" in the library domain [9]. However, given the variety of collections, as well as the simplicity of the current metadata, it is deemed more realistic to consider a wider range of object relations: duplication (recognizing records that describe a same object), depiction/representation, derivation (an object has been created by reworking another), succession (an object continues another one), *etc.*

In this paper, we try to answer the following research questions: (1) can we apply clustering to find semantic groups at different similarity levels? (2) what types of useful relationships can we extract with this technique?

To this end, we propose a framework for hierarchically structuring objects at different similarity levels in Section 2, including a fast and scalable clustering algorithm and an automated field selection method for finding focal clusters. In Section 3, we report a qualitative evaluation on the cluster categories based on records from the United Kingdom and a quantitative evaluation on the results from the complete Europeana dataset.

2   Hierarchical Structuring Based on Levels of Similarity

We aim at finding related Europeana objects at different levels of similarity, which potentially reflect different semantic relations between them. As depicted in Fig. 1, we provide clusters at five similarity levels. A user could thus explore the collections to find CH objects with five different levels of relatedness. We now describe our framework in three parts: (1) fast clustering based on minhashes and compression similarity (Section 2.1), (2) automatically selecting important fields

---

[2] http://pro.europeana.eu/edm-documentation
[3] http://wiki.apache.org/solr/MoreLikeThis

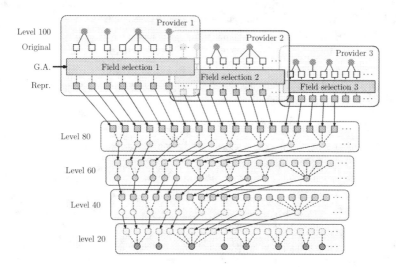

Fig. 1. Hierarchical structuring of CHOs at different similarity levels. White squares indicate original records which are clustered at level 100. Based on genetic metadata field selection, the original records are represented by selected fields and clustered at level 80. Then clusters at a level (circles) are summarised into new artificial records (rounded squares at the level below). These are then clustered at the lower level, together with the objects that were not yet clustered.

based on genetic algorithm to generate *focal semantic clusters* (Section 2.2), and finally (3) hierarchically structuring records at different similarity levels (Section 2.3).

2.1   Clustering Based on Minhashes and Compression Similarity

Grouping Records Using Combined Minhashes. Records should be clustered based on certain kinds of similarity. Because of the sheer amount of records in the dataset, calculating the pair-wise similarity between all records is practically impossible and also unnecessary. Therefore we first group records which could potentially be further clustered based on a *bag-of-bits* approach.

For each record, the metadata from all fields is combined and divided into words, with numbers removed. Long words (>8 characters) are transformed into 8-grams [13].[4] A set of minhashes [4] from these words and 8-grams are calculated and randomly put into 4 groups.[5] The logical operation exclusive disjunction (XOR) is applied to each minhash group, producing 4 combined

---

[4] Necessary for more precise grouping, although at the cost of recall.

[5] The size of groups depends on the desired similarity level. At level 100, 16 minhashes are randomly chosen for each group, while at level 20, only 2 minhashes are chosen. Thus clusters at higher similarity levels have higher probability to be precise than those at lower levels. We could use more groups and minhashes, but our general design alleviates this need: we only need reasonable similarity values and can afford finding, *e.g.*, different duplicates at the highest levels, as in Table 4.

minhashes. Thus, every Europeana record is represented by four combined min-hashes. Records with the same combined minhashes are grouped together, as they are the ones that are most likely to be clustered further on.

Iterative Parallel Clustering Based on Compression Similarity. The clustering process is iterative as follows:

Step 1 Choose a similarity level and set the maximum iteration.[6]

Step 2 Group records based on combined minhashes, as described above, and put the groups on a stack

Step 3 Get a group of records from the stack if the stack is not empty, otherwise, go to Step 7

Step 4 From the group, randomly select up to 10 records as *cluster heads* that are not closer than the required similarity.[7]

Step 5 Assign each record within this group to its closest cluster head, which, after all records are assigned, creates candidate clusters.

Step 6 For each candidate cluster, if the average similarity between the cluster head and the rest of the records is lower than the required similarity, put this group of records on the group stack to be further divided. Otherwise, this cluster is considered to be a real cluster. All the records are considered as *clustered* to the cluster head and will not join the next iteration.

Step 7 Collect all the records which are not clustered, together with the current cluster heads, repeat Step 3 to 6, until no more records can be clustered or the maximum iteration has been reached.

The similarity between records is calculated using a formula from the Normalised Compression Distance (NCD) [5]. Let x and y be two records, $C(xy)$ the compressed size of the concatenation of x and y, $C(x)$ and $C(y)$ the compressed size of x and y. Then the similarity between x and y is defined as $sim(x,y) = 1.0 - \frac{C(xy) - min(C(x), C(y))}{max(C(x), C(y))}$.

Note, a large part of the clustering process (steps 3 to 6) is implemented as multi-thread computing, making it very fast and scalable to all Europeana data.

2.2 Field Selection at Level 80 for Focal Semantic Clusters

As shown in Fig. 1, all metadata fields are used to find (near-)duplicates. Checking a set of clusters at level 80, one can easily find that some are of specific interest, *e.g.*, pages of the same book, parts of a same building, *etc.* These clusters are often in a collection from one data provider. They are more loosely connected than clusters of (near-)duplicates, because they gather different cultural objects. Yet their records collectively represent a small cultural entity. We

---

[6] In our experiments, the maximum iteration is set at 5 as this allows the program to reach the desired recall. This can be set higher but at the cost of performance.

[7] Experiments show no strong relation between this value and cluster quality; 10 proved better in terms of run time.

name these clusters *focal semantic clusters* (FSC). These FSCs can be further clustered at lower similarity levels as described in Section 2.3.

However, detecting such FSCs is not easy. The Europeana data is obtained from a wide range of providers. The information associated with each record is not uniform, since providers use different metadata schemes originally and enrich their records with different amounts of textual information. Take the example of digitised book pages. One provider may assign exactly the same metadata to all the pages of the same book while another may give a detailed description of each page of an illuminated manuscript. For the latter, if all the metadata fields were used for clustering, the large body of descriptive texts could falsely separate pages of the same book into different smaller clusters. It is therefore important to select the most important metadata fields for clustering these FSCs. As shown in Fig. 1, such selection is done on a data provider basis.

For each data provider, we aim at the selection of metadata fields which gives the best FSCs. We apply a genetic algorithm (GA) to automatically select important fields, that is, taking an evolutionary approach to select the optimal solution based on a fitness function [15]. This algorithm handles candidate solutions as binary sequences, "1" when a metadata field is selected and "0" otherwise. For example, if a given institute provides metadata records with dc:title, dc:contributor, dc:subject and dc:source, then a candidate solution 1010 indicates clustering on dc:title and dc:subject only. In the Europeana dataset, dc:title is the most used and often the only descriptive field. Given its importance, we therefore decided to set it as compulsory for each data provider's solutions.[8]

The fitness function is to evaluate how good a solution, *i.e.*, a selection of metadata fields, is to produce reasonable clusters. We adapted a measure of variance ratio clusterability [1] as our fitness function: Let X be a dataset, and C a set of clusters over X. The fitness function is defined as following: $f(C, X) = log(Avg(C)) \times \frac{B_C(X)}{W_C(X)}$, where $B_C(X)$ is the between-cluster distance, $W_C(X)$ is the within-cluster distances and $Avg(C)$ is the average size of the set of clusters. This function gives higher fitness (*i.e.*, a higher chance to be selected for the next generation) to tightly connected clusters that are relatively big and far apart.

For the genetic evolution, clustering is set at level 80: first insights (see Sec. 3.1) hinted that it was the "sensitive level" for finding such FSCs. Original records are represented by the metadata from the fields selected in the best GA solution, and clustered again at level 80. Clustering at level 60 and lower uses all fields again: it invites broadly linked records to be clustered and potentially corrects the bias towards links within individual providers at level 80.

2.3   Hierarchically Structuring Records Based on Similarity

Duplicates and FSCs can be further clustered at lower similarity levels. *E.g.*, different pictures of buildings could be clustered, and these pictures could be clustered with census records on the same area at an even lower level.

---

[8] Note, either dc:title or dc:description are mandatory for data input in Europeana; when dc:title is not available, we take dc:description as the compulsory field.

Therefore, after calculating the FSCs at level 80, we generate an artificial record from each cluster, gathering in each metadata field its values for all clustered records. These artificial records, together with all the records which could not be clustered at level 80, will join the clustering process at level 60. We again cluster at level 40 and 20 in the same way. In the end, hierarchies of records are generated, so that one can have some structural information about these records, instead of quickly getting drowned in the sheer amount of data.

3   Results and Evaluation

3.1   Qualitative Evaluation and Categorisation of Clusters

To prepare formal evaluation, while tuning our method, we qualitatively discussed hundreds of intermediate results generated from 1.1M records from UK. We started by looking at the representation and metadata of the clustered records on `Europeana.eu`. We also browsed the hierarchy of clusters produced, giving specific attention to how smaller clusters combine into bigger clusters and allowing us to find meaningful clusters for a given (set of) object(s), independently from their level in the hierarchy.

At that stage, the clusters were still sometimes rough and our evaluation not wide enough for us to claim that they were representative. However, this semi-principled analysis offered us precious insight on the typology of groupings, which looked both useful and relatively complete as it covers a broad extent of the relations that EDM covers.

Same Objects/Duplicate Records. This is the strongest similarity relationship found in clusters. Europeana datasets come via different channels: individual institutions, European projects, thematic portals... It is possible to receive multiple records for the same object from the same institution.[9] A quality control failure during the data ingestion process can let duplicates be published in the Europeana portal. Clustering allows us to identify these duplicates with a high degree of accuracy; often the exact same metadata appears in many fields.

Views of the Same Object. Digitisation practices often lead providers to create different views of the same CHO. These views happen to be provided as different CHOs but they are actually different views on the same "real object," see Fig. 2. Such clusters usually share exactly the same descriptive metadata.

Parts of an Object. CHOs provided to Europeana can have a hierarchical structure: they are composed of other objects or parts. However, digitisation and description choices by providers, or the barrier of a simplified data format can result in the data describing this structure not being provided to Europeana. The clustering process allows us to find clusters of objects linked by such relationships. In principle relations between different parts of a CHO or between

---

[9] For   example,   see   `http://www.europeana.eu/resolve/record/09307/` `2FFD07620AFC6500C005DAC1D0AFCF6A31778A88` and `http://www.europeana.eu/` `resolve/record/09307/772B1D83F4727C4DEEEF763C300D5315FC1EBEAA`

Fig. 2. (a) Different views of the same portrait (Mary of Teck) – (b) Derivative prints

Table 1. Parts of a CHO—a music piece made of different individual music scores

Shared metadata	Record
dcterms:spatial : City of London	The Oil Shop part 01
dcterms:medium : Lithograph	The Oil Shop part 03
dc:creator : Composer: Dallas, John	The Oil Shop part 04
dc:date : [1873]	The Oil Shop part 05
dcterms:isPartOf : Victorian popular music. Collect Britain	The Oil Shop part 06
dc:format : jpeg	The Oil Shop part 07
dc:type : Cover Illustrated Music Printed StillImage	The Oil Shop part 08

CHOs should be expressed in relation fields (dc:relation) but the clusters indicate that providers often use dc:title, see Table. 1. In the latter case, an automatic procedure would have difficulty making the distinction with other types of relations.

Derivative Works. These are objects which are derived from another one, such as reprint. Fig. 2 shows two different prints created from the same master.[10] Some cases can be analysed in terms of FRBR relationships, where an original *work* leads to a range of *expressions, manifestations* and/or *items*. The metadata of the concerned records are often the same, except the dc:description field, which usually indicates that the object is a copy or other type of derivative.

Collections. Clusters can represent coherent collections. They group objects of a specific type, gathered by one individual, for a specific goal. For example, the letters shown in Fig. 3 were written by one specific WWI soldier and contributed by a family member to the *Europeana1914-1918* project. Object metadata is often similar, with the dc:relation field expressing membership in a specific collection.

Thematic Groupings. These clusters gather objects about a similar topic, location or event, which link them to the other collections above. However, they often lack the size or an explicit unity criterion such as common provenance (*e.g.*, a collector) that would allow them to be assessed as complete collections. In fact we have found such individual clusters included in bigger ones, which have been

---

[10] http://www.europeana.eu/resolve/record/09405a1/
49EADC41C49A4C6F14C626EB067EB7D3F9131632 and
http://www.europeana.eu/resolve/record/09405a1/
1A3460CBB5FE76A1CD4433F7FFA052C34A982934

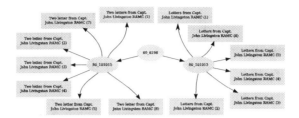

Fig. 3. An example of collection clusters

Table 2. Field selection for FSCs (clusters at level 80)

	#Providers	metadata field		#Providers	field combination
1	2358	dc:title	1	1521	dc:title
2	436	dc:type	2	37	dc:title dc:type
3	328	dc:language	3	28	dc:title dc:creator
4	315	dc:rights	4	23	dc:title dc:identifier
5	309	dc:subject	5	20	dc:description

(a) Top 10 most selected fields   (b) Top 5 most selected field combinations

classified as collections in the sense above. These clusters have in common some metadata fields that are related to a similar theme, most often dc:subject.

Conclusion. During our qualitative evaluation, we observed that clusters of "closely related" objects, such as duplicates or parts of a CHO are easier to assess. Recognising clusters describing broader links, such as topical relationships, seems a more difficult, error-prone process, both for human evaluators and the machine. In order to check our finished clustering method, we proceeded further with a more complete, quantitative evaluation over the entire dataset.

3.2   Quantitative Manual Evaluation on the Full Europeana Dataset

Working Dataset. The entire Europeana data was made available as a dump on February 2013. It contains 23,6M records from 2428 data providers (defined by europeana:dataProvider field, or europeana:provider when it is not present).

Field Selection for FSCs. 1198 individual data providers provided more than 100 records and cover 99.9% of the entire dataset. We applied the genetic algorithm to select the important fields over these providers.

We used a python package Pyevolve,[11] setting the number of individuals at each generation to 50 and the maximum number of generations to 100. The time taken by field selection depends on the number of records one provider has. For the 10 providers with most records (covering 35% of the whole Europeana dataset), it takes 161 minutes in average, while datasets with 200-250 records require 21 minutes in average. Table 2 lists the top 5 most selected metadata fields and the most selected field combinations. For an overwhelming majority

---
[11] http://pyevolve.sourceforge.net/

Table 3. Clustering performance (* Level 80 is clustered differently due to the field selection based on GA, see Section 2.2 for more detail)

Similarity level	#Records to be clustered	#Clusters	Time
100	23,595,555	200,245	6m2.82s
80	23,595,555	1,476,089	*
60	6,407,615	382,268	3m35.26s
40	2,431,753	212,389	2m28.79s
20	1,068,188	84,554	1m20.99s

of data providers, dc:title carries the most distinguishing information. In the end, we use the metadata from the selected fields for each provider to generate the FSCs at level 80. For the rest of the data providers, we select dc:title directly. This leads to 1,476,089 clusters in total.

Hierarchical Structuring of Records. The clustering was carried out on a server with two Intel XEON E5-2670 processors and 256G memory. Table 3 gives the clustering time per level. As described in Section 2.3, clusters generated at higher levels lead to artificial records replacing the *clustered* records for the lower levels. This greatly reduced the amount of items to be clustered at lower levels.

Clusters are hierarchically ordered across similarity levels. In Fig. 4, at the record level (the bottom grey boxes), one can see the sibling records. These can be closely clustered at level 80 (in pink), or more vaguely connected (at level 40 in blue). These clusters can again be clustered at level 20 (brown). When more records are involved (the size of level 20 clusters ranges from 2 to 456,155, with an average size of 190), such structural information is crucial to make sense out of a large amount of records.

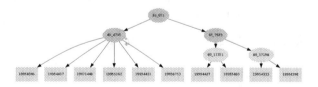

Fig. 4. Hierarchical view of records

Manual Evaluation. For lack of resources, we could not build a gold standard of manually clustered collections for evaluation. Picking "small" collections (hundreds of objects) may bias our effort towards specific domains or subjects: Europeana lacks the collection survey tools that would warrant their representativity. On the other hand, manually clustering cross-institution national aggregators like Hispana.mcu.es (2M objects) is out of reach and perhaps also biased by the country or language. To evaluate our method and the categories from Section 3.1 on the full Europeana dataset, we randomly chose 100 clusters at each level and asked 7 evaluators to categorise them.

Table 4. Manual evaluation results

Cluster Category	Similarity Level				
	100	80	60	40	20
Same objects/duplicate records	11	10	1	0	0
Views of the same object	61	33	6	2	5
Parts of an object	10	11	3	1	2
Derivative works	2	1	0	0	0
Collections	1	4	27	13	43
Thematic grouping	9	34	36	29	22
Nonsense	2	3	30	57	28

Clusters were assigned to evaluators so that each cluster is checked at least by two evaluators. For each cluster, the evaluators assigned one of the six categories from Sec. 3.1 or indicated if it did not make any sense. Evaluators could leave comments and propose new categories if necessary. Many comments were given but no new category was proposed. We measured for each level the average number of clusters that are assessed as belonging to each category.

As shown in Table 4, duplicate records and views or parts of the same CHO are mostly clustered at levels 100 and 80. At these levels we also found different editions of the same work, different volumes of the same book, pictures of the same event, *etc.* Note that the latter illustrates how thematic groupings also appear as clusters at the highest level. Derivative works are rare and only occur at high levels. Lower levels lead to bigger, more heterogeneous clusters, many of which fall into the categories of collections or thematic groupings while many of which do not make much sense any more. These big clusters could contain views of different buildings, issues of the same journal, different books by the same author, pictures taken at the same place but at different time, pictures of different sarcophagi and ships, collections of religious or folk music, theses of the same university, specimen of birds, posters about movies or Communist movements, or more vaguely, collections of furniture or Spanish books, *etc.*

The general impression from the evaluators is that most clusters make sense. At level 60, it is often clear that the records form a "collection" according to some implicit logic; but in most cases the original provider sites did not present them as explicit collections. So the clustering was being creative and yet correct.

However, assessing clusters gets more difficult as the similarity level lowers. It is often difficult to recognise any specific logic beyond more general and over-arching rules like: "belonging to same data provider", "being of the same type", *etc.* This is especially so at level 20, where the average size of the evaluated clusters is 3442, ranging from 2 to 60,204, with 11 clusters having more than 10,000 records. It is not possible to manually go through them one by one. Many clusters are also in a language which the evaluators are not familiar with, which made them even more difficult to assess. The evaluators only selected as many sub-clusters as possible to explore the rough structure within such big clusters.

Of course, not every cluster at level 20 is too big to judge. For example, one is composed of two (higher-level) sub-clusters that each corresponds to an edition of a multi-volume book. While these are represented as hierarchical objects on the provider's site[12] this information could not reach Europeana. Solr's More-LikeThis returns the volumes of both editions, but as a flat, mixed list that includes other books—some tests on Europeana even fail to bring all volumes of both editions as suggestions when one of them is explored.

In summary, our evaluation shows the clusters are rather relevant. The two highest levels, especially, could directly provide meaningful subsets for users of a "similar items" browsing feature. However, clusters, especially at lower similarity levels, are much more heterogeneous than we initially thought. We need to make more detailed distinction between these clusters. The next step of detecting these different categories automatically is a more challenging task.

4   Related Work

Providing similar objects for access to large collections is not novel. Europeana itself uses Solr's "MoreLikeThis." But such standard search engine features are designed for full-text documents and suffer from the heterogeneity and sparseness of the metadata, resulting often in lists that seem random and unidimensional. Clustering can provide more structured query-dependent snippets [16], but such work focus on grouping objects *after* a search, and often for smaller and/or homogeneous collections. Amazon.com exploits users' input to infuse more relevance in similar items. But the necessary user data is not available for cultural aggregators yet. Others have explored using image similarity instead [6] or next to [2] descriptive metadata. However, digitized content is not available consistently in cross-domain aggregations, where media types and quality vary greatly.

Tuning textual similarity to CH metadata is therefore still relevant. [3,11] have used the standard corpus-based similarity measures of [13]. Recently, researchers started looking at using external knowledge bases such as Wikipedia [7] or WordNet [14] to help measuring similarities between objects. Different similarity measures were compared [8,3] but most existing works explore a single dimension of similarity, which does not take into account the multidimensionality of CH collections; it also focuses on smaller-scale collections. The extraction of FRBR-like relations, a topic researched for more than a decade [9,12,17], has been a clear source for inspiration for us. It requires however collections from well-bounded domains with extensive and consistent metadata, and would need to be completed with techniques with a broader application scope. Our work tries to complement these efforts, further exploring the aspects of scalability and the typing and organizing of clusters of similar objects.

5   Conclusion

Identifying semantic links and groups of CH objects is desirable for data enrichment in large cultural aggregations. Finding similar objects is the first step

---

[12] See `http://www.biodiversitylibrary.org/bibliography/14916#/summary` and `http://www.biodiversitylibrary.org/bibliography/931#/summary`

towards such semantic links. Our approach avoids too much dependence on metadata fields and the multidimensionality they denote. Instead, we try to hierarchically structure Europeana objects at different levels, starting with a rather simple similarity measure. We developed a fast and scalable clustering algorithm and applied a genetic algorithm to select important fields for generating focal semantic clusters. We qualitatively evaluated intermediate results from UK records before carrying out a larger-scale quantitative evaluation of the results obtained from the entire Europeana dataset.

We found that clusters at higher similarity levels are usually accurate and make sense to evaluators, *e.g.*, as duplicates or parts of a CHO. The relevance of lower-level clusters is much more difficult to judge. Even at higher levels, our evaluation shows that based on a single dimension of similarity we generate highly heterogeneous clusters. We need to investigate more multidimensional similarity measures while maintaining the performance levels for clustering large amounts of data. Future work shall of course include the practical evaluation of hierarchical structuring for improving end-user navigation.

References

1. Ackerman, M., Ben-David, S.: Clusterability: A theoretical study. Journal of Machine Learning Research - Proceedings Track, 1–8 (2009)
2. Aletras, N., Stevenson, M.: Computing similarity between cultural heritage items using multimodal features. In: Proc. 6th EACL Workshop on Language Tech. for Cultural Heritage, Social Sciences and Humanities, pp. 85–92 (2012)
3. Aletras, N., Stevenson, M., Clough, P.: Computing similarity between items in a digital library of cultural heritage. J. Comput. Cult. Herit. 5(4), 16:1–16:19 (2013)
4. Broder, A.Z.: On the resemblance and containment of documents. In: Compression and Complexity of Sequences (SEQUENCES 1997), pp. 21–29. IEEE Computer Society (1997)
5. Cilibrasi, R., Vitanyi, P.M.B.: Clustering by compression. IEEE Transactions on Information Theory 51, 1523–1545 (2005)
6. Gennaro, C., Amato, G., Bolettieri, P., Savino, P.: An Approach to Content-Based Image Retrieval Based on the Lucene Search Engine Library. In: Lalmas, M., Jose, J., Rauber, A., Sebastiani, F., Frommholz, I. (eds.) ECDL 2010. LNCS, vol. 6273, pp. 55–66. Springer, Heidelberg (2010)
7. Grieser, K., et al.: Using ontological and document similarity to estimate museum exhibit relatedness. J. Comput. Cult. Herit. 3(3), 10:1–10:20 (2011)
8. Hall, M., Clough, P., Stevenson, M.: Evaluating the Use of Clustering for Automatically Organising Digital Library Collections. In: Zaphiris, P., Buchanan, G., Rasmussen, E., Loizides, F. (eds.) TPDL 2012. LNCS, vol. 7489, pp. 323–334. Springer, Heidelberg (2012)
9. Hickey, T.B., O'Neill, E.T., Toves, J.: Experiments with the IFLA Functional Requirements for Bibliographic Records (FRBR). D-Lib Magazine 8(9) (2002)
10. Hyvönen, E.: Publishing and Using Cultural Heritage Linked Data on the Semantic Web. Synthesis Lectures on The Semantic Web. Morgan & Claypool (2012)
11. Knoth, P., Novotny, J., Zdrahal, Z.: Automatic generation of inter-passage links based on semantic similarity. In: The 23rd International Conference on Computational Linguistics (COLING 2010), Beijing, China (2010)

12. Manguinhas, H., Freire, N., Borbinha, J.: FRBRization of MARC records in multiple catalogs. In: Joint International Conference on Digital Libraries (JCDL), pp. 225–234 (2010)
13. Manning, C.D., Raghavan, P., Schtze, H.: Introduction to Information Retrieval. Cambridge University Press (2008)
14. Mihalcea, R., Corley, C., Strapparava, C.: Corpus-based and knowledge-based measures of text semantic similarity. In: Proc. 21st National conference on Artificial intelligence (AAAI 2006), vol. 1, pp. 775–780 (2006)
15. Mitchell, M.: An Introduction to Genetic Algorithms (Complex Adaptive Systems). A Bradford Book, MIT Press (1999)
16. Papadakos, P., Armenatzoglou, N., Kopidaki, S., Tzitzikas, Y.: On exploiting static and dynamically mined metadata for exploratory web searching. Knowl. Inf. Syst. 30(3), 493–525 (2012)
17. Takhirov, N., Duchateau, F., Aalberg, T.: Supporting FRBRization of Web Product Descriptions. In: Gradmann, S., Borri, F., Meghini, C., Schuldt, H. (eds.) TPDL 2011. LNCS, vol. 6966, pp. 69–76. Springer, Heidelberg (2011)

Methodology for Dynamic Extraction of Highly Relevant Information Describing Particular Object from Semantic Web Knowledge Base

Krzysztof Sielski, Justyna Walkowska, and Marcin Werla

Poznań Supercomputing and Networking Center,
ul. Noskowskiego 12/14, 61-704 Poznań, Poland
{sielski,ynka,mwerla}@man.poznan.pl

Abstract. Exploration and information discovery in a big knowledge base that uses a complex ontology is often difficult, because relevant information may be spread over a number of related objects amongst many other, loosely connected ones. This paper introduces 3 types of relations between classes in an ontology and defines the term of RDF Unit to group relevant and closely connected information. The type of relation is chosen based on association strength in the context of particular ontology. This approach was designed and implemented to manipulate and browse data in a cultural heritage Knowledge Base with over 500M triples, created by PSNC during the SYNAT research project.

Keywords: Semantic Web, ontology, OWL, RDF, CIDOC CRM, FRBRoo, RDF Unit, RDF Molecule, knowledge base.

1   Introduction

Semantic Web is often conceptualized as a big graph consisting of billions of edges and vertices. Exploring such a graph by its direct visualization is appealing, but often inconvenient due to the graph's overwhelming size and high density around some vertices. A popular way of accessing information stored in such a base is via a SPARQL interface, which is very powerful, but requires detailed knowledge about the chosen ontology and the SPARQL language itself. In case of very complex ontologies, extracting composite pieces of relevant information about a particular object is difficult.

During the SYNAT[1] project we built the Knowledge Base using the FRBRoo ontology [1]. This base contains metadata of several million cultural heritage objects

---

[1] SYNAT project, financed by Polish National Center for Research and Development (grant number: SP/I/1/77065/10), is aimed to conduct a research task titled "Creation of universal, open, repository platform for hosting and communication of networked resources of knowledge for science, education and open society of knowledge", which is a part of Strategic Research Programme "Interdisciplinary system of interactive scientific and technical information".

T. Aalberg et al. (Eds.): TPDL 2013, LNCS 8092, pp. 260–271, 2013.
© Springer-Verlag Berlin Heidelberg 2013

aggregated from tens of Polish institutions using the Clepsydra system[2] [2]. The purpose of this Knowledge Base is to serve as an advanced data source for implementation of new features in Polish Digital Libraries Federation (http://fbc.pionier.net.pl/) – a national cultural heritage metadata aggregator [3].

The data in the Knowledge Base originates from heterogeneous sources, such as libraries and museums. It was originally represented in various xml-based flat or hierarchical metadata formats and had to be normalized and mapped to fit the ontology model. Single input metadata record e.g. in MARC XML or PLMET schema after mapping to FRBRoo creates an RDF graph consisting of tens of URIs and even hundreds of triples. After mapping all the data from our sources, enhancing it with additional information from external data sources, aligning it with Linked Open Data (such as VIAF, Geonames or Lexvo), and adding inferred relations between resources, the resulting Knowledge Base is represented by a large coherent graph [4]. In such a graph the actual boundaries of a single record are often fuzzy, and deciding which information is relevant for the final user is not obvious. For this reason, a methodology for dynamic and automatic extraction of subgraphs from the Knowledge Base was introduced. The aim was to achieve a subgraph which contains: all highly relevant information about one resource, all references to another relevant resources and relations to other, loosely associated resources.

The remainder of the paper is organized as follows. Section 2 describes a classification of relations between classes in any OWL ontology into three groups: dependent, attribute and loose. On the ground of these concepts, in Section 3 a new term RDF Unit is introduced as a new level of information in RDF-based knowledge base. The implementation of this methodology is described in Section 4. The application of developed concepts in manipulating data and knowledge exploration is presented in Section 5. The paper ends with a short summarization of the achieved results and with conclusions.

The described methodology is meant to be of generic purpose, but was originally built over FRBRoo and hence all the examples in this article use classes and relations from this ontology. For this reason, the next subsection presents a few comments on FRBRoo.

1.1   FRBRoo

FRBRoo [5] is an event-centric ontology which extends the cultural heritage-oriented CIDOC CRM [6] ontology with FRBR [7] concepts representing bibliographic records. It is made up of 119 classes and 178 properties. The OWL implementation of both CIDOC CRM and FRBRoo is available as Erlangen CRM / OWL [8]. One considerable feature of this implementation is that almost all the properties have their inverse equivalents. There are only two exceptions to this rule: a symmetric P133_is_separated_from and asymmetric P139_has_alternative_ form. Thanks to this, describing a resource involves examining only triples where

---

the resource is used as an subject, not an object (contrary to the default SPARQL DESCRIBE query behavior which returns all triples where the passed resource is either subject or object).

2   Metaproperties for Relations between OWL Classes

OWL allows to express qualified or unqualified cardinality constraints for properties. Such constraints are defined in FRBRoo, for instance P4_has_time-span is quantified as many to one, necessary, dependent (1,1 : 1,n). It means that every E2_Temporal_Entity must have at least one E52_Time-Span and every E52_Time-Span must have exactly one E2_Temporal_Entity. This is a fact about the universe but – due to the Open World Assumption – the actually stored data can be incomplete and there might exist an instance of E52_Time-Span not connected with an instance of E2_Temporal_Entity and vice versa, while the knowledge base remains consistent.

In order to ensure that the knowledge base contains comprehensible information about objects, some additional constraints about the data should be maintained. Incomplete information in such systems is inevitable, but for some applications deficient data is not valuable: e.g. a E52_Time-Span object that is not describing any E2_Temporal_Entity carries no information. To describe relations between concepts in the ontology, 3 metaproperties for ObjectProperties are proposed (presented below in order of descending association strength, with FRBRoo based examples):

Dependent Relations – link main resources to subsidiary objects which cannot exist without the main resource. An example of such property is P4_has_time-span where object of range E52_Time-Span exists only to express time information about subject of domain E2_Temporal_Entity. It is similar to the foreign key constraint with cascade delete from relational database vocabulary. The set of all dependent properties in the ontology is denoted as D.

Attribute Relations – they add important information about the subject but object and subject are independent resources. An example of such property is P14_carried_out_by which links an instance of E7_Activity with instance of E39_Actor – a participant of the activity which can exist on its own. The set of all attribute properties in the ontology is denoted as A.

Loose Relations – they link loosely related objects. Example is P129i_is _subject_of which links E1_CRM_Entity with E89_Propositional_Object. The set of all loose properties in the ontology is denoted as L.

Every ObjectProperty in the ontology must be qualified as either dependent, attribute or loose. The three sets D, A and L are mutually disjoint.

By default, metaproperties are inherited in property hierarchy, but a subproperty can override the relation type, specifying a stronger one: a subproperty of a loose property can be of any type, a subproperty of an attribute property might be either attribute or dependent and a subproperty of a dependent property must be dependent.

There is no correlation between the metaproperty of a property and the metaproperty of inverse property. There are examples of all relation type transitions after inverting (except for loose relations that are inverse of dependent relations – such case does not exist in our interpretation of FRBRoo):

- `R16_initiated` and `R16i_was_initiated_by` are both dependent
- `P88_consists_of` and `P88i_forms_part_of` are both attribute
- `R1_is_logical_successor_of` and `R1i_has_successor` are both loose
- `P72_has_language` is attribute but `P72i_is_language_of` is loose
- `P131_is_identified_by` is dependent but `P131i_identifies` is attribute

The assignment of metaproperties for ontology relations may differ in various applications depending on the intended purpose and the specificity of the data. Particularly, the distinction between attribute and loose relations is non-obvious in some cases. For instance, one may argue that `R1_is_logical_successor_of` is an attribute relation, which is contrary to our interpretation where it is loose. Such classification decisions based on semantic nuances would have an effect on the amount of information which would be collected to describe a certain resource by using the methodology described in the remaining part of this paper.

3   RDF Unit

By using the relation metaproperties introduced in the previous section, a new granularity level in RDF graph can be introduced to enhance analyzing content of Semantic Web knowledge base: RDF Unit. This concept represents a set of triples from RDF graph that comprehensively and relevantly describe a particular resource. The RDF Unit for the resource R (identified by URI) includes:

- all triples $(R\ p\ o)$ where p is a DataProperty,
- all relations to closely related concepts i.e. triples $(R\ p\ o)$ where p is an attribute property,
- all RDF Units of dependent concepts, i.e. triples $(R\ p\ R')$ where p is an dependent property and RDF Units of resource R'.

RDF Unit does not include references to loosely related concepts.

Definition 1 (RDF Unit). Let G be an RDF graph defined as a set of triples $G = \{(s\ p\ o)\}$, $IODP$ – set of DataProperties in ontology, D – set of dependent properties, A – set of attribute properties. RDF Unit $U_G(R)$ of a resource R in graph G is defined as follows:

$$U_G(R) = \{(R\ p\ o) \in G : p \in IODP \vee p \in A\} \cup \bigcup_{R':(R\ p\ R') \in G \wedge p \in D} U_G(R')$$

The RDF Units are not necessarily mutually disjoint or equal. This is a consequence of the fact that inverse properties often have different metaproperties and RDF Units of closely related resources might be overlapping in any degree. Particularly, according to the definition, dependent relations imply recursive inclusion of RDF Units for objects of triples. For this reason, RDF Units that are not proper subsets of any other RDF Unit will be called maximal because they carry the maximum amount of connected information. Formally:

Definition 2 (Maximal RDF Unit). $U_G(R)$ is maximal $\Leftrightarrow \neg \exists_{R'} U_G(R) \subset U_G(R')$

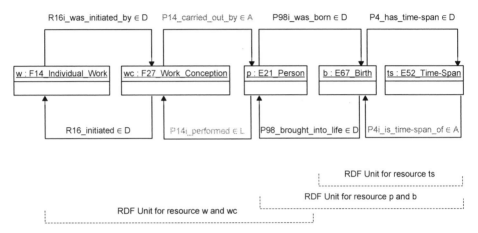

Fig. 1. Sample data modeled in FRBRoo and represented as a graph. It consists of 5 instances of different classes connected by 8 relations of different association strength. Boundaries of RDF Units for each resource are marked. Subgraphs $U_G(w) = U_G(wc)$ and $U_G(p) = U_G(b)$ are maximal but $U_G(ts)$ is not maximal because $U_G(ts) \subset U_G(p)$

3.1 Note on Terminology

RDF Molecule is a term used to describe behavior of RDF indexing feature in Owlim triplestore [9] and is defined as a sub-graph including starting node and its neighboring nodes that are reachable via the specified number of predicate arcs. This feature proved to be helpful and appropriate in full text search over the triplestore and was the base to the concept of RDF Unit, which has similar purpose but does not take into consideration the distance between nodes (only types of properties) and is more semantically than structurally grounded.

The same term *RDF Molecule* was proposed in [10]. That article defines RDF molecules as lossless and finest subgraphs of RDF graph according to a particular decomposition. RDF Units introduced in this article are indeed lossless (i.e. it is possible to restore original graph without adding new triples) but not finest (i.e. they can be further decomposed into lossless subgraphs because some molecules can include other molecules). Moreover, RDF Molecules address the problem of merging graphs with blank nodes, which is beyond the scope of this paper.

RDF Molecule definitions in the above mentioned articles stand for particular subgraph of RDF graph, but both have slightly different meaning and purpose. RDF

Unit has only some features common to any of them. Therefore, to avoid confusion, the new term was introduced.

4   Implementation

The vocabulary that allows to qualify each ObjectProperty from an OWL ontology into one of three classes was implemented as of two functional DataProperties with boolean values: isAttribute and isCascade. Each ObjectProperty in FRBRoo ontology has both properties assigned. The types of relations are defined using the two mentioned properties in the following way (expressed in the Manchester Syntax):

```
Class: DependentRelation
EquivalentTo:
    ObjectProperty and
    isAttribute value "true"^^xsd:boolean and
    isCascade value "true"^^xsd:Boolean

Class: AttributeRelation
EquivalentTo:
    ObjectProperty and
    isAttribute value "true"^^xsd:boolean and
    isCascade value "false"^^xsd:Boolean

Class: LooseRelation
EquivalentTo:
    ObjectProperty and
    isAttribute value "false"^^xsd:boolean and
    isCascade value "false"^^xsd:Boolean
```

Following the constraints of metaproperty inheritance in property hierarchy, the ontology is not consistent if any of the following conditions occur (here DL notation $R \sqsubseteq R'$ is used to denote that R is a subproperty of R'):

- $\exists_R$ R isAttribute false and R isCascade true
- $\exists_{R,R':R \sqsubseteq R'}$ R isAttribute false and R' isAttribute true
- $\exists_{R,R':R \sqsubseteq R'}$ R isCascade false and R' isCascade true.

The presented implementation of metaproperties with only two functional DataProperties is simple and does not require any modifications to the ontology. Collecting triples that form an RDF Unit for any resource can be achieved by directly following the definition of RDF Unit.

Another important operation on data in a triplestore is *delete*. This operation on a resource in knowledge base includes removal of the whole RDF Unit for that resource so that no orphaned dependent resources are left. The *delete* operation means removing all triples where the resource is a subject or object (including triples with loose relations as predicate, which do not belong to the RDF Unit) and recursive *delete* operation of dependent objects, i.e. resources *R'* such that a triple *(R p R')* exists and *p* is a dependent relation: *(p isCascade true)*. This behavior is somehow similar to removing a row in a table in relational database, which references a row in another table, if foreign key constraint with cascade delete exists (all URIs and blank nodes in triples can be regarded as equivalents to foreign keys in databases as they are unique identifiers of resources).

5   Application in Knowledge Base Browser

Each property from FRBRoo was individually analyzed and assigned metaproperties. This process involved making decisions that were dependent primarily on relation semantics and quantifiers described in the ontology documentation. Apart from this, the quantity of information obtained from our sources, its structure implied by mapping rules designed by us and the predicted expectations of Knowledge Base users were taken into consideration.

The data in the Knowledge Base comes from heterogenic sources such as library catalogues (NUKAT), digital libraries (DLF), museum catalogues (The National Museum in Warsaw, The National Museum in Krakow), authority files (VIAF, KABA) and other databases (e.g. Geonames). The process of information integration begins with mapping data into FRBRoo ontology using the jMet2Ont tool [11] with mapping rule sets individually designed for each provider and format. A sample bibliographic record from source data provider is shown in Fig. 2.

```
<plmet:metadata>
<dc:title>Figliki albo rozlicznych ludzi przypadki dworskie
      [...]</dc:title>
<dc:creator>Rej, Mikołaj (1505-1569)</dc:creator>
<dc:contributor>Pencz, Georg (ca 1500-1550). Il.</dc:contributor>
<dc:description>Dzieło pierwotnie współwydane z dziełem: Zwierziniec W
      ktorym rozmaitich</dc:description>
<dc:publisher>Drukarnia Macieja Wirzbięty</dc:publisher>
<plmet:placeOfPublishing>Kraków</plmet:placeOfPublishing>
<dc:date>1574</dc:date>
<dc:language>pol</dc:language>
<dc:coverage>16 w.</dc:coverage>
<dc:subject>starodruki 16 w.</dc:subject>
<dc:type>starodruk</dc:type>
<dc:format>image/vnd.djvu</dc:format>
<plmet:locationOfPhysicalObject>Biblioteka
      Jagiellońska</plmet:locationOfPhysicalObject>
<dc:rights>Domena publiczna (public domain)</dc:rights>
<plmet:digitisationSponsor>EFRR POIiŚ 11.1</plmet:digitisationSponsor>
</plmet:metadata>
```

Fig. 2. Sample bibliographic record in the PLMET schema

This record would be mapped to 78 triples which form a graph consisting of 33 nodes and 16 literals (the structure of objects and relations between them is shown on Fig. 3). After mapping all the data from our sources, different URIs that represent the same objects (the same places, works etc.) are linked together and merged. In case of the record from Fig. 2, linked objects include:

- the place of publishing named *"Kraków"* – would be recognized to be the same as resource identified by URI *http:/www.geonames.org/3094802*
- author named *"Rej, Mikołaj (1505-1569)"* – would be recognized to be the same as resource identified by URI *http://viaf.org/viaf/61585459*.

The information from the record can also be extended by another record that is a copy (in FRBR terminology: another item) of the same book. The resulting knowledge base is highly connected and information about objects is enriched in comparison to the original data from single source. This situation is highly desirable but creates a problem: which facts should be presented to a user, if there are no record boundaries? A reasonable solution would be to present the information originating from the source record together, probably enriched with references to resources with deeper information (which can mean e.g. information about place including its population, geographical coordinates or administrative division) and links to another related resources. This is the granularity of information that is meant to be stored in one RDF Unit.

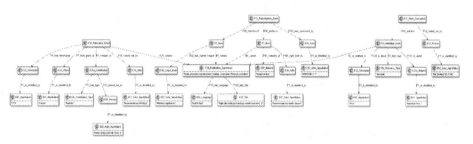

Fig. 3. A structure of graph representing single bibliographic record in FRBRoo ontology

5.1   RDF Unit as a Rooted Tree

Representation of RDF Unit as directed graph as shown in Fig. 3 can be unclear and difficult to understand – it has often complex structure and a big diameter. For that matter, a more approachable graph structure is used in presentation: a rooted tree where the described resource is the root. In general, RDF Units are coherent, but not required to be acyclic, so some conversion might be needed. If a presented RDF Unit has a cycle, it is eliminated by removing the arc that is the most distant from the root. A sample RDF Unit represented as a tree is pictured in Fig. 4. In such a tree, each triple from the RDF Unit becomes a node. Internal nodes (non-leafs) represent triples with dependent properties and are labeled with property label and object class. Leafs represent DataProperties or attribute properties. In the former case they are labeled with property label and object literal value, in the latter they are labeled with property label and object label. Each URI resource from the presented RDF Unit can be further examined in another linked view.

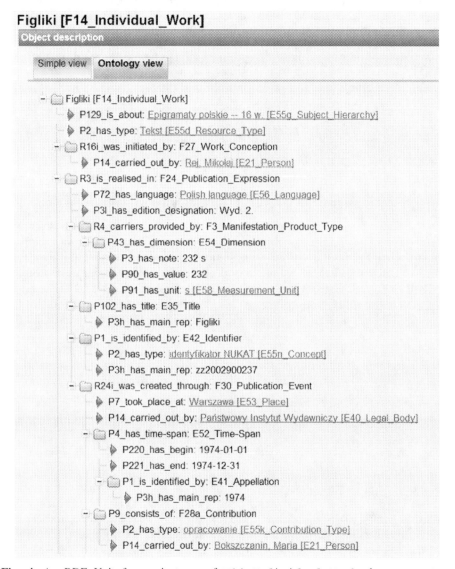

Fig. 4. An RDF Unit for an instance of `F14_Individual_Work` shown as a tree. Underlined expressions link to descriptions of attribute resources

The view is completely dynamic, there are no restrictions about the class of described resource and the process of gathering information and building the graph to be displayed is based entirely on the metaproperties. Since RDF Units of closely related resources can overlap or even be equal, the information presented for them would be similar or the same but because of the rooted tree view, they would be presented in slightly different perspectives e.g. a bibliographical record can be viewed starting from a Work or Work Conception or Item. If presented RDF Unit is not maximal (see definition 2), it can be presented to user, but it often would be reasonable to switch (or at least suggest switching) the view to the maximal RDF Unit to show more relevant information.

A view of the RDF Unit tree is further transformed and simplified to clarify the view by introducing context dependent labels for relations and merging some ontology paths. An example of such view is presented in Fig. 5 (methodology of such conversion is not in the scope of this paper). Although loose relations are not part of RDF Unit, they are very important in Semantic Web and are also presented next to object description tree so that users can browse the Knowledge Base further through them.

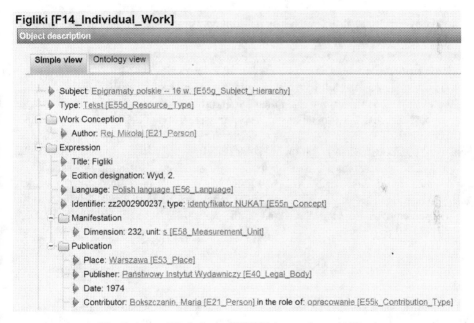

Fig. 5. A simplified view of RDF Unit tree shown in Fig. 4

6   Conclusions

Exploring a dataset represented as a graph which has both sparse and dense components is a challenging issue. In order to obtain all relevant information about a certain resource, it is not enough to analyze its neighboring nodes – for example, in the FRBRoo ontology the place of publication is 4 arcs away from a work entity (it can be reached via the predicate path: R16i_was_initiated_by / R3_is_realised_in / R24i_was_created_through / P7_took_place_at). On the other hand, the set of all neighboring nodes can be superfluous – for example, resources that represent cities would be connected by triples of predicate `P7i_witnessed` to all publication events that took place in that city, which in some cases would be an overwhelming number of loosely connected resources.

Information can be retrieved from a triplestore using `SPARQL` `SELECT` or `CONSTRUCT` queries. While it is a very powerful feature for advanced users who need unrestricted inspection into the knowledge base to find uncommon relationships between objects, it requires good familiarity with the ontology and precisely specified needs.

To facilitate retrieving and exploring information, an application has been built. The first attempt to browse data relied on a set of predefined static `SPARQL` queries which would extract sufficient information about objects. A separate query string had to be prepared for every significant class in the ontology. This approach appeared to be difficult to maintain as successive data sources were introduced and graph structure became more and more complex. In a system where information about any resource is never exhaustive, there is no common graph pattern that would describe all resources in the triplestore, even for instances of the same class. Dynamic construction of RDF Units relying on generic metaproperties proved to be a satisfying solution to this problem.

The presented methodology using simple metaproperties was sufficient to describe relations between classes in our application and in the chosen ontology. However, in some more specific cases it might not be expressive enough because it depends only on properties. The context of a relation determined by subject and object types can change semantics of the relation and conversely – a proper metaproperty of the property. In such situations, a subproperty with stronger association type should be introduced, but this is not always possible in case of predefined ontologies. OWL has a notion of qualified cardinality constraints that can be used to precisely describe property quantifiers that are dependent on the class of object and a similar model can be introduced to the presented methodology to increase its expression.

References

1. Mazurek, C., Sielski, K., Walkowska, J., Werla, M.: From MARC21 and Dublin Core, through CIDOC CRM: First Tenuous Steps towards Representing Library Data in FRBRoo. CIDOC (2012),
   http://www.cidoc2012.fi/en/File/1611/mazurek.pdf
2. Mazurek, C., Mielnicki, M., Nowak, A., Stroiński, M., Werla, M., Węglarz, J.: Architecture for Aggregation, Processing and Provisioning of Data from Heterogeneous Scientific Information Services. In: Bembenik, R., Skonieczny, Ł., Rybiński, H., Kryszkiewicz, M., Niezgódka, M. (eds.) Intell. Tools for Building a Scientific Information. SCI, vol. 467, pp. 529–546. Springer, Heidelberg (2013), http://link.springer.com/chapter/10.1007/978-3-642-35647-6/_32
3. Mazurek, C., Werla, M.: Network of Digital Libraries in Poland as a Model for National and International Cooperation. In: IATUL 2011 Conference: Libraries for An Open Environment: Strategies, Technologies and Partnerships (2011), http://www.bg.pw.edu.pl/iatul2011/proceedings/ft/Werla/_M.pdf

4. Mazurek, C., Sielski, K., Stroiński, M., Walkowska, J., Werla, M., Węglarz, J.: Transforming a Flat Metadata Schema to a Semantic Web Ontology: The Polish Digital Libraries Federation and CIDOC CRM Case Study. In: Bembenik, R., Skonieczny, L., Rybiński, H., Niezgodka, M. (eds.) Intelligent Tools for Building a Scient. Info. Plat. SCI, vol. 390, pp. 153–177. Springer, Heidelberg (2012)
5. Bekiari, C., Doerr M., Le Boeuf, P.: FRBR object-oriented definition and mapping to FRBRER (Version 1.0.2) (2012), http://www.cidoc-crm.org/docs/frbr_oo/frbr_docs/FRBRoo_V1.0.2.pdf
6. Crofts, N., Doerr, M., Gill, T., Stead, S., Stiff, M.: Definition of the CIDOC Conceptual Reference Model, 5.0.2 edition (June 2005), http://www.cidoc-crm.org/docs/cidoc_crm_version_5.0.2.pdf
7. Functional requirements for bibliographic records. Final report, http://www.ifla.org/files/cataloguing/frbr/frbr_2008.pdf
8. Görz, G., Oischinger, M., Schiemann, B.: An Implementation of the CIDOC Conceptual Reference Model (4.2.4) in OWL-DL. In: Proceedings of CIDOC 2008 — The Digital Curation of Cultural Heritage. ICOM CIDOC, Athens (2008)
9. Bishop, B., Kiryakov, A., Ognyanoff, D., Peikov, I., Tashev, Z., Velkov, R.: OWLIM: A family of scalable semantic repositories. In: Semantic Web – Interoperability, Usability, Applicability (2010), http://www.semantic-web-journal.net
10. Ding, L., Finin, T., Peng, Y., Pinheiro da Silva, P., Deborah, L.: Tracking RDF Graph Provenance using RDF Molecules. In: Proceedings of the 4th International Semantic Web Conference (November 2005)
11. Walkowska, J., Werla, M.: Advanced Automatic Mapping from Flat or Hierarchical Metadata Schemas to a Semantic Web Ontology. In: Zaphiris, P., Buchanan, G., Rasmussen, E., Loizides, F. (eds.) TPDL 2012. LNCS, vol. 7489, pp. 260–272. Springer, Heidelberg (2012)

Personalizing Keyword Search on RDF Data

Giorgos Giannopoulos[1,2,*], Evmorfia Biliri[1], and Timos Sellis[3]

[1] School of ECE, NTU Athens
[2] IMIS Institute, "Athena" Research Center
[3] RMIT University, Australia

Abstract. Despite the vast amount on works on personalizing keyword search on unstructured data (i.e. web pages), there is not much work done handling RDF data. In this paper we present our first cut approach on personalizing keyword query results on RDF data. We adopt the well known Ranking SVM approach, by training ranking functions with RDF-specific training features. The training utilizes historical user feedback, in the form of ratings on the searched items. In order to do so, we join netflix and dbpedia datasets, obtaining a dataset where we can simulate personalized search scenarios for a number of discrete users. Our evaluation shows that our approach outperforms the baseline and, in cases, it scores very close to the ground truth.

1 Introduction

Web search personalization is a well known IR problem that has been tackled by a great amount of works over the years. It lies in changing users' search result list (re-ranking, filtering or suggesting new results) so that the presented results fit their specific information needs. There have been studies on user search behavior and feedback [1], [2], as well as works introducing or improving machine learning techniques for learning ranking functions [1], [2], [4]. Researchers have focused on exploiting users' short/long-term search history [5], [6], context [3], [5] or applying collaborative techniques to personalize search results on users with common interests/search intents [6], [7].

In this paper, we extend the classical setting of personalizing keyword search results on unstructured data, into the scenario where the searched entities are structured, related and organized under a common schema (e.g. RDFS or OWL). Consider the following motivating example: A user wants to search about movies related to Woody Allen in DBpedia, a large RDF dataset. Then, she would pose a keyword query of the form $Q = \{film, woody\ allen\}$. However, the user is a big fan of Scarlett Johansson and this is reflected in her search/rating history, where she has searched and clicked results about Johansson or has consistently rated movies of Johansson with high scores. So, a personalized result list should contain on the top positions results for Woody Allen films that somehow involve Johansson. The problem is not trivial, since:

* This research has been co-financed by the European Union (European Social Fund ESF) and Greek national funds through the Operational Program "Education and Lifelong Learning" of the National Strategic Reference Framework (NSRF) - Research Funding Program: Heraclei-tus II. Investing in knowledge society through the European Social Fund.

T. Aalberg et al. (Eds.): TPDL 2013, LNCS 8092, pp. 272–278, 2013.

(a) Relations between searched entities and the schema that characterizes them imposes the construction of new, structure and schema specific training features, beyond the classical IR features. Defining training features is a critical part of the personalization process because it is through them that the quality of a result is *quantified* and *assessed*, w.r.t. the specific user information needs and search history.

(b) While a result list in the classical setting consists of autonomous documents, this does not apply in the setting of keyword search on RDF, where a result may consist of several entities, **along with** the relations that connect them. Thus, issues of combining partial entities to form a complex (graph) result or computing a representative personalization score out of partial scores from the respective entities have to be handled.

In this work, we focus on the first issue, of defining novel, RDF-specific training features and applying the Ranking SVM Model [2] on the RDF search scenario. The experimental results show that our method improves the baseline ranking method and, in cases, performs very close to the ground truth. We note that the second issue is still a subject of our ongoing work.

The paper is organized as follows. Dataset analysis is presented in Section 3. We present our method for training RDF-specific ranking functions and combining them with a keyword search engine to retrieve personalized RDF entities, in Section 4. Section 5 reports on the evaluation. Section 2 reviews related work and Section 6 concludes.

2   Related Work

To the best of our knowledge, most existing works either handle implicitly/indirectly the problem of ranking function training on RDF data or build memory based models to personalize search on RDF. Our work is the first one to propose a model based approach.

The most relevant to our work is [8], where user profile is constructed as a snippet of the knowledge graph and the ontological facts of the knowledge base are utilized to propagate scores from user-accessed entities and facts, thus creating a probabilistic personalized ranking model. In [10] the authors use spreading activation techniques combined with classical search in order to improve the search process in a certain semantic domain. In [12] a statistical approach is applied to learn a user ontology model from a domain ontology. Spreading activation is used for inferencing in the user ontology.

In [9] the authors address the semantic query suggestion task and automatically link queries to DBpedia concepts. Relevant concepts are retrieved for the full query and for each n-gram in the query and then supervised machine learning methods are used to decide which of the retrieved concepts should be kept and which should be discarded. The approach in [11] uses features which can be grouped into dataset specific or dataset independent features. Dataset specific features are extracted from the RDF graph. Dataset independent features are extracted from external sources like web search engines or N-gram databases.

In [13], an extended set of conceptual preferences is derived for a user based on the concepts extracted from search results and clickthrough data. Then, a concept-based user profile is generated and given as input to a support vector machine to learn a concept preference vector for adapting a personalized ranking function.

3   Dataset Pre-processing and Analysis

To be able to train personalization models, it is crucial to have some knowledge about the user's historical needs and preferences. To extract user feedback, we consider user film ratings from the Netflix dataset. In order to enrich the available information, we find the corresponding DBpedia resources for the films in Netflix. Next, we give a brief introduction of the two datasets.

DBpedia knowledge base is a community effort to extract structured information from Wikipedia. The facts are extracted from Wikipedia infoboxes and stored as RDF triples. The triple subject is a resource and the object can be either a resource or a string literal. The DBpedia version we used is characterized by the following statistics: It describes more than 3.64 million things, 1.83 million of which are classified in a consistent ontology. It includes 416,000 persons, 526,000 places, 106,000 music albums, 60,000 films, 17,500 video games, 169,000 organizations, etc. Its ontology consists of 320 ontology classes, 750 object properties and 893 datatype properties. Netflix dataset contains more than 100 million datestamped movie ratings performed by anonymous Netflix users between Dec 31, 1999 and Dec 31, 2005. This dataset gives ratings about 480,189 users and 17,770 movies.

We joined the two datasets in order to exploit the user feedback in the form of movie ratings from Netflix and the RDF structure schema of DBpedia. The join is performed on the Films of each dataset. For a match to be considered valid, we demand exact string matching of the film's title and year of release. We ended up with 5179 matches.

Along with the available OWL ontology for DBpedia concepts, we used Wikipedia categories which are described using the SKOS vocabulary. Through SKOS categories we can obtain useful information such as the film's genre, topics related to film, filming technique, director, decade of release etc. Similarly, we used the YAGO ontology, also available in the DBpedia dataset. In Section 4 we describe how we utilize the aforementioned ontologies to produce training features.

User selection was made according to the following criteria: (a) Number of films the user has rated, to ensure adequate size of training/testing set, (b) Percentage of rated films that were matched against dbpedia entries against total rated films by the user, to ensure consistency of the user profile, (c) Rating distribution: The ratings are integer numbers from 1 to 5. Users that give consistently high or low ratings are considered outliers and, thus, are excluded. Table 1 presents the final set of users divided into two groups: (a) A1-A14 users with many ratings and (b) B1-B11 users with few ratings.

Table 1. Users' rating statistics

user ID	A1	A2	A3	A4	A5	A6	A7	A8	A9	A10	A11	A12	A13	A14	B1	B2	B3	B4	B5	B6	B7	B8	B9	B10	B11
#ratings	2185	2206	1649	1770	1752	1726	1656	2092	2440	1935	1840	1675	1635	1890	200	167	164	180	177	264	154	174	291	513	151
mean rating	2.84	2.68	2.93	2.57	3.18	2.91	3.08	3.1	2.57	2.88	3.15	3.16	2.84	3.04	3.61	3.23	3.48	3.29	2.42	3.13	3.06	3.07	3.05	3.63	3.2
#(rating=5)	17	10	17	17	55	27	16	31	7	29	28	19	17	69	3	0	5	0	0	3	2	0	6	2	
#(rating=4)	107	75	102	50	89	71	64	81	44	49	72	97	71	66	8	11	10	12	6	8	6	14	11	31	9
#(rating=3)	236	129	140	133	121	105	112	216	149	143	151	156	122	87	25	12	7	12	12	43	12	10	40	59	15
#(rating=2)	64	149	62	124	71	85	114	70	162	103	92	58	96	111	2	6	8	8	1	6	7	7	6	4	
#(rating=1)	13	78	8	30	14	57	25	20	126	63	25	5	21	45	2	3	4	4	9	0	3	1	0	0	0

4   RDF-Specific Ranking Function Training and Personalization

We apply Ranking SVM to train user personalization models. Because of the restrictions imposed by our limited user feedback, we use a large number of features to describe all the information we were able to infer from the film ratings. We were only able to construct query independent features, since there are no training queries in the dataset, so that relations between queries and results can be quantified and learned by our model. We treat all films rated by a user as results to the single keyword query "film" and their ratings as representatives of the desired rank in which the search engine should present them to the user (user feedback). This way, we simulate a process where the user searches for e.g. movies and clicks on some of the results (since we lack data of this kind). The features used for the Ranking SVM method are related to the user search history and the structure of the RDF graph. Actors and Directors are considered closely related to a user's opinion about a film, even though the training involves only resources of the first kind (Films). In order to achieve this, we construct a set of features that can be applied to all three kinds of resources. Next, we present the categorization of training features that we implemented.

1. Actors based on dbpedia property *starring*. Each actor is represented by a separate boolean feature.
2. Directors based on dbpedia property *director*. Each director is represented by a separate boolean feature.
3. SKOS categories on films. For a film, a feature of this kind has value 1 if the film belongs to the category and 0 otherwise. For actors and directors the feature's value is the number of the category films in which they participated.
4. SKOS categories on actors/directors. For actors/directors feature values are boolean depending on whether they are related to a category. For films, the value is the number of actors/directors that participate in the film and belong to the category.
5. Film genre from imdb. Feature values are calculated in the same way as in 3.
6. Film genre from imdb and skos combined. For films, the feature has boolean values, where 1 means that the film is of the specified genre and/or belongs to the specified skos category. For actors/directors the feature's value is the number of films in which they participated that have value 1 in the feature.
7. Yago classes for films. The features represent all classes of the YAGO ontology that have as direct member any film of our dataset. Feature values are calculated in the same way as in 3.
8. Yago classes for actors and directors. The features represent all classes of the YAGO ontology that have as direct member any actor/director of our dataset. Feature values are calculated in the same way as in 4.
9. Entity's degree: both incoming and outgoing properties of the entity.
10. Total number of *starring/director* properties.

We implement a baseline keyword search engine by indexing resources, classes, properties and literals of our dataset with lucene. We consider as query a comma delimited series of keywords or keyword phrases, where the comma symbol delimits keywords (phrases) meant to search different entities. For example, query $Q = \{film, woody\ allen\}$ means that we search for separate entities about "film" and separate

Algorithm 1. RDF results retrieval for keyword queries

for each keyword K_i **do**

    Retrieve the full result list RL_i of size N_i and the respective scores S_{ij} for each result r_{ij}

    Normalize scores S_{ij} in the interval $[0, 1]$

    For each result r_{ij} search whether the rest keywords K_k $k \neq i$ are found in its abstract textual description. If so, double its score.

    For each result r_{ij} search whether it has been retrieved using the *label* property of the entity. If so, double its score.

    Input the final result list into RSVM and retrieve the personalized, re-ranked list PRL_i

    Prune the result list of each keyword according to a given threshold.

end for

entities about "woody allen". For each of the keywords (keyword phrases), multiple resources are retrieved as possible results to the user's search intention. Algorithm 1 describes the retrieval process, that incorporates the personalized re-ranking of retrieved entities.

5   Evaluation

In this section we compare the effectiveness of our approach for search personalization as compared (a) to the ground truth given by Film ratings in the dataset and (b) to the baseline entity ranking given by the retrieval engine, **without** personalization. For our experiments, we considered 80% of the available dataset as training set and the rest 20% as test set. We note that the ground truth is given exclusively from the test set, that does not participate in the training process. The evaluated users are given in Table 1.

Figure 1 shows the average rating score of results at each position, for each approach. Graph *ground truth* represents the ideal ranking of the highest rated results at the top, followed by decreasingly rated results. *personalization* gives our ranking and graph *baseline ranking* the ranking of the search engine without personalization.

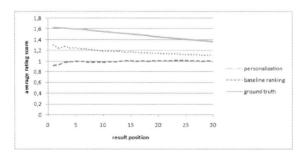

Fig. 1. Average rating scores for each approach

As we can see, our personalization method, first of all, outperforms the baseline ranking, by returning in higher positions more highly rated results. Secondly, the graph is almost constantly decreasing, meaning that there are not significant outliers, e.g. many results with low rating at the top positions, that could cause the graph to suddenly decrease and then increase back. Finally, although the ground truth is consistently better (as expected) than our method, the two graphs demonstrate almost the same behavior, that is, our graph decreases almost in the same way the ground truth does. Part of our ongoing work is to examine whether the size of the training set (i.e. the size of user's feedback) significantly affects the personalization effectiveness, by performing separate analysis for users with many and users with few ratings.

In Figure 2 we show the effect on personalization of training ranking functions with different groups of training features (for clarity, we present two different graphs, due the large amount of feature combinations). Note that this is a preliminary study, aiming to just give an intuition of the effect. That's why we present results for only one random user (B3). A more thorough evaluation is part of our ongoing work.

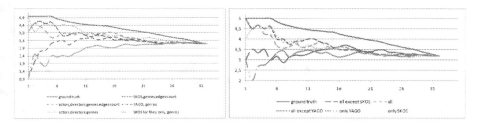

Fig. 2. Effect of different training features use on the personalization

We can see that the performance greatly varies for different feature groups. For example, for this particular user, features representing YAGO classes seem to have a negative effect, although, when **all** features are combined, the YAGO features influence is smoothed and the graph approximates the ground truth graph. On the other hand, using only SKOS features seems, in general, to favor personalization. As future work, we intend to examine if there exists user information that can be inferred from film ratings that can help us predict which features would be more appropriate for each user.

We should note here that the presented results regard Film entities, on which we have explicit user ratings. Similar experiments on ranking Actor and Director entities gave us poor results which are not reported in graphs due to lack of space. Improving the ranking of entities with only implicit feedback available is part of our ongoing work.

6   Conclusion

In this paper, we presented a methodology for personalizing keyword queries on RDF data. We defined a series of RDF-specific ranking function training features and used Ranking SVM to build personalization models. In order to do so, we joined utilized information from two datasets (DBpedia, Netflix) producing a proper dataset to be able to simulate user feedback on keyword search on RDF data. We applied our method on a baseline entity ranking engine and demonstrated its effectiveness.

Our ongoing and future work involves extending the current methods in order to be able to personalize complete graph results and not just separate entities. The challenges are (a) to be able to efficiently combine separate entities in order to obtain meaningful results, (b) to examine which groups of training features and why are more effective and (c) how entities with implicit user feedback can be effectively personalized.

References

1. Agichtein, E., Brill, E., Dumais, S.: Improving web search ranking by incorporating user behavior information. In: Proc. of the ACM SIGIR Conference (2006)
2. Joachims, T.: Optimizing search engines using clickthrough data. In: Proc. of the ACM SIGKDD Conference (2002)
3. Kim, J.-W., Candan, K.-S.: Skip-and-prune: cosine-based top-k query processing for efficient context-sensitive document retrieval. In: Proceedings of the ACM SIGMOD Conference (2009)
4. Qin, T., Zhang, X.-D., Wang, D.-S., Liu, T.-Y., Lai, W., Li, H.: Ranking with multiple hyperplanes. In: Proceedings of the ACM SIGIR Conference (2007)
5. Shen, X., Tan, B., Zhai, C.: Context-sensitive information retrieval using implicit feedback. In: Proceedings of the ACM SIGIR Conference (2005)
6. Sugiyama, K., Hatano, K., Yoshikawa, M.: Adaptive web search based on user profile constructed without any effort from users. In: Proceedings of the ACM WWW Conference (2004)
7. Giannopoulos, G., Brefeld, U., Dalamagas, T., Sellis, T.: Learning to rank user intent. In: Proceedings of the CIKM Conference (2011)
8. Dudev, M., Elbassuoni, S., Luxemburger, J., Ramanath, M., Weikum, G.: Personalizing the Search for Knowledge. In: 2nd PersDB (2008)
9. Meij, E., Bron, M., Hollink, L., Huurnink, B., de Rijke, M.: Learning Semantic Query Suggestions. In: Bernstein, A., Karger, D.R., Heath, T., Feigenbaum, L., Maynard, D., Motta, E., Thirunarayan, K. (eds.) ISWC 2009. LNCS, vol. 5823, pp. 424–440. Springer, Heidelberg (2009)
10. Rocha, C., Schwabe, D., Poggi, M.P.: Hybrid approach for searching in the semantic web. In: Proc. of the 13th International Conference on World Wide Web, pp. 374–383 (2004)
11. Dali, L., Fortuna, B., Duc, T.T., Mladenić, D.: Query-independent learning to rank for RDF entity search. In: Simperl, E., Cimiano, P., Polleres, A., Corcho, O., Presutti, V. (eds.) ESWC 2012. LNCS, vol. 7295, pp. 484–498. Springer, Heidelberg (2012)
12. Jiang, X., Tan, A.H.: Learning and inferencing in user ontology for personalized Semantic Web search. Information Sciences: An International Journal 179(16), 2794–2808 (2009)
13. Leung, K.W.-T., Lee, D.L., Ng, W., Fung, H.Y.: A Framework for Personalizing Web Search with Concept-Based User Profiles. ACM Transactions on Internet Technology 11(4), Article 17 (2012)

Providing Meaningful Information in a Large Scale Digital Library – A Case Study

Laura Rueda[1], Sünje Dallmeier-Tiessen[1], Patricia Herterich[1], Samuele Carli[1], Salvatore Mele[1] for the INSPIRE Collaboration, and Simeon Warner[2]

[1] CERN Scientific Information Service, CH-1211 Geneva 23, Switzerland
{laura.rueda,sunje.dallmeier-tiessen,patricia.herterich,
samuele.carli,salvatore.mele}@cern.ch
[2] Cornell University Library, Ithaca, NY 14850, USA
simeon.warner@cornell.edu

Abstract. Emerging open science practices require persistent identification and citability of a diverse set of scholarly materials, from paper based materials to research data. This paper presents a case study of the digital library INSPIRE digital library and its approach to connecting persistent identifiers for scientific material and author identification. The workflows developed under the ODIN project, connecting DataCite DOIs and ORCIDs, can serve as a best practice example for integrating external information into such digital libraries.

Keywords: persistent identifier, digital library, interoperability model, open science.

1 Introduction

The tradition of scholarly communication has existed for centuries and has not changed much in that time. Nevertheless, with the advent of the Internet, the community practices are evolving and new opportunities are appearing for digital preservation, workflows and dissemination. Much more than just the text publication can be shared, and open research requests that new resources made accessible.

This paper focuses on the challenges faced by the large-scale digital library INSPIRE[1] in developing new services to facilitate the sharing of meaningful scholarly information. In particular, it is addressed how research data and other supplementary material is being integrated and how these contents can be shared openly. INSPIRE comprises over a million (metadata) records, half of them with fulltext. It is the successor to the SPIRES bibliographic database which served the High-Energy Physics (HEP) community for more than two decades. In this case study, special emphasis is also given to the INSPIRE involvement in the cross-disciplinary research being conducted within the international ODIN project.

---

[1] http://inspirehep.net

T. Aalberg et al. (Eds.): TPDL 2013, LNCS 8092, pp. 279–284, 2013.

Community discussions are emerging and will expand the horizon of INSPIRE to more varied materials. Forthcoming challenges will increase the complexity of the data management and raise the requirements of the service. Moreover, the HEP community demands their full scientific record to be available as a whole, from preprints or published articles to their newest research data, and they require these materials to be fully citable. Statistics on the publication output and citation metrics for each individual researcher are also a key feature, and high accuracy is vital. Those statistics have a very high visibility and are used in career and research assessments.

2   The ODIN Project and Its Impact on INSPIRE

The international project ODIN[2] (ORCID and DataCite Interoperability Network) targets an enhanced interoperability of persistent identification beyond single systems or community boundaries. The consortium consists of partners representing research organisations, libraries, data centres, repositories, and the service providers DataCite[3] and ORCID[4]. Through the latter, the consortium works closely with publishers so the whole scholarly communication and open science life cycle is covered. The project comprises a dedicated workpackage focused on previously divergent case studies: High-Energy Physics and Humanities and Social Sciences. These steps guide INSPIRE to a shared path with other disciplines.

INSPIRE supports persistent identifiers (PI) for publications. In the framework of this project, it has extended them by minting new PIs for objects, as datasets, using Digital Object Identifiers (DOIs) obtained from the cross disciplinary initiative DataCite. The persistent identification support is essential to ease the citability of the datasets.

On the author identification side, INSPIRE already had a specific hybrid author disambiguation approach[3]. To improve the process, CERN helped found ORCID (Open Researcher and Contributor ID), aiming to establish global persistent identifiers for researchers to address the ambiguity problems.

The integration of both systems, DOIs for objects and ORCIDs for authors, will clarify the technical aspects of the open science challenges. This close look at the similarities and differences between cases done by the ODIN project will result in common workflows.

3   In Practice: The INSPIRE Approach

The association of DOIs and ORCIDs, unique and interoperable identifiers among several systems, will avoid problems such as errors comparing metadata, deviations on disambiguation processes and useless data exchange.

---

[2] http://odin-project.eu/
[3] http://datacite.org/
[4] http://orcid.org/

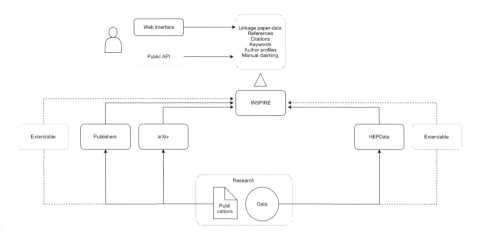

Fig. 1. INSPIRE as a content aggregator

INSPIRE has focused its efforts on extending DOI use to datasets and ancillary material. Its first provider is HepData[5], a data repository hosted by Durham University (UK), which manages up to 7000 datasets[1]. DOIs enable direct citation of dataset and ORCID iDs grant credit to their authors.

In addition, the implementation of similar processes in multiple systems will considerably ease the data and metadata exchange in the near future (Figure 1). Under the ODIN project, INSPIRE and arXiv[6] have joined forces to offer a proof of concept of meaningful information exchanged.

Previously, the only connection between them was the periodical harvest done by INSPIRE to obtain new articles from arXiv. Now, using persistent identifiers, both systems have defined a RDF representation and are developing public open APIs to exchange information. This way, each one will be able to find and share articles, datasets, ancillary files and authors, as well as to process them and enhance the information exposed to the users. Additionally, interested third-parties can build on the INSPIRE/arXiv expertise and interface.

3.1 DOIs and DataCite Services on INSPIRE

In order to implement the DOI identifiers, INSPIRE uses the service provided by DataCite[4], which is also a member of the ODIN project. Given that the published articles already have a DOI assigned by the publisher, INSPIRE mints additional DOIs for datasets, so they became fully citable and can be retrieved and reused by the scientific community (see Figure 2). Those datasets are obtained from the HepData initiative, currently in charge of matching data and publications.

---

[5] http://durpdg.dur.ac.uk/
[6] http://arxiv.org/

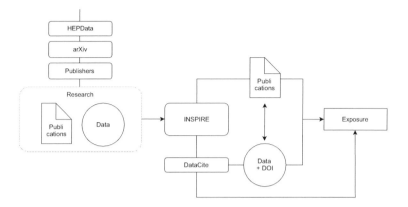

Fig. 2. Data exposure follows the same model as publications

This simple workflow is generic and applicable to different identifiers. Data-Cite's metadata schema includes relations with a property called 'RelatedIdentifier'. This property supports the use of different identifiers: not only DOIs, but also ISBNs[7], URNs[8], ARKs[9], etc. This way, even if the original publication was not identified by a DOI, the relationship can be kept. Other properties as clear as "is supplemented to/by", "is documented by", "is continued by" are implemented in the schema.

When a researcher makes use of a dataset, he or she will be able to cite it using its DOI. This way, the reference will be easily traceable, will grant credit to the original authors and will provide other researchers with accessible information. Nevertheless, a common framework and author matching is necessary in run these services. ORCID offers the infrastructure for such author identification.

3.2 ORCIDs and Sharing Authorship Data on INSPIRE

The service of author identification was launched by ORCID during the last months of 2012[5]. Since then, many publishers and public organisations have supported the initiative, seen as a general, non-restricted and practical way to manage authorship information. Based on, different services have been established.

ORCID offers each person the possibility to create a profile and get an identification number, to include information about affiliation, names and publications, and even to import them automatically from external systems[6]. A strict security policy is in place, different levels of privacy exist to guarantee the author that only the chosen information will be public.

---

[7] http://isbn-international.org/
[8] http://ietf.org/rfc/rfc2141.txt
[9] https://wiki.ucop.edu/display/Curation/ARK

ORCID services are implemented in INSPIRE in two different processes. The first includes user interaction, where each member can create an ORCID and add it to their profile. INSPIRE itself encourages users to do it. Once both systems are connected, through the OAuth protocol[10], the user will see an automatic profile matching if possible, or a manual interface to select the correct one, if not. By that time, INSPIRE will start offering the public information received on its RDF data representation, so external systems, such as arXiv, can be updated.

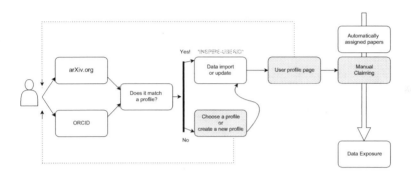

Fig. 3. Author information ingestion and exposure

The second way INSPIRE can receive ORCIDs for authors is via partner systems, such as arXiv or the American Physical Society[11], for example. Those systems, which prior to the exchange have developed similar infrastructures, will provide their own knowledge using the common identification framework based on DOIs and ORCIDs. Matching the information received, INSPIRE will enhance the accuracy of the content. It will also avoid the manual process of linking systems by the user. These workflows are shown in Figure 3, in grey for the interactions with the users and in white for the automatic tasks.

4   Future Work on INSPIRE: Managing the Information Obtained

Beyond the basic identification of users, ORCID offers the added-value service of centralised preservation, a place to manage all the disseminated information. Authors are able to define the sharing policy, correct errors or include extra information about themselves such as affiliations, alternative names, etc. For its part, the DataCite metadata schema is vast and flexible and provides a realistic way of metadata sharing. Systems can share DOIs and its metadata can be queried directly from DataCite.

---

[10] http://oauth.net/
[11] http://aps.org/

As the adoption of both systems is at an early stage, many developments will follow. INSPIRE will move from the restricted internal use to show all new publications received. This will be an important step for the crowdsourced curation, as the community will be able to suggest the inclusion of new articles in an easier way. Then, internal mechanisms, such as author disambiguation will be improved with extended information. New services will be explored, based on the users needs such as expanded searches, automatic claim or validation.

5   Conclusions

New trends in research, data sharing and open access are redrawing the scene of scholarly communication. As community needs are changing and new ways of sharing research material are being established, the role of persistent information management tools become crucial. Given the demands of the different scientific communities, generic workflows and interoperable networks are the way to reach the best scenario and offer suitable services.

Initiatives such as the ODIN Project, as well as efforts from companies, funders and communities point in the same direction. The correct use and linkage of persistent identifiers fills the thin layer of interoperability needed to provide support to the new needs, such as data reuse and citation tracking.

INSPIRE, as a case of study and proof of concept of the new developments, serves as an example on how to take advantage of the possibilities offered by different interoperable networks to offer added-value services to a community, i.e. linked to the incentive system. Following this path of open sharing and cross-disciplinary efforts will guide the scientific community to a better situation to face the challenges of the growing data needs, and will offer researchers new incentives to engage them in the process.

References

1. Praczyk, P., Nogueras-Iso, J., Dallmeier-Tiessen, S., Whalley, M.: Integrating Scholarly Publications and Research Data-Preparing for Open Science, a Case Study from High-Energy Physics with Special Emphasis on (Meta) data. Semantics Research 343, 146–157 (2012), doi:10.1007/978-3-642-35233-1_16
2. Piwowar, H.: Altmetrics: Value all research products. Nature 493, 159 (2013), doi:10.1038/493159a
3. Brooks, T.C., Carli, S., Dallmeier-Tiessen, S., Mele, S., Weiler, H.: Proceedings of the ACM Web Science Conference WebSci 2011 (2011)
4. Brase, J.: DataCite - A Global Registration Agency for Research Data. In: Fourth International Conference on Cooperation and Promotion of Information Resources in Science and Technology, pp. 257–261 (2009), doi:10.1109/coinfo.2009.66
5. Haak, L., Fenner, M., Paglione, L., Pentz, E., Ratner, H.: ORCID: a system to uniquely identify researchers. Learned Publishing 25(4), 259–264 (2012), doi:10.1087/20120404
6. Fenner, M.: ORCID: Unique Identifiers for Authors and Contributors. Information Standards Quarterly 23(3), 10–13 (2011), doi:10.3789/isqv23n3.2011.03

Context-Sensitive Ranking Using Cross-Domain Knowledge for Chemical Digital Libraries

Benjamin Köhncke[1] and Wolf-Tilo Balke[2]

[1] L3S Research Center, Hannover, Germany
[2] TU Braunschweig, Germany
koehncke@L3S.de, balke@ifis.cs.tu-bs.de

Abstract. Today, entity-centric searches are common tasks for information gathering. But, due to the huge amount of available information the entity itself is
often not sufficient for finding suitable results. Users are usually searching for
entities in a specific search context which is important for their relevance assessment. Therefore, for digital library providers it is inevitable to also consider
this search context to allow for high quality retrieval. In this paper we present
an approach enabling context searches for chemical entities. Chemical entities
play a major role in many specific domains, ranging from biomedical over biology to material science. Since most of the domain specific documents lack of
suitable context annotations, we present a similarity measure using cross-
domain knowledge gathered from Wikipedia. We show that structure-based similarity measures are not suitable for chemical context searches and introduce a
similarity measure combining entity- and context similarity. Our experiments
show that our measure outperforms structure-based similarity measures for
chemical entities. We compare against two baseline approaches: a Boolean retrieval model and a model using statistical query expansion for the context term.
We compared the measures computing mean average precision (MAP) using a
set of queries and manual relevance assessments from domain experts. We were
able to get a total increase of the MAP of 30% (from 31% to 61%). Furthermore, we show a personalized retrieval system which leads to another increase
of around 10%.

Keywords: Chemical Digital Libraries, Personalization, Context Search.

1 Introduction

Throughout the sciences the information gathering process is to a large degree based
on Web sources today. Considering the exponentially growing amount of information
on the Web it is thus essential for large-scale information providers, such as digital
libraries, to build effective systems allowing for easy and flexible access to information relevant for specific user needs. Especially entity-centric searches have become
common tasks for many researchers across almost all scientific domains. Considering
for instance the domain of chemistry information gathering is prominently focused on
chemical entities. However, the actual search for chemical entities is by no means

T. Aalberg et al. (Eds.): TPDL 2013, LNCS 8092, pp. 285–296, 2013.
© Springer-Verlag Berlin Heidelberg 2013

restricted to the chemical domain: in medicine it is important to find active ingredients of drugs, e.g., against infectious diseases. In biology chemical substances are important to understand complex metabolism processes. And in materials science chemical entities play a major role in developing novel materials like polymers or nanomaterials.

Thus throughout this paper we focus on chemical entities as an important example of entity-based searches. The problem for such entity-based searches is usually two-fold: one central complex is markup and disambiguation (which also included detecting synonyms), the other complex deals with similarity-based searches to find in some respect similar entities. The first complex for chemical entities is quite well researched and already actively used in portals, e.g., SMILES or InCHI code for representation, the OSCAR framework [1] for chemical markup, chemical search engine for formulae [2], or building enriched index pages for synonymy in chemical documents [3]. In contrast, the second complex has yet to make the step from laboratory usage to a widespread use in digital portals. The main problem is how to actually compute similarity between chemical entities?

Generally speaking, chemical entities are transformed into so-called fingerprint representations based on their chemical structures. A fingerprint is a sequence of bits where each bit represents the occurrence of a special chemical feature. Of course, there are different possibilities to encode chemical properties in a bit-sequence leading to different fingerprint representations. Also for the subsequent similarity computations different well-known measures are used, like e.g. Cosine, or Russell-Rao. [4] analyzed these different measures and found that they often produce entirely uncorrelated result lists. Thus, it seems that larger contexts or specific tasks may strongly influence the individual perception of the entities' similarity and relevance.

The problem is that none of the structural measures takes context information into account. But this is very important, because the similarity of two chemical substances is actually heavily related to the search context. Consider for instance the chemical entities *Zanamivir* and *Ibuprofen*. Both are used in the treatment of flu and are therefore similar regarding this pharmacological activity context. *Ibuprofen* is also used to treat inflammatory diseases such as rheumatoid arthritis. But, regarding this context both entities are very dissimilar: *Zanamivir* is a neuraminidase inhibitor and thus not at all useful for the treatment of rheumatoid arthritis. It is therefore necessary to personalize measures for entity similarity to the task or search context a user is currently engaged in. In brief, context used to disambiguate the user's explicit query can be expected to lead to focused and relevant retrieval results.

Most users perform the *contextualization* of searches manually by adding additional terms to their actual query, if the retrieval results have not yet been satisfying (query refinement) [5]. There are also first approaches *automatically enriching* a user's query with terms related to user's context, see e.g. [6]. However, for using context terms in document retrieval most approaches require documents to be annotated or classified with the related context terms using a fixed (controlled) vocabulary. For example, in the biomedical domain documents are annotated by terms from the well-known MeSH ontology. Since it is maintained manually, the offered terminology is of high quality. But the almost completely MeSH-indexed MEDLINE digital library is a rare case and its manual curation is expensive, while automatic classification is still error-prone. Moreover, most document collections miss both, suitable annotations and the funds to add them. Considering for instance the linked open data community, hardly any collection dealing with chemical entities is properly annotated. Examples are *Linking Open Drug Data*, a task force within the World Wide Web Consortium's Health Care and Life Sciences Interest Group, or *clinical trials* describing relationships between active ingredients and diseases tested in clinical studies around the world.

In this paper we present an approach enabling *context searches for chemical entities using cross-domain knowledge* harvested from Wikipedia as a major knowledge base. One advantage of our approach is that every term occurring in Wikipedia can be used as context term. Instead of using a fixed vocabulary of predefined classes, we thus use the 'wisdom of the crowd' which is dynamic and ever-growing. The derived similarity measure is therefore not purely based on structural information of chemical entities, but extracts different features of chemical entities using common knowledge in the community. All features are combined in enriched profiles of chemical entities. These profiles are then used for similarity computations resulting in a personalized ranking function considering both, context as well as entity similarity. Our experiments show that it is indeed sensible to combine cross-domain features: the average precision is increased from 31% when using a Lucene fulltext filter for contextualization to up to 71% for personalized queries using our measure.

The rest of the paper is organized as follows: the next section gives an overview of related work. In section 3 we introduce our novel similarity measure based on chemical profiles incorporating cross-domain knowledge followed by a detailed evaluation in section 4. Finally, section 5 concludes the paper with an outlook on future work.

2 Related Work

Today there are different groups of approaches using context information. The area of contextual search tries to proactively capture the information need of a user by automatically extending the user's query with information from the user's search. An approach using information from raw query search logs to discover context terms is described in [7]. The detected terms are included in user preferences used to optimize search results. It was shown that in terms of top-k search quality a system using context information outperforms existing personalization approaches without context information. In [6] three different algorithms are compared considering contextual search for the Web, i.e. query rewriting, rank-biasing and iterative filtering metasearch (IFM). The experimental results have shown that the query rewriting approach performs surprisingly well. Therefore, we will compare against a quite similar approach using query expansion for the context term in our evaluation.

Another famous ranking algorithm considering context information for Web searches is the topic-sensitive PageRank [8]. For each Webpage multiple importance scores with respect to various topics are computed. These scores are combined at query time dependent on the topics stated in the query. Afterwards they can be combined with different IR measures to produce a suitable ranking. In [9] it was shown that context-sensitive ranking improves the retrieval quality for domain experts remarkably, compared with conventional ranking models. The proposed ranking model uses keyword statistics collected from the specified contexts to rank the documents. In comparison to our approach, here, it is still necessary to pre-classify the documents to their respective context terms. Since they are working on the MEDLINE corpus and all given documents are annotated with MeSH terms this classification is given.

But, such a corpus as MEDLINE where each document is indexed with several MeSH terms is a rare case and is actually curated manually with expensive efforts. In the domain of chemistry for example, no such ontology for annotating chemical documents with context information is available. Indeed, in the chemical domain only a few highly specialized controlled vocabularies are openly available, e.g. *Chemical Entities of Biological Interest* (ChEBI [10]). But our experiments with domain experts in [11] have shown that Wikipedia categories are more useful to describe the documents' context. The reason is that ChEBI focuses exclusively on a small subset of molecules, namely small molecules, which are either natural products or synthetic products used to intervene in processes of living organisms. The approach presented in [12] also propose to use Wikipedia to enable cross-domain search. But their main focus is on analyzing tags used in Web 2.0 systems like Flickr and connect them to concepts in Wikipedia.

Beside the query context, of course, it is also necessary to consider the actual query term for retrieving suitable search results. In the chemical domain similarity search is centered on chemical entities. In previous work we have shown how to use structural information to create enriched index pages [3]. Indexing different unambiguous representations we were able to reach the retrieval quality of a chemical structure search using a common Google text search. Based on these index pages we analyzed how similarity between chemical entities is computed [4]. We analyzed the different possible combinations of fingerprints and similarity measures computing the k-tau correlation coefficient. We figured out that there are many uncorrelated measures. As a straight forward idea, we assumed that the uncorrelated combinations can be assigned to different chemical search tasks. But our experiments have shown that this is not possible and structure-based similarity measures are not useful for context searches.

3   Computing Context Similarity in Chemistry

In this section we introduce a similarity measure using external knowledge sources independent of chemical structures. Our measure considers both, entity- as well as context similarity. Finally, we are interested in documents including the query entity (or similar entities) in the sense of the specified context.

In our system a document, further denoted by d, is represented as the bag of words of its included chemical entities $E_d \subseteq E$, where E is the set of all chemical entities in the collection. Let D denote the collection of documents. A query for a context search is composed of two parts: $q = e_q \mid q_c$, where e_q is a chemical entity and q_c is the desired context specification. q_c specifies a sub-collection $D_c \subseteq D$ such that $\forall d \in D_c, d$

satisfies q_c. A chemical entity is defined as the trivial name of a chemical structure. The first necessary step is to extract all chemical entities from the documents. We use the OSCAR framework for an automatic extraction [1]. Next the similarity between these entities is computed.

3.1 Entity Similarity

To find a suitable similarity measure we use external knowledge from different information sources, create profiles of chemical entities containing different features, and finally compute the similarity based on these profiles. Since it was shown in [11] that Wikipedia is a reliable source for representing chemical documents we also used it here as main information source. For each chemical entity $e \in E_d$ we analyzed its corresponding Wikipedia page and extracted suitable features used in the chemical profiles. From each page we extracted a set of the assigned Wikipedia categories, a set of all other entities that are cited in the Wikipedia page (outgoing links), and a set of all other entities pointing to the respective page (incoming links).

Beside Wikipedia we also use another tool to automatically detect important entities in text, named OpenCalais. OpenCalais is a free Web service from Thomson-Reuters that does named entity recognition to extract events and relationships from text. It uses natural language processing and machine learning techniques to recognize instances of named entities. Since OpenCalais uses surface features, like e.g. capitalization, and is not based on handcrafted databases of entities it can detect new entities that may not be included in any knowledge base like Wikipedia.

For each chemical entity we analyze its Wikipedia page using OpenCalais and add the retrieved information to its chemical profile. In detail, we use the detected Calais entities, topics and tags. The Calais entities are further divided into several different types, ranging from types like e.g. medical treatment or medical condition, to types like e.g. person or operating system. The social tags are not really semantic features, but emulate how a person would tag a specific piece of content. The topics describe a category that the input content is about. They are based on the Calais categorization taxonomy. But, it is also possible that no topic is assigned to the input content.

To summarize, each chemical profile contains six different features. Each feature is used to compute the similarity between the query entity e_q and the entity $e_a \in E$.

Calais Entity Similarity: Let ts_q be the type set for e_q and ts_a the type set for e_a. Each type $t \in ts_x$ where $x \in \{q, a\}$ is associated with a set of related Calais entities, $t_n es_q$ and $t_n es_a$, where $1 \leq n \leq |ts_x|$. The similarity is computed using the Jaccard coefficient.

$$ts = \frac{ts_q \cap ts_a}{ts_q \cup ts_a} \tag{1}$$

The ts coefficient describes how many types the given chemical entities have in common. For each type they have in common the entity similarity is computed and normalized by the number of types e_q and e_a have in common.

$$es = \frac{\sum_{t \in ts_q \cap ts_a} \frac{t_t es_q \cap t_t es_a}{t_t es_q \cup t_t es_a}}{|ts_q \cap ts_a|} \tag{2}$$

The Calais entity similarity is computed as follows:

$$ces = (\gamma * ts) + ((1 - \gamma) * es)$$
(3)

where γ is a weighting factor and $0 \leq \gamma \leq 1$.

Calais Tag and Topic Similarity: For tag and topic similarity the same measure is used. For each detected term (tag or topic term) a relevance score in the range of 0 to 1, further denoted as rs, is computed, describing the importance of each unique term.

Let tsm_q be the term set for e_q, and tsm_a the term set for e_a. The tag and topic similarity is computed using the following equation:

$$tsm = \beta * \frac{tsm_q \cap tsm_a}{tsm_q \cup tsm_a}$$
(4)

β is called the regulation factor which is computed as follows:

$$\beta = \frac{\sum_{t \in tsm_q \cap tsm_a} \frac{rsa_t + rsq_t}{2}}{|ts_q \cap ts_a|}$$
(5)

where rsa_t is the relevance score of term t for e_a and rsq_t the relevance score of t for e_q. The relevance scores are in the range of 0 to 1 and are assigned by OpenCalais. The regulation factor is used to give lower similarity scores to entities that indeed have many terms in common, but which have low relevance scores for the entity itself.

Wikipedia Category Similarity: For the Wikipedia category similarity we defined a quite similar formula as for the Calais tag and topic similarity. Let wc_q be the categories set for e_q and wc_a the categories set for e_a. For each Wikipedia category also a weighting factor (wf) is assigned describing how general the respective category is regarding the Wikipedia category graph. We use this factor to give more specific categories a higher score. The category similarity is computed using the following formula:

$$wc = wf * \frac{wc_q \cap wc_a}{wc_q \cup wc_a}$$
(6)

The weighting factor wf is defined as

$$wf = \frac{\sum_{wc \in wc_q \cap wc_a} dt_{wc}}{|wc_q \cap wc_a|}$$
(7)

where dt is the length of the shortest path from the respective Wikipedia category to the root category.

Wikipedia Related Entities Similarity: Furthermore, we use the Jaccard coefficient to compute the similarity based on the related entities. For related entities we distinguish between entities linking to the Wikipedia page of e_a and e_q (further denoted as res_{in}) and entities that are linked from the Wikipedia pages of e_a and e_q (further denoted as res_{out}). Let res_q be the set of related entities for e_q and res_a the set of related entities for e_a. The similarity is computed as follows:

$$res_{in/out} = \frac{res_q \cap res_a}{res_q \cup res_a} \tag{8}$$

Entity Similarity: To compute the entity similarity of e_a and e_q we combine the different feature similarities in a linear fashion.

$$entSim = \omega * ces + \vartheta * tsm_{tag} + \sigma * tsm_{topic} + \vartheta * wf + \rho * res_{in} + \tau * res_{out} \tag{9}$$

Each feature is multiplied with a Boolean variable, i.e. $\omega, \vartheta, \sigma, \vartheta, \rho, \tau$, having the value 0 or 1. These variables are used for personalizing the entity similarity measure by switching features on and off. As we will see in the experiments it depends on the user preferences which combination of features leads to best retrieval results.

3.2   Context Similarity

The context similarity is also based on the knowledge covered by Wikipedia. We use the Wikipedia Miner [13] to access the Wikipedia corpus and compute the semantic similarity between the context term and all chemical entities in our corpus using the relatedness measure described in [14]:

$$contextSim(c, e) = \frac{\log(\max(|A|,|B|)) - \log(|A \cap B|)}{\log(|W|) - \log(\min(|A|,|B|))} \tag{10}$$

where c and e are the Wikipedia pages for the context term c and the entity e, C and E are the sets of pages that link to c, respectively e, and W is the set of all pages in Wikipedia.

A drawback of this measure is that we need to compute the semantic similarity between the context term and all other chemical entities in our collection. After computation the scores are stored in a database meaning that we only need to compute the similarity once for every context term. In case a new context term is entered in the system this computation has to be performed. The next time the context term is entered no computation is necessary and the scores can be directly retrieved from the database.

3.3   Combined Similarity

Our goal is to find the most similar entities for the query entity e_q in the given context q_c. The entity similarity computes the most similar entities for e_q and the context similarity finds the most related entities to the context term. The total similarity for query q is computed as follows:

$$totalSim = (\alpha * contextSim)\frac{+((1-\alpha) * entSim)}{|EF|} \tag{11}$$

where EF is the set of features used for entity similarity computation and α is a weighting factor with $0 \leq \alpha \leq 1$.

4   Evaluation

For our experiments we used a data set of 44660 clinical studies[1]. We choose 10 different context terms which are all diseases, i.e. Malaria, Tuberculosis, Mumps, Tinnitus, Hypertension, Hepatitis A and C, Influenza, Dengue and Cancer. We automatically extracted all chemical entities using the OSCAR framework [1]. In total 1.573.264 entities have been annotated in the documents, 79223 of them are distinct.

OSCAR also uses a name-to-structure algorithm which associates chemical structures to the found entities. Since we want to compare against the fingerprint-based similarity measures we filtered out all found entities that do not have structural information (in this case a SMILES code). This leads to a total of 721 distinct chemical entities independent of the documents' context. Since our measure relies on Wikipedia we analyzed how many of the chemical entities can be found. We used the WikipediaMiner [13] to search for the chemical entities in Wikipedia. For 92.6% (668) we found a matching Wikipedia page.

4.1   Correlation Analysis

In this experiment we analyzed if we need all cross-domain features in the chemical profile for similarity computation or if some of them are correlated. We randomly chose around 10% of all chemical entities as query terms, resulting in 72 queries in total. Using these terms we computed the rankings to all other chemical entities in our set based on the six feature similarities introduced in section 3.

Since we can interpret the similarity value as a value in a ranking vector, we used the Kendall rank correlation coefficient (KTau) [15] to determine the correlation of the different measures. We calculated the correlation coefficient for each ranking vector and the arithmetic mean over 72 queries. A KTau of 1 means that the agreement of two rankings is perfect, -1 indicates a perfect disagreement and for independent rankings one would expect the coefficient to be *approximately* 0. For each pairwise comparison of two rankings we averaged the Ktau values over all queries. We only considered those queries which are significant meaning having a p-Value less than 0.05. The highest correlation is found between the Wikipedia in-links and the Wikipedia categories, followed by the Open Calais topic ranking and the Wikipedia categories. However the values are still very small (< 0.45) so that we consider the rankings as uncorrelated. Therefore, all features deliver different rankings and are used in our similarity measure.

4.2   Comparing Different Rankings

In this experiment we compare the rankings of the different similarity measures. As stated earlier, a query is defined as follows: A query for a context search is composed of two parts: $q = e_q \mid q_c$, where e_q is a chemical entity and q_c is the desired context specification. Basically, we compared the feature similarity against the fingerprint-

---

[1] http://clinicaltrials.gov/ct2/home

based similarity measures. Since the relevance ratings for two entities differ between different context terms it is not sensible to evaluate the entity ranking without considering the search context. For considering the context in the fingerprint-based measures we used the following procedure. The documents in our collection, further denoted by D, are filtered and only those related to q_c are retrieved. From this document set, denoted by D_c, the chemical entities are extracted and ranked using the different similarity measures. We evaluated different possibilities for building D_c. First, we use a Boolean approach where D_c contains all documents including the context term q_c. Second, we use an approach using statistical query expansion where q_c is expanded using the most co-occurring terms.

For building a ground truth to compare the different rankings against, we randomly choose a set of 10 chemical entities and related context terms as queries. In order to make manual relevance assessment feasible, we pooled together the top-20 entities retrieved for each query and similarity metric. The relevance assessment was done manually by domain experts. The experts marked for each query all chemical entities from the sampling sets that are relevant for the query in a Boolean fashion. To evaluate the rankings we computed the mean average precision (MAP) based on the relevance assessments.

First, we analyze the results of the Boolean retrieval model. The document set is filtered using q_c, meaning only documents are included containing q_c in the fulltext. The filtering was done using a Lucene fulltext index. The highest MAP of 31% is reached using the Forbes similarity measure based on the Substructure fingerprint. The average recall using the Boolean approach is 82.7%. That means some relevant entities are filtered out. The reason is that not all relevant documents contain the context term in the fulltext.

For the second baseline approach we use a retrieval model including statistical query expansion. We computed a term-to-term co-occurrence matrix based on our document set. We also considered the position of the term in the document, meaning two terms that are close together will get a higher score. Furthermore, we used popularity thresholds defining a required minimum and maximum popularity. Terms not fulfilling these thresholds are not used as context terms. Finally, the context term q_c is expanded with the top-10 co-occurring terms. We used the following retrieval model: Let $C=\{q_c,c_1,...,c_n\}$ be the set including q_c and all expanded terms. The expanded context query is formulated as q_c OR c_1 OR ... OR c_n, meaning all documents are returned containing q_c or any of the expanded terms. The highest MAP of 23% is reached using the Yule similarity measure based on the Extended fingerprint. The MAP is even lower than for the Boolean approach. The reason is that using query expansion the set of entities is getting bigger. This is also proved if we take a look at the recall. It has increased up to 89.5%. These results confirmed the experiments in [4] showing that fingerprint-based measures are not suitable for context searches.

For our feature-based approach we combine context- and entity similarity in one single measure. Since our measure computes the similarities for all chemical entities the recall is always 100%. To regulate the weighting between context- and entity similarity a variable *alpha* is used (see 3.3). If alpha is 0 no context similarity is used and if it is 1 no entity similarity is used. Fig.1 shows the MAP results for the cross-domain similarity measure for varying alpha values.

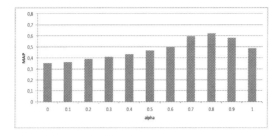

Fig. 1. MAP values dependent on alpha

The best result of a MAP of 61% is reached for alpha equals 0.8. That means the context similarity is slightly higher weighted. Using this measure we were able to increase the MAP from 31% for the Boolean approach to 61%. Since this result is an average over all chemists and all queries we tried to further increase it by personalizing the similarity measure.

4.3   Personalized Ranking

The idea is to build a personalized retrieval system where each individual user trains the system and the system will learn the best similarity measure for the user. The system includes a simple feedback step where the user marks the chemical entities most relevant for him. Therefore, we conducted a user study with domain experts from the area of drug design and synthesis. For the user study, we have randomly chosen ten queries consisting of chemical entity and context. Each query represents a feedback cycle in the system.

Since the measure for computing the entity similarity is composed of six different features, we analyzed which feature combination is the best for the individual chemist. The goal is to find a suitable feature combination for computing the entity similarity within the feedback cycles. Thus, we need to compute all possible combinations and analyze which leads to the best results. Let us consider we have a finite set EF containing n features. The number of different subsets we need to combine is computed using the power set, $|P(EF)| = 2^n$. Since we have 6 different features we can combine them in $2^6 - 1 = 63$ different ways. We need to subtract 1 since we do not need to compute the empty set which is also contained in the power set.

For each chemist and each query we computed the 63 different rankings and compared them to the manual relevance judgments by computing the average precision. For each query we analyzed which feature combinations lead to the best result. Unfortunately it was not possible to find the optimal solution for each chemist. But we found out that in average 4 different feature combinations are enough to always find the most suitable ranking. These combinations have been found after 7 feedback cycles in average. That means that we only need to compute 4 different rankings instead of 63 and have a high probability that the most suitable solution is found.

Fig.2 (left) shows the number of top rankings for the different feature combinations over all chemists. It is interesting to see that more than half of the combinations never lead to the best ranking. Of course, this statistic will change over time depending on the different users submitting queries to the system, but it is useful to overcome the well known *new user problem*. For new users it seems to be a good choice to use the overall best measure as global starting point, i.e. tsm_{tag} and tsm_{topic} or res_{in} (see 3.1).

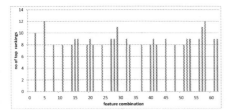 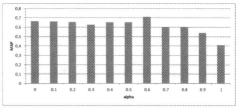

Fig. 2. Number of top rankings for different feature combinations (left) Example: MAP values for varying alpha for one chemist over 10 queries (right)

Now, that we found the best feature combinations we use them to analyze which weighting between entitiy- and context similarity is the best by varying the alpha value. For each chemist and each query we took the best feature combination and compute the average precision using the chemist's relevance vector. Fig.2 (right) shows the MAP results for one chemist for varying alpha over 10 queries. For this chemist, the best results are retrieved using an alpha of 0.6. Compared to the imperso-nalized measure the mean average precision is increased of up to 71%. In average over all users the mean average precision increases about 9% using personalization.

5   Conclusion and Future Work

For digital library providers it is important to allow for context searches to assure high quality retrieval. Our experiments showed that structure-based similarity measures cannot retrieve suitable results for context searches. Therefore, we presented an ap-proach using cross-domain knowledge gathered from Wikipedia to enable context searches in the chemical domain. The beauty of the presented approach is that digital library providers can easily integrate it into their workflow of metadata enrichment. The necessary steps are the extraction of chemical entities, creation of enriched chem-ical profiles using Wikipedia and the similarity computation using the profiles. Each profile consists of six different features, i.e. Wikipedia categories, in- and out-links, and three additional features extracted using OpenCalais. The features are combined in a linear fashion and used to compute entity similarities. For context similarity we also relied on Wikipedia and computed the semantic similarity of each chemical enti-ty for the specific query context. Finally entity- and context similarity are combined in one similarity measure.

Our experiments have shown that the cross-domain similarity measure outperforms the structure-based measures. We compared our measure against two baselines: a Boolean retrieval model and a model using statistical query expansion for the context terms. We computed the mean average precision (MAP) using a set of queries and manual relevance assessments from domain experts. We were able to get a total in-censement of the MAP of 30% (from 31% to 61%). To further increase the precision we introduced a personalized retrieval system based on user feedback by varying the features used for entity similarity and the weighting between context and entity similarity. Using the best feature combination for each query we were able to further increase the MAP up to 71%.

For our future work we plan to generalize our approach and use it in other domains. It will be interesting to see if cross-domain knowledge from Wikipedia is also useful in domains using different entities, like e.g. genes in biology. There, we can also compare against classification approaches, like e.g. SVM, since we can rely on a fixed set of context terms, like e.g. provided by the MeSH ontology. Furthermore, instead of using Boolean variables in the entity similarity measure, it might be interesting to learn the weighting parameters using a learning to rank framework.

References

1. Corbett, P., Murray-Rust, P.: High-throughput identification of chemistry in life science texts. In: Berthold, M., Glen, R.C., Fischer, I. (eds.) CompLife 2006. LNCS (LNBI), vol. 4216, pp. 107–118. Springer, Heidelberg (2006)
2. Sun, B., et al.: Identifying, Indexing, and Ranking Chemical Formulae and Chemical Names in Digital Documents. ACM Transactions on Information Systems 29 (2011)
3. Tönnies, S., Köhncke, B., Koepler, O., Balke, W.-T.: Exposing the Hidden Web for Chemical Digital Libraries. In: Proc. of the Joint Conf. on Digital Libraries (JCDL) (2010)
4. Tönnies, S., et al.: Taking Chemistry to the Task – Personalized Queries for Chemical Digital Libraries. In: Proc. of the Joint Conf. on Digital Libraries (JCDL) (2011)
5. Kraft, R., Zien, J.: Mining anchor text for query refinement. In: Proc. of the Int. Conf. on World Wide Web (WWW) (2004)
6. Kraft, R., Chang, C.C., Maghoul, F., Kumar, R.: Searching with context. In: Proc. of the Int. Conf. on World Wide Web (WWW) (2006)
7. Jiang, D., et al.: Context-aware search personalization with concept preference. In: Proc. of Conf. on Information and Knowledge Management (CIKM) (2011)
8. Haveliwala, T.: Topic-sensitive pagerank: A context-sensitive ranking algorithm for web search. IEEE Transactions on Knowledge and Data Engineering 15 (2003)
9. Chen, L., Papakonstantinou, Y.: Context-sensitive ranking for document retrieval. In: Proc. of ACM SIGMOD Conf. (2011)
10. Degtyarenko, K., et al.: ChEBI: A database and ontology for chemical entities of biological interest. Nucleic Acids Research 36, Database issue (2008)
11. Köhncke, B., Balke, W.-T.: Using Wikipedia categories for compact representations of chemical documents. In: Proc. of Conf. on Information and Knowledge Management (CIKM) (2010)
12. Liu, C., Wu, S., Jiang, S., Tung, A.K.H.: Cross Domain Search by Exploiting Wikipedia. In: Int. Conf. on Data Engineering (ICDE) (2012)
13. Milne, D., Witten, I.H.: An open-source toolkit for mining Wikipedia. Artificial Intelligence 194 (2012)
14. Milne, D., Witten, I.: Learning to link with wikipedia. In: Proc. of Conf. on Information and Knowledge Management (CIKM) (2008)
15. Kendall, M.G.: A New Measure of Rank Correlation. Journal of Biometrika 30(1-2) (1938)

Topic Cropping: Leveraging Latent Topics for the Analysis of Small Corpora

Nam Khanh Tran[1], Sergej Zerr[1], Kerstin Bischoff[1],
Claudia Niederée[1], and Ralf Krestel[2]

[1] Leibniz Universität Hannover / Forschungszentrum L3S, Hannover, Germany
{NTran,zerr,bischoff,niederee}@L3S.de
[2] Bren School of Information and Computer Sciences, University of California, Irvine
krestel@uci.edu

Abstract. Topic modeling has gained a lot of popularity as a means for identifying and describing the topical structure of textual documents and whole corpora. There are, however, many document collections such as qualitative studies in the digital humanities that cannot easily benefit from this technology. The limited size of those corpora leads to poor quality topic models. Higher quality topic models can be learned by incorporating additional domain-specific documents with similar topical content. This, however, requires finding or even manually composing such corpora, requiring considerable effort. For solving this problem, we propose a fully automated adaptable process of *topic cropping*. For learning topics, this process automatically tailors a domain-specific Cropping corpus from a general corpus such as Wikipedia. The learned topic model is then mapped to the working corpus via topic inference. Evaluation with a real world data set shows that the learned topics are of higher quality than those learned from the working corpus alone. In detail, we analyzed the learned topics with respect to coherence, diversity, and relevance.

Keywords: digital humanities, qualitative data, topic modeling.

1 Introduction

For social sciences, sharing qualitative primary data like interviews and re-using it for secondary analysis is very promising as data collection is very time consuming. Moreover, some qualitative data sources capture valuable information about attitudes, beliefs, etc. as people had them at other times – "realities" that cannot be captured anymore. Enabling secondary analysis of data not collected by oneself, analyzing it with new research questions in mind, imposes a lot of challenges though. In this paper, we focus on the aspect of advanced techniques for facilitating exploration of such data and for improving findability in digital data archives. Supporting intelligent access to and exploration of data shared for re-use is also a main goal within the digital humanities as expressed, for example, in the theme of the Digital Humanities 2013 conference: "Freedom to Explore".

By exploiting information retrieval and topic modeling techniques we can mine additional knowledge about themes discussed in primary qualitative data.

T. Aalberg et al. (Eds.): TPDL 2013, LNCS 8092, pp. 297–308, 2013.

This way, interview contents can be visualized by means of extracted topics to give a quick overview. For example, topics extracted from a collection of studies, or samples show the commonalities of themes while comparing topics of individual studies, or samples sheds light on the specifics. Interview topics as well aid an enhanced (automatic) content analysis and retrieval of similar documents. This is especially interesting as qualitative documents are often long, and thus it is hard to grasp their thematic coverage – let alone to manually analyze them.

Due to the enormous resources required for conducting qualitative research by means of interviews (holding the interview, transcription, document coding/analysis), the primary data resulting from such qualitative studies is usually limited to a small number of interviews per study case or sample. Topic models, however, are based on statistics and thus perform better on big data sets (see, e.g. [1]). Here, we present a generalizable framework for using topic modeling given such corpora restrictions as they occur in qualitative social science research. Our fully automated adaptable process tailors a domain-specific Cropping corpus by collecting relevant documents from a general corpus or knowledge base, here Wikipedia. The topic model learned on this substitute corpus is then applied to the original collection. Hence, we exploit state-of-the-art IT-methods adapting and integrating them for usage as research tools for the digital humanities. In detail, the contributions of this paper are:

- We propose a process for *topic cropping* and proof its improved performance for small corpora by analyzing diversity, coherence, and relevance.
- By integrating the automatic evaluation of topic quality we take a first step towards a self-optimizing process of selecting parameters for topic cropping in different settings.

2   Related Work

Tools for (Secondary) Analysis of Qualitative Data: Regarding software tools and techniques for supporting the (re-)analysis of qualitative data usually three groups are differentiated. Qualitative data analysis (QDA) tools like AT-LAS.ti, MaxQDA, or Nvivo are well developed products enabling the manual coding, annotation, and linking of data in a variety of formats. Other common features are simple search procedures, the definition of variables, automatic coding of specified text strings, and word frequency or co-occurrence counts.

More advanced are tools for (quantitative) content analysis, e.g., General Inquirer, Diction, LIWC, TextPack, WordStat. Software in this category usually builds upon large dictionaries to analyze vocabulary use also semantically. Besides word frequencies, category frequency analysis as well as statistics or filtering for keywords in contexts (KWIC / concordance) are typical features. Programs may offer co-occurrence or correlation analysis of categories or words, ideally accounting for synonyms via the built-in dictionaries. Related is cluster analysis and multidimensional scaling for visualizing word or category correlations. Dictionaries can also be used for normative comparison, i.e., to find specifics of vocabulary usage in a document or a collection [2].

Text mining and statistical analysis are advanced techniques exploited to automatically find themes and trends in qualitative data. Tasks are, for example, supervised document classification requiring human input for the label or variable value to be learned, unsupervised clustering of similar documents, or document summarization. Various algorithms as well as standard data preprocessing procedures (stemming, stop word removal, etc.) exist. Information extraction, e.g., of sentiment, can be achieved via lexicons, patterns, and rules. To name just a few – mostly commercial – tools that (claim to) provide additional text mining capabilities: Catpac, SAS Text Miner, SPSS TextSmart, WordStat.

In [3], the usage of unsupervised learning methods for qualitative data analysis is discussed, here a self-organizing map (SOM) build upon manually selected terms from interviews. The authors argue that such text mining procedures can aid both data-driven, inductive research by finding emergent concepts as well as theory-driven, deductive research by checking the adequacy and applicability of defined schemes. The next section reports in detail on work regarding the related goal of topic modeling for qualitative data – the focus of this paper.

Topic Modeling: Topic modeling is a generative process that introduces latent variables to explain co-occurrence of data points. Latent Dirichlet allocation (LDA) [4] is a further development of probabilistic latent semantic analysis (PLSA) [5]. LDA was developed in the context of large document collections, such as scientific articles, news collections, etc. The success of LDA led to the application in other domains, such as image processing, as well as other types of documents, e.g. tweets [6] or tags [7]. Some work applies topic modeling to transcribed text. In [8], the standard LDA model is extended to identify not only topics but also topic boundaries within longer meeting transcripts. The authors show that topic modeling can be used to detect segments in heterogeneous text. Howes et al. [9] investigate the use of topic models for therapy dialog analysis. More specifically, LDA is applied to 138 transcribed therapy sessions to then predict patient symptoms, satisfaction, and future adherence to treatment using latent topics detected vs. hand coded topics. The authors find only the manually assigned topics to be indicative. Human assessment of the interpretability of the automatically learned topics showed high variance of topic coherence.

Using topic models where there is only limited data, e.g., very short documents or very few documents, has been studied as well. Micro-blogging services, such as Twitter, limit single documents to 140 tokens. Hong and Davison [6] study different ways to overcome this limitation when training topic models by aggregating these short messages based on users or terms. The resulting longer documents yield better topic models compared to training on short, individual messages. Unfortunately, this method only works if the number of short texts is sufficiently large. Using additional long documents to improve topics used for classification was proposed in various approaches: Learning a topic model from long texts and then applying it to short text [10] improves significantly over learning and applying it on short texts only. Learning it on both [11] and applying it on short texts improves performance further. Jin et al. [12] present their Dual LDA model to model short texts and additional long text explicitly, which outperforms standard LDA on long and short texts for classification. Our focus is not on classification of short documents but we use topic modeling to analyze (long) individual documents and focus more on a careful selection of the corresponding training corpus. Incorporating domain knowledge for topic transition detection using LDA as described in [13] addresses this problem using manual selection of training corpora. A topic model is trained using auxiliary textbook chapters and is used to compare slide content and transcripts of lectures. Because of sparse text on slides and possible speech recognition errors in the transcripts training a topic model on long, related documents improves alignment of slides and transcript significantly. In contrast, our method does not rely on a manual selection of a training set as cropping is performed as an automated process.

3   A General Approach for Topic Cropping

The goal of our approach is to enable the exploitation of the advantages of topic models, e.g., with respect to capturing latent semantics, even if the considered corpus is too small for their direct application. Smaller corpora such as qualitative studies in the humanities result in topic models of restricted quality. The approach we are following in this work is to use another larger corpus (the Cropping corpus) for learning the topic model. Subsequently, the learned topic model is applied to the study under consideration via topic inference. Qualitative studies are often very focused, which makes finding a good Cropping corpus a difficult task. Since we are looking for an approach, which is applicable in different settings (i.e., for studies in different application domains), there are two requirements to be satisfied: (1) having a Cropping corpus that is specific enough to produce a good and useful coverage of the topics in the study under consideration (2) while avoiding the effort of searching for an adequate Cropping corpus whenever working with studies in a new application domain.

For this purpose, we decided to include into the automated process of topic cropping a phase for analyzing the working corpus coverage and a phase of automatic corpus tailoring. The tailoring phase creates a tailored domain-specific corpus from a large corpus with a very wide coverage such as Wikipedia. This implies a four step process for topic cropping (see also Figure 1):

1. Analyzing working corpus coverage by selecting characteristic terms
2. Tailoring a Cropping corpus by collecting relevant documents
3. Learning a topic model from the Cropping corpus
4. Applying topic inference to the working corpus

This process is embedded into a generalizable framework, which can be adapted to different settings via parameters. The final aim is to learn those parameters of the process steps in a self-optimizing loop.

Analyzing Working Corpus Coverage: For tailoring the Cropping corpus, we first have to understand the topical coverage of the corpus under consideration. At first glance, this might look like a hen-egg problem: we need to know the main topics of the corpus for building a corpus for learning those topics.

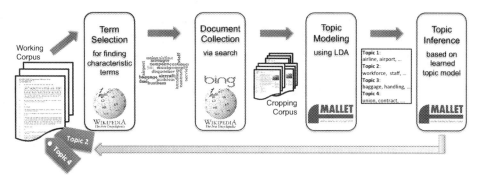

Fig. 1. Workflow for Topic Modeling on a Cropping corpus

For overcoming this, we relied on a method for determining the most relevant terms by using a counter corpus. Starting from a particular case in the study under consideration and a random subset of pages selected from Wikipedia, we used the metric of Mutual Information (MI) [14], which measures how much the joint distribution of terms deviates from a hypothetical distribution in which features and categories (working corpus and Wikipedia corpus in our case) are independent of each other. The measure ranks higher terms which are frequent in the working corpus but not in general. They are used as representative terms for corpus coverage.

Tailoring a Cropping Corpus: The top-ranked subset of those terms is used for tailoring the Cropping corpus. In our approach, we used a general Web search engine to identify the set of highest ranked Wikipedia pages for each of the terms. The Cropping corpus is created from the set union of all those pages. Wikipedia has been selected as the starting point for Cropping corpus creation because of its broad coverage providing information on seemingly every possible topic. Of course it is also possible to use large domain specific corpora or combinations of several corpora.

Learning the Topic Model: For learning the topic model, we made use of the Mallet topic modeling toolkit [15], namely the class ParallelTopicModel. This class offers a simple parallel threaded implementation of LDA (see [16]) together with SparseLDA sampling scheme and data structure from [17]. LDA models documents as probabilistic combinations of topics $P(z|d)$, with each topic described by terms following another probability distribution i.e. $P(w|z)$.

$$P(w_i) = \sum_{j=1}^{T} P(w_i|z_i = j)P(z_i = j)$$

where $P(w_i)$ is the probability of the ith word for a given document and z_i is the latent topic. $P(w_i|z_i = j)$ is the probability of w_i within topic j. $P(z_i = j)$ is the probability of picking a word from topic j in the document. These probability distributions are specified by LDA using Dirichlet distributions. The number of latent topics T has to be defined in advance and allows to adjust the degree of specialization of the latent topics. For inference and parameter estimation, Gibbs sampling iterates multiple times over each word w_i in document d_i, and samples a new topic j for the word based on the probability $P(z_i = j|w_i, d_i, z_{-i})$ until the LDA model parameters converge.

Applying the Topic Model: In this step the topic model learned from the Cropping corpus is applied to the working corpus using topic inference as offered by the Mallet toolkit (cc.mallet.topics.TopicInferencer). It is not expected that the set of topics learned from the Cropping corpus is exactly the set of topics inherently included in the working corpus. Rather, the set of topics learned from the Cropping corpus is roughly a superset of the working corpus topics. Learned topics that are not available in the working corpus will however have no major impact on the topic inference process as long as the "real" working corpus topics are also in the learned topic model. Topic inference will assign to each of the topics in the topic model a probability of it being relevant for a study document.

4   Experiments

4.1   Dataset

For our experiments, we re-used qualitative data shared via the ESDS Qualidata / the UK Data Service. We selected four out of the eight cases from the case study on "Changing Organizational Forms and the Re-shaping of Work" [18]. Each case has verbatim transcriptions or summaries of in-depth Face-to-face interviews conducted in England and Scotland between 1999 and 2002.

1. *Airport case*: four airlines, engineering department, airport security, baggage handling, full handling, cleaning company, fire service (30 files)
2. *Ceramics case*: five ceramics manufacturers (32 files)
3. *Chemicals case*: a pigment manufacturing plant, two Suppliers, two Transportation specialists, two Business Service Contractors (28 files)
4. *PFI case*: Hotel Services Company, Facilities Design Company, Special Purpose Vehicle, NHS Trust Monitoring Team (41 files)

Interviews were held in semi-structured form given guidelines for questions along the main research themes of managing, learning and knowledge development, experience of work, and performance – particularly investigating the links between these topics and changing organizational forms[1]. Participants were managers and employees at all levels, sometimes also union representatives. The number of pages per document varies between two and 32 for verbatim transcripts, summaries are usually of two to ten pages in length. These interview documents consist of transcribed spoken, natural language with answers being usually short, often elliptic, and requiring co-text and context for interpretation.

4.2   Experimental Settings

For tailoring the Cropping corpus we used the top 20 most representative terms as identified in the working corpus analysis phase. The Bing Search engine was

---

[1] For more details see: `http://discover.ukdataservice.ac.uk/catalogue?sn=5041`

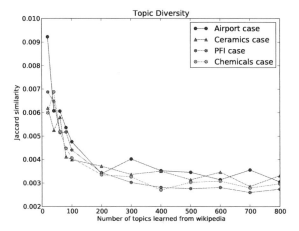

Fig. 2. Topic diversity, measured via Jaccard similarity for various number of topics learned from the Cropping corpus

queried for each of those terms individually to retrieve relevant Wikipedia pages. This resulted in a Cropping corpus of about 10,000 documents.

An important parameter in learning the topic model is the number of topics to be learned. With an increasing number of topics – a parameter of the topic model learning process – the topics get more fine-grained. The challenge here is to find a number, which results in good topic coverage for the study (all relevant topics are in) and in sufficiently fine-grained topics to help exploring unknown qualitative material while still being useful for human understanding and for spotting areas with similar topics. There is no general notion of a "good" number of topics since this strongly depends on the corpus and the application. We decided to take topic diversity as a measure for an appropriate number of topics, more precisely the diversity of the topics assigned to the study based on the topics learned from the Cropping corpus. The intuition behind this is that we need a sufficiently large topic model to cover all aspects of the study. Once the diversity stops increasing substantially the newly added topics are either not relevant for the study or they just provide subtopics by splitting topics, which does not substantially add to the diversity. Figure 2 shows the increase in topic diversity for various numbers of topics learned from the Cropping corpus. For this topic inference we used a threshold of 0.01 to cut out "noisy" topics with very low probabilities. Figure 2 is discussed in more detail in the next section.

5   Evaluation

We judge the quality of the automatically detected topics exploiting both, internal (intrinsic) and external (extrinsic) evaluation [14,19]. In topic analysis an internal evaluation prefers low similarity between topics whilst within a topic high similarity is favored. We adopt this idea by measuring *topic diversity* capturing variance between the different topics in a model and *topic coherence* within the single topics respectively. We additionally measure *topic relevance* externally by comparing with human annotators. In this section, we evaluate both the topics learned directly from the working corpus and those from the Cropping corpus with the same setting and analyze them with respect to these quality dimensions.

5.1   Topic Diversity

Topic diversity is an important criterion for judging the quality of a learned model. The more diverse, i.e. dissimilar, the resulting topics are, the higher will be the coverage regarding the various aspects talked about in our interview data. It has been shown in earlier work that the Jaccard Index is an adequate proxy for diversity [20] and its output value correlates with a number of clusters (topics in our case) within the dataset. Thus, to estimate the average similarity between produced clusters, we employ the popular Jaccard coefficient [14]. Given two topic models T_i and T_j, i.e. set of terms, their Jaccard similarity $JS(T_i, T_j)$ is defined as follows:

$$JS(T_i, T_j) = \frac{|T_i \cap T_j|}{|T_i \cup T_j|}.$$

Given a collection of topic models $T_1, \ldots, T_n$, the refined (excluding self-similar pairs) average Jaccard similarity [20] is defined as follows ($1 \leq i < j \leq n$):

$$sim = \frac{2}{n(n-1)} \sum_{i<j} JS(T_i, T_j),$$

For alle available cases, Figure 2 plots topic diversity with respect to the number of inferred topics. We observe that similarity values sharply decrease until the number of topics reaches the range 80-100. They do not substantially change in the tail. This may be an indicator for a reasonable number of topics for our datasets. Similarly, Figure 3 shows the change of the average Jaccard similarity, comparing the diversity of topics learned from the working and the Cropping dataset. We observe that topics learned from the Cropping corpus are generally more diverse in the beginning of the curve, indicating that our approach covers more aspects of the data even for smaller number of topics.

5.2   Topic Coherence

We tackle the task of topic coherence evaluation by rating coherence or interpretability based on an adaptation of the Google similarity distance, which performs effectively in measuring similarity between words [21]. The more similar, i.e less distant, the representative words within a topic, the higher or easier is its interpretability. Cilibrasi and Vitanyi's *normalized Google distance* (**NGD**) function measures how close word x is to word y on a zero to infinity scale using the formula:

$$\mathbf{NGD}(x, y) = \frac{max\{log f(x), log f(y)\} - log f(x, y)}{log M - min\{log f(x), log f(y)\}}$$

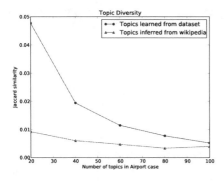 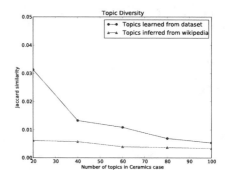

Fig. 3. Topic diversity, measured via Jaccard similarity, and its variance for different numbers of topics learned during topic modeling

Table 1. Example topics with coherence measured via normalized Google distance (NGD), topics inferred from the working corpus (W) or the Cropping corpus (C)

Corpus	Topics	NGD
W	bag day company baggage ramp	0.44
W	airline service issue baggage handling	0.38
C	workers labor work employment workforce	0.19
C	employee employees tax employer pay	0.19

Table 2. Average (Avg) and standard deviation (SD) of topic coherence of three cases, measured via normalized Google distance (NGD). Topics are inferred from the working corpus (W) or the Cropping corpus (C).

Case	AvgNGD$_W$	SD$_W$	AvgNGD$_C$	SD$_C$
Airport	0.34	0.07	0.21	0.08
Ceramics	0.32	0.08	0.25	0.09
Pfi	0.35	0.1	0.22	0.08

where $f(x)$ and $f(y)$ are the number of hits of words x and y, respectively, $f(x, y)$ is the page-counts for the query $x\ AND\ y$ and M is the total number of web pages that Google indexes. A NGD of zero indicates that word x and word y are practically the same. They are independent when their distance reaches approximately one.

Given a topic T which is represented by its top-m words (we set m=5 in this experiment) denoted by $\mathbf{w} = (w_1, ..., w_m)$, its normalized Google distance is:

$$\mathbf{NGD}(T) = \frac{2}{m(m-1)} \sum_{w_i, w_j \in \mathbf{w}} \mathbf{NGD}(w_i, w_j)$$

To estimate overall topic coherence, we randomly choose a list of 30 learned topics per case ($T = (T_1, ..., T_n)$), compute NGD for each T_j, and then take the average of the list $\mathbf{AvgNGD}(T) = \frac{1}{n}\mathbf{NGD}(T_j)$.

Table 2 reports the average normalized Google distances and their deviations for topics inferred for three cases. For all cases evaluated, we obtain consistent improvement. Specifically, evaluating over the 90 topics of these three cases, we improve 32% in terms of normalized Google distance. This indicates that the topics inferred from the Cropping corpus are significantly more coherent than those learned directly from the working corpus (significance of a t-test $p < 0.001$).

5.3   Topic Relevance

While topic diversity and topic coherence can help to estimate the quality of the topics with respect to information-theoretic considerations, validity of our results, i.e., the usefulness of the derived topics for the working corpus, needs to be assessed by human evaluation of topic relevance. Here, we decided to compare our inferred topics with topics assigned by human annotators. For this evaluation, we randomly selected 16 documents from the study to be manually annotated by four users. Each document was split into smaller units – typically question and answer pairs – resulting in about 60 units per document. Thus, a total of 1000 units was annotated. We asked users to define topics discussed in each given unit. Each unit could have one or more topics and there were no restrictions on how topics are to be phrased. Typically the topics assigned were single words or short phrases.

Topic relevance is then assessed by automatically matching user defined topics with the learned ones. For this, the terms used by the user for a topic are matched with the top terms learned for a topic by the topic model. We consider it a match if the term used by the user appears in the top terms of the respective topic. By design, this evaluation gives preference to the topic model learned directly from the working corpus since the users tend to use terms that appear in the text. Similarly, the topic models learned directly on the working corpus use exactly those terms for their topics. In order to even out this terminology disadvantage, we made use of word synonyms from WordNet [22] to extend sets of topic words before matching. A learned topic T is considered to be relevant if its representative words and their synonyms $\mathbf{w} = (w_1, ..., w_k)$ share one or more terms with user defined topics $\mathbf{t} = (t_1, ..., t_r)$

$$\mathbf{Rel}(T) = \begin{cases} 1 & \text{if } |\mathbf{w} \cap \mathbf{t}| > 0 \\ 0 & \text{otherwise} \end{cases}$$

There are two reasons to use this type of evaluation in spite of its weakness: First, the alternative solution of showing the user the learned topic together with the text for relevance assessment puts a high burden on the user since it is not trivial to judge automatically learned topics. In addition, there is the risk that the user also unintentionally assesses topic quality in terms of coherence at the same time. Second, we are aiming for a self-optimizing loop, where parameters of the process are adapted iteratively through learning based on quality assessment. In this context, the evaluation of topic relevance chosen here only has to be done once and can be re-used in every iteration. The alternative manual evaluation of the relevance of each learned topic as a whole would have to be repeated in every loop to assess the newly learned topics.

For two example documents, Figure 4 compares topics learned from the working and Cropping corpus with respect to the number of relevant topic at rank

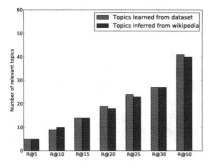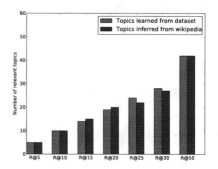

Fig. 4. Topic relevance as the number of relevant topics at rank k, for two documents

k $\mathbf{R}@k = \sum_{i=1}^{k} \mathbf{Rel}(T_i)$, where the rank is determined by the probability of the topic assignment (resulting from topic inference). We achieve similar results for other documents. On average, at rank 10 we obtain 9.8 relevant topics with a deviation of 0.35 for the working topics and 9.2 with a deviation of 1.0 for the Cropping topics. It can be seen from the results that the topics learned from Wikipedia reach a comparable level of relevance as those learned directly from the corpus, while being more coherent and diverse.

6   Conclusion and Future Work

In this paper we propose a method for a *fully automated* and adaptable process of tailoring a domain-specific sub-corpus from a general corpus such as Wikipedia and exploiting it to increase the topic model quality for limited size corpora such as studies in sociology and other qualitative material in the digital humanities. Our experiments show substantial improvements in diversity as well as in internal coherence of inferred topics compared to a naive approach using the limited size corpora exclusively. At the same time our method keeps the topic relevance high as confirmed by human annotators. We believe that our approach can be further improved by exploiting the automatic evaluation for adjusting the input parameters of the algorithm. In future work, we plan to modify the approach towards a self-optimizing automatic cycle. One important task, therefore, is to develop a more precise automatic evaluation of topic relevance through matching the user-annotated and the automatically inferred topics.

Acknowledgments.   We are greatly thankful to M. Marchington, J. Rubery, and H. Willmott for sharing their primary data and to the UK Data Archive for making qualitative data available for (secondary) research. The work was supported by the project *"Gute Arbeit" nach dem Boom (Re-SozIT)* funded by the German Federal Ministry of Education and Research (BMBF) under mark 01UG1249C and by the European projects ForgetIT (GA600826) and AR-COMEM (GA270239). Responsibility for the contents lies with the authors.

References

1. Newman, D., Bonilla, E.V., Buntine, W.: Improving topic coherence with regularized topic models. In: Proceedings NIPS, pp. 496–504 (2011)
2. Leetaru, K.H.: Data Mining Methods for the Content Analyst: An Introdution to the Computational Analysis of Content. Routledge, New York (2012)
3. Janasik, N., Honkela, T., Bruun, H.: Text mining in qualitative research: Application of an unsupervised learning method. Organizational Research Methods 12(3), 436–460 (2009)
4. Blei, D.M., Ng, A.Y., Jordan, M.I.: Latent dirichlet allocation. Journal of Machine Learning Research 3, 993–1022 (2003)
5. Hofmann, T.: Probabilistic latent semantic analysis. In: Proceedings UAI, pp. 289–296 (1999)
6. Hong, L., Davison, B.D.: Empirical study of topic modeling in twitter. In: Proceedings 1st Workshop on Social Media Analytics, SOMA, pp. 80–88 (2010)
7. Krestel, R., Fankhauser, P., Nejdl, W.: Latent Dirichlet Allocation for Tag Recommendation. In: Proceedings RecSys, pp. 61–68 (2009)
8. Purver, M., Körding, K.P., Griffiths, T.L., Tenenbaum, J.B.: Unsupervised topic modelling for multi-party spoken discourse. In: Proceedings ACL, pp. 17–24 (2006)
9. Howes, C., Purver, M., McCabe, R.: Investigating topic modelling for therapy dialogue analysis. In: Proceedings IWCS Workshop on Computational Semantics in Clinical Text (CSCT), pp. 7–16 (2013)
10. Phan, X.-H., Nguyen, L.-M., Horiguchi, S.: Learning to classify short and sparse text & web with hidden topics from large-scale data collections. In: Proceedings WWW, pp. 91–100 (2008)
11. Xue, G.R., Dai, W., Yang, Q., Yu, Y.: Topic-bridged plsa for cross-domain text classification. In: Proceedings SIGIR, pp. 627–634 (2008)
12. Jin, O., Liu, N.N., Zhao, K., Yu, Y., Yang, Q.: Transferring topical knowledge from auxiliary long texts for short text clustering. In: Proceedings CIKM, pp. 775–784 (2011)
13. Zhu, X., He, X., Munteanu, C., Penn, G.: Using latent dirichlet allocation to incorporate domain knowledge for topic transition detection. In: Proceedings INTERSPEECH, pp. 2443–2445 (2008)
14. Manning, C.D., Raghavan, P., Schütze, H.: Introduction to Information Retrieval. Cambridge University Press (2008)
15. McCallum, A.K.: Mallet: A machine learning for language toolkit (2002), http://mallet.cs.umass.edu
16. Newman, D., Asuncion, A.U., Smyth, P., Welling, M.: Distributed algorithms for topic models. Journal of Machine Learning Research 10, 1801–1828 (2009)
17. Yao, L., Mimno, D., McCallum, A.: Efficient methods for topic model inference on streaming document collections. In: Proceedings KDD, pp. 937–946 (2009)
18. Marchington, M., Rubery, J., Willmott, H.: Changing organizational forms and the re-shaping of work: Case study interviews, 1999-2002 (computer file) (2004)
19. Newman, D., Lau, J.H., Grieser, K., Baldwin, T.: Automatic evaluation of topic coherence. In: Proceedings Human Language Technologies, HLT, pp. 100–108 (2010)
20. Deng, F., Siersdorfer, S., Zerr, S.: Efficient jaccard-based diversity analysis of large document collections. In: Proceedings CIKM, pp. 1402–1411 (2012)
21. Cilibrasi, R.L., Vitanyi, P.M.B.: The google similarity distance. IEEE Trans. on Knowl. and Data Eng. 19(3), 370–383 (2007)
22. Miller, G.A.: Wordnet: a lexical database for english. Communications of the ACM 38(11), 39–41 (1995)

A Domain Meta-wrapper Using Seeds for Intelligent Author List Extraction in the Domain of Scholarly Articles

Francesco Cauteruccio and Giovambattista Ianni

Dipartimento di Matematica e Informatica,
Università della Calabria,
I87036, Rende (CS), Italy

Abstract. In this paper we investigate about automated extraction of author lists in the domain of scientific digital libraries. It is given a list of known "seed" authors and we aim to extract complete lists of co-authors from Web pages in arbitrary format. We adopt a methodology embedding domain knowledge in a unique "meta-wrapper", not requiring training, with negligible maintenance costs and based on the combination of several extraction techniques. Such methods are applied at the structural level, at the character level and at the annotation level. We describe the methodology, illustrate our tool, compare with known approaches and measure the accuracy of our techniques with proper experiments.

1 Introduction and Motivation

The world research community has nowadays great interest towards numerically estimating the impact of whole institutions, research authors and individual papers thereof [17, 19, 22]. In order to ease this process, involving also quantitative analysis, many search engines for scholar literature introduced bibliometric tools in their online interfaces [20, 21, 24, 25]. The Google Scholar portal is renowned for its recall and stimulated the development of many systems which perform automated bibliometrics estimates computed on top of its information [10, 12, 18, 23]. Specialized wrapping techniques are unfortunately necessary for extracting information from this portal, and the available information is incomplete: for instance, author lists are partial. Despite interest of the research community [2], incomplete lists prevent an accurate estimate of bibliometric indices which take into account normalizations based on the number of co-authors of a given paper, such as the *multi-authored h-index* [13].

Our Scholar H-Index Calculator [23], allows users to interact using their browser with the Google Scholar web site; result pages are transparently enriched with bibliometrics information related to the displayed page hits, starting from the well-known h-index [11], to more specialized ones. The tool includes many specialized features for advanced bibliometrics analysis, including the possibility of defining custom formulas and the recently introduced capability to refine incomplete author lists, which is the subject of this paper. The problem

T. Aalberg et al. (Eds.): TPDL 2013, LNCS 8092, pp. 309–314, 2013.

of reconstructing full author lists can be solved by visiting web pages containing paper descriptions linked by Google Scholar: these description pages normally contain detailed author lists, but are in arbitrary HTML format, whose structure depends on the digital library the paper at hand has been indexed from (see Figure 1). In order to face the above issue, we developed a sub-module of our tool, implementing what we called TPI-S techniques (*Tree Pattern Induction with Seeds*). The contributions of this paper are the following:

▶ we suggest a "meta-wrapper" approach aimed at completing partial information from scholar digital libraries. Our techniques need only a small amount of input information (seed data, i.e., incomplete author lists), do not require user interaction nor preliminary bootstrapping and are independent from the page structure of specific digital libraries.
▶ the ability to automatically reconstruct full author lists on top of a scholarly digital library with large recall, enables the possibility to perform accurate measurement of bibliometric impact indices, over a large corpus of indexed data, even when such measures depend on the number of co-authors and considerably reducing the burden of manual assessment;
▶ Information is automatically extracted at run-time and our technique works transparently also when a new digital library enters the collection of interest, or it changes its HTML shape; it has been not necessary to take the burden of designing a battery of information extraction wrappers, nor to allocate resources for training wrappers over sample instances at design-time;

2   The TPI-S Methodology

In the following we assume we are given a tree-structured document D, a *seed list* of strings L and a *hidden list* $L^* \supseteq L$. L^* and L are connected by some semantic relationship, which is usually defined in a informal way only (e.g., *lists of recipes' ingredients, etc.*). In our setting, we look for lists of co-authors of scientific articles. In general, hidden lists are encoded within documents according to two main categories: either *i)* elements of L^* appear as individual nodes in a DOM structure (i.e., a HTML table, a list, etc.), or *ii)* L^* appears as encoded within the same textual node (e.g., a textarea, the text content of a single `<span>` node, etc.). Accordingly, our approach combines the two following techniques.

XPath Resolution. The XPR method aims at constructing a XPath expression E which should capture L^* over D. Our technique takes into account that usually *i)* lists of co-authors can be found in the textual content of a group of nodes each having the same distance from a common ancestor node, called *Lowest Common Ancestor* (LCA); and *ii)* among the sub-nodes of the LCA, those having the same level depth of seeds and correspond on a subset of their attributes values, usually contain remaining hidden authors names. The XPR method is based on iterating over couples (p, R), for p a candidate XPath expression and R a list of author names; a candidate couple (p, R), is ranked according to the fraction of

Fig. 1. An example for the XPR technique

seeds appearing in R. A threshold value is used for excluding expressions of poor quality. Candidate XPath expressions are built by looking at balanced couples of nodes containing seed values in their text content; a XPath expression is built for their LCA, then it is concatenated with a second expression which captures the path downwards to unknown elements of L^*.

An example for XPR. An instance example is shown in Figure 1, which depicts a portion of a Web document encoded in HTML and containing a list of authors of a scientific publication. We have 2 seeds, $l_1 = $ "AM Turing" and $l_2 = $ "J von Neumann". The candidate elements e_1 and e_2 for which we achieve the maximum score value are framed with a solid line, where the dotted frame encloses an unknown element h_1. When running XPR over the above document and considering e_1, e_2 as candidate nodes, we obtain a corresponding XPath expression /tbody/tr/td/a[@title='Author'] which is then concatenated with the proper LCA expression. Note that unbalanced couples of candidates are filtered and excluded from scoring, consider e.g., the couple w_1 and e_2. Also, note that XPR is elastic with respect to changes in the substructure of elements candidate for matching seeds: for instance, e_2 would be unbalanced with respect to e_1 whenever surrounded by some additional markup (e.g., some nesting within a <div> element, etc.). It is worth mentioning that nearly 100% of the experimental corpus respected this balancing principle, no matter of the presence of optional tags attached to some author names (e.g. superscripts), which are correctly handled by the XPR method.

Text Node Resolution. Whenever XPR can't be applied, we assume that the author list is encoded as raw text with little or no markup. We thus work at the character level, i.e., processing the textual content l_n of a single element of $n \in D$. Author lists have often a specific structure in which names are separated by some fixed delimiter, except the last element, which is easy to be confused

```
A Vendittil, A BattagliaZ, F Buccisanol,        #1, #Z, #1,
L Maurillol, A Tamburinil, B Del Morol,         #1, A Tamburinil, B Del Morol,
A M Epicenol, M Martiradonnal, T Caravital,     A M Epicenol, M Martiradonnal, T Caravital,
S Santinellil, G Adornol, A Picardil, F Zinnol, S Santinellil, G Adornol, A Picardil, F Zinnol,
A Lantil, A Brunol, G Suppol, A Franchil,       A Lantil, A Brunol, G Suppol, A Franchil,
G Franconil and S Amadoril                      G Franconil and S Amadoril
```

Fig. 2. An input example for TNR and the same input after placeholder substitution

with a portion of a last name: think e.g,. at the list "AM Turing, GW Leibniz, J von Neumann and N Tesla.". Note however, that it is not possible to build a simple extraction module which relies on looking for standard separators like "," and "and". We found indeed that author lists are represented in a quite heterogeneous number of ways, think e.g,. at "G. Paratinik, M.Sc. and D. Knuth, Ph.D.", a usual case in fields other than computer science.

To this end, we generate and then try to apply two types of patterns, expressed in terms of a regular expression: one is aimed at describing author names (the *element regular expression*, or EREG), and the other aimed at describing groups of delimiters between names (the *glue characters regular expression* or GREG). We attempt to extract author names both by means of matches of the generated EREG, or extracting the text appearing in between two matches of a GREG. For space reasons we describe here our TNR technique with an example.

An example for TNR. Suppose we have extracted a textual content t from a node $d \in D$ and suppose we have a set of seeds $L =\{$ "A Venditti", "A Battaglia", "F Buccisano", "L Maurillo" $\}$. t is shown in Fig. 2: it is straightforward to see that each name is followed by a comma a space and a number, except for the last one. First a EREG is generated based on the first seed available; in this case, we have $l_1 = $ "A Venditti" and the generated EREG is /[A-Z]\s[A-Z][a-z]+/[1]. We iteratively substitute EREG matches with placeholders in t (see Fig. 2). Then a GREG is computed by analysing text within two placeholders, obtaining in this case /(.*?)[0-9],?\s?/. Eventually, we apply the GREG (or the EREG regular expression when the GREG fails to find a match), on the original value of t, obtaining $I = \{$"A Venditti", "A Battaglia", "F Buccisano", ..., "G Franconi", "S Amadori"$\}$. Note how the last name is extracted by applying the EREG instead of the generated GREG.

3   Evaluation, Related Work and Conclusions

We tested our tool by exploiting, as seed information, the partial author lists reported when querying Google Scholar. The evaluation document collection (C in the following) has been constructed by taking the set of publications of professors and researchers in Applied Physics officially enrolled in Italian Universities as of the end of 2012 and extracting from Google Scholar their list of publications. We pragmatically used for our assessment the restricted set of

---

[1] We herein use the Perl/Javascript regular expression syntax.

Table 1. Summary of the evaluation for TPI-S techniques

Origin	#	XPR Acc.	TNR Acc.	Total Acc.
ScienceDirect	1738	98.8%	0%	98.8%
IEEE Xplore	542	99.8%	100%	100.0%
Physical Review D	258	100.0%	N.A.	100.0%
IOPscience	218	7.3%	100%	100.0%
DSpace@MIT	184	0.0%	100%	100.0%
SAO/NASA ADS	176	88.6%	0%	88.6%
Taylor & Francis	135	100.0%	N.A.	100.0%
Wiley Online	164	100.0%	N.A.	100.0%
ACS Publications	111	98.2%	100%	100.0%
SPIE Digital Library	55	100.0%	N.A.	100.0%
Cambridge Journals	55	100.0%	N.A.	100.0%
Others	466	59.7%	6%	62.2%
Total	**4102**	**85.0%**	**65.0%**	**94.7%**

documents for which the full author lists as reported by Microsoft Academic Search Portal (MSA) were available. After data cleaning we obtained a set of about 4000 items, containing documents with an average of 145 co-authors per paper, with a peak number of 2887 co-authors.

The outcome of our evaluation is shown in Table 1, where percentages of success are reported for the two methods. We classified documents in C according to the digital library of provenance and we aggregated results accordingly: roughly, each row reflects a family of documents with similar structure. In order to test our data extraction method, we ignored the, anyway limited, availability of machine-readable metadata, which is instead exploited in our publicly available system. The evaluation shows that the overall accuracy of TPI-S is satisfactory and that TNR is a fair complement of XPR[2], except for the *others* category, which contained mostly unstructured and heterogenous documents, not coming from a public digital library, like lecture announcements, or conference schedules.

Concerning related work, this can be categorized into two main streams: *a) structural approaches*, in which the goal is to induce an extraction expression (written in XPath or another tree extraction language) for extracting information [4–7, 9, 15]. This approach category takes advantage of document markup and is related mostly to our XPR resolution method; and, *b) unstructured approaches*, in which documents are seen at the character level and is more related to our TNR method [14, 16]. Note that our approach cannot be directly compared with the setting of [8] in that extraction is made from Postscript and PDF documents and with the differing goal of extracting citations and clustering related documents. The TPI-S module has been deployed in our tool enlarging its pool of data extraction and bibliometric analysis features. The Scholar H-Index Calculator, containing a publicly accessible version of TPI-S features is available from [23]. A longer discussion of algorithms, related work and of the experimental setting can be found in [3].

---

[2] Note that TNR has been applied only *incrementally* on the relatively small fraction of documents which XPR has failed to find an expression above threshold. For instance, TNR has not been applied at all when XPR reached 100% of accuracy.

References

1. ATLAS Collaboration, The: The ATLAS experiment at the CERN large hadron collider. Journal of Instrumentation 3(08) (2008)
2. Carbone, V.: Fractional counting of authorship to quantify scientific research output. arXiv preprint arXiv:1106.0114 (2011)
3. Cauteruccio, F., Ianni, G.: A Domain Meta-wrapper Using Seeds for Intelligent Author List Extraction in the Domain of Scholarly Articles. Technical Report, http://www.mat.unical.it/ianni/storage/HCalc-TR-2013-1-Long.pdf
4. Cohen, W.W., Fan, W.: Web-collaborative filtering: recommending music by crawling the web. Computer Networks 33(1-6), 685–698 (2000)
5. Cohen, W.W., Hurst, M., Jensen, L.S.: A flexible learning system for wrapping tables and lists in HTML documents. In: WWW 2002, pp. 232–241 (2002)
6. Doorenbos, R.B., Etzioni, O., Weld, D.S.: A scalable comparison-shopping agent for the world-wide web. In: AGENTS, pp. 39–48 (1997)
7. Etzioni, O., Cafarella, M., Downey, D., et al.: Unsupervised named-entity extraction from the web: An experimental study. Artificial Intelligence 165, 91–134 (2005)
8. Giles, C.L., Bollacker, K.D., Lawrence, S.: CiteSeer: An Automatic Citation Indexing System. In: ACM DL, pp. 89–98 (1998)
9. Gupta, R., Sarawagi, S.: Answering table augmentation queries from unstructured lists on the web. VLDB Endow. 2(1), 289–300 (2009)
10. Harzing, A.: Publish or Perish (2007), http://www.harzing.com/pop.htm
11. Hirsch, J.: An index to quantify an individual's scientific research output. PNAS 102(46), 16569 (2005)
12. Kaur, J., Hoang, D., Sun, X., et al.: Scholarometer: A social framework for analyzing impact across disciplines. PloS One 7(9) (2012)
13. Schreiber, M.: A modification of the h-index: The hm-index accounts for multi-authored manuscripts. Journal of Informetrics 2(3), 211–216 (2008)
14. Talukdar, P.P., Brants, T., Liberman, M., Pereira, F.: A context pattern induction method for named entity extraction. In: CoNLL-X 2006, pp. 141–148 (2006)
15. Urbansky, D., Feldmann, M., Thom, J.A., Schill, A.: Entity extraction from the web with webKnox. In: Snášel, V., Szczepaniak, P.S., Abraham, A., Kacprzyk, J. (eds.) Advances in Intelligent Web Mastering - 2. AISC, vol. 67, pp. 209–218. Springer, Heidelberg (2010)
16. Wang, R.C., Cohen, W.W.: Language-independent set expansion of named entities using the web. In: ICDM 2007, pp. 342–350 (2007)
17. ASN: Italian National Scientific Habilitation (Abilitazione Scientifica Nazionale) (2012), http://abilitazione.miur.it/
18. Citations gadget for Google Scholar, http://code.google.com/p/citations-gadget/
19. ERA: Excellence in Research for Australia (2012), http://www.arc.gov.au/era/
20. Google Scholar, http://scholar.google.com
21. Microsoft Academic Search, http://academic.research.microsoft.com/
22. REF: Research Excellence Framework (2012), http://www.ref.ac.uk/
23. Scholar H-Index Calculator (2010), http://scholarcalculator.gibbi.com/
24. Sciverse Scopus, http://www.scopus.com/
25. Thomson Reuters Web of Knowledge, http://wokinfo.com/

Securing Access to Complex Digital Artifacts – Towards a Controlled Processing Environment for Digital Research Data

Johann Latocha[1], Klaus Rechert[1], and Isao Echizen[2]

[1] University of Freiburg,
Hermann-Herder Str. 10, 79104 Freiburg, Germany
[2] National Institute of Informatics
2-1-2 Hitotsubashi, Chiyoda-ku, Tokyo 101-8430, Japan

Abstract. Providing secured and restricted access to digital objects, especially access to digital research data, for a general audience poses new challenges to memory institutions. For instance, to protect individuals, only anonymized or pseudonymized data should be released to a general audience. Standard procedures have been established over time to cope with privacy issues of non-interactive digital objects like text, audio and video. Appearances of identifiers and potentially also quasi-identifiers were removed by a simple overlay, e.g. in text documents such appearances were simply blackened out. Today's digital artifacts, especially research data, have complex, non-linear and even interactive manifestations. Thus, a different approach to securing access to complex digital artifacts is required. This paper presents an architecture and technical methods to control access to digital research data.

1 Introduction

Management of research data is becoming a crucial service of memory institutions and university-libraries in particular. In order to foster scientific innovation and simultaneously reduce redundant spending on data generation, efficient access to research results as well as their fundamental data is indispensable. Re-using research data is not only economically worthwhile, but convenient access to research data may also spur new research ideas and interdisciplinary collaboration. Furthermore, with the rise of networked functional services, e.g. Cloud offerings such as software-as-a-service and data services (Big Data), a process-oriented, holistic approach to research data management becomes more important.

Recently, public replication and verification of published scientific results has been intensely discussed.[1] However, if research data contains personal data, quasi-identifiers etc., access to research data has to be restricted to ensure the privacy of individuals, e.g. protecting personal information of study participants, or in some cases to protect trade secrets or intellectual property. Furthermore, to

---

[1] http://www.nature.com/news/independent-labs-to-verify-high-profile-papers-1.11176, version 3/20/2013.

T. Aalberg et al. (Eds.): TPDL 2013, LNCS 8092, pp. 315–320, 2013.
© Springer-Verlag Berlin Heidelberg 2013

process such data, toolchains are necessary and in some cases even a distributed networked setup is required. There might also be concerns about disclosing implementation details since not only data has to be made available for verification but also the complete toolchain for its processing.

Hence, today's digital artifacts pose new challenges to memory institutions. Research data is usually kept in dedicated file formats and stored in databases or specialized repositories, mostly as complex aggregates composed of sensitive and non-sensitive data. In contrast to linearly structured media like text, audio or video, sensitive content is more difficult to identify and even more difficult to protect. A simple privacy overlay, e.g. blacken out sensitive data, is in general not a suitable strategy if an authentic replication of a scientific process is required, but also the digital artifact's functional utility is most probably lost. For such scenarios, a different strategy is desired to protect sensitive information. In this article we tackle the problem of securing access to complex research data, first, by a developing decentralized architecture for rendering and interactive usage, providing a complete controlled access environment. This allows restricting access while simultaneously allowing the user to replicate and to verify scientific results to a certain extent. As an example, we propose a generic privacy auditing tool, to verify privacy-policy compliant behavior of the user.

2   Related Work

Privacy-preserving data publishing has become a hot research topic. Large amounts of data are published for various reasons, e.g. California hospitals are required by regulation to publish certain demographic data [1], or Netflix published their subscribers' movie rating and recommendation database for research purposes. [2] Since such data-sets may contain sensitive or person-specific data, appropriate strategies are required to ensure individual privacy. One goal usually is to "sanitize," i.e. anonymize, the data set, without losing the data-set's utility [2,3]. However, these methods usually need domain specific adaption in order to provide the desired privacy guarantees. For a comprehensive overview and discussion on privacy preserving data publishing cf. [4].

A different approach is to rely on retrospective privacy audits. In this case, tools and methods are required to track potential privacy violations, for instance by including cryptographic watermarks. Various frameworks for retrospective privacy audits have been proposed, e.g. in the domain of health-records allowing a complete reconstruction of disclosure chains [5].

Usually these strategies are either purpose or data specific. A generic memory institution may not have privacy experts for all kinds of data-sets available. Thus, at least for generic purposes, a technology neutral approach is required in order to provide a generic, base-line protection for rather simple access patterns like replication of research results or casual data search.

---

[2] Netflix price, `http://www.netflixprize.com/community/viewtopic.php?id=1537`, version of 3/20/2013.

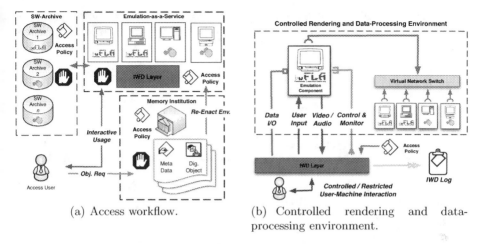

(a) Access workflow.

(b) Controlled rendering and data-processing environment.

Fig. 1. bwFLA Emulation-as-a-Service architecture providing access to complex digital artifacts using their original system environment for rendering and processing

3   Architecture of a Restricted Access-Framework

In most cases, the best way to re-enact a digital scientific process and its data is using its original environment since this should cover all aspects of the artifact's significant properties, and thus, provide an authentic and possibly an interactive rendered result. Hence, emulation and virtualization provide the key strategy to re-enact and access a digital object's native environment.

While technical challenges of developing emulators are not considered in this paper, usability and accessibility of emulators for non-technical users are crucial. Since the number of different ancient and current computer systems (i.e. hardware architectures) is limited, the number of required emulator-setups is limited, too. Hence, providing access to emulation is suitable for standardized service offers. In order to allow a large, non-technical user-group to interact with virtual computer systems, an abstract *emulation-component* has been developed to standardize usage and to hide individual system complexity. Each emulation component provides a uniform API. Up to now, emulation components for all major past and present desktop systems, e.g. PPC, m68k, x86, etc., and major operation systems, e.g. OS/2, MS Windows, Mac OS 7 and newer, etc., have been deployed. Currently, the user is able to interact with emulated environments using either an HTML5-based web-client or a JAVA-based desktop client. Data-I/O and machine interaction, such as attaching/detaching removable media (e.g. floppies, CD/DVDs) and connecting storage sites to the emulation component, is made possible through dedicated interfaces. In general, emulation-components are designed as atomic units suitable to be run in a distributed setup, e.g. computing grids or clusters. A detailed technical description of an emulation-as-a-service (EaaS) framework can be found in earlier work [6].

To re-enact digital data as well as the required software environment in a distributed setting, three distinct entities have to cooperate: the local memory institution managing individual digital artifacts, a software archive and finally an EaaS site providing suitable emulation components. Usually, the access workflow starts with a user querying his or her local memory institution's catalogue for digital objects of interest. If we assume that for these objects suitable technical meta-data is available, the software archive provides all necessary software components for the environment requested to the EaaS. Finally, the EaaS site initiates the emulator rendering of the requested digital object in its original system environment. Fig. 1(a) illustrates the aforementioned access workflow.

4 Securing User-Machine Interaction

Due to the design of the EaaS access model, the user is never able to access sensitive objects directly. Instead the user interacts through controlled and potentially restricted interfaces with an emulated computer system. This setup allows, for instance, "guided tours," where the user is only able to observe actions he or she has requested but which are actually carried out by a trusted third person, e.g. a library employee. Furthermore, the requested data-processing environment may consist of more than a single computer-system. In this case, several emulation components are initialized simultaneously and connected through a virtual network switch (cf. Fig. 1(b)). Since any external events are sent through a single, monitored interface, only emulation components with direct user-interaction need to be monitored.

Hence, by controlling the execution environment and all aspects of user-machine interaction, different technical options become available to secure and/or restrict access to archived data. Firstly, all user-inputs can be monitored and logged, such that any user action could be reproduced if required, i.e. enabling retrospective privacy audits. Another option to protect sensitive data is to limit user interaction to certain, pre-defined steps in data-processing workflows. In this case, the user is not allowed to directly interact with the machine, but will be able to provide parameters or similar input to the process. Such input is then translated to user-machine interactions and executed on the user's behalf. While auditing a user's behavior is a generic option, restricted (guided) user-interaction requires careful preparation.

4.1 Example: Auditing Privacy Compliant Behavior

To monitor user behavior any user-interaction either directly with the running system or with the emulator is processed by the interaction workflow description (IWD) layer (cf. Fig. 1(b)). IWD was originally designed as an abstract user-machine interaction description to capture and replay system-configuration or format-migration workflows in a platform- and system-independent way [7]. In contrast to so-called macro-recorder, the IWD-system does not interact directly with the emulated OS and thus, is platform independent and extensible to cover new, upcoming interaction paradigms. Having a rendering and data processing environment with controlled user interaction, such a system could be extended to track potential privacy violations. IWD in combination with a fully controlled computing environment allows for a complete reproduction of the user's actions, e.g. in case the user has signed a privacy policy or non-disclosure agreement.

In a first step, the actual runtime-configuration of the emulation components as well as hash-values of all attached media are collected. This way, the rendering and data-processing environment can be exactly reconstructed. Further, an IWD interaction-log consists of an ordered list of captured events ev_i, each describing an interaction between user and machine. A single event is described through a precondition, i.e. the system has to be in a specific, pre-defined state pc, an action a, e.g. mouse or keyboard input, and the expected outcome eo of the user-action ($ev_i := < pc, a >_i \rightarrow eo_i$). Both, pre- and postcondition of each interaction are verified by using the emulator's visual output and the emulator's internal machine state. Currently, these conditions are automatically generated, rather simply, by fingerprinting the emulators output. This way, IWDs are independent of the emulation-component's general execution speed.

The user's behavior could also be recorded as a video-stream or similar. However, in this case only the visible results of the user's actions become observable. To fully capture the effects of a user's interaction with a system environment, all communication channels have to be observed, e.g. network connection and other data I/O interfaces. This is especially crucial if several distinct environments are involved, e.g. in a client-server setup. Alternatively, the (secured) system may collect access-logs, for example to databases. However, such logs are usually restricted to certain access patterns and therefore are neither able to capture the user's actual actions nor indirect interactions between machines in a networked setup.

4.2 Preliminary Results, Limitations and Discussion

For reliable and authentic reconstruction of the user's behavior, different IWD-logs have been captured and analyzed. By capturing all user interactions with the machine, an audit file consists of N user-actions ev. To verify the authenticity of the audit log, first, none of the user interaction have been missed at capturing time, none of the user-events are missed at reproduction time and finally, $eo_i^{captured} = eo_i^{reproduced}$ for all events captured.

For the following tests an x86 QEMU-based emulation with Microsoft Windows 98 SE has been used. In a first test-case the user started a web browser and navigated to a special purpose web site. The pages shown to the user consist of a 3×3 table with a single text-input field and a single check-box. The user is then requested to select the text-input field, fill-in the field's location within the table and to activate the check-box. This procedure has been repeated for ten pages with random cell layout. Finally, the form data is submitted to the web server. In total, 4496 mouse events and 46 key events were captured and successfully reproduced. To verify that the IWD-event synchronization works correctly, the IWD has been replayed over a high latency wireless network (avg. 350 ms).

To verify that each event produces the same outcome as at capturing time, a second test has been made, asking the user to open a bitmap file found on a virtual floppy disk attached to the emulator with an image drawing application (in our case MS Paint). The bitmap has been modified by the user, using some of the available drawing tools. Finally, the result is saved again on the disk. For this, 3475 mouse events and 14 key events have been captured. After each replay the bitmap's MD5 sum has been calculated and verified against the user's original result, to verify that the recreated interactions produced exactly the same results, i.e. no user-event has been lost nor altered at replay time. For both test-cases reproduction runs have been repeated at least ten times and in both cases no failure occurred.

5   Conclusion and Outlook

Having a generic, controlled and secured setup for data-rendering and data-processing lays the foundation to implement privacy and security techniques protecting sensitive data in complex digital artifacts. While the aforementioned test-cases show that in principle the system is able to capture and replay user-events in a reliable way, the system so far only allows a simple reconstruction of user-behavior. Based on this e.g. proactive privacy protection systems could be built, detecting specific, not allowed user actions or to dynamically control data release. However, as a next step, robustness and practicality have to be proven using real workloads and real users.

References

1. Carlisle, D.M., Rodrian, M.L., Diamond, C.L.: California inpatient data reporting manual, medical information reporting for california (5th ed). Tech. rep., Office of Statewide Health Planning and Development (2007)
2. Kifer, D., Gehrke, J.: Injecting utility into anonymized datasets. In: Proceedings of the 2006 ACM SIGMOD International Conference on Management of Data, SIGMOD 2006, pp. 217–228. ACM, New York (2006)
3. Li, T., Li, N.: On the tradeoff between privacy and utility in data publishing. In: Proceedings of the 15th ACM SIGKDD International Conference on Knowledge Discovery and Data Mining, KDD 2009, pp. 517–526. ACM, New York (2009)
4. Fung, B.C.M., Wang, K., Chen, R., Yu, P.S.: Privacy-preserving data publishing: A survey of recent developments. ACM Comput. Surv. 42(4), 14:1–14:53 (2010)
5. Wohlgemuth, S., Echizen, I., Sonehara, N., Müller, G.: Tagging disclosures of personal data to third parties to preserve privacy. In: Rannenberg, K., Varadharajan, V., Weber, C. (eds.) Security and Privacy – Silver Linings in the Cloud. IFIP AICT, vol. 330, pp. 241–252. Springer, Heidelberg (2010)
6. Rechert, K., Valizada, I., von Suchodoletz, D., Latocha, J.: bwFLA – a functional approach to digital preservation. PIK – Praxis der Informationsverarbeitung und Kommunikation 35(4), 259–267 (2012)
7. von Suchodoletz, D., Rechert, K., Welte, R., van den Dobbelsteen, M., Roberts, B., van der Hoeven, J., Schroder, J.: Automation of flexible migration workflows. International Journal of Digital Curation 2(2) (2010)

Restoring Semantically Incomplete Document Collections Using Lexical Signatures

Luis Meneses, Himanshu Barthwal, Sanjeev Singh,
Richard Furuta, and Frank Shipman

Center for the Study of Digital Libraries and Department of Computer Science and Engineering
Texas A&M University
College Station, TX 77843–3112, USA
{ldmm,shady3025,sanjekus,furuta,shipman}@cse.tamu.edu

Abstract. Unexpected changes create a problem when managing missing resources in a digital collection. In decentralized and distributed collections such as Walden's Paths, a missing point or an incomplete resource is of grave importance as it can potentially interrupt the continuity in the narration and render the collection semantically incomplete. We can foresee two possible scenarios occurring when resources cannot be found. First, we have access to a copy of the missing document or to its lexical signatures, which allows us to find the missing resource. The second case is more interesting to us. What happens if we don't have any valid metadata associated to the missing resource? To solve this problem, we used the lexical signatures of valid documents within a collection to find suitable replacements for absent resources. As results we found that traditional similarity metrics do not adequately convey the relationships between the elements in the collections. Our analyses also showed that our procedures were able to restore the semantic integrity of incomplete document collections.

Keywords: Semantic replacements, Web resource management, distributed collections.

1   Introduction

Change is inevitable. In our role as researchers, we strive to manage and minimize the impact of unexpected changes in document collections. More specifically, our work has been motivated to mitigate the impact of unexpected change in documents stored in decentralized collections. Examples of decentralized collections include, but are not limited to, Walden's Paths [1] and the Ensemble Computing Portal [2].

Electronic resources can change, intentionally and unintentionally, because of different factors and circumstances. Change may be because of deliberate actions on part of the collector – for example, reorganization of the structure of the collection, switching to a different content management system, or changing jobs and institutions. They may be due to unexpected events – earthquakes, power outages, disk failures, and the like. They may be due to uncontrollable factors, as McCown et al. point out [3] – for example, death, seizure of computers by law enforcement, or termination of an ISPs services.

T. Aalberg et al. (Eds.): TPDL 2013, LNCS 8092, pp. 321–332, 2013.

Great strides have been made to characterize and manage change within collections of documents. Klein and Nelson argued that digital documents do not disappear from the Web, but they leave artifacts that can be used to reconstruct them [4, 5]. Bar–Yosseff et al. carried out experiments to measure the decay of the Web [6]. SalahEl-deen argued that nearly 11% of shared resources will be lost one year after being pub-lished and that this decay will continue to lose 0.02% per day [7]. Additionally, our research group has investigated the characterization of change in collections of admi-nistratively–decentralized Web–based resources [8-10]. Lately we have focused on addressing issues raised when a Web server reports change in a human–readable, but not in machine–readable format [11].

However, managing missing resources can still be problematic. Taking into account the infrastructure of Walden's Paths, where decentralized collections are stored as traversable paths containing multiple nodes and documents, we can foresee two possible scenarios occurring when resources cannot be found. First, we have access to a copy of the missing document or to its lexical signatures – which are de-fined as a set of key identifying terms. Previous research by Dalal et al. has already addressed this case [12], thus finding the missing resource is trivial. The second sce-nario is more interesting to us at this point: What happens if we don't have any meta-data associated to the missing resource? A missing document is of grave importance, because each resource contributes to the overall meaning of the collection and to the continuity of the narration. Therefore, a missing document can potentially interrupt the flow of the collection and make it semantically incomplete. Figure 1 shows an example of a "soft 404" error, where a server masks a "404: not found" HTTP re-sponse with a standard page and a different response code, which in this case causes a collection in Walden's Paths to become semantically incomplete. Given that the re-source URL is part of the metadata describing the node, gathering the documents that point to the missing resource could be proposed to solve this problem [4]. However, we believe that this solution would not render adequate results when taking into ac-count that some of the URLs point to outdated resources that are no longer included in search indexes or harvested by preservation services such as the Internet Archive.

To solve this problem, we propose to use the lexical signatures of the other "valid" documents (i.e. that are not missing) within the collection to find a suitable replace-ment for the absent resource. In the best–case scenario, we would expect to be able to find the actual resource that is missing. However, the main focus of our research is to find similar resources that can act as a surrogates or placeholders, contribute towards the continuity of the narration and restore the semantic completeness of the collection.

Therefore, finding document surrogates for a document collection raises three questions. First, what characteristics should a digital resource have to be considered a suitable replacement? Second, what mechanisms and processes should we use to find a suitable surrogate? And third, how can we measure the quality of the replacement document? We will explore these research questions in the following sections.

Fig. 1. Example of a "soft 404" error viewed through the Walden's Paths user interface. This missing document makes the collection semantically incomplete.

2   Previous Work

Previous work on finding missing resources is based around the premise that documents and information are not lost but simply misplaced [13] as a consequence of the lack of integrity in the Web [14-17]. Other studies have also focused on finding the longevity of documents in the Web [18] and in distributed collections [19, 20].

Phelps and Wilensky pioneered the use of lexical signatures to locate missing content in the Web [21]. They claimed that if a Web request returned a 404 error, querying a search engine with a five–term lexical signature could retrieve the missing content. Park et al. used Phelps and Wilensky's previous research to perform an evaluation of nine lexical signature generators that incorporate term frequency measures [22]. Additionally, Klein and Nelson have extracted lexical signatures from titles and backlinks to find missing Web resources [4, 5, 23]. However, we believe that we must use more active measures that do not rely on "lazy preservation" [24] to ensure the integrity of the collections in Walden's Paths over time.

The research problem that we are describing in this paper shares some similarities with identifying near–duplicate documents. Near–duplicate documents are identical in terms of content, but have differences in their formatting, minor corrections, advertisements, logos and timestamps. Finding near–duplicate documents is difficult because single web resources usually convey many semantic components. Despite the inherent difficulty associated with this problem, the Shingling [25] and Simhash [26] algorithms are considered the state of the art in near–duplicate document detection. The Shingling algorithm uses a subset of "shingles", which are n–grams extracted from the text, to create a signature for the document. The similarity of two documents is then calculated with the Jaccard coefficient between the common signatures.

Another approach used to identify near–duplicates is based on creating a digital fingerprint for a document. A digital fingerprint is a stream of integers that represent the key content in a given document. Early proponents of this approach include Manber [27]; along with Shivakumar and Garcia–Molina [28]. Along the same lines, Brin, Davis and Garcia–Molina also proposed a system that detected documents that overlapped in "significant ways" [29].

Forman et al. identified near–similar technical support documents [30]. Interestingly, they chose to rely only on the contents of the documents because of missing and corrupted metadata. Their approach was defined by the document corpus, as support documents can contain illustrations and diagrams and cannot be broken into semantic sections. Instead they chose to break the documents in a consistent way that was not dictated by semantics and then detect collisions between near–duplicates.

Although detecting near–duplicates shares some similarities with our research, ours has a different scope. Near–duplicates are documents that share the same content but have different presentation characteristics. The purpose of our research is finding documents that can serve as replacements for missing items to restore the semantic integrity of a path. Moreover, finding near–duplicates of missing documents would require a cached or archived copy of the lost document – which we assume that we don't have – and a very specific crawl of the web that is also beyond the scope of our approach.

Our research aims to enhance and complement the methods used by Dalal et al. to find appropriate replacements for missing resources from the web that belonged to a collection in the Walden's Paths Project [12]. Their approach was based on a two–step process. First, metadata was extracted when the path was created thus preserving the author's intent and vision. Second, the extracted metadata was used to find pages when they cannot be retrieved. In the specific case of collections such as Walden's Paths, each node in a path is destined to make a contribution towards the overall concept and the continuity in the narration. Therefore, finding replacements becomes a critical factor to maintain the integrity of the collections and preserve their semantic meaning.

3 Methodology and Results

3.1 Experiment Setup

At its backend, the Walden's Paths project uses a Mysql database. This database stores the metadata for each path and its nodes. Title, abstract and language describe each path; while metadata for the nodes includes the resource URL and general notes. Given that users of Walden's Paths created all the paths in the database, it is safe to assume that the nodes share semantic ideas and follow a stream of thought. Moreover, for our experiment a replacement was considered suitable if it shared similarities with the missing resource and it conveyed the semantic meaning of the rest of the path. We initially considered paths that fulfilled three requisites: First, they must contain at least one node. Second, the nodes must have links to web resources; and third, the paths must be in English. Thus, our initial sample from the collection consisted of 948 paths that fit these criteria.

The documents from the resource URLs for each node were retrieved using seven steps. First, we attempted to fetch the "absolute URL" for each given URL. Our methods allowed 10 redirects per URL entry: if it exceeds 10 redirects the URL entry was discarded and not used in the study. Second, the web resources were downloaded using Python's HTTP protocol client with a timeout value of 10 seconds and a 54Mbps connection. Third, and because of the diversity of documents in the web, we decided to focus only on HTML files. Thus, the retrieved documents were then identified as HTML files using Python–magic and non–HTML files were discarded. Fourth, we checked the HTML documents for "soft 404" errors using the procedure based on lexical signatures that we described in our previous work [11]. Fifth, we removed the HTML elements using Python's Beautiful Soup libraries. Sixth, we eliminated the stop words using Python's Natural Language Toolkit (NLTK), removed punctuation using string translation functions, converted to lowercase and then stemmed each remaining term using a Lancaster stemmer. Finally, the resulting lexical signatures were stored as individual documents in a folder structure, where each folder represented a different path.

To run our experiment, we assumed that the paths were "incomplete" meaning that one of the resource URLs from the nodes could not be retrieved. We did this by pretending that the document referenced in the metadata from one of the nodes was "missing" and could not retrieved. The node that referenced the missing resource was randomly selected from each path. This allowed us to compare the original missing document and its replacement.

The replacements for the missing resources in the nodes were found using a search engine. We decided to use the Microsoft Bing Search API because it allowed us to run 5000 queries per month for free. Also, Bing is based on MSN Search and its document index and top results are known to be updated more frequently when compared to other search engines [31]. We gathered the five most significant lexical signatures – which describe and characterize each incomplete path, and then used them to create a query string taking into account Phelps and Wilensky's previous work [21]. Then we retrieved the resources from the URLs of the five top results. This retrieval was done at run time and followed the seven–step procedure that was used for the resource URLs in the path nodes.

3.2 Results

We proceeded to narrow down our sample to paths that contained at least three nodes with retrievable HTML documents. This condition was enforced to provide contextual information to the retrieval algorithms for our experiment. However, it further reduced our sample to a working set of 447 paths. Paths with three and four nodes were the most common cases. At this point we hypothesized that a better notion of context, provided by a larger number of nodes and documents, would allow our processes to obtain better replacements for missing resources.

We commenced the analysis by validating the assumption that the nodes within a path share semantic ideas and follow a stream of thought. For this, we calculated the cosine similarity between the resource in the incomplete node and the rest of the documents in the path. We found that the vectors formed with the documents within a same path are not identical, but they do share some similarities. Figure 2 shows the average cosine similarity between a missing document and the other valid documents within the path.

We also calculated the link similarity between the missing and the valid documents, but this measure did not provide us any statistical evidence of similarity.

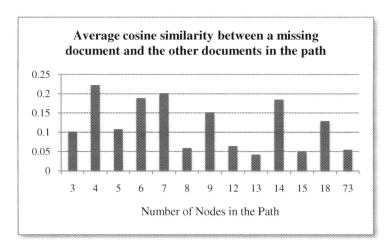

Fig. 2. Average cosine similarity between a missing document and the other valid documents within the path.

We selected the replacements using two procedures. In the first, we proceeded to use the top–ranked result from the search engine API. For convenience, we will refer to this method as the "top–ranked" approach. For the second, which we will refer to as the "top–similar" method, our goal was to evaluate if the most similar documents from the search results could be used as suitable placeholders. For this method, we calculated the cosine similarity between the documents in the top five search results and selected the two that had the shortest distance between them. We then chose the topmost–ranked result from the resulting pair. We evaluated our algorithms using the resemblance measure, which was defined in the Shingling algorithm [25], and the cosine similarity between the original document and its surrogate. The cosine similarity was calculated using NumPy.

The average resemblance and cosine similarity were very close for both methods. For resemblance, the average values were 0.735 for "top–ranked" and 0.738 for the "top–similar" method. With resemblance, optimal cases are closer to one. Likewise, the average values for calculated the cosine similarity were 0.148 for "top–ranked" and 0.166 for the "top–similar" method. For cosine similarity, optimal values are closer to zero. Given the magnitude of these values, we found that using resemblance as a similarity measure was more accurate when expressing the relationships and common ground between documents. However, the results vary greatly when we consider the number of documents in each path that were used for the calculations. Figure 3 and 4 show the distribution of the average resemblance and cosine similarity when grouped by the number of nodes in each path. When we analyzed the data represented in these figures we realized that they do not truly represent the relationship between the number of documents used to extract the lexical signatures and the replacements we obtained. We decided to perform further analysis.

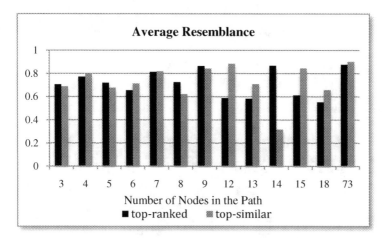

Fig. 3. Average Resemblance grouped by the number of nodes in each analyzed path

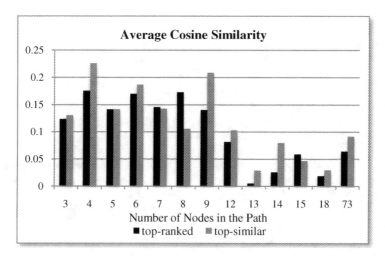

Fig. 4. Average cosine similarity grouped by the number of nodes in each analyzed path

Then we proceeded to calculate the quadratic mean between the similarity matrix of the original documents in the path, and the similarity matrix of the original documents with a replacement resource in place. We calculated the quadratic mean between the similarity matrices to get a sense of how the surrogates would fit among the original documents and if they would restore the semantic meaning of the path. We performed this calculation for the "top–ranked" and the "top–similar" methods. Given that we are using two similarity matrices, the best–case scenario would be to encounter values closer to zero. Figure 5 shows the Average Quadratic Mean between the original and modified similarity matrices grouped by the number of nodes on each analyzed path.

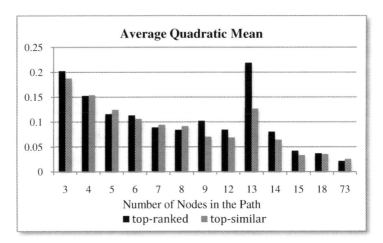

Fig. 5. Average Quadratic Mean between the original and modified similarity matrices grouped by the number of nodes on each path

Using the quadratic mean between the two matrices, we observed that there is correlation between the number of nodes in the path and the quality of the document surrogates. If a path has more nodes, the extraction algorithm has more information available and it is able to obtain more significant lexical signatures, thus retrieving better document surrogates in the end. Figure 5 shows that there is a tendency leaning towards zero as more nodes are present in a path collection. However, we observed an irregular spike in the group of paths that contained 13 nodes. In this case, the algorithm was unable to find any suitable replacements, which caused the quadratic measure to augment drastically. Looking closely at the source documents, we believe that the lack of a main theme in these paths caused the algorithm to be unable to extract relevant lexical signatures from these documents.

3.3   User Testing

To further test the validity of our findings we conducted a quick user evaluation. We randomly populated two test servers with a replacement document within a node in each path. The replacement nodes were found using the "top–ranked" and "top–similar algorithms". Then we requested six members of our research group to go over 10 preselected paths and check for inconsistencies: replacement documents that were out of context. These inconsistencies were then labeled and tagged using a browser extension for Google Chrome that we developed for this specific purpose. On average, we found that users viewed the replacement documents as valid with a precision value of 0.917 and a recall of 0.947.

4   Discussion

Finding documents that can semantically restore a document collection is not an easy task. Thus, we faced three obstacles for this task. First, the variability in the documents served as Web pages makes content fluctuate greatly across the Web. Second, the combined probabilities of occurrence from the terms in a Web page can have a tendency to introduce false positives. Although we minimized this tendency when we stemmed and streamlined the contents of the documents, we believe that our approach would work better in a specialized domain. And third, capturing user intent can be problematic when dealing with a diverse corpus of documents.

We relied on resemblance and cosine similarity to quantify the relationship between the original document and its possible replacement. Likewise, we also wanted to quantify the relationship between the surrogate and the rest of the documents in the path. Calculating the determinant of the similarity matrices was an obvious choice, but it was not a good option. We looked at the determinant as a measure that represents the volume formed by the vectors in n dimensions, where n is the number of nodes in the path. However, we found cases where the determinant had a value of zero. This was caused because the algorithm retrieved a document with the same lexical signatures as one already present in the path; thus causing rows and columns in the matrix to be equal. Therefore, we decided to use the quadratic mean instead between the original similarity matrix and the one derived from the modified document set.

An important result from our work was the realization that traditional similarity measures were not adequate to quantify the relationships between documents in the collections and their replacements. We can point out two cases. First, the link similarity between the assumed missing document and the other valid resources in the collection did not provide any statistical evidence of similarity. We believe this was caused by the high variability in the documents' structural markup and their associated metadata. And second, our analysis showed that cosine distance as a similarity measure made it difficult to fully express the associations and connections between a missing document and its replacement. We believe this difficulty stems from the fact that a missing document in a narrative–based collection not only depends on the resource that is replacing, but also depends on its neighboring documents. On the other hand, using resemblance as a similarity measure gave us a better idea of the relationships between documents because it is based on the combined probability of occurrence of n–grams.

We must also address if using a different search engine could have changed the outcome of our study. We believe a different search engine could have probably shifted the results on the paths with fewer nodes. However, the resemblance and cosine similarity measures would not have varied significantly for more populated paths.

5   Future Work

We consider our work a starting point rather than an end result. We plan to continue exploring the semantic relationships between documents in digital collections. We believe that this exploration will allow us to devise other methods to replace missing resources. We plan to focus on three points. First, we would like to explore the semantic relationships between documents in collections where the narrative is important, but the collection lacks the boundaries that a path–based collection provides. In these collections, the documents still share a semantic meaning. However the continuity and semantics are set by the curator and not by the infrastructure of the collection.

Second, we would like to explore different methods for finding replacements. More specifically, we would expand our algorithms into a two–step iterative process where a designated user ultimately evaluates replacements.

Finally, we would carry out more extensive user testing involving a larger sample size. Using a larger sample size will increase the statistical significance of our methods. Additionally, in some cases the replacement we found through our methods had some differences with the missing document. Although this was completely expected, it caused some confusion when users could only label the document surrogate as "right" or "wrong". To solve these cases, we will be using Likert scales during the user testing of future iterations.

6   Conclusions

Distributed collections were envisioned to allow curators to organize resources without having the burden of managing and maintaining them over time. This model works well in theory. However, documents in the Web are known to decay over time. In this paper, we have described our approach towards identifying replacements for missing documents in distributed collections where the continuity in the narration and the semantics of the collection are important factors. Additionally, we have documented cases where similarity measures fail to quantify the relationships between resources within the same collection. In the end, we believe that our research brings forth new possibilities for curators on how to manage and alleviate unexpected and problematic changes in digital collections.

Acknowledgements. This work was supported in part by National Science Foundation grants DUE–0840715 and DUE–1044212. We would also like to thank Jeremy Tzou for his involvement and help in this work.

References

[1] Bogen, P.L., Pogue, D., Poursardar, F., Li, Y., Furuta, R., Shipman, F.: WPv4: a reimagined Walden's paths to support diverse user communities. In: Proc. of the 11th Annual International ACM/IEEE Joint Conference on Digital Libraries, Ottawa, Ontario, Canada, pp. 419–420 (2011)

[2] Cassel, L., Fox, E., Shipman, F., Brusilovsky, P., Fax, W., Garcia, D., Hislop, G., Furuta, R., Delcambre, L., Potluri, S.: Ensemble: enriching communities and collections to support education in computing: poster session. Journal of Computing Sciences in Colleges 25, 224–226 (2010)

[3] McCown, F., Marshall, C.C., Nelson, M.L.: Why web sites are lost (and how they're sometimes found). Communications of the ACM 52, 141–145 (2009)

[4] Klein, M., Ware, J., Nelson, M.L.: Rediscovering missing web pages using link neighborhood lexical signatures. In: Proc. of the 11th Annual International ACM/IEEE Joint Conference on Digital libraries, Ottawa, Ontario, Canada (2011)

[5] Klein, M., Nelson, M.L.: Evaluating methods to rediscover missing web pages from the web infrastructure. In: Proc. Of The 10th Annual Joint Conference on Digital Libraries, Gold Coast, Queensland, Australia (2010)

[6] Bar-Yossef, Z., Broder, A.Z., Kumar, R., Tomkins, A.: Sic transit gloria telae: towards an understanding of the web's decay. In: Proc. of the 13th International Conference on World Wide Web, New York, NY, USA (2004)

[7] SalahEldeen, H.M., Nelson, M.L.: Losing My Revolution: How Many Resources Shared on Social Media Have Been Lost? In: Zaphiris, P., Buchanan, G., Rasmussen, E., Loizides, F. (eds.) TPDL 2012. LNCS, vol. 7489, pp. 125–137. Springer, Heidelberg (2012)

[8] Francisco-Revilla, L., Shipman, F., Furuta, R., Karadkar, U., Arora, A.: Managing change on the web. In: Proc. of the 1st ACM/IEEE-CS Joint Conference on Digital Libraries, Roanoke, Virginia, United States (2001)

[9] Francisco-Revilla, L., Shipman, F., Furuta, R., Karadkar, U., Arora, A.: Perception of content, structure, and presentation changes in Web-based hypertext. In: Proc. of the 12th ACM Conference on Hypertext and Hypermedia, Arhus, Denmark (2001)

[10] Logasa Bogen, P., Francisco-Revilla, L., Furuta, R., Hubbard, T., Karadkar, U.P., Shipman, F.: Longitudinal study of changes in blogs. In: Proc. of the 7th ACM/IEEE-CS Joint Conference on Digital Libraries, Vancouver, BC, Canada (2007)

[11] Meneses, L., Furuta, R., Shipman, F.: Identifying "Soft 404" Error Pages: Analyzing the Lexical Signatures of Documents in Distributed Collections. In: Zaphiris, P., Buchanan, G., Rasmussen, E., Loizides, F. (eds.) TPDL 2012. LNCS, vol. 7489, pp. 197–208. Springer, Heidelberg (2012)

[12] Dalal, Z., Dash, S., Dave, P., Francisco-Revilla, L., Furuta, R., Karadkar, U., Shipman, F.: Managing distributed collections: evaluating web page changes, movement, and replacement. In: Proc. of the 4th ACM/IEEE-CS Joint Conference on Digital Libraries, Tuscon, AZ, USA, pp. 160–168 (2004)

[13] Baeza-Yates, R., Pereira, I., Ziviani, N.: Genealogical trees on the web: a search engine user perspective. In: Proc. of the 17th International Conference on World Wide Web, Beijing, China (2008)

[14] Ashman, H.: Electronic document addressing: dealing with change. ACM Computing Surveys 32, 201–212 (2000)

[15] Ashman, H., Davis, H., Whitehead, J., Caughey, S.: Missing the 404: link integrity on the World Wide Web. In: Proc. of the Seventh International Conference on World Wide Web, Brisbane, Australia (1998)

[16] Davis, H.C.: Hypertext link integrity. ACM Computing Surveys 31, 28 (1999)

[17] Davis, H.C.: Referential integrity of links in open hypermedia systems. In: Proc. of the Ninth ACM Conference on Hypertext and Hypermedia, Pittsburgh, Pennsylvania, United States (1998)

[18] Kahle, B.: Preserving the Internet. Scientific American 276, 82–83 (1997)

[19] Koehler, W.: Web page change and persistence—a four-year longitudinal study. Journal of the American Society for Information Science and Technology 53, 162–171 (2002)

[20] Spinellis, D.: The decay and failures of web references. Communications of the ACM 46, 71–77 (2003)

[21] Phelps, T.A., Wilensky, R.: Robust Hyperlinks Cost Just Five Words Each. University of California at Berkeley (2000)

[22] Park, S.-T., Pennock, D.M., Giles, C.L., Krovetz, R.: Analysis of lexical signatures for improving information persistence on the World Wide Web. Transactions on Information Systems 22, 540–572 (2004)

[23] Klein, M., Shipman, J., Nelson, M.L.: Is this a good title? In: Proc. of the 21st ACM Conference on Hypertext and Hypermedia, Toronto, Ontario, Canada (2010)

[24] McCown, F., Smith, J.A., Nelson, M.L.: Lazy preservation: reconstructing websites by crawling the crawlers. In: Proc. of the 8th Annual ACM International Workshop on Web Information and Data Management, Arlington, Virginia, USA, pp. 67–74 (2006)

[25] Broder, A.Z., Glassman, S.C., Manasse, M.S., Zweig, G.: Syntactic clustering of the Web. Computer Networks 29, 1157–1166 (1997)

[26] Charikar, M.S.: Similarity estimation techniques from rounding algorithms. In: Proc. of the Thiry-fourth Annual ACM Symposium on Theory of Computing, Montreal, Quebec, Canada (2002)

[27] Manber, U.: Finding similar files in a large file system. In: Proc. of the USENIX Winter 1994 Technical Conference, San Francisco, California (1994)

[28] Shivakumar, N., Garcia-Molina, H.: Finding Near-Replicas of Documents and Servers on the Web. In: Atzeni, P., Mendelzon, A.O., Mecca, G. (eds.) WebDB 1998. LNCS, vol. 1590, pp. 204–212. Springer, Heidelberg (1999)

[29] Brin, S., Davis, J., Garcia-Molina, H.: Copy detection mechanisms for digital documents. In: Proc. of the 1995 ACM SIGMOD International Conference on Management of Data, San Jose, California, USA, pp. 398–409 (1995)

[30] Forman, G., Eshghi, K., Chiocchetti, S.: Finding similar files in large document repositories. In: Proc. of the eleventh ACM SIGKDD International Conference on Knowledge Discovery in Data Mining, Chicago, Illinois, USA (2005)

[31] McCown, F., Nelson, M.L.: Search engines and their public interfaces: which apis are the most synchronized? In: Proc. of the 16th International Conference on World Wide Web, Banff, Alberta, Canada (2007)

Resurrecting My Revolution

Using Social Link Neighborhood in Bringing Context to the Disappearing Web

Hany M. Salaheldeen and Michael L. Nelson

Old Dominion University, Department of Computer Science
Norfolk VA, 23529, USA
{hany,mln}@cs.odu.edu

Abstract. In previous work we reported that resources linked in tweets disappeared at the rate of 11% in the first year followed by 7.3% each year afterwards. We also found that in the first year 6.7%, and 14.6% in each subsequent year, of the resources were archived in public web archives. In this paper we revisit the same dataset of tweets and find that our prior model still holds and the calculated error for estimating percentages missing was about 4%, but we found the rate of archiving produced a higher error of about 11.5%. We also discovered that resources have disappeared from the archives themselves (7.89%) as well as reappeared on the live web after being declared missing (6.54%). We have also tested the availability of the tweets themselves and found that 10.34% have disappeared from the live web. To mitigate the loss of resources on the live web, we propose the use of a "tweet signature". Using the Topsy API, we extract the top five most frequent terms from the union of all tweets about a resource, and use these five terms as a query to Google. We found that using tweet signatures results in discovering replacement resources with 70+% textual similarity to the missing resource 41% of the time.

Keywords: Web Archiving, Social Media, Digital Preservation, Reconstruction.

1 Introduction

Microblogging services like Twitter have evolved from merely posting a status or quote to an intra-user interaction tool that connect celebrities, politicians, and others to the public. They have also evolved to act as a narration tool and an information exchange describing current publicly recognized events and incidents. In 2011, during the Egyptian revolution, thousands of posts and resources were shared during the 18 days of the uprising. These resources could have crucial value in narrating the personal experience during this historic event, acting as a first draft of history written by the public.

In our previous work, we proved that shared resources on the web are prone to loss and disappearance at nearly constant rate [17]. We found that after

T. Aalberg et al. (Eds.): TPDL 2013, LNCS 8092, pp. 333–345, 2013.

only one year we lost nearly 11% of the resources linked in social posts and continued to lose an average of 7.3% yearly. In some cases, this disappearance is not catastrophic as we can rely on the public archives to retrieve a snapshot of the resource to fill into the place of the missing resource. In another study we measured how much of the web is archived and found that 16%–79% of URIs have at least one archived copy [1]. Unfortunately, there is still a large percentage of the web that is not archived and thus a huge amount of resources are not archived and prone to total loss upon disappearance from the live web.

This evolution in the role of social media and the ease of reader interaction and dissemination could be used as a possible solution to metigate or prevent the loss of the unarchived shared resources. Fortunately, when a user tweets or shares a link, it leaves behind a trail of copies, links, likes, comments, other shares. If the shared resource is later gone these traces, in most cases, still persist. Thus, in this paper we investigate if the other tweets that also linked to the resource can be mined to provide enough context to discover similar resources that can be used as a substitute for the missing resource. To do this, in this study we extract up to the 500 most recent tweets about linked URIs and we propose a method of finding the social link neighborhood of the resource we are attempting to reconstruct. This link neighborhood could be mined for identifiers and alternative related resources.

2   Related Work

Social media has been the focus of numerous studies in the last decade. Twitter, for example, was analyzed by Kwak et al. where they aimed to identify the characteristics of the Twittersphere, retweeting, and the diffusion speed of posts by using algorithms like PageRank in ranking users [10]. Bakshy et al. investigated 1.6 million users along with the tweet diffusion events to identify influencers on Twitter and their effect in content spread [2]. To answer questions in regards to the production, flow, and consumption of information on Twitter, Wu et al. analyzed the intra-user interactions and found that nearly 20K elite users are responsible for generation of nearly 50% of URLs shared [18]. Intuitively, this shows that popularity plays an important role in the content disseminated. They also found that type of the content published and the type of users broadcasting this content affect the lifespan of the tweet activity.

Along with understanding the nature of the social media, researchers analyzed user behavior on the social networks in general. By analyzing user activity click logs, Beneventu et al. aimed to get a better understanding of social interactions social browsing patterns [5]. Zhao and Rosson aimed to explore the reasons of how and why people use Twitter and this use's impact on informal communication at work [23]. Following the how and the why, Gill et al. attempted to answer the next question of what is the user-generated content is about by investigating personal weblogs to detect the effects of personality, topic type, and the general motivation in published blogs [7]. Yang and Counts investigated the information diffusion speed, scale and range in Twitter and how they could be predicted [22].

This in-depth analysis and study of the social media, its nature, the information dissemination patterns, and the user behavior and interaction paved the way for the researchers to have a better understanding of how the social media played a major role in narrating publicly significant events. These studies prove that user-generated content in social media is of crucial importance and can be considered the first draft of history. Vieweg et al. analyzed two natural hazard events (the Oklahoma grass fires and the red River floods in 2009) and how microblogging contributed in raising the situational awareness of the public [21]. Starbird and Palen analyzed how the crowd interact with politically sensitive context regarding the Egyptian revolution of 2011 [20]. Starbird et al. in another study utilized collaborative filtering techniques for identifying social media users who are most likely to be on the ground during a mass disruption event [19]. Mark et al. investigated weblogs to examine societal interactions to a disaster over time and how they reflect the collective public view towards this disaster [11].

In our previous work we showed that this content is vulnerable to loss. Similar to regular web content and websites, there are several reasons explaining this loss. McCown et al. analyzed some of the reasons behind the disappearance and reappearance of websites [12]. McCown and Nelson also examined several techniques to counter the loss prior to its occurrence in social networking websites like Facebook [13]. As for regular web pages, Klein and Nelson analyzed the means of using lexical signatures to rediscover missing web pages [9]. Given that the web resource itself might not be available for analysis or might be costly to extract, several studies investigated other alternatives to having the resource itself. Other studies investigated the use of the page's URL to aid web page categorization without resorting to the have the webpage itself [4, 8]. Xiaoguang et al. utilized class information from neighboring pages in the link graph to aid the classification [15].

3   Existence and Stability of Shared Resources

We start our analysis by revisiting the experiment conducted in March of 2012, in which we modeled the existence of shared resources on the live web and the public archives. In that experiment, we examined six publicly-recognized events that occurred between June 2009 and March 2012, extracting six sets of corresponding social posts. Each of the selected posts include an linked resource and hashtags related to the events. Consequently, we tested the existence of the embedded resources on the live web and in the public archives. After calculating the percentages lost and archived we estimated the existence as a function of time. In this paper, we start by revisiting this year-old estimation model and checking its validity after a year before proceeding with our analysis of reappearance and extracting the social context of the missing resources. Then we investigated how this context could be utilized in guiding the search in extracting the best possible replacement for the missing resource.

3.1 Revisiting Existence

In the 2012 model, we found a nearly linear relationship between the number of resources missing from the web and time (equation 1), and a less linear relationship between the amount archived and time (equation 2).

$$Content\ Lost\ Percentage = 0.02(Age\ in\ days) + 4.20 \tag{1}$$

$$Content\ Archived\ Percentage = 0.04(Age\ in\ days) + 6.74 \tag{2}$$

As a year has passed, we need to analyze our findings and the estimation calculated to see if it still matches our prediction. For each of the six datasets investigated, we repeat the same experiment of analyzing the existence of each of the resources on the live web. A resource is deemed missing if its HTTP responses terminate in something other than 200, including "soft 404s" [3]. Table 1 shows the results from repeating the experiment, the predicted calculated values based on our model, and the corresponding errors. Figure 1 illustrates the measured and the estimated plots for the missing resources. The standard error is 4.15% which shows that our model matched reality.

Table 1. Measured and predicted percentages for missing and archived content in each dataset

	MJ		Iran		H1N1		Obama		Egypt		Syria
Missing Measured	37.10%	37.50%	28.17%	30.56%	26.29%	31.62%	32.47%	24.64%	7.55%		12.68%
Predicted	31.72%	31.42%	31.96%	30.98%	30.16%	29.68%	29.60%	28.36%	19.80%		11.54%
Error	5.38%	6.08%	3.79%	0.42%	3.87%	1.94%	2.87%	3.72%	12.25%		1.14%
									Average Prediction Error		**4.15%**
Archived Measured	48.61%	40.32%	60.80%	55.04%	47.97%	52.14%	48.38%	40.58%	23.73%		0.56%
Predicted	61.78%	61.18%	62.26%	60.30%	58.66%	57.70%	57.54%	55.06%	37.94%		21.42%
Error	13.17%	20.86%	1.46%	5.26%	10.69%	5.56%	9.16%	14.48%	14.21%		20.86%
									Average Prediction Error		**11.57%**

To verify the second part of our model we calculate the percentages of resources that are archived at least once in one of the public archives. Table 1 illustrates the archived results measured, predicted, and the corresponding standard error. Figure 1 also displays the measured and predicted corresponding plots for the archived resources. While the archived content percentages had a higher error percentage of 11.57% and proceeded to become further less linear with time. This fluctuation in the archival percentages convinced us that a further analysis is needed.

3.2 Reappearance and Disappearance

In measuring the percentage of resources missing from the live web, we assumed that when a resource is deemed missing it remains missing. It was also assumed that if a snapshot of the resource is present in one of the public archives the resource is deemed archived and that this snapshot persists indefinitely. Utilizing

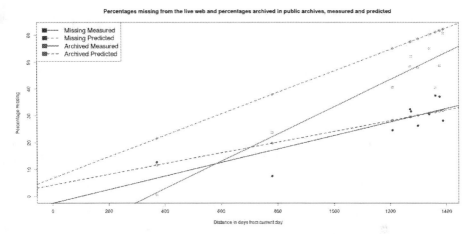

Fig. 1. Measured and predicted percentages of resources missing and archived for each dataset and the corresponding linear regression

the response logs resulting from running the existence experiment in 2012 and in 2013 we compare the corresponding HTTP responses and the number of mementos for each resource. As expected, portions of the datasets disappeared from the live web and were labeled as missing. An interesting phenomena occurred as several of the resources that were previously declared as missing became available again as shown in table 2. A possible explanation of this reappearance could be a domain or a webserver being disrupted and restored again. Another possible explanation is that the previously missing resources could be linked to a suspended user account that was reinstated. To eliminate the effect of transient errors, the experiment was repeated three times in the course of two weeks.

The dotted line in figure 2 shows resources missing in 2012 that reappeared in 2013. Given those percentages we notice a linear relationship with time. By applying linear regression we reach equation 3 describing the reappearance of resources as a function of time.

$$LiveContent\ Reappearing = 0.01(Age\ in\ days) - 1.42 \qquad (3)$$

In the same previous study, we modeled the archival existence or the percentage archived as a function of time. The phenomena analyzed in the previous section showed the instability of the resources in the web which influenced us to investigate

Table 2. Percentages of resources reappearing on the live web and disappearing from the public archives per event

Event	MJ	Iran	Obama	H1N1	Egypt	Syria	Average
% Re-appearing on the web	11.29%	11.48%	6.63%	3.68%	4.21%	1.97 %	6.54%
% Disappearing from archives	9.98%	11.17%	15.65%	5.46%	2.81%	2.25 %	7.89%
% Going from 1 memento to 0	2.72%	2.89%	4.24%	1.96%	0.23%	0.28%	2.05%

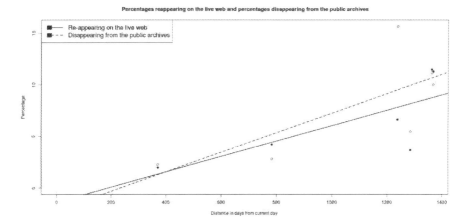

Fig. 2. Percentages of resources reappearing on the live web and the resources disappearing from the public archives

the archived resources as well. We deemed a resource to be archived if there existed at least one publicly available memento of the resource in the archives. For each resource we extracted the memento timemaps and recorded the number of available mementos. The resources are expected to have the same number of mementos or more indicating more snapshots taken into the archives or unarchived resources started to exist in the archives. We notice another interesting phenomena, the number of available mementos of several resources have actually descreased indicating disappearance from the archives as shown in table 2.

Brunelle and Nelson have shown that timemaps shrink 20% of the time [6]. Another possible explanation is that in 2012 the memento aggregator included search engine caches as archives but no longer does so in 2013. We estimate search engine cache only timemaps by measuring the number of resources whose timemaps went from 1 memento to 0 as shown in table 2 as well. Similarly, we plot the percentages of archival disappearance in figure 2. Equation 4 results from applying linear regression in curve fitting. Inspecting figure 2 verifies to a certain degree our explanation of the archival disappearance phenomena as the regression line maintains the same slope of the estimated model as shown in figure 1 while it differs in the Y-intercept. This explains to a certain degree the uniform variation in the estimated function. Unfortunately, we cannot verify this precisely as we do not have the past timemaps of the resources in the datasets.

$$Mementos\ Disappearing = 0.01(Age\ in\ days) - 2.22 \qquad (4)$$

3.3   Tweet Existence

After focusing on the embedded resources shared in posts in social media another question arouse, what about the existence of the social post itself? In collecting the dataset that we utilized in our analysis we focused on the embedded resource and the creation dates. Also the Stanford Network Analysis Platform (SNAP)

Table 3. Percentages of missing posts averages

Event	MJ	Iran	Obama	H1N1	Egypt	Syria	Average
Average % of missing posts	14.43%	14.59%	10.03%	7.38%	15.08%	0.53%	10.34%

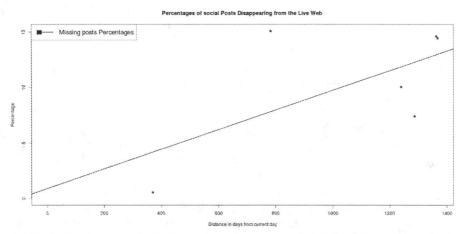

Fig. 3. Percentages of missing posts averages curve fitted using linear regression

dataset we used provides only the tweet text, the author's username, and the creation date with no further information about the tweet or its URI. A social post could face the same fate of the embedded resource by being deleted, service hosting it discontinued, or the author's account getting suspended. Similarly to the resource existence testing, we check the existence of the posts by examining the HTTP response headers. Unfortunately, the datasets we used do not include all the fields and parameters of a tweet, among which is the tweet's URI. To work around the absence of the social post URI we utilized Topsy, a service that mines social media websites like Twitter to provide analytics and insight to topics and resources. Using the API, we can extract all the available tweets that incorporate a given URI with a maximum of 500 tweets. For each resource in the dataset we extract all the tweets and check their existence on the live web accordingly. Given a URI, we can estimate the percentage of social posts that are missing. This number could give an insight to what is the probability that the post itself is missing. Table 3 shows the results for each dataset. Figure 3 illustrates the collective percentages through time. Equation 5 shows the result of curve fitting the percentages of loss as a function of time.

$$SocialPosts\ Missing = 0.01(Age\ in\ days) + 0.88 \qquad (5)$$

4   Context. Discovery and Shared Resource Replacement

A web resource can fall into one of the categories as shown in table 4. These categories were adopted from the work of McCown and Nelson [14].

Table 4. Web resource categories in regards to archivability and availability

	Archived	**Not Archived**
Available	Replicated	Vulnerable
Missing	Endangered	Unrecoverable

If a resource is available on the live web and also archived in public archives then it is considered replicated and safe. The resource is considered vulnerable if it persists on the web but has no available archived versions. If a resource is not available on the live web but has an archived version then it is considered endangered as it relies on the stability and the persistence of the archive. The worst case scenario occurs when the resource disappears from the live web without being archived at all thusly, be considered unrecoverable. In our study we focus on the latter category and how we can utilize the social media in identifying the context of the shared resource and select a possible replacement candidate to fill in the position of the missing resource and maintain the same context of the social post.

A shared resource leaves traces even after it ceases to exist on the web. We attempt to collect those traces and discover context for the missing resource. Since Twitter for example restricts the length of the posts to be 140 characters only, an author might rely mostly on the shared resource in conveying a thought or an idea by embedding a link in the post and resorting to limiting the associated text. Thusly, obtaining context is crucial when the resource disappears. To accomplish that, we try to find the social link neighborhood of the tweet and the resource we are attempting this context discovery. When a link is shared on Twitter for example, it could be associated with describing text in the form of the status itself, hashtags, usertags, or other links as well. These co-existing links could act as a viable replacement to the missing resource under investigation while the tags and text could provide better context enabling a better understanding of the resource.

4.1   Social Extraction

Given the URI of the resource under investigation, we utilize Topsy's API to extract all the available tweets incorporating this URI. In social media, a resource's URI can be shared in different forms with the aid of URL shortening. To elaborate, a link to Google's web page http://www.google.com could be shared also in several forms like http://goo.gl/xYMol, http://bitly.com/XeRH58, and http://t.co/XFiAkbHnp3. Each of these forms redirects to the same final destination URI. Fortunately, Topsy's API handles this by searching their index for the final target URL rather than the shortened form. A maximum of 500 tweets of

```
Reconstruction:
{
  "URI": "http://ws-dl.blogspot.com/2012/02/2012-02-11-losing-my-revolution-year.html",
  "Related Tweet Count": 290,
  "Related Hashtags": "#history #jan25 #sschat #arabspring #jrn112 #archives #in #revolution
  #iipc12 #mppdigital #egypt #recordkeeping #twitter #egyptrevolution #digitalpreservation
  #preservation #webarchiving #or2012 #1anpa #socialmedia",
  "Users who talked about this": "@textfiles @jigarmehta @blakehounshell] @jonathanglick
  @daensen404: @ryersonjourn @chanders @theotypes) @jwax55 @marklittlenews @ndiipp ...",
  "All associated unique links:": "http://t.co/ZRASTg5o http://t.co/eXhlSTRF
  http://t.co/3GIb6oI3 http://t.co/ArVqCqfP ...",
  "All other links associated:": "http://www.cs.odu.edu/~mln/pubs/tpdl-2012/tpdl-2012.pdf
  http://dashes.com/anil/2011/01/if-you-didnt-blog-it-it-didnt-happen.html",
  "Most frequent link appearing:": "http://t.co/0A1q2fzz",
  "Number of times the Most frequent link appearing:": 19,
  "Most frequent tweet posted and reposted:": "@acarvin You may have seen this already.
  Arab Spring digital content is apparently being lost.",
  "Number of times the Most frequent tweet appearing:": 23,
  "The longest common phrase appearing:": "You may have seen this already Arab Spring
  digital content is apparently being lost",
  "Number of times the Most common phrase appearing:": 28
}
```

Fig. 4. Social Content Extraction using Topsy API

the most recent tweets posted could be extracted from the API regarding a certain URL. The content from all the tweets is collected to form a social context corpus.

From this corpus we extract the best replacement tweet by calculating the longest common N-gram. This represents the tweet with the most information that describes the target resource intended by the author. Within some tweets, multiple links coexist within the same text. These co-occurring resources share the same context and maintain a certain relevancy in most cases. A list of those co-occurring resources are extracted and filtered for redundancies. Finally, the textual components of the tweets are extracted after removing usertags, URIs, social interaction symbols like "RT". We named the document composed of those text-only tweets in the form of phrases the *"Tweet Document"*.

Figure 4 illustrates the JSON object produced from social mining the resource as described above.

4.2 Resource Replacement Recommendation

From the social extraction phase above we gathered information that helps us to infer the aboutness and context of a resource. Given this context, can we utilize it in obtaining a viable replacement resource to fill in the missing one and provide the same context?

To answer this, we utilize the work of Klein and Nelson [9] in defining the lexical signatures of web pages as discussed earlier. First, we extract the tweet document as described above. Next, we remove all the stop words and apply Porter's stemmer to all the remaining words [16]. We calculate the term frequency of each stemmed word and sort them from highest occurring to the lowest. Finally, we extract the top five words to form our tweet signature.

On the one hand, and using this tweet signature as a query, we utilize Google's search engine to extract the top 10 resulting resources. On the other hand, we collect all the other co-occurring pages in the tweets obtained by the API. These pages combined produce a replacement candidate list of resources. One or more of which can be utilized as a viable replacement of the resource under investigation.

To choose which resource is more relevant and a possibly better replacement we utilize once more the tweet document extracted earlier. For each of the extracted pages in the candidate list, we download the representation and utilize the boilerpipe library in extracting the text within[1]. The library provides algorithms to detect and remove the "clutter" (boilerplate, templates) around the main textual content of a web page. Having a list of possible candidate textual documents and the tweet document, the next step is to calculate similarity. The pages are sorted according to the cosine similarity to the tweets page describing the resource under reconstruction.

At this stage we have extracted contextual information about the resource and a possible replacement. The next step is to measure how well the reconstruction process was undergone and how close is this replacement page is to the missing resource.

5   Evaluation

Since we cannot measure the quality of the discovered context or the resulting replacement page to the missing resource, we have to set some assumptions. We extract a dataset of resources that are currently available on the live web and assume they no longer exist. Each of these resources are textual based and neither media files nor executables. Each of these resources has to have at least 30 retrievable tweets using Topsy's API to be enough to build context.

We collect a dataset of 731 unique resources following these rules. We perform the context extraction and the replacement recommendation phases. We download the resource under investigation ($R_{missing}$) and the list of candidate replacements from the search engines (R_{search}) and the list of co-occurring resources ($R_{co-occurring}$). For each we use the boilerpipe library to extract text and use cosine similarity to perform the comparisons. For each resource, we measure the similarity between the ($R_{missing}$) and the extracted tweet page. For each element in (R_{search}) we calculate the cosine similarity with the tweet page and sort the results accordingly from most similar to the least. We repeat the same with the list of co-occurring resources ($R_{co-occurring}$). Then we calculate the similarity between ($R_{missing}$) and ($R_{search}(first)$) indicating the top result obtained from the search engine index. Then, we compare ($R_{missing}$) with each of the elements in (R_{search}) and ($R_{co-occurring}$) to demonstrate the best possible similarity. Figure 5 illustrates the different similarities sorted for each measure and shows that 41% of the time we can extract a significantly similar replacement page ($R_{replacement}$) to the original resource ($R_{missing}$) by at least 70% similarity. Finally, we needed to validate the effectiveness of using the tweet signature as a query string to the search engine. Using the tweet signature extracted from tweets associated with an existing resource against the search engine API and locating the rank in which the resource appear in the results list, we calculate the mean reciprocal rank to be 0.43.

---

[1] http://code.google.com/p/boilerpipe/

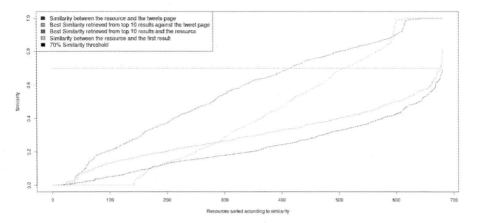

Fig. 5. Similarities with the original resource $R_{missing}$

6   Conclusions and Future Work

In this study we verify our previous analysis and estimation of the percentage missing of the resources shared on social media. The function in time still holds in modeling the percentage disappearing from the web. As for the model estimated for the amount archived it showed an alteration. The slope of the regression line in the model stayed the same while the y-intercept varied. We deduce that a possible explanation to this phenomena is due to timemap shrinkage. Previously, timemaps incorporated search engine caches as mementos which was removed in the most recent Memento revision. Next, we classified web resources into four different categories in regards to existence on the live web and in public web archives. Then we considered the unrecoverable category where the resource is deemed missing from the live web whilst not having any archived versions. Since we cannot perform a full reconstruction or retrieval, we utilize the social nature of the shared resources by using Topsy's API in discovering the resource's context. Using this context and the co-occurring resources we apply a range of heuristics and comparisons to extract the most viable replacement to the missing resource from its social neighborhood. Finally, we performed an evaluation to measure the quality of this replacement and found that for 41% of the resources we can obtain a significantly similar replacement resource with at least 70% similarity. For our future work, we would like to expand our investigation to incorporate other resources of different types like images and videos. A further investigation is crucial to better rank the results and account for the different types of resources.

Acknowledgments. This work was supported in part by the Library of Congress and NSF IIS-1009392.

References

1. Ainsworth, S.G., Alsum, A., SalahEldeen, H., Weigle, M.C., Nelson, M.L.: How Much of the Web Is Archived? In: Proceedings of the 11th Annual International ACM/IEEE Joint Conference on Digital Libraries, JCDL 2011, pp. 133–136 (2011)
2. Bakshy, E., Hofman, J., Mason, W., Watts, D.: Identifying 'Influencers' on Twitter. In: Proceedings of the 4th ACM International Conference on Web Search and Data Mining, WSDM 2011 (2011)
3. Bar-Yossef, Z., Broder, A.Z., Kumar, R., Tomkins, A.: Sic Transit Gloria Telae: Towards an Understanding of the Web's Decay. In: Proceedings of the 13th International Conference on World Wide Web, WWW 2004, pp. 328–337 (2004)
4. Baykan, E., Henzinger, M., Marian, L., Weber, I.: Purely URL-based topic classification. In: Proceedings of the 18th International Conference on World wide web, WWW 2009, pp. 1109–1110 (2009)
5. Benevenut, F., Rodrigues, T., Cha, M., Almeida, V.: Characterizing User Behavior in Online Social Networks. In: Proceedings of ACM SIGCOMM Internet Measure- ment Conference, SIGCOMM 2009, pp. 49–62 (2009)
6. Brunelle, J.F., Nelson, M.L.: An Evaluation of Caching Policies for Memento TimeMaps. In: Proceedings of the 13th ACM/IEEE-CS Joint Conference on Digital Libraries, JCDL 2013 (2013)
7. Gill, A.J., Nowson, S., Oberlander, J.: What are they blogging about? Personality, topic and motivation in blogs. In: Proceedings of the International AAAI Conference on Weblogs and Social Media, ICWSM 2009 (2009)
8. Kan, M.-Y.: Web page classification without the web page. In: Proceedings of the 13th International World Wide Web Conference on Alternate Track Papers & Posters, WWW Alt. 2004, pp. 262–263 (2004)
9. Klein, M., Nelson, M.L.: Revisiting lexical signatures to re-discover web pages. In: Christensen-Dalsgaard, B., Castelli, D., Ammitzbøll Jurik, B., Lippincott, J. (eds.) ECDL 2008. LNCS, vol. 5173, pp. 371–382. Springer, Heidelberg (2008)
10. Kwak, H., Lee, C., Park, H., Moon, S.: What is Twitter, a Social Network or a News Media? In: Proceedings of the 19th International Conference on World Wide Web, WWW 2010, pp. 591–600 (2010)
11. Mark, G., Bagdouri, M., Palen, L., Martin, J., Al-Ani, B., Anderson, K.: Blogs as a collective war diary. In: Proceedings of the ACM 2012 Conference on Computer Supported Cooperative Work, CSCW 2012, pp. 37–46 (2012)
12. McCown, F., Marshall, C.C., Nelson, M.L.: Why web sites are lost (and how they're sometimes found). Communications of the ACM, 141–145 (November 2009)
13. McCown, F., Nelson, M.L.: What happens when facebook is gone. In: Proceedings of the 9th ACM/IEEE-CS Joint Conference on Digital Libraries, JCDL 2009, pp. 251–254 (2009)
14. McCown, F., Nelson, M.L.: A framework for describing web repositories. In: Proceedings of the 9th ACM/IEEE-CS Joint Conference on Digital Libraries, JCDL 2009, pp. 341–344 (2009)
15. Qi, X., Davison, B.D.: Knowing a web page by the company it keeps. In: Proceedings of the 15th ACM International Conference on Information and Knowledge Management, CIKM 2006, pp. 228–237 (2006)
16. Porter, M.F.: An algorithm for suffix stripping. Program: electronic library and information systems 14, 313–316 (1980)

17. SalahEldeen, H.M., Nelson, M.L.: Losing my revolution: how many resources shared on social media have been lost? In: Zaphiris, P., Buchanan, G., Rasmussen, E., Loizides, F. (eds.) TPDL 2012. LNCS, vol. 7489, pp. 125–137. Springer, Heidelberg (2012)

18. Wu, S., Hofman, J.M., Mason, W.A., Watts, D.J.: Who Says What to Whom on Twitter. In: Proceedings of the 20th International Conference on World Wide Web, WWW 2011, pp. 705–714 (2011)

19. Starbird, K., Muzny, G., Palen, L.: Learning from the Crowd: Collaborative Filtering Techniques for Identifying On-the-Ground Twitterers during Mass Disruptions. In: Proceedings of the 9th International ISCRAM Conference, ISCRAM 2012 (2012)

20. Starbird, K., Palen, L. (How) will the revolution be retweeted?: information diffusion and the 2011 Egyptian uprising. In: Proceedings of the ACM 2012 Conference on Computer Supported Cooperative Work, CSCW 2012, pp. 7–16 (2012)

21. Vieweg, S., Hughes, A.L., Starbird, K., Palen, L.: Microblogging during two natural hazards events: what twitter may contribute to situational awareness. In: Proceedings of the SIGCHI Conference on Human Factors in Computing Systems, CHI 2010, pp. 1079–1088 (2010)

22. Yang, J., Counts, S.: Predicting the Speed, Scale, and Range of Information Diffusion in Twitter. In: 4th International AAAI Conference on Weblogs and Social Media, ICWSM 2010 (2010)

23. Zhao, D., Rosson, M.B.: How and Why People Twitter: The Role that Micro-blogging Plays in Informal Communication at Work. In: Proceedings of the ACM 2009 International Conference on Supporting Group Work, GROUP 2009, pp. 243–252 (2009)

Who and What Links to the Internet Archive

Yasmin Alnoamany, Ahmed Alsum, Michele C. Weigle, and Michael L. Nelson

Old Dominion University, Department of Computer Science
Norfolk VA 23529, USA
{yasmin,aalsum,mweigle,mln}@cs.odu.edu

Abstract. The Internet Archive's (IA) Wayback Machine is the largest and oldest public web archive and has become a significant repository of our recent history and cultural heritage. Despite its importance, there has been little research about how it is discovered and used. Based on web access logs, we analyze what users are looking for, why they come to IA, where they come from, and how pages link to IA. We find that users request English pages the most, followed by the European languages. Most human users come to web archives because they do not find the requested pages on the live web. About 65% of the requested archived pages no longer exist on the live web. We find that more than 82% of human sessions connect to the Wayback Machine via referrals from other web sites, while only 15% of robots have referrers. Most of the links (86%) from websites are to individual archived pages at specific points in time, and of those 83% no longer exist on the live web.

Keywords: Web Archiving, Web Server Logs, Web Usage Mining, Language Detection.

1 Introduction

A variety of research has been conducted for studying web archives in order to answer questions related to user needs and to present web archive data to users [12,5]. However, no previous work has been carried out to answer these questions: What content languages are web archive users looking for? Why do users come to web archives? Where do web archive users come from? Who links to web archives? How do sites link to web archives? Do sites link deeply to specific archived pages or link to the repository? Why do sites link to the past?

The Internet Archive [11] is the first web archiving initiative attempting global scope and currently holds over 240 billion web pages with archives as far back as 1996 [8]. It allows traveling back in time for traversing archived versions of web pages through the Wayback Machine [18]. This paper provides a study of the requests of web archive users, both humans and robots, to gain insight into what users look for, in the context of the language of the requested pages, through an analysis of the server logs of the Internet Archives' Wayback Machine. We also provide an analysis of referring pages of human users to investigate how humans discover the Wayback Machine, why the referrers link to web archives, and how they link to web archives.

T. Aalberg et al. (Eds.): TPDL 2013, LNCS 8092, pp. 346–357, 2013.
© Springer-Verlag Berlin Heidelberg 2013

We found that users of Internet Archive's Wayback Machine request English pages the most, followed by several European languages. We also found that most human users come to the Wayback Machine via links or direct address presumably because they did not find the requested pages on the live web. Of the requested archived pages, 65% do not currently exist on the live web. From analyzing the referrers, we found that more than 82% of human sessions have referrers, while only 15% of robot sessions have referrers. We also found that 86% of the referrers are deep links to archived pages.

2   Related Work

To the best of our knowledge, no prior study has analyzed where web archive users come from nor what they look for in terms of the linguistic context. Furthermore, the usage of web archives in general has not been widely studied. The characterization of search behavior and the information needs of web archive users have been studied by Costa et al. [4,5] based on quantitative analysis of the Portuguese Web Archive (PWA) search logs. In a previous study [1], we provided the first analysis of user access to a large web archive. We discovered four basic access patterns for web archives through analysis of web server logs from the Internet Archive's Wayback Machine. In the study, we applied heuristics for robot detection after data filtering and found that robot sessions outnumber human sessions 10:1. Robots outnumber humans in terms of raw, unfiltered requests 5:4, and 4:1 in terms of megabytes transferred.

Many studies have investigated what is missing from digital libraries and web archives, in addition to the effect of this on the satisfaction of users' needs and expectations [17,3,22,16]. In [17], the Internet Archive's coverage of the web was investigated. The results showed an unintentional international bias through uneven representation of different countries in the archive. Carmel et al. [3] suggest a tool to dynamically analyze the query logs of the digital library system, identify the missing content queries, and then direct the system to obtain the missing data. We investigate what is missing through an analysis of requests with an HTTP 404 status in the Wayback Machine web server logs.

Memento Terminology

In this section, we explain the terminology we adopt in the rest of the paper. Memento [20] is an HTTP protocol extension which enables time travel on the web by linking the current resources with their prior state. Memento defines the following terms:

- URI-R identifies the original resource. It is the resource as it used to appear on the live web. A URI-R may have 0 or more mementos (URI-Ms).
- URI-M identifies an archived snapshot of the URI-R at a specific datetime, which is called Memento-Datetime, e.g., URI-M_i= URI-R@t_i.
- URI-T identifies a TimeMap, a resource that provides a list of mementos (URI-Ms) for a URI-R with their Memento-Datetimes, e.g., $URI - T(URI - R) = \{URI - M_1, URI - M_2, ..., URI - M_n\}$.

Although we use Memento terminology, the logs we analyze are from the Internet Archive's Wayback Machine and not the Memento API.

3 Methodology

We use the Internet Archive's Wayback Machine server logs in our analysis. We constructed our sample by combining three different slices of 2M records each (covering approximately 30 minutes) at times 03:00, 13:00, and 18:00 UTC on February 2, 2012, for a total dataset of 6M records. Because we are checking the language of the content accessed by the web archive users, we cover the peak time of Internet traffic periods for several countries with different language speakers to avoid biasing the results. According to many studies, the hours between 6 p.m. to 12 a.m. are considered to be peak times for Internet traffic [14,6,21]. We picked samples from the log file that were representative of the peak time for several cities around the world, as shown in Figure 1.

Table 1 contains the features of the sample. The features, from left to right, are the percentage of requests that used the GET method, were for embedded resources of web pages (such as images and CSS files), had null referrers (i.e., they do not identify a URI that links to a page at the Internet Archive), were successful requests (2xx status code), were redirections (3xx status code), were client errors (4xx status code), were server errors (5xx status code), remained

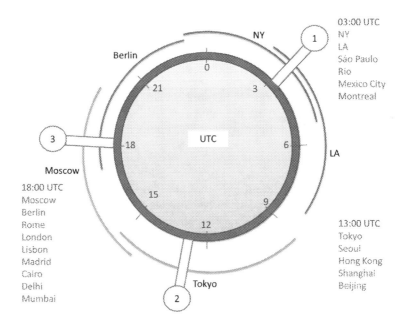

Fig. 1. The dataset of 6M HTTP requests is constructed from slices of 2M each from 03:00, 13:00, and 18:00 UTC on February 2, 2012

Table 1. Data set statistics based on 6M requests. Note that the last two columns are the percentage of humans and robots remaining after cleaning (removing the irrelevant requests to the analysis, e.g., embedded resources).

GET	Embedded	Null Ref	2xx	3xx	4xx	5xx	Humans	Robots
98.7%	42.9%	46.6%	33.1%	51.4%	12.0%	3.5%	1.5%	18.8%

from human requests after cleaning (removing the irrelevant requests to the analysis, e.g., embedded resources), and remained from robot requests after cleaning. The characteristics are consistent with our previous analysis of web archives [1].

Preparing the Wayback access logs for usage mining starts with transforming the raw log file into server sessions through web log preprocessing (data cleaning, user identification, and session identification) [13]. A session is the group of consecutive requests performed by a user [10]. We apply the same methodology as in our previous work for preprocessing the logs and web robot detection [1].

4   What Do Wayback Machine Users Look for?

In this section, we give insight into what web archive users look for in terms of the content language of requested pages. We used the language detection library created by Shuyo [15] for detecting the language.

4.1   Archived Web Pages

Distribution of Languages Used in the Wayback Machine. We extracted the successful requests (HTTP 200 status code) from humans and robots to detect the language distributions for the content of the requested pages. These successful requests represent 93.1% (85,909 out of 92,204) of all human requests and 56.7% (639,684 out of 1,127,204) of all robots requests. The request can be for a URI-T or a URI-M. For the URI-Ts, which represent 13% of human requested pages and 80.8% of robot requested pages, we estimated the language by using the most recent URI-M from the TimeMap. We identified 52 different languages from the successful requests. The left two columns of Table 2 show the top 10 languages which accounted for 94.8% of human and 93.4% of robot requests. For both human and robot users, English contributes the most to the successful requests, reflecting the high web archive penetration rate in English speaking countries. Japanese is the second most frequent language with 5.5% for humans, but Russian is the second most frequent language for robots at 7.0%. We also notice that despite of the existence of web archives in Europe, the requests to the IA from speakers of European languages contribute 13% of the top 10 list for human requested pages and 18.5% of the top 10 list for the robot requests.

Existence on the Live Web. From all 85,909 successful human requests, we checked the existence of the 40,791 unique URI-Rs on the live web. The robots

Table 2. The top 10 languages for URI-Ms with HTTP 200 (on the left) and for the URI-Rs of unarchived requested pages (on the right)

URI-Ms with HTTP 200				URI-Rs with HTTP 404			
Language	Humans	Language	Robots	Language	Humans	Language	Robots
English	71.7%	English	72.4%	English	66.9%	English	62.2%
Japanese	5.5%	Russian	7.0%	Russian	7.9%	Russian	11.1%
German	3.6%	German	3.1%	German	5.4%	German	3.8%
Vietnamese	2.9%	Spanish	1.9%	Japanese	5.1%	Indonesian	3.1%
Russian	2.3%	French	1.8%	Spanish	2.5%	Polish	2.5%
Portuguese	2.1%	Vietnamese	1.7%	Polish	2.3%	Vietnamese	2.2%
French	2.1%	Japanese	1.5%	Romanian	1.6%	Spanish	2.0%
Spanish	1.9%	Polish	1.5%	French	1.2%	Thai	1.9%
Bengali	1.8%	Portuguese	1.3%	Italian	0.8%	French	1.8%
Italian	0.9%	Thai	1.1%	Portuguese	0.7%	Dutch	1.1%

Table 3. The existence of the requested archived pages on the live web. Available represents the requests which ultimately return "HTTP 200", while missing represents the requests that return HTTP 4xx, HTTP 5xx, HTTP 3xx to others except 200, timeouts, and soft 404s.

	Found in Archive		Unarchived	
	Humans	Robots	Humans	Robots
URI-Rs available on live web	36.4%	62.5%	25.4%	33.2%
URI-Rs missing from live web	63.6%	37.5%	74.6%	66.8%
Uniq. URI-Rs	**40,791**	**331,573**	**2,441**	**209,384**

generated 639,684 successful requests, in which there are 331,573 unique URI-Rs whose existence on the live web were also checked. We also checked the pages that give "soft 404s", which return HTTP 200, but do not actually exist, based on the algorithm in [2]. Table 3 contains the results of checking the status of the web pages on the live web.

We believe humans access the Wayback Machine because they do not find web pages on the live web. Table 3 shows that for the requested pages that were found in the archive (returned HTTP 200 status), the percentage of the available pages on the live web for human requests is 36.4%. On the other hand, the percentage of the available pages on the live web for robot requests is 62.5%.

4.2   Unarchived Web Pages

Of the 6M requests in our sample, 12% returned HTTP 404 status, as shown in Table 1. Not all of these are actually unarchived; approximately 2% of the unique URI-Rs are malformed (e.g., http://http://cnn.com) and were removed. We used the remaining valid URI-Rs (209,348 robots and 2,441 humans) to detect content language, check live web status, and check existence in other archives.

Table 4. The number of the found URI-Rs and the corresponding URI-Ms of the missing pages (211,825 unique URI-Rs) on the web archives

Web Archive	Archive Web Site	#URI-R	#URI-M
Internet Archive (2013)	web.archive.org	56,503	1,657,264
The National Archives	webarchive.nationalarchives.gov.uk	787	15,354
ArchiefWeb	www.archiefweb.eu	47	18,347
Archive-It	archive-it.org	41	4,682
UK Web Archive	www.webarchive.org.uk	38	12,277
Library of Congress	webarchive.loc.gov	35	1,092
WebCite	webcitation.org	29	1,104

Existence on the Live Web. The current state of the requested URI-Rs that had HTTP 404 status was determined by testing their existence on the live web. Of the URI-Rs that were not found in the Wayback Machine, 66.8% of those requested by robots and 74.6% of those requested by humans do not exist on the live web. To compensate for transient errors we repeated the requests several times for a week before declaring a URI-R non-existent.

Distribution of the Content-Language for Unarchived Web Pages. We detected the content language of available URI-Rs on the live web, which represent 25.4% (620 out of 2,441) of the unique URI-Rs for humans and 33.2% (69,510 out of 209,384) for robots. The total number of requested URI-Rs is 227,450 for robots and 1,578 for humans. The two rightmost columns of Table 2 have the results for robots and humans separately. For the web pages that were not archived in IA's Wayback Machine, English is the most requested language with 66.9% of the human-requested web pages and 62.2% of the robot-requested web pages. The top 10 languages compromised 94.5% of all the content-language of the requested pages. European languages made up 22.5% of the human-requested pages and 22.4% of the robot-requested pages.

Existence in Other Web Archives. We checked the 211,825 unarchived pages for existence in other archives at the time of the experiment. The existence in the web archives was tested by querying Memento proxies and aggregator [19]. For completeness and fairness, we also included the results from IA's Wayback Machine in March 2013. This resulted in 56,503 out of 211,825 URI-Rs that were unarchived in Feb. 2012 now being available in the archive. Table 4 contains the number of URI-Rs found in the web archives and the number of covered URI-Ms. The Internet Archive has the most coverage at the time of experiment as they have increased their repository recently [8].

5 Where Do Wayback Machine Users Come from?

We used the referrer field, which contains the web page that links to the resource, for the logs in our sample to determine how people discover the Wayback

Table 5. The top 10 referrers

Web Site	Percentage	Description
en.wikipedia.org	12.9%	Wikipedia
archive.org	11.9%	IA Home Page
reddit.com	10.2%	Social News Web Site
google.TLD	9.9%	Search Engine
info-poland.buffalo.edu	1.5%	Polish Studies
de.wikipedia.org	1.4%	Wikipedia
cracked.com	1.2%	Humor Site
snopes.com	1.1%	Urban Legends Reference Pages
facebook.com	0.9%	Social Media
crochetpatterncentral.com	0.9%	Crocheting Hobbies

Machine. In terms of sessions, 84.8% of robot sessions do not have referrers while only 18.1% of human sessions do not have referrers (i.e., they reached the Wayback Machine by a link in an email, direct address, or direct bookmark). An empty referral field is a strong indicator of a robot.

In this section, we provide a detailed analysis of the referrer field of human users to gain insight into who links to the Wayback Machine and how they link to it. Robots are not included in the analysis of referrers because the majority of robots do not have referrers and if they do, we do not necessarily trust their values.

5.1   Who Links to Wayback Machine?

The percentage of human sessions with referrers is 81.9%. We eliminated the sessions that were referred by a URI-M or URI-T because they started prior to our sample. Of the sessions that started with an external referrer, 9.6% came from Google. The users who came from the home page of the IA contributed to 11.9% of the sessions with referrers. That means that many people start with the IA to access the Wayback Machine.

Top Referrers. Table 5 contains the top 10 referrers that link to IA's Wayback Machine. The list of top 10 referrers represents 51.9% of all the referrers. As the table shows, en.wikipedia.org outnumbers all other sites including the search engine and the home page of Internet Archive (archive.org). Note that "google.TLD" represents Google search and 24 other pages from Google (e.g., http://www.google.com/about/company/history.html). Since the majority are from Google search, we describe it as search engine. Facebook also appears as a top referrer, which indicates that many people share links to the past.

Classification of Referrers. Table 6 presents the distribution of Top Level Domains (TLD) for the URIs that link to the IA's Wayback Machine (only the top 10 are shown). It can be noticed that most of the connections are from the

Table 6. The top 10 TLDs of the referrers

TLD	.com	.org	.net	.jp	.ru	.de	.edu	.to	.uk	.info
Percentage	45.4%	33.9%	8.4%	1.8%	1.4%	1.4%	1.1%	0.7%	0.6%	0.5%

Table 7. The top 10 ccTLDs of Google search referrers

ccTLD	.com	.uk	.de	.ca	.jp	.pl	.nl	.ru	.fr	.br
Percentage	56.7%	6.0%	5.3%	4.8%	3.7%	2.2%	1.9%	1.7%	1.5%	1.4%

.com, .org, .net, .jp, .edu, and .ru domains. Despite of the existence of many web archives in Europe, there are many European domains linking to the IA, such as .ru (Russia), .de (Germany), .fr (France), and .it (Italy). Note that .to is the TLD for a Russian language site (http://lurkmore.to/).

For the referrers from Google search, we extracted the country code top-level domain (ccTLD) of the URIs to discover the countries of the users who came to the Wayback Machine through the search engine. The results are shown in Table 7. English-speaking countries are in the lead, followed by the European language countries.

5.2 Inter-Linking between Languages

From the analysis of the content languages of the referrers and the archived pages which have been linked by the referrers, English represents 80.7% of the referrers' content languages and 80.2% of all referred pages. English referrers link to English archived pages 92% of the time. A small percentage of English referrers link to pages in other languages. The top 5 languages that English pages link to are (in decreasing order) Portuguese, Vietnamese, French, and German. Figure 2 contains a directed weighted graph, which is created using Circos [9], for the relationship between the languages of the referrers and referees. We exclude English from the graph to be able to analyze the rest of the languages and see what they are linking to. For a particular language, the length of the outer arc represents the sum of the number of referrer pages and the number of referee pages in that language. Moving toward the center, the next arc represents the percentage of referees, and the third arc represents the percentage of referrers in that language. For example, links to Japanese archived web pages denote 46% (160 out of 357) of all the Japanese language pages for referrers and archived pages all together. The inner circle shows the relationships between languages of the referrers and referees. Ribbons of different widths connect the languages. The direction is represented by a gap between the line and the incoming language (referrer language). For example, there are 30 links from Japanese (ja) pages to Bengali (bn) pages, which are shown as a fairly broad blue line. The languages where the relative number of referrer and referee together is less than 20 have been excluded to remove noise from the graph.

The figure shows that the languages are mainly linking to themselves with a few inter-language links. Though, recall that we have excluded English from the

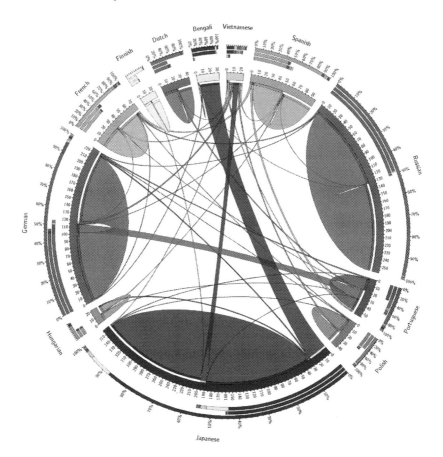

Fig. 2. Most languages self-link, with the notable exceptions of Japanese → {Bengali, Vietnamese} and German → Portuguese

figure. Many of the top ranked languages of human-requested pages appear in the top ranked list of referrers, such as Japanese, German, Russian, Spanish, French, Polish, Dutch, Bengali, etc. It is surprising to find many European referrers to IA's Wayback Machine in spite of the existence of European web archives.

5.3   How Do Web Pages Link to the Wayback Machine?

We found that 86.4% of the web pages that link to the Wayback Machine are pointing to mementos, which means they link to web pages at a specific time. There are 12.8% of web pages that point to TimeMaps. The percentage of web pages that point to the repository (e.g., http://web.archive.org) is 0.8%. Google search links to the top level URI, because Google does not crawl the archive based on the robots.txt exclusion protocol.

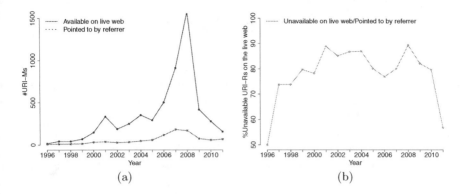

Fig. 3. (a) The temporal distribution of URI-Ms pointed to by the referrers and the number of relative URI-Rs of these URI-Ms that are currently available on the live web. (b) The percentage of unavailable URI-Rs of these URI-Ms on the live web.

Temporal Distribution of the Referred URI-Ms. Figure 3(a) shows the total number of mementos which were pointed to by the referrers, grouped by the year of their Memento-Datetime. There is a significant bias toward 2008, then 2007, and then a bias against the more distant past. We found 14 URI-Ms all from a single web site that link to a datetime in 2099. We assume that the referrer wants to redirect the site's visitors to the most recent copy of the linked web page.

Why Do Web Sites Link to the Wayback Machine? The nature of the web is ephemeral, and the expected lifetime of a web pages is short [7]. So, web archives are important to webmasters and third parties for preserving and saving many web sites. Figure 3(b) clarifies that most people link to the Wayback Machine because they did not find the pages on the live web. The figure shows that for most of the years, more than 70% of the referred pages on the archive no longer exist on the live web. About 83% of all referred-to URI-Rs do not currently exist on the live web.

6   Future Work and Conclusions

We plan to extend our analysis for investigating if the destination of users affects the session length and the behavior of web archive users. Furthermore, we will investigate the behavior of robots in web archives more and contrast it with the behavior of robots on the live web to distinguish their behaviors.

From the analysis of Internet Archive's Wayback Machine server logs, we conclude that most humans come to the Wayback Machine to find missing pages from the live web. The percentage of the requested archived pages which currently do not exist on the live web is 65%. We provided analysis for the distributions of languages to gain insight about what users look for. We found that

English is the most used language on the Wayback Machine, followed by many European languages. European languages represent about 22% of the web pages that were not found on the Wayback Machine, for both human and robot requests. The large percentage of European languages among the unarchived pages can be a good indicator for archival demand for European web pages. We also provided analysis for the human referrers to discover where Wayback Machine users come from. We discovered that wikipedia is the most frequent referrer of pages to IA's Wayback Machine. From analyzing the TLDs of the referrers, we found many European domains (.ru, .de, .fr, etc.) in the top list of the referrers. English represents 80.2% of the referrer languages, followed by European languages. We found that the languages are linking mainly to themselves and to English. We also found that 86% of the referrer web pages link deeply to mementos. More than 82% of the links to these mementos are because their corresponding URI-Rs do not exist on the live web.

Acknowledgment. This work was supported in part by the NSF (IIS 1009392) and the Library of Congress. We thank Kris Carpenter Negulescu (Internet Archive) for access to the anonymized Wayback Machine logs.

References

1. AlNoamany, Y., Weigle, M.C., Nelson, M.L.: Access patterns for robots and humans in web archives. In: Proceedings of the 13th ACM/IEEE-CS Joint Conference on Digital Libraries, JCDL 2013 (2013)
2. Bar-Yossef, Z., Broder, A.Z., Kumar, R., Tomkins, A.: Sic transit gloria telae: towards an understanding of the web's decay. In: Proceedings of the 13th International Conference on World Wide Web, WWW 2004, pp. 328–337. ACM (2004)
3. Carmel, D., Yom-Tov, E., Roitman, H.: Enhancing digital libraries using missing content analysis. In: Proceedings of the 8th ACM/IEEE-CS Joint Conference on Digital Libraries, JCDL 2008, pp. 1–10. ACM (2008)
4. Costa, M.J. Silva, M.: Characterizing Search Behavior in Web Archives. In: Proceedings of Temporal Web Analytics Workshop. TWAW (2011)
5. Costa, M., Silva, M.J.: Understanding the information needs of web archive users. In: Proc. of the 10th International Web Archiving Workshop, pp. 9–16 (September 2010)
6. Fukuda, K., Cho, K., Esaki, H.: The impact of residential broadband traffic on Japanese ISP backbones. SIGCOMM Comput. Commun. Rev. 35(1), 15–22 (2005)
7. Harrison, T.L., Nelson, M.L.: Just-in-time recovery of missing web pages. In: Proceedings of the 17th Conference on Hypertext and Hypermedia, HYPERTEXT 2006, pp. 145–156. ACM (2006)
8. Kahle, B.: Wayback Machine: Now with 240,000,000,000 (January 2013), http://blog.archive.org/2013/01/09/updated-wayback/
9. Krzywinski, M.I., Schein, J.E., Birol, I., Connors, J., Gascoyne, R., Horsman, D., Jones, S.J., Marra, M.A.: Circos: An information aesthetic for comparative genomics. Genome Research (2009)
10. Markov, Z., Larose, D.T.: Data Mining the Web: Uncovering Patterns in Web Content, Structure, and Usage. John Wiley & Sons, Inc. (2007)

11. Negulescu, K.C.: Web Archiving @ the Internet Archive. Presentation at the 2010 Digital Preservation Partners Meeting (2010), http://1.usa.gov/XSjDG8
12. Padia, K., AlNoamany, Y., Weigle, M.C.: Visualizing digital collections at archive-it. In: Proceedings of the 12th ACM/IEEE-CS Joint Conference on Digital Libraries, JCDL 2012, pp. 15–18 (2012)
13. Reddy, K.S., Varma, G.P.S., Babu, I.R.: Preprocessing the web server logs: an illustrative approach for effective usage mining. ACM SIGSOFT Software Engineering Notes 37(3), 1–5 (2012)
14. Reisinger, D.: Netflix gobbles a third of peak Internet traffic in North America. CNET(2012), http://goo.gl/2cVPg
15. Shuyo, N.: Language Detection Library for Java (2012), http://code.google.com/p/language-detection/
16. Silva, A.J.C., Gonçalves, M.A., Laender, A.H.F., Modesto, M.A.B., Cristo, M., Ziviani, N.: Finding what is missing from a digital library: A case study in the computer science field. Inf. Process. Manage. 45(3), 380–391 (2009)
17. Thelwall, M., Vaughan, L.: A fair history of the web? examining country balance in the internet archive. Library & Information Science Research 26(2), 162–176 (2004)
18. Tofel, B.: Wayback for Accessing Web Archives. In: Proceedings of International Web Archiving Workshop. IWAW (2007)
19. Van de Sompel, H., Nelson, M.L., Sanderson, R.: HTTP framework for time-based access to resource states – Memento (2012), https://datatracker.ietf.org/doc/draft-vandesompel-memento/
20. Van de Sompel, H., Nelson, M.L., Sanderson, R., Balakireva, L.L., Ainsworth, S., Shankar, H.: Memento: Time Travel for the Web. Technical Report arXiv:0911.1112 (2009)
21. Wasserman, T.: Netflix takes up 32.7% of Internet bandwidth. Marshable (2011), http://goo.gl/2FtWa
22. Zhuang, Z., Wagle, R., Giles, C.: What's there and what's not?: focused crawling for missing documents in digital libraries. In: Proceedings of the 5th ACM/IEEE-CS Joint Conference on Digital Libraries, JCDL 2005, pp. 301–310 (2005)

A Study of Digital Curator Competencies – A Delphi Study

Anna Maria Tammaro[1] and Melody Madrid[2]

[1] University of Parma, Italy
annamaria.tammaro@unipr.it
[2] National Library of the Philippines
mmmadrid@nlp.gov.ph

Abstract. The aim of this research was to define competencies for digital curators, and to validate them through a Delphi process in the context of Library, Archives, Museum curriculum development. The objective for the study was to obtain consensus regarding competence statements for Library, Archives and Museum digital curators.

Keywords: Digital Curation, Digital Curator Competencies, Delphi Method.

1 Introduction

In today's data center-centric world, the development of digital technologies, cloud and big data has dramatically changed the way people create, access, share and store data. It has produced significant sets of data that promotes rapid improvements across many subject fields. These sets of data come in many different forms, for example, "the measurements recorded by environmental monitoring satellites, the products of collisions between fundamental particles, the sequences of entire genomes, the results of social science surveys and interviews, the annotated images of ancient Greek inscriptions or the annotated videos of innovative dance routines" [1]. These data can be useful in other parts of the world now or can be a wealthy source of information for future researchers. Libraries, archives, museums (LAM) is at the center of this digital innovation. LAM provides platform that allows the use of digital technologies in improving access of complex objects and enriching the experience users get from cultural resources. However, technological developments in LAM context bring not only new opportunities; they come also with corresponding challenges.

One of the challenges brought by digital innovation is that of digital curation, this is because if data are not properly curated and kept in well-managed data centers, they really do not have the potential to be accessible and reusable either now or in the future and that makes the very existence of LAM useless because it makes research a failure. Digital curation is a relatively new domain emerged as a result of overall changes in creation, distribution and use of data. Several authors from Library and Information Science, Archival and Records Management, Computer Science fields have discussed the development and the nature of the concept of Digital curation in

T. Aalberg et al. (Eds.): TPDL 2013, LNCS 8092, pp. 358–361, 2013.
© Springer-Verlag Berlin Heidelberg 2013

general, for example Beagrie [1], Yakel [2], Williams [3], Ray [4], Duranti [5], Harvey [6], Cunningham [7], Tibbo, et al [8] and Lord and MacDonald [9, 10].

Although the concept of digital curation is still young, what it can do has been eyed as very beneficial not only in short term period but in long-term period too. The aim of this research was to define competencies for digital curators, and to validate the competencies in the context of library, archives and museum curriculum development. The objective for the study was to obtain consensus regarding competence statements for library, archives and museum digital curators.

2   Methods

The Delphi method, a research technique, typically used to develop a consensus of opinion for topic areas in which there is little previously documented knowledge, was used in specifying the digital curator competencies in LAM context. And since digital curator has to combine knowledge, skills, attitude and understanding in performing their important tasks, this study used the term "competencies" which is viewed as characteristic of the task or job which an individual can do . And because this study is aiming to define competence for digital curator for educational reason, it is better to write competencies using the bottom-up approach and to be written in holistic way. The panel was consisting of a number of experts chosen based on their experience and knowledge and the following criteria: (1) Familiarity with digital curation and preservation; (2) Conducts research, lectures, or practice digital curation activities; (3) Has a deep interest in the role of digital curation in LAM context.

3   Results

The definition of Digital Curator which has been agreed by the experts participating to the Delphi study is:

"Digital curators are individuals capable of managing digital objects and collections for long-term access, preservation, sharing, integrity, authenticity and reuse. In addition, they have a range of managerial and operating skills, including domain or subject expertise and good IT skills"

The list of the 20 statements is divided into two kinds, Operational and Managerial competencies for maintaining the structure of this research, the statements were the result of a holistic approach.

Operational Competencies

1. Selects and appraises digital documents for long-term preservation.
2. Have an expert knowledge on the purpose of each kind of digital entities used within the designated community and its impact on preservation.

3. Knows data structure of different digital objects and determines appropriate support it needs.
4. Understands storage and preservation policies, procedures and practices that ensure the continuing trustworthiness and accessibility of digital objects.
5. Is aware of requirements to information infrastructure in order to ensure proper access, storage and data recovery.
6. Diagnoses and resolves problems to ensure continuous accessibility of digital objects, in collaboration with IT professionals.
7. Monitors the obsolescence of file formats, hardware and software and the development of new ones (e.g. using such tools as PRONOM registry)
8. Ensures the use of methods and tools that support interoperability of different applications and preservation technologies among users in different locations.
9. Verifies the provenance of the data to be preserved and ensures that it is properly documented.
10. Has the knowledge to assess the digital objects' authenticity, integrity and accuracy over time.

Managerial Competencies

1. Plans, implements, and monitors digital curation projects.
2. Understands and communicates the economic value of digital curation to existing and potential stakeholders, including administrators, legislators, and funding organizations.
3. Formulates digital curation policies, procedures, practices, and services and understands their impact on the creators and (re)users of digital objects.
4. Establishes and maintains collaborative relationships with various stakeholders (e.g., IT specialist, information professionals inside and outside the institution, data creators, (re)users and other stakeholders like vendors, memory institutions and international partners) to facilitate the accomplishment of digital curation objectives.
5. Organizes personnel education, training and other support for adoption of new developments in digital curation.
6. Is aware of the need to keep current with international developments in digital curation and understands the professional networks that enable this.
7. Understands and is able to communicate the risk of information loss or corruption of digital entities.
8. Organizes and manages the use of metadata standards, access controls and authentication procedures.
9. Is aware of relevant quality assurance standards and makes a well considered choice whether to employ them or not.
10. Observes and adheres to all applicable legislation and regulations when making decisions about preservation, use and reuse of digital objects in collaboration with legal practitioners.

4   Conclusion

The initial required competencies for digital curators set in motion one component of the agenda for digital curation research. The result of this study – a preliminary set of competencies for LAM digital curators can be used in curriculum development and training programs for digital curators at pre-doctoral and postdoctoral level. As this list of competencies will be use into practice, it is likely that gaps will be identified or that one or more of these competence statements will be shown to be unnecessary. For that reason, critical and regular evaluation of these digital curator competence statements should be instituted. The regular review of competencies would provide digital curation curriculum and training programs with the evolving tools necessary to keep pace with the learning opportunities taking place in centers across the academic enterprise. In addition, these competence statements can be very useful in setting research agendas for next generation of LAM digital curators.

References

1. Beagrie, N.: Digital curation for science, digital libraries, and individuals. International Journal of Digital Curation 1(1) (2006)
2. Yakel, E.: Digital curation. OCLC Systems & Services 23(4), 335–340 (2007)
3. Williams, A.: On the Tip of Creative Tongues. The New York Times. Fashion & Style, http://www.nytimes.com/2009/10/04/fashion/ (October 4, 2009) (retrieved)
4. Ray, J.: Managing the Digital World: The role of Digital Curation (2009), http://www.imls.gov/pdf/JRay_Edinburgh.pdf (retrieved)
5. Duranti, L.: The Long-Term Preservation of Accurate and Authentic Digital Data: The INTERPARES Project. Data Science Journal 4 (2006), http://www.jstage.jst.go.jp/article/dsj/4/0/4_106/_article (retrieved)
6. Harvey, R.: Digital curation: a how-to-do-it manual. Neil Schuman Publishers, Inc., New York (2010)
7. Cunningham, A.: Digital Curation/Digital Archiving: A View from the National Archives of Australia. American Archivist 71(2), 530–543 (2008)
8. Tibbo, H., Hank, C., Lee, C.A.: Challenges, curricula, and competencies: Researcher and practitioner erspectives for informing the development of a digital curation curriculum. Archiving, 234–238 (2008), https://www.asis.org/asist2012/proceedings/Submissions/283.pdf (retrieved)
9. Lord, P., Macdonald, A.: Digital Data Curation Task Force. Report of the Task Force Strategy Discussion Day Tuesday, Centre Point, London WC1 (2003) http://www.jisc.ac.uk/uploaded_documents/CurationTaskForceFinal1.pdf (November 26, 2002) (retrieved)
10. Lord, P., Macdonald, A.: E-Science curation report: Data curation for e-science in the UK – an audit to establish requirements for future curation and provision. Report prepared for the JISC Support of Research Committee, JCSR (2003), http://www.jisc.ac.uk/uploaded_documents/e-ScienceReportFinal.pdf (retrieved)

Large Scale Citation Matching
Using Apache Hadoop

Mateusz Fedoryszak, Dominika Tkaczyk, and Łukasz Bolikowski

Interdisciplinary Centre for Mathematical and Computational Modelling,
University of Warsaw
{m.fedoryszak,d.tkaczyk,l.bolikowski}@icm.edu.pl

Abstract. During the process of citation matching links from bibliography entries to referenced publications are created. Such links are indicators of topical similarity between linked texts, are used in assessing the impact of the referenced document and improve navigation in the user interfaces of digital libraries. In this paper we present a citation matching method and show how to scale it up to handle great amounts of data using appropriate indexing and a MapReduce paradigm in the Hadoop environment.

Keywords: citation matching, approximate indexing, MapReduce, Hadoop, CRF, SVM.

1 Introduction

Since Hitchcock et al. [1] demonstrated a proof-of-concept system that performed autonomous linking within Cognitive Science Open Journal, the problem of citation matching (i.e. linking citation strings referencing the same paper) has been tackled in countless papers by means of various methods [2]. Considering the rapid growth of the number of scientific publications, we need to seek new ways of dealing with large amounts of data. Recently, a MapReduce paradigm [3] and Apache Hadoop, its open-source implementation, have been gaining popularity. It has already been used for entity matching by Paradies et al. [4]. In this paper we present our own approach to citation matching in the Hadoop environment[1].

2 Small Scale Disambiguation

First of all, let us look on how reference disambiguation is performed when working on a small scale. Since amount of data is not large in this case, one can afford to count the similarity between every citation string pair. Having pairwise similarities, one can apply any clustering algorithm.

The whole process consists of two parts: citation parsing and matching. The aim of the first part is to extract metadata fields from a citation string; it is

---

[1] Extended version is available as arXiv:1303.6906 [cs.IR].

T. Aalberg et al. (Eds.): TPDL 2013, LNCS 8092, pp. 362–365, 2013.
© Springer-Verlag Berlin Heidelberg 2013

done using CRF-based [5] parser supplied with CERMINE — a metadata and content extraction tool [6]. Extracted information is then used in the matching step. As citations tend to contain spelling errors and differ in style, there is a need to introduce fuzzy similarity measures fitted to the specifics of various metadata fields. Most of them compute a fraction of tokens or trigrams [7] that occur in both fields. When comparing journal names, we have taken LCS (longest common subsequence) of two strings into consideration. For author matching, being especially difficult task involving abbreviations and token transposition, we have developed a similarity measure based on finding the heaviest matching of tokens. This can be seen as an instance of an assignment problem [8] with some refinements added. The overall similarity of two citation strings is obtained by applying a linear SVM using field similarities as features.

The evaluation was conducted on the CORA-ref data set [9]. It contains several citation clusters (each cluster consisting of citations referencing the same article). The clusters were randomly distributed into 3 slices and used to perform cross validation. The half of training set for each fold was used in the CRF parser training and the other half was used for the SVM training. Finally, pairwise similarities between citation strings were computed. The results were binarised by setting the similarity threshold at 50%. In order to obtain clusters, a single-link algorithm was applied. As can be seen in Tab. 1, the results are close to those achieved by Joint MLN method, reported in [10], outperforming them in terms of pairwise recall.

Table 1. Matching results. *Cluster recall* is the percentage of correct clusters that were recovered by a matcher. *Pairwise precision* and *recall* are, respectively, the percentage of links returned by a matcher that are correct and the percentage of correct links that were returned by a matcher. *Pairwise F_1* is their harmonic mean.

	Fold0	Fold1	Fold2	Average	Joint MLN
cluster recall	65.82%	72.50%	77.53%	71.95%	78.10%
pairwise precision	95.21%	97.51%	94.98%	95.90%	97.00%
pairwise recall	93.91%	93.06%	97.43%	94.80%	94.30%
pairwise F_1	94.56%	95.23%	96.19%	95.33%	95.63%

3   Heuristic: Author Indexing

The main scalability issue in the presented solution is its quadratic runtime. It would, therefore, be beneficial to limit the number of necessary pairwise comparisons. We have decided to use heuristic based on indexing that for each citation retrieves only metadata records that have the biggest number of author tokens in common with it. On the other hand, spelling errors occur commonly in citation strings. That is why an index supporting non-exact matches was desired. We have decided to implement ideas presented by Manning et al. in Chapter 3 of [11] to support retrieval of tokens with edit distance less than or equal 1.

Instead of putting as a key an exact word w, we put all the rotations of $w\$$ (where $\$$ is a character not present in an alphabet). In a similar manner, to retrieve a word from the index, we create all its rotations and for each rotation r of length n, all the keys of length $\leq n$ that match at least $n-1$ first letters of r and keys of length $\leq n+1$ that match first n letters are returned.

4 Hadoopisation

Fig. 1 presents the map-reduce steps of the algorithm described above. Note that those transforming one entry into many can be implemented as map tasks and those transforming many into one as reduce. A special data structure called *MapFile* is used to store our index and enable fast entity retrieval.

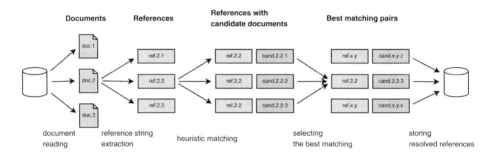

Fig. 1. Citation matching steps. The documents are read and references are extracted from their metadata. Then, the actual matching occurs: in the first step heuristic is used to find documents that may match citations, in the next step the best match is selected for each citation. Eventually, the results are persisted.

We have evaluated efficiency of our solution using PMC Open Access Subset[2] document set. It consists of over 450 thousand documents containing 12 million citations. The benchmark was performed on our Hadoop cluster [12] which consists of four 'fat' slave nodes, each containing 48 cores. The time spent in each phase is presented in Tab. 2.

Table 2. The time spent in individual phases

Phase		Time spent [hrs:mins:secs]	Task No. Map	Reduce
Index building	All	0:00:57	13	2
Matching	Citation extraction	0:00:46	13	0
	Heuristic matching	3:01:38	745	0
	Selecting the best match	2:51:00	996	1

[2] http://www.ncbi.nlm.nih.gov/pmc/tools/openftlist/

5   Conclusions and Future Work

In this paper we have presented an efficient citation matching solution which scales up to handle millions of citations by means of Apache Hadoop. We have also built an index enabling approximate entity retrieval. Future work will include refining the heuristic to achieve better results, e.g. by indexing other fields besides the author name. It would also be beneficial to study Hadoop technicalities to find the best way of using the index as the current process involves performing many small requests causing plenty of random disk reads.

References

[1] Hitchcock, S.M., Carr, L.A., Harris, S.W., Hey, J.M.N., Hall, W.: Citation Linking: Improving Access to Online Journals. Proceedings of Digital Libraries 97, 115–122 (1997)

[2] Fedoryszak, M., Bolikowski, L., Tkaczyk, D., Wojciechowski, K.: Methodology for Evaluating Citation Parsing and Matching. In: Bembenik, R., Skonieczny, L., Rybiński, H., Kryszkiewicz, M., Niezgódka, M. (eds.) Intell. Tools for Building a Scientific Information. SCI, vol. 467, pp. 145–154. Springer, Heidelberg (2013)

[3] Dean, J., Ghemawat, S.: MapReduce: Simplified Data Processing on Large Clusters. Communications of the ACM 51(1), 1–13 (2004)

[4] Paradies, M., Malaika, S., Siméon, J., Khatchadourian, S., Sattler, K.-U.: Entity matching for semistructured data in the Cloud. In: SAC 2012, p. 453. ACM Press (2012)

[5] Lafferty, J., McCallum, A., Pereira, F.: Conditional random fields: Probabilistic models for segmenting and labeling sequence data. In: ICML 2001, pp. 282–289. Citeseer (2001)

[6] Tkaczyk, D., Bolikowski, L., Czeczko, A., Rusek, K.: A modular metadata extraction system for born-digital articles. In: Proceedings of the 10th IAPR International Workshop on Document Analysis Systems (2012)

[7] Ukkonen, E.: Approximate string-matching with q-grams and maximal matches. Theoretical Computer Science 92(1), 191–211 (1992)

[8] Kuhn, H.W.: The Hungarian method for the assignment problem. Naval Research Logistics Quarterly 2(1-2), 83–97 (1955)

[9] McCallum, A.K., Nigam, K., Rennie, J.: Automating the construction of internet portals with machine learning. Information Retrieval, 127–163 (2000)

[10] Poon, H., Domingos, P.: Joint Inference in Information Extraction. In: Artificial Intelligence, vol. 22, pp. 913–918. AAAI Press (2007)

[11] Manning, C.D., Raghavan, P., Schtze, H.: Introduction to Information Retrieval. Cambridge University Press, New York (2008)

[12] Kawa, A., Bolikowski, L., Czeczko, A., Dendek, P.J., Tkaczyk, D.: Data Model for Analysis of Scholarly Documents in the MapReduce Paradigm. In: Bembenik, R., Skonieczny, L., Rybiński, H., Kryszkiewicz, M., Niezgódka, M. (eds.) Intell. Tools for Building a Scientific Information. SCI, vol. 467, pp. 155–170. Springer, Heidelberg (2013)

Building an Online Environment
for Usefulness Evaluation

Jasmin Hügi and René Schneider

Haute Ecole de Gestion de Genève, 7 route de Drize, CH-1227 Carouge
{jasmin.hugi,rene.schneider}@hesge.ch

Abstract. In this paper we present a methodological framework for usefulness evaluation of digital libraries and information services that has been tested successfully in two case studies before developing a corresponding tool that may be used for further investigations. The tool is based on a combination of a knowledge base with exploitable and modifiable questions and an open source tool for online-questionnaires.

Keywords: Digital Libraries, Usefulness Evaluation, Quality metrics.

1 Introduction

Recent years have seen a considerable increase in evaluating the usability of digital libraries and several methods (e.g. heuristic evaluations, user acceptance testing) have been established. Unfortunately the matter of usefulness, which has the same importance in the realm of online libraries and information services, is less investigated. In the context of a research project named PECI (= Plateforme d'Evaluation pour les Centres d'Information) a framework that allows an adjustable elaboration of a survey concerning usefulness was built. Persons interested in evaluating the usefulness of a digital library or its content will be able to quickly create a survey without having to consult an expert.

2 Case Studies

Tsakonas and Papatheodorou [1] developed a model named interaction triptych framework on which the work presented in this paper is based upon. This framework investigates the relationship between three major components: system, user, and content provided, whereas the relationship between the user and the content defines the evaluation axis of usefulness.

Based on this model, two case studies were executed, one for infoclio.ch, the Swiss portal of the historical sciences (www.infoclio.ch), and one for the Swiss national sound archives (www.fonoteca.ch). In both cases, all services are digital and there is no direct contact between the institution and the users. The study concerning infoclio.ch was based on an online survey (with incentives for participants) in order to

T. Aalberg et al. (Eds.): TPDL 2013, LNCS 8092, pp. 366–369, 2013.
© Springer-Verlag Berlin Heidelberg 2013

evaluate the usefulness of the information portal's components. The study concerning the Swiss National Sound Archives was focused on listening spots for copyrighted audio files and started with ethnographic interviews in three institutions housing a listening spot. In addition to the interviews, an online survey was made, which contained questions focusing on the usefulness and the usage of the listening spots and questions regarding the satisfaction of the content provided on the website of the Swiss National Sound Archives.

The usefulness dimension of the Interaction Triptych Framework contains five attributes: relevance, format, reliability, level and coverage. As it is rather rare to obtain the questions used in other usefulness studies, it has been decided to develop new questions going into detail for every attribute. These questions were then discussed with the stakeholder who added new ones or deleted some of them. After discussions with the stakeholders, the model developed by Tsakonas et al. has been extended and two more attributes have been added in order to correspond to their expectations, namely satisfaction and competition. Satisfaction was added because whenever a digital library is of use to a user and when there are no major problems with the usability, it should positively and measurably influence the user's degree of satisfaction. Therefore, the attribute of satisfaction represents an indirect way to measure the usefulness of a system. In the case of a non-satisfactory attitude of a user, it is very important to identify the source of this non-satisfaction. The attribute of competition provides knowledge about competitive services which may be consulted by a user. This attribute allows going beyond the hermetic view of a system in order to not only compare it with the users' needs and preferences, but to take its environment into account in the analysis. Any given system is always exposed to competitors, as competitive services influence the users' expectations and model their behavior. Questions about competition allow as well comparing the proposed contents and services with similar systems.

In order to make the concept usefulness as visual and understandable as possible, a mind map was created (see: http://campus.hesge.ch/id_bilingue/doc/Usefulness_en.bmp) containing usefulness as the core concept, followed by the dimensions (or attributes), which are detailed in simple and general questions that could also show up in a survey. This concretization of parameters helped the stakeholders to understand the concept of usefulness and to see which aspects of usefulness could be explored and as a consequence made it easier for the stakeholders to decide what aspects are to investigate and what aspects are to ignore. The stakeholders were invited at several points of time to modify, add or delete questions according to the specific objectives of their evaluation. Finally, the questions were transferred into an online questionnaire and disseminated. The evaluation process finished with the analysis of the data obtained and further explanations on them together with some recommendations for improving the service and a last meeting with the stakeholders involved in the evaluation process. To make similar evaluations easier, the whole evaluation process, which can be interpreted as an assessment process, was subsumed in an eleven step approach as described in detail in [2].

3   Practical Implementation

One of the main objectives of this study was the transfer of the gained knowledge to librarians. As a consequence, the study was supposed to develop a framework which librarians can follow in order to conduct their own usefulness evaluation. Based on the case studies, we built a framework for the whole evaluation process that allowed us to extract mesoscopic question on the base of the specific questionnaires, which represented the most difficult undertaking. The mesoscopic approach tried to respond the demand to keep the questions specific enough so that their purpose is still understandable and adaptable to every one's own context with minimum effort.

In order to make the process and the collection of mesoscopic questions available to the public, an online platform has been developed to provide a usefulness evaluation tool (usefulness.ch). This tool is based on the open source web application Lime-Survey which is dedicated to the creation of questionnaires and the conduct of online surveys. LimeSurvey is mainly based on PHP and MySQL and currently the most complete open source software concerning surveys with an active community [www.limesurvey.org]. LimeSurvey provides an enormous amount of functionalities and allows parameterizing surveys in detail. This leads inevitably to a high complexity within the interface. As many of the provided functionalities of this software were not used for the usefulness.ch platform, a new interface which works as a layer on top of the software has been created.

The platform usefulness.ch provides in addition to the online survey software a template questionnaire which contains all mesoscopic level questions. After the creation of an account on the platform, the user has access to the template questionnaire. The user can choose from this template questionnaire the questions which are to be integrated in his own questionnaire. In a further step, he may then modify the chosen questions to the context of his evaluation purposes and add his own questions. After having completed the questionnaire, it is possible to either conduct the survey directly on the usefulness.ch platform or to export the survey. If the survey is conducted via the online platform, a link is provided which can be sent to potential participants or integrated on a website for example. The responses are collected on the platform and may be exported once the survey has ended. The results can be downloaded in the .lsv format which is readable by any table processing program like Excel. The usefulness.ch platform is available in German and French and its use is free of charge.

4   Conclusions

It seems clear that after decades of putting emphasis on the evaluation of a system's usability, the exploration of its usefulness, i.e. the usefulness of a digital library's content is about to gain more and more interest. There is still much work to be done to establish this relationship and to build a solid methodological fundament. The work described in this paper shall be considered as a contribution for a further step in this process.

References

1. Tsakonas, G., Papatheodorou, C.: Analysing and evaluating usefulness and usability in electronic information services. Journal of information science 32(5), 400–419 (2006)
2. Birri Blezon, R., Hügi, J., Schneider, R.: "Sieht gut aus, aber was bringt es mir?": zur Evaluation der Nützlichkeit digitaler Inhalte. In: Bekavac, B., Schneider, R., Schweibenz, W. (eds.) Benutzerorientierte Bibliotheken im Web, pp. 55–73. de Gruyter, Berlin (2011)

Topic Modeling for Search and Exploration in Multivariate Research Data Repositories

Maximilian Scherer[1], Tatiana von Landesberger[1], and Tobias Schreck[2]

[1] TU Darmstadt, 64283 Darmstadt, Germany
{maximilian.scherer,tatiana.von_landesberger}@gris.tu-darmstadt.de
[2] University of Konstanz, 78457 Konstanz, Germany
tobias.schreck@uni-konstanz.de

Abstract. Huge amounts of multivariate research data are produced
and made publicly available in digital libraries. Little research focused
on similarity functions that take multivariate data documents as a whole
into account. Such similarity functions are highly beneficial for users, by
enabling them to browse and query large collections of multivariate data
using nearest-neighbor indexing. In this paper we tackle this challenge
and propose a novel similarity function for multivariate data documents
based on topic-modeling. Based on a previously developed bag-of-words
approach for multivariate data, we can then learn a topic model for a
collection of multivariate data documents and represent each document
as a mixture of topics. This representation is very suitable for efficient
nearest-neighbor indexing and clustering according to the topic distribution of a document. We present a use-case where we apply this approach
to retrieval of multivariate data in the field of climate research.

Keywords: multivariate data, content-based retrieval, bag-of-words, lda.

1 Introduction

Multivariate data arises in many areas of research, industrial production and
other commercial applications. Due to increasing efforts in the digital library
community over the last decade, such data, particularly data obtained for research purposes, is made publicly available is specialized research data repositories and annotated with high-quality meta-data. Similar to the search and access
schemes for multimedia databases, content-based access to such repositories has
started to receive attention from the digital library community.

Assessing the similarity between two arbitrary multivariate documents is a
challenging problem. Such documents are very heterogeneous, as they vary in
their respective number of columns, as well as their respective column types
(based on meta-data annotations). The top part of Figure 1 shows an example
of this challenge.

In this paper, we propose a novel approach for computing a similarity measure
between multivariate data documents, by learning a topic model for this type
of data and representing each document as a mixture of topics. Topic modeling originates from textual information retrieval [3], and has also shown to be

T. Aalberg et al. (Eds.): TPDL 2013, LNCS 8092, pp. 370–373, 2013.

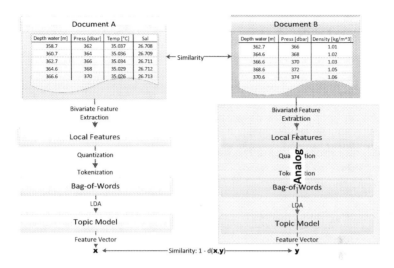

Fig. 1. Our approach for topic modeling of multivariate research data documents

the state-of-the-art for content-based multimedia retrieval applications [6]. We provide a case-study of our proposed approach by building a topic model for multivariate data documents in the domain of climate research.

2   Related Work

There are several recent examples of digital library systems that provide means of content-based access. These systems specialize in different retrieval domains, ranging from 3D models and classical music [2] and images [8] to research data documents that contain time-series data [1] or bivariate data [9].

Topic modeling is a generative learning process that models documents as a mixture of a small number of topics [3]. In the domain of non-textual documents, Topic modeling has been shown to yield state-of-the-art retrieval performance for image retrieval [6] as well as 3D models and 3D scenes [5] and time-series data [7]. In this paper we transfer it for the first time to the domain of multivariate research data by extending our previous work on bag-of-words representations for multivariate research data [10].

3   Approach

Multivariate research data documents consist of tabular data with n columns (measurement variables / parameters) and m rows (observations) along with annotated meta-data for each column (usually parameter name and base unit, e.g. *Depth water [m]*). Our goal is to compute a similarity score between two

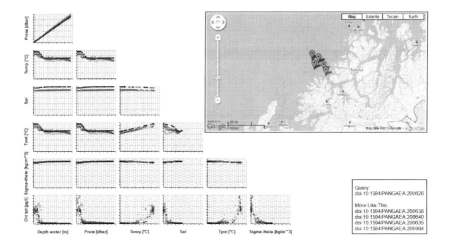

Fig. 2. Example of our similarity function for multivariate data documents

arbitrary such documents. Based on the bag-of-words representation for multi-variate research data we recently developed [10], our approach consists of several steps shown in Figure 1.

The basic approach is to first extract a bag-of-words representation of the data by extracting local features, and quantizing these features via k-means or other suitable clustering methods. We use this bag-of-words representation for the multivariate data documents under concern to compute a topic model. Using our own implementation of the *latent-Dirichlet-analysis* (LDA) [3], and the (normalized and rescaled) word histograms from our bag-of-words representation as input, we compute a topic model consisting of $k = 100$ topics.

Each multivariate data document is now represented by a k-dimensional feature vector containing the topic activations for the document. For distance computation we propose to use the cosine similarity, though other metrics can be used as well.

4   Use Case

We show the applicability of our topic modeling approach to multivariate real-world data from the *PANGAEA* Data Library [4]. *PANGAEA* is a digital library for the environmental sciences. It archives, publishes, and distributes geo-referenced primary research data from scientists all over the world. For our experimental setup, we acquired every document available under the Creative Commons Attribution License 3.0 from http://www.pangaea.de. Each document is uniquely identified with a DOI and consists of a table of multivariate measurements. We obtained 98,416 such documents in total and built a nearest-neighbor index using our proposed feature extraction and similarity computation scheme.

We implemented a "Related Documents" approach that presents the four nearest neighbors to the document we are currently viewing (thus, the four most similar documents with respect to our approach). Figure 2 shows a screen-shot of this approach in action. Scatter-plot-matrices are used for result visualization. They show the pair-wise relationship between every variable in the dataset. We can see that the four nearest neighbors to the query document all contain the same dimensions (although the search was not restricted to that), and that the scatter-plot-matrices of all retrieved documents are very similar to the scatter-plot-matrix of the query object. This indicates that all five documents describe a similar climate pattern. Additionally, we visualized the geo-location where the documents were originally measured. All document were obtained in the Norwegian Sea near the coast of Tromso, and as such, were indeed measured in the same maritime climate zone.

References

1. Bernard, J., Ruppert, T., Scherer, M., Kohlhammer, J., Schreck, T.: Content-based layouts for exploratory metadata search in scientific research data. In: Boughida, K.B., Howard, B., Nelson, M.L., de Sompel, H.V., Sølvberg, I. (eds.) JCDL, pp. 139–148. ACM (2012)
2. Berndt, R., et al.: The PROBADO project - approach and lessons learned in building a digital library system for heterogeneous non-textual documents. In: Lalmas, M., Jose, J., Rauber, A., Sebastiani, F., Frommholz, I. (eds.) ECDL 2010. LNCS, vol. 6273, pp. 376–383. Springer, Heidelberg (2010)
3. Blei, D., Ng, A., Jordan, M.: Latent dirichlet allocation. The Journal of Machine Learning Research 3, 993–1022 (2003)
4. Diepenbroek, M., Grobe, H., Reinke, M., Schindler, U., Schlitzer, R., Sieger, R., Wefer, G.: Pangaea–an information system for environmental sciences. Computers & Geosciences 28(10), 1201–1210 (2002)
5. Eitz, M., Richter, R., Boubekeur, T., Hildebrand, K., Alexa, M.: Sketch-based shape retrieval. ACM Trans. Graph (Proc. SIGGRAPH) 31(4), 31:1–31:10 (2012)
6. Lew, M., Sebe, N., Djeraba, C., Jain, R.: Content-based multimedia information retrieval: State of the art and challenges. ACM Transactions on Multimedia Computing, Communications, and Applications (TOMCCAP) 2(1), 1–19 (2006)
7. Lin, J., Khade, R., Li, Y.: Rotation-invariant similarity in time series using bag-of-patterns representation. J. of Intelligent Information Systems, 1–29 (2011)
8. Rowley-Brooke, R., Pitié, F., Kokaram, A.: A ground truth bleed-through document image database. In: Zaphiris, P., Buchanan, G., Rasmussen, E., Loizides, F. (eds.) TPDL 2012. LNCS, vol. 7489, pp. 185–196. Springer, Heidelberg (2012)
9. Scherer, M., Bernard, J., Schreck, T.: Retrieval and exploratory search in multivariate research data repositories using regressional features. In: Proceeding of the 11th Annual International ACM/IEEE Joint Conference on Digital Libraries, JCDL 2011, pp. 363–372. ACM Press, New York (2011)
10. Scherer, M., von Landesberger, T., Schreck, T.: Visual-interactive querying for multivariate research data repositories using bag-of-words. In: Proceedings of the 13th ACM/IEEE-CS Joint Conference on Digital Libraries, JCDL 2013, pp. xx–xx (to appear 2013)

Time-Based Exploratory Search in Scientific Literature

Silviu Homoceanu, Sascha Tönnies, Philipp Wille, and Wolf-Tilo Balke

IFIS TU Braunschweig, Mühlenpfordstraße 23, 38106 Braunschweig, Germany
{silviu,toennies,wille,balke}@ifis.cs.tu-bs.de

Abstract. State-of-the-art faceted search graphical user interfaces for digital libraries provide a wide range of filters perfectly suitable for narrowing down results for well-defined user needs. However, they fail to deliver summarized overview information for users that need to familiarize themselves with a new scientific topic. In fact, exploratory search remains one of the major problems for scientific literature search in digital libraries. Exploiting a user study about how computer scientists actually approach new subject areas we developed ESSENCE, a system for empowering exploratory search in scientific literature.

Keywords: Digital Libraries, User Interface, Exploratory Search, Timeline.

1   Introduction

A short survey we conducted among fellow researchers in computer science pointed to a surprising insight: entry points for today's literature search are no longer (digital) library portals, but search engines like Google Scholar or Microsoft Academic Search. Indeed indexing a wide variety of digital libraries, such systems are perfect for exact match searches like looking for a paper, where the title is known, or all recent publications of some author. However, an important part of literature search involves familiarizing oneself with some topic of interest. This kind of search, known as exploratory search, is difficult with any search engine: Starting from rather general keywords one manually has to explore many of the resulting documents and iteratively refine the search in order to get a sufficient overview of the topic. Therefore, in most practical digital library interfaces exploratory search on scientific material is supported through faceted interfaces ([1]). But besides a selection of relevant venues, prolific authors or in the best case, frequent co-occurring keywords for a query, no overview of the field is actually conveyed. Ideally, for a general query like "database systems" exploratory search systems should provide an overview like: In the '60s research focused on hierarchical DBMS, in the '70s relational DBMS were the dominant topic, in the '80s, expert systems and object oriented databases emerged and so on.

We conducted a more detailed user study to analyze how computer scientists approach new subject areas. The main result showed that participants paid special attention to authors' keywords and how they changed over time. Thus, based on sophisticated measures for novelty detection ([2]) we developed ESSENCE (Exploratory Search for SciENCE) a system that extracts emerging keywords from topically focused document collections and presents them on a timeline.

T. Aalberg et al. (Eds.): TPDL 2013, LNCS 8092, pp. 374–377, 2013.

2   User Study – Exploratory Search in Scientific Literature

We conducted a study to understand how scientists become acquainted with a new subject area. All participants (15) had a background in computer science with different levels of expertise, ranging from master students to senior researchers. They were asked to describe their approach on performing literature search on a subject they had low expertise in. All participants proposed to perform a keyword search of this exact term. The tools they used show some differences: While students and young researchers proposed starting with either a Google or Wikipedia search, more experienced researchers chose Google Scholar, Microsoft Academic Research, or Mendeley. The next step they took was to look through the metadata for the found papers: Keywords were generally the first stop, followed by title, time of publication and abstract. Independent of the tools two different strategies were adopted by the participants when exploring an unknown field: The first one was to find "overview" papers. Soon enough it became clear that just one overview paper would not suffice: While early overview papers miss out on what we today refer to as state-of-the-art, recent overview papers focus on the state-of-the-art without covering history or evolution of a field. In consequence, for a complete coverage one needs to consider multiple overview papers published in different time periods. Criteria for identifying overview papers were hints in the paper title e.g., "state-of-the-art", "survey", "overview". However, this approach generates many 'false alarms' while often missing out on actual state-of-the-art papers. The second approach focused on identifying hot topics and how they changed over time. For example, for early papers on "semantic web", keywords like "RDF" or "Metadata" were common. For recently published papers "Linked Data" emerged. Both strategies take important metadata like the keywords and publication time into consideration. But while in the first case participants still had to read at least some of the found overview papers, the second approach already provides an overview by grasping the evolution of keywords over time.

Examining the distribution of keywords' frequencies over time, one can differentiate keywords with high variance in their distribution vs. keywords showing a "flat" distribution. On manual inspection on the results for multiple queries we observed that keywords with low variance in their relative frequency are either general keywords, 'popular' for most fields, or the field itself. In contrast, keywords that were picked up as hot topics for some time interval by study participants, show higher degree of variance over time. They deviate from the expected for the respective time periods appearing more frequent than average. Consistent with the theory of *novelty detection* presented in [2], this observation allowed us to isolate hot topics.

3   System Description

Starting from a paper collection, ESSENCE identifies those papers that are relevant for a scientific field provided as query and extracts those keywords showing high novelty on a yearly basis. Together with other scientific literature metadata they are integrated in summarized form in a GUI (presented in [3]) that facilitates exploratory search. The UI is focused on the two central elements whose importance we identified during the user study: A timeline with query-relevant year span and a tag cloud comprising selected authors' keywords.

A query is a term that best represents a field of interest. For our running example, a possible query would be "semantic web". Throughout this paper we repeatedly make use of the *term* and *document* concepts. By *term* we understand a word or group of ordered words. In accordance with the document metadata that study participants found particularly useful, a *document* is a 5-tuple comprising a document *title*, a set of *keywords* (each keyword is a *term*), an *abstract* a *publication year* and a list of *authors*. Starting with the query term, the system finds those documents that are relevant for the query. A document is a *hit* for a query or any term for that matter, if the term is included in any of the document components: Given a term *t* and a document *d* we define *hit* as a function, hit : (Terms × Documents) → {0, 1} with:

$$hit(t,d) = \begin{cases} 1 \text{ iff } t \text{ is contained in } title, keywords \text{ or } abstract \text{ of } d \\ 0 \text{ } otherwise \end{cases} \quad (1)$$

All authors' keywords that annotate documents representing hits for the query are possible feature candidates for the overview. Given a query term *q*, and a set of documents *H* representing hits for the query term, with $H = \{d \mid hit(q,d) = 1\}$, we define the set of feature candidates for *q* denoted by FC_q as:

$$FC_q = \{k \mid k \text{ is a keyword of } d, \forall d \in H\}. \quad (2)$$

Publication dates are also extracted in the process since they are needed for computing the publication time span (year of publication of the earliest published paper - year of publication of the latest published paper) for the query. Given a query *q*, we define the *query years set* for *q* denoted by Y_q as:

$$Y_q = \{y \mid |D_{q,y}| \geq \theta\}, \quad (3)$$

where $D_{q,y} = \{d \mid hit(q,d) = 1 \wedge d \text{ was published in year } y$. The lower the value of θ the less significant are the resulting estimations.

For each year in the publication time-span, a yearly term weight is computed for all extracted keywords: Given a query *q*, a publication year *y*, and a term *t* we define the *yearly term weight* for term *t* under query *q* in year *y*, denoted by $w_{q,y}(t)$ *as* a function, $w_{q,y}(t)$: Terms → [0, 1] with:

$$w_{q,y}(t) = \begin{cases} \frac{1}{|D_{q,y}|} \cdot \sum_{i=1}^{|D_{q,y}|} hit(t, d_i), with \ d_i \in D_{q,y}, \ iff \ D_{q,y} \neq \emptyset; \\ 0, \qquad\qquad\qquad otherwise; \end{cases} \quad (4)$$

where $D_{q,y} = \{d \mid hit(q,d) = 1 \wedge d \text{ was published in year } y\}. \quad (5)$

The yearly term weight seems like a good mechanism for determining which feature candidates show high weight variance. But computing a measure of variance like the standard deviation of the weights for each feature candidate favors mainstream keywords: The standard deviation of mainstream keywords is much bigger than the standard deviation of more specific, lower frequency keywords. Despite representing important features, keywords with low frequencies would never be considered relevant. For this purpose, normalizing the standard deviation by the average (known as the coefficient of variation) is necessary: Given a query q, and a set of feature candidates FC_q for q, we define the set of features for q denoted by F_q as:

$$F_q = \{f \mid f \in FC_q \land \frac{stdev\left(\cup_{i=1}^{|Y_q|} w_{q,y_i}(f)\right)}{avg\left(\cup_{i=1}^{|Y_q|} w_{q,y_i}(f)\right)} \geq \gamma \}, \; with \; y_i \in Y_q, \tag{6}$$

where *stdev* and *avg* represent the standard deviation and average of all weights for f under query q and γ regulates the lowest acceptable frequency distribution.

F_q comprises a list of features that are relevant for query q, but the relevance of each feature on a yearly basis still has to be determined. The *yearly term weight* is not suitable since it favors mainstream features. Instead, a function that captures the normalized positive deviations on a yearly basis is necessary: Given a query q, a publication year y, and a term t, we define the *yearly term novelty* for term t under query q in year y, denoted by $n_{q,y}(t)$ as a function, $n_{q,y}(t)$:Terms $\rightarrow [0; \infty)$ with:

$$n_{q,y}(t) = \begin{cases} \frac{w_{q,y}(t) - avg_{w_q}(t)}{avg_{w_q}(t)}, & iff \; w_{q,y}(t) > avg_{w_q}(t) > 0; \\ 0, & otherwise. \end{cases} \tag{7}$$

$$where \; avg_{w_q}(t) = avg \left(\cup_{i=1}^{|Y_q|} w_{q,y_i}(t) \right), with \; y_i \in Y_q. \tag{8}$$

Finally, the relevance of features (from F_q) for a given query q over time, is computed as the *yearly term novelty* of the feature for the corresponding relevant years (from Y_q).

4   Conclusion

Systems like Google Scholar, or Microsoft Academic Research, favoring simple yet effective interfaces are the first stop when searching for literature in computer science. However, for exploratory search, even the more sophisticated faceted search interfaces don't perform to the users' satisfaction. Learning from the way users familiarize themselves with new scientific areas, we discovered that their approach is consistent with the theory of novelty detection successfully implemented in online news mining. ESSENCE adapts these techniques to the particularities of scientific literature for extracting overview information.

References

1. Diederich, J., Balke, W.-T.: FacetedDBLP - Navigational Access for Digital Libraries. In: TCDL (2008)
2. Ma, J., Perkins, S.: Online Novelty Detection on Temporal Sequences. In: KDD (2003)
3. Homoceanu, S., Tönnies, S., Wille, P., Balke, W.-T.: ESSENCE- Time-Based Exploratory Search in Scientific Literature (2013),
   http://dx.doi.org/10.6084/m9.figshare.710918

Crowds and Content:
Crowd-Sourcing Primitives for Digital Libraries

Stuart Dunn and Mark Hedges

Centre for e-Research, Department of Digital Humanities, King's College London,
26-29 Drury Lane, London WC2B 5RL
{stuart.dunn,mark.hedges}@kcl.ac.uk

Abstract. This poster reports on a nine month scoping survey of research in the arts and humanities involving crowd-sourcing. This study proposed a twelve-facet typology of research processes currently in use, and these are reported here, along with the context of current research practice, the types of research assets which are currently being exposed to crowd-sourcing, and the sorts of outputs (including digital libraries and collections) which such projects are producing.

Keywords: crowd-sourcing, typology, humanities.

1   Introduction

Crowd-sourcing is the process of leveraging public participation in or contributions to projects and activities. It is relatively new to the academy and especially to the world of digital libraries; and is even newer in the domains of the humanities. However, at a time when the web is simultaneously transforming the way in which people collaborate and communicate, and merging the spaces which the academic and library communities inhabit, the contribution of crowd-sourcing as a means of creating and curating digital libraries is of increasing importance. The Trove project in Australia for example [1] has leveraged public participation in correcting imperfect Optical Character Recognition in scans of Australian newspapers; and the British Library's Georeferencer project has allowed members of the public to create metadata for the Library's historic map archive by associating places marked on the maps with the correct latitude/longitude geometries [2]. The purpose of this poster is to present the high level outcome of a review of research literature of crowd-sourcing's contributions to digital libraries the academic humanities domains, and to propose how it might be visualized. This outcome takes the form of a new typology of crowd-sourcing methods which captures the different approaches which have emerged is presented.

The visualization derives from a study the authors undertook in 2012 for the UK's Arts and Humanities Research Council (AHRC). It consisted of four components: a literature review of academic research in the humanities which has drawn on crowd-sourcing, as well as papers detailing research into crowd-sourcing itself as a method;

T. Aalberg et al. (Eds.): TPDL 2013, LNCS 8092, pp. 378–381, 2013.

two workshops held at King's College London in May and October 2012 facilitating discussion between, respectively, academics in the humanities who use crowd-sourcing, and members of the public with records of contributing to such projects; a set of interviews with both academics and contributors, and an online survey of contributors exploring their backgrounds, histories, and motivations for participating. We also conducted an extensive web crawl, identifying projects using crowd-sourcing that may not yet have produced a tangible academic outcome; tools that facilitate crowd-sourcing, and relevant blogs and Twitter feeds.

2   Terminology

Crowd-sourcing as an epistemic model is a complex and wide-ranging area, and it is necessary at the outset to define terms and the boundaries of the review. Public involvement in the humanities can take many forms – transcribing handwritten text into digital form; tagging photographs to facilitate discovery and preservation; entering structured or semi-structured data; commenting on content or participating in discussions, or recording one's own experiences and memories in the form of oral history – and the relationship between the public and the humanities is convoluted and poorly understood. This being so, it is unsurprising that the term crowd-sourcing is frequently used as a convenient label for a diverse range of activities. It was originally coined in 2006, when a parallel was drawn between businesses farming out labour to cheaper markets in the developing world, and companies utilising 'the productive potential of millions of plugged-in enthusiasts' [3], with similar reduction in labour costs. In recent years, academics have come to use the power of the crowd to achieve research aims, in what may be considered as an *epistemic model* [4]. As a method of undertaking academic research, however, the term 'crowd-sourcing' is problematic. It is certainly less easy to define than the analogous term 'citizen science', which is commonly understood to refer to activities whereby members of the public undertake well-defined and (individually) small-scale tasks as part of much larger-scale scientific projects, but which, in the past, has also been used to refer to more passive forms of participation such as making available unused CPU power of desktop machines for harvesting by research teams.

3   Typology

Our typology seeks to bring together a wide range of these approaches. It does not seek to provide an alternative set of categories or labels specifically for humanities crowd-sourcing; rather it recognizes that there are a set of fluid and interchangeable categories within four key typological areas: **asset type**, **process type**, **task type**, and **output type**.

   The main conclusion of this poster is that crowd-sourcing projects in the humanities – including the motivations of the participating communities and individuals – can best be understood by analysing them in terms of these four 'primitive' facets and of the relationships between them, and in particular by observing how the categories applicable in one facet are dependent on those in others.

Of course, not all projects will map straightforwardly onto single categories under of the four facets. Historypin (http://www.historypin.com), for example, is involved with georeferencing, images, metadata, impact, engagement and recording. While it operates outside the academic sector, it has developed strong links with the GLAM sector by providing a set of tools to allow embedding of Historypin content in cultural collections (see http://wearewhatwedo.org/press-releases/historypin-unleashes-new-tools). Such examples constantly challenge this typology, and provide the impetus that will guide its future evolution.

3.1   Types of Process

At the core of the typology are the processes, defined as a sequence of tasks, through which an output is produced by modifying asset. It is conditioned by the kind of asset involved, and by the questions that are of interest to project stakeholders (both organizers and volunteers) and can be answered, or at least addressed, using information contained in the asset.

Table 1. Process types defined in the crowd-sourcing scoping study

PROCESS
Collaborative tagging
Linking
Correcting/modifying content
Transcribing[1]
Recording and creating content
Commenting, critical responses and stating preferences
Categorising
Cataloguing
Contextualisation
Mapping
Georeferencing
Translating

Any robust set of replicable methodologies for creating or processing information by or for humanistic scholarship must be framed in the terms of these processes.

Depending on the project or activity, and what it aims to achieve, some processes will be combined. Outputs might be original knowledge, or they might be more

---

[1] This category also includes marked-up transcriptions, e.g. as TEI XML.

ephemeral and difficult to identify: however, considering the processes of both know-ledge and resource creation as comprising of these four facets gives a meaningful context to every piece of research, publication and activity we have uncovered in the course of this review. We hope the lessons and good practice we have identified here will, along with this typology, contribute to the development of new kinds of humanities crowd-sourcing in the future.

The most significant finding of the research review is that most humanities scholars who have used crowd-sourcing in its various forms now agree that it is not simply a form of cheap labour for the creation or digitization of content; indeed in a cost-benefit sense it does not always compare well with more conventional means of digitization and processing. In this sense, it has truly left its roots, as defined by Howe [3] behind. The creativity, enthusiasm and alternative foci that communities outside that academy can bring to academic projects is a resource which is now ripe for tap-ping in to, and the examples shown in this report illustrate the rich variety of forms that tapping can take.

For the specific issue of digital libraries, there are two immediate challenges for a review of crowd-sourcing as a research method. Firstly, in purely semantic terms, where should the boundaries of what is considered to be crowd-sourcing lie? And secondly, since humanities crowd-sourcing is in its very early stages, there is relative-ly little academic literature dealing with its application and outcomes to allow any firm judgments to be made about its potential to produce academically credible know-ledge[2]. Given this lack of evidence, we therefore do not seek to make value judgments on any individual cases, and we stress that equally this report does not seek to evan-gelize or promote crowd-sourcing as a method. It simply seeks to identify what, on present evidence, seems to work and what does not. Moreover, this underlines the need to examine other, less formal, sources of information, such as blogs and inter-views, and emphasizes that at this early stage, it is just as important to consider the academic validity of processes as well as outcomes.

References

1. Holley, R.: Many Hands Make Light Work: Public Collaborative OCR Text Correction in Australian Historic Newspapers. National Library of Australia (2009), http://www.nla.gov.au/ndp/project_details/documents/ANDP_ManyHands.pdf
2. Fleet, C., Kowal, K.C., Pridal, P.: Forthcoming: Georeferencer – crowdsourced georeferenc-ing for map library collections. Forthcoming in D-Lib Magazine
3. Howe, J.: The Rise of Crowdsourcing. Wired 14(06) (June 2006), http://www.wired.com/wired/archive/14.06/crowds.html
4. Dunn, S., Hedges, M.: Forthcoming: How the crowd can surprise us: Humanities crowd-sourcing and the creation of knowledge

---

[2] The desk research for this review identified around sixty papers of potential relevance.

Regional Effects on Query Reformulation Patterns

Steph Jesper, Paul Clough, and Mark Hall

Information School, University of Sheffield, United Kingdom

Abstract. This paper describes an in-depth study of the effects of geographic region on search patterns; particularly query reformulations, in a large query log from the UK National Archives (TNA). A total of 1,700 sessions involving 9,447 queries from 17 countries were manually analyzed for their semantic composition and pairs of queries for their reformulation type. Results show country-level variations for the types of queries commonly issued and typical patterns of query reformulation. Understanding the effects of regional differences will assist with the future design of search algorithms at TNA as they seek to improve their international reach.

1   Introduction

The user's context, including individual differences and search task, are known to affect the way people search for information [1]. In this paper we focus on whether users searching from different countries exhibit different search patterns, in particular when reformulating queries. Query reformulation is a common part of users' information retrieval behavior [2] whereby search queries are adapted until the user fulfills their information need, or they abandon their search. Although query reformulation has been extensively studied, there has been little investigation into the effects of regional variances on query reformulation, even though users' demographics, such as their cultural background and language abilities are known to affect their searching behavior [3, 4]. In this paper we investigate the effects of geographical region (country) on the queries issued and typical patterns of query reformulation for searches at The National Archives (TNA), the UK government's physical and digital repository for all government documents. Understanding how people reformulate queries under different situations can help improve search results [5].

2   Related Work

Query reformulation has been extensively studied in various contexts from web search to library catalogue usage. Approaches to study reformulations are typically based on manually analyzing the transitions between query pairs in a session [2, 6]. Alternatively, automatic techniques have also been used to learn types of query reformulation [5]. Query reformulations have commonly been grouped into three main types: specialization, generalization and parallel moves. The first type reflects the situation in which a user refines a query to be more specific, typically by adding terms to a query. The second type reflects a user generalizing the query, typically by removal of query terms. The final type indicates where a user changes to a new aspect of the

T. Aalberg et al. (Eds.): TPDL 2013, LNCS 8092, pp. 382–385, 2013.

same topic. Findings from previous studies have generally shown that parallel moves are the most common form of reformulation, followed by specializations and then generalizations [4-7]. Various studies have also explored the effects of cultural background on search behaviors. This includes comparing queries originating from different locations [5, 8], as well as users searching with varying language ability [3]. Most relevant to this paper are the studies by Spink et al. [4] and Boldi et al. [5]. Spink et al. analyzed the searching behavior of European users of FAST compared with US users of Excite. Results highlighted clear differences in the topics searched and search behaviors across the two countries, such as the vocabulary of queries used and query lengths. Boldi et al. compared query reformulation patterns identified in query logs from Yahoo! UK and Yahoo! US. Differences in query reformulation patterns could be observed between the UK and US search engine logs, with the UK data displaying higher proportions of specializations and parallel moves.

3   Methodology

Sessions comprising ≥ 3 queries were extracted from a 2009 search log from TNA containing ~1.9 million queries. These were derived from web logs at TNA that record search interactions with various resources accessed through various search functionalities, including an online catalogue (http://discovery.nationalarchives.gov.uk). Sessions were demarcated as interactions from the same IP address with a time interval between each interaction of <30 mins. The originating country of IP addresses was determined using the Maxmind Geolite geo-location database, which has an accuracy of 99.5% for country-lookup. The first 100 sessions for each region were extracted and analyzed manually providing 1,700 sessions and 9,447 queries for analysis. Queries were analyzed with respect to their linguistic structure and semantic composition (Person, Location, Specific item/object, Organization, Event and Other). Following the analysis of individual queries, the transitions between query pairs, Q_n and Q_{n+1}, were analyzed and categorized regarding type of query reformulation: *New* (N) Q_n and Q_{n+1} have no words in common (or $Q_n=Q_0$), *Specialization* (S) Q_n and Q_{n+1} are mostly identical but with more specific concepts used or material added, *Generalization* (G) Q_n and Q_{n+1} are mostly identical but with more general concepts used or material removed, *Parallel* (P) at least one phrase in Q_n is exchanged for a different phrase in Q_{n+1}, *Revision* (R) Q_n and Q_{n+1} contain the same information, but re-ordered, re-formatted or spelt differently and *Back* (B): Q_{n+1} is exactly identical to Q_{n-1}.

4   Results

Table 1 summarizes the proportion of queries containing particular semantic entities. Overall, 55.1% of all queries contain a Person element, 30.4% a Location and 21.5% reference to a Specific item/object. Person searches constitute over 50% of all queries submitted, and are the most popular element for all but five of the regions. Latin America shows a particularly strong preference for names of people (92% of South American searches and 90% of Central American). This corresponds to previous findings showing query topics may vary based on cultural background [4].

Table 1. Percentage of queries containing semantic entities

	Per. (%)	Loc. (%)	Item (%)	Org. (%)	Event (%)	Other (%)
Australia & New Zealand	64.4	20.0	24.8	15.3	4.8	11.2
British Isles	65.0	22.4	20.3	13.9	3.2	11.2
Caribbean	51.4	49.3	26.1	14.2	9.0	16.1
Central Africa	39.2	48.7	28.6	16.4	6.9	22.4
Central America	90.1	9.0	4.2	2.9	2.4	5.9
East Asia	32.1	43.3	32.0	16.6	11	14.7
Eastern Europe	56.8	11.4	20.1	24.1	2.4	13.4
Middle East	40.7	44.8	23.6	22.3	17	24.0
Nordic Countries	64.5	16.6	15.2	15.4	2.6	15.6
North America	63.6	21.7	17.4	13.7	2.6	11.3
Northern Africa	31.9	56.6	19.6	14.4	3.6	24.9
South America	92.1	4.0	3.5	7.0	0.2	1.2
South-Central Asia	49.8	30.1	33.3	16.3	6.1	25.2
Southeast Asia	49.8	38.7	24.5	19.4	7.9	14.1
Southern Africa	69.2	21.2	13.0	18.2	10	17.5
Southern Europe	54.4	29.5	23.7	15.0	7.6	14.8
Western Europe	51.0	22	24.2	27.9	4.4	16.0
OVERALL	55.1	30.4	21.5	16.4	6.5	15.8

Table 2. Percentage of reformulation types and most frequent reformulation path

	N (%)	S (%)	G (%)	P (%)	R (%)	B (%)	Modal path
Australia & New Zealand	24.4	19.1	15.2	18.9	9.7	12.8	N→ S→B
British Isles	24.7	22.6	10.0	13.9	15.8	13.0	N→ S→B
Caribbean	19.9	19.9	7.6	22.1	15.6	14.9	N→ R→R
Central Africa	25.3	18.9	6.9	25.8	12.3	10.8	N→ R→R
Central America	23.7	15.4	9.4	12.1	25.9	13.6	N→ R→R→R→R
East Asia	20.7	17.2	10.7	20.7	15.2	15.6	N→ S→B
Eastern Europe	22.7	13.6	3.7	22.1	31.4	6.5	N→ R→R
Middle East	18.1	16.7	8.8	26.8	20.0	9.6	N→ S→P
Nordic Countries	24.6	15.0	5.8	14.4	24.6	15.8	N→ R→R
North America	23.6	16.7	10.6	23.6	16.9	8.5	N→ S→B
Northern Africa	21.3	18.3	10.3	22.3	15.4	12.4	N→ S→P
South America	23.5	6.5	7.9	8.8	43.0	10.2	N→ R→R
South-Central Asia	22.6	18.3	7.7	21.3	18.1	12.0	N→ S→B
Southeast Asia	19.9	19.3	7.0	24.2	20.0	9.6	N→ S→P
Southern Africa	20.3	21.5	11.3	20.8	11.7	14.3	N→ S→P
Southern Europe	22.1	19.0	8.5	16.5	21.2	12.6	N→ R→R→R→R
Western Europe	22.4	17.8	10.1	23.3	15.2	11.2	N→ S→B
OVERALL	22.2	17.6	9.0	20.4	18.9	12.0	N→ R→R

Table 2 shows the proportion of reformulation types for each of the regions and across all queries. Ignoring the results for New, overall the most common query reformulation is Parallel (20.4%), Revision (18.9%), Specialization (17.6%), Back (12%) and Generalization (9%). The results are similar to previous findings where results showed that parallel is the most common form of reformulation and specializations are performed more often than generalizations [2]. In this dataset we observe a high proportion of revision reformulations. This is partly explained by the high number of person searches, which commonly exhibit revision moves. Revisions are also generally higher for regions where English is not the first language. The final column in Table 2 shows the most frequent reformulation paths taken through the sessions. In most cases the session length consists of 3 queries and the most frequent path is N→ R→R due to the high number of revisions. Another dominant pattern is to start with a more general query and then specialize.

5 Conclusions

In this paper we investigate differences in search patterns that arise from users around the world searching for information from the UK National Archives. Similar to previous findings, regional variations are shown to exist in the semantic composition of queries and reformulation types. For example, visitors from the Middle East use longer queries and sessions, and seek locations more than they seek people; visitors from Latin America have a particularly high interest in people. Analyzing query logs enables a better understanding of how people interact with search engines and can be used to improve retrieval performance and enhance user interaction. For example, in this study the high proportion query revisions, particularly for countries that frequently search for person names, highlights the need for improvements in name matching.

References

1. Ford, N., Miller, D., Moss, N.: The role of individual differences in Internet searching: an empirical study. Journal of the American Society for Information Science and Technology 52(12), 1049–1066 (2001)
2. Rieh, S.Y., Xie, H.: Analysis of multiple query reformulations on the web: The interactive information retrieval context. Information Processing & Management 42(3), 751–768 (2006)
3. Zoe, L.R., DiMartino, D.: Cultural diversity and end-user searching: An analysis by gender and language background. Research Strategies 17(4), 291–305 (2000)
4. Spink, A., Ozmutlu, S., Ozmutlu, H.C., Jansen, B.J.: US versus European Web searching trends. ACM SIGIR Forum 36(2) (2002)
5. Boldi, P., Bonchi, F., Castillo, C., Vigna, S.: From "Dango" to "Japanese Cakes": Query Reformulation Models and Patterns. In: Proceedings of the 2009 IEEE/WIC/ACM International Conference on Web Intelligence, WI 2009, pp. 183–190 (2008)
6. Jansen, B.J., Zhang, M., Spink, A.: Patterns and transitions of query reformulation during web searching. International Journal Web Information Systems 3(4), 328–340 (2007)
7. Huang, J., Efthimiadis, E.N.: Analyzing and Evaluating Query Reformulation Strategies in Web Search Logs. In: Proceeding of the 18th ACM Conference on Information and Knowledge Management, pp. 77–86 (2009)
8. Weber, I., Castillo, C.: The demographics of web search. In: Proceedings of the 33rd International ACM SIGIR Conference on Research and Development in Information Retrieval, pp. 523–530 (2010)

Persistence in Recommender Systems: Giving the Same Recommendations to the Same Users Multiple Times

Joeran Beel[1], Stefan Langer[1], Marcel Genzmehr[1], and Andreas Nürnberger[2]

[1] Docear, Germany
{beel,langer,genzmehr}@docear.org
[2] Otto-von-Guericke University, Dept. of Computer Science, DKE Group, Magdeburg, Germany
andreas.nuernberger@ovgu.de

Abstract. How do click-through rates vary between research paper recommendations previously shown to the same users and recommendations shown for the very first time? To answer this question we analyzed 31,942 research paper recommendations given to 1,155 students and researchers with the literature management software Docear. Results indicate that recommendations should only be given once. Click-through rates for 'fresh', i.e. previously unknown, recommendations are twice as high as for already known recommendations. Results also show that some users are 'oblivious'. It frequently happened that users clicked on recommendations they already knew. In one case the same recommendation was shown six times to the same user and the user clicked on it each time again. Overall, around 50% of clicks on reshown recommendations were such 'oblivious-clicks'.

Keywords: recommender systems, persistence, re-rating, research paper.

1   Introduction

Recommender systems became popular in many domains during the past decades and content-based and collaborative filtering became the two most dominant approaches. Some researchers in the field of collaborative filtering analyzed the effect of letting users re-rate items. They found that correlation between original ratings and new ratings was low and only 60% of users gave the same rating as before [1]. Amatriain et al. showed that it might be better to letting users re-rate items than showing new ones. By doing so accuracy of recommender systems increased by around 5% [2].

We wonder whether re-showing recommendations might make sense in general. For instance, a user might miss a recommendation the first time, simply because he was in a hurry and did not pay attention to the recommendation. In this case it would make sense for a recommender to be persistent and to display the same recommendation again. To the best of our knowledge 'recommendation persistence' has not been studied so far.

2   Research Objective and Methodology

Our goal was to find out if and how often it makes sense to display the same recommendations to the same users. To answer this question we analyzed empirical data from the

T. Aalberg et al. (Eds.): TPDL 2013, LNCS 8092, pp. 386–390, 2013.

literature management software Docear [4] which features a research paper recommender system [3]. The recommender system recommends research papers to users regardless of whether papers were previously recommended to the users or not. We analyzed how click-through rates (CTR) between recommendations shown only once and CTR of recommendations shown multiple times differed. CTR expresses how much percent of the delivered recommendations were clicked. For instance, if 12 recommendations were clicked out of 1,000 delivered ones, CTR would be 1.2%. CTR basically measures the 'precision' of the recommendation algorithm under the assumption that a clicked recommendation is a 'good', i.e. useful, recommendation. For further details on Docear and its recommender system (e.g. how recommendations are generated and displayed) see [3, 4].

3   Results

31,942 recommendations were shown to 1,155 users for the first time and from the 31,942 recommendations 1,677 were clicked, which equals a click-through rate of 5.25% (Table 1). From the 31,942 recommendations 2,466 were shown a second time to 375 distinct users and 154 recommendations were clicked (CTR 6.24%). From the 2,466 recommendations 574 were displayed a third time and CTR was 6.97%. Also for the fourth iteration CTR was still rather high (6.55%). Based on these results one might conclude that it could make sense to display recommendations at least two or three times because for these reiterations CTR was significantly higher than for the first one ($p < 0.05$).

Table 1. Reiterations and click-through rate (CTR)

		Reiteration								
		1	2	3	4	5	6	...	11	...	21
	Users	1,155	375	97	38	12	6		-		1
	Impressions	31,942	2,466	574	229	112	71		2		1
	No clicks	30,265	2,312	534	214	100	68		2		1
	Clicks	1,677	154	40	15	12	3		-		-
	CTR, overall	5.25%	6.24%	6.97%	6.55%	10.71%	4.23%		0.00%		0.00%
Obliv.-clicks	1st click	1,677	97	14	8	7	-		-		-
	2nd click	-	57	13	1	2	1		-		-
	3rd click	-	-	13	3	2	1		-		-
	4th click	-	-	-	3	-	-		-		-
	5th click	-	-	-	-	1	-		-		-
	6th click	-	-	-	-	-	1		-		-
	Σ Obliv. clicks	-	57	26	7	5	3		-		-
	% Obliv. clicks	0%	37%	65%	47%	42%	100%		-		-
	CTR, 1st click	5.25%	3.93%	2.44%	3.49%	6.25%	0.00%		0.00%		0.00%

The picture changes when looking at more detail into the data: around 50% of all clicks on reshown recommendations are 'oblivious-clicks' (Table 1, lower part). We define an 'oblivious click' as a click on a recommendation that the user should know already, because he clicked it previously. For instance, 574 recommendations were shown three times. 40 of these recommendations were clicked which equals a CTR of

6.97%. However, only 14 were clicked for the first time – the other 26 (2x13) were clicked for the second or even third time. In one case a recommendation was even shown six times to the same user and the user clicked it each time. Ignoring the oblivious-clicks, i.e. considering only 1st clicks, CTR decreases the more often recommendations are shown. Therefore, results may indicate that CTR increases when showing recommendations multiple times but only because users sometimes clicked on recommendations they have clicked before.

In addition, CTR increased in general the more recommendations were shown previously to a user (Figure 1). For instance, CTR did not only increase for reshown recommendations but also for 'fresh' recommendations, i.e. recommendations being displayed to a user for the very first time. This is not surprising because users who receive many recommendations probably are using the software for a longer time than users receiving their first recommendations. And for users using the software for a longer time, better user models can be created and hence better recommendations can be given (although this is not always the case as shown in [5].

	1	2	3	4	5	>5
Rshwn; new	5.25%	3.93%	2.44%	3.49%	6.25%	2.11%
Rshwn; obl.		2.31%	4.53%	3.06%	4.46%	5.91%
Rshwn; all	5.25%	6.24%	6.97%	6.55%	10.71%	8.02%
Fresh	5.25%	6.44%	9.59%	8.67%	12.83%	21.74%

Number of Reiterations (no delay)

Fig. 1. Redisplayed recommendations vs. fresh ones

To get a better understanding of how good re-shown recommendations performed, we compared their CTR with CTR of fresh recommendations. If a recommendation was shown the second time, it received a CTR of 6.24% on average – a CTR of 3.93% for reshown recommendations not being clicked before and a CTR of 2.31% for reshown recommendations being clicked before (Figure 1). In contrast, fresh recommendations being displayed at the same time achieved a CTR of 6.44% and hence performed better than the reshown recommendations. This is true for all iterations: fresh recommendations always performed better than reshown recommendations at the same time (including oblivious-clicks). Considering only new clicks on reshown recommendations (i.e. ignoring oblivious clicks), fresh recommendations performed even two to three times as good.

Based on the presented numbers one could conclude that reshowing recommendations would never make sense. However, we did the same analysis for recommendations that were reshown with at least one day delay (Figure 2). That means we ignored all recommendations in the analysis that were reshown to the same user within 24 hours. In this case, CTR of reshown recommendations is often better than for fresh recommendations (with oblivious-clicks included). For instance, for the second iteration CTR for fresh recommendations was 6.69% but for reshown recommendations 7.72%. However, when ignoring oblivious-clicks again fresh recommendations always perform better than reshown recommendations. We also conducted the same analysis with a longer delay (three, seven, and fourteen days). Results were similar to the ones presented. Due to space restrictions we omit further details.

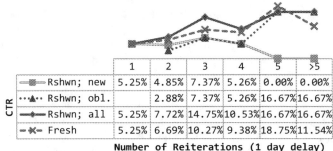

	1	2	3	4	5	>5
Rshwn; new	5.25%	4.85%	7.37%	5.26%	0.00%	0.00%
Rshwn; obl.		2.88%	7.37%	5.26%	16.67%	16.67%
Rshwn; all	5.25%	7.72%	14.75%	10.53%	16.67%	16.67%
Fresh	5.25%	6.69%	10.27%	9.38%	18.75%	11.54%

Number of Reiterations (1 day delay)

Fig. 2. Fresh recommendations vs. redisplayed ones with at least one day delay

4   Interpretation and Outlook

Our results indicate that it makes no sense to generally display recommendations multiple times to the same users – fresh recommendations usually perform better. Nevertheless, about 2-3 % of recommendations shown the second or third time were clicked by the users for the first time. By showing recommendations only once, researchers would miss this 2-3% of interesting articles. In further research it should be studied why users sometimes click recommendations only when they were shown multiple times and whether users eventually found those recommendations useful or not. If they found the recommendations useful, then it should be studied how to find out which recommendations to show multiple times and how often. For instance, it might be that the interest of a user has changed – maybe even due to the recommendations he has seen – and on first display the recommendation simply was not relevant for him. That means if a strong concept drift was determined by the recommender system, recommendations shown previously (before the concept drift) might be given again.

In addition, it should be studied why users click several times on the same recommendations. We assumed that users were just oblivious. In this case it probably would be of little benefit for the user to see the same recommendations several times. But maybe obliviousness is not the only reason for clicking recommendations multiple times.

It is also quite interesting that it made a difference whether a recommendation was reshown before or after 24 hours of a previous impression. In latter case (delay of one day or more), click through rates were significantly higher than for recommendations being re-shown within 24 hours and CTR of the reshown recommendations was even higher than for fresh recommendations. Under the assumption that oblivious clicks are desirable, reshowing recommendations could make sense. It might also make sense to transfer this finding to collaborative filtering and study how long to set a delay before letting users re-rate their items.

Open Data. Due to space restrictions, some data and graphs were omitted in this paper. For those being interested in more details (or validating our research), we publish our data on http://labs.docear.org.

References

1. Cosley, D., Lam, S.K., Albert, I., Konstan, J.A., Riedl, J.: Is seeing believing?: how recommender system interfaces affect users' opinions. In: Proceedings of the SIGCHI conference on Human factors in computing systems, pp. 585–592. ACM (2003)
2. Amatriain, X., Pujol, J.M., Tintarev, N., Oliver, N.: Rate it again: increasing recommendation accuracy by user re-rating. In: Proceedings of the third ACM conference on Recommender systems, pp. 173–180. ACM (2009)
3. Beel, J., Langer, S., Genzmehr, M., Nürnberger, A.: Introducing Docear's Research Paper Recommender System. In: Proceedings of the ACM/IEEE Joint Conference on Digital Libraries (JCDL) (2013)
4. Beel, J., Gipp, B., Langer, S., Genzmehr, M.: Docear: An Academic Literature Suite for Searching, Organizing and Creating Academic Literature. In: Proceedings of the 11th International Joint Conference on Digital Libraries, pp. 465–466. ACM (2011)
5. Beel, J., Langer, S., Nürnberger, A., Genzmehr, M.: The impact of demographics (age and gender) and other user-characteristics on evaluating recommender systems. In: Aalberg, T., Papatheodorou, C., Dobreva, M., Tsakonas, G. (eds.) TPDL 2013. LNCS, vol. 8092, pp. 396–400. Springer, Heidelberg (2013)

Sponsored vs. Organic (Research Paper) Recommendations and the Impact of Labeling

Joeran Beel, Stefan Langer, and Marcel Genzmehr

Docear, Germany
{beel,langer,genzmehr}@docear.org

Abstract. In this paper we show that organic recommendations are preferred over commercial recommendations even when they point to the same freely downloadable research papers. Simply the fact that users perceive recommendations as commercial decreased their willingness to accept them. It is further shown that the exact labeling of recommendations matters. For instance, recommendations labeled as 'advertisement' performed worse than those labeled as 'sponsored'. Similarly, recommendations labeled as '*Free* Research Papers' performed better than those labeled as 'Research Papers'. However, whatever the differences between the labels were – the best performing recommendations were those with no label at all.

Keywords: recommender systems, organic search, sponsored search, labeling.

1 Introduction

In the Web community there is lots of discussion about organic and sponsored search. 'Organic search' is the classic search where users enter search terms and search engines return a list of relevant web pages. 'Sponsored search' describes additional 'results' that are often shown beside the organic results. Usually these results are related to the search terms but companies pay for them to be displayed (in other words, 'sponsored search' is a nice paraphrase for personalized advertisement). While typical online advertisement has click-through rates (CTR) around 0.5% [1], sponsored search achieves CTRs around 2% and sometimes even more than 30% [2]. CTR is a common performance measure in online advertisement. It describes how many ads were clicked relative to the delivered ones. For instance, if 1,000 ads were delivered, and users clicked 61 of them, CTR was 6.1%. The higher the CTR the better is the algorithm behind the search results.

In academia, there are several academic recommender systems which typically only show organic recommendations [3, 4]. However, we were interested which CTR was to expect for sponsored recommendations in academia and more importantly, how much, or how little, users would like recommendations in general that were displayed for profit-making.

T. Aalberg et al. (Eds.): TPDL 2013, LNCS 8092, pp. 391–395, 2013.
© Springer-Verlag Berlin Heidelberg 2013

2   Methodology

Our academic literature management software '*Docear*' [6] features a research paper recommender system [5]. Every third start Docear displays ten recommendations that can be freely downloaded (Figure 1). We modified Docear's recommender system and analyzed the effects of the modifications on click-through rates (overall, 22,452 recommendations were delivered to 587 users). Modifications were related to a label describing the nature of the recommendations (organic or commercial) and the way of presenting recommendations (Figure 1). More information on the recommender system can be found in [5, 6].

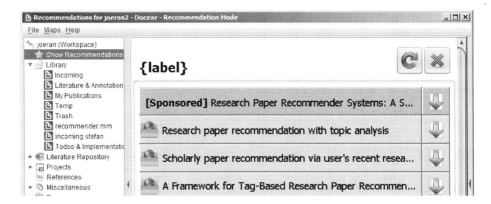

Fig. 1. Recommendations in Docear (top recommendation 'sponsored' and highlighted)

Recommendations in Docear were 'labeled' to explain the 'nature' of the recommendations (Figure 1). The 'basic' label was 'Research Papers'. We modified this label for each user by randomly choosing whether to add a prefix such as 'Free' or 'Free Full-text' (Table 1) or a suffix such as '(Advertisement)' or '(Sponsored)' which resulted in labels like 'Free Research Papers', 'Research Papers from our partners', or 'Free Full-text Research Papers (Sponsored)'. When a suffix was chosen, user must have assumed that the recommendations had a commercial background. When no suffix was chosen, users must have assumed that recommendations were organic. In addition, when no suffix was chosen it was randomly chosen whether to mark the first recommendation as '[Sponsored]' and whether to highlight this recommendation or not (Figure 1). Whatever label was displayed, recommendations were always calculated with the same algorithms and always linked to freely downloadable PDFs.

Table 1. Labels for the recommendations

Prefix				Suffix		
Free	Free Full-text	Full-text	None	(Sponsored)	(Advertisement)	From our partners

We selected two metrics to measure the effectiveness of recommendations and determine differences between the labels. With click-through rate (CTR) we measured how many recommendations out of the displayed ones were clicked overall. For instance, if 1,000 recommendations with a certain label were shown and 50 were clicked, CTR was 5%. If CTR for recommendations with another label was, for instance, 3.2%, the first label performed better. CTR is a common measure on advertisement but it suffers from one problem, especially when recommendations of only a few users are analyzed. In this case, a few users could spoil the results. For instance, one user receiving and clicking many recommendations would strongly increase overall CTR, although maybe all other users hardly clicked on any recommendations. Therefore, we also used mean average precision (MAP) for users' click-through rates. That means, for each user we calculated his average CTR and then we calculated the mean CTR over all users. For instance, if one user had seen 50 recommendations and clicked all of them, and 95 other users had each seen 10 recommendations but clicked none, CTR for the first user was 100% but CTR for the 95 others were 0% each. Hence, MAP was $\frac{100\%+0\%+0\%+\cdots+0\%}{96} = 1.04\%$.

3   Results

Based on CTR organic recommendations clearly outperform commercial ones with a CTR of 8.86% vs. 5.86% (Figure 2, blue line). This is probably what most people would expect. However, it is still interesting to have it quantified that only because recommendations are labeled as some kind of commercial, users are far less likely to click on them. Based on CTR, recommendations with the first recommendation being labeled as '[Sponsored]', but not highlighted, also clearly outperform those being highlighted (8.38% vs. 5.16%). However, the evaluation based on MAP shows a different picture (Figure 2, beige line). Here, organic (MAP=5.21%) and commercial recommendations (4.91%) perform very much alike. In addition, recommendations with the first one being labeled as sponsored *and* being highlighted (MAP=7.47%) outperform those being not highlighted (5.25%). What is evident with both metrics is that completely unlabeled recommendations performed better than all other label variations (CTR=9.87%; MAP=8.76%).

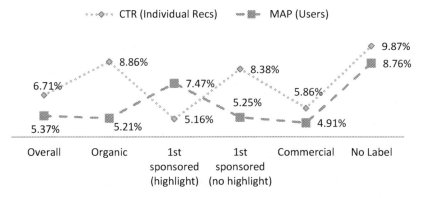

Fig. 2. CTR and MAP of different labels

For organic recommendations the 'free' and 'free full-text' labels clearly outperformed those labels not indicating that the recommended papers were free to download (Figure 3). This is true for both metrics CTR and MAP[1]. However, for commercial recommendations results differed. Here, using no suffix at all (MAP=6.51%; CTR=7.26%) performed better than any of the suffixes. We cannot explain this difference. For suffixes, both CTR and MAP indicate that 'Advertisement' leads to the lowest performance (Figure 4). Based on MAP 'Sponsored' recommendations (5.95%) performed better than 'partner' recommendations (4.85%). Based on CTR, 'partner' recommendations performed better (6.79%) than 'sponsored' ones (5.93%).

Summarized, the most surprising result was that recommendations with no label at all performed best, and that based on MAP commercial and organic recommendations performed about alike. Our study also showed that click-rates on recommendations varied strongly based on how they were labeled (although they were all based on the same algorithms). In particular recommendations labeled as 'advertisement' were least liked by the users. Results based on CTR often contradicted those based on MAP and also using certain prefixes had different effects on commercial and organic recommendations. More research is needed to clarify these contradictions. In some cases a small sample size might have caused the contradictions. For instance, for some labels (e.g. 'Free Research Papers') results were only based on twelve users. However, other results were based on larger samples and still contradict each other.

Open Data. Due to space restrictions, some data and graphs were omitted in this paper. For those readers being interested in more details, e.g. exact numbers of users per label, or validating our research, we publish additional data on http://labs.docear.org.

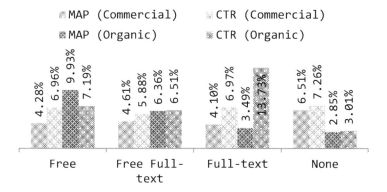

Fig. 3. MAP and CTR for prefixes (commercial and organic)

---

[1] For 'full-text' CTR is an outlier. We investigated the result and found that in this case few users had extremely high CTRs based on few received recommendations they almost all clicked.

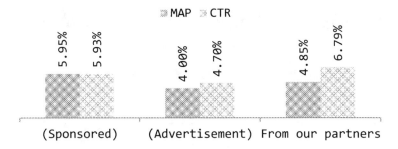

Fig. 4. MAP and CTR for suffixes (commercial only)

References

1. Manchanda, P., Dubé, J.P., Goh, K.Y., Chintagunta, P.K.: The effect of banner advertising on internet purchasing. Journal of Marketing Research 43 (2006)
2. Schwartz, B.: Google AdWords Click Through Rates: 2% is Average But Double Digits is Great. Search Engine Round Table Blog (2010),
   http://www.seroundtable.com/archives/021514.html
3. Gori, M., Pucci, A.: Research paper recommender systems: A random-walk based approach. In: Proceedings of the International Conference on Web Intelligence (2006)
4. Zhang, M., Wang, W., Li, X.: A Paper Recommender for Scientific Literatures Based on Semantic Concept Similarity. In: Buchanan, G., Masoodian, M., Cunningham, S.J. (eds.) ICADL 2008. LNCS, vol. 5362, pp. 359–362. Springer, Heidelberg (2008)
5. Beel, J., Langer, S., Genzmehr, M., Nürnberger, A.: Introducing Docear's Research Paper Recommender System. In: Proceedings of the ACM/IEEE Joint Conference on Digital Libraries, JCDL (2013)
6. Beel, J., Gipp, B., Langer, S., Genzmehr, M.: Docear: An Academic Literature Suite for Searching, Organizing and Creating Academic Literature. In: Proceedings of the 11th ACM/IEEE Joint Conference on Digital Libraries, pp. 465–466. ACM (2011)

The Impact of Demographics (Age and Gender) and Other User-Characteristics on Evaluating Recommender Systems

Joeran Beel[1], Stefan Langer[1], Andreas Nürnberger[2], and Marcel Genzmehr[1]

[1] Docear, Germany
{beel,langer,genzmehr}@docear.org
[2] Otto-von-Guericke University,
Dpt. of Computer Science, DKE Group, Magdeburg, Germany
andreas.nuernberger@ovgu.de

Abstract. In this paper we show the importance of considering demographics and other user characteristics when evaluating (research paper) recommender systems. We analyzed 37,572 recommendations delivered to 1,028 users and found that elderly users clicked more often on recommendations than younger ones. For instance, 20-24 years old users achieved click-through rates (CTR) of 2.73% on average while CTR for users between 50 and 54 years was 9.26%. Gender only had a marginal impact (CTR males 6.88%; females 6.67%) but other user characteristics such as whether a user was registered (CTR: 6.95%) or not (4.97%) had a strong impact. Due to the results we argue that future research articles on recommender systems should report detailed data on their users to make results better comparable.

Keywords: recommender systems, demographics, evaluation, research paper.

1 Introduction

There are more than one hundred research articles on research paper recommender systems, and even more on recommender systems in general. Many of them report on new recommendation approaches and their effectiveness. For instance, *Papyrus* is supposed to have a precision around 20% [1]; Quickstep's approach is supposed to have a precision around 10% [2]; and Jomsri et al. claim an accuracy of 91.66% for their research paper recommender system [3]. Unfortunately, results cannot be compared with each other because researchers used different evaluation methods, metrics, and data sets.

We believe there is another factor influencing the comparability which has received too little attention: users' demographics and characteristics. In other disciplines it is well known that results from one study cannot be used to draw conclusions for a population if the study's user sample differs too much from that population. For instance, in marketing you cannot draw reliable conclusions about how elderly people in Germany will react to a product if a study about that product was conducted in France with university students. Evaluations of recommender systems widely ignored

T. Aalberg et al. (Eds.): TPDL 2013, LNCS 8092, pp. 396–400, 2013.

differences in user samples. Some studies report to have asked their participants for demographic data, but they do not report on them in their papers [4]. Another paper reports that age and gender had no impact on the accuracy of recommendations but test subjects were all students [5]. With students typically being all in the same age-range, it is no surprise that the study could not find any differences between different ages.

We analyzed empirical data collected with Docear's research paper recommender system [6] to find out whether users' demographics and characteristics influence the outcome of the recommender system evaluation.

2   Methodology

Docear users can register an account and provide demographic information such as year of birth and gender if they like. They may also opt-in for receiving research paper recommendations (even without registration). Recommendations are shown on request or automatically every three days of use, ten at a time. During March and Mai 2013 1,028 users received 37,572 recommendations. Details on the recommendation process may be found in [6]. For the evaluation we used click-through rate (CTR) which expresses how many out of the displayed recommendations were clicked. For instance, when 37,572 recommendations were shown, and 2,361 were clicked, CTR is 6.28%. CTR is a common measure in online advertisement and equivalent to "precision" in information retrieval.

3   Results

From a total of 1,028 users who received recommendations, 38.62% did not register and 61.38% registered. 21.79% registered but did not provide information about their gender, 33.17% registered and were males, and 6.42% registered and were females (Figure 1, left pie). Looking only at those users who specified their gender, 83.79% were male, and 16.22% were female (Figure 1, right pie). Among the genders there is only a marginal difference in CTR with 6.88% for males and 6.67% for females (Figure 2). However, there is a significant difference between registered users (6.95%) and unregistered users (4.97%). Interestingly, those users who registered and did not specify their gender have the highest CTR with 7.14%. Another interesting difference between genders relates to the willingness of accepting recommendations. From all male users, 38.09% activated recommendations while only 34.74% of women did and even less (28.72%) of the users who did not specify their gender during registration (Table 1). This might indicate that these users are concerned about privacy issues when receiving recommendations [7].

From the registered users, 39.62% did not specify their age. From those who did, around one quarter (24.15%) were 25 to 29 years of age (Figure 3, bar chart). 11.29% were between 20 and 24 years and only two users were younger than 20, namely 17 and 18. The vast majority (88.19%) was older than 25 years. 4.46% of the users were 60 or older. The mean age was 36.56 years, the median was 33. Of course, it might be that some users did not provide their correct age and the true ages slightly differ from the ones presented.

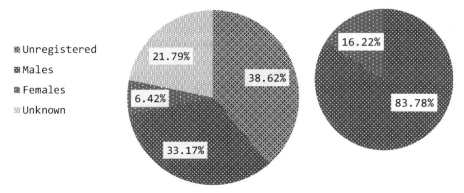

Fig. 1. Gender and user type (registered/unregistered) distribution

Looking at click-through rate by age shows that the older a user is the higher CTR becomes (Figure 3, dotted line). While younger users (20-24 years) have the lowest CTR of only 2.73% on average, CTR for users older than 60 is the highest with 9.92%. Overall, a clear linear trend is recognizable (Figure 3, dotted line). CTR for users who registered but did not provide their age was 7.66% on average (not shown in Figure 3).

Table 1. Percentage of activated recommendations by gender

	Male	Female	n/a
Recs. Activated	38.09%	34.74%	28.72%
Recs. Deactivated	61.91%	65.26%	71.28%

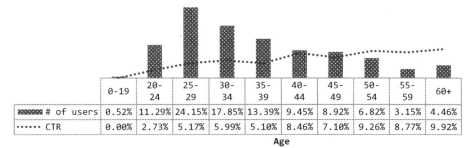

Fig. 2. Click-through rate (CTR) by user type and gender

Age	0-19	20-24	25-29	30-34	35-39	40-44	45-49	50-54	55-59	60+
# of users	0.52%	11.29%	24.15%	17.85%	13.39%	9.45%	8.92%	6.82%	3.15%	4.46%
CTR	0.00%	2.73%	5.17%	5.99%	5.10%	8.46%	7.10%	9.26%	8.77%	9.92%

Fig. 3. Age distribution and click-through rate (CTR) by age

The analysis also indicates that the number of days on which a user started Docear impacts CTR (Figure 4). For the first 20 times a user starts Docear, CTR increases. For instance, users who started Docear on one to five days had a CTR of 5.62% on average while users having started Docear on 11-20 days had a CTR of 7.30% on average. This is not surprising assuming that the more often users start Docear, the more information they enter, the better the user models become, and hence the recommendations. However, for users having started Docear on more than 20 days, CTR decreased. For instance, users having started Docear on more than 100 days achieve a CTR of 4.92% on average.

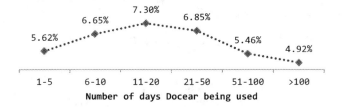

Fig. 4. Click-through rate by the number of days Docear being used

Another analysis brings even more confusion. We analyzed how CTR changes based on the number of recommendations a user received. Based on the above results we assumed that the more recommendations a user received, the lower the CTR would become because users starting Docear often also receive more recommendations. Our assumption was not correct. There is a trend that the more recommendations users see, the higher the CTR becomes (Figure 5, dotted line). Users who received only one recommendation set (i.e. typically ten recommendations) had a CTR of 4.13% while users who saw 21-50 sets had a CTR of 9.91% on average.

	1	2	3	4	5	6-10	11-20	21-50	51-100
# of users	32.00%	19.46%	13.52%	9.34%	6.81%	13.42%	3.99%	1.17%	0.29%
CTR	4.13%	4.56%	4.03%	4.39%	6.07%	6.32%	7.74%	9.91%	12.67%

Number of delivered recommendation sets (10 recs per set)

Fig. 5. User distribution and CTR by number of delivered recommendation sets

4   Conclusion

The analysis showed that demographics and user-characteristics may have a significant impact on click-through rates on (research paper) recommender systems. Although gender had only a marginal impact, age impacted CTR strongly. It made also a difference for CTR whether users were registered or not, how many recommendations they had seen before and how often users had started Docear. However, to fully understand the effects and correlations between the last two factors, more research is required.

We suggest that future evaluations should report on their users' demographics and characteristics in order to create valid and comparable results of recommender systems. Some of these are registered vs. unregistered; intensity of the software being used; and amount of previously shown recommendations. There are certainly further demographics and characteristics that might impact an evaluation such as nationality, field of research, and profession, whose impact should be researched.

Open Data. Due to space restrictions, some data and graphs were omitted in this paper. For those being interested in more details (or validating our research), we publish our data on http://labs.docear.org.

References

1. Naak, A., Hage, H., Almeur, E.: A multi-criteria collaborative filtering approach for research paper recommendation in papyres. E-Technologies: Innovation in an Open World (2009)
2. Middleton, S.E., Shadbolt, N.R., De Roure, D.C.: Ontological user profiling in recommender systems. ACM Transactions on Information Systems (TOIS) 22, 54–88 (2004)
3. Jomsri, P., Sanguansintukul, S., Choochaiwattana, W.: A framework for tag-based research paper recommender system: an IR approach. In: 2010 IEEE 24th International Conference on Advanced Information Networking and Applications Workshops, WAINA (2010)
4. Bonhard, P., Harries, C., McCarthy, J., Sasse, M.A.: Accounting for taste: using profile similarity to improve recommender systems. In: Proceedings of the SIGCHI Conference on Human Factors in Computing Systems, pp. 1057–1066. ACM (2006)
5. Parsons, J., Ralph, P., Gallagher, K.: Using viewing time to infer user preference in recommender systems. In: Proceedings of the AAAI Workshop on Semantic Web Personalization Held in Conjunction with the 9th National Conference on Artificial Intelligence (2004)
6. Beel, J., Langer, S., Genzmehr, M., Nürnberger, A.: Introducing Docear's Research Paper Recommender System. In: Proceedings of the ACM/IEEE Joint Conference on Digital Libraries, JCDL (2013)
7. Stober, S., Steinbrecher, M., Nürnberger, A.: A Survey on the Acceptance of Listening Context Logging for MIR Applications. In: Proceedings of the 3rd Workshop on Learning the Semantics of Audio Signals (LSAS), pp. 45–57 (2009)

PoliMedia

Improving Analyses of Radio, TV
and Newspaper Coverage of Political Debates

Max Kemman and Martijn Kleppe

Erasmus University Rotterdam, The Netherlands
{kemman,kleppe}@eshcc.eur.nl

Abstract. Analysing media coverage across several types of media-outlets is a challenging task for academic researchers. The PoliMedia project aimed to showcase the potential of cross-media analysis by linking the digitised transcriptions of the debates at the Dutch Parliament (Dutch Hansard) with three media-outlets: 1) newspapers in their original layout of the historical newspaper archive at the National Library, 2) radio bulletins of the Dutch National Press Agency (ANP) and 3) newscasts and current affairs programs from the Netherlands Institute for Sound and Vision. In this paper we describe generally how these links were created and we introduce the PoliMedia search user interface developed for scholars to navigate the links. In our evaluation we found that the linking algorithm had a recall of 67% and precision of 75%. Moreover, in an eye tracking evaluation we found that the interface enabled scholars to perform known-item and exploratory searches for qualitative analysis.

Keywords: political communication, parliamentary debates, newspapers, radio bulletins, television, cross-media analysis, semantic web, information retrieval.

1   Introduction

Analysing media coverage across several types of media-outlets is a challenging task for academic researchers. Up until now, the focus has been on newspaper articles: being generally available in digital, computer-readable format, these can be studied relatively easily. Analyses of visual material like photos or television programs are however rarely undertaken. We expect that both researchers of political communication (e.g. [1]) as well as researchers on television (e.g. [2]) would benefit from a cross-media comparison, providing a better overview of the choices that different media outlets make.

The PoliMedia project[1] aimed to showcase the potential of cross-media analysis by linking the digitised transcriptions of the debates at the Dutch Parliament (Dutch Hansard) with three media-outlets: 1) newspapers in their original layout of the historical newspaper archive at the National Library, 2) radio bulletins of the Dutch National Press Agency (ANP) and 3) newscasts and current affairs programmes from the Netherlands Institute for Sound and Vision.

---

[1] http://www.polimedia.nl

T. Aalberg et al. (Eds.): TPDL 2013, LNCS 8092, pp. 401–404, 2013.

The PoliMedia search user interface (SUI) allows researchers to browse the debates by date and analyse the related media coverage, as well as search by name of a politician or any keyword and evaluate the debates in which the politician appeared and how he or she was covered in the press. The SUI consists of three main levels: 1) the landing page where researchers can enter search terms, 2) the results page (figure 1) with the search results, facets for refinements and a search bar for new queries and 3) the debate page (figure 2) which shows the whole debate and the linked media items. An advantage of PoliMedia is that the coverage in the media is incorporated in its original form, enabling analyses of both the mark-up of news articles as well as the photos in newspapers and the footage of the televised programmes. The main research question that can be addressed using the datasets and technology provided by the project is: *What choices do different media make in the coverage of people and topics while reporting on debates in the Dutch parliament since the first televised evening news in 1956 until 1995?*

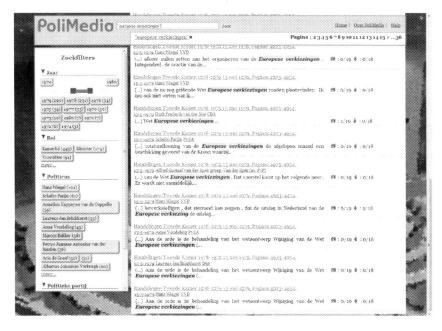

Fig. 1. Screenshot of the PoliMedia search results page

2   Method

The basis of PoliMedia lies in the minutes of Dutch parliament from 1814-1995, containing circa 2.5 million pages of debates with speeches that have been OCR'd and thus allow full-text search. The minutes have been converted to structured data in XML form in previous research [3]. For each speech (i.e. a fragment from a single speaker in a debate), we extract information to represent this speech; the speaker, the date, important terms (i.e. named entities) from its content and important terms from the description of the debate in which the speech is held. This information is then combined to create a query with which we search the archives of the newspapers, radio bulletins and television programmes. Media items that correspond to this query are retrieved, after which a link is created between the speech and the media item, using semantic web technologies [4].

In order to navigate these links, a SUI was developed in which the parliamentary debates are presented with links to the media coverage. The development was based on a requirements study with five scholars in history and political communication, leading to a faceted SUI as depicted in figure 1. Facets allow the user to refine search results, they support the searcher by presenting an overview of the structure of the collection, as well as provide a transition between browsing and search strategies [5]. During development, an initial version of this SUI was evaluated in an eye tracking study with 24 scholars performing known-item and exploratory search tasks [6].

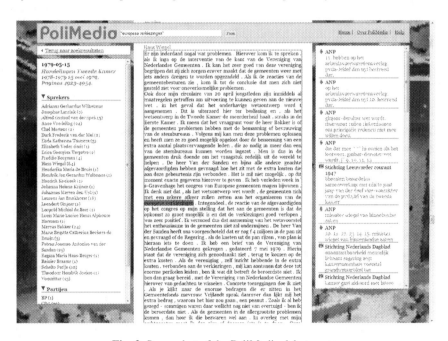

Fig. 2. Screenshot of the PoliMedia debate page

3   Results

From an evaluation of a set of links to newspaper articles, it was found that the recall of the algorithm is approximately 62%, with a precision of 75% [4]. In this context, relevance is indicated as a newspaper article referring to a specific speech or to the entire debate.

From the eye tracking evaluation we found that the faceted SUI enabled users to perform both known-item searches, as well as exploratory searches to analyse a topic over time. However, navigating the debates themselves proved to be rather difficult;

as debates can be dozens of pages long, users had difficulty gaining an overview of the debate. To address this issue, the faceted search available on the search results page (figure 1) was also introduced on the debate page (figure 2) in the final version of the interface.

4   Discussion

In the evaluation of the links we found a satisfying balance of recall and precision. However, no links to television programmes could be made. At this point we can make no conclusions about whether this was due to the size of the television dataset, the lack of full-text search or due to lack of suitability of the linking algorithm. The lack of links to television programmes thus remains a question for future research.

We found that the search user interface enabled scholars to navigate the debates and find links to related media coverage. However, the user interface focusses on qualitative research and requires scholars to make an overview themselves by trying several queries and using a combination of facets. The use of these links for quantitative scholarly research has not yet been touched, and is an application we would like to experiment with in future research.

Acknowledgements. We are grateful for the financial support from the CLARIN-NL project PoliMedia – *Interlinking multimedia for the analysis of media coverage of political debates.*

References

1. Van Santen, R.A., Van Zoonen, L.: The personal in political television biographies. Biography 33, 49–67 (2010)
2. Bignell, J., Fickers, A.: A European Television History. Wiley-Blackwell, Oxford (2008)
3. Gielissen, T., Marx, M.: Exemelification of parliamentary debates. In: Proceedings of the 9th Dutch-Belgian Workshop on Information Retrieval (DIR 2009), pp. 19–25 (2009)
4. Juric, D., Hollink, L., Houben, G.-J.: Discovering links between political debates and media. In: Daniel, F., Dolog, P., Li, Q. (eds.) ICWE 2013. LNCS, vol. 7977, pp. 367–375. Springer, Heidelberg (2013)
5. Kules, B., Capra, R., Banta, M., Sierra, T.: What do exploratory searchers look at in a faceted search interface? In: Proceedings of the 2009 Joint International Conference on Digital Libraries - JCDL 2009, vol. 313 (2009)
6. Kemman, M., Kleppe, M., Maarseveen, J.: Eye Tracking the Use of a Collapsible Facets Panel in a Search Interface. In: Aalberg, T., Papatheodorou, C., Dobreva, M., Tsakonas, G. (eds.) TPDL 2013. LNCS, vol. 8092, pp. 405–408. Springer, Heidelberg (2013)

Eye Tracking the Use of a Collapsible Facets Panel in a Search Interface

Max Kemman, Martijn Kleppe, and Jim Maarseveen

Erasmus University Rotterdam, The Netherlands
kemman@eshcc.eur.nl

Abstract. Facets can provide an interesting functionality in digital libraries. However, while some research shows facets are important, other research found facets are only moderately used. Therefore, in this exploratory study we compare two search interfaces; one where the facets panel is always visible and one where the facets panel is hidden by default. Our main research question is *"Is folding the facets panel in a digital library search interface beneficial to academic users?"* By performing an eye tracking study with N=24, we measured search efficiency, distribution of attention and user satisfaction. We found no significant differences in the eye tracking data nor in usability feedback and conclude that collapsing facets is neither beneficial nor detrimental.

Keywords: eye tracking, facets, information retrieval, usability, user studies, digital library, user behaviour, search user interface.

1 Introduction

In the development of search interfaces for digital libraries, an interesting functionality is the availability of filters, or facets. Not only do facets help to refine the search results, they can also support the searcher by presenting an overview of the structure of the collection, as well as provide a transition between browsing and search strategies. In previous eye tracking studies, it was found that facets played an important role in the exploratory search process. However, the authors stated that *"it is possible that the visual layout influenced searchers – people click on what they see and what is most visible"*, leaving room for different results when implementing the facets differently [1]. In our previous research, academic researchers indicated that facets are not an important factor in their search process [2]. Facets could thus also be an unnecessary complexity in the interface. To research this, we created a simplified search interface with a collapsible facets panel. The panel is collapsed to a minimized form, until the user actively opens it. However, when hiding the facets, the opposite of *"people click on what they see"*, namely *"out of sight is out of mind"* [3] might occur. Therefore, in this exploratory study we compare two search interfaces; one where the facets panel is always visible and one where the facets panel is collapsible and thus hidden by default. Our main research question is *"Is folding the facets panel in a digital library search interface beneficial to academic users?"* In order to address this question, we performed an eye tracking study with academic users to evaluate the two

T. Aalberg et al. (Eds.): TPDL 2013, LNCS 8092, pp. 405–408, 2013.
© Springer-Verlag Berlin Heidelberg 2013

search interfaces by analysing search efficiency, distribution of attention and user satisfaction. In doing so, we will test the hypothesis that collapsing the facets panel will be a detrimental user experience due to the *"out of sight is out of mind"* issue.

2   Related Work

The benefit of using eye tracking for evaluating an interface are twofold [4]. First, eye tracking provides a more thorough insight in the interactions users have with the interface. Not only is data collected on user click behaviour, but also what users look at. As such, additional insight into the way attention is divided across the screen and the way information is processed can be acquired [5]. For example, a large number of eye movements across the screen can indicate a suboptimal layout, resulting in a less efficient search [6]. Other measures such as the amount of time spent on, or number of visits to, a certain area of the screen can provide information about the attention-grabbing properties of such an area. This can serve a useful role in judging whether a certain aspect of the user interface is looked at, understood or is distracting the user. Second, it complements other qualitative data such as user feedback and think-aloud, as it provides a real-time insight in how users experience the interface. As such, eye tracking can be used to track down the source of usability issues found with traditional usability metrics [7].

3   Method

The interface we used to evaluate the collapsing of the facets panel is the PoliMedia system. This system is a search interface for the minutes in the Dutch parliament, linked to the media coverage of those debates [8]. Facets present in the interface are *role* (i.e. the role of the politician; parliamentary member or minister), *politician* (i.e. name), *political party* and *year*. We then created two versions of the system; 1) where the facets panel is visible and 2) where the facets panel is collapsible, see figure 1. In the collapsible panel version, the facets panel collapsed up into a button called "Filters". The button was large enough and clearly marked so that users could easily recognize where the facets panel was, in order to address the *"out of sight is out of mind"* issue. We evaluated with a total of 24 participants, of which 11 participants received the visible version of the interface, while 13 received the collapsible version. Of these participants, 15 were male and 9 female. The average age was approximately 30, in the range of 22-45. Participants received a verbal introduction and completed five known item search (KIS) tasks and three exploratory search tasks, for which they recorded their answers on an answer sheet. Their eye movements were recorded using the Mirametrix S2 Eye Tracker. To test the effect of collapsing the facets panel on the users' interaction with this panel, we divided the interface into five separate areas of interest (AOI's) based on their functionality: 1) search bar, 2) facets, 3) search results, 4) page-search (via ctrl+f command) and 5) other, containing remaining parts of the screen.

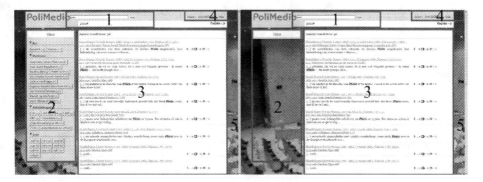

Fig. 1. Screenshots of the visible facets version (left) and the collapsible facets version (right) with Areas of Interest drawn on top of the screenshots

The eye tracking data was quantitatively analysed separately for both the KIS and the exploratory search sessions using the OGAMA[1] statistical module and SPSS. After the recording errors were removed by manually checking video recordings of outliers we calculated the total number of fixations (NF) and total viewing duration (VD) overall and per AOI, to analyse respectively search efficiency and distribution of attention, as discussed in the related work. These measurements were analysed with four MANOVA's; for both the KIS and exploratory search sessions we used the viewing data (NF or VD) for each AOI as dependent variables and version (visible or collapsible facets) as the independent variable.

4   Results[2]

We found that participants with the visible interface spent more total fixations (NF) and more total viewing duration (VD) on the KIS tasks than participants with the collapsible interface. However, for the exploratory tasks, this is the other way around. For the KIS tasks, participants with the visible version spent 18.2% of NF on the facets panel, and 20.2% of VD. Participants with the collapsible version spent 20.8% of NF and 22.3% of the VD on the facets panel. For the exploratory tasks, participants with the visible version spent 9.3% of the NF and 11.7% of VD on the facets panel. Participants with the collapsible version spent 8.5% of NF and 11.1% of VD on the facets panel. Comparing between the visible and collapsible facets versions using MANOVA with Pillai's trace, we found no significant differences for any of the metrics used. In other words, we found no significant differences in search efficiency, nor in distribution of attention. Moreover, we found no significant differences in users' satisfaction during the post-experiment discussion.

---

[1]   OpenGazeAndMouseAnalyzer: http://www.ogama.net/

[2]   All data minus the videos of the recordings are available open access through http://www.persistent-identifier.nl/?identifier=urn:nbn:nl:ui:13-1vo4-9k

5   Conclusion

It appears that the facets were heavily used during searching in both versions of the search interface. We assume that the more moderate figures in the exploratory search can be explained by the users interacting much more with the speeches themselves, increasing the interaction with the search results AOI. Given the lack of significant differences between the two versions of the interface in users' eye tracking data nor in users' satisfaction between the two groups, we conclude that collapsing the facets panel did not introduce the usability issue *"out of sight is out of mind"*, meaning it can provide a viable alternative to showing the facets at all times. We can thus reject our hypothesis. However, having the facets visible at all times did not introduce usability issues either. To answer our research question *"Is folding the facets panel in a digital library search interface beneficial to academic users?"* we conclude that folding the facets panel is neither necessarily beneficial nor detrimental.

Acknowledgements. We are grateful for the financial support from the EU FP7 project AXES[3] – *Access to Audiovisual Archives* ICT-269980 and from the CLARIN-NL project PoliMedia[4] – *Interlinking multimedia for the analysis of media coverage of political debates.*

References

1. Kules, B., Capra, R., Banta, M., Sierra, T.: What do exploratory searchers look at in a faceted search interface? In: Proceedings of the 2009 Joint International Conference on Digital Libraries, JCDL 2009, pp. 313 (2009)
2. Kemman, M., Kleppe, M., Scagliola, S.: Just Google It - Digital Research Practices of Humanities Scholars. Studies in the Digital Humanities (2013)
3. Nielsen, J., Pernice, K.: Eyetracking Web Usability. New Riders (2010)
4. Balatsoukas, P.: An eye-tracking approach to the evaluation of digital libraries. In: Dobreva, M., O'Dwyer, A., Feliciati, P. (eds.) User Studies for Digital Library Development, pp. 95–104. Facet Publishing (2012)
5. Poole, A., Ball, L.: Eye tracking in human-computer interaction and usability research: Current status and future prospects. In: Ghaoui, C. (ed.) Encyclopedia of Human-Computer Interaction, Idea Group, Inc., Pennsylvania (2005)
6. Goldberg, J.H., Kotval, X.P.: Computer interface evaluation using eye movements: methods and constructs. International Journal of Industrial Ergonomics 24, 631–645 (1999)
7. Pretorius, M., Calitz, A., Greunen, D.: van: The added value of eye tracking in the usability evaluation of a network management tool. SAICSIT 2005, 1–10 (2005)
8. Kemman, M., Kleppe, M.: PoliMedia: Improving Analyses of Radio, TV & Newspaper Coverage of Political Debates. In: Aalberg, T., Papatheodorou, C., Dobreva, M., Tsakonas, G. (eds.) TPDL 2013. LNCS, vol. 8092, pp. 401–404. Springer, Heidelberg (2013)

---

[3] http://www.axes-project.eu
[4] http://www.polimedia.nl

Efficient Access to Emulation-as-a-Service – Challenges and Requirements

Dirk von Suchodoletz and Klaus Rechert

Institute of Computer Science, Albert-Ludwigs University Freiburg, Germany

Abstract. The shift of the usually non-trivial task of emulation of obsolete software environments from the end user to specialized providers through Emulation-as-a-Service (EaaS) helps to simplify digital preservation and access strategies. End users interact with emulators remotely through standardized (web-)clients on their various devices. Besides offering relevant advantages, EaaS makes emulation a networked service introducing new challenges like remote rendering, stream synchronization and real time requirements. Various objectives, like fidelity, performance or authenticity can be required depending on the actual purpose and user expectations. Various original environments and complex artefacts have different needs regarding expedient and/or authentic performance.

1 Motivation

Using emulation strategies provides access over long time periods to a wide range of deprecated object types and complete original environments. Especially for complex digital artefacts, interactive media, pieces of digital art or computer games of various types emulation is the only viable long-term access strategy. Nevertheless, Emulation-as-a-Service (EaaS, [1]) introduces new challenges as it requires that emulators be network-aware applications. The core of the emulated machine is split from the user frontend for the in- and output part. EaaS changes both, the *interaction of the user with the original environment* and the *requirements toward the emulators as applications*. The emulation core running at the service provider's side has no direct access either to the user input nor to the output device. The client application on the user's device controls the actual rendering and adapts to the local machine capabilities. The in-between network link may add round trip time, jitter, bandwidth limitations and de-synchronization of data streams. For EaaS the adaptation of various current and past in- and output streams is required. This includes the mapping of together different keyboard layouts. A comparably new challenge to long-term preservation is posed by mobile devices like tablet computers or smartphones. They feature new types of input like (multi-)touch or swipe gestures and new sensors like gyroscope, position sensors or GPS.

EaaS can be deployed for a wide range of scenarios starting from traditional textual or graphical office documents, spreadsheets or access to databases. More challenging artefacts include multimedia objects, primarily audio and video (AV)

T. Aalberg et al. (Eds.): TPDL 2013, LNCS 8092, pp. 409–412, 2013.

streams of online learning material, electronic encyclopedias or, in a couple of cases for the access to web-archives. Further up artefacts that have high demands on screen rendering coupled with near real time feedback to user input, like computer games or certain pieces of digital art.

2   Stream De-multiplexing and Remote Emulation

The performance of various artefacts, especially ones with multimedia components, has several implications as the object is not directly rendered within the end user's environment but send through additional layers (Fig. 1). Other than with direct rendering where the artefact is (uncompressed and) de-multiplexed (1) and where streams are directly send to the devices like screen and loudspeaker, it is moderated through the emulator executing the original environment. The emulator itself runs as a normal application within a hosting environment. This step may already de-synchronize the original performance as different buffers can be in place for screen and audio output. It can be worsened

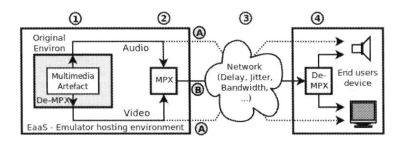

Fig. 1. AV Stream De-/Multiplexing Challenges in Remote Emulation

in scenario A where independent streams are sent over an (uncontrollable) network channel to the end users device (3). The transport layer protocol might add additional buffers. Various AV protocols optimize quality, reliability or low-latency and thus add to end-to-end delay. System buffers in (2,4) can influence the end-to-end delay and skew significantly. In the other approach B the previously separated AV streams get re-multiplexed within the EaaS environment and send as a single stream. The second de-multiplexing takes place in a better controllable environment of the the end user's device (4). Nonetheless, the stream is prone to network delays and limitations. Emulators have to provide APIs for local and/or remote AV output.

3   Evaluation of Different Remote Access Methods

We analyzed currently available technologies to evaluate their applicability for EaaS interactive access looking at hardware requirements, the possibility of integration into EaaS services and implemented features. Different implementations of streaming protocols are already known from Thin Client Computing. A bandwidth optimized, platform-independent protocol for remote desktop access is Virtual Network Computing (VNC) that uses the Remote Frame Buffer (RFB) protocol. To achieve the significant compression VNC needs to run over small bandwidth connections, it tiles the desktop into regions, and transfers only the differences between two consecutive images. Those are usually pretty small in standard desktop interaction. Furthermore, the protocol normally runs within the operating system whos desktop is accessed over the net. Thus it can make heavy use of the knowledge if e.g. a window is moved, resized or gets partially hidden to efficiently redraw the remote end. Optimizations like special codecs to update parts of the screen or well understood content are discussed and algorithmically improved in [2] and [3]. A significant limitation for multimedia artefacts is the missing audio channel in VNC. The latter limitation is overcome by RDP, a proprietary protocol designed by Microsoft. A different trend, completely agnostic of the actual underlying operating systems and specific screen content, are various hardware solutions directly attached to the device output. Further options in that domain like Apple Airplay, and similar mirror device render output by using specialized external hardware and encode the screen updates (and audio streams) into a wireless H.264 stream. In contrast to the remote framebuffer solutions the screen content is treated as a movie and transmitted at a fixed update rate. Only slightly different are the comparably recent Gaikai and OnLive proprietary streaming services primarily focusing on cloud-based gaming. They require a previously installed Java, Flash or client application. The encoding of the actual AV stream takes place within specialized 3D graphic adaptors capable of handling high resolution and frames per second.

Besides having some proven implementations even for large resolution, fast screen update available, the number of actually working solutions for EaaS is much smaller. To start with, proprietary solutions like Gaikai or OnLive demonstrate very well the feasibility of fast remote access to multimedia objects, but require very special hardware setups, high bandwidth with low delay and are not yet available to external third parties. External screen capture at the output device is conceptually near to the aforementioned approach with similar characteristics, but is not suitable for the envisioned EaaS deployment as it requires a dedicated setup (machine with a particular emulator) per accessed instance. While RDP clients exist for a wide range of operating systems, support in emulators or virtual machines is available for Virtual Box only.

Emulators are a perfect source for remote AV streaming from a cloud service as they implement both the output devices in software and do not require special hardware. More than a single instance without particular restrictions regarding the emulator easily run on a single machine. As VNC is the defacto-standard for remote machine interaction and control, we chose it for our experiments to access EaaS. A VNC interface is directly implemented into Qemu or Virtual Box. We started to evaluate the remote performance of Qemu and SheepShaver. It performed well for comparably small desktop sizes and screen resolutions, tested with Windows 3.11 till 98 and MacOS 8.5 for several standard static digital objects but failed on artefacts requiring fast refresh and an audio channel. To mitigate the missing audio stream we looked both into non-proprietary audio additions to VNC (variant B in Fig. 1) and separate channels (A). In contrast to the normal application VNC has no particular knowledge of the screen layout as it merely gets the content of the machine's frame buffer. The input events from remote keyboard and mouse are translated to raw machine input, producing key code translation issues and mismatches of the real and virtual mouse pointer on screen on the remote end.

In search for a general emulator API the Simple DirectMedia Layer library (SDL), which is is a cross-platform multimedia library designed to provide fast access to the graphics frame buffer and audio device and is a quasi-standard for open source emulators, becomes the next focus of research. SDL supports different virtual framebuffer implementations. We extended them with an unofficial VNC patch available, thus making several additional emulators remotely accessible. We achieved reasonable results for e.g. Qemu and SheepShaver, but failed e.g. for SNES. Nevertheless, a couple of severe issues with key translations remain. As this approach still does not solve the missing audio channel, Guacamole, an HTML5 remote desktop gateway, got our attention. It translates remote desktop protocols like RDP or VNC for direct browser access without the need of a special browser plugin. Guacamole thus makes EaaS accessible independent of the actual hardware platform used to a wide range of end user devices without particular software requirements. Instead we started to implement a Guacamole interface to SDL.

Depending on the expected outcome proper EaaS access solutions exist. VNC and similar protocols offer reasonable access for static objects and complete original environments (without audio) and they are suitable for general curation tasks, e.g. of digital art or early computer games. The SDL-Guacamole approach looks promising as it provides a generic interface to remotely interact with emulators. Both SDL and Guacamole are Open Source and well established methods for AV and input handling. With the development of Gaikai and OnLive alternate AV streaming optimized methods may become available for the future. Remote access performance measuring [4] should be considered to compare the different options and protocols.

References

1. von Suchodoletz, D., Rechert, K., Valizada, I.: Towards emulation-as-a-service – cloud services for versatile digital object access. In: Proceedings of the 8th International Digital Curation Conference, IDCC 2008. Amsterdam (2013)
2. Chandra, S., Biehl, J.T., Boreczky, J., Carter, S., Rowe, L.A.: Understanding screen contents for building a high performance, real time screen sharing system. In: Proceedings of the 20th ACM International Conference on Multimedia. MM 2012, pp. 389–398. ACM, New York (2012)
3. Baratto, R.A., Kim, L.N., Nieh, J.: Thinc: a virtual display architecture for thin-client computing. SIGOPS Oper. Syst. Rev. 39, 277–290 (2005)
4. Nieh, J., Yang, S.J., Novik, N.: Measuring thin-client performance using slow-motion benchmarking. ACM Trans. Comput. Syst. 21, 87–115 (2003)

RDivF: Diversifying Keyword Search on RDF Graphs

Nikos Bikakis[1,2], Giorgos Giannopoulos[1,2,*], John Liagouris[1,2,*],
Dimitrios Skoutas[2], Theodore Dalamagas[2], and Timos Sellis[3]

[1] National Technical University of Athens, Greece
[2] "Athena" Research Center, Greece
[3] RMIT University, Australia

Abstract. In this paper, we outline our ongoing work on diversifying keyword search results on RDF data. Given a keyword query over an RDF graph, we define the problem of diversifying the search results and we present diversification criteria that take into consideration both the content and the structure of the results, as well as the underlying RDF/S–OWL schema.

Keywords: Linked Data, Semantic Web, Web of Data, Structured Data.

1 Introduction

As a growing number of organizations and companies (e.g., *Europeana*, *DBpedia*, *data.gov*, *GeoNames*) adopt the *Linked Data* practices and publish their data in RDF format, going beyond simple SPARQL endpoints, to provide more advanced, effective and efficient search services over RDF data, has become a major research challenge. Especially, since users prefer searching with plain keywords, instead of using structured query languages such as SPARQL, there has been an increasing interest on keyword search mechanisms over RDF data [1,2,3].

Most of the proposed works return the *most relevant* RDF results, in the form of *graphs* or *trees*. Relevance, in this case, is typically defined in terms of (a) *content similarity* between the elements comprising a result and the query terms and (b) *result compactness*, which means that smaller trees or graphs are preferred. The drawback is that this leads to result sets that are often characterized by a high degree of redundancy. Moreover, significant information is often lost, since graph paths that connect two entities and might denote a significant relation between them are omitted to satisfy the compactness requirement. Moreover, most approaches do not consider the rich *structure* and *semantics* provided by the RDF data model. For instance, an effective RDF keyword search method should treat RDF properties (edges) as first-class citizens, since properties may provide significant information about the *relations* between the entities being searched.

* This research has been co-financed by the European Union (European Social Fund ESF) and Greek national funds through the Operational Program "Education and Lifelong Learning" of the National Strategic Reference Framework (NSRF) - Research Funding Program: Heracleitus II. Investing in knowledge society through the European Social Fund.

T. Aalberg et al. (Eds.): TPDL 2013, LNCS 8092, pp. 413–416, 2013.

As an example, consider a user searching for *"Scarlett Johansson, Woody Allen"* over the DBpedia dataset. An effective approach should, at least initially, consider *all* the possible ways these two entities are related. Since there exist various roles and relations between these two entities, e.g., Woody Allen may appear as either a director or an actor, this leads to a large and complex result set, containing several overlapping or similar results. The plethora of different relation combinations requires a mechanism that reduces information redundancy, allowing the system to return to the user a more concise and also more meaningful and informative result set. This can be achieved by introducing a diversification step into the retrieval and ranking process. Ideally, the system should return to the user results that cover different aspects of the existing connections between these entities, e.g., a movie where they played together, a movie directed by Woody Allen where Scarlett Johansson appears, an award they shared, etc.

Although the diversification problem has been extensively studied for document search [7,8,9], the structured nature of RDF search results requires different criteria and methods. Most of the approaches regarding keyword search on graphs [1,2,5] limit their results to trees (particularly, variations of Steiner trees); only few allow subgraphs as query answers [3,4]. Among them, [3] is the most relevant to our work; however, it does not address the diversification problem and it also does not consider the schema of the data. A different perspective is followed in [6], where a keyword query is first interpreted as a set of possible structured queries, and then the most diverse of these queries are selected and evaluated.

In this paper, we introduce a diversification framework for keyword search on RDF graphs. The main challenges arise from the fact that the structure of the results, including additional information from the underlying schema, needs to be taken into account. This is in contrast to the case of diversifying unstructured data, where the factor of content (dis)similarity is sufficient. In our framework, called RDivF (<u>RDF</u> + <u>Div</u>ersity), which we are currently developing, we exploit several aspects of the RDF data model (e.g., resource content, RDF graph structure, schema information) to answer keyword queries with a set of diverse results. To the best of our knowledge, this is the first work addressing the issue of result diversification in keyword search on RDF data.

2   Diversifying RDF Keyword Search

Assume an *RDF graph* $G(V, E)$, where V is the set of *vertices* and E the set of *edges*. Optionally, G may be associated with an RDF schema, defining a hierarchy among classes and properties. Let $q = \{\{t_1, t_2, \ldots, t_m\}, k, \rho\}$ be a *keyword query* comprising a set of m *terms* (i.e., keywords), a parameter k specifying the *maximum number of results* to be returned, and a parameter ρ that is used to restrict the *maximum path length* between keyword nodes (i.e., vertices), as will be explained later. Assume also a function $\mathcal{M}: t \to V_t$ that maps a keyword t to a set of graph nodes $V_t \subseteq V$.

Definition 1. (Direct Keyword Path). Assume two nodes $u, v \in V$ that match two terms t, s of a query q, i.e., $u \in V_t$ and $v \in V_s$. Let P be a path between u and v. P is called a *direct keyword path* if it does not contain any other node that matches any keyword of the query q.

Definition 2. (Query Result). Assume an RDF graph G and a query q. A subgraph G_q of G is a *query result* of q over G, if: (a) for each keyword t in q, there exists exactly one node v in G_q such that $v \in V_t$ (these are called *keyword nodes*), (b) for each pair of keyword nodes u, v in G_q, there exists a path between them with length at most ρ, (c) for each pair of keyword nodes u, v in G_q, there exists at most one direct keyword path between them, and (d) each non-keyword node lies on a path connecting keyword nodes.

The above definitions leed to query results that contain pair-wise connections among all the terms in the query. That is, in our framework, we are interested in results that can be graphs and not only spanning trees, which is the typical case in previous approaches. This is based on the intuition that we want to emphasize on the completeness of relationships between query terms rather than on the criterion of minimality. Note that the aspect of minimality is still taken into consideration in our definition by means of the conditions (c) and (d) above.

Now, assume a function $r \colon (G_q, q) \to [0, 1]$ that measures the *relevance* between the query q and a result G_q, and a function $d \colon (G_q, G'_q) \to [0, 1]$ that measures the *dissimilarity* between two query results G_q and G'_q. Let also $f_{r,d}$ be a monotone objective function that combines these two criteria and assigns a score to a result set $\mathcal{R}$ w.r.t. the query q, measuring how relevant the included results are to the query and how dissimilar they are to each other. We assume that $|\mathcal{R}| > k$. Then, the goal of the diversification task is to select a subset of k results so that this objective function is maximized. Formally, this can be defined as follows.

Definition 3. (Diversified Result Set). Assume an RDF graph G, a query q, and the functions r, d, and $f_{r,d}$ as described above. Let $\mathcal{R}$ denote the result set of q over G. The *diversified result set* $\mathcal{R}_k$ is a subset of the results $\mathcal{R}$ with size k that maximizes $f_{r,d}$, i.e., $\mathcal{R}_k = \underset{\mathcal{R}' \subseteq \mathcal{R}, |\mathcal{R}'| = k}{\operatorname{argmax}} f_{r,d}(\mathcal{R}')$.

Following this approach, in order to select a diversified result set for keyword queries over RDF graphs, one needs to determine appropriate functions for r, d, and $f_{r,d}$. Regarding the latter, [8] presents several objective function and studies their characteristics. The same functions can also be used in our case, since this aspect is independent from the nature of the underlying data. Therefore, we focus next on specifying the relevance and dissimilarity functions, r and d, in our setting.

3   Diversification Criteria

The main challenge for diversifying the results of keyword queries over RDF graphs, is how to take into consideration the semantics and the structured nature of RDF when defining the relevance of the results to the query and the dissimilarity among results. In this section, we outline a set of criteria for this purpose, which can be used for specifying the functions r and d, as described above.

The relevance of a result to the query takes into consideration two main factors. The first factor refers to text-based matching between the nodes in the result graph and the keywords in the query. This aspect is essentially covered by the function $\mathcal{M}$ that maps query terms to graph nodes. This function can be modified to return, for each graph node, a degree of match $m \in [0, 1]$ between this node and a corresponding query keyword. In addition, a threshold τ can be specified in the query, so that only nodes with $m \geq \tau$ are returned. The second factor refers to the fact that results should be concise and coherent. One step to ensure this is the minimality criterion included in Definition 2. Furthermore, we need to consider structural and semantic homogeneity of the result, so that the results can be more meaningful to the user. This is an intra-result measure, capturing the homogeneity among the nodes, edges and paths in the result graph. For example, this would assign a higher score to a path where all the edges are labelled with the same property. Moreover, RDF schema information can be taken into account, i.e., scoring based on class or property hierarchy and least common ancestors.

The dissimilarity among results can be defined by comparing paths between corresponding pairs of keyword nodes. This takes into account both structural properties, e.g., path lengths or common subpaths, and semantic information, i.e., classes and properties corresponded to the nodes and edges along the path. The main objective here is, for each result, to obtain paths that are similar to other paths in the result, but dissimilar to paths in other results. This objective is not restrained to textual similarity only, but takes also into account the semantic similarity of classes and properties inferred by the schema.

References

1. Tran, T., Wang, H., Rudolph, S., Cimiano, P.: Top-k Exploration of Query Candidates for Efficient Keyword Search on Graph-Shaped (RDF) Data. In: ICDE (2009)
2. Zhou, Q., et al.: SPARK: Adapting Keyword Query to Semantic Search. In: Aberer, K., et al. (eds.) ASWC 2007 and ISWC 2007. LNCS, vol. 4825, pp. 694–707. Springer, Heidelberg (2007)
3. Elbassuoni, S., Blanco, R.: Keyword Search over RDF Graphs. In: CIKM (2011)
4. Li, G., Ooi, B.-C., Feng, J., Feng, J., et al.: EASE: An Effective 3-in-1 Keyword Search Method for Unstructured, Semi-structured and Structured data. In: SIGMOD 2008 (2008)
5. He, H., Wang, H., Yang, J., Yu, P.: BLINKS: Ranked Keyword Searches on Graphs. In: SIGMOD 2007 (2007)
6. Demidova, E., Fankhauser, P., Zhou, X., Nejdl, W.: DivQ: Diversification for Keyword Search over Structured Databases. In: SIGIR 2010 (2010)
7. Drosou, M., Pitoura, E.: Search Result Diversification. In: SIGMOD Rec., vol. 39(1) (2010)
8. Gollapudi, S., Sharma, A.: An Axiomatic Approach for Result Diversification. In: WWW (2009)
9. Stefanidis, K., Drosou, M., Pitoura, E.: PerK: Personalized Keyword Search in Relational Databases through Preferences. In: EDBT 2010 (2010)

Evolution of eBooks on Demand Web-Based Service:
A Perspective through Surveys

Õnne Mets[1], Silvia Gstrein[2], and Veronika Gründhammer[2]

[1] National Library of Estonia, EOD dissemination, Tallinn, Estonia
onne.mets@nlib.ee
[2] University of Innsbruck Library, EOD coordinator, Innsbruck, Austria
{silvia.gstrein,veronika.gruendhammer}@uibk.ac.at

Abstract. In 2007 a document delivery service eBooks on Demand (EOD) was launched by 13 libraries from 8 European countries. It enables users to request digitisation of public domain books. By 2013 the self-sustained network has enlarged to 35 libraries in 12 countries and generated thousands of PDF e-books. Several surveys have been carried out to design the service to be relevant and attractive for end-users and libraries. The current paper explores the EOD service through a retrospective overview of the surveys, describes the status quo including ongoing improvements and suggests further surveys. The focus of the surveys illustrates the benchmarks (such as user groups and their expectations, evaluation of the service environment and form of outcomes, business to business opportunities and professional networking) that have been achieved to run an effective library service. It aims to be a possible model for libraries to start and develop a service.

Keywords: user surveys, evaluation, library services, digital library services, digitisaton on demand, online environments, ebooks.

1   Introduction

In 2007 a document delivery service *eBooks on Demand* (EOD) was launched by 13 libraries from 8 European countries. The EOD service enables users to request digitisation of public domain books via library catalogues or via the common EOD search engine. The outcome is a single PDF file, mostly with full-text search option, which is later incorporated into the participating library's digital library and thus becomes accessible on the Internet.

By 2013 the self-sustained service network has enlarged to 35 libraries in 12 European countries. Several thousand PDF e-books have been generated in the past years and delivered to users from over 30 countries worldwide. According to the current paper the evolution of the EOD service can be divided into the following phases: submitted surveys, current situation and service development, further possible action.

1.1   Description of the EOD Service

For users, the EOD service start-point is the button „Digital on request" by the records of public domain books not yet digitised in the e-catalogues of participating libraries

T. Aalberg et al. (Eds.): TPDL 2013, LNCS 8092, pp. 417–420, 2013.

or in the EOD search engine (http://search.books2ebooks.eu). An IT infrastructure has been designed for efficient processing of orders. The EOD network provides its partners a web-based software which allows for order management, automated customer communication, e-book production, delivery and electronic accounting.

The next step is scanning the book by the library who received the order. The digitised books and all related output files (such as OCR XML, RTF) belong to the delivering library. The outcomes of the service are always EOD e-books and may additionally be reprints. A customer can choose how to get the e-book – online, CD/DVD-ROM, and/or reprint.

Usually in a few months after completing the digitisation order, the item is also made available via the repository of the library. The link to the full-text is incorporated into the EOD search engine.

2   Retrospective Overview of Surveys

Majority of the surveys have taken place during preparation and launching of the EOD service.

In 2007 Customer Service Website Accessibility Audit was carried out within TENUTA. The aim of the audit was to test accessibility and usability of the service. Not only was the website evaluated, but also the order forms and the order process.

In 2007 also Online Market Survey was carried out (Institut für Marketing – Strategieberatung GmbH). It introduced the service and identified user expectations. The survey clearly showed that users tend to search for old books via the internet instead of printed or online library catalogues.

In 2008 Customer Survey was carried out to collect feedback on the service. Telephone interviews were held with end-users who had ordered eBooks via test installations. The survey aimed to evaluate the satisfaction of the end-users who have already used the eBooks on Demand service, to identify key consumer expectations and the potential of the improvement. It revealed important information concerning:

- Profile of the users: as expected, the overwhelming majority of the users are either researchers or readers requiring e-books for professional or scientific use (over 60%). The second largest category (16%) is book collectors and readers from special interest groups such as amateur historians, collectors, or ethnographers.
- Need for the service: when asked why they had opted for the service, almost half of the interviewees answered that without EOD the book would have been impossible or difficult to access. This shows that EOD has achieved one of its main goals of being a practical alternative to accessing printed books in library collections.
- Pricing: 30% of the customers felt the price of the service to be high or very high, but overall value for money was still found to be acceptable by the majority. The price per an e-book was calculated by starting with a minimum fee (on average 10 EUR) and adding the cost per page scanned (generally 0.15 to 0.30 EUR). The price-policy varies a little by EOD service providers.
- Outcome of the service: 60% of customers said that they usually print out selected pages or even the whole book. Thus, there was an obvious demand for the re-materialization of the digital material [1].

That finding was assured by an independent survey. It was found that 65% of Cambridge academics would be interested in a print facsimile [2]. In response to that, the EOD network began to offer reprints on demand: historical books on paper supplementing the digital file. This option can be selected during the ordering process, in addition to requesting the PDF [3].

Library User Survey was implemented online in parallel to the customer survey. It was similar to the market survey in 2007 by structure and content, but differed by the sample. The aim was to examine the expectations of library users towards the service, its design and possibilities it offers. 550 000 library users were targeted.

Structured interviews on business to business scale were carried out with potential adopter libraries. The interest in offering the service was to be identified across Europe. The interviews are repeated.

3   Status quo

From May 2009 until April 2013, EOD is co-financed by the EC under the Culture Programme. 20 libraries from 10 European countries take part in this follow-up project which focuses mainly on the three objectives: enlarging the EOD network; taking the EOD as a best practice model for a Europe-wide cooperation and training stakeholders (libraries, museums, or other cultural operators) to run a multinational cultural service based on state-of-the-art information technologies; to support intercultural dialogue among users of historical books with the help of web 2.0 technology.

In 2011 the **EOD search engine** was launched. It enables users to submit information retrieval among items from 22 libraries across Europe. The idea for the development was supported by the Market Survey 2007 and the current feedback. According to the survey there was a need to promote digital collections on the internet. According to other feedback, which was collected via participating libraries, there was a need for a multiple search option.

For even better visibility of old books on the internet, an **interaction between Europeana and EOD search engine** has been established. For every record displayed in the EOD search engine a query is carried out using the API of the Europeana database to find out whether this record has already been digitised and displayed in Europeana. If the query is positive, the links to the digitised items are displayed. It helps to avoid double digitisation and is seen as a crucial and additional service by the search engine.

In 2013 the user-centricity of EOD was tested by using the NET-EUCEN indicators [4]. It was noted that already the definition of the EOD service includes users. The development of the service is documented and available. The assessment activities are mostly described in Part 2 of the current paper.

4   Further Challenges

Monitoring the trends in user behaviour in general, it is evident that users need a personalised service and appreciate social networking.

An account option has been added to the EOD search engine for personalised information management. It allows users to leave comments and add tags to items. But the full potential of the feature in the EOD service context is to be examined.

An interaction with web 2.0 is established between Wikipedia and EOD search engine. Whenever there is an article about an author in Wikipedia, it is shown in the search engine.

In order to include the information concerning the EOD service in the social networks, a twitter feed of all digitised items has been set up (https://twitter.com/eod_ebooks), facebook pages created in English (http://www.facebook.com/eod.ebooks), German, Czech, Slovenian and Hungarian, and slides and videos shared accordingly in SlideShare and YouTube. But again, the full potential within the EOD service is to be examined and implemented.

5   Conclusion

The number of orders and new EOD network members prove EOD to be a useful library service. The surveys held as well as professional networking have led path to it step-by-step, given confidence, and even more importantly, given ideas to implement new features.

Acknowledgements. This work program has been funded with support from the European Commission. This publication reflects only the views of the authors, and the Commission cannot be held responsible for any use which may be made of the information contained therein.

References

1. Gstrein, S., Mühlberger, G.: Producing eBooks on Demand - A European Library Network. In: Price, K., Havergal, V. (eds.) E-Books in Libraries, pp. 37–52. Facet Publishing, London (2011)
2. Chamberlain, E.M.: Digitisation-on-Demand in Academic Research Libraries (2010), http://www.dspace.cam.ac.uk/bitstream/1810/240492/1/on_demand_report.pdf
3. Mühlberger, G., Gstrein, S.: EBooks on Demand (EOD): a European Digitization Service. IFLA Journal (Official Journal of the International Federation of Library Associations and Institutions) 35(1), 35–43 (2009)
4. Network of European Stakeholders for Enhance User Centricity in eGovernance: Measuring user centricity in services (2013), http://95.110.228.151/elgg/file/view/2969/indicators-for-user-centricity-in-public-services

Embedding Impact into the Development of Digital Collections: Rhyfel Byd 1914-1918 a'r Profiad Cymreig / Welsh Experience of the First World War 1914-1918

Lorna Hughes

University of Wales Chair in Digital Collection,
National Library of Wales,
Aberystwyth,
Wales, SY23 3BU
lorna.hughes@llgc.org.uk

Abstract. This poster describes a mass digitisation project led by the National Library of Wales to digitize archives and special collections about the Welsh experience of the First World War. The digital archive that will be created by the project will be a cohesive, digitally reunified archive that has value for research, education, and public engagement in time for the hundredth anniversary of the start of the First World War. In order to maximize impact of the digital outputs of the project, it has actively sought to embed methods that will increase its value to the widest audience. This paper describes these approaches and how they sit within the digital life cycle of project development.

1   Introduction

Rhyfel Byd 1914-1918 a'r profiad Cymreig / Welsh experience of the First World War 1914-1918 (cymruww1.llgc.org.uk) is led by the National Library of Wales (NLW) and funded by the UK's Joint Information Systems Committee (JISC) from February 2012-October 2013. The project will digitize archives, manuscripts, photographs, art works, and oral histories held by the NLW; Bangor University; Cardiff University; Aberystwyth University; Swansea University; the University of Wales Trinity Saint David's; local archives in the Archives and Records Council, Wales (ARCW); and the archive of BBC Cymru Wales. These include 190,000 pages of archival materials (including photographs, manuscripts, artworks, and newspapers); 30 hours of audio and 12 hours of audio-visual material. Approximately 30% of the content is in the medium of Welsh. These source materials are presently fragmented, frequently inaccessible, and difficult to access, yet collectively they form a unique resource of vital interest to researchers, students, and the public of Welsh life, language and culture. The project will create a coherent, consolidated digital collection revealing the often hidden history of the impact of the War: an invaluable resource for teaching, research, and public engagement in time for the 100th anniversary of the start of the War.

T. Aalberg et al. (Eds.): TPDL 2013, LNCS 8092, pp. 421–424, 2013.

2   Creating Digital Resources with Widest Impact

Digital cultural heritage content is becoming an essential component of the contemporary scholarly and research infrastructure. However, digital collections are expensive to develop and sustain, and there is increasing pressure to document and demonstrate their impact and value, and to better document their use. The creators of digital resources need to develop a more inclusive view of the 'value' and 'impact' that extends beyond numbers of users to a more qualitative understanding of the way that this content is having a transformative effect on scholarship and public engagement.

NLW has invested significant resources in the development of large scale digital collections, including *Welsh Wills Online (*www.llgc.org.uk/?id=487*)*, *Welsh Journals Online (*www.welshjournal.llgc.org.uk*)*, and *Welsh Newspapers Online* (www.welshnewspapers.llgc.org.uk), and digitization of the Library's photographic and art collections. The Library's Research Programme in Digital Collections (www.llgc.org.uk/research) is currently investigating the impact of this content using the qualitative (interviews, focus groups, surveys) and quantitative (web analytics and log analytics, and metrics) methods that are part of the TIDSR (Toolkit for the Impact of Digital Resources) developed by the Oxford Internet Institute (http://microsites.oii.ox.ac.uk/tidsr/welcome). This research builds on earlier investigations into the use of digital collections in the humanities, including The Log Analysis of Digital Resources in the Arts and Humanities (LAIRAH) project,[1] the evaluation of MIT's OpenCourseWare in 2006 [2]; Diane Harley's report on "Use and Users of Digital Resources in 2006 [3]; Lisa Spiro's study in 2007, "Impact of Digital Resources on the Humanities"[4], and the OII report on the use of TIDSR for digital humanities collections (2009)[5].

The research carried out at NLW revealed methods to maximize the impact of the of *Rhyfel Byd 1914-1918 a'r profiad Cymreig / Welsh experience of the First World War 1914-1918*. These have been incorporated throughout its development, including: the selection of collections for digitization; the development of the project's user interface; and dissemination and stakeholder involvement.

3   Selection of Content for Digitisation

An extensive scoping process of the Library, Archive and Special Collections of Wales was the basis for selecting content that could be included in this project. This analysis was conducted in three ways: assessing demand for the analogue archive materials; seeking advice and recommendations of researchers in several disciplines; and conducting bibliographic research to identify citations of key source materials. The final refinement assessed content against considerations of IPR and copyright.

The collections to be digitised – and some of the research questions they address – demonstrate the importance of the content for research. They include *The records of the Welsh Army Corps*, which are sources for recruitment, including demographic information, mobilisation of public attitudes, and propaganda; *Welsh newspapers 1913-1919* that include news and literary content, letters from soldiers, and poetry; *Manuscripts,* including diaries, journals and letters, contemporary writings and oral histories; *Literary Archives*, especially of the "Welsh War Poets", notably Edward Thomas, David Jones and Hedd Wyn (Ellis Humphrey Evans); and artists including David Jones; and *Official documents* including Church and chapel records; records of official organisations, businesses and trade unions.

4   Interface Development

As studies have shown that users appreciate clean, straightforward user interfaces with few 'bells and whistles"[6], our aim was to create a simple interface that provides material in a variety of formats and at varying levels of archival complexity, while retaining the hierarchical structures of archives that increase usability – through familiarity – of digital resources [7].   This included scoping, designing and developing a fully bilingual and accessible user interface in collaboration with stakeholders, and iterative testing and refinement.

In order to make the Welsh language materials accessible to the widest possible audience, we worked with the Canolfan Bedwyr Language Technologies Unit at the University of Bangor (www.bangor.ac.uk/ar/cb/), who developed methods for enrichment of the content via the utilization of Natural Language Processing (NLP) methods and tools to enable cross-lingual free text search of Welsh Language content.

5   Stakeholder Engagement and Dissemination

Stakeholder engagement was conducted via a process of collaboration with, and outreach to, researchers, students, teachers, government officials, museums staff, the public, technical and computer science researchers, the creative industries and businesses, and the media and military organisations. We also understood that key stakeholders can also be close to home: the archivists, librarians, and technical staff of all partner institutions were also invited to become involved.

Representatives of these communities were involved in iterative process of engagement and input through several workshops, including a workshop with academic researchers, asking them to critique and comment on existing websites for research in the humanities; a participatory design workshop, organized by the Humanities Research Institute at the University of Sheffield [8]; and an education workshop targeting teachers and developers of teaching materials that will feed into the Welsh Government online educational resource, Hwb (https://hwb.wales.gov.uk/Home/). *We also supported a* research network of academics using the content, and community engagement workshops with the People's Collection Wales (*www.peoplescollectionwales.co.uk/*).

Widest dissemination of the project as it developed was favoured by the timing of the project – during the project life cycle, the First Minister of Wales announced a committee to oversee Welsh activities to commemorate the First World War [9]. We collaborated with other projects and initiatives creating digital content relating to the War, including the Strategic Content Alliance; the Imperial War Museum, Europeana, the British Library, and the National Library of Scotland.

6   Conclusion

Incorporating considerations of use and impact of digital resources at the outset of a digitization project is crucial: impact is a crucial component of the entire digital life cycle, and should be considered at every stage: selection, digitization, curation, preservation, and, most importantly, sustainability over the long term. In many respects, the actions taken to promote use, uptake and embedding of the resource can support future sustainability: digital collections that are used are more likely to be sustained over the log-term if they are invaluable to education, research, and community building [10].

References

[1] Warwick, C., Terras, M., Huntington, P., Pappa, N., Galina, I.: The LAIRAH Project: Log Analysis of Digital Resources in the Arts and Humanities Final Report to the Arts and Humanities Research Council. University College London, London (2006),
     http://www.ucl.ac.uk/infostudies/
     claire-warwick/publications/LAIRAHreport.pdf
[2] Carson, S.: 2005 Program Evaluation Findings Report: MIT OpenCourseWare. Massachusetts Institute of Technology, Cambridge MA (2006),
     http://ocw.mit.edu/ans7870/global/
     05_Prog_Eval_Report_Final.pdf
[3] Harley, D.: Why study users? An environmental scan of use and users of digital resources in humanities and social sciences undergraduate education. First Monday, 12(1) (2007)
[4] Spiro, L., Segal, J.: The Impact of Digital Resources on Humanities Research. Fondren Library, Rice University (2007),
     http://library.rice.edu/services/dmc/about/projects/
     the-impact-of-digital-resources-on-humanities-research
[5] Meyer, E.T., Eccles, K., Thelwall, M., Madsen, C.: Usage and Impact Study of JISC-funded Phase 1 Digitisation Projects & the Toolkit for the Impact of Digitised Scholarly Resources (TIDSR). Oxford Internet Institute (2009),
     http://microsites.oii.ox.ac.uk/tidsr/
[6] Hughes, L.M., Ell, P., Dobreva, M., and Knight, Gareth, K.: Assessing and measuring impact of a digital collection in the humanities: An analysis of the SPHERE (Stormont Parliamentary Hansards: Embedded in Research and Education) Project. Literary and Linguistic Computing, Oxford (forthcoming, 2013)
[7] See Dobreva, M., O'Dwyer, A., Konstantelos, L.: In: Hughes, L.M. (ed.) Digital Collections: Use, Value and Impact. Facet, London (2011)
[8] Wessels, B., Dittrich, Y., Ekelin, A., Eriksen, S.: Creating synergies between participatory design of e-services and collaborative planning. International Journal of E-planning Research 1(3) (2012)
[9] http://wales.gov.uk/newsroom/firstminister/2012/120808ww1/
     ?lang=en
[10] Hughes, L.M.: Digital Collections: Use, Value and Impact. In: Hughes, L.M. (ed.) ICT Methods for Digital Collections Research. Facet, London (2011)

Creating a Repository of Community Memory in a 3D Virtual World: Experiences and Challenges

Ekaterina Prasolova-Førland, Mikhail Fominykh, and Leif Martin Hokstad

Program for learning with ICT, Norwegian University of Science and Technology, Norway
{ekaterip,mikhail.fominykh,leif.hokstad}@ntnu.no

Abstract. In this paper, we focus on creation of 3D content in learning communities, exemplified with a Virtual Gallery and Virtual Research Arena projects in the virtual campus of our university in Second Life. Based on our experiences, we discuss the possibilities and challenges of creating a repository of community memory in 3D virtual worlds.

Keywords: repository of community memory, learning communities, 3D virtual worlds.

1   Introduction

In this paper, we focus on affordances of 3D Virtual Worlds (VWs) for facilitating collaborative creation of repositories of community memory. From an epistemological perspective, knowledge resides in and is accessible from these repositories. The choice of 3D VWs is motivated by the potential and capability of such environments to support collaborative activities and work with various types of content [1,2]. Most VWs allow creating, manipulating, and sharing 3D objects and other media.

In order to better understand the notion of community memory we refer to the seminal work on communities of practice [3] and the theory behind organizational memory [4]. Continuous negotiation of meaning is the core of social learning and involves two processes: participation and reification [3]. The collection of artifacts appeared in these processes comprises the shared repertoire and history of the community. We describe learning process and creation of knowledge as characterized by narratives, collaboration, and social constructivism [5,6]. Narratives are used for the diagnosis of problems and as repositories of existing knowledge, be that tacit of explicit [7]. They contain the tacit knowledge of a given domain and field of practice, and provide a bridge between tacit and explicit knowledge [8]. Through collaboration in shared practices, knowledge may be created as well as distributed among the participants. Such a socialization process may give the learning access the *episteme* or *underlying game* of a discipline, the most difficult knowledge to access [9].

Walsh and Ungson propose that interpretations of the past can be embedded in systems and artifacts as well as within individuals through the narratives they may convey [10]. An important concept for community memory is 'boundary objects' that exist on the practice and social boundaries and are used across them. They contain sufficient details to be understandable by both parties, after the information they

T. Aalberg et al. (Eds.): TPDL 2013, LNCS 8092, pp. 425–428, 2013.

contain is de-contextualized [4]. To conclude, organizational and community memory consists of mental and structural artifacts [10], but it can also be thought of as a process and representational states [4]. In addition, an integral part of community memory is the histories and trajectories of its members as expressed in narratives that are represented as the community's shared repertoire.

Further, we present our prototypes and discuss how 3D VWs can be used not only as place of enactment, but also for accessing data to be enacted or collaborated into knowledge. In this way, our idea of a repository is more connected to narratives, artifacts, and boundary objects than to traditional data.

2   Prototypes: Virtual Research Arena and Virtual Gallery

The Virtual Gallery (VG) was intended to assist constructing, presenting, and storing student 3D visualization projects in a shared repository and designed based on the results of a case study [11]. A library of pre-made 3D objects, scripts, and textures could allow concentrating more on the creativity instead of technical details. In addition, student 3D visualizations occupied considerable amount of space in our virtual campus in Second Life (SL), and a better storage solution required.

The VG prototype was implemented, including a realistically reconstructed building (modeled after an existing student society house), a gallery for storing and presenting 3D constructions, and a library of pre-made resources (Fig. 1). In two other studies [12,13], we collected student feedback on the VG and its functions. Most of the student groups stressed the importance of having access to previous students' constructions for inspiration. Some of the groups stated that they get additional motivation from exhibiting their construction for other people.

We studied further the possibilities of 3D VWs for educational visualizations and supporting learning communities that can form around them. We developed a framework, Virtual Research Arena (VRA), for creating awareness about educational and research activities, promoting cross-fertilization between different environments and engaging the public [12] that was later implemented as a prototype in SL. It provides appropriate atmosphere, tools, and facilities for the community activities (seminars, meetings, and discussions). VRA is a place, where students and researchers can express themselves trying out, visualizing and sharing their ideas (using VG resources). It should accumulate 'reifications'/traces of community activities over time, thus becoming a community repository, containing different layers of community activities.

VRA prototype functions as a virtual extension of the Norwegian Science Fair festival where research projects are presented to the public in a set of pavilions (Fig. 2). A city landmark – King Olav Tower was reconstructed on the virtual 'central square' that serves as a venue for the fair in reality, to create a familiar atmosphere and a meeting place for the online visitors. While the physical pavilions at the fair were deconstructed at the end of the event, the virtual ones and the student constructions with activities traces have been preserved. The feedback collected in a case study [12] showed that most of the students and visitors acknowledged the potential of 3D VWs and VRA for supporting social networks and collaboration among various groups of participants as well as the importance of preserving their own constructions.

Fig. 1. Virtual Gallery prototype   **Fig. 2.** Virtual Research Arena prototype

3   Discussion and Future Work

Our experiences show that collaborative 3D content creation has enriched the reflective dialog in the communities with innovative expression forms. It has contributed to creation of a shared repository of community knowledge, consisting of such elements as narratives, boundary objects, and virtual places. The total knowledge of a community consists of the tacit and explicit knowledge that reside in the objects, places, and relations developed by the participants. The prototypes we presented afford the learner to develop knowledge through explorative and constructive methodologies, and through access to narratives and the development of relations. This implies that 3D VWs may thus offer richness in available resources for learning rarely found in a real-life situation alone. The epistemological landscape is in this perspective augmented with sources for knowledge commonly not included. At the same time, the situated, contextualized, and partly ephemeral nature of these repositories suggests the following challenges, especially when comparing to 'traditional' repositories.

- *Platform and context dependence*: storing and transferring 3D constructions between different platforms is not always possible. In addition, even when technically possible, the 3D content in the repository might lose its context and connections, e.g. when 'storing' a virtual place without the activity that gives meaning to it.
- *Rights management*: clearly showing the ownership of the created content is important for both visualizing trajectories/activities of community members as well as addressing the copyright issues. However, managing rights in SL and other VWs are often in the conflict with flexibility of constructing and storing the content.
- *Indexing and annotating* of a repository containing 'narratives/ crystallizations/ traces of community activities' is complicated due to the fluid nature of the learning communities, but also to the ambiguity of the content which might be interpreted differently depending on the context and the background of the visitors.
- *Shared sense of place:* though many of the challenges are associated with contextualization of the content, it could in some cases be seen as an advantage, as it provides community members with a shared understanding and shared sense of place.

There is still a need to explore further the affordances of 3D VWs for supporting such 'fluid' repositories of community knowledge as well as developing methodologies for managing and annotating such repositories. It is important to take interdisciplinary nature of such repositories into account, since they contain both tangible and non-tangible artifacts, as well as the different types of media and content they contain.

References

1. Atkins, C.: Virtual Experience: Observations on Second Life. In: Purvis, M., Savarimuthu, B.T.R. (eds.) ICCMSN 2008. LNCS, vol. 5322, pp. 7–17. Springer, Heidelberg (2009)
2. van Nederveen, S.: Collaborative Design in Second Life. In: de Ridder, H.A.J., Wamelink, J.W.F. (eds.) 2nd International Conference World of Construction Project Management (WCPM), pp. 1–6. Delft, The Netherlands (2007)
3. Wenger, E.: Communities of Practice: Learning, Meaning, and Identity. Cambridge University Press, New York (1998)
4. Ackerman, M.S., Halverson, C.: Considering an organization's memory. In: Conference on Computer Supported Cooperative Work (CSCW), pp. 39–48. ACM, Seattle (1998)
5. Lave, J., Wenger, E.: Situated Learning: Legitimate Peripheral Participation. Cambridge University Press, Cambridge (1991)
6. Brown, J.S., Duguid, P.: Organizational Learning and communities of Practice: Towards a Unified View of Working, learning, and innovation. Organization Science 2(1), 40–57 (1991)
7. Polanyi, M.: The Tacit Dimension. Peter Smith, Glouchester (1966)
8. Linde, C.: Narrative and social tacit knowledge. Journal of Knowledge Management 5(2), 160–171 (2001)
9. Entwistle, N.: Learning outcomes and ways of thinking across contrasting disciplines and settings in higher education. Curriculum Journal 16(1), 67–82 (2005)
10. Walsh, J.P., Ungson, G.R.: Organizational Memory. The Academy of Management Review 16(1), 57–91 (1991)
11. Prasolova-Førland, E., Fominykh, M., Wyeld, T.G.: Virtual Campus of NTNU as a place for 3D Educational Visualizations. In: Abas, Z.W., Jung, I., Luca, J. (eds.) 1st Global Conference on Learning and Technology (Global Learn Asia Pacific), Penang, Malaysia, pp. 3593–3600. AACE, Chesapeake (2010)
12. Fominykh, M., Prasolova-Førland, E.: Virtual Research Arena: Presenting Research in 3D Virtual Environments. In: Barton, S.-M., Hedberg, J., Suzuki, K. (eds.) 2nd Global Conference on Learning and Technology (Global Learn Asia Pacific), Melbourne, Australia, pp. 1558–1567. AACE, Chesapeake (2011)
13. Fominykh, M., Prasolova-Førland, E., Divitini, M.: Learning Computer-Mediated Cooperation in 3D Visualization Projects. In: Luo, Y. (ed.) CDVE 2012. LNCS, vol. 7467, pp. 65–72. Springer, Heidelberg (2012)

Social Navigation Support
for Groups in a Community-Based Educational Portal

Peter Brusilovsky[1], Yiling Lin[1], Chirayu Wongchokprasitti[1], Scott Britell[2],
Lois M.L. Delcambre[2], Richard Furuta[3], Kartheek Chiluka[4],
Lillian N. Cassel[4], and Ed Fox[5]

[1] University of Pittsburgh, Pittsburgh, PA, USA
[2] Portland State University, Portland OR, USA
[3] Texas A&M University, College Station, TX, USA
[4] Villanova University, Villanova, PA, USA
[5] Virginia Tech., Blacksburg, VA, USA

Abstract. This work seeks to enhance a user's experience in a digital library using group-based social navigation. Ensemble is a portal focusing on computing education as part of the US National Science Digital Library providing access to a large amount of learning materials and resources for education in Science, Technology, Engineering and Mathematics. With so many resources and so many contributing groups, we are seeking an effective way to guide users to find the right resource(s) by using group-based social navigation. This poster demonstrates how group-based social navigation can be used to extend digital library portals and how it can be used to guide portal users to valuable resources.

Keywords: social navigation, digital library, portal, navigation support.

1   Introduction: Social Navigation in Ensemble

It has been recognized that users of digital libraries might need help locating interesting and relevant resources. In real libraries this help is usually provided by librarians but digital libraries typically rely on various automatic guidance approaches such as resource recommendation and adaptive navigation support. Social navigation [4] - a specific kind of social information access [1] - has been recognized as one approach for automatic guidance in digital libraries [2]. Social navigation collects traces of past users' interactions with the system and uses it to provide navigation support to current users. For example, a relatively simple, yet useful social navigation approach known as traffic-based social navigation [3], collects and displays the browsing behavior of past users to indicate the popularity of resources. This kind of social navigation has been used and explored in the context of our work developing the *Ensemble* educational digital library [2].

Ensemble is a portal for computing educators in the US National Science Digital Library[1] (NSDL): www.computingportal.org. The portal presents easy access to

---

[1] http://nsdl.org/

T. Aalberg et al. (Eds.): TPDL 2013, LNCS 8092, pp. 429–433, 2013.

recognized collections and tools. It is also a central meeting place for communities who are interested in various aspects of computing education; over thirty communities are now active. Collections and communities are equally important for the portal. The original focus of Ensemble social navigation efforts was providing navigation support to *educational resources* in the portal collections. Since resources form a relatively straightforward and homogeneous space, the traditional traffic-based social navigation approach worked reasonably well. However, our attempts to expand the same social navigation approach to the *community* part of the portal faced additional challenges.

The source of these challenges was the diversity of Ensemble. Different groups feature different kinds of pages (pages, books, resources, blog posts, forums, etc.) and have very different proportions of these resources. For example, some groups are more resource oriented with a relatively large number of resource-type pages, while other groups focus more on communication with few if any resources. Also, groups have very different sizes and activity levels. This diversity created two problems. First, the traditional approach to provide social navigation between groups (i.e., helping visitors to select most relevant or interesting groups) was not sufficient in a heterogeneous group space. Adding a traffic indicator to the top-level links leading to group pages offered too little help since it couldn't explain which type(s) of pages each group hosted, which of these pages took the majority of user visits, and how frequent were these visit with respect to the size of the groups' total postings. Second, due to very different traffic levels in different groups, a portal-level separation of pages into low-, medium-, and high-traffic pages failed to distinguish pages within group spaces. In large, active groups all page links had high traffic "dark green" annotation, while in smaller and less active groups, all links were annotated white since their traffic did not exceed a portal-level threshold for medium-level traffic. To address these two problems and to provide better support for groups within Ensemble, we developed two extensions to our social navigation approach, presented below.

2   Choosing the Right Group: Group-Level Social Navigation

Given the number of active groups and their differing styles of interaction, a newcomer might find it hard to distinguish communities by relying on the description of the group, number of members, and number of posts. Even for existing users, it may be hard to catch all the information about the communities without extensive exploration. To help portal users distinguish different groups hosted by Ensemble and pick the most appropriate groups we offered a treemap-based social navigation.

Using a treemap, we were able to uncover and visualize two levels of hierarchy for the portal group. The first level of the treemap represents different *groups* while the second shows the kinds of *information pages* that are hosted in each group's space. The treemap represents the group's information by adapting its three elements: cell size, color, and labels. Since the size and color dimensions are correlated with the number of posts and views of resources within the group, one can easily distinguish the differences among resources without any difficulty. In Fig. 1, the size of a rectangle corresponding to a specific kind of page represents the number of pages of this kind in a group space (a larger space represents more posts) and the color of the rectangle represents the average traffic-based popularity of this area (a darker color represents a greater number of views, with three levels of darkness being used). This visualization shows many important things at once.

With the treemap, users can easily recognize large groups and small groups as well as groups with high and low levels of activity. Moreover, the second level visualization points to the nature of the group by showing which type of resources dominate and which type is most actively used (e.g., it is easy to see that "book" has been posted 24 times more frequently than the other resources in the Ensemble Design and Development group). In addition, it is quite easy to recognize resource-oriented groups (such as Tech, with a large and actively used collection component and a small low-traffic blog part) and discussion-oriented groups (such as CS2013, with a large and active forum page and a small, low-traffic resource part).

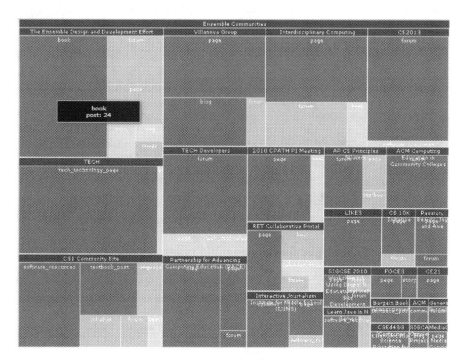

Fig. 1. An overview of TreeMap group social navigation in Ensemble

3   Navigating within a Group: Group-Adjusted Social Navigation

In the past, Ensemble provided global-level social navigation support for any list of links to resources in the portal with social visual cues. The list of links was collected and classified by the portal for each group of similar resources. Social visual cues annotated links with the popularity of the resource by color intensity. The more intense the color was, the more popular was the resource in the portal. However, we recognized that global-level social navigation was not able to provide a clear view of the local popularity within each group. Recently created communities or communities with fewer members might only get social cues with lowest color intensity since the resources in such a group are relatively new likely with fewer visits than the resources in an older or larger group. To extend the social navigation support for groups, we adjusted the original global-level social navigation support to a local-level one. The social visual cues are now generated based on the local popularity of the resources *for each group*. Fig. 2 shows the group-adjusted social navigation support in the group, *RET Collaborative Portal*. This is a relatively small group with 7 members. Within the group, we show a list of resources grouped by resource type, such as Event, Page, and Book page, inside the group. The social visual cues are applied based on the viewing frequency of each resource within the group. We assess the group-adjusted popularity of the resource by calculating the ratio of the resource's views within the group to the maximum of the group views over the group resources. Three thresholds are used to distinguish different levels of group popularity: resources with the adjusted popularity over 50% of the group maximum are considered very popular and receive dark-green visual cues, resources with popularity between 10% and 50% are considered moderately popular and receive light-green visual cues, and resources with relative popularity lower than 10% are considered low-popularity and receive light cues. Users can easily see which resources garnered the most attention in a group.

Fig. 2. Content-level group-adjusted social navigation support

4 Discussions and Conclusion

This work argues in favor of group social navigation to extend digital libraries and demonstrated two types of group social navigation mechanisms implemented in Ensemble: group-level social navigation based on a social treemap and group-adjusted social navigation within group pages shown as link annotations. We will observe two features' usage on the portal and gain more insights of how to apply group social navigation in the large educational digital library.

Acknowledgments. This material is based upon work supported by the National Science Foundation under Grant Numbers 0534762, DUE-0840713, 0840719, 0840721, 0840668, 0840597, 0840715, 0511050, 0836940, 0937863, and 1044212.

References

1. Brusilovsky, P.: Social Information Access: The Other Side of the Social Web. In: SOFSEM 2008. LNCS, vol. 4910, pp. 5–22. Springer, Heidelberg (2008)
2. Brusilovsky, P., Cassel, L., Delcambre, L., Fox, E., Furuta, R., Garcia, D.D., Shipman III, F.M., Bogen, P., Yudelson, M.: Enhancing Digital Libraries with Social Navigation: The Case of Ensemble. In: Lalmas, M., Jose, J., Rauber, A., Sebastiani, F., Frommholz, I. (eds.) ECDL 2010. LNCS, vol. 6273, pp. 116–123. Springer, Heidelberg (2010)
3. Brusilovsky, P., Chavan, G., Farzan, R.: Social adaptive navigation support for open corpus electronic textbooks. In: De Bra, P.M.E., Nejdl, W. (eds.) AH 2004. LNCS, vol. 3137, pp. 24–33. Springer, Heidelberg (2004)
4. Dieberger, A., Dourish, P., Höök, K., Resnick, P., Wexelblat, A.: Social navigation: Techniques for building more usable systems. Interactions 7(6), 36–45 (2000)

Evaluation of Preserved Scientific Processes

Rudolf Mayer[1], Mark Guttenbrunner[1], and Andreas Rauber[1,2]

[1] Secure Buisness Austria, Vienna, Austria
[2] Vienna University of Technology, Austria

Abstract. Digital preservation research has seen an increased focus is on objects that are non-deterministic but depend on external events like user input or data from external sources. Among those is the preservation of scientific processes, aiming at reuse of research outputs. Ensuring that the preserved object is equivalent to the original is a key concern, and is traditionally measured by comparing *significant properties* of the objects. We adapt a framework for comparing emulated versions of a digital object to measure equivalence also in processes.

1 Introduction

Digital data is in its nature volatile, and always needs an environment in which it is rendered to a form that makes it useful. The interpretation of the bitstream is the subject of digital preservation (DP) research. Two strategies have evolved as the most promising. *Migrating* a digital object means continuously changing its format to one that is not obsolete at the time of use. *Emulation* keeps the original digital object but changes the rendering environment, by modifying the application used to render the object, or replacing the original hardware by introducing a virtual layer, using the original software-stack for rendering. It is necessary to evaluate that the result of the digital preservation action produces a rendering that is similar to the original in its "significant properties", i.e., the properties of the object deemed important for future use by the designated community. For migration, the significant properties of the object extracted from the original and migrated form are compared. With emulation, one has to compare the rendering of the digital object in the two environments. Traditionally DP research concentrated on objects that behave deterministic, i.e., are rendered similarly on the same system during each rendering, such as text-documents, videos, images, or database content. Objects that are rendered non-deterministic change their rendering depending on user input, hardware values, or random values, e.g. digital art or computer games. The preservation and curation of scientific data is important to ensure reuse and long-term usability of data that has been the basis to scientific experiments. Data, however, does also require information about its context and the processes involved in its creation and usage, e.g., the setting where it was created or interpreted. It may be impossible to recreate the original experiment, and thus a preserved process that allows to reproduce and trace how results and analysis were obtained is important. eScience processes are depending on specific software or hardware, thus facing digital obsolescence.

T. Aalberg et al. (Eds.): TPDL 2013, LNCS 8092, pp. 434–437, 2013.

To preserve a process, one needs to go beyond capturing single files and meta-data, up to including complete computer systems. From a high level perspective, organizational parameters need to be described, down to the technical description of the systems the process depends on, including hardware, software, and third-party services. To describe these, a context model identifying relevant aspects of a process has been created [2].

2 Preservation Actions for Processes and Evaluation

The preservation of a process will in most cases be a mixture of currently available techniques. Documentation relevant to the understanding of the process and technical environment can be migrated to different formats. Also data and documents used within or in the transition between process steps need to be preserved. They can both be interpreted by humans, or machines, which has an impact on the significant properties. For software systems forming the execution environment supporting the process, emulation of both hardware and software (especially operating systems) is a viable option. Virtualization can aid to abstract the system from the physical hardware. Migration of the software supporting the process to another environment is a viable option, e.g. by migration to a different programming language supported in the new environment, or cross-compilation to a different platform. One strategy for external systems employed, such as web services, is in contractual agreements, which will obligate the providers to perform preservation efforts themselves. When that is not possible, an external system has to be replaced by a system controlled by the process owner. This can be a reimplementation (migration) of the system, or simply a simulation of the behavior of the system, e.g. by recording and replaying messages previously exchanged. Of course, this is not a valid strategy for non-deterministic servicess, e.g. for which the output dependends also on the time of invocation (and thus a *state*). In all cases, it is important to evaluate that the preserved process is still equivalent to the originally executed process.

A framework to determine the effects of an emulated environment on the rendering of objects is presented in [1]. It suggests methods to automate the evaluation, and methods to automate input to ensure that changes in manual handling of the digital object can be ruled out as a cause for changes. To apply this framework to the evaluation of processes we have to take the following steps:

(1) *Description of the original environment*, using the context model.

(2) *External events* Typical events that will influence the behavior of a process are external data used as input to the process, either manually supplied by a user, or data that is read from sources connected to the system, e.g., web services, or sensors. To enable evaluation, we have to record the data supplied to the process so that it can be reapplied on a re-run. As not every possible combination of data can be evaluated, significant test cases are defined.

(3) *Level to compare* Depending on the process and the type of "output" it creates, we have to decide where to capture the rendered data (cf. Figure 1(a)). For an automatically running process that does not produce any rendered screens

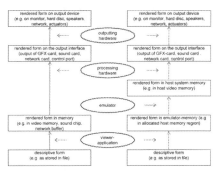
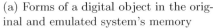

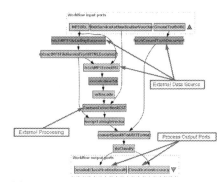

(a) Forms of a digital object in the orig-   (b) Scientific workflow modeled in the
inal and emulated system's memory   Taverna Workflow engine

Fig. 1.

for users we can compare on the interface where the output is provided, e.g. a
file. If user output is created and that triggers a response from the user, then
extraction from the video memory e.g. in the form of a screenshot is necessary.

(4) *Recreating the environment* A typical recreation of a process would happen
either in a virtualized or a fully emulated environment. Alternatively the process
could also be executed in a different process execution engine.

(5) *Standardized input* External data that has been captured during the test
case-recordings of the rendering of the process has to be provided to the new
rendering of the process, to ensure a deterministic rendering.

(6) *Extracting data* During the execution of a process intermediary data is generated, handed between different steps of the process and discarded afterwards.
From an evaluation point of view we are interested in all data that is provided
outside of the system. We thus identify these "Significant States" in the process
and at these extract both in the original rendering and the emulated version.
If the original process is executed in a workflow engine, i.e. an application that
orchestrates processes, the single processing steps are well defined and allow for
capturing the data exchanged. For other processes, a viable strategy is to move
the execution environment into a virtual machine environment, which enables
capturing data from the interface between the virtual machine and the host system. Capturing data in the original environment is also possible to some extent.

(7) *Comparing data* The data extracted during the run of the process in the original environment is compared to the data extracted from the re-run. Using the
same input data for a process the assumption is that the process behaves similar
to the original rendering, producing the same results if we extract the data in the
same significant states of the process. Otherwise, a difference in the rendering
environment is likely the reason for the failed verification of the process.

3   Case Study – A Music Classification Experiment

We test our method on a scientific experiment where the researcher performs
an evaluation of an algorithm for automatic classification of music into a set of

predefined categories, which is a standard scenario in music information retrieval research, and is used for numerous evaluation settings, ranging from ad-hoc experiments to benchmark evaluations. An implementation of the process is shown in Figure 1(b), a detailed description and context model thereof can be found in [2]. In the experiment, music data is acquired from external sources (e.g. online content providers), and genre assignments for the pieces of music from ground truth registries. Features describing characteristics of the audio files are extracted using an external web service. The service needs the input in MP3 format, Base64 encoded to allow for a data exchange via XML. The service returns an ASCII file, that after conversion from SOMLib to ARFF format forms the basis for learning a machine learning model. The numeric metric "accuracy" and a detailed description are the output.

Of particular interest for evaluation are those steps where the process communicates with the system it is embedded in, i.e., all the steps where external data influences the rendering of the process, or where data is provided to external interfaces. To create a deterministic rendering we need to make sure that for every evaluation cycle the same data influencing the process is provided. In the music classification process there are several process steps that have a connection to an external service, annotated in Figure 1(b). As such, fetchMP3FileListing, fetchGroundTruth and fetchMP3 get data from an external web server. Communication with the web service includes the music files as well as parameters controlling the extraction. The process in turn receives as input the extracted features. Finally, there are two end results where data is provided by the process.

To enable evaluation of the workflow results we need to provide either a connection to the original external web server, or create a simulation of the service. Capturing the data on the output ports of the process lets us then compare different cycles of the same process steps with the same data. If the captured data is identical even if the rendering environment has been changed, we have a strong indication that the process is executed correctly in the new environment. If the captured data is different, even if the process has been executed with the exact same input parameters, then the rendering environment changes the execution of the process and thus can not be considered a proper preservation of the process. Also internal intermediary results after each step can be compared, to check how far in the process the results are unchanged. Differences can be introduced by internal dependencies, e.g., due to differences in versions of libraries, or different versions of the Java Virtual Machine. Comparing intermediary results can thus help us identify differences in the rendering environment leading to changes in the result of the process.

References

1. Guttenbrunner, M., Rauber, A.: A measurement framework for evaluating emulators for digital preservation. ACM Trans. on Information Systems 30(2) (2012)
2. Mayer, R., Rauber, A., Neumann, M.A., Thomson, J., Antunes, G.: Preserving scientific processes from design to publications. In: Zaphiris, P., Buchanan, G., Rasmussen, E., Loizides, F. (eds.) TPDL 2012. LNCS, vol. 7489, pp. 113–124. Springer, Heidelberg (2012)

An Open Source System Architecture
for Digital Geolinguistic Linked Open Data

Emanuele Di Buccio, Giorgio Maria Di Nunzio, and Gianmaria Silvello

Dept. of Information Engineering, University of Padua
{dibuccio,dinunzio,silvello}@dei.unipd.it

Abstract. Digital Geolinguistic systems encourages collaboration between linguists, historians, archaeologists, ethnographers, as they explore
the relationship between language and cultural adaptation and change.
These systems can be used as instructional tools, presenting complex
data and relationships in a way accessible to all educational levels. In
this poster, we present a system architecture based on a Linked Open
Data (LOD) approach the aim of which is to increase the level of interoperability of geolinguistic applications and the reuse of the data.

1 Introduction

In the last two decades, several large-scale databases of linguistic material of
various types have been developed worldwide. The World Atlas of Languages
Structures (WALS) [1] is one of the largest projects, with 160 maps showing
the geographical distribution of structural linguistic features,[1] and it is the first
linguistic feature atlas on a world-wide scale. The Common Language Resources
and Technology Infrastructure project (CLARIN, [2]) is a European initiative
the aim of which is to create an infrastructure which makes language resources
(annotated recordings, texts, lexica, ontologies) and technology (speech recog-
nisers, lemmatisers, parsers, summarisers, information extractors) available and
readily usable to scholars of all disciplines. Language resources that have been
made publicly available can vary in the richness of the information they contain.
Bird et al. [3] discuss three important points about the design and distribution
of language resources: (i) How do we design a new language resource and ensure
that its coverage, balance and documentation support a wide range of uses? (ii)
When existing data is in the wrong format for some analysis tool, how can we
convert it into a suitable format? (iii) What is a good way to document the
existence of a resource we have created so that others can easily find it?

In this poster, we present a system architecture based on a current project
named Atlante Sintattico d'Italia, Syntactic Atlas of Italy (ASIt) based on the
LOD paradigm with the aim of enabling interoperability at a data-level. The
LOD paradigm refers to a set of best practices for publishing data on the Web[2]

---

[1] http://www.wals.info/

[2] http://www.w3.org/DesignIssues/LinkedData.html

T. Aalberg et al. (Eds.): TPDL 2013, LNCS 8092, pp. 438–441, 2013.

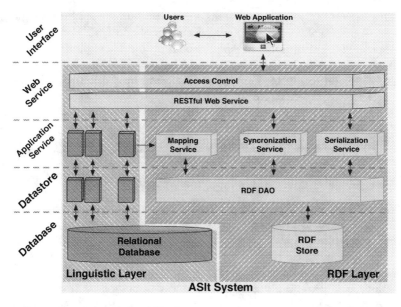

Fig. 1. The architecture of the ASIt System in which we highlight the diverse constituting levels and the RDF Layer

and it is based on a standardized data model, the Resource Description Framework (RDF). RDF is designed to represent information in a minimally constraining way and it is based on the following building blocks: graph data model, URI-based vocabulary, data types, literals, and several serialization syntaxes.

2 System Architecture

We present the architecture of the ASIt system composed by the *linguistic layer* and the *RDF layer*, as shown in Figure 1.

2.1 Linguistic Layer

The *linguistic layer* [4] has been designed to be modular, thus reducing the dependency on a particular implementation of its constituting modules. It can be framed in four different levels: *database*, *datastore*, *application service*, and *Web service*. The *database* level is constituted by a relational database, the schema of which is based on the ASIt conceptual model; the currently adopted DataBase Management System (DBMS) is PostgreSQL.[3] The *datastore* is responsible for the persistence of the linguistic resources and provides an interface to store and access linguistic data. The *application service* is responsible for the interaction with the linguistic resources; it provides an Application Program Interface (API)

---

[3] http://www.postgresql.org/

to perform operations on the resources – e.g. list sentences in a document, or list words in a sentence, and add tags to sentences and words. When linguistic resources are created or modified, the application service exploits the datastore API for the persistence of data. The *Web service* provides functionalities to create, modify and delete resources, and gather their descriptions through appropriate HTTP requests based on a RESTful Web service [5]. This level is also responsible for access control which is necessary to preserve the quality of the data maintained in the ASIt database. Indeed, only allowed users can create or modify resources, whereas there is no restriction to access resource descriptions.

2.2 RDF Layer

The *RDF layer* is responsible for persistence and access to RDF triples of linguistic data instantiated on the basis of the ontology. The RDF layer has been developed by exploiting the functionalities of the open source library Apache Jena.[4] Jena was adopted because of the variety of solutions for persistence of the RDF/S instantiation, the support of a number of RDF output formats, and the functionalities for reasoning with RDF and Ontology Web Language (OWL) data sources. A *mapping service* has been developed to instantiate the ontology starting from the data stored in the ASIt relational database. A request for creation, deletion or modification of a resource is processed by the linguistic layer that, through the proper module of the *application service*, allows the interaction with the resource and stores its new state. In parallel, by means of the *syncronization service*, the RDF layer processes the request and updates the RDF triples instantiating the ASIt ontology. This service allows for the interaction with the *RDF datastore* which is responsible for the persistence of the RDF triples in the RDF store. Therefore, the operations required by resource creation, deletion or modification are performed in parallel for each request to guarantee the synchronzation between the relational database and the RDF store. When a request for accessing a resource is submitted to the system, the RDF *serialization service* retrieves information on the requested resource from the RDF store and it returns the result in the requested output format.

3 Web Application and Final Remarks

The architecture presented in this poster allows us to expose the linguistic resources as a Linked Open Dataset. By exploiting the synchronisation services, the ASIt Geolinguistic Linked Open Dataset size grows proportionally to the size of the database.[5] Table 1 reports the statistics about the evolution of the data in ASIt in the last two and a half years. This dataset has been exposed following the guidelines in [6]. The linguistic dataset created with this architecture can be easily linked to other open datasets. As an example, the ASIt dataset is linked to DBpedia; indeed, the instances of the geographical classes Region,

---

[4] http://incubator.apache.org/jena
[5] The details of this dataset can be found here: http://purl.org/asit/alld

Table 1. Statistics about the growth of main entities/relationships of the ASIt curated database

	Jan '11	Jul '11	Jan '12	Jul '12	Jan '13
tags	524	530	532	532	532
documents	462	468	512	540	510
sentences	47,973	48,575	51,256	54,091	54,195
tags/sentences	10,364	16,731	18,080	18,369	18,371
tags/words	0	5,411	18,509	27,046	27,271

`Province`, and `Town` are linked to the corresponding instances of the dbpedia.org class `Place` through the property `owl:sameAs`.

A GUI to submit queries to the ASIt Linguistic Linked Open Dataset[6] and to dynamically produce maps on the basis of the user requests[7] are already available and publicly accessible.

One of the key points of this approach is the decoupling between the system which manages the data and the one which provides services over those data. In fact, this system has been adopted to develop a geolinguistic application build upon the presented dataset providing linguists with a tool for investigating variations among closely related languages. We also developed a graphical user interface on top of this application that dynamically produces maps on the basis of the user requests. Finally, we imagine the use of the Geolinguistic Linked Open Dataset by third-party linguistic projects in order to enrich the data and build-up new services over them.

References

1. Haspelmath, M., Dryer, M.S., Gil, D., Comrie, B.: The World Atlas of Language Structures. Oxford University Press, United Kingdom (2005)
2. Odijk, J.: The CLARIN-NL Project. In: LREC, European Language Resources Association (2010)
3. Bird, S., Klein, E., Loper, E.: Natural Language Processing with Python. O'Reilly Media (2009)
4. Di Buccio, E., Di Nunzio, G.M., Silvello, G.: A system for exposing linguistic linked open data. In: Zaphiris, P., Buchanan, G., Rasmussen, E., Loizides, F. (eds.) TPDL 2012. LNCS, vol. 7489, pp. 173–178. Springer, Heidelberg (2012)
5. Fielding, R.T., Taylor, R.N.: Principled design of the modern web architecture. ACM TOIT 2, 115–150 (2002)
6. Heath, T., Bizer, C.: Linked Data: Evolving the Web into a Global Data Space. In: Synthesis Lectures on the Semantic Web. Morgan & Claypool Publishers (2011)

---

[6] http://purl.org/asit/rdf/sparqlGui
[7] http://purl.org/asit/rdf/search

Committee-Based Active Learning
for Dependency Parsing

Saeed Majidi[1] and Gregory Crane[2]

[1] Department of Computer Science, Tufts University, Medford, MA, USA
saeed.majidi@tufts.edu
[2] Perseus Project, Tufts University, Medford, MA, USA
gregory.crane@tufts.edu

Abstract. Annotations on structured corpora provide a foundational instrument for emerging linguistic research. To generate annotations automatically, data-driven dependency parsers need a large annotated corpus to learn from. But these annotations are expensive to collect and require a labor intensive task. In order to reduce the costs of annotation, we provide a novel framework in which a committee of dependency parsers collaborate to improve their efficiency using active learning.

Keywords: active learning, corpus annotation, dependency parsing.

1 Introduction

Annotations on structured corpora provide a foundational instrument for emerging linguistic research, comparable to that of genomic databases in the life sciences. For students of language, linguistic annotations identifying features such as part of speech and syntactic function of the words in a corpus are increasingly important. These annotations are, however, expensive to collect.

Dependency graph of a sentence is a tree in which every word is represented as a node and the directed arcs between the nodes show syntactic modifiers of the words. *Data-driven dependency parsing* techniques use an annotated corpus and learn to generate dependency graphs automatically from it. In this work we explore the hypothesis that active learning techniques can be used for dependency parsing to help us reach better performance on parsing with cheaper annotation cost.

2 Active Learning

One of the mostly used applied machine learning techniques is active learning. In active learning, the learner has the control of data it uses to learn a model. This control is in the form of asking an oracle, a domain expert, about the annotations of only those unlabeled instances that could help the learner to improve itself.

One of the basic scenarios is *pool-based sampling* [1]. It is used when there is a large collection of unlabeled data. In pool-based sampling, one assumes that

T. Aalberg et al. (Eds.): TPDL 2013, LNCS 8092, pp. 442–445, 2013.

there is a small set of labeled data $\mathcal{L}$ and a large pool of unlabeled data $\mathcal{U}$. Queries are drawn from $\mathcal{U}$ according to a selection strategy. Then the labels of the chosen instances are asked from an oracle and are added to $\mathcal{L}$. This process is repeated until there are enough annotated data at $\mathcal{L}$. *Uncertainty sampling* and *query-by-committee* are two commonly used query selection scenarios.

In uncertainty sampling [1], after training a model using existing labeled data in $\mathcal{L}$, it is used to predict the labels of instances in $\mathcal{U}$. Then the learner selects the instances about whose labels it is less confident. In query-by-committee [2] (QBC), the system contains a committee of competing models. All models are trained on the current labeled data set $\mathcal{L}$. Then each of the committee members votes on the label of examples in $\mathcal{U}$. The query contains the samples about which committee members most disagree.

3   QBC for Dependency Parsing

For the task of dependency parsing, we use a committee of c parsers. Each parser, trained on $\mathcal{L}$, generates a separate model. Each model predicts the head node and the relation to the head of every instance in $\mathcal{U}$. $h(P_i, w)$ shows the head prediction of parser P_i for token w, and $r(P_i, w)$ shows its relation prediction. Here we assume that the head and relation of token w are predicted independently. We also apply the models generated by the parsers on a separate test set $\mathcal{T}$ and for each parser we compute its accuracy on $\mathcal{T}$. We indicate the unlabeled accuracy of parser P_i as $UA(P_i)$ and its labeled accuracy as $LA(P_i)$. *Unlabeled accuracy* is the percentage of correct head dependencies, and *labeled accuracy* is the percentage of correct relations for the correct dependencies that the parser predicts. To select the next tokens to be queried, we calculate two entropy measures $HE(w)$ and $RE(w)$ as the confidence score for each token w as follows:

$$HE(w) = -\sum \frac{V(h_j, w)}{\sum_{i=1}^{c} UA(P_i)} \cdot \log \frac{V(h_j, w)}{\sum_{i=1}^{c} UA(P_i)}$$

$HE(w)$ is the head vote entropy of token w in which h_j varies over all of the head values assigned to token w and $V(h_j, w)$ indicates the number of votes assigned to h_j as the head of token w and is calculated as follows:

$$V(h_j, w) = \sum_{\forall i, h_j = h(P_i, w)} UA(P_i)$$

In a same way, we calculate the relation vote entropy, $RE(w)$, for token w. We compute the entropy measure of token w as the mean value of the head entropy and relation entropy:

$$WE(w) = \frac{HE(w) + RE(w)}{2}$$

Finally, for a sentence S we assign the average entropy value of all its n tokens as the sentence entropy:

$$SE(S) = \sum_{i=1}^{n} \frac{WE(w_i)}{n}$$

After computing the confidence score of each token and sentence in $\mathcal{U}$, we select k sentences with most entropy value. For each chosen sentence, we ask the expert to annotate l tokens that has the highest entropy. Here, we select one of the parsers as the main parser and use it to annotate the rests of the words of those k selected sentences and add them all to $\mathcal{L}$.

4   Experimental Results

To evaluate the proposed method, we setup 3 different experiments. In the first one, we select the tokens that should be annotated randomly. A committee of parsers vote about the annotations of the rests of the words of sentences that should be added to the labeled pool. In the second experiment, we try the query by uncertainty sampling based on the method proposed by Mirroshandel and Nasr [3]. We setup these two experiments as baselines with which we compare the proposed method. The last experiment is the QBC active learning. We use MSTParser [4] as the main parser. To setup the QBC experiments, we make a committee of three parsers. Besides MSTParser, we add up Anna parser [5] and DeSR parser [6] as the rests of committee members.

In our experiments we use data sets from TUT corpora [7]. TUT corpora has been organized in five sections, and consists of 2,860 Italian sentences. Here we use the Wiki section that includes 459 sentences, randomly chosen from the Italian version of the Wikipedia. There are 14747 tokens in this corpus. The corpus has been divided in two parts. Test set $\mathcal{T}$ made of 25% of sentences and training set made of 75% of the sentences of the text. Initially we put 10% of training data in $\mathcal{L}$ as the labeled pool and the rests go to unlabeled pool $\mathcal{U}$.

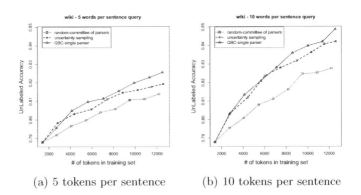

(a) 5 tokens per sentence   (b) 10 tokens per sentence

Fig. 1. Learning curves for dependency parsing of the Wiki data set

Figure 1 shows the learning curve for unlabeled dependency parsing of the Wiki data set when (a) 5 and (b) 10 tokens per sentence are selected for annotation. x arrow grows with the number of tokens in training set, and y arrow shows the test set accuracy that the main parser, MSTParser, can achieve. In both plots of figure 1 the methods that use an active query strategy do a better job than the one which is based on random selection strategy. Here QBC method performs better than uncertainty sampling. One reason could be the fact that different parsers generate different models that make different types of errors. Hence when a query is selected by the committee it is the one that most of the members have difficulty on predicting it and is more informative.

5   Conclusions and Future Work

We have proposed an active learning framework based on a committee of parsers for dependency parsing. The experimental results show that it can help the parser to reach better accuracy with less annotation cost. We are currently working on a model that instead of a single oracle we have a committee of experts with different levels of expertise.

Acknowledgments. This material is based upon work supported by the National Science Foundation under Grant No. IIS-0910165 and by a Tufts Collaborates 2011 seed grant.

References

1. Lewis, D.D., Gale, W.A.: A sequential algorithm for training text classifiers. In: The 17th Annual International ACM-SIGIR Conference on Research and Development in Information Retrieval, pp. 3–12 (1994)
2. Sebastian Seung, M.O., Sompolinsky, H.: Query by committee. In: The 5th Annual ACM Workshop on Computational Learning Theory, pp. 287–294 (1992)
3. Mirroshandel, S.A., Nasr, A.: Active learning for dependency parsing using partially annotated sentences. In: The 12th International Conference on Parsing Technologies, pp. 140–149 (2011)
4. McDonald, R., Pereira, F., Ribarov, K., Hajič, J.: Non-projective dependency parsing using spanning tree algorithms. In: Proc. of the Conference on Human Language Technology and Empirical Methods in Natural Language Processing, pp. 523–530 (2005)
5. Bohnet, B.: Top accuracy and fast dependency parsing is not a contradiction. In: Proc. of the 23rd International Conference on Computational Linguistics, pp. 89–97 (2010)
6. Attardi, G.: Experiments with a multilanguage non-projective dependency parser. In: Proc. of the Tenth Conference on Computational Natural Language Learning, pp. 166–170 (2006)
7. Bosco, C., Lombardo, V., Vassallo, D., Lesmo, L.: Building a treebank for italian: a data-driven annotation schema. In: Proc. of the 2nd International Conference on Language Resources and Evaluation, pp. 99–105 (2000)

PoliticalMashup Ngramviewer
Tracking Who Said What and When in Parliament

Bart de Goede[1,2], Justin van Wees[1,2], Maarten Marx[1], and Ridho Reinanda[1]

[1] ISLA, Informatics Istitute, University of Amsterdam
{maartenmarx,r.reinanda}@uva.nl
[2] Dispectu
bart@dispectu.com,
justin@dispectu.com

Abstract. The PoliticalMashup Ngramviewer is an application that allows a user to visualise the use of terms and phrases in the "Tweede Kamer" (the Dutch parliament). Inspired by the Google Books Ngramviewer[1], the PoliticalMashup Ngramviewer additionally allows for *faceting* on politicians and parties, providing a more detailed insight in the use of certain terms and phrases by politicians and parties with different points of view.

1 Introduction

The Google Books Ngramviewer [2] allows a user to query for phrases consisting of up to 5 terms. The application visualises the relative occurrence of these phrases in a corpus of digitised books written in a specific language over time.

Inspired by the Google Books Ngramviewer, the PoliticalMashup Ngramviewer[2] allows the user to query phrases consisting of up to 7 terms spoken in the Dutch parliament between 1815 and 2012, and visualise the occurrence of those phrases over time. Additionally, the PoliticalMashup Ngramviewer allows the user to facet on politicians and parties, allowing for comparison of the use of phrases through time by parties with different ideologies.

In this demonstration paper we describe the data used in this application, the approach taken with regard to analysing and indexing that data, and examples of how the application could be used for agenda setting-, framing- or linguistic research.

2 Ngramviewer

2.1 Data

The PoliticalMashup project [1] aims to make large quantities of political data, such as the proceedings of the Dutch parliament, available and searchable. In

---

[1] http://books.google.com/ngrams
[2] http://ngram.politicalmashup.nl

T. Aalberg et al. (Eds.): TPDL 2013, LNCS 8092, pp. 446–449, 2013.

Table 1. Distribution of unique n-grams in the Ngramviewer corpus for all terms, and with all *hapaxes* (terms that occur only once in the corpus) removed

n-gram	unique terms	without hapaxes
1-grams	2.773.826	992.291
2-grams	38.811.679	12.852.501
3-grams	170.314.738	38.648.440
4-grams	358.360.166	48.621.948
5-grams	498.848.849	36.838.184
6-grams	573.197.917	22.737.318
7-grams	606.867.133	13.655.460
total	2.249.174.308	174.346.142

addition, a goal of the project is to combine (or *mash up*) political data from different sources, in order to provide for *semantic search*, such as queries for events or persons.

This Ngramviewer is an example of why linking raw text to entities such as persons or parties can be useful: for each word ever uttered in the Dutch parliament, we know who said it, when it was said, to which party that person belonged at that time, and which role that person had at that point in the debate. By linking text to speakers, faceting on persons and parties is enabled.

The data this application uses originates from three sources: Staten-Generaal Digitaal[3], Officiële Bekendmakingen[4] and Parlementair Documentatiecentrum Leiden[5]. PoliticalMashup collected, analysed and transformed data from these sources, determining which speaker said what when, and to which party that speaker belonged at the time. This dataset is freely available via DANS EASY[6].

2.2 Indexing

The PoliticalMashup Ngramviewer is built on top of an Apache Lucene[7] index. We defined a document as *every word* of a specific *politician* spoken on a *particular day*. This allows for comparison of term frequencies per person, per day, which can be aggregated to words spoken by all members of a particular party in a particular time period (week, month, year, etcetera).

---

[3] Project of the Koninklijke Bibliotheek (http://kb.nl/en/), digitising all Dutch parliamentary proceedings between 1814 and 1995 (http://statengeneraaldigitaal.nl/overdezesite).

[4] Portal of the Dutch government, providing a search interface to all govermental proclamations, including parliamentary proceedings since 1995 (https://zoek.officielebekendmakingen.nl/).

[5] Biographical information on politicians and parties (http://www.parlement.com/).

[6] http://www.persistent-identifier.nl/urn:nbn:nl:ui:13-k2g8-5h

[7] http://lucene.apache.org/core/

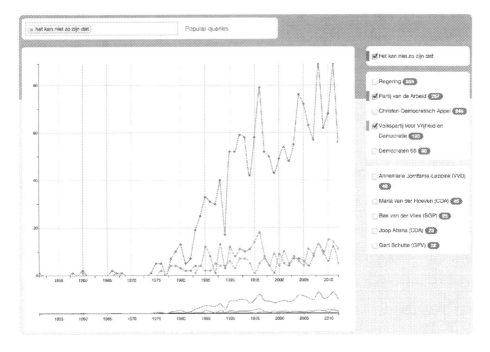

Fig. 1. The PoliticalMashup Ngramviewer interface showing results for "het kan niet zo zijn dat", with facets on PvdA and VVD, illustrating the rise of the phrase since the eighties

We used standard tokenisation and analysis on these documents; lowercasing, character folding and removal of punctuation, but *keeping* stopwords, in order to facilitate search on phrases containing common words such as articles or determiners. Additionally, we constructed word n-grams ($1 \leq n \leq 7$), respecting sentence boundaries.

The index contains data from 4 April 1815 to 9 September 2012, with 326.315 documents (where a document is all the text one person said on one day), 18.572 days for which there are documents, for in total 3.085 politicians which are members of 119 parties or the government. Table 1 shows the distribution of n-grams in the corpus. The second column shows the distribution of n-grams that occur more than once in the corpus, yielding a reduction of the vocabulary size of one order of magnitude. This is partly due to OCR errors (all proceedings predating 1995 are scans of paper archives).

2.3   Architecture

We constructed an inverted index in Lucene, storing the document frequency for each n-gram, and the term frequency for each document that n-gram occurs in.

Additionally, each document has attributes, such as the date the terms of that document were spoken, and identifiers that resolve to politicians and parties[8].

At query time, these identifiers are used to obtain information on persons and parties at query time, which are subsequently cached in a Redis key-value store. This Redis store is also used to cache query results and keep track of popular queries. Also, date frequencies are aggregated to frequencies per year at query time.

2.4 Examples

"Het kan niet zo zijn dat"[9] is a popular phrase used by (Dutch) politicians, lending their statement a more urgent feeling, (unconsciously) trying to manipulate their audience, while the person is just ventilating an opinion. Figure 1 shows the rapid increase in use since the eighties, and the use of the Ngramviewer for linguistic research.

3 Demonstration

The demonstration will show how the PoliticalMashup Ngramviewer can be used, displaying a graph of how often the entered phrases occur over time in the proceedings of the Dutch parliament. Also, it will demonstrate faceting on politicians and parties, showing the occurrence of the entered phrases over time for specific politicians and parties.

Future Extension.   We are planning to extend our Ngramviewer for digitized news articles from the Dutch Royal Library (84 millions articles). With such a large collection, performance and response time would definitely be an issue. Our strategy is to have the ngrams aggregation per year pre-computed beforehand. This way, displaying the frequency would simply be a matter of file lookup.

Acknowledgments. This research was supported by the Netherlands Organization for Scientific Research (NWO) under project number 380-52-005 (PoliticalMashup).

References

[1] Marx, M.: Politicalmashup,
   http://politicalmashup.nl/over-political-mashup/ (retrieved March, 2013)
[2] Michel, J.-B., Shen, Y.K., Aiden, A.P., Veres, A., Gray, M.K., Pickett, J.P., Hoiberg, D., Clancy, D., Norvig, P., Orwant, J., et al.: Quantitative analysis of culture using millions of digitized books. Science 331(6014), 176–182 (2011)

---

[8] PoliticalMashup maintains a resolver that maps identifiers to persons parties and proceedings.
[9] In English: "It is unacceptable that ... "

Monitrix – A Monitoring and Reporting Dashboard for Web Archivists

Rainer Simon[1] and Andrew Jackson[2]

[1] AIT - Austrian Institute of Technology, Donau-City-Str. 1,
1220 Vienna, Austria
rainer.simon@ait.ac.at
[2] The British Library,
Boston Spa, Wetherby
West Yorkshire, LS23 7BQ, UK
andrew.jackson@bl.uk

Abstract. This demonstration paper introduces *Monitrix*, an upcoming monitoring and reporting tool for Web archivists. Monitrix works in conjunction with the Heritrix 3 Open Source Web crawler and provides real-time analytics about an ongoing crawl, as well as summary information aggregated about crawled hosts and URLs. In addition, Monitrix monitors the crawl for the occurrence of suspicious patterns that may indicate undesirable behavior, such as crawler traps or blocking hosts. Monitrix is developed as a cooperation between the British Library's UK Web Archive and the Austrian Institute of Technology, and is licensed under the terms of the Apache 2 Open Source license.

Keywords: Web Archiving, Quality Assurance, Analytics.

1 Introduction

One of the most challenging aspects of Web Archiving is quality assurance. Current harvesting technology does not deliver 100% replicas of Web resources; and a long list of known technical issues exists that hamper the task of Web preservation [2]. One aspect is the complexity of Web content, being a mix of different content types, embedded scripts and streaming media, as well as content that is dynamically generated (the "deep Web" [4]). Another aspect is the scale of the task: the .uk top-level domain alone, for example, consists of more than 10 million hosts. Practical limitations such as finite computing resources and time, as well as limited legal mandates to libraries impose restrictions on the size and scope of the crawl. This forces decisions on aspects such as: suitable starting points ("seeds") for the crawl; criteria for curtailing the crawl of a particular host; the exclusion of specific hosts to those curtailing rules; or relevant and eligible domains outside the targeted domain which should be included in the crawl nonetheless, e.g. URL shorteners. (For a survey of of practices in various Web archiving initiatives worldwide refer to [1]).

To enable effective reporting, it is important to identify metrics by which the impact of such decisions can be measured, and to implement tools that

T. Aalberg et al. (Eds.): TPDL 2013, LNCS 8092, pp. 450–453, 2013.

capture these metrics automatically. State-of-the-art crawler software such as Heritrix[1], or archiving services such as Archive-It[2] offer a number of reports out of the box – e.g. on crawled seeds, hosts and URLs, downloaded file types, etc. However, these are rarely in a form that is suitable for wider dissemination to stakeholders outside the technical team. (E.g. Heritrix 3 provides reports in a bare-bones text format[3], Archive-It offers lists of comma-separated values for further processing in spreadsheet applications[4]. Additionally, it is often desirable to generate derivative metrics from the original raw numbers (such as histograms of specific properties), and to produce graphical visualizations in order to make the data useful enough to answer fundamental questions (*"are we making best use of our resources?"*, *"are we collecting what we want to collect"* [3]), identify gaps and issues early, and inform estimates of the current rate of completion.

In this TPDL 2013 demonstration, we introduce *Monitrix*, an Open Source Web crawl reporting tool currently being developed by the Austrian Institute of Technology under the guidance of the British Library's Web Archiving team. Monitrix works in conjunction with the Heritrix 3 Web crawler, and generates crawl analytics which it makes available in graphical form, in a browser-based user interface. Monitrix is licensed under the terms of the Apache 2 License, and available at https://github.com/ukwa/monitrix.

2   System Overview

Monitrix is a self-contained Web application which tracks the logs of one or more Heritrix 3 Web crawler instances. Based on the log data, it provides (i) **summary views** which expose aggregate information about different aspects of the crawl as a whole, (ii) **alerts** that flag up suspicious behavior observed during the crawl, and (iii) **search functionality** which allows a detailed inspection of specific hosts or crawled URLs.

2.1   Summary Views

In addition to global status information (e.g. time since start or last activity, total no. of URLs crawled, momentary values for no. of URLs crawled or MBytes downloaded per minute, etc.) Monitrix provides three distinct summary views:

The **crawl timeline** (Fig. 1, left) shows timeseries graphs for the total number of URLs crawled, the total download volume, the total number of new hosts visited, and the total number of hosts completed over time, either as standard or cumulative graphs.

The **hosts summary** (Fig. 1, right) shows the number of successfully crawled hosts and their distribution across top-level domains, lists the hosts that have

---

[1] https://webarchive.jira.com/wiki/display/Heritrix/Heritrix
[2] http://www.archive-it.org/
[3] https://webarchive.jira.com/wiki/display/Heritrix/Reports
[4] https://webarchive.jira.com/wiki/display/ARIH/
    Listing+of+Reports

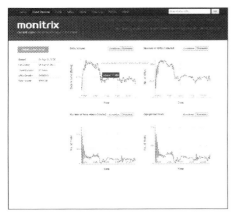 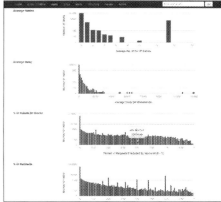

Fig. 1. Monitrix screenshots

reached the *crawl cap* (i.e. the maximum allowed download limit), and provides a number of histograms to help identify slow or otherwise problematic hosts: e.g. for average delay, number of HTTP retries, or percentage of requests blocked due to robots.txt rules. The user can "drill down" into the histograms to inspect the hosts represented through a particular bar by clicking on it.

The **virus log** summarizes the results of the virus check (which is usually conducted as part of the crawl).

2.2   Alerts

In order to gather requirements prior to the development of Monitrix, a workshop was conducted with experienced Web crawl coordinators from different institutions. As one part of this workshop, participants discussed heuristics which could be used to detect crawler traps and other undesirable crawler behaviour, e.g:

- hosts with many sub-domains (500+) are likely either to be "spammy" or to be sites with virtual sub-domains (e.g. blogs).
- very long URLs – i.e. where the number of path segments exceeds a certain threshold, or where there are multiple identical path segments - may be indicative of a problem.
- if a host is not serving any non-text resources any more, there is most likely a problem.

These heuristics have been implemented in Monitrix. They will trigger alerts which are then shown in the user interface. It is also foreseen that alerts will trigger E-Mail notifications to the crawl operator at a later stage.

2.3   Search

Monitrix' search feature not only supports search by URL or hostname, but also offers advanced search options to search by specific properties. It is, for example, possible to retrieve hosts by their average fetch delay, or URLs that were logged with a specific crawl annotation, e.g. one indicating a virus infection. For host searches, Monitrix generates pages summarizing all information collected about a specific host. These pages include, among other parameters: the time spent crawling the host; a graph showing the number of URLs crawled over time at this host (which allows a quick visual appraisal of whether the host has likely been completed); and distribution pie charts of the HTTP response codes, the content types and the virus scan results observed at this host.

3   Technical Architecture

The key technical challenge that Monitrix faces is the massive amount of data it needs to aggregate. The initial design has been dimensioned for a target size of 1 Terabyte of crawler log data – which corresponds to more than 3 billion log lines. In order to support reporting on such a scale with reasonable response times, Monitrix performs a number of pre-processing steps during ingest, and stores interim results (along with the raw log information) in a MongoDB NoSQL database. For example, all timeseries values (e.g. the number of URLs or hosts crawled over time, etc.) are pre-aggregated into a fixed base resolution raster, which can later be resampled into live timeseries visualizations on the screen with relatively low processing overhead. Monitrix also maintains a number of aggregated records and indexes on crawled hosts and alert conditions in the database. The frontend is implemented as standalone Java Web application, which is to be deployed alongside Heritrix. It also offers a JSON API, which enables loosely-coupled integration with external systems. Along with extensive testing and trial operation, additional work on integration options are expected to be the next steps in our future work.

References

1. Gomes, D., Miranda, J., Costa, M.: A survey on web archiving initiatives. In: Gradmann, S., Borri, F., Meghini, C., Schuldt, H. (eds.) TPDL 2011. LNCS, vol. 6966, pp. 408–420. Springer, Heidelberg (2011),
   http://dl.acm.org/citation.cfm?id=2042536.2042590
2. Hockx-Yu, H.: How good is good enough? quality assurance of harvested web resources (October 2012), http://britishlibrary.typepad.co.uk/
   webarchive/2012/10/how-good-is-good-enough-quality-assurance-
   of-harvested-web-resources.html
3. ISO Technical Committee 46 Working Group on Statistics and Quality Indicators for Web Archiving: Statistics and Quality Indicators for Web Archiving - Draft Technical Report (November 2012),
   http://netpreserve.org/sites/default/files/resources/
   SO_TR_14873_E_2012-10-02_DRAFT.pdf
4. Olston, C., Najork, M.: Web crawling. Found. Trends Inf. Retr. 4(3), 175–246 (2010),
   http://dx.doi.org/10.1561/1500000017

SpringerReference:
A Scientific Online Publishing System

Sebastian Lindner, Christian Simon, and Daniel Wieth

Dept. of Computer Science, University of Würzburg, Germany
{lindner,simon,wieth}@informatik.uni-wuerzburg.de

Abstract. This paper presents an online publishing system with focus on scientific peer reviewed content. The goal is to provide authors and editors with a platform to constantly publish and update content well in advance of their print editions across every subject. The techniques in this paper show some of the main components of the implemented document lifecycle. These include a custom document workflow to cope with HTML- and file-based content, an online editing platform including LaTeX formula generation, automatic link insertion between different documents, the generation of auto suggests to simplify search and navigation and a Solr-based search engine.

Keywords: digital library, semi structured data, dynamic scientific content, data mining, document workflow, collaboration.

1 Introduction

To keep up with the growing scientific developments, there is a need for a short time span between new content being available and its publication. In order to maintain high quality while publishing new articles at the pace of current research, the main focus of the document workflow lies on a peer reviewing process of new content.

SpringerReference[1] is a modern publishing system developed in cooperation with Springer Science+Business Media. The platform's goal is to collect documents in different formats like HTML or text documents (e.g. Microsoft Word) to simplify the workflow for authors and editors. Thus they can produce new online content and are able to publish selected chapters in book form. In this section we compare our online publishing platform to other currently available digital libraries (Greenstone, EPrints and DSpace) and an object repository system (Fedora[2]).

The articles of SpringerReference are protected by an IP address based authorization in addition to a user/password login system. Fedora also supports this, Greenstone, EPrints and DSpace use LDAP, Shibboleth and User/Group-based authentications [8]. In order to attract more visitors via search engines like Google and Bing, a small teaser of each article can be accessed without subscription.

Other publishing systems mostly work file-based, while the focus of SpringerReference is on HTML-based content [8]. Therefore an HTML editor with image upload functionality, LaTeX formula generation, HTML sanitization to prevent XSS and CSRF

---

[1] http://www.springerreference.com/
[2] http://www.wikipedia.org/, http://fedora-commons.org/

T. Aalberg et al. (Eds.): TPDL 2013, LNCS 8092, pp. 454–457, 2013.

attacks [11] and an automatic PDF generation are available on SpringerReference. In addition, available online editors extended with some custom plugins greatly simplify working on articles. On top of that a link generation process is used to find links between articles. These features are not available in EPrints, Greenstone or DSpace.

Similar to EPrints a reviewing process is integrated in the publishing workflow to achieve high quality content [2]. Greenstone and DSpace lack a reviewing process before the publishing of new content. Just like in DSpace, Solr/Lucene is used for searching [3]. Greenstone also offers the option to use Lucene to provide an incremental indexing capable search engine, but by default MG (Managing Gigabytes) is used [9].

2   Document Workflow

The document lifecycle is designed to collect and publish high quality content. The goal here is to accelerate the process of authors producing and editors reviewing content. Once an article is published, an author has the possibility to edit the article and create a new version. An updated article needs to pass the entire reviewing process again.

In order to encourage authors to create appealing content, a WYSIWYG editor based on the CKEditor and CKFinder software[3] is enhanced with state-of-the-art multimedia tools. Both can be extended by a plugin system. Uploaded images are automatically converted into suitable file formats (PNG, JPEG), re-encoded and resized for optimal compression. Additionally, plugins for on-the-fly LaTeX preview generation help the author to include mathematic formulas. Depending on its complexity, a formula is rendered as HTML by texvc or as image by JLaTexMath/LaTeX[4]. If JLatexMath is not able to render the formula correctly, a full-featured LaTeX system produces the image. This results in 112.000 HTML, 132.000 JLatexMath and 52.000 LaTeX generated formulas.

Besides the online editing workflow, the platform offers the possibility to upload document manuscript files. However both workflows are bound to the same reviewing process. While an HTML article is directly published on the website, file-based submissions must be converted to HTML first.

All published versions of an article remain accessible and have a DOI-based permanent link [6] like in Greenstone [10], DSpace [7] and Fedora[4].

3   Automatic Link Generation

Besides the possibility to insert links between documents manually with the help of a CKEditor plugin, an automatic link generation is done every time an article is published. This process uses the Apache UIMA[5] framework and tries to find article titles in other documents with a certain fuzziness. First of all, punctuation characters are removed from the article titles and the order of short articles titles (two or three words) is discarded to capture links like 'Stem Cells, Muscle'.

---

[3] "What you see is what you get", http://ckeditor.com/,
http://cksource.com/ckfinder
[4] http://www.mediawiki.org/wiki/Texvc,
http://forge.scilab.org/index.php/p/jlatexmath/
[5] Unstructured Information Management Architecture, http://uima.apache.org

If some titles are equal or similar, a disambiguation page with all alternative link results is shown. In this case the membership of an article to a book and a library is used as a ranking criteria. Other approaches use the intersection of all links pointing to two articles to calculate a ranking value [5]. In the following table you can see that most of the generated links have a single, definite target, while only a small amount of links need to be disambiguated (see Table 1).

Table 1. Distribution of entries per link disambiguation page

Disambiguation entries per link	1	2	3	4	5	6
Number of link targets affected	112975	6954	1642	547	200	74

To avoid excessive linking to the same document, the number of links to the same destination is restricted to a certain window of words. By collecting the frequency of all one word and two word combinations and removing the intersection of the most common ones with article titles from link generation, too frequent links like 'AND' in the library computer science are avoided.

In SpringerReference 135.000 of 230.000 documents are the target of at least one link. The other titles did not appear in any article or are specifically excluded from linking (ca. 85.000). Altogether a total amount of 2.200.000 links is placed in the corpus with an average of 16 links in articles that have automatically generated links.

4   Indexing and Search

In addition to a hierarchical navigation on libraries, books and chapters, the system offers a full-featured, well adapted search engine with OpenSearch support. Because of the access restriction (see Sect. 1), the content of the plattform is invisible for guest users, which prevents search engines like Google or Bing from indexing the content. Therefore a custom search engine is required. Like SpringerReference, DSpace uses Solr/Lucene for searching [8], Greenstone provides it optionally [1]. Fedora implements a graph search with SQL-like syntax to query the object repository [4].

The platform assists users with formulating meaningful search queries and typing them completely by offering auto suggestion of titles and section titles. To further improve ranking calculations, a semantic category indicating the quality of the article is also stored as a non-searchable metadata field.

$$\text{ranking Value} = (\text{fl\_title} \cdot 50.0 + \text{fl\_subtitle} \cdot 10.0 + \text{fl\_text}) \cdot f \qquad (1)$$

Equation (1) shows a slightly simplified version of the applied ranking function. The variables fl_* denote the TF/IDF ranking value of the search terms within the corresponding field, $\cdot N$ is a multiplicative boost value for the field. Since articles on Springer-Reference are of scientific nature, their titles are meaningful in most cases. The factor f is $\frac{1}{10}$, if the ranked article is just a short introductory article and 1 otherwise.

On change of an article, the system triggers a Solr delta update, so added or altered documents are indexed.

5 Conclusion and Future Work

As shown previously, SpringerReference has similar features compared to other publishing platforms like Greenstone, EPrints and DSpace. On top of that, the platform assists authors with a set of unique features to produce high quality articles. This includes an easy to use HTML editor, LaTeX and link generation and image processing. This helps submitting several hundred articles per month. Additionally the system makes the content available to search engines. It provides navigation functionality, auto suggestion and a search engine to support users to find the most relevant content.

In future, the current capabilities will be extended to use the platform as a general purpose workflow tool for content creation. The main focus will be to better support XML based import and export of content and meta information. File-based content and editing is expected to play a more significant role on the system. In these days publishing latest scientific developments becomes more and more important. Springer-Reference offers this kind of functionality, while further supporting the workflow for traditional book generation. We expect exactly this type of dual workflow to be relevant in the future.

References

1. Bainbridge, D., Osborn, W., Witten, I.H., Nichols, D.M.: Extending Greenstone for Institutional Repositories. In: Sugimoto, S., Hunter, J., Rauber, A., Morishima, A. (eds.) ICADL 2006. LNCS, vol. 4312, pp. 303–312. Springer, Heidelberg (2006)
2. Beazley, M.R.: Eprints Institutional Repository Software: A Review. Partnership: the Canadian Journal of Library and Information Practice and Research 5(2) (2011)
3. Biswas, G., Paul, D.: An evaluative study on the open source digital library softwares for institutional repository: Special reference to Dspace and greenstone digital library. International Journal of Library and Information Science 2(1), 1–10 (2010)
4. Lagoze, C., Payette, S., Shin, E., Wilper, C.: Fedora: an architecture for complex objects and their relationships. International Journal on Digital Libraries 6(2), 124–138 (2006)
5. Milne, D., Witten, I.H.: Learning to link with wikipedia. In: Proceedings of the 17th ACM Conference on Information and knowledge Management, pp. 509–518. ACM (2008)
6. Paskin, N.: Digital object identifier (DOI) system. Encyclopedia of Library and Information Sciences 3, 1586–1592 (2008)
7. Smith, M., Barton, M., Bass, M., Branschofsky, M., McClellan, G., Stuve, D., Tansley, R., Walker, J.H.: DSpace: An Open Source Dynamic Digital Repository. D-Lib Magazine 9(1) (2003)
8. Tramboo, S., Humma, Shafi, S.M., Gul, S.: A Study on the Open Source Digital Library Software's: Special Reference to DSpace, EPrints and Greenstone. International Journal of Computer Applications 59(16) (Dezember 2012)
9. Witten, I.H., Bainbridge, D., Boddie, S., Don, K.J., McPherson, J.R.: Inside Greenstone Collections. Greenstone Digital Library (2003)
10. Witten, I.H., Boddie, S.J., Bainbridge, D., McNab, R.J.: Greenstone: a comprehensive open-source digital library software system. In: Proceedings of the Fifth ACM Conference on Digital Libraries, pp. 113–121. ACM (2000)
11. Zeller, W., Felten, E.W.: Cross-Site Request Forgeries: Exploitation and Prevention (2008)

Data Searchery
Preliminary Analysis of Data Sources Interlinking

Paolo Manghi and Andrea Mannocci

Consiglio Nazionale delle Ricerche
Istituto di Scienza e Tecnologie dell'Informazione "A. Faedo"
name.surname@isti.cnr.it

Abstract. The novel e-Science's data-centric paradigm has proved that interlinking publications and research data objects coming from different realms and data sources (e.g. publication repositories, data repositories) makes dissemination, re-use, and validation of research activities more effective. Scholarly Communication Infrastructures are advocated for bridging such data sources, by offering tools for identification, creation, and navigation of relationships. Since realization and maintenance of such infrastructures is expensive, in this demo we propose a lightweight approach for "preliminary analysis of data source interlinking" to help practitioners at evaluating whether and to what extent realizing them can be effective. We present Data Searchery, a configurable tool enabling users to easily plug-in data sources from different realms with the purpose of cross-relating their objects, be them publications or research data, by identifying relationships between their metadata descriptions.

Keywords: Interoperability, Interlinking, Research Data, Publications.

1 Introduction

The Research Digital Libraries (RDLs) ecosystem is ever growing since creating and publishing a proprietary *publication repository* is essentially mandatory for any institution striving to gain a modicum of visibility and relevance. In addition, the advent of e-Science and data-intensive research [1] has fired a similar trend for research data. *Data repositories* for persisting and publishing research data are becoming common in many scientific communities [2].

In such a scenario, being able to correctly infer relationships among objects belonging to different domains, i.e. publication-publication, publication-data and data-data interlinking, becomes crucial in order to: (*i*) foster multi-disciplinarity by looking at adherences among distinct disciplines; (*ii*) enable a better review, reproduction and re-use of research activities [3]. Identifying which *data sources* are worth bridging in such a plethora of publication and data repositories from different scientific domains is not an easy task. Nonetheless, understanding which kind of relationships can be inferred across objects of different data sources is yet another challenge. Finally, interoperability issues generally arise, since access protocols, metadata formats and object models are likely to differ for different data sources, due to technological and scientific domain peculiarities. Scientific

T. Aalberg et al. (Eds.): TPDL 2013, LNCS 8092, pp. 458–461, 2013.
© Springer-Verlag Berlin Heidelberg 2013

communities cope with these needs by realizing *Scholarly Communication Infrastructures* (SCIs). These provide tools and services to aggregate objects coming from different data sources and realms and enable both humans and machinery to interconnect such objects by identifying relationships via user-interfaces or advanced inference-by-mining algorithms (e.g. OpenAIRE [4]).

Since requirements change both from case to case and over time, SCIs have to specifically address ever changing requirements and therefore must be planned and designed very carefully. Additionally, once deployed they have to undergo a continuous and expensive process of extension, optimization and maintenance. Thus, their cost in terms of time and skills tends to be generally high and sometime prohibitive for the smallest communities. For such reasons, planning the realization of a SCI would benefit from tools permitting a lightweight preliminary analysis of data source interlinking possibilities. In this demo we present the prototype of Data Searchery, a tool aiding practitioners willing to realize SCIs to evaluate whether and to what extent the intended SCI could be effective for the community. The tool offers user interfaces to run and cross advanced metadata searches over data sources and therefore identify relationships between their objects. Data Searchery may also be useful for scientific user communities willing to identify relationships between objects between data sources not yet aggregated and interconnected in the context of a SCI.

2 Data Searchery Overview

Data Searchery enables users to surf and (best-effort) correlate metadata coming from two different data sources, here referenced as *origin* and *target* data sources, which may contain publication or research data objects. A data source can be either a sole repository serving a single institution or an aggregative data infrastructure serving a research community; e.g. DataCite[1] for research data. The approach relies on the metadata descriptions of the data source objects. The more metadata are accurate and thorough, the more the recall of the approach tends to be accurate, but in general, poor or incomplete metadata content does not necessarily invalidate the generic reasoning behind the approach. As shown in Fig.1, the prototype guides the user in a two-step process: (*i*) querying an origin data source of preference; (*ii*) starting from one record of interest returned by the first query, drafting a second query on a target data source of preference. The user drafts the first query by typing keywords and (optionally) by narrowing down to one or more collections made available by the origin data source. The second query is drafted by automatically extracting keywords from one metadata record of interest, chosen among the ones returned by the first query. Keywords are extracted by applying one or more *extraction filters* selected by the user from a list; as in the first step, the user can narrow the query down to one or more collections exposed by the target data source.

Harvesting, storing and cleaning metadata falls out the scope of Data Searchery which on the contrary relies solely on "live-queries" over remote data sources;

---

[1] The DataCite Initiative, `http://datacite.org/`

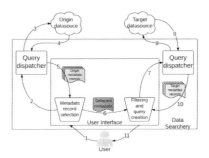

Fig. 1. Data Searchery interlinking session

no standard protocol such as OAI-PMH or OAI-ORE is thus involved. The only requirement is the availability of a search API at the data source (e.g. Solr API). Relevant information is extracted from results and rendered onto the screen as the search API provides it (e.g. ordered by field relevance in the case of Solr index) without any additional re-ordering or proximity-scoring policy. Data Searchery is designed to be a general-purpose tool handling the abstractions: *data source*, i.e. an API capable of responding to keyword queries and collection queries, *data source sub-collections*, i.e. an API returning the list of possible data source collections, and *extraction filters*, i.e. functions inferring a set of keywords from an input record (e.g. identifying and extracting given ontology terms from the *abstract* field). The user interface adapts itself seamlessly to additions, changes, or removal of such abstractions. Data Searchery is open source and developed in Java, thus developers can easily add instances of data sources and extraction filters as new implementations of corresponding Java classes.

A running instance of the Data Searchery prototype with some built-in data sources and extraction filters can be found here: http://datasearchery-prototype.research-infrastructures.eu/datasearchery#/search.

3   The Demonstration

During the demo, users will first be driven through explanatory and meaningful interlinking sessions, then given free access to the tool. Fig.2 shows the tool's UI, the search panel on the left-side. The user has selected DataCite as original data source and the OpenAIRE infrastructure [4] as target data source, choosing from a drop down menu of available data sources. Her/his first search is on DataCite with the keywords *"Abyssal brown algae"*. The search results are fetched and rendered on the left side of a two-column layout. then the user is interested in finding cross-links between the dataset *"n-Alkanes and phenols in bottom. . . "* with publications in OpenAIRE. To this aim, she/he selects both keywords and organisms extraction filters from the record drop-down menu[2] and fires the search. The results are displayed on the right-side column in the screen and dynamically adapt to changes in the search parameters.

---

[2] WhatIzIt - EBI, http://www.ebi.ac.uk/webservices/whatizit/

It must be noticed that the prototype relies entirely on dynamic interaction with data sources, hence the same interlinking session, run at different times, may return different number of hits or results ordering depending on the changes to the original content.

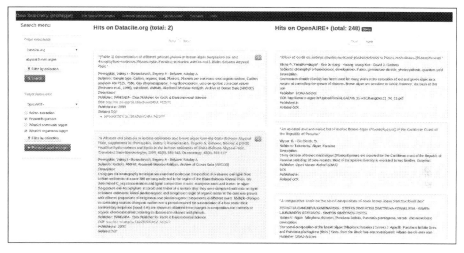

Fig. 2. Screenshot of Data Searchery web app

4   Conclusions and Future Work

The ability to correlate either data or publications hosted in different data sources and realms is becoming a key aspect in modern scholarly communication. SCIs advocate this new trend, but their realization and maintenance raises serious sustainability issues. Data Searchery is a configurable tool allowing for lightweight and preliminary evaluation of the existence of meaningful links between objects from different data sources. Currently the tool is being extended with functionalities to elaborate extensive statistical reports on the overall degree of correlation between two data sources w.r.t. a set of user queries (e.g. a pool of authors and/or keywords).

References

1. Gray, J.: A transformed scientific method. In: The Fourth Paradigm: Data-Intensive Scientific Discovery. Microsoft Research (2009)
2. Callaghan, S., Donegan, S.: Making data a first class scientific output: Data citation and publication by NERC's environmental data centres. International Journal of Digital Curation (2012)
3. Reilly, S., Schallier, W., Schrimpf, S., Smit, E., Wilkinson, M.: Report on integration of data and publications. ODE Opportunities for Data Exchange
4. Manghi, P., Bolikowski, L., Manola, N., Shirrwagen, J., Smith, T.: Openaireplus: the european scholarly communication data infrastructure. D-Lib Magazine 18(9-10) (September-October 2012)

PATHSenrich: A Web Service Prototype for Automatic Cultural Heritage Item Enrichment

Eneko Agirre, Ander Barrena, Kike Fernandez, Esther Miranda,
Arantxa Otegi, and Aitor Soroa

IXA NLP Group, University of the Basque Country UPV/EHU
arantza.otegi@ehu.es

Abstract. Large amounts of cultural heritage material are nowadays available through online digital library portals. Most of these cultural items have short descriptions and lack rich contextual information. The PATHS project has developed experimental enrichment services. As a proof of concept, this paper presents a web service prototype which allows independent content providers to enrich cultural heritage items with a subset of the full functionality: links to related items in the collection and links to related Wikipedia articles. In the future we plan to provide more advanced functionality, as available offline for PATHS.

1 Introduction

Large amounts of cultural heritage (CH) material are now available through online digital library portals, such as Europeana[1]. Europeana hosts millions of books, paintings, films, museum objects and archival records that have been digitised throughout Europe. Europeana collects contextual information or metadata about different types of content, which the users can use for their searches.

The main strength of Europeana lays in the vast number of items it contains. Sometimes, though, this quantity comes at the cost of a restricted amount of metadata, with many items having very short descriptions and a lack of rich contextual information. One of the goals of the PATHS project[2] is precisely to enrich CH items, using a selected subset of Europeana as a testbed[1].

Whithin the project, this enrichment will make possible to create a system that acts as an interactive personalised tour guide through Europeana collections, offering suggestions about items to look at and assist in their interpretation by providing relevant contextual information from related items within Europeana and items from external sources like Wikipedia. Users of such digital libraries may require information for purposes such as learning and seeking answers to questions. This additional information supports users in fulfilling their information need, as the evaluation of the first PATHS prototype shows [2].

In this paper we present a web service prototype which allows independent content providers to enrich CH items. Specifically, the service enriches the items

---

[1] http://www.europeana.eu/portal/
[2] http://www.paths-project.eu

T. Aalberg et al. (Eds.): TPDL 2013, LNCS 8092, pp. 462–465, 2013.

with two types of information. On the one hand, the item will be linked to similar items within the collection. On the other hand, the item will be linked to Wikipedia articles which are related to it.

There have been many attempts to automatically enrich cultural heritage metadata. Some projects (for instance, MIMO-DB[3] or MERLIN[4]) relate CH objects with terms of an external authority or vocabulary. Some others (like MACE[5] or YUMA [6]) adopt a collaborative annotation paradigm for metadata enrichment. To our knowledge, PATHS is the first project using semantic NLP processing to link CH items to similar items or external Wikipedia articles.

The current service has limited bandwidth, and provides a selected subset of the enrichment functionality available internally in the PATHS project. The quality of the links produce is also slightly lower, although we plan to improve it in the short future. However, we think that the prototype is useful to demonstrate the potential to construct a web service for automatically enriching CH items with high quality information.

2   Demo Description

The web service takes as input one CH item represented following the Europeana Data Model (EDM) in JSON format, as exported by the Europeana API v2.0[7] (a sample record is provided in the interface). The web service returns the following:

- A list of 10 closely related items within the collection.
- A list of Wikipedia pages which are related to the target item.

Figure 1 shows a snapshot of the web service. The service is publicly accessible following the URL `http://ixa2.si.ehu.es/paths_wp2/paths_wp2.pl`.

The enrichment is performed by analyzing the metadata associated with the item, i.e., the title of the item, its description, etc. The next sections briefly describe how this enrichment is performed.

2.1   Related Items within the Collection

The list of related items is obtained by first creating a query with the content of the title, subject and description fields (stopwords are removed). The query is then posted to a SOLR search engine[8]. The SOLR search engine accesses an index created with the subset of Europeana items already enriched offline within the PATHS project. In that way, the most related Europeana items in the subset are obtained, and the identifiers of those related items are listed. Note that the related items used internally in the PATHS project are produced using more sophisticated methods. Please refer to [1] for further details.

---

[3] `http://www.mimo-international.com`
[4] `http://www.ucl.ac.uk/ls/merlin`
[5] `http://www.mace-project.eu`
[6] `http://dme.ait.ac.at/annotation`
[7] `http://preview.europeana.eu/portal/api-introduction.html`
[8] `http://lucene.apache.org/solr/`

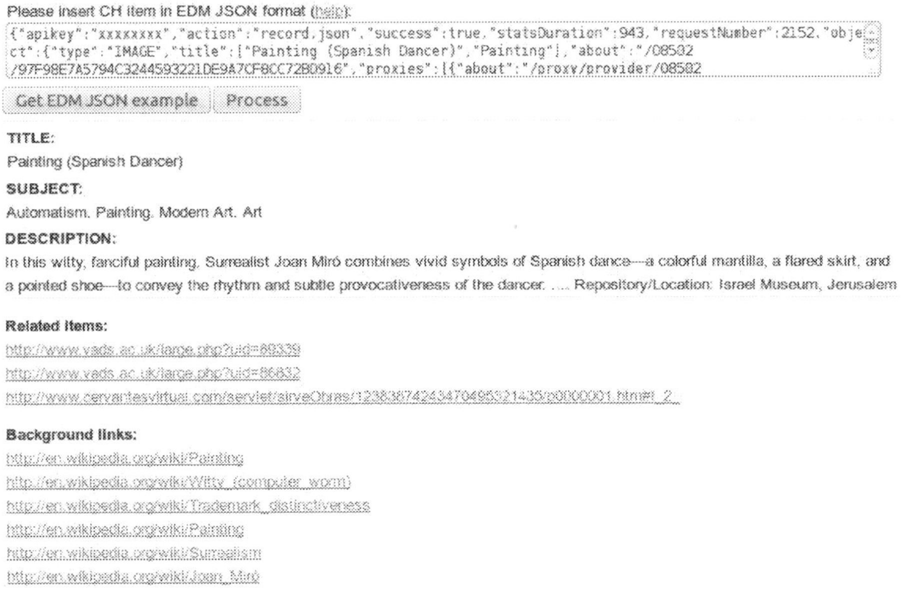

Please insert CH item in EDM JSON format (help):

{"apikey":"xxxxxxxx","action":"record.json","success":true,"statsDuration":943,"requestNumber":2152,"obje
ct":{"type":"IMAGE","title":["Painting (Spanish Dancer)","Painting"],"about":"/08502
/97F98E7A5794C3244593221DE9A7CF8CC72B0916","proxies":[{"about":"/proxy/provider/08502

Get EDM JSON example   Process

TITLE:
Painting (Spanish Dancer)
SUBJECT:
Automatism. Painting. Modern Art. Art
DESCRIPTION:
In this witty, fanciful painting, Surrealist Joan Miró combines vivid symbols of Spanish dance—a colorful mantilla, a flared skirt, and
a pointed shoe—to convey the rhythm and subtle provocativeness of the dancer. ... Repository/Location: Israel Museum, Jerusalem

Related Items:
http://www.vads.ac.uk/large.php?uid=88339
http://www.vads.ac.uk/large.php?uid=86832
http://www.cervantesvirtual.com/servlet/sirveObras/12383874243470495321435/p0000001.htm#I_2_

Background links:
http://en.wikipedia.org/wiki/Painting
http://en.wikipedia.org/wiki/Witty_(computer_worm)
http://en.wikipedia.org/wiki/Trademark_distinctiveness
http://en.wikipedia.org/wiki/Painting
http://en.wikipedia.org/wiki/Surrealism
http://en.wikipedia.org/wiki/Joan_Miró

Fig. 1. Web service interface. It consists of a text area to introduce the input item
in JSON format (top). The "Get EDM JSON example" button can be used to get an
input example. Once a JSON record is typed, click "Process" button to get the output.
The output (bottom) consists on a list of related items and background links.

2.2   Related Wikipedia Articles

For linking the items to Wikipedia articles we follow an implementation similar
to the method described in [3]. This method creates a *dictionary*, an association
between string mentions with all possible articles the mention can refer to. Our
dictionary is constructed using the title of the Wikipedia article, the redirect
pages, the disambiguation pages and the anchor texts from Wikipedia links.
Mentions are lower-cased and all text between parenthesis is removed. If the
mention links to a disambiguation page, it is associated with all possible articles
the disambiguation page points to. Besides, each association between a mention
and article is scored with the prior probability, estimated as the number of
times that the mention occurs in the anchor text of an article. Note that such
dictionaries can disambiguate any mention, just returning the highest-scoring
article for this particular mention.

   Once the dictionary is built, the web service analyzes the title, subject and
description fields of the CH item and matches the longest substring within those
fields with entries in the dictionary. When a match is found, the Wikipedia article
with highest score for this entry is returned. Note that the links to Wikipedia
in the PATHS project are produced using more sophisticated methods. Please
refer to [1] for further details.

3   Conclusions and Future Work

This paper presents a web service prototype which automatically enriches CH items with metadata. The web service is inspired in the enrichment work carried out in the PATHS project, but, contrary to the batch methodology used in the project, this enrichment is performed online. The prototype has been designed for demonstration purposes, to showcase the feasibility of providing full-fledged automatic enrichment.

Our plans for the future include moving the offline enrichment services which are currently being evaluated in the PATHS project to the web service. In the case of related Wikipedia articles, we will take into account the context of the matched entities, which improves the quality of the links [4], and we will include a filtering algorithm to discard entities that are not relevant. Regarding related items, we will classify them according to the type of relation [5]. In addition we plan to automatically organize the items hierarchically, according to a Wikipedia-based vocabulary [6].

Acknowledgements. The research leading to these results was carried out as part of the PATHS project (http://www.paths-project.eu) funded by European Communitys Seventh Framework Programme (FP7/2007- 2013) under grant agreement no. 270082. The work has been also funded by the Basque Government (project IBILBIDE, SAIOTEK S-PE12UN089).

References

1. Otegi, A., Agirre, E., Soroa, A., Aletras, N., Chandrinos, C., Fernando, S., Gonzalez-Agirre, A.: Report accompanying D2.2: Processing and Representation of Content for Second Prototype. PATHS Project Deliverable (2012),
   http://www.paths-project.eu/eng/content/download/2489/18113/version/2/file/D2.2.Content+Processing-2nd+Prototype-revised.v2.pdf
2. Griffiths, J., Goodale, P., Minelli, S., de Polo, A., Agerri, R., Soroa, A., Hall, M., Bergheim, S.R., Chandrinos, K., Chryssochoidis, G., Fernie, K., Usher, T.: D5.1: Evaluation of the first PATHS prototype. PATHS Project Deliverable (2012),
   http://www.paths-project.eu/eng/Resources/D5.1-Evaluation-of-the-1st-PATHS-Prototype
3. Chang, A.X., Spitkovsky, V.I., Yeh, E., Agirre, E., Manning, C.D.: Stanford-UBC entity linking at TAC-KBP. In: Proceedings of TAC 2010, Gaithersburg, Maryland, USA (2010)
4. Han, X., Sun, L.: A Generative Entity-Mention Model for Linking Entities with Knowledge Base. In: Proceedings of the ACL, Portland, Oregon, USA (2011)
5. Agirre, E., Aletras, N., Gonzalez-Agirre, A., Rigau, G., Stevenson, M.: UBC_UOS-TYPED: Regression for typed-similarity. In: Second Joint Conference on Lexical and Computational Semantics (*SEM), Atlanta, Georgia, USA (2013)
6. Fernando, S., Hall, M., Agirre, E., Soroa, A., Clough, P., Stevenson, M.: Comparing Taxonomies for Organising Collections of Documents. In: Proceedings of COLING 2012, Mumbai, India (2013)

Leveraging Domain Specificity
to Improve Findability in OER Repositories

Darina Dicheva and Christo Dichev

Winston-Salem State University, 601 S. Martin Luther King J. Drive,
Winston Salem, NC 27110, USA
{dichevad,dichevc}@wssu.edu

Abstract. This paper addresses the problem of improving the findability of open educational resources (OER) in Computer Science. It presents a domain-specific OER reference repository and portal aimed at increasing the low OER use. The focus is on enhancing the search and navigation capabilities. A distinctive feature is the proposed *query-by-navigation* method.

Keywords: Open Educational Resources, Information Retrieval, Search.

1 Introduction

As the OER movement emerges into a mainstream, it is evident that the findability of OER is one of the major barriers towards their wider use and reuse. The problem of finding open content resources of interest is complex. One of the reasons is that the open content is distributed across many different institutional repositories and individual sites. Identifying these repositories and sites and searching in each of them is a significant barrier for the large-scale uptake and reuse of OER [1]. This motivated our work. We developed a Reference Repository and Portal for accessing Computer Science OER – the CS OER Portal[1]. It is based on Drupal, an open source content management system. We adopted Drupal for its security, rapid evolution, modular architecture, and abundance of contributed modules that meet a wide array of needs. Although the repository is in a testing phase, it is functional and offers references to a significant number of Computing OER.

2 Support for Resource Findability

Our preliminary user studies [2, 3] were critical to ensuring that the proposed reference repository will gain acceptance. They indicated several reasons for the low OER use, with the dominating one being the insufficient support for finding relevant open content. We distinguish between two levels of helping users to find needed content stored in repositories. The first one is to bring the users to the repository and the second one starts after their landing there. The latter includes helping users locate

---

[1] http://iiscs.wssu.edu/drupal/csoer

T. Aalberg et al. (Eds.): TPDL 2013, LNCS 8092, pp. 466–469, 2013.

relevant content with minimal search and navigation efforts. To achieve this, we focused on using the subject-orientation of the portal for making the search more efficient and providing intuitive navigation mechanisms for stimulating content exploration. The three guiding principles for categorizing resources are: *predictability* (organize resources in predictable groups); *discoverability* (provide multiple ways for locating resources); *typicality* (provide support for common resource needs).

Among the primary design objectives were: (1) creating an environment where categorization and search play complementary roles; and (2) exploiting common types of users' searching behavior in the chosen domain-specific environment in order to predict possible navigational steps. It is known that in certain situations, the search often follows common patterns. This can be exploited for bringing content that would result from an anticipated search beforehand, which can eliminate further searches. The implemented multi-strategy approach includes: navigation (structural and tag-based), search (standard search, faceted search and advanced text search extended with faceted search), topical recommendation, and 'query-by-navigation' search.

2.1   Searching for Courses by Course Topics

Our studies indicate that searching for a course relevant to an instructor's task by typing the course title in the search box of a conventional search tool usually brings many irrelevant or duplicated results. There is no standard or agreement in naming courses. For example, similar content can be found under "Introduction to Programming" and "Introduction to Computer Science". Even with established courses, such as "Operating Systems", the course content and structure may vary from campus to campus. Thus finding a useful course involves mapping an intended structure of topics and corresponding instructional materials occurring in the mind of the searcher to a course from a set of courses in a repository. One of the aims of our work was to simplify this task by reducing it to a comparison of two metadata sets. Our approach is based on the assumption that users who look for courses are guided by a certain *descriptive topical framework*. Instances of such framework are included in course documents under names, such as "course outline", "topics covered", "schedule", etc. Accordingly, in the CS OER Portal all courses are represented by descriptive metadata including the course name, a list of topics and a set of tags.

Assume that we have a search engine providing a search box with sufficient space, where the user can enter as a query the title of a course along with the course topics. The expectation is that the search engine will retrieve all courses matching the query and will display them ranked based on their similarity to the input. Unfortunately, the standard Drupal search could not be used for implementing this scenario. It is based on the Boolean query model, where the predictor of relevance is whether all query terms occur in the document. In addition, long queries are problematic since search tools typically impose certain limits on the query length.

2.2   Query-by-Navigation

It turned out that the above scenario for easing the search for relevant courses could be implemented within a framework with suitable organization by replacing the classic search with a version of a *query by navigation* [4]. Our idea was to create a directory-like interface for query formulation reflecting the current knowledge structure in Computer Science education. Although there is no such standard structure, an agreed upon set of topics is emerging with the maturation of Computer Science, which is forming the core of a curricula. This process is shaped by authoritative scholars and textbook authors. The *ACM/IEEE Curriculum Recommendation*[2] is an effort intended to tailor the CS curriculum to the dynamic landscape of computing. The result is a *model curriculum* incorporating a consensus view of the Computer Science community. The identified body of knowledge for Computer Science Undergraduate Programs is topically organized in a set of "Knowledge Areas" (CS subjects), each of which provides a list of learning outcomes. Thus the ACM/IEEE Curriculum Recommendation was chosen to provide a structural framework for our directory-like interface.

If we store the components of the *knowledge areas-units-topics* hierarchy defined by the Curriculum Recommendation as searchable units in the repository, by navigating the hierarchy we can land on a knowledge area of interest. We can use then the listed topics to search for matching courses from the repository. With this approach the users can also find resources of interest hidden under alternative course names (for example, course topics typically found in "Human-Computer Interaction", may be listed under "User Interface Design and Implementation"), since the relevance is measured based on the proportion of matching topics rather than just on course titles.

The rationality of this approach rests on the following heuristics: (1) in CS many course-related queries can be anticipated; (2) if search is predictable, then it is avoidable in its traditional sense. Our studies indicated that users often search for course content by typing the course title in the search box. If a set of common course and topic titles is known, then we can: (i) eliminate the process of entering them; (ii) improve the search relevance and ranking for such courses and resources. While the first gain looks simple, it eliminates one of the major challenges of searching - choosing what terms to use in the search query. In addition, materials traditionally part of a certain course can be found in the resources for another course. Searching by topics is aimed at locating relevant resources independently of their course grouping.

The realization of the above principles resulted in an interface, which is a combination of navigation and search. The idea behind this realization was to present the user with an interface that looks similar to that of a (link) directory. In our case however the clickable links incorporate a combined semantics of a directory and search engine input. When a user activates a link, it opens the next level of the hierarchy showing the corresponding body of topics and at the same time sending these topics as a query to the search engine. This way we can capitalize on users' familiarity with directories and relieve them from guessing the appropriate search terms associated with the proverbial search box, while harnessing the power of the search engines.

The implementation of this approach required the creation of a *transparent* document collection, mapping the ACM/IEEE Curriculum Recommendation structure. Each document in this collection contains the name of the corresponding hierarchy component along with its description and is accessible through a link appearing in the page corresponding to its parent in the topic hierarchy. When appropriate, the titles of the stored documents were extended to include alternative names. Having this document collection

---

[2] http://www.acm.org//education/curricula/ComputerScience2008.pdf

in place, the search for relevant courses and resources in the repository was realized as a two-step process. When a user selects "Browse Courses/Resources based on the ACM/IEEE CS Curriculum" from the front portal page, they are presented with the top level of the Curriculum and can select any course listed there. If, for example, they select "Operating Systems", the algorithm returns the corresponding list of course topics. In parallel, the retrieved list of topics is passed as an input to the algorithm described in Section 2.1, which retrieves and displays the set of courses in the repository matching the input that is, matching the topical structure as defined by the ACM/IEEE Curriculum Recommendation. If the user further selects a topic, the system will present all resources relevant to the selected topic. This search capability combined with the simplicity of its use is what makes the CS OER Portal different from other OER reference repositories, such as OER Commons[3].

3   Conclusion

The concept of resource findability includes two tasks: locating the repository and locating the content of interest inside the repository. While the focus of the presented work is on the second task, the created reference repository incorporates features addressing both of them. The task of locating resources locally has also two sides: support for navigation and support for search. We addressed the navigation challenges by organizing resources in predictable groupings (to make navigation intuitive) and by introducing query-by- navigation user interface, which combines the search and navigation functionality. The quality of the search depends on knowing what search terms to use and on the implemented search strategies. The support for internal search was addressed by utilizing a domain specific vocabulary on different levels of the employed search mechanisms. The challenge of what terms to use was addressed partially by removing it within the proposed query-by-navigation search method.

Acknowledgments. This material is based upon work supported by the NSF Grant No. DUE-1044224 "NSDL: Social Bookmarking for Digital Libraries: Improving Resource Sharing and Discoverability".

References

1. Glahn, C., Kalz, M., Gruber, M., Specht, M.: Supporting the Reuse of Open Educational Resources through Open Standards. In: Workshop Proc. of the 18th Int. Conference on Computers in Education, ICCE 2010 (2010)
2. Dichev, C., Dicheva, D.: Open Educational Resources in Computer Science Teaching. In: Proceedings of the ACM SIGSE 2012, Raleigh, NC, pp. 619–624 (2012)
3. Dichev, C., Dicheva, D.: Is It Time to Change the OER Repositories Role? In: Proceedings of the ACM/IEEE Joint Conference on Digital Libraries, JCDL 2012, Washington, DC, June 10-14, pp. 31–34 (2012)
4. ter Hofstede, A.H.M., Proper, H.A., van der Weide, T.P.: Query formulation as an information retrieval problem. The Computer Journal 39(4), 255–274 (1996)

---

[3] http://www.oercommons.org/

VirDO: A Virtual Workspace for Research Documents

George E. Raptis, Christina P. Katsini, and Stephen J. Payne

Department of Computer Science, University of Bath, Bath, UK
{george.e.raptis,christina.katsini}@bath.edu, s.j.payne@bath.ac.uk

Abstract. We report the design of a system which integrates a suite of tools to allow scholars to manage related documents in their personal digital stores. VirDO provides a virtual workspace in which pdfs can be placed and displayed, and which allows these documents to be manipulated in various ways that prior literature suggests to be useful. Particularly noteworthy are the various maps that support users in uncovering the inter-relations among documents in the workspace, including citation relations and flexible user-defined tags. Early evaluation of the system was positive: especially promising was the increasing use of maps by two participants who used VirDO for their own research over a period of a week, as well as the extensive use by all participants of sticky notes.

Keywords: sensemaking, document mapping, annotation, scholarship.

1 Introduction

Managing academic documents from the literature is a vital task for researchers everyday life. We present a system, VirDO (for Virtual Document Organizer) designed to help scientists manage a local store of downloaded documents, providing tools to support sensemaking.

Many tools have already been developed to support easier organization of digital documents [1,4]. However, only a few support sensemaking from local, individual document stores, which in the case of research is complicated by research literature having unique characteristics such as citations networks, particular categories of articles, pre-defined keywords etc. Scientists use some distinct processes in order to build their local research libraries, such as tracing citations, evaluating articles in terms of citation frequency, or relying on other peoples comments so they can decide whether a paper is worth reading or not.

Modjeska et al. [8] proposed five features for an effective bibliographic visualization. Briefly, an effective bibliographic visualization tool should provide full bibliographic information, such as title and author(s); filter data; display chronology and citations of the articles; allow for detailed view of information supporting different levels of details and be capable of visualizing large search sets. These authors describe the BIVTECI system, which incorporated these features and influenced our own design, which nonetheless differs in several details.

T. Aalberg et al. (Eds.): TPDL 2013, LNCS 8092, pp. 470–473, 2013.

As its name (Bibliographic Visualization Tool with enhanced Citation Inter-activity) suggests BIVTECI attempts to support sensemaking through visual-ization of document spaces, with particular reference to citation links. A large number of systems have similarly explored these issues [4,8] including techniques such as growing polygons between related documents [4], family tree networks [7] and hypertext co-citation maps [3]. However, these tools have focused on computation and display of properties of very large document collections rather than limited local filestores. The provision of an interactive workspace to replace a standard document folder is our focus.

In this respect VirDO is also similar to CiteSense [10], which is similar in intent to BIVTECI but additionally allows personal annotations, which facility we also provide through tags. File or document tagging has been widely studied recently, most often as an alternative retrieval mechanism to hierarchical folder structures [5]. In our system, tags provide an additional basis for mapping the document space, reflecting our focus on the organization of a local workspace. This is another issue that has seen a great deal of exploratory research, including studies of offices and real desks [6]. To very briefly summarize, this research has shown the importance of: (a) document location: Digital resources can be organized spatially too and location is used in retrieval [2]; (b) notes: people attach noted to paper documents and find this feature useful in electronic environments [9]; (c) filing and piling: people adapt their strategies to their task, and should be allowed to store documents in ad hoc piles which are better for some tasks [6]; (d) working versus archived documents: documents are important to their users over different timescales, from ephemeral to long-term [2,9]; (e) virtual workspaces: a promising idea is the creation of virtual workspaces, where the documents are organized in a more realistic manner [1].

2   VirDO

VirDO allows users to organize their electronic documents spatially, as they would with paper documents on their desks. It provides them with a virtual workspace, where they can perform various operations, such as re-arrangement of the documents, importing of new documents, deletion of documents they do not need any more, creation of spatial maps which show various relations between the documents and attachment of sticky notes. The virtual workspace consists of the following elements:

- **Incoming Box:** This is a place for all the documents of the project folder which the user has not yet placed on his workspace, because they are new and/or unclassified. The user can move these into the workspace either by dragging and dropping each of them, or by using the multiple import feature.
- **Trash Bin:** where the user can place whatever exists on his workspace and is not useful anymore; including digital documents, sticky notes, etc.
- **Virtual Document:** A virtual instance of a document can be placed into the workspace. Each is a 3-D box displaying a thumbnail of the first page of

the actual document. Its length and height have fixed-size, but its depth is related to its number of pages, giving the user an immediate sense of document length. Moreover, each virtual document provides the user with more information about it. In particular two ways of representing such information are provided: a vertical bar indicating the number of the citations the documents has, and a popup menu offering a variety of choices

- The vertical bar is updated regularly by web services, such as Google Scholar. The height of the bar indicates the number of citations as a proportion of the highest number of citations for any paper in the collection (which is fixed to the maximum-height bar).
- Through the popup menu, the user can view the whole document with an integrated pdf viewer offering document navigation, markup, zoom, etc. The user can also view additional document properties: title, author(s), user-assigned tags, references and the papers that cite that document, along with the number of citations of each reference or citation-source. Moreover, the user can mark a document as read or not-read, post personal notes, or create any of four interrleation maps: by author(s), by citations, by tag(s) or by publciation year.

Considering the maps, documents related by the chosen attribute are connected with lines showing the inter-relations. When Author is selected, that authors documents are connected; when Tags is enabled, the documents with that tag in common are connected; for Year, the documents published in the selected year are connected. Finally, Citations shows a selected document linked both with its references and its citations. The maps are created in the main workspace and in a new tab window of VirDO , where only the interrelated documents are displayed, re-arranged in the space.

An additional feature of VirDO is the creation and use of notes. The user can create sticky notes and place them anywhere in the workspace or even on the documents, as he would normally do with the paper documents, creating in that way piles, or spatially-close clusters of interrelated documents.

3   Evaluation Study

For the first evaluation of VirDO we conducted two small empirical studies, a shorter and a longer term study, in which participants used the system to consider a small sub-part of an academic literature. Participants in both studies were given a brief training session, by watching a video-tutorial of the system in use, and all interactions with VirDO were recorded.

In the shorter-term study, thirteen graduate students had already each used Google Scholar to download a set of pdfs (5 to 35) on a topic provided by the investigators. They spent 20 minutes using VirDO to organize these pdfs. - we observed extensive use of tags and sticky notes by all participants. Only five participants used the maps, most commonly the Tags map. In the longer-term study, two graduate students were invited to use VirDO to organize their pre-existing locally stored set of academic documents, as well as any new documents they retrieved during the study. Their use of VirDO was recorded for a full week.

In the later stages of this study, both participants made use of maps, and their use gradually increased. Tag maps and Citation maps were used regularly, whereas Author and Year maps were used less often. The longer-term participants commented on the visualization of the document relationships. They found connecting lines useful and effective, but advocated colour-coding lines. Finally, opening a new tab when a new map was generated was found to be useful.

4 Conclusion

Our main aim in this work has been to explore the idea that the academic sensemaking process can fruitfully be considered in the context of relatively small local collections of academic documents. The iterative building of local document stores requires incremental, iterative sensemaking of document spaces, and this cyclical process might be supported by a variety of mapping tools and note-taking resources.

References

1. Agarawala, A., Balakrishnan, R.: Keepin' it real: pushing the desktop metaphor with physics, piles and the pen. Paper presented at the Proceedings of the SIGCHI Conference on Human Factors in Computing Systems, Montreal, Quebec, Canada (2006)
2. Barreau, D., Nardi, B.A.: Finding and reminding: file organization from the desktop. SIGCHI Bull. 27(3), 39–43 (1995), doi:10.1145/221296.221307
3. Chen, C., Carr, L.: Trailblazing the literature of hypertext: author co-citation analysis (1989-1998). Paper presented at the Proceedings of the tenth ACM Conference on Hypertext and Hypermedia: Returning to Our Diverse Roots: Returning to Our Diverse Roots, Darmstadt, Germany (1999)
4. Elmqvist, N., Tsigas, P.: CiteWiz: a tool for the visualization of scientific citation networks. Information Visualization 6(3), 215–232 (2007), doi:10.1145/1375939.1375943
5. Farooq, U., Zhang, S., Carroll, J.M.: Sensemaking of scholarly literature through tagging. In: CHI 2009 Sensemaking Workshop, pp. 4–9 (April 2009)
6. Malone, T.W.: How do people organize their desks?: Implications for the design of office information systems. ACM Transactions on Information Systems (TOIS) 1(1), 99–112 (1983)
7. Matejka, J., Grossman, T., Fitzmaurice, G.: Citeology: visualizing paper genealogy. Paper presented at the CHI 2012 Extended Abstracts on Human Factors in Computing Systems, Austin, Texas, USA (2012)
8. Modjeska, D., Tzerpos, V., Faloutsos, P., Faloutsos, M.: BIVTECI: a bibliographic visualization tool. Paper presented at the Proceedings of the 1996 Conference of the Centre for Advanced Studies on Collaborative Research, Toronto, Ontario, Canada (1996)
9. Sellen, A.J., Harper, R.H.R.: The Myth of the Paperless Office. MIT Press, Cambridge (2003)
10. Zhang, X., Qu, Y., Giles, C.L., Song, P.: CiteSense: supporting sensemaking of research literature. Paper presented at the Proceedings of the SIGCHI Conference on Human Factors in Computing Systems, Florence, Italy (2008)

Domain Search and Exploration with Meta-Indexes

Michael Huggett and Edie Rasmussen

University of British Columbia
Vancouver, B.C. Canada
{m.huggett,edie.rasmussen}@ubc.ca

Abstract. In order to facilitate navigation and search of large collections of digital books, we have developed a new knowledge structure, the meta-index, which aggregates the back-of-book indexes within a subject domain. Using a test collection of digital books, we demonstrate the use of the meta-index and associated metrics that characterize the books within a digital domain, and explore some of the challenges presented by the meta-index structure.

Keywords: Indexes, Meta-indexes, Bibliometrics, Visualization, Search, User interfaces.

1 Introduction

Although millions of digital books are available on the Web as a result of mass digitization projects (for example, the Gutenberg Project, the Million Books Project, the Open Content Alliance, and Google Books) [1, 2, 3], relatively little research has explored ways to ensure that these collections are useful and used. Given their widespread availability, digital books offer the potential to change the way scholars interact with texts; Henry and Smith [4] suggest that "[t]he challenge before scholars now is to make connections among and within huge sets of digitized data and to create new knowledge from them" (p. 108). As the scholar's work migrates from print to the digital realm, new ways of browsing, navigating and searching collections of digital books are needed [5].

In the Indexer's Legacy Project, we are exploring the potential of the back-of-book index (BoBI) as a knowledge structure for domain exploration and navigation. We have built a test collection of about 700 books, from a convenience sample chosen equally from non-copyrighted books in each of seven subject areas or domains, in the arts (art history, music), humanities (cooking, economics), and sciences (anatomy, geology, Darwin). We have created a suite of programs that extracts the back-of-book index for each book in our test collection, expands each index entry to its canonical form, stems and stop-words index terms, combines and sorts all index entries across a subject domain, and then aggregates a well-structured meta-index for the entire domain [6]. The meta-index is a new knowledge structure that allows users to explore the collection at the domain level, and can be explored using our Meta-Dex User Interface (MUI) [7]. The initial response of users to the functionality offered by meta-index navigation and search has been positive [8].

T. Aalberg et al. (Eds.): TPDL 2013, LNCS 8092, pp. 474–477, 2013.

2   The Challenges of Meta-Index Data

The literature on BoBIs suggests that they serve a critical role in locating information in print and digital books, and that the indexing process generates a vocabulary that is more structured and more concentrated than that found in the book itself [9, 10]. Because the BoBI is carefully crafted by a human domain expert, it is a rich source of information for the vocabulary and concepts in individual books, and if aggregated across multiple books, in a subject domain as a whole. However, building the meta-index and finding the best way to present it to users presents a number of interesting challenges.

The Meta-Dex software suite aggregates the indexes of individual books in a domain subject area to generate a single meta-index that, for each index entry, points to specific books and pages. These meta-indexes tend to be large, on the order of 100,000 lines of text. The more popular meta-entries in a domain can be thousands of lines long when aggregated. Thus despite the inherent utility of indexes, there is still the difficulty of navigating large amounts of information to find items of interest.

A related problem concerns the statistics compiled during meta-index aggregation. Aside from basic term, token, and entry counts, there are many other factors that can be used to typify and differentiate domains. First, structural metrics measure the count ratio of main entries to sub-entries, and the number of references per entry, across the domain as a whole and as averaged between books. Other measures indicate how the structure changes: how much the individual indexes are 'compressed' as they are aggregated into a meta-index.

Second, there are comparisons of book index versus content (i.e. chapter text): how large each tends to be, how similar are their language models, and what terms appear in one but not the other: the 'value-added' terms of the index that indicate a potential lexical bias in a domain, and the popular words in the content that are somehow not reflected in the index.

Third, books of a domain are 'connected' to a greater or lesser degree by the terms and entries that they share. Some domains show more 'coherence' by sharing a greater proportion of entries among their books. Other domains have higher proportions of 'singleton' entries that appear in only one book. From these measures we can rank books by how 'representative' they are of a domain, how much they contribute to domain coherence, and how well they fit the global language model of the domain.

Domains vary on all these dimensions, and navigating this wealth of tabular statistical data can itself be overwhelming.

3   A System for Visualizing and Editing Meta-Indexes

To meet the challenges of navigating large meta-indexes, we have developed a graphical meta-index user interface (MUI) with a connected series of interactive 'views' on the data [7]. The primary component is a **Search View** that provides keyword search of domain meta-indexes, returning a list of main entry titles (e.g. *ophthalmic nerve*) ranked first by the proportion of books that contain them, and second by their number of references. Clicking on an entry title opens the **Entry View**, which displays the main entry including all of its sub-entries and references. Since the entries are sometimes quite large, the display is initially folded to show only the terms of the entry title. Clicking on the ellipses exposes the hidden sub-entries. The references on each line show both the book ID and the page number. Clicking either of these opens the **Book View** to display the book's meta-data (title, author, year, source, etc.) and the text of the referenced book page with the search terms highlighted. Users can then browse to previous and following pages to read the context of the result.

As a complementary tool, we also offer a standard keyword-based **Content Search** tool indexed on all of the domain's book chapters. A keyword search returns ten snippets from across the domain, ranked by relevance. Clicking on a snippet opens the snippet's page in the **Book View**, with an additional list of all pages in the same book that contain the search terms. The Content Search tool is intended to be used in user studies as a control condition to compare to the meta-index search views.

To help users navigate the large amount of tabular statistical data, we provide several graphical aids. First, the basic data tables are enhanced with heat-map coloration to highlight the maxima and minima of the many values. Such highlighting makes it easier to analyze trends and quickly identify the relative strengths and weaknesses of different subject domains. To give users a sense of when the books of the domain were written (which has a direct impact on vocabulary and turns of phrase), we provide a **Domain Years** view that shows a histogram timeline of publication years, with longer lines representing more books published in that year. Since our books all come from the public domain, we see a concentration of publications prior to 1925 that became immediately obvious across all domains once the view was developed.

Following creation of a meta-index by automatic aggregation of a domain's book indexes, the meta-index is still fairly 'loose', primarily due to all the different ways that words and names can be spelled. Clearly, one way to address this would be to edit manually the indexes of the source books. However, due to the amount of text involved this would be an enormous task. To compress the meta-index more efficiently, we have implemented a system of *synonyms* that allows a user to specify manually a canonical term or phrase, along with all of its equivalent variations. The variations are then substituted by the canonical phrase where encountered during processing. Synonyms can be applied across the entire meta-index, or just within a specific entry. We find that this approach greatly reduces the amount of effort required to generate a viable meta-index.

4   Future Work

There are further enhancements to come in both user interfaces and meta-index editing. First, since we have already compiled language models within each domain, domain-based auto-completion of search keywords is an obvious enhancement that would better cue users as they enter search terms. A related enhancement will be a *most-correlated terms* mechanism that, given a user's search term, can suggest other related terms based on their co-location in the text. Here we see parallels with the presentation used by Chi et al. [11] in their conceptually-reorganizing ScentIndex system, and will be looking at incorporating this approach.

Second, the synonyms mechanism could be upgraded to provide *chained synonyms* that specify that if a given term is found in an entry then a different given term should be found and replaced, and *negative synonyms* that specify that a substitution should be attempted only if a specific term is *not* present. A more ambitious sub-project of *structural synonyms* will take an NLP approach to matching different, equivalent turns of phrase that mean the same thing: wherever the terms of two equivalent phrases match, the user will be given the option of accepting the transformation into the canonical word pattern. We expect these synonym upgrades to enhance further the compressibility of the meta-indexes.

Finally, we intend to perform in-depth user studies. Our user interface includes an option for a standard keyword search, so we will compare performance on search tasks with the meta-index and with keyword search in the text of books in the domain. Our initial pilot studies have been encouraging [8], and we look forward to a more solid basis to justify meta-indexes for semantic search of large collections of digital books.

References

1. Quint, B.: Microsoft launches book digitization project—MSN Book Search. Information Today (October 31, 2005)
2. Choudhury, G.S., DiLauro, T., Ferguson, R., Droettboom, M., Fujinaga, I.: Document recognition for a million books. D-Lib Magazine 12(3) (March 2006)
3. Coyle, K.: Mass digitization of books. J. Academic Librarianship 32(6), 641–645 (2006)
4. Henry, C., Smith, K.: Ghostlier demarcations: Large-scale text digitization projects and their utility for Contemporary Humanities Scholarship. In: The Idea of Order: Transforming Research Collections for 21st Century Scholarship, pp. 106–115. CLIR, Washington, DC (2010)
5. Crane, G.: What do you do with a million books? D-Lib Magazine 12(3) (March 2006)
6. Huggett, M., Rasmussen, E.: Creating meta-indexes for digital domains. In: Proceedings of the 2011 ACM IEEE Joint International Conference on Digital Libraries, pp. 423–424. ACM, New York (2011)
7. Huggett, M., Rasmussen, E.: Dynamic online views of meta-indexes. In: Proceedings of the 12th ACM/IEEE-CS Joint Conference on Digital Libraries, pp. 233–236. ACM, New York (2012)
8. Huggett, M., Rasmussen, E.: Using digital book metrics for navigation and browsing. In: iConference 2013, Fort Worth, Texas (February 2013)
9. Anderson, J.D., Pérez-Carballo, J.: The Nature of indexing: how humans and machines analyze messages and text for retrieval. Part I: Research, and the nature of human indexing. Information Processing & Management 37, 231–254 (2001)
10. Mulvany, N.C.: Indexing Books. University of Chicago Press, Chicago (1994)
11. Chi, E.H., Hong, L., Heiser, J., Card, S.K., Gumbrecht, M.: ScentIndex and ScentHighlights: productive reading techniques for conceptually reorganizing subject indexes and highlighting passes. Information Visualization 6(1), 32–47 (2007)

COST Actions and Digital Libraries: Between Sustaining Best Practices and Unleashing Further Potential

Matthew J. Driscoll[1], Ralph Stübner[2], Touradj Ebrahimi[3], Muriel Foulonneau[4],
Andreas Nürnberger[5], Andrea Scharnhorst[6], and Joie Springer[7]

[1] Den Arnamagnæanske Samling, Københavns Universitet, Denmark
[2] European Cooperation in Science and Technology (COST), Belgium
[3] Ecole Polytechnique Fédérale de Lausanne, EPFL/STI/IEL/GR-EB, Switzerland
[4] Knowledge Intensive Systems and Services, Henri Tudor Research Centre, Luxembourg
[5] Faculty of Computer Science, Otto von Guericke University Magdeburg, Germany
[6] Data Archiving and Networking Services (DANS), The Netherlands
[7] Knowledge Societies Division, United Nations Educational,
Scientific, and Cultural Organization (UNESCO), France

1   Background and Participants

The panel brings together chairs or key participants from a number of COST-funded[1] Actions from several domains—Individuals, Societies, Cultures and Health (ISCH), Information and Communication Technologies (ICT) — as well as a Trans-Domain Action), a Science Officer from the COST Office and will be complemented by a representative of the Memory of the World programme of UNESCO.

The panel aims to look into the links between on-going digital library research and emerging new areas from the point of view of multi-national cooperation focused on particular research domains. Some of the participating actions are aiming to deepen particular subject domain knowledge, for example mediaeval heritage or world documentary heritage. Others look at novel methods and tools, for example web-based data collection, or quality in multimedia systems.

The list of actions which will be discussed during the panel follows.

- From the Individuals, Societies, Cultures and Health (ISCH) Domain:
  — IS1004 WebDataNet: Web-based data-collection, methodology and implementation challenges[2]
  — IS1005: Medieval Europe—Medieval Cultures and Technological Resources[3]
- From the Information and Communication Technologies (ICT) Domain:

---

[1] COST, European Cooperation in Science and Technology, is a programme facilitating cooperation among scientists and researchers across Europe (http://www.cost.eu/).

[2] http://www.cost.eu/domains_actions/isch/Actions/IS1004; represented by Muriel Foulonneau.

[3] http://www.cost.eu/domains_actions/isch/Actions/IS1005; represented by Matthew Driscoll.

T. Aalberg et al. (Eds.): TPDL 2013, LNCS 8092, pp. 478–479, 2013.

- IC1002 Multilingual and Multifaceted Interactive Information Access (MUMIA)[4]
- IC1003 European Network on Quality of Experience in Multimedia Systems and Services (QUALINET)[5]
- Trans-Domain Action:
  - TD1210: Analyzing the Dynamics of Information and Knowledge Landscapes (KNOWeSCAPE)[6]
- Additional International Cooperation Programme: Memory of the World[7]

2 Key Discussion Issues

COST currently is funding about 300 networks; those selected for this panel are only some of those Actions which either create new digital resources, or look at new methods for creating, exploring and safe-guarding digital content. This panel seeks to achieve several goals:

- Raise the awareness on ongoing COST cooperation relevant to digital libraries research.
- Showcase the use of digital library research within the particular Actions—and identify any useful patterns which illustrate the synergies of the digital library community with professional from other domains.
- Outline what new areas of research emerge or and need support from the digital libraries community.
- Discuss the specific role such cooperation actions play in sustaining best practices in digital library research and fostering new research agendas or roadmaps relevant to the digital library domain.

---

[4] http://www.mumia-network.eu/; represented by Andreas Nürnberger.

[5] http://www.qualinet.eu; represented by Touradj Ebrahimi.

[6] http://www.cost.eu/domains_actions/mpns/Actions/TD1210; represented by Andrea Scharnhorst.

[7] http://www.unesco.org/webworld/en/mow; represented by Joie Springer.

e-Infrastructures for Digital Libraries… the Future

Wim Jansen[1], Roberto Barbera[2], Michel Drescher[3], Antonella Fresa[4],
Matthias Hemmje[5], Yannis Ioannidis[6], Norbert Meyer[7],
Nick Poole[8], and Peter Stanchev[9]

[1] DG Connect, European Commission
[2] Dipartimento di Fisica e Astronomia & INFN Sezione di Catania, Italy
[3] European Grid Infrastructure (EGI), The Netherlands
[4] PROMOTER, Italy
[5] FernUniversität Hagen, Germany
[6] University of Athens, Greece
[7] Poznań Supercomputing and Networking Center, Poland
[8] Collections Trust, UK
[9] Kettering University, USA

1 Background

The digital ICT revolution is profoundly changing the way knowledge is created, communicated and is being deployed. New research methods based on computing and "big data" enable new means and forms for scientific collaboration also through policy measures supporting open access to data and research results. The exponential growth of digital resources and services is supported by the deployment of e-Infrastructure, which allows researchers to access remote facilities, run complex simulations or to manage and exchange unprecedented amounts of digital data.

This panel will bring together leading e-Infrastructure experts coming from different subject domains addressing a range of different types of digital materials, services and collaborative tools supporting a variety of research communities to discuss with the Digital Libraries community the challenges modern research brings in terms of efficiency and relevance for an open research society.

2 Cultural Heritage Perspective

The numerous digitisation initiatives carried out by memory institutions (museums, libraries, archives) in Europe and world-wide have produced a large amount of cultural content\data, which is continuously growing. The existing services – e.g. the metadata aggregators, such as Europeana and the national cultural portals, play a key role to mobilise attention and resources on the general theme of the digitisation of cultural heritage. On the other hand, the research infrastructures (like DARIAH) are currently missing most of the cultural heritage data, including the data that are hold by local institutions.

The idea of a digital cultural heritage e-Infrastructure is to set-up a "common pot", where institutions can deliver safely their content, which can be seen as a

T. Aalberg et al. (Eds.): TPDL 2013, LNCS 8092, pp. 480–481, 2013.

"continuum" by the users. On the cultural heritage side, the panel will showcase such initiatives as DCH-RP (Digital Cultural Heritage Roadmap for Preservation). It will also benefit from the analysis of evidence done within the ENUMERATE project which is gathering evidence and analysing the current state in digitisation, accessibility online and preservation across the cultural heritage institutions in Europe.

These examples will provide a basis to discuss how cultural institutions could be more proactive in expressing their needs in terms of e-Infrastructures, and how they could benefit in a bigger extent from the already established e-Istructures.

3   Research Data Perspective

The panel will also discuss recent development within e-Infrastructures targeting support for the research communities. It will look into EUDAT, a project that brought together data infrastructure providers and practitioners to discuss current data infrastructure challenges and solutions, with a focus on interoperability, cross-disciplinary and cross-border collaboration; OpenAIREplus project which aims at bridging the missing link between the research articles, the data and the project funding. Building on the OpenAIRE portal and OpenAIRE compatible repositories, and EGI.eu which is a not-for-profit foundation established under Dutch law to coordinate and manage the European Grid Infrastructure (EGI) federation on behalf of its participants: National Grid Initiatives (NGIs) and European International Research Organisations (EIROs), as well as the "Coordination & Harmonisation of Advanced e-Infrastructures for Research and Education Data Sharing" (CHAIN-REDS) project and its activities to foster and support worldwide data infrastructures. Furthermore, Projects like APARSEN and SCIDIP-ES are bringing the perspectives of research data and cultural heritage infrastructures together.

4   Key Questions

The experts in the panel will provide their perspective on the following matters:

- What is the relation between the e-Infrastructure they are involved in and digital libraries research and development?
- What is their expectation on the capacity building impact of their e-Infrastructure?
- What support is needed for various stakeholders in relation to future e-Infrastructure developments?
- Which are the most critical factors for the success of e-Infrastructures' deployment?

The Role of XSLT in Digital Libraries, Editions, and Cultural Exhibits

Laura Mandell[1] and Violeta Ilik[2]

[1] Department of English, Texas A&M University
[2] Texas A&M University Libraries

We offer a half day tutorial that will explore the role of XML and XSLT (eX-tensible Stylesheet Language Transformations, themselves XML documents) in digital library and digital humanities projects. Digital libraries ideally aim to pro-vide both access and interaction. Digital libraries and digital humanities projects should foster edition building and curation. Therefore, this tutorial aims to teach librarians, scholars, and those involved in cultural heritage projects a scripting language that allows for easy manipulation of metadata, pictures, and text. The modules in this tutorial will help participants in planning for their own orga-nizations digital efforts and scholarly communications as well as in facilitating their efforts at digitization and creating interoperability between document edi-tions. In five instructional modules, including hands-on exercises, we will help participants gain experience and knowledge of the possibilities that XSLT offers in transforming documents from XML to HTML, from XML to text, and from one metadata schema to another.

Introduction to Working with XML and XSLT

Using provided examples, attendees will be taught to identify well-formed XML documents. These examples will also provide for quick discussions of the XML tree, beginning with the logic of parent-child-sibling element relationships and ending with a tutorial on XPath 2.0 (atomic values, path expressions, name-spaces, and referencing nodes). This introduction will proceed quickly and as-sume a general knowledge of HTML markup and a basic understanding of XML markup and XSLT technologies. The first module will conclude with a tour of the <oXygen> XML editor and the various XML application templates provided by the software.

How to Display XML Data in an HTML Page

Focusing on writing XSLT transformations and using the <oXygen> XML editor software, attendees will be directed to generate HTML pages of sample data. This module will expand upon the particular concepts of the previous module, using the transformation of XML to HTML to provide a detailed tutorial on the XML DOM, avoiding XML data islands, and why XSLT is the preferred style sheet language of XML.

T. Aalberg et al. (Eds.): TPDL 2013, LNCS 8092, pp. 482–483, 2013.
© Springer-Verlag Berlin Heidelberg 2013

Extracting Metadata from and Injecting Metadata into Digital Objects

Scholars who create digital archives and editions may either curate images or a combination of images, text, and metadata. We will explore existing metadata schemas, XML templates, and XSLT transformations for associating metadata with all digital objects, and then for extracting metadata in order to replicate it from metadata-rich documents (e.g., TEI headers). We will focus on the use of the XML/TEI document as a master, one that can be created for images and artifacts as well as for text. Using TEI to structure an archive provides a foundation for using XSLT transformations to generate OPDS, COINS, Dublin Core, RDF, and other kinds of metadata that usefully propagate links on the web. For our main example, we will generate metadata wrappers for images (as an accompaniment to posting a jpeg online) with the following steps: formatting an XML/TEI master, placing the image link in this document, using XSLT to transform the XML document into HTML, and proofing the generated HTML. We will then extract metadata in the various forms mentioned above from these TEI image wrappers and text files.

How to Structure Searching and Extract Searchable Files from Encoded Documents

Because digital archives are moving towards a semantic web model, we will explore how XSLT transformations can make digital objects searchable in both relational and semantic databases. Following up on the discussion of digital editions, exhibits, and collections, this module will present how XSLT can be used to associate metadata in a Linked Data system. Next, we will discuss how XSLT can be used to extract plain-text files from encoded documents which can then be used in keyword searches and collocation tools (e.g., Voyant). For our main example, we will produce database entry csv files, rdf, and text files from a series of encoded documents, creating the data needed for a relational database, a linked database, and plain texts.

How to Build a Crosswalk between Multiple Metadata Formats

Libraries, archives, and museums constantly manage heterogeneous data while documenting the cultural heritage information. The heterogeneous types of material create collections described by different metadata schemas. Many well-known metadata standards are expressed as XML schemas, including MARCXML, Dublin Core, MODS, METS, EAD, to name a few. A crosswalk can be built between various schemas that defines the semantic mapping of the elements of a source metadata schema to the elements of an output metadata schema. The flexible structure of XML makes it possible to convert data from one metadata standard to another. Specific examples will be shown, such as stylesheet for transforming MARCXML document into Dublin Core.

Mapping Cross-Domain Metadata
to the Europeana Data Model (EDM)

Valentine Charles[1], Antoine Isaac[1], Vassilis Tzouvaras[2], and Steffen Hennicke[3]

[1] Europeana Foundation, Den Haag, The Netherlands
valentine.charles@kb.nl, aisaac@few.vu.nl
[2] National Technical University of Athens, Athens, Greece
tzouvaras@image.ntua.gr
[3] HU-Berlin-Berlin School of Library and Information Science, Berlin, Germany
steffen.hennicke@ibi.hu-berlin.de

Keywords: Interoperability, EDM, mapping, MINT.

1   Introduction

With the growing amount and the diversity of aggregation services for cultural heritage, the challenge of data mapping has become crucial.

Europeana[1], as one of the major European aggregation services has to face the issues of data integration and data interoperability. Europeana provides a common access point to digital cultural heritage objects across cultural domains. It has established a professional knowledge-sharing network[2] and platform to introduce, document and promote the adoption of standardized practices.

2   The Europeana Data Model (EDM)

In order to provide a service based on richer and more interlinked data, Europeana has moved to a new data model: The *Europeana Data Model* [1]. EDM is designed as a framework for collecting, connecting and enriching the descriptions provided by Europeana data providers. Therefore it is not built on any particular domain standard. It rather reuses well-known and cross-domain standards from the Semantic Web and related communities, such as the Resource Description Framework (RDF), the OAI Object Reuse and Exchange (ORE), Dublin Core with additional properties from SKOS, RDA or CIDOC-CRM. This way, the model is able to articulate links between "provided cultural heritage objects" (painting, books, monuments) and their digital representations, as well as between objects and metadata records describing them. EDM also supports contextual resources which will help building a "semantic layer" (concepts, thesauri...) on top of the aggregated objects. EDM tries to minimize its semantic commitment, focusing mainly in gathering data for access points such as the Europeana service.

---

[1] http://www.europeana.eu
[2] http://pro.europeana.eu/network

T. Aalberg et al. (Eds.): TPDL 2013, LNCS 8092, pp. 484–485, 2013.
© Springer-Verlag Berlin Heidelberg 2013

However the need for data exchange requires work on data mapping and alignment from domain specific schemas to more common ones such as EDM. Thematic aggregators around Europeana have developed or adopted domain standards (e.g. LIDO in museums, EAD in archives, EBUcore etc.) and help their providers to create mappings from their proprietary metadata sets to those standards. To ingest the resulting metadata in Europeana, mappings from each of those standards to EDM are thus required. In some cases, the cross-domain nature of EDM can lead to a loss of data during mapping. Refinements and extensions of EDM have been proposed to accommodate the domain needs. They are in the form of subclasses and sub-properties that specialise the "standard" EDM concepts and properties [2].

Creating such specialisations has a cost for data providers. The refinement of mappings also depends on the existence of appropriate tools which will enable the linking of domain specific data at the level of elements sets. A good knowledge of mapping patterns will also benefit the design of such tools.

3   A Mapping Tool: MINT

MINT (Metadata Interoperability services [3]) participates in aggregation, digitization, technology-enabling projects and initiatives for digital cultural heritage. These typically involve the design, implementation and execution of an ingestion strategy, according to a specific domain(s) and scope. MINT is a web-based platform that supports workflows involving the ingestion, the (manual) mapping, the transformation and enrichment of metadata records. .It is being used by a growing number of data providers (including Europeana) that align proprietary data structures to a variety of standard or aggregation-specific models, and in that way establish and maintain interoperability with aggregators and Europeana.

4   Conclusion

The tutorial invites metadata and data experts from the Gallery, Library, Archive and Museum (GLAM) community to a discussion on the modeling, semantic, and technical challenges brought by EDM and mapping of cross-domain activities in general. The tutorial also highlights the guiding principles in mapping and data alignment exercises.

References

1. EDM. Definition of the Europeana Data Model elements, version 5.2.3 (2012),
   http://pro.europeana.eu/edm-documentation (retrieved May 13, 2013)
2. EDM case studies, http://pro.europeana.eu/case-studies-edm
3. MINT. MINT Metadata Interoperability Services (2013),
   http://mint.image.ece.ntua.gr/ (retrieved May 13, 2013)

State-of-the-Art Tools for Text Digitisation[*]

Bob Boelhouwer[1], Adam Dudczak[2], and Sebastian Kirch[3]

[1] Instituut voor Nederlandse Lexicologie, Netherlands
[2] Poznan Supercomputing and Networking Center, Poland
[3] Fraunhofer-Institut für Intelligente Analyse- und Informationssysteme IAIS, Germany

Abstract. The goal of this tutorial (organised by the Succeed project) is to introduce participants to state-of-the-art tools in digitisation and text processing which have been developed in recent research projects. The tutorial will focus on hands-on demonstration and on the testing of the tools in real-life situations, even those provided by the participants.

Keywords: Digitisation, OCR, Image Enhancement, Enrichment, Lexicon, Ground Truth, NLP.

1 Introduction

Tools developed in research projects to improve the quality and efficiency of the digitisation workflow can help to accelerate the production of high quality digital content. However, these tools seldom progress beyond working prototypes and their implementation in actual production environments is hindered by the limited awareness of the results and the lack of resources for their adaptation, maintenance or further development. This tutorial will offer participants an opportunity to gain firsthand knowledge of the latest advances this field. Conversely, researchers will benefit from practitioner comments and suggestions. The learning objectives are:

- Gain practical insight into the most recent developments in text digitisation techniques.
- Identify strengths and usability weaknesses of existing tools.
- Reach a better knowledge on the effect of new tools and resources on the productivity.
- Discuss the requirements and effects of their integration in production workflows.

2 Programme

2.1 Introduction to the Digitisation Process

The tutorial will start with a general introduction to the digitisation process where the necessary steps and best practices when starting a mass digitisation project will be

---

[*] A complete list of tools will be updated on http://www.succeed-project.eu/wiki

T. Aalberg et al. (Eds.): TPDL 2013, LNCS 8092, pp. 486–487, 2013.

discussed. In this introduction, we will overview the areas in which significant improvement in the digitisation workflow can be achieved and discuss the evaluation criteria which led to the selection of the tools showcased.

2.2   Overview of Available Tools

After the introductory section, every tool will be presented, briefly followed by a practical demonstration and a discussion on how they can be deployed within the library digitisation infrastructure. The tools showcased will cover the most relevant steps of the digitisation process:

Image Enhancement. These tools enhance the quality of scanned documents, both for visual presentation in digital libraries and eBooks and to improve the results of the subsequent steps such as segmentation and OCR. We will showcase tools for binarisation and colour reduction, noise and artefact removal, and geometric correction.

Optical Character Recognition (OCR). OCR is defined as automatic transcription of the text represented on an image into machine-readable text. From this area, we will discuss and demonstrate the latest developments in both commercial and open source OCR. In this section we will also include tools for document segmentation.

Logical Structure Analysis. Documents such as newspapers or magazines are a composition of various structural elements such as headings or articles. Here we will present tools that are able to automatically detect and reconstruct these structural elements from scanned documents.

Post-correction and Enrichment. Approaches to both interactive (e.g. crowdsourcing) and fully automatic post-correction of the digitised text will be demonstrated.

Lexicon-Building and Deployment. The purpose of tools in this area is to make digitised text more accessible to users and researchers by applying linguistic resources and language technology. The tutorial will show how lexical resources for retrieval and OCR can be constructed and how they can be exploited in retrieval and OCR.

2.3   Hands-On Session

The tutorial will be continued with an extended hands-on session for those attendees who are interested in further training or testing.

ResourceSync: The NISO/OAI Resource Synchronization Framework

Herbert Van de Sompel[1], Michael L. Nelson[2],
Martin Klein[1], and Robert Sanderson[1]

[1] Los Alamos National Laboratory, Los Alamos, NM, USA
{herbertv,mklein,rsanderson}@lanl.gov
[2] Old Dominion University, Norfolk, VA, USA
mln@cs.odu.edu

Abstract. This tutorial provides an overview and a practical introduction to **ResourceSync**, a web-based synchronization framework consisting of multiple modular capabilities that a server can selectively implement to enable third party systems to remain synchronized with the server's evolving resources. The tutorial motivates the ResourceSync approach by outlining several synchronization use cases including scholarly article repositories, OAI-PMH repositories, linked data knowledge bases, as well as content aggregators. It details the concepts of the ResourceSync capabilities, their discovery mechanisms, and their serialization based on the widely adopted Sitemap protocol. The tutorial further hints at the extensibility of the synchronization framework, for example, for scenarios to provide references to mirror locations of synchronization resources, to transferring partial content, and to offering historical data.

Description

The tutorial introduces ResourceSync, a web-based synchronization framework resulting from a project launched by the National Information Standardization Organization (NISO) and the Open Archives Initiative (OAI). The project aims to design an approach for resource synchronization that is aligned with the Web Architecture and that has a fair chance of adoption by different communities.

The tutorial starts with a presentation of our perspective on the problem of resource synchronization and the conceptual approach taken by ResourceSync. It initially introduces the ResourceSync terminology such as a Source (a server that hosts resources subject to synchronization) and a Destination (a system that synchronizes itself with the Source's resources). It then goes on to motivate for a standardized web resource synchronization framework by analyzing several synchronization use cases and their requirements in terms of synchronization latency and accuracy. After a general walkthrough of the framework, it introduces the concepts behind the separate ResourceSync capabilities in detail. It offers a brief recap of the Sitemap protocol as sanctioned by major search engines as all ResourceSync capability documents are based on the Sitemap format.

T. Aalberg et al. (Eds.): TPDL 2013, LNCS 8092, pp. 488–489, 2013.
© Springer-Verlag Berlin Heidelberg 2013

The tutorial provides technical insights into the serialization of the capability documents and outlines the ResourceSync specific extensions to the Sitemap format. The technical discussion focuses on pull-based approaches to obtain the capability documents but it does also include an outlook to push-based approaches that are currently under investigation to be adopted by the project team.

The tutorial gives attention to the extensibility of the framework. In particular, the ability to link to resources that are related to resources subject to synchronization, for example, resources at mirror locations, alternate representations of resources, and metadata records describing synchronization resources.

A key aspect of the framework is for Destinations to discover all capabilities offered by a Source. The tutorial covers multiple discovery approaches and outlines our view on best-practices to address this issue. Archives of various capabilities constitute an additional part of the framework and the tutorial gives a brief insight into their use and discovery.

The tutorial concludes with current implementation examples, pointers to available libraries and the ResourceSync specification, which will support attendees of the tutorial in adopting the framework.

Audience

The tutorial is intended for an audience that includes technologists, programmers, and managers with some technical knowledge. It assumes a basic level of familiarity with notions of digital data repositories, Web resources, and XML but is presented in a way that no prior experience with synchronization protocols or the Sitemap format is required.

Participants of the tutorial not only gain an understanding of the motivations for the ResourceSync synchronization framework and the roles of Sources and Destinations in the synchronization process but also close familiarity with the underlying concepts of the individual modular ResourceSync capabilities and how they can be concerted. Tutorial attendees afterwards have a thorough understanding of the Sitemap-based format of the framework's capability documents and understand the integration with existing systems and discoverability issues.

From Preserving Data to Preserving Research: Curation of Process and Context

Rudolf Mayer[1], Stefan Pröll[1], Andreas Rauber[1,2],
Raul Palma[3], and Daniel Garijo[4]

[1] Secure Buisness Austria,
Vienna, Austria
[2] Vienna University of Technology,
Austria
[3] Poznan Supercomputing and Networking Center,
Poland
[4] Universidad Politecnica de Madrid,
Spain

Abstract. In the domain of eScience, investigations are increasingly collaborative. Most scientific and engineering domains benefit from building on top of the outputs of other research: By sharing information to reason over and data to incorporate in the modelling task at hand.

This raises the need to provide means for preserving and sharing entire eScience workflows and processes for later reuse. It is required to define which information is to be collected, create means to preserve it and approaches to enable and validate the re-execution of a preserved process. This includes and goes beyond preserving the data used in the experiments, as the process underlying its creation and use is essential.

This tutorial thus provides an introduction to the problem domain and discusses solutions for the curation of eScience processes.

Awareness for the need to provide digital preservation solutions is spreading from the core memory institutions to other domains, including government, industry, SME and consumers. Likewise, in the domain of eScience, the documentation and preservation of research processes, to allow later understanding and re-execution of e.g. experiments that may be the basis of scientific discoveries, is understood as an important part of the research, and thus gaining more interest. However, comprehensive solutions are still rarely applied. This tutorial is therefore aimed at providing a holistic view on the challenges and solutions of preservation of eScience processes.

As the very core of eScience, *data* forms the basis of the results of many research publications. It thus needs to be referenced with the same accuracy as bibliographic data. Only if data can be identified with high precision, it can be reused, validated, falsified, verified and reproduced. Citing a specific data set is however not always a trivial task. Research and business data exist in a vast plurality of specifications and instances. Additionally, data sets can be potentially

T. Aalberg et al. (Eds.): TPDL 2013, LNCS 8092, pp. 490–491, 2013.

huge in size, and their location might change as they are transferred between different institutions. This tutorial thus starts with an overview of current data citation practices.

In some scenarios, the data base itself is *dynamic*, e.g. new data gets added on a regular basis, or existing elements were changed or deleted. Such settings pose new challenges to citation, as the cited source should be unchanged over time. We thus provide an introduction into the topic of dynamic data citation and present potential solutions for this area.

On top of the research data, the re-usability and traceability of *workflows and processes* performed thereon is vital for preservation. The processes creating and interpreting data are complex objects. Curating and preserving them requires special effort, as they are dynamic, and highly dependent on software, configuration, hardware, and other aspects. These aspects form the *contextual information* of the processes, and are thus the primary concern of preservation. This tutorial presents these challenges in detail, and provides an introduction to two complementary approaches to alleviate them.

The first approach is based on the concept of Research Objects, which adopts a workflow-centric approach and thereby aims at facilitating the reuse and reproducibility. It allows packaging the data and the methods as one Research Object to share and cite it, and thus enable publishers to grant access to the actual data and methods that contribute to the findings reported in scholarly articles.

A second approach focuses on describing and preserving a process and the context it is embedded in. The artefacts that may need to be captured range from data, software and accompanying documentation, to legal and human resource aspects. Some of this information can be automatically extracted from an existing process, and tools for this will be presented. Ways to archive the process and to perform preservation actions on the process environment, such as recreating a controlled execution environment or migration of software components, are presented. Finally, the challenge of evaluating the re-execution of a preserved process is discussed, addressing means of establishing its authenticity.

Throughout the tutorial, the challenges and problem domain are demonstrated on practical examples taken from eScience research workflows. On these examples, the tools and methods presented earlier are applied, and the solutions are discussed for the adequacy.

Linked Data for Digital Libraries

Uldis Bojārs[1], Nuno Lopes[2], and Jodi Schneider[2]

[1] National Library of Latvia
[2] Digital Enterprise Research Institute, National University of Ireland, Galway
uldis.bojars@gmail.com,
{nuno.lopes,jodi.schneider}@deri.org

This tutorial will empower attendees with the necessary skills to take advantage of Linked Data already available on the Web, provide insights on how to incorporate this data and tools into their daily workflow, and finally touch upon how the attendees' own data can be shared as Linked Data.

Linked Data has been embraced as the way to bring complex information onto the Web, enabling accessibility while maintaining the richness of the original data, making it ideal for digital libraries that want to increase their search visibility and interoperability. Thus digital libraries are giving increasing importance to Linked Data in a variety of ways – by creating metadata models (such as the Europeana Data Model and the Library of Congress Bibliographic Framework) and by publishing Linked Data from digital library projects (such as LC's Chronicling America Historic Newspapers, WGBH's public television video archives, ...), authority files (e.g. VIAF), and bibliographic catalogs (used by many national libraries, pioneered by the Swedish LIBRIS project since 2008). Other types of Linked Data available include crowdsourced information from Wikipedia and OpenStreetMap, published as Linked Data by the DBpedia and LinkedGeoData projects, respectively. Meanwhile, library-created Linked Data has been reused by Wikipedia: biography articles in the English and German-language Wikipedia projects now link to the VIAF.org name authorities.

Commonly used software systems (such as Evergreen, Hydra, and Omeka) are beginning to automatically produce Linked Data, and a deeper understanding of the principles of Linked Data is beneficial for making best use of these systems. For practitioners, this tutorial provides a greater understanding of what Linked Data is, and how to prepare digital library materials for conversion to Linked Data. For researchers, this tutorial updates the state of the art in digital libraries, while remaining accessible to those learning Linked Data principles for the first time. For library and iSchool instructors, the tutorial provides a valuable introduction to an area of growing interest for information organization curricula. For digital library project managers, this tutorial provides a deeper understanding of the principles of Linked Data, which is needed for bespoke projects that involve data mapping and the reuse of existing metadata models.

The introduction will start by explaining the motivation for using Linked Data for digital libraries, then will provide an overview of Linked Data and the concepts involved, including links as the basis for the Web, URIs as identifiers for objects, and the RDF data representation model. We will highlight some of

T. Aalberg et al. (Eds.): TPDL 2013, LNCS 8092, pp. 492–493, 2013.

the most widely used RDF vocabularies and ontologies, for example the Bibliographic Ontology, Dublin Core, FOAF (short for 'Friend of a Friend', for data
about persons) and NeoGeo (for describing geographical data). Turning our focus to digital libraries we will explore the uptake of Linked Data in the cultural
heritage sector and will look at some examples including the metadata standards
and technologies used.

The second part of the tutorial will present tools that can be used to visualize,
validate, and transform Linked Data. Participants will learn to discover and
analyze existing Linked Data sets, with special focus on Library Linked Data.
We will look in some detail at library information contained in the Linked Data
cloud (`http://lod-cloud.net/`), for instance the Open Library data, as well
as how Linked Data is used in a growing number of national libraries. We will
provide examples of tools for translating MARC records to RDF as well as tools
for translating spreadsheets to RDF (e.g. MARiMbA and the RDF extension to
Google Refine). We will also present existing library and repository software that
are using Linked Data. Also relevant for the third part of the tutorial, we will look
at existing providers of geographical data like LinkedGeoData, which exports
user-generated data from OpenStreetMap. We will briefly introduce participants
to the SPARQL query language for RDF and show how public Web data can be
integrated into your Linked Data applications.

The final part of the tutorial will pull together the information presented in
the first two parts. We will explore in more detail two use cases: (1) the VIAF
international authority file project and how it is being used outside libraries; and
(2) how to publish and use Linked Data about maps.

In the first use case, we will look at a large-scale Linked Data project, VIAF,
which is integrating multilingual information contributed by national libraries
from every continent. We will also highlight how VIAF is being used outside
libraries. In particular, we will look at how the Wikipedia Authority Control
initiative acts as an entry-point to the web of linked authority data. The second
use case will explore enhancing library records, using the online database of Irish
place names, Logainm (`http://logainm.ie`), as an example of how Geographic
Linked Data can be used as a controlled vocabulary for place names, for example
to avoid misspellings or to disambiguate place names. We describe the creation
of a new Linked Data dataset, pointing out the steps needed to build Linked
Data applications. We will show how we can automatically leverage the resulting
Linked Data version to enhance metadata records by searching for place names
that are represented in digital maps.

Author Index